PROPHETS
AND
PRINCES

PROPHETS AND PRINCES

Saudi Arabia
from Muhammad to the Present

MARK WESTON

John Wiley & Sons, Inc.

Copyright © 2008 by Mark Weston. All rights reserved

Published by John Wiley & Sons, Inc., Hoboken, New Jersey
Published simultaneously in Canada

Maps © D. L. McElhannon

Illustration Credits: p. 289 (top), courtesy of the FDR Library; p. 289 (bottom), the Middle East Centre Archive, St. Antony's College, Oxford, England; pp. 290, 292, 293 (bottom), 296, 297, 300, courtesy of the Royal Embassy of Saudi Arabia; p. 291 (top), UN photo/MB; p. 291 (bottom), LBJ Library photo by Yoichi Okamoto; p. 293 (top), UN photo/Maluwa Williams-Myers; p. 294, UN photo/Michelle Poiré; p. 295 (top), 299 (top), Saudi Aramco World/PADIA; p. 295 (bottom), UN photo; p. 298, by Kent Howell; p. 299 (bottom), by Ali Zhang Hua

For general information about our other products and services, please contact our Customer Care Department within the United States at (800) 762-2974, outside the United States at (317) 572-3993 or fax (317) 572-4002.

Wiley also publishes its books in a variety of electronic formats. Some content that appears in print may not be available in electronic books. For more information about Wiley products, visit our web site at www.wiley.com.

Library of Congress Cataloging-in-Publication Data:

Weston, Mark, date.
    Prophets and princes : Saudi Arabia from Muhammad to the present / Mark Weston.
       p.   cm.
    Includes bibliographical references and index.
    ISBN 978-0-470-18257-4 (cloth : alk. paper)
       1. Islamic Empire—History.   2. Saudi Arabia—History—20th century.
    3. September 11 Terrorist Attacks, 2001—Influence.   I. Title.
    DS232.W47   2008
    953.8—dc22
                                                            2008019095

Printed in the United States of America

10 9 8 7 6 5 4 3 2 1

To my mother,
Marybeth Weston Lobdell,
with love

Contents

Photo gallery begins on page 289.

Author's Note

Regarding the word *prophet* in this book's title, dictionary definitions of the word include "a person gifted with profound moral insight and exceptional powers of expression." By this definition, at least half a dozen people in the first five chapters were prophets.

Muslims, however, consider Muhammad to be the last prophet, preceded by Adam, Noah, Abraham, Jacob, Joseph, Moses, Aaron, David, Solomon, Jonah, John the Baptist, and Jesus. The leaders who followed Muhammad did not call themselves prophets but "successors."

Foreword

by Wyche Fowler Jr.

As a former U.S. ambassador to Saudi Arabia, I welcome *Prophets and Princes* as a balanced and comprehensive history of this vital, oil-rich nation. Many excellent (and some dreadful) works have been written about the kingdom, but the scope of *Prophets and Princes* is particularly ambitious. In one volume, Mark Weston describes the development of the Arabian peninsula from the era of Muhammad and his successors and the beginnings of the Sunni-Shia split in the seventh century to the strategic importance and the many social and economic changes that characterize the Saudi kingdom today. This is a rare work of fact and analysis, a guide to understanding Saudi Arabia's policies, politics, and application of Islam to modern life.

For centuries, Arabia was isolated from the world. Even the Ottoman Turks had no desire to govern the hundreds of miles of harsh desert east of Mecca. As a result, the Arabian people were left alone to develop a unique society that assigns the highest priority to honor, family, and a strict separation of the sexes.

It is easy to stereotype people whose customs are so different from our own, but preconceptions are often misconceptions. When President Bill Clinton asked me to serve as the U.S. ambassador to Saudi Arabia, I sought the advice of the late John West, the former governor of South Carolina, who was our ambassador to the kingdom during Jimmy Carter's presidency. "You will like the Saudis,"

Wyche Fowler Jr. was a member of the U.S. House of Representatives from Georgia (1977–1986), United States senator (1987–1993), and U.S. ambassador to the Kingdom of Saudi Arabia (1996–2001). Currently, he is chairman of the Board of Governors of the Middle East Institute in Washington, D.C.

Governor West told me. "They are a lot like Southerners—religious, family-oriented, conservative. They will be suspicious at first but will respond warmly if you show you are interested in them. And once you win their trust, they are loyal friends." During my time at my post, I found his observations to be accurate.

Today, it is distressing to see the tragedy of September 11, 2001, aggravated by uninformed commentary about Saudi Arabia in many Western publications and broadcasts and from members of Congress whose criticism ignores our countries' long history of cooperation and friendship. A common mistake, Weston says, is to attribute al-Qaeda's violence primarily to the Saudi form of Islam, Wahhabism. This religious movement, which dates from the 1740s, is motivated mainly by monotheism, not by *jihad*, for it emerged as a reaction to the idolatry and the superstition of the times. *Prophets and Princes* asserts that the chief ideological influence on al-Qaeda is Sayyid Qutb, an Egyptian who wrote for the Muslim Brotherhood. In his chapter on the rise of Muslim fundamentalism and the emergence of Osama bin Laden, Mark Weston documents the political difficulties the Saudi monarchy faced because of its alliance with the United States, which was a mutually beneficial friendship in times of war and peace for more than half a century.

Having lived in Saudi Arabia for almost five years, I share Weston's sense of wonder at how far the kingdom has come in just two generations. Sixty years ago, most of the country's people were illiterate and lived in mud-brick houses. Today the majority enjoys a first-world infrastructure, modern conveniences, and at least a high school education. Certainly, there is more progress to be made. The Saudi government, under its widely respected new king, Abdullah, has recognized the need to diversify its economy, expand opportunities for women, and improve the quality of education by minimizing religious prejudice in the classroom, adopting a more rigorous academic curriculum, and disciplining teachers (and preachers) who use their authority for political purposes. This will help the kingdom to gradually democratize, enforcing human rights and the rule of law and opening its society to enhanced economic opportunity.

I share Weston's optimism that if Muslims and Westerners can avoid a "clash of civilizations" brought on by extremists' acts and extreme reactions, the Saudis can reconcile Islam with modern life and different religious traditions. Saudi Arabia may be the West's best hope for Muslim moderation. As the custodian of Islam's holiest places, the Saudi hierarchy—both clerics and princes—has an enormous influence over whether deeds done in the name of Islam are accepted or reviled. We should all pray for the Saudi leaders' wisdom and success.

Prophets and Princes is an essential book in these dangerous times. It will widen the knowledge of serious students of history and theology and will reward the lay reader who seeks a deeper understanding of the long and often misunderstood friendship between the West and Saudi Arabia.

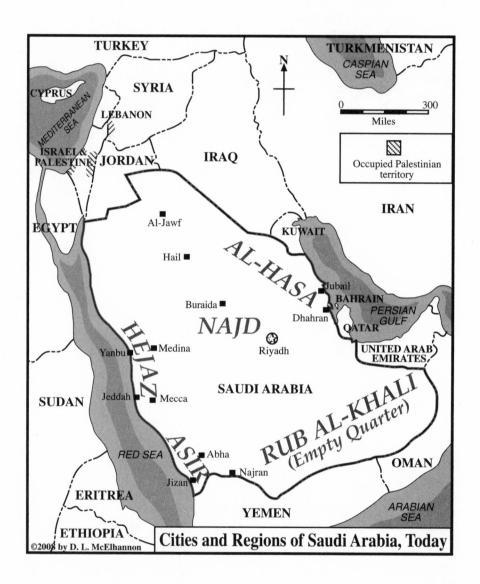

Cities and Regions of Saudi Arabia, Today

©2008 by D. L. McElhannon

The Men of the
AL-SAUD FAMILY

(Birth years are approximate)

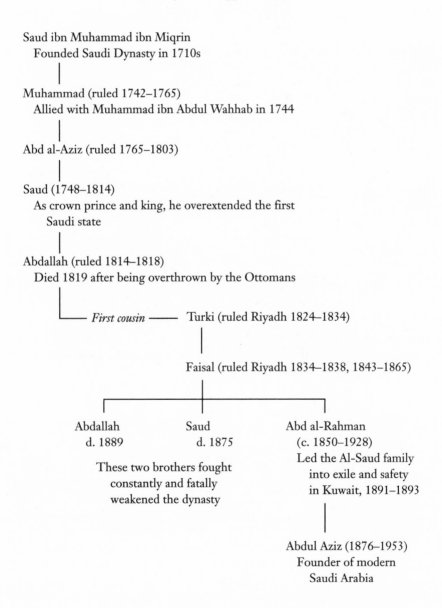

Saud ibn Muhammad ibn Miqrin
  Founded Saudi Dynasty in 1710s

|

Muhammad (ruled 1742–1765)
  Allied with Muhammad ibn Abdul Wahhab in 1744

|

Abd al-Aziz (ruled 1765–1803)

|

Saud (1748–1814)
  As crown prince and king, he overextended the first
    Saudi state

|

Abdallah (ruled 1814–1818)
  Died 1819 after being overthrown by the Ottomans

└── *First cousin* ── Turki (ruled Riyadh 1824–1834)

|

Faisal (ruled Riyadh 1834–1838, 1843–1865)

| Abdallah | Saud | Abd al-Rahman |
| d. 1889 | d. 1875 | (c. 1850–1928) |

These two brothers fought
constantly and fatally
weakened the dynasty

Abd al-Rahman (c. 1850–1928)
Led the Al-Saud family
into exile and safety
in Kuwait, 1891–1893

|

Abdul Aziz (1876–1953)
Founder of modern
Saudi Arabia

Prominent Sons and Grandsons of
King Abdul Aziz
(1876–1953)
Founder of Modern Saudi Arabia

(Birth years are approximate)

43 sons: 9 died in infancy, childhood, or adolescence
1 adult had no sons
1 adult's two sons died as young men (one of them was beheaded after assassinating King Faisal)
32 sons have produced approximately 200 grandsons

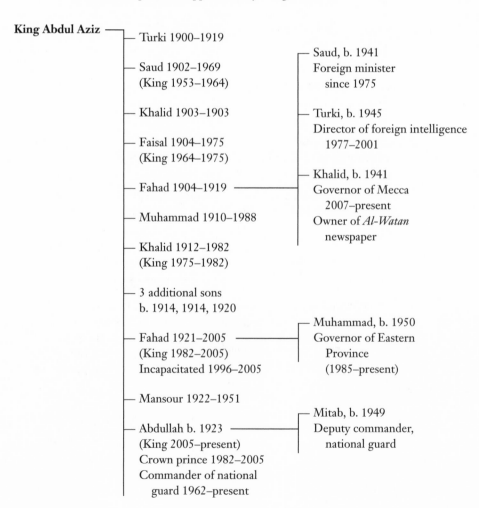

King Abdul Aziz

— Turki 1900–1919

— Saud 1902–1969
(King 1953–1964)

— Khalid 1903–1903

— Faisal 1904–1975
(King 1964–1975)

— Fahad 1904–1919

— Muhammad 1910–1988

— Khalid 1912–1982
(King 1975–1982)

— 3 additional sons
b. 1914, 1914, 1920

— Fahad 1921–2005
(King 1982–2005)
Incapacitated 1996–2005

— Mansour 1922–1951

— Abdullah b. 1923
(King 2005–present)
Crown prince 1982–2005
Commander of national
guard 1962–present

— Saud, b. 1941
Foreign minister
since 1975

— Turki, b. 1945
Director of foreign intelligence
1977–2001

— Khalid, b. 1941
Governor of Mecca
2007–present
Owner of *Al-Watan*
newspaper

— Muhammad, b. 1950
Governor of Eastern
Province
(1985–present)

— Mitab, b. 1949
Deputy commander,
national guard

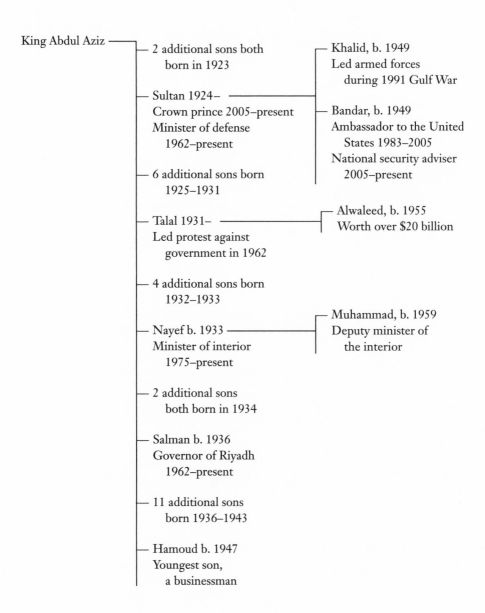

King Abdul Aziz

— 2 additional sons both
  born in 1923

— Sultan 1924–
  Crown prince 2005–present
  Minister of defense
  1962–present

— 6 additional sons born
  1925–1931

— Talal 1931–
  Led protest against
  government in 1962

— 4 additional sons born
  1932–1933

— Nayef b. 1933
  Minister of interior
  1975–present

— 2 additional sons
  both born in 1934

— Salman b. 1936
  Governor of Riyadh
  1962–present

— 11 additional sons
  born 1936–1943

— Hamoud b. 1947
  Youngest son,
  a businessman

— Khalid, b. 1949
  Led armed forces
  during 1991 Gulf War

— Bandar, b. 1949
  Ambassador to the United
  States 1983–2005
  National security adviser
  2005–present

— Alwaleed, b. 1955
  Worth over $20 billion

— Muhammad, b. 1959
  Deputy minister of
  the interior

Introduction

SAUDI ARABIA is both the economic and the spiritual center of the Middle East and a crucial ally of the West. It has a quarter of the world's oil; the United States has just 2 percent. At present, if the United States were forced to rely on its own resources, it could run out of oil in less than five years.

Three families control more than 40 percent of the Earth's oil reserves: the al-Saud of Saudi Arabia, the al-Sabah of Kuwait, and the al-Nahayan of Abu Dhabi. By far the most powerful of these families is the al-Saud, the rulers of Saudi Arabia, the world's only country that is named after a family. Their desert kingdom is almost as large as the United States east of the Mississippi River.

Saudi Arabia is also the cradle of Islam, the monotheistic but misunderstood faith of almost a quarter of the world's people. When one and a half billion people from Morocco to Indonesia kneel to pray, they pray facing Mecca, Islam's holiest city, in western Saudi Arabia. There are 25 percent more Muslims than Catholics in the world, three times as many Muslims as Protestants, and more than eighty Muslims for every Jew.

The Saudi kingdom is a paradox. It has been a breeding ground for al-Qaeda, but it has also been a reliable friend of the United States for more than sixty years. After September 11, 2001, for example, when oil buyers were nervous, Saudi Arabia pumped millions of barrels of extra oil to keep the price down, and it did the same in

March 2003, when the United States invaded Iraq. The kingdom has also been a force for moderation in the Arab world, periodically proposing a plan for peace between Israel and Palestine and denouncing Hezbollah as "irresponsible" when the militia's guerrillas crossed into Israel and killed eight Israeli soldiers in July 2006.

A balanced view of Saudi Arabia is vital if Americans are to avoid more of the miscalculations that so often lead to violence in the Middle East. The kingdom's duality needs to be acknowledged and explored, but many recent books about the country have been polemics. In fact, since 2001, it has been open season on Saudi Arabia in newspapers, magazines, and especially books with titles such as *Hatred's Kingdom: How Saudi Arabia Supports the New Global Terrorism*; *Princes of Darkness: The Saudi Assault on the West*; and *The Two Faces of Islam: The House of Saud from Tradition to Terror*. Most of these attacks are one-sided and written by people who have never been to the country.

Saudi Arabia is easy to criticize. Women cannot drive, work with men, or travel without a man's permission. The religious police, though less assertive than they used to be, still harass women if they see the slightest bit of hair, arm, or ankle but never arrest a Saudi man for abusing his Indonesian or Sri Lankan housemaid. In business, corrupt princes have taken "commissions" on large contracts and squandered the money on luxuries, even while 30 percent of the nation's young men are unemployed. In schools, students spend almost a third of their time on Islamic studies and often graduate without the skills they need to compete with the nine million foreigners who live in the kingdom and do much of the country's work.

Worst of all, until 9/11 the Saudis sent millions of dollars abroad to schools that taught Muslim extremism and to charities that turned out to be fronts for al-Qaeda. Even today, 10 to 20 percent of the members of al-Qaeda are Saudi, including its leader, Osama bin Laden. On September 11, 2001, as everyone knows, nineteen of bin Laden's followers hijacked four U.S. passenger jets and slammed three of them into the World Trade Center and the Pentagon, killing almost three thousand people. Fifteen of these murderers were from Saudi Arabia, eleven from a single region.

Yet Saudi Arabia has also been a steadfast ally of the West since 1915, first of Britain and then of the United States. The kingdom has huge oil reserves but is dependent on the United States for its security, and for decades it has kept its end of the energy-for-security bargain. The Saudis often pump much more oil than their own need for income requires in an effort to keep both the price of oil and the world's economy stable. If the Saudis did not provide this cushion of extra oil, the world's oil supplies would be much more prone to disruption, and markets would be a lot more jittery. Americans might easily be paying a dollar or two more for a gallon of gasoline than they already do.

After 9/11, it took the Saudi people more than a year to fully appreciate the fact that homegrown terrorism had become a major problem. Since 2002, however, the Saudis have killed more than 150 terrorists and captured more than 1,000 others, shared valuable information with the FBI and the CIA, stopped all Saudi charities from sending any money abroad, fired or retired 1,300 extremist clerics and forbidden them to preach at their mosques, and begun the lengthy process of replacing millions of schoolbooks in the one subject, "Monotheism," in which the textbooks contained numerous hostile references to Christians and Jews.

Despite these efforts, two-thirds of Americans have an unfavorable view of Saudi Arabia, according to one Gallup poll. Misunderstanding, of course, is a two-way street. In Riyadh, an old man waiting in line at a bank asked me, "Why are you in Iraq? Why do you help Israel? You are a great people. You make planes. You make cars. Then I watch television and see what you are doing nearby, and I don't understand it." (I just nodded, having learned within days of my arrival that it was futile to try to change Saudi minds about Israel.)

In the United States, harm is done by grossly misleading magazine articles such as "The World's 10 Worst Dictators," a piece David Wallechinsky updates each year for *Parade*. In 2006, he put Saudi Arabia's King Abdullah seventh on his list, although, as this book makes clear, Abdullah has been an excellent monarch, and a Saudi king is not a dictator. The king is subject to Muslim law, receives many petitions, and seldom makes a decision without the support of his brothers, the senior clergy, and experts with PhDs.

Thomas Lippman, a former Middle East bureau chief for the *Washington Post* and the author of *Inside the Mirage*, an excellent book on America's relationship with Saudi Arabia, correctly called *Parade*'s inclusion of King Abdullah on its list of the world's worst dictators "ridiculous" and asked, "What planet do these people dwell on?"

Yet in a sign of how deeply suspicious many Americans are toward the kingdom, *Parade* ignored Lippman's criticism and moved King Abdullah up to fourth place in 2008, ahead of Zimbabwe's Robert Mugabe, a brutal tyrant who has killed his opponents and has robbed his people of a generation of economic progress. (*Parade*'s three worst dictators were the leaders of North Korea, Sudan, and Burma.)

Saudi Arabia's unfair ranking comes from the fact that the kingdom justifiably gets a zero in religious freedom. Non-Muslims are forbidden to build houses of worship in Saudi Arabia and can hold services only inside their homes. This is because when Muhammad was dying, he said, "Let there not be two religions in Arabia." Today, the Saudis say, building a church in Saudi Arabia, the home of Islam, is as unthinkable as building a synagogue would be in Vatican City.

Like an F on a report card, the kingdom's zero in religious freedom pulls down what is otherwise a fairly decent human rights record. Even Amnesty International, one of the kingdom's harshest critics, concedes that no one has ever disappeared in Saudi Arabia, as so many have in Iraq, and it estimates that the number of political prisoners in Saudi Arabia, a nation of twenty-seven million people, is fewer than two hundred. While the Saudis are not free to demonstrate against their government, their right to petition the royal family is absolute because the Quran commands rulers to seek advice. As a result, clerics and professors routinely sign petitions, with impunity, that ask the king to give up his power and form a constitutional monarchy.

In the last decade, the Saudi people have begun to speak freely, but, out of residual caution, most of the Saudis I met still asked me not to use their names in this book. I never heard anyone make fun of the king or crack a joke about the senior princes, but people did not hesitate to call some uneducated, although most Saudis see them as conscientious administrators who consult many experts before making a decision.

King Abdullah has worked especially hard to integrate his country into the world economy. Recently, Saudi Arabia has signed thirty-eight trade agreements and enacted forty-two commercial laws so that in 2005, it could be the 149th nation to join the World Trade Organization and exchange goods and services more freely and cheaply with the other 148 countries.

By then, 91 percent of the Saudis had satellite television, with access to more than 150 Arabic-language channels. Saudis today get their news from many sources and have also begun to see how women live in less gender-segregated societies. Nearly every Saudi agrees that women, who outnumber men almost three-to-two at Saudi universities, will have more rights soon. But even educated young women seem content to move cautiously, because the goal, many say, is not to free themselves *from* men, but *with* men.

Although Saudi Arabia is a U.S. ally making genuine social progress, many Americans, from right-wing media mogul Rupert Murdoch to left-wing film director Michael Moore, want the House of Saud to fall. They ignore the fact that unlike Iran, where the people are more progressive than their rulers, in Saudi Arabia the royal family is more progressive than its people. Day after day, I asked almost every Saudi I met the same question: If three political parties competed in elections tomorrow—one representing the royal family, a second representing conservative clerics, and the third representing Western-educated reformers—how would the Saudi people vote? The answer was always about the same: 50 to 55 percent for the royal family, 35 to 45 percent for the Islamist clerics, and just 5 to 10 percent for the Western-oriented reformers.

The alternative to Saudi Arabia's royal family today is not some Arabic-speaking version of the Swedish parliament, but a militantly Islamist regime, which, even if it were democratically elected, would almost certainly be far more troublesome and anti-Western than the royal family is. (In Kuwait, Muslim fundamentalists won 34 percent of the seats in parliament in 2006, and the Saudis are more devout than the people of Kuwait.)

The Saudi princes "are the only ones in the position to stop the extremists from controlling our lives," a blogger, Saudi Jeans, wrote to me, "and liberals need them to implement the reforms they are looking for." Even Patrick Buchanan, the ultraconservative U.S. columnist, has rightly asked, "Can anyone believe that should the 7,000 princes go to the wall, 7,000 liberal democrats will replace them?"

The harshest critics of Saudi Arabia are ill-informed. They ignore the country's long traditions, pro-Western history, and undeniable recent progress and treat the whole kingdom as if it were a rogue state where everyone supports terrorism. The truth is that the overwhelming majority of the Saudi people, including all but one of the Saudis I talked with, hate terrorism, and the police have been able to raid dozens of terrorist hideouts because of tips, as one officer said, from "disgusted neighbors." A 2005 poll of ten thousand Saudis found that only 4.7 percent of them wanted Osama bin Laden to have political power. Ninety-two percent thought it was a "bad idea."

Critics of Saudi Arabia face a dilemma. If the majority of Saudis are Islamic militants, then we are lucky the House of Saud is in power because the alternative would be an anti-American theocracy that has billions of petrodollars to spend opposing U.S. interests. But if most Saudis are against extremism and most princes and police officers want to help us fight terrorism, then it is foolish and counterproductive to demonize their country just because their culture is so different from our own.

It is easy to disparage the Saudis. It is harder to try to see them as they see themselves: as champions of monotheism and modesty, under a monarchy that is subject to Islamic law. Saudis know that their royal house has many corrupt princes, but the al-Saud family also has a 260-year tradition of ruling the country, a 60-year alliance with the United States, and a current king, Abdullah, who is widely considered to be accessible, prudent, and broad-minded.

As for Saudi women, few of the ones I talked with would trade places with their American sisters and give up the protection of their extended families. To women in Saudi Arabia, the possibility of raising children as a single mother without any money from brothers, uncles, and cousins seems as demeaning as having to wear a full veil and not being able to drive seem to us.

Appearances are deceiving in Saudi Arabia. "Outside, everything is dusty," said an American nurse who has lived in Riyadh for years. "The only colors are beige, brown, tan, and cream. But inside, everything is air-conditioned, well-furnished, and beautiful." Similarly, "Western journalists covering our kingdom only show extremists and the royal family," a petrochemical salesman complained, "but everyone I know just wants to make money, raise a good family, and live a peaceful life. We are more like the Americans than different."

Riyadh is dusty because it is surrounded on every side by hundreds of miles of desert, so if there is the slightest breeze, the blue sky turns half-brown, particles of sand brush against one's cheeks, and contact lenses become hard to wear. The cities and towns of Saudi Arabia are oases in an unrelentingly harsh desert, where vast seas of off-white sand reflect so much sunlight that without dark glasses, it is difficult to see until about five in the afternoon. There is not even much scrub in Saudi Arabia. Compared to the almost lifeless Arabian Desert, the American Southwest is a garden. In fact, much of the kingdom looks more like Mars than like the Mojave. It is amazing that anyone ever settled Arabia's interior, and it is not surprising that until the twentieth century, fewer than a dozen Europeans had ever been to Riyadh.

As late as 1950, Riyadh and every other Saudi city except Jeddah were just clusters of mud-walled homes, with no restaurants, parks, electricity, or running water. Saudi Arabia did not have a high school until the 1930s or a girls' school until the 1950s. Today, in many Saudi families, although the grandmothers and the great-grandparents are illiterate, the grandfathers attended only elementary school, and the parents have just a high school education, the sons and the daughters are attending universities. It is easy for an American to think that Saudi Arabia is backward, but the Saudis themselves feel as if they are rocketing into the future.

My curiosity about Islam began in 1990, when I was writing my first book, *The Land and People of Pakistan*, a few years after I had made some Pakistani friends at the London School of Economics. Two things struck me about the Muslims: their numbers and their fervor. While churches in the United States may fill up once or twice a week, mosques in Pakistan (and in Saudi Arabia) fill up five times a day.

In Islamabad, Pakistan's capital, there was a wonderful store called Mr. Books that sold biographical pamphlets about the early Muslims for ten rupees, about fifty cents. The booklets told the stories of not only Muhammad, but also his immediate successors, favorite wives, smartest daughter, son-in-law, and two grandsons, among others. Historically, these men and women are as important to Muslims as Jesus, Mary, Joseph, Peter, and Paul are to Christians.

I realized that the prophets, the saints, the rulers, and the martyrs whom the Muslims learn about in childhood are alien to us. Yet if we in the West are to understand the thinking of our allies and the motives of our adversaries, it is important that more of us begin to know some of these dramatic Muslim stories. Greedily, I bought twenty of the pamphlets. "Someday," I promised myself, "I will write about them."

Eleven years later, after the attacks of 9/11, that time had come. I wrote the first four chapters of this book in 2002, trying to combine the liveliness of the Pakistani pamphlets with the rigor of the more scholarly books on Muslim history that I found in university libraries.

Americans are typically more concerned with the present than with the past, and many busy people may have the time to read only my book's final chapters on Saudi Arabia today. But almost every Saudi would agree that if you have time to read just one chapter in this book, you will learn much more about Saudi Arabia by reading the first chapter on Muhammad than you will by reading the last chapter on relations with Iran and the future of the royal succession.

When I lived in Saudi Arabia and had already decided to write a much longer book, I sometimes showed the Saudis my table of contents so they could see what I was writing. They were always pleased that this book begins with chapters on Muhammad and his successors. Once, when I interviewed Prince Abdullah bin Faisal bin Turki, the former director of the Saudi Arabian General Investment Authority (roughly the equivalent of the secretary of commerce), he had originally agreed to see me for fifteen minutes. After taking a long look at my table of contents, he changed his mind and talked to me for an hour and a half.

The Middle East dominates the news almost every day, yet only 7 percent of Americans claim to have any knowledge of Islam's core beliefs. Few Americans realize that Muslims revere Genesis, Exodus, Psalms, and even parts of the Gospels as holy scripture and honor Noah, Abraham, Moses, and Jesus as prophets of God. It is news to most Americans that Muslims believe in the virgin birth, miracles, and the resurrection of Jesus (for there is no miracle, Muslims say, that Allah cannot perform). Muslims do not believe that Jesus is the Son of God. To them, the Trinity is a deviation from monotheism.

Few Americans know that Muhammad was a reformer who loved the company of women and greatly improved their lives. The Quran, the scripture he recited, prohibits the killing of girls at birth and commands that a woman inherit half of what a man inherits, a revolutionary idea anywhere in the world until the nineteenth century. It was also Muhammad's personal opinion that a woman should be educated and have a major say in choosing her husband. Indeed, his first wife was a businesswoman who proposed to him.

Some influential Americans display an astonishing ignorance about Islam. In 2003, Lieutenant General William Boykin, the deputy undersecretary of defense for intelligence, said that the Muslims he fought in Somalia worship "an idol." Similarly, Franklin Graham, the son of Billy Graham, told NBC News in 2002 that "the God of Islam is . . . a different God," and Islam "is a very evil and wicked religion." Jerry Vines, a former president of the Southern Baptists, told a Baptist convention in 2001 that "Allah is not Jehovah." In fact, Allah and Jehovah are one and the same. *Al-lah* is simply Arabic for "the God," and Islam began as and continues to be a movement against idol worship.

Fox News commentator Bill O'Reilly compared the University of North Carolina's assignment of a book about the Quran to incoming freshmen in 2002 to a requirement that they read Hitler's *Mein Kampf* and asked why Americans should study "our enemy's religion." O'Reilly's question has two answers. First, America's enemy is terrorism, not Islam. Second, the growth of terrorism has shown that it is not possible to fully understand the twenty-first century without knowing something about the seventh century, the period when Muhammad began the spread of Islam.

Millions of Muslims, including many Saudis, see the seventh century, when Islam grew so rapidly, as a golden age when saints ruled the world, a utopia that they want to restore. In the "smoking gun" videotape that U.S. soldiers found in Afghanistan in 2001, Osama bin Laden and his black-turbaned Saudi dinner companion discuss their destruction of the World Trade Center, then talk about reviving the spirit of early Islam.

Why are Muslims so fervent about their religion? Muhammad and his followers introduced a way of life that was more just and equitable than anything the Arabs had known before, and this spurred them to spread their faith from Spain to India. Muslim civilization became the most advanced in the world until the time of the European Renaissance. In the 1030s, for example, one Arab scientist, ibn al-Haytham, closely observed the twilight and correctly determined that the air peters out (and space begins) about sixty miles up. It would be almost nine hundred years before Western scientists discovered the ionosphere and reached a similar conclusion.

The many English words that come from Arabic are a constant reminder that for centuries, Europeans borrowed from the Muslims—not the other way around. Words derived from Arabic include *coffee, sugar, soda, candy, alcohol, magazine, orange, lemon, lime, rice, spinach, cotton, sofa, mattress, admiral, average, canal, cannon, jacket, jar, sheriff, traffic,* and *zero.* Muslims led the world in astronomy, mathematics, medicine, and even home furnishings for more than four hundred years, until a combination of reactionary clerics and Mongol invasions drained Islamic civilization of its dynamism in the twelfth and thirteenth centuries.

By the time I had finished writing about early Islam, I had also become interested in Wahhabism, the strict Saudi form of Islam that began in the 1740s as a movement against superstition, magic, and idolatry. After 9/11, because most of the hijackers were Saudi, some writers began to call Wahhabism a totalitarian ideology, comparing it to Nazism and communism, and said that it was America's next great enemy. But as chapter 5 makes clear, Wahhabism was simply a puritanical religious revival, rather like Calvinism in our own past.

Arabia had regressed and become a superstitious backwater when Wahhabism began. People prayed at tombs and sacred palm trees instead of in mosques, and they pursued astrology and ancestor worship instead of monotheism. The Saudis themselves call this time a "period of ignorance." Then, in 1744, ibn Abdul Wahhab, a fiery preacher and a strict monotheist, joined forces with Muhammad ibn Saud a few miles outside what is now the city of Riyadh. Together, they formed a military and spiritual alliance that conquered and briefly ruled most of the Arabian peninsula. The kingdom fell but reappeared in the twentieth century as modern-day Saudi Arabia, and the Saudi-Wahhabi alliance, after 260 years, is still one of the key pillars of the royal family's legitimacy.

Today, the most pressing question in Saudi Arabia is whether the kingdom can control its population growth, find work for its unemployed, and create an economy based on manufacturing and services before its oil runs out by the end of the century. If it is left alone, Saudi Arabia will have a bright future. It earns huge oil revenues, has a business-friendly government, and is making slow but steady social progress. Turmoil in the Middle East, however, could easily spill into the kingdom, particularly if a "clash of civilizations" developed between the West and the Muslim world.

Whether the Saudi people choose to be moderate or militant in the future depends on whether they believe globalization can enrich their lives without endangering their faith. Do they feel that Islam is secure in the face of the Western world's many influences? Whatever the Saudis decide, their influence on the rest of the Muslim world will be enormous, both because of their immense oil wealth and because of their moral authority as the guardian of Islam's two holiest cities, Mecca and Medina.

Most of my friends read more fiction than nonfiction, and the art of reading the two genres is quite different. A novel is a work of art that needs to be taken whole. A nonfiction book is a buffet; the reader has only to read what interests him or her. To make it easy for readers to jump and skip, I have divided each chapter into many subchapters. Some are obviously more interesting than others. The boyhood of Osama bin Laden, for example, is a more interesting topic for most people than are monthly fluctuations in the price of oil, and women's issues are generally more interesting than budget cutbacks and petrochemical plants are. Although a book on Saudi Arabia would not be complete without detailed discussions of the price of oil, no one ever said that you have to read every page of a nonfiction book.

When I was a sophomore in college, I was struck by the second paragraph of Niccolo Machiavelli's introduction to *The Discourses*:

> And if my poor talents, my little experience of the present and insufficient study of the past, should make the result of my labors defective

and of little utility, I shall at least have shown the way to others, who will carry out my views with greater ability, eloquence, and judgment, so that if I do not merit praise, I ought at least not to incur censure.[1]

At nineteen, I pitied Machiavelli. One of the great political thinkers of all time had to humble himself before his patrons. Now I read the same paragraph with envy. Machiavelli did not have to claim to have written "the one indispensable book on the subject," as so many authors do to sell their wares today. He simply hoped that he had done some useful work, as I do with this book.

No one can spend six years on a project without being deeply aware of its deficiencies. The ideal author for this book would have gone to college pursuing a double major in Arabic literature and petroleum engineering, worked in the Saudi kingdom for twenty years, come to know many Saudi families extremely well, and then, with a novelist's eye, woven the history of the kingdom back and forth between the sweep of national events and the daily lives of his friends. If we are lucky, perhaps someone this talented is writing such a book now.

In the meantime, there is room for a new and sympathetic survey of Saudi Arabia that highlights its reforms since 2001 instead of only its shortcomings. Unlike other works about the kingdom, the purpose of this book is not to criticize the Saudis, although often I do, but to try to understand them. In a region as explosive, exasperating, and hostile to the United States as the Middle East, America's sixty-year friendship with Saudi Arabia is worth preserving.

PART ONE

THE BIRTH OF ISLAM IN THE SEVENTH CENTURY

THE DRAMATIC LIVES of Muhammad and his successors are the "Bible stories" taught to every Muslim child from Morocco to Indonesia. They inspire an equally large number of adults, millions of whom uncritically look back to the seventh century as a golden age when saints ruled the world.

Muhammad first started to recite the Quran in 610. In 622, when the people of Medina invited him to govern their city, Muhammad and his followers created a way of life that was more equitable and just than anything the Arabs had known before, inspiring them later to spread their faith from Spain to India.

Muhammad's first four successors, who ruled from 632 to 661, are known as the "Rightly Guided Caliphs." The first, Abu Bakr, ruled only two years but preserved Arabia's newly won unity and the caliph's right to tax the wealthy to help the poor. Under the second caliph, Umar, Muslim soldiers took Syria, Palestine, and Egypt away from the Byzantines and overthrew the Persian Empire in 642. The third caliph, Uthman, was pious and kind, but his nepotism led to a civil war in the late 650s, during the rule of the fourth caliph, Ali, Muhammad's adopted son.

The fifth caliph, Muawiya, was an exceptionally skillful ruler, but Muslims dislike him because he turned the great Islamic theocracy into an ordinary hereditary dynasty. Muawiya kept the Muslims united, however, and expanded their frontiers to include Tunisia and Afghanistan. In 680, soldiers loyal to Muawiya's son, Yazid, the sixth caliph, murdered Muhammad's grandson, Hussein, who soon became the leading martyr of the new Shi'ite branch of Islam.

I

Muhammad: Islam's Prophet

A S THE EARTH TURNS and dawn moves west from Indonesia to Bangladesh, Pakistan, the Middle East, and North Africa, nearly one-fourth of the world's people start their day with prayer. The call to this prayer begins, "There is but one God, Muhammad is His Messenger." One and a half billion Muslims believe Muhammad to be the last and the greatest of all prophets. Muhammad vastly increased the number of people who believe in one God, and he made a violent society far more humane. He called his religion Islam, an Arabic word meaning "submission" (to God). A Muslim is "one who submits."

For fourteen hundred years, Islam has given meaning to the lives of generations of men, educated and illiterate alike, and to women, too. Muhammad loved the company of women and greatly improved their lives. The Quran (Arabic for "recitation," also spelled Koran), the scripture of Islam, gives a woman the right to divorce her husband if he treats her badly, and it commands that a woman receive a half-share of her family's property, a revolutionary idea in any part of the world until modern times. Muhammad also taught that a woman should be educated and have a say in choosing her husband.

Muslims consider the Quran to be the literal word of God, transmitted through Muhammad. But unlike Jesus and Buddha, Muhammad was a ruler as well as a teacher, and he made political and military decisions. The fact that Muhammad sometimes went to war does not diminish his achievement. He founded one of the world's most widespread religions, dictated its scripture, and unified the Arabs.

The common Western belief that Islam is "a religion of the sword" is mistaken. Muslim conquerors allowed Christians, Jews, and Hindus to keep their faith because the Quran forbids conversion by force. The millions of Hindus, Zoroastrians, and Syrian and Coptic Christians who converted to Islam in the eighth, ninth, and tenth centuries did so freely because their Muslim conquerors governed more justly than any rulers they had known before.

Muhammad (570–632) was born in Mecca, a city in one of the world's bleakest deserts, fifty miles inland from the Red Sea, in what is now Saudi Arabia. The name *Muhammad* means "the praised one." His father, Abdullah, died before he was born, and his mother, Amina, gave her baby to a nomad who raised Muhammad outdoors in the open desert. (This was the custom of urban women then, because cities were full of disease.) When Muhammad was six, his nurse, Halimah, returned him to his mother, but his mother died just a few months later. Orphaned at seven, Muhammad entered the home of his uncle, Abu Talib, although he and Halimah visited each other often.

When Muhammad was a child, he tended goats and camels, wrestled with other boys, and learned to shoot with a bow and arrow. Later, he accompanied his uncle on caravans north to Syria during the summer and south to Yemen in the winter. The trips took a month each way, and hundreds of camels carried loads of up to four hundred pounds each. The value of a caravan's merchandise was enormous.

Muhammad had no education, but he loved poetry, and during his travels to Syria, he learned many of the stories of the Jewish and Christian faiths. The Arabs at this time worshipped many gods and goddesses, represented by roughly 360 idols in and around the Kaaba (Arabic for "cube"). This stone cube in Mecca is almost forty feet high, with corners facing north, south, east, and west. The Kaaba is said to have been built (or rebuilt) centuries earlier by the prophet Abraham and his son Ishmael, long before the Arabs put idols inside it, and a black meteorite was placed in its southeastern wall. Among the Kaaba's idols were statues of the Greek goddess Aphrodite, the Egyptian god Isis, and three Arabian goddesses: al-Lat, al-Uzza, and al-Manat.

For years, Muhammad could work only for others on caravans because he was too poor to do any trading himself. Gradually, he earned the nickname al-Amin, "the trustworthy." In his early twenties, Muhammad began to work for a woman named Khadija, a rich trader.

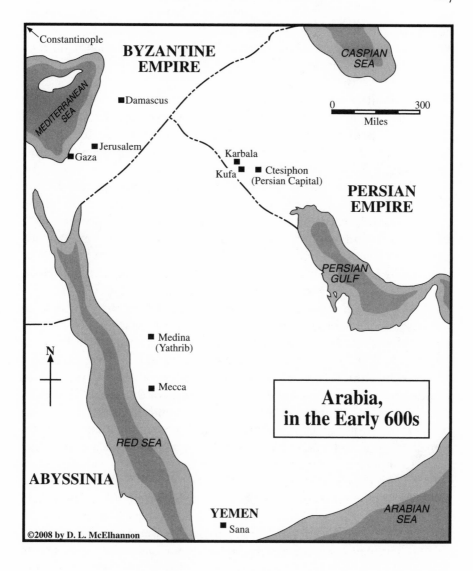

Her first two husbands had died, and now she owned their businesses. At first, she hired Muhammad to look after a single caravan, but soon she put him in charge of all her caravans.

In time, Khadija fell in love with her employee. Muhammad was a determined worker but kind and gentle in manner, and he was strong, with broad shoulders and a lean, sturdy build. He had dark expressive eyes, thick black hair, a full beard, a fair complexion, and a winning smile. After two years, Khadija proposed marriage and Muhammad accepted. Tradition has it that Muhammad was twenty-five and Khadija was forty when they married. They had two sons, who died in infancy, and four daughters, so it is more likely that she was only a few years older than he was.

As a wealthy man, Muhammad gave to the poor and now also had more time to devote to spiritual matters. He escaped the heat of the desert and spent several weeks each year in a cave on Mount Hira, high above Mecca. He stared at the star-filled sky of the desert nights and thought deeply about the condition of his city.

In the sixth century, Mecca had transformed from a tribal town into a great trading center. War between the Byzantine and Persian empires had disrupted the land routes between Europe and Asia. Chinese silk, Indian spices and cotton, and African ivory and ostrich plumes all began to arrive by sea at Yemen, where the Red Sea meets the Indian Ocean. (One of Yemen's ports is Al-Mukha, from which we get our English synonym for coffee, *mocha*.)

From Yemen, well-armed caravans carried their cargoes north to the bazaars of Damascus and Gaza and brought back gold, wine, and grain. Mecca grew in size not only because it was halfway between Yemen and Syria, but because it was a sanctuary where merchants could trade freely without fear of violence. For four months of the year, it was forbidden to avenge a blood feud in the vicinity of the Kaaba.

Some Meccan traders became rich beyond the wildest dreams of their nomadic ancestors. Others, especially widows and orphans, remained poor and hungry. Until Muhammad's lifetime, a tribal chief helped the poorer members of his clan as a matter of honor, but the merchants of Mecca had not grown rich from tribal raids but from their own shrewdness in the marketplace. They therefore felt no obligation to help anyone not connected with their businesses, not even hungry members of their own clan. Wealth had become more important than honor.

Muhammad, an orphan himself, had compassion for the poor. He was angry that the rich ignored their tribal duty to help others, and he was troubled by the lack of moral feeling among the people in his city. Most Meccans still prayed to local idols, but the only thing they really believed in was the power of their own wealth.

Muhammad's First Years as a Prophet

One night on Mount Hira, when Muhammad was about forty, he felt a powerful, crushing presence. He believed it to be the archangel Gabriel, and the angel commanded him to "Recite!" three times.

Each time Muhammad, who was illiterate, replied, "I cannot recite." Gabriel then appeared a fourth time, commanded Muhammad to "Recite in the name of the Lord," and later said, "Muhammad! Thou art the Messenger of God."

Muhammad was greatly disturbed. He was afraid that he was possessed by an evil demon and even considered killing himself by jumping off a cliff. His wife reassured him with the words "You speak the truth and help anyone in need. God would not allow you to be led astray."

Khadija then asked her elderly Christian cousin Waraqa about Muhammad's vision. Waraqa said that God had approached Muhammad as he had once approached Moses, and Waraqa predicted that Muhammad would be "the prophet of his people." He also warned Muhammad that his preaching would make him many enemies.

The first Muslims were members of Muhammad's own family: his wife, Khadija; his cousin Waraqa; a ten-year-old cousin and adopted son named Ali; a freed slave, Zayd ibn Haritha; and Muhammad's four daughters, Zaynab, Ruqayyah, Umm Kulthum, and Fatima.

The first non–family member to convert to Islam was Muhammad's best friend, Abu Bakr. A moderately successful cloth trader, Abu Bakr was well known in Mecca for being wise, honest, and kind and for his skill in interpreting dreams. Abu Bakr, two or three years younger than Muhammad, persuaded several other men to become Muslims, including a few from wealthy families. But most of the early converts to Islam (as with Christianity) were poor and female, and several were slaves.

At first, Muhammad preached only to his family, friends, and a few followers. There are no spirits and demons to be afraid of, Muhammad said, Allah is the one and only God. (*Al-lah* is Arabic for "the God.") He is the source of all creation and is merciful to those who worship him. On Judgment Day, Allah will decide the fate of every man and woman, and no friend or relative will be able to intervene. Those who lead good lives and are generous to the poor will live forever in the gardens of paradise, attended by youths of great beauty. Those who are evil and too selfish to help others will suffer hellfire for eternity, growing new skin to feel new pain even as their old skin burns. The people of Mecca and especially its merchants, Muhammad said, should realize that there are things more important than credits and debts. Everyone should fear the power of Allah, the creator of life, and be kind to the poor.

Islam borrows heavily from Judaism. It often comes as a surprise to Westerners that Muslims revere Adam, Noah, Abraham, and Moses as major prophets and honor Joseph, Job, Jonah, David, Solomon, and many other biblical figures. They regard the Torah and the Psalms as divine scripture and also revere Jesus as a leading prophet.

Muslims believe that Jesus was born to the Virgin Mary and that he healed the sick, walked on water, and was resurrected after his crucifixion. They say there is no miracle that Allah cannot perform. Muslims, however, do not believe that Jesus is the son of God. In its 112th chapter, the Quran says explicitly, "He is God Alone: God the Eternal! He begets not, and He is not begotten."[1] Muslims believe that in the four Gospels (Matthew, Mark, Luke, and John), the word of God has been distorted by the writings of men. To Muhammad and his followers, the belief in the Christian Trinity (Father, Son, and Holy Ghost) was only somewhat better than a belief in the 360 idols in the Kaaba. Indeed, Muslims believe that on Judgment Day, Jesus himself will rebuke Christians for worshipping him as a god.

A simple belief in one God is what Muhammad wished to give to his followers, and in order to keep that faith simple, Muhammad was careful to emphasize, "I am a man like you, only the Word of God has been revealed to me." Muhammad considered himself to be just one more messenger in a long series of prophets; his mission was to bring God's word to the Arab people.

After three years of preaching among friends, Muhammad began to preach in public, but the people of Mecca rejected his message. Meccans made money from pilgrims who came to worship and trade at the Kaaba, and they did not like to hear the gods inside referred to as idols of stone. The Meccans particularly scoffed at Muhammad's claim to be a Messenger of God since he did not perform any miracles, and they mocked him as a "mad poet."

Muhammad said that he was just a "warner" about Judgment Day and his only miracle was receiving the Quran. From the time of his first vision on Mount Hira until his death twenty-two years later, Muhammad had many revelations, usually oral rather than visual. He would shake for a while and sometimes moan. He once said that he had never received a revelation without feeling as if his soul were being torn away. When it was finished, however, he calmly told his followers what God or one of God's angels had said to him. Because Muhammad was illiterate (although he was quick with numbers), one of his followers wrote down the verses on parchment if it were available or, if not, on wood, leather, or the shoulder-blade bone of a camel or a sheep. Then the congregation memorized the new verses. Muhammad was careful to distinguish between the Quran and his own thoughts, for he sincerely believed that his revelations came directly from God.

After Muhammad's death, his followers collected all of the verses into the book we know as the Quran. In length, it is about the same size as the New Testament. Muhammad's followers also recorded the Prophet's sayings, which became known as the *hadith*, and his deeds (and his explanations of his deeds), which became known as the *sunnah*. Together, the Quran, the *hadith*, and the *sunnah* form the core of Islamic law, the *sharia*.

In Arabic, much of the Quran is in rhyme, giving it a power and a majesty that no translation can convey. Even the most basic tenet of Islam, "There is but one God," is melodious in Arabic: *"La ilaha illa Allah."* This is why hundreds of millions of Muslims whose native language may be Persian, Bengali, Malay, or Swahili nevertheless recite the Quran each day in its original Arabic.

The Quran is not a narrative book like Genesis or Matthew. It is a collection of lyric appeals to virtue and stern warnings of judgment, rather like Isaiah or some of the Psalms. It was the beauty of the Quran that converted Umar (also spelled Omar) to Islam; he later presided over the conquests of Persia, Syria, and Egypt.

Umar had been a strong young pagan with a fierce temper. One day he decided to kill Muhammad, whom he regarded as a troublemaker. But on the way, a friend suggested that perhaps Umar should talk to his sister first. The friend knew that Umar's sister and her husband had secretly become Muslims. Umar immediately marched to their house and heard them reciting a new verse of the Quran. In a fit of anger he hit his brother-in-law; then, when his sister tried to stop him, he hit her, too. The sight of his sister's blood brought Umar to his senses. Ashamed and slightly calmer, he asked to read the pages of the Quran that she had been reciting, but his sister insisted that he wash his hands first. Then, having washed himself, Umar read the opening verses of Sura (chapter) 20:

> Not to sadden thee have we sent down this Quran to thee,
> But as a warning for him who fears,
> It is a message from Him Who has made the earth and the lofty
>   heavens!
> The God of Mercy sits on His throne:
> His, what is in the heavens and what is in the earth,
> and what is between them both, and what is beneath the humid soil!
> Thou need not raise thy voice, for He knows the secret whisper, and
>   the yet more hidden.[2]

"What noble and beautiful words," Umar exclaimed, and he promptly went to see Muhammad and become a Muslim.

For a decade, conversions to Islam came slowly. Typical was that of Muhammad's uncle Hamza. In an angry argument with someone who had insulted Muhammad, Hamza shouted, "And I also do not believe in your gods of stone." Hamza, recognizing his true feelings for the first time, walked to Muhammad's home and became a Muslim.

Another young man, Khalid ibn Sa'id, hesitated to convert to Islam because he did not want to quarrel with his father. One night he dreamed that his father was pushing him off a cliff into hell and that Muhammad rescued him at the last moment. When Khalid woke the next morning, he became a Muslim.

Intelligent men gave Muhammad their loyalty not only because of his message, but because of the man himself. Everyone who knew Muhammad recalled how kind and down-to-earth he was. He insisted that servants, slaves, and animals be well-treated, and he gave old peasant women the same full attention that he gave to a tribal chief.

Muhammad tried to lead by gentle example. Once, when Abu Bakr was about to beat a servant who had let a camel go astray, Muhammad laughed and said, "Just look at what he is doing." The hint was enough for Abu Bakr, who stopped immediately.

Muhammad himself could also feel shame. When a girl had neglectfully allowed a prisoner to escape after a battle, Muhammad exploded, "May Allah cut off your hand!" Later, when he saw the girl staring sadly at her hands, wondering which one Allah was going to cut off, Muhammad apologized for his outburst and told her he would pray for Allah to bless everyone he had ever cursed.

Around the year 614, not long after Muhammad began to preach in public, he recited the "Satanic Verses," lines made famous in the West by Salman Rushdie's controversial novel. Muhammad was dismayed by how many people in Mecca were hostile to his religion, and he wondered how he could win them over. One day he had a revelation that three local goddesses, al-Lat, al-Uzza, and al-Manat, would take the form of high-flying swans and mediate between God and man on Judgment Day. The revelation delighted the people of Mecca because it confirmed the faith of their ancestors who had worshipped the three deities. Many Meccans even began to join the Muslims in their prayers.

Muhammad quickly saw that something was terribly wrong. Suddenly, there were four gods—Allah and the three goddesses— instead of one and three priests at local shrines who could dispute

Muhammad's revelations. Perhaps most galling, rich sinners now had the hope that if their offerings to the goddesses were lavish enough, the offenders could negotiate their way out of hell on Judgment Day.

In a few weeks, Muhammad had a new revelation. Satan had tricked him into reciting the verses about the goddesses, and now God refuted these lines. The three goddesses were "mere names" and had "no authority."

When the people of Mecca learned that Muhammad would not compromise with their religious beliefs, they felt betrayed and began to oppose Islam more vigorously. Some threw dirt, garbage, and even sheep innards at Muhammad. Others spread thorns on his doorstep. Pagan masters began to beat Muslim slaves so brutally that Abu Bakr had to buy and free several slaves to rescue them from further beatings. One freed slave was an African, Bilal, who soon became famous for his beautiful prayer calls.

No one dared injure Muhammad because he enjoyed the protection of his clan, the Hashim, headed by his uncle Abu Talib. Although many Hashim were not Muslims, they still felt a duty to defend Muhammad as a matter of tribal honor.

Muhammad's enemies tried a different strategy. The merchants of Mecca declared a boycott against the entire Hashim clan and a related family, the Muttalib, and refused to do any business with them. Khadija, Abu Bakr, and others lost a large part of their fortunes. It is a tribute to Muhammad's leadership that his followers stuck with him despite their financial losses. The boycott lasted more than two years before the coalition behind it broke up. The Muslims could trade only with nomads from the desert and a few of the poorest families in Mecca.

In 619, soon after the end of the boycott, Muhammad's wife, Khadija, died. Muhammad grieved. He had been a faithful husband for twenty-two years, and she had been his first supporter. She had stood by him steadfastly, even when his preaching hurt her business. Then, only a few days later, Muhammad's uncle Abu Talib also died.

The new chief of the Hashim clan vigorously opposed Muhammad's preaching. To trap Muhammad with a trick question, Abu Lahab asked whether his own father, a former chief, was in hell because he had worshipped other gods besides Allah. Muhammad tried to avoid the question but finally said that yes, the new chief's father was in hell. Abu Lahab took the answer as an insult and was able to withdraw his protection from Muhammad without a loss of honor. Muhammad was suddenly without any shield from physical harm and had to stop preaching in public.

uring this difficult time, Muhammad dreamed one night that ... archangel Gabriel put his (Muhammad's) spirit (not his body) on a winged horse that flew to Jerusalem. There he met Abraham, Moses, Aaron, Joseph, Jesus, and other prophets. Muhammad prayed with them a while, then soared through seven levels of heaven and saw the prophets again, this time as beautiful heavenly beings. On Muhammad's way back through the heavens, Moses told him that it was God's will that Muslims did not need to pray constantly; five times a day was enough.

Muslims call this journey the "Night Flight to Jerusalem," but at the time, the people of Mecca mocked Muhammad for having such a grandiose dream. Seventy-two years later, however, the Muslims who ruled Jerusalem built the huge Dome of the Rock over the stone near the Temple Mount where they believed that Muhammad had left a footprint when he made a second trip to Jerusalem, just before he died and ascended to heaven.

In 620, Muhammad's fortunes improved. Six men arrived from Yathrib, an oasis 220 miles to the north that would soon be renamed Medinat al-Nabi ("the City of the Prophet") or, more simply, Medina. The six sheikhs had long talks with Muhammad and were impressed by his message and his character. Medina was a collection of orchards, fields, and palm groves where eleven tribes lived together, although they often quarreled violently. Three of the tribes were Jewish, so the Arabs there were familiar with the idea that there was just one God, and sometimes they felt inferior to the Jews because they did not have a scripture of their own. The men from Medina were thrilled to meet an Arab prophet with an Arabic scripture, and they thought that perhaps Muhammad was the Messiah whom the Jews said would come one day.

The six leaders also realized that because Muhammad was an outsider and not aligned with any tribe in Medina, he could probably settle disputes and make life there much more peaceful. These men became Muslims at once and told Muhammad they would return the next year.

The following year, five of them did return to Mecca, along with seven others whom they had converted. The twelve men represented most of the Arab tribes of Medina, and they solemnly promised to worship Allah exclusively, to obey Muhammad, and to avoid adultery and other sins.

During 621 and the spring of 622, whole clans in Medina became Muslim. In an age where poetry was a means of communication as important as television and movies are today, the beauty of the Arabic Quran won many hearts and minds.

Muhammad also tried to win the support of the Jews of Medina, who spoke Arabic, owned most of the city's palm groves, and made swords, clothes, and wine. He told his followers to stop eating pork, to fast on Yom Kippur, to pray in the direction of Jerusalem, and to hold prayers on Friday afternoons when the Jews were about to begin their Sabbath. (Friday has been the Muslim Sabbath day ever since.)

Finally, in June 622, the eight Arab tribes of Medina invited Muhammad and his followers to live in Medina. They pledged to obey him as the Messenger of God and to fight for him against any enemies. Because this was a promise by different tribes to give protection to a group unrelated by blood, it was a revolutionary social arrangement, unprecedented in Arabia.

During the summer, Muhammad asked his followers to leave their homes and possessions behind and begin new lives in Medina. He could not command them to take such a drastic step, and several Muslims chose to stay in Mecca. But quietly, a few at a time so as not to draw any attention, seventy Muslim families made the scorching, ten-day trek through the desert to Medina.

By September, the people of Mecca finally realized what was happening. They worried that the Muslims in Medina would threaten their trade route to Syria, and they decided that they had to kill Muhammad. The plan was for one member of every major clan in Mecca to stab Muhammad to death. This would make revenge impossible because no one could declare a vendetta against the entire city.

Muhammad got word of the plot and left Mecca in the middle of the night with his friend Abu Bakr, who had camels and food ready for the journey. To make the Meccans think that Muhammad was still at home, Muhammad's cousin Ali wrapped himself in Muhammad's green cloak and slept in the Prophet's bed with the window open. Not until morning did the Meccans learn of Muhammad's escape and set out in pursuit.

For Muhammad, it was the end of a difficult era. After twelve long years of preaching in his home city, he had almost no following in Mecca. He was fleeing for his life.

The Years in Medina

Muhammad and Abu Bakr headed south, in the opposite direction from Mecca, and hid in a cave for three days while the Meccans hunted for them, spurred by an offer of a hundred female camels as a reward for the Prophet's capture. According to traditional legends, several Meccans found the cave, but they did not go in because a spider had covered the entrance with a large web. At last, Muhammad and Abu Bakr traveled north toward Medina, zigzagging along rarely traveled routes through particularly harsh desert. This journey is known as the *hijrah* (also spelled "hegira") or "emigration," and the Muslim lunar calendar dates from this year, 622, when the Muslims first began to be a self-governing community.

Muhammad arrived in Medina at the end of September. At first, he was just one of a dozen tribal leaders in the city, with some extra prestige that allowed him to arbitrate disputes. To remain impartial and to avoid having to accept the hospitality of any one particular tribe, Muhammad let his camel loose and made his home where the camel stopped and rested. He offered to buy the land from its owners, but they insisted on giving the plot to Muhammad. He then built two mud-brick huts, with palm-thatched roofs and dirt floors, and laid out a small courtyard for prayer and business.

Like his followers, Muhammad lived simply. He slept on a mat, cobbled his own shoes, mended his own clothes, and tended goats. He ate mostly dates and milk, but some nights, if dates were not in season and there was not enough food, he and his wives went hungry. He was careful about his personal hygiene. Muhammad washed before prayer, kept his teeth clean by using a root as a toothpick, and rubbed oil on his sun-baked body. He looked quite young for a man in his fifties.

During their first months in Medina, the Muslims from Mecca were completely dependent on the hospitality of their new converts. The trading skills that had served the Muslims so well in Mecca were of limited use in Medina, a much more fertile oasis where there was less need to trade. The Muslims knew little about farming, and it would be several years before they were fully self-sufficient.

In the spring of 623, the Muslims built a large mud-brick mosque next to Muhammad's courtyard. At last, they had a temple of their own where they could pray in public. Muhammad loved prayer and compared it to bathing in a fresh river. He said that the archangel Gabriel had shown him the proper movements and prostrations of a Muslim prayer.

Once, when Muhammad spent the night at the home of a friend, ibn Abbas, he recited a long prayer that included these lines:

> My Lord, to You belongs all praise. You are the light of heaven and
>   earth and all therein;
> Praise be to You, the true Lord; Your promise is true; Whatever You
>   say is true;

The meeting with You is true; Heaven is true; Hell is true; t
 Prophets are true;
and the Hour is true.
I submit myself to You; I believe in You and depend on You. To You
 I return.[3]

Devout Muslims pray five times a day: at dawn, noon, midafternoon, sunset, and early evening. At the first light of dawn, the prayer
caller, or *muezzin*, wakes up the faithful by shouting "*Allahu Akbar*"
("God is great!") three times, followed by the profession of faith,
"There is but one God, Muhammad is His Messenger." The *muezzin*
also says, "Prayer is better than sleep!" When Muhammad was alive,
men and women prayed side by side. Later, when Medina became a
bigger city, prayers were segregated to prevent the mingling of strangers of the opposite sex.

Muhammad did not expect to convert the Jews of Medina to
Islam. He deeply admired Judaism and hoped only that the Jews
would acknowledge him as another messenger in their long line of
prophets. Instead, the Jews pointed out that Muhammad's knowledge
of the Bible was limited, denied the sanctity of the Quran, and challenged his claim to be a prophet.

In the course of his discussions with Jews, Muhammad became
more familiar with the Torah. He learned that the Jews had rejected
many prophets throughout their history, and he claimed that they
were doing so again. He also learned more about Abraham and
concluded that Abraham had not been a Jew, for Judaism did not
really begin until after his lifetime. Abraham became the prophet
Muhammad admired most because Abraham was not a religious
scholar but simply an ordinary man who believed in one God and in
Judgment Day. Muhammad said that Islam was a return to the simple
faith of Abraham, a faith untarnished by the many arguments between
Jews and Christians.

After a year and a half in Medina, Muhammad gave up trying to
win the acceptance of the Jews. One day early in 624, after some Jews
had scoffed at his prayers, Muhammad turned his body in the middle
of a service, and instead of bowing toward Jerusalem, he bowed
toward the Kaaba, the stone cube in Mecca that Abraham and his
son Ishmael were said to have built long ago. Later, Muhammad
also changed the time of fasting from Yom Kippur to the month of
Ramadan. Because of Islam's 354-day lunar calendar, Ramadan moves
backward through the seasons eleven days every year, so the fast is
not associated with any one season or its decorations.

The Muslims from Mecca desperately wanted to make their own living. Since they were not farmers, they began to raid caravans traveling to and from Mecca. Caravan raiding was a common practice in Arabia, something of a sport, and was not considered wrong as long as no one was killed. The Muslims' first raids were unsuccessful because enemies in Medina leaked information about the raids to the merchants of Mecca. But in January 624, Muhammad gave sealed instructions to his raiders, and this time they captured a small caravan, taking two Meccans as prisoners in the process. One prisoner was so impressed by the happy egalitarian community in Medina that he chose to stay and become a Muslim himself. Later, other prisoners made the same decision.

Two months later, a huge caravan of a thousand camels passed near Medina on its way from Gaza to Mecca. With 320 men, Muhammad tried to raid the caravan at a desert crossroad called Badr. The leader of the caravan, Abu Sufyan, scouted the path himself in advance of his caravan, and seeing camel droppings, he rubbed them and found date seeds inside. He concluded that the camels must have come from Medina because it was the only place nearby where dates were so plentiful that people fed them to camels. He realized that Muhammad's men were scouting this crossroad, too. Abu Sufyan quickly moved his caravan away from Badr and safely down the coast of the Red Sea.

The people of Mecca were outraged that Muhammad would try to attack the biggest caravan of the year. They decided to send more than nine hundred men to Badr, including a hundred in armor, to teach Muhammad a lesson. The Muslims were outnumbered three to one, but they reached Badr first and filled all of its wells with sand except one. When the thirsty Meccans arrived at the well that the Muslims had left intact, they were at the bottom of a hill, with the morning sun shining in their eyes.

Battles in ancient Arabia began with the strongest men on each side fighting in hand-to-hand combat, but soon everyone joined in a wild free-for-all of swords, javelins, and bows and arrows. The Muslims were more disciplined than the Meccans, and their archers shot volley after volley of arrows. The chief difference between the two armies was in their fighting spirit—Muhammad had told his soldiers that death in battle would lead to paradise, and they believed him.

The fearless Muslims routed the Meccans. They killed about fifty men, took seventy prisoners, including two of Muhammad's cousins, and lost only fourteen men of their own. The prisoners were held for ransom, but Muhammad insisted that they be treated kindly and they should eat the same food the Muslims ate. Today, when Muslim extremists mistreat their hostages, they are violating one of the traditional laws of Islam.

The battle at Badr was the first Muslim victory, and it was against the strongest city in Arabia. To the Muslims, it was proof that Muhammad was indeed the Messenger of God. Within weeks, almost all of the Arabs in Medina became Muslims; Medina now became a religious, rather than a tribal, community.

Meanwhile, in Mecca, Abu Sufyan swore that he would not sleep with women until he had his revenge against the Muslims, and he persuaded his fellow merchants to devote the entire profit of their large caravan to preparations for war. The following year, three thousand Meccans rode to Medina, two hundred on horseback and the rest on camels, and seven hundred of them wore coats of armor. They camped on a hill outside Medina called Uhud and let their animals graze in the Muslims' fields. Against this force, the Muslims had only seven hundred men, including fifty archers, and just two horses. When the battle started, Muhammad himself fired arrows. He ordered the archers not to break ranks, but at some point they began to plunder the dead, and the Meccans seized their opportunity to advance. The Meccans killed seventy Muslims, wounded Muhammad with a blow to his head, and lost only about twenty-five of their own.

The Meccans could not follow up on their gains, however, because most of their horses had arrow wounds and because Medina was a well-fortified city. So despite their efforts, Muhammad remained in power. The Meccans had to be content with revenge, and it was grisly. Some Meccan women made necklaces out of the ears and the noses of dead Muslims, and one woman, whose father died at Badr, chewed the liver of Muhammad's uncle Hamza. "Today is in exchange for Badr," Abu Sufyan shouted at the Muslims. "War is like a well-bucket, sometimes up, sometimes down."

Although the battle of Uhud was a draw, many Muslims counted their dead and saw it as a defeat. Like certain biblical prophets before him, Muhammad assured his followers that God was still on their side but was testing their faith. Still, the Muslims were in an angry mood. Muhammad accused one of the Jewish tribes in Medina of plotting to kill him, and he demanded that they leave the city. At first, the Jews refused to go, but when the Muslims began to cut down the tribe's palm trees, they agreed to leave. They moved to Khaybar, a city ninety miles to the north where they owned some land. Muhammad gave the Jews' palm groves to the seventy Muslim families who had left Mecca. For the first time, these Muslims were owners of land and no longer dependent on anyone for support.

After the battle of Uhud, there were dozens of widows in Medina. It was at this time that Muhammad received the revelation that men could marry up to four wives, provided that they could support and genuinely care for each one. Although this portion of the Quran may seem sexist to Westerners today, it was a reform at the time. In ancient Arabia, a man sometimes married a widow for her property and then treated her with indifference; according to the Quran, a man can marry again only if he treats his new wife equitably.

Muhammad himself exceeded the limit of four wives, eventually taking a total of ten wives (and one concubine) in his lifetime. His followers did not see this as unusual because in the Middle East, until recently, most rulers had many wives. Solomon, for example, had more than seven hundred. Nor does the number of Muhammad's wives bother Muslims today. Even Muslim women will say with pride that Muhammad was the most human of the world's religious leaders.

As Muhammad took more wives, the possibilities for gossip grew. One wife's hand accidentally brushed against the hand of a male guest while she was serving him food. Another wife who was outdoors one evening received a bawdy comment from a non-Muslim. Soon there were two new verses in the Quran: one commanded women to dress modestly; the other required that the Prophet's wives stay at home, behind a curtain.

The practice of keeping women in *purdah*, or "seclusion," which still continues today in some Muslim countries, thus began as a sign of status, reserved for the wives of Muhammad. *Purdah* was already widespread, however, among upper-class women in Persia and in the eastern half of the Byzantine Empire. When the Muslims conquered these regions soon after Muhammad died, thousands of soldiers remained there, married, and adopted the "elite" new custom.

Muhammad's relationships with his wives and daughters were easygoing and informal; they were not afraid to talk back to him. Muhammad also wanted a son, but none of his sons lived beyond infancy. Because of this, he particularly loved his two grandsons, Hasan and Hussein, and even let them climb on his back during prayers.

Usually, the reason for a marriage was political. Muhammad married the daughters of his closest followers, the daughters of chiefs who had converted to Islam, and several widows of followers who had died in battle. Only about half of the Prophet's wives were thought to be attractive.

In general, Muhammad preferred mature women. Eight of Muhammad's ten wives were widows, and one was a divorcee. Each wife had her own hut next to Muhammad's courtyard, and Muhammad slept one night in turn with each of them, except that the elderly Sawdah, a housekeeper to whom Muhammad had given his protection, voluntarily yielded her turn to Aisha, the daughter of his best friend, Abu Bakr.

Aisha was nine when she married the fifty-year-old Muhammad, but she continued to live with her parents and play with dolls and toy horses. The marriage was not consummated for another four years. Aisha was the only virgin among the ten wives Muhammad ultimately married. She was mature for her age, beautiful, intelligent, and full of laughter. She remained Muhammad's favorite until he died.

One evening the wives flew into an uproar when Muhammad slept with a Christian concubine named Mary on a night that had been reserved for another wife. Greatly annoyed by the quarreling, Muhammad moved away from his harem and said that he would not sleep with any of his wives for a month. It was a tense time as each wife wondered whether Muhammad might ask for a divorce. Finally, after four weeks, Muhammad returned to Aisha's hut with a stern look. "I thought you said you would be away for a month," Aisha said with a smile. Muhammad had to laugh, "Well, this month has just twenty-eight days."

In 626, Muhammad made several raids against desert tribes allied with Mecca. During one raid, Aisha lost a necklace, and while she was looking for it, several soldiers put her curtained carriage back on her camel without realizing that she was not inside. When Aisha found the necklace and returned to the campsite, the soldiers and the camels were gone.

Eventually, a handsome young man named Sufwan rode by, put Aisha on his camel, and walked in front of the beast, pulling the rein. When they arrived at the new campsite, people immediately gossiped about what the young couple had or had not done together.

Muhammad did not know what to think. Most of the young people in Medina continued to believe in Aisha's virtue, but Muhammad's cousin and adopted son, Ali, coolly said that women were plentiful and could easily be replaced.

After a month, Muhammad asked Aisha directly to confess any sin, assuring her that God would forgive her. Aisha calmly said that she had nothing to confess. Finally, Muhammad had a revelation that Aisha was innocent and that three men who had slandered Aisha should be punished with eighty lashes each. Aisha resumed her role as

Muhammad's favorite wife, but she never forgave Ali for his unkind remark, and the enmity between them contributed to a civil war thirty years later.

In March 627, the Meccans marched toward Medina with almost ten thousand soldiers, an unheard-of number in Arabia. Their forces included many desert nomads and also the Jewish tribe that Muhammad had expelled from Medina.

Medina is surrounded by cliffs and lava formations on three sides, but the lower, northern portion of the city was vulnerable to attack. Fortunately for Muhammad, a recent convert from Persia named Salman suggested an idea that was new to Arabia: that the Muslims build a deep trench wide enough to stop horses. Muhammad himself started to dig. The entire city joined in, singing as they worked. They also harvested their grain early so that they would have plenty to eat. They completed the trench in six days, just in time.

When the horde from Mecca arrived, they halted in complete surprise just outside the range of the Muslim archers. They had never seen a trench before. Bewildered, they stared at it and shook their heads. They shouted insults at the Muslims and called the trench dishonorable and un-Arabic. But after three weeks, their camels and horses began to run out of grass to eat. When a driving rainstorm blew out their campfires, the massive army went home.

The unsuccessful siege of Medina was a great victory for Muhammad because it proved to everyone in Arabia that the Muslims could not be defeated by force. But during the three weeks of siege, the Muslims had been quite fearful. The last of the large Jewish tribes in Medina, the Qurayzah, had talked with the Meccans about the possibility of letting them into Medina through one of the lava formations on the south side of the city. The negotiations broke down over the issue of guarantees for the Jews' safety, but to the Muslims, any contact at all with the Meccans was treason.

As soon as the Meccan army left Medina, Muhammad ordered his soldiers to surround the Jews and demanded that they surrender unconditionally. The Jews asked to be allowed to go to the city of Khaybar, as other Jews had done two years earlier, but Muhammad saw no reason to swell the ranks of his enemies. He suggested instead that the dispute be settled by Saad ibn Muad, the leader of the Aws, an Arab tribe in Medina that had long been allied to the Jews.

The Jews agreed to the arbitration, but to their horror, Saad ordered that all of the Jewish men be executed and all of the women and the children sold into slavery. The Aws chief, who was dying from a painful battle wound, had ruled far more harshly than anyone had expected.

Before each execution, the Muslims gave the Jews a chan[ce to] profess the Muslim faith, and when someone did, he was immediately accepted by the Muslims as an equal. But few chose this path. Almost all of the Jews chose to die. Five or six hundred men were beheaded, about six at a time. Most of the women and the children, fortunately, were bought and freed by their relatives in Khaybar.

As biographer Karen Armstrong has observed,

> It is probably impossible for us to disassociate this story from Nazi atrocities and it will inevitably alienate many people irrevocably from Muhammad. But . . . this was a very primitive society, far more primitive than the Jewish society in which Jesus had lived and promulgated his gospel of mercy and love some 600 years earlier. . . . Medina was probably more like the Jerusalem of King David, who was a mighty slayer of enemies.[4]

Muhammad ordered the killing of the Jews because he thought they were a serious threat to Medina's security. He was not anti-Semitic. Once, for example, Muhammad stood up as a Jewish funeral procession passed by. When a companion asked him why he was paying respects to a non-Muslim, Muhammad answered, "Was he not a living being?" Another time, Muhammad became angry when a young Muslim beat a Jew because the Jew had sworn an oath, "By Him Who chose Moses above all mankind," which implied that Moses was superior to Muhammad. Muhammad, however, had no objection to the oath and scolded his follower, "Don't ever say that I am better than Moses."

Muhammad had enormous respect for Jews and Christians as "People of the Book [Bible]," and the Quran mentions Moses 130 times and Jesus dozens more. Later, as Islam spread throughout the world, tens of thousands of Jews prospered in Alexandria, Cordoba, Constantinople, and many other cities. Even in Medina, hundreds of Jews, unaffiliated with the large Jewish tribes, lived in peace among the Muslims for generations. Muhammad cannot be charged with personal bigotry; one of his wives, Safiyah, had been Jewish before her marriage. *[Safiyah Jewish wife]*

In 628, one year after the siege, Muhammad dreamed that he was making a pilgrimage to the Kaaba in Mecca. When he awoke, he invited his followers to come with him. Wearing white cloth and armed only with swords during a traditional month of truce, Muhammad took fifteen hundred men and women to the outskirts of Mecca. There, he asked Mecca's leaders to allow the Muslims to make the pilgrimage to the Kaaba, which by tradition was the right of all Arabs. The Meccans refused.

After much talk, Muhammad and the Meccans agreed to a treaty. The Muslims had to go home that year, but they could return in future years and pray at the Kaaba. Umar and many other of Muhammad's impatient soldiers were outraged and wanted to march to Mecca right then, but Muhammad restrained them. He had won the right to enter Mecca soon enough, and he knew this was a great victory.

Muhammad also agreed not to attack any Meccan caravans for ten years, and in turn, the Meccans agreed to give up their monopoly on trade with Syria and other nations. The older men of Mecca were content to win a decade of peace, but the young men knew that Medina was now the stronger and more dynamic city, and many of them began to convert to Islam. An interesting provision of the treaty was that if a young Meccan arrived in Medina to embrace Islam without permission from his father, the Muslims would have to send him back to Mecca. Muhammad made these concessions because he was not interested in conquering the Meccans but in converting them. Muhammad wanted to unify *all* of the Arabs under Islam, and he knew that he would soon need the administrative skills of the well-educated Meccan merchants.

The following year, Muhammad went to Mecca again with more than two thousand Muslims. Many Meccans left the city for several days but watched the Muslims from the hillsides. To their amazement, Bilal, the African they had known as a lowly slave, climbed to the top of the sacred Kaaba and gave the prayer calls.

Muhammad circled the Kaaba seven times, as was the tradition, and ignored the idols. The Muslims, back in Mecca after six and a half years, impressed the Meccans with their manners and their discipline and made conversions by the hundreds. The people of Mecca began to feel that they had nothing to fear from the Muslims because, even under Islam, the lucrative pilgrimages to the Kaaba were going to continue.

In January 630, the patience and diplomacy that Muhammad had shown two years earlier paid off. With new converts from desert tribes, Muhammad surrounded Mecca with ten thousand men. For several days, he assured the people of Mecca that no one would harm them if they stayed in their homes. Finally, he and his followers entered the city.

Muhammad walked around the Kaaba seven times, then smashed the 360 idols, saying, "Truth has come. The lies shall stop." Muhammad spared a statue of Mary and Jesus and a painting of Abraham. Soon, it seemed as if the entire city of Mecca was converting to Islam. Encouraged by Muhammad, who offered an amnesty to his former enemies, the Meccans even destroyed the idols inside their own homes. Only seven years earlier, Muhammad had fled Mecca for his life. Now the people of his home city acknowledged him as the Messenger of God.

During the next several weeks, Muslim soldiers destroyed the shrines of two of the goddesses mentioned in the Satanic Verses. But the people of the city of Taif, east of Mecca, quickly assembled an army of thousands of nomads to defend the shrine of the third goddess, al-Lat.

To confront this force, twelve thousand Muslims rode to Taif, including two thousand of the newly converted Meccans. The disciplined Muslims easily defeated the unorganized nomads, and from then on, tribes all over Arabia sent delegations to Muhammad to ask him for protection. Muhammad demanded that each tribe convert to Islam and pay an annual tax of one-fortieth of their crops and herds to help the poor. The tribesmen knew that paying this tax, called *zakat*, was preferable to being subject to raids. Even in faraway Bahrain, an island in the Persian Gulf, tribal chiefs sought a political alliance with Muhammad. For the first time in history, the Arabs were united.

One chief in central Arabia also claimed to be a prophet. When Muhammad's power grew, this chief wrote, "From Musailama the Messenger of God to Muhammad the Messenger of God, let us divide the earth between us." Muhammad replied with scorn, "From Muhammad the Messenger of God to Musailama the Liar, the earth belongs to Allah. He causes His servants to inherit it as He pleases."

In March 632, Muhammad made his last pilgrimage to Mecca, taking all of his wives along. On a hillside, he spoke to tens of thousands of his followers and reviewed the main points of Islam. He reminded everyone that all Muslims are brothers and sisters, whatever their tribe or race. He concluded by asking the crowd, "Have I delivered my message?" and when the Muslims roared their approval, Muhammad said, "Oh God, bear witness."

Muslims summarize Islam by its five "pillars":

- To make the profession of the faith: "There is but one God, Muhammad is His Messenger."
- To pray toward Mecca five times a day
- To fast during daylight during the month of Ramadan
- To give one-fortieth of one's income-producing assets to the needy each year
- To make at least one pilgrimage to Mecca during one's life, if possible

Three months after his last pilgrimage, Muhammad suffered a terrible fever and headache and died, possibly of pneumonia, with his head in Aisha's lap in her hut in Medina, on June 8, 632. Before dying, he insisted several times that only his old friend Abu Bakr lead the prayer services. His last words were, "Lord grant me pardon and join me to the companionship in Paradise." He was sixty-two.

When the fiery Umar heard the news, he did not believe that Muhammad had died. For twenty-two years, the Muslims had felt that the revelation of the Quran through Muhammad was a direct connection to God. Now Umar and others could not believe that this contact had ended. "Muhammad will return as Moses returned from Mount Sinai," Umar told a crowd, "and if anyone says the Messenger of God is dead, I will cut off his hands and feet!" But Abu Bakr arrived, told Umar to stop, and said to the crowd, "If anyone worships Muhammad, let him know now that Muhammad is dead. But if anyone worships God, let him know that God is alive and lives forever."

Within twelve years, the Muslims, led by Umar, conquered all of the land from Libya to Iran. Within eighty years, the Muslim Empire stretched from Spain to India. Today, after nearly fourteen hundred years, Islam remains the dominant religion from Morocco to Indonesia, the faith of almost one-fourth of humanity.

Muhammad's thousands of sayings (*hadith*) were carefully recorded by his followers after his death. Here are seven of them:

Seven Sayings of Muhammad[5]

- Truly, reducing pride and conceit to nothing is a task of seventy years.

- Second only to faith in God is love for people.

- A father can give his children no possession more precious than good manners.

- On Resurrection Day the ink of the scholar will weigh more heavily than the blood of martyrs.

- No one ever suffered from seeking advice, nor gained by being willful.

- God helps His servant to the extent that His servant helps others.

- God's pardon exceeds your guilt.

Five Excerpts from the Quran[6]

Sura (Chapter) 1

Praise be to God, Lord of the worlds!
The compassionate, the merciful!
King on the day of reckoning!
Thee only do we worship, and to Thee do we cry for help.
Guide Thou us on the straight path,
The path with those to whom Thou hast been gracious;
With whom Thou art not angry, and who go not astray.

Sura 29, Verse 45

Dispute not, unless in a kindly sort,
With people of the Book [Christians and Jews];
Save with such of them as have dealt wrongfully with you:
And say ye, "We believe in what has been sent down
To us and has been sent down to you.
Our God and your God is one,
And to Him we surrender our selves."

Sura 107

What thinkest thou of him who treats our religion as a lie?
He it is who thrusts away the orphan,
And stirs not to feed the poor.
Woe to those who pray,
But in their prayer are careless;
Who make a show of devotion,
But refuse help to the needy.

Sura 112

Say: He is God Alone:
God the Eternal!
He begets not, and He is not begotten;
And there is none like unto Him.

Sura 56, Verses 22–23, 29–35, and 92–97

And theirs shall be the Houris [virgins], with large dark eyes,
Like pearls hidden in their shells,
In recompense of labors past. . . .
And in exalted shade,
And by flowing waters,
And with abundant fruits,
Unfailing, unforbidden,

And on lofty couches
Of a rare creation we created the Houris,
And we have made them ever virgins. . . .
But for him who shall be of those who treat the prophets
as deceivers,
And of the erring,
His entertainment shall be scalding water,
And the broiling of hell-fire.
Verily this is a certain truth:
Praise therefore the name of thy Lord, the Great.

2

The Successors Who Preserved the Faith and Began the Conquests: Abu Bakr and Umar (632–644)

AFTER MUHAMMAD DIED, the Prophet's two best friends led the Muslims for twelve years as they spread their faith north to Iraq and Syria, east to Persia, and west to Egypt. Abu Bakr (c. 572–634) ruled only two years before he died, but he defeated a dozen rebellious tribes, silenced their would-be prophets, and reunified Arabia. Then, in one dramatic decade, Umar (c. 583–644) destroyed the Persian Empire; took Syria, Palestine, and Egypt away from the Byzantines; and made the Muslims the most powerful community on Earth for almost a millennium.

Abu Bakr and Umar called themselves *khalifa*, Arabic for "successor." In English, the word is *caliph*. Muslims call the Prophet's first four successors (Abu Bakr, Umar, Uthman, and Ali) "The Rightly Guided Caliphs" because all four were early followers of Muhammad, totally devoted to Islam, and indifferent to money or the trappings of power.

The Quran makes no mention of how Muslims should govern themselves, and Muhammad never spoke of having a successor. Once Muhammad died, there were several possibilities. Some people thought that Muhammad's son-in-law Ali should be caliph, but most Muslims felt that at thirty-two, he was too young to be their leader, and they also had an instinctive dislike of anything resembling a monarchy.

In Medina, the people wanted their own caliph. After ten years of hosting Muhammad and his followers, they were tired of taking direction from them. "Let's have two chiefs," they said, "one for the people from Mecca, and one for the people from Medina."

Abu Bakr and Umar both knew this was a dangerous idea. Muslims would never stay united if they had two caliphs from different cities. The two men went to a tribal meeting to convince Medina's citizens of the need for unity. Upon arriving, though, the gentle Abu Bakr turned to his blunt, hot-tempered friend and said, "Umar, please stay silent."

Patiently, Abu Bakr reminded the people of Medina of the need for unity if they were going to keep the fiercely independent tribesmen in other parts of Arabia from abandoning Islam. He also assured them that he and the other men from Mecca would never make an important decision without consulting them first. The Medinans were pleased to hear this because if Abu Bakr made a promise, they knew he would keep it. His nickname was the *Siddiq* ("Truthful"). Finally, Abu Bakr shouted, "You, the people of Medina, should choose whether our caliph will be Umar or Abu Ubeida."

Umar broke in. "No, I could never rule over you. You were in the cave with Muhammad on the journey to Medina, and you are the one the Prophet chose to lead the prayers last week. You shall be caliph!" The Medinans hailed their approval, for they knew from experience that the *Siddiq* was also a man of sound judgment.

Abu Bakr, the First Caliph (632–634)

Abu Bakr was about sixty and frail, and he walked with a stoop. A successful cloth merchant, he nevertheless wore simple clothes, although he liked to dye his beard red. The new caliph was soft-spoken but was considered a good speaker because his words were always worth hearing.

Abu Bakr was by far the most loyal of Muhammad's followers. A friend of the Prophet's since childhood, Abu Bakr was the first grown man to accept Muhammad's teaching. "Everyone I called to Islam had to think about it for a while," Muhammad once said, "but Abu Bakr accepted it without any hesitation." When Muhammad dreamed his night flight to Jerusalem, even some Muslims had trouble accepting it. By contrast, Abu Bakr said, "I believe anything the Messenger of God says."

Once, before the battle of Tabuk, Muhammad asked his followers for money to pay for the battle. Umar gave Muhammad half of his fortune, but Abu Bakr gave the prophet all that he had. "Have you left anything for your wife and children?" Muhammad asked. "Yes," Abu Bakr replied, "we still have Allah and His Prophet."

Still handsome despite his age, the new caliph was the father of Aisha, Muhammad's favorite and prettiest wife. Abu Bakr had four wives during his life but divorced one because she wouldn't accept Islam. Another wife died young. He had three sons and three daughters, but one son did not convert to Islam until the conquest of Mecca in 630. Later, this son said, "Father, at the battle of Badr I had the opportunity to kill you but held back." Abu Bakr looked at him sternly and said, "Son, if I had had the chance, I would not have spared you."

In his first speech as caliph, Abu Bakr declared, "The weak shall be strong with me, until they get what is due them, and the strong shall be weak with me, until they have yielded to the rights of others. . . . Obey me as long as I obey Allah and His Prophet, but if I disobey them, then obey me not."

Abu Bakr's first act as caliph was to continue with a raid that Muhammad had ordered against some frontier fortresses of the Byzantine Empire in Syria. The purpose of the raid was to avenge a previous defeat and also to carry off plunder. To lead this new army of seven hundred men, Muhammad chose a nineteen-year-old whose father had been killed by Byzantine soldiers. The boy's name was Osama.

Before the troops left, Abu Bakr cautioned them, "Do not kill women, children, or old people. Do not burn crops or orchards . . . and if you see monks praying in Christian monasteries, leave them alone."

Osama's raid was successful; he and his men returned to Medina in only six weeks. It was not a moment too soon. More than a dozen tribes were rejecting Islam; they especially hated the annual tax of one-fortieth (2.5 percent) of one's wealth that Muslims paid to help the poor. Many tribesmen said that they liked Islam and objected only to the tax.

Some of Abu Bakr's advisers, including Umar, said that since there were many clans to subdue, perhaps it would be better to compromise on the tax. But Abu Bakr refused to let Muslims pick and choose among their obligations. "Umar," the caliph asked, "you were such a harsh man when you were young. Are you so mild now that you will allow our faith to be mutilated? By Allah, if the tribes withhold even a piece of rope from their taxes, I will go to war against them."

Several tribes rejected not only the poor-tax, but Islam itself. Interestingly, no tribe rejected monotheism. Once a tribe abandoned its idols, there was no going back. But a number of clans developed prophets of their own and saw no reason to follow the commands of a dead man from Mecca. One new prophet was a woman, Sajah, who combined forces and married another prophet, Musailama, the impostor whom Muhammad had denounced as a liar.

For the first time, Muslims began to insist that Muhammad was the last and the greatest of the prophets. They cited Sura 33, verse 40, of the Quran, which says, "Muhammad is . . . the Apostle of God and the seal of the prophets." To back up this claim, Abu Bakr raised eleven armies to attack rebellious tribes in every part of Arabia. Often, the mere sight of a Muslim army was enough to intimidate a wayward clan back into the faith. In such cases, no one was punished, and a Quran reciter was left behind to teach the Arab tribesmen the tenets of their new religion.

Other tribes fought fiercely. The best Muslim general was Khalid ibn al-Walid, also known as "the Sword of Allah." Khalid had defeated the Muslims at the battle of Uhud but later converted to Islam when the Muslims took Mecca. He was an excellent rider, a fearless fighter, and a skillful tactician, especially in the sudden, surprising use of rearguard troops. Sometimes he divided his army by tribes, to encourage rivalry as to which one could fight the most bravely.

In battle, horsemen galloped heedlessly into enemy lines carrying lances and javelins, while infantrymen fired bows and arrows. The soldiers spurred each other on with shouts such as "Adorn the Quran with deeds!" or "Look, Muslims! An attack is made like this."

Khalid's army killed the false prophet Musailama and thousands of his soldiers but lost twelve hundred of its own men, a far greater loss than any Muslim army had ever suffered before. After this carnage, a smaller Muslim army subdued remote tribes in Bahrain, Oman, and Yemen.

Within one year of Abu Bakr's becoming caliph, all of the would-be prophets had been defeated and Arabia was entirely Muslim. This unity, tested by battle, was far stronger than it had been during the last year of Muhammad's life.

Khalid was a hero, but he had made a powerful enemy: Umar. Once, when Khalid's soldiers had killed a prisoner named Malik, Khalid promptly married Malik's widow, Leila, an unusually beautiful woman. Her husband had fought the Muslims but still claimed to be a Muslim, and this made Khalid liable for murder. Umar was especially angry. "You murdered a believer to take his wife and are unfit for command!" he shouted. Khalid replied that his orders concerning prisoners had been misunderstood. Abu Bakr was doubtful but let it pass, saying, "I will not sheathe a sword which Allah has drawn for His service."

Khalid rejoined his army and shouted insults at Umar before he left Medina. Later, after the battle with Musailama, he married Musailama's granddaughter right on the battlefield where hundreds of his soldiers were freshly buried. Abu Bakr wrote to Khalid of his disapproval. Umar, whose brother had died in this battle, seethed with silent anger.

Seven hundred of the Muslim warriors who died at the Garden of Death had been able to recite at least part of the Quran, and the number of people who knew the entire work by heart was now probably less than a dozen. Umar worried that after another such battle, parts of the Quran would be lost forever, and he suggested that the Quran's verses be collected into a single volume. Abu Bakr assigned the task to Zaid ibn Thabit. A careful man, Zaid checked every line with Muhammad's friends and relatives. The work took more than twelve years.

Between 602 and 628, the Persian and Byzantine empires had fought a series of wars that left both powers exhausted. Persia (which included Iraq) was particularly weak because a power struggle had resulted in the massacre of almost every man of royal blood in 628. Persia then suffered through nine rulers in just four years. Christian Arabs who lived along the Euphrates River were especially unhappy because the Persian kings frequently raised taxes to pay for the wars. With Arabia united and Persia vulnerable, Abu Bakr ordered his army to raid Iraq in 633.

Khalid and his army first marched to the rich port of Ubulla, on the Persian Gulf, from whence ships carried silver to India and spices back home. The general offered the city a choice: convert to Islam, pay an annual tribute, or fight. The town chose to pay tribute.

For centuries, this three-pronged alternative was the standard offer whenever a Muslim army approached a new city and its surrounding farms. If townsmen chose to become Muslims, the soldiers immediately accepted them as brothers (although if the citizens backed away from their new faith later, they were killed as apostates). Until the ninth century, however, non-Arabs could not serve in the army or govern a province. In fact, the early Muslims often preferred their subjects to remain Christian or Jewish because they paid higher taxes than Muslims did.

If a city agreed to pay tribute, Muslims promised in return to protect the town's buildings, fields, churches, and synagogues, an obligation they took very seriously. If a Muslim army was forced to abandon a city, it usually returned the tribute to its citizens since it had failed to provide the protection the townspeople had paid for.

Jews and Christians were free to worship unmolested. It was forbidden, however, for Christians to build new churches, proselytize, ring church bells, or carry a cross in a street procession. And the penalty for belittling Muhammad or the Quran was death.

Typically, a city dweller's annual tribute was several gold pieces and a certain amount of wheat and olive oil. Usually, this was more than the 2.5 percent tax a Muslim paid but somewhat less than the tax the Christian or the Jew had paid the year before to the city's previous ruler. Many townsmen therefore welcomed Muslim rule.

Finally, if a city chose to fight the Muslims and lost, the Arab soldiers felt free to kill the men, carry off the women, and sell the children into slavery.

Muslim law required that soldiers send one-fifth of whatever they collected in tribute or plunder to the caliph, who used it to take care of the poor and to buy weapons and horses for the army. The other four-fifths of the booty served as income for the soldiers since no one paid them a salary.

Beginning with the raids against Persia, vast amounts of gold, jewels, carpets, and grain poured into Medina, yet Abu Bakr had no armed guards and kept no ledgers or accounts. When money arrived, he spent it. The treasury remained empty, a vivid example of his unshakable faith that Allah would provide for the future.

Abu Bakr was utterly indifferent to money and luxury. He never wore jewelry, leather, or fine cloth. When he first became caliph, he still spent his mornings selling cloth in Medina's dusty market, but as his duties took more time, he finally stopped and reluctantly accepted an income that was no more than that of an average citizen. As caliph, Abu Bakr continued to help neighbors milk their goats, but what impressed the Muslims most was that he never once appointed a son or any other relative to public office.

In the spring of 633, Abu Bakr ordered Khalid to lead an army to the west bank of the Euphrates. There, Khalid wrote a letter to the local Persian governor, Hormuz, offering him the choice of Islam, tribute, or war. Khalid cautioned him that if he chose war, "My men love fighting and death as much as you love pleasure and life." Despite this warning, Hormuz chose war and challenged Khalid to personal combat. Khalid accepted and killed him quickly. Then his men slew thousands of Persian soldiers, including those they had taken prisoner, in a massacre known as the Battle of the River of Blood.

One town along the Euphrates had a moat. Khalid stared at it for a while, then ordered his men to kill the weakest camels in the army and fill up one part of the moat with their carcasses. The soldiers stepped over the dead camels and took the town the same day.

Khalid's men crossed the Euphrates briefly and even advanced to the banks of the Tigris, but they did not remain between these two rivers long because the Muslim horsemen did not know how to ride in a land crisscrossed with irrigation ditches. They preferred to stay close to the desert. This is where the Muslims had won most of their battles—and where, if necessary, they could make a hasty retreat.

Most Muslims, including Abu Bakr, were far more interested in taking Syria than Iraq, since they had traded with Syria all their lives and often had traveled there. In 633, Abu Bakr sent four armies of several thousand men each to raid Syria and Palestine, but the Byzantine emperor Heraclius responded by sending four much larger armies of his own.

The Muslim commanders merged their troops into one force, which prompted the Byzantines to combine their armies, too. To meet this new threat, Abu Bakr ordered Khalid and his men to leave Iraq immediately and get to Syria as fast as they could.

In two months, Khalid rushed nine thousand of his soldiers across hundreds of miles of desert. Before entering a two-hundred-mile stretch with no water at all, Khalid first allowed a herd of thirsty camels to gorge themselves with water. Then every few miles, he killed a camel, emptied its bladder, and had his horses drink the water.

After arriving in Syria, Khalid took command of the other Muslim armies and tightened their discipline. The Muslims skirmished with the Byzantines east of Damascus and again outside Gaza. Finally, in August 634, the two forces met by the Yarmuk River, a deep gorge east of the Sea of Galilee. Khalid led a charge that cut the Byzantine cavalry off from its infantry, then used most of the Muslim army to annihilate the cavalry. The Byzantines retreated to the coast, leaving the inland city of Damascus defenseless.

In the middle of this battle, a messenger gave Khalid a letter from Medina. Abu Bakr was dead, and Umar, in his first act as the new caliph, had relieved Khalid of command. Khalid showed the order to his new commander, Abu Ubeida, who quietly put the note in his pocket until the end of the battle. When asked later whether the letter had dampened his fighting spirit, Khalid replied, "I was not fighting for Umar, I was fighting for Allah."

An able warrior himself, Abu Ubeida deeply admired Khalid and constantly sought his advice. The two men had become good friends during the Syrian campaign and continued to work as a team, which took the sting out of Umar's demotion.

Abu Bakr died from a fever he may have caught while taking a bath on a chilly day. During the last two weeks of his life, he talked with many longtime Muslims, and most agreed that the best way to avoid a division among the Muslims was for Abu Bakr to choose the next caliph by himself. Most Muslims also thought that Umar was a more experienced and energetic man than Ali, Muhammad's son-in-law, who was only thirty-four at the time. They also worried that appointing Ali would make the caliphate a hereditary office.

One old man asked, "Abu Bakr, you know how severe Umar is in your service. What will he be like when he rules alone?" The dying caliph replied, "When he bears the burden of office, he will be less fierce. I know his heart is good."

With difficulty, one of Abu Bakr's wives helped the caliph to a window that overlooked Medina's mosque. "I appoint Umar ibn al-Khattab as my successor," Abu Bakr told the congregation. "If he does justice, that will be what I expect and know of him. . . . Will you obey?" the caliph asked. "Yes!" roared hundreds. Later, in private, Abu Bakr gave Umar his parting advice: fear Allah, make truth and the Quran your guide, use persuasion when possible, send more troops to Iraq, and, most important—watch your temper.

Before he died, Abu Bakr repaid two debts, a camel to one friend and a piece of cloth to another. He also sold some land to reimburse the state for the salary it had paid him. At the end of his life, the caliph had no wealth at all.

Abu Bakr asked to be buried next to Muhammad, at his daughter Aisha's hut, and insisted that his body be wrapped in old cloth because "new cloth can be better used by the living." His last words were, "Allah, I pray to Thee that I might die as a Muslim and join the virtuous." He was probably sixty-two when he died on August 23, 634.

Abu Bakr was caliph for only two years and three months, but during this brief period, he unified Arabia without compromising any of the basic principles of Islam, such as paying a tax to help the poor. Tribesmen who had no idea what Islam was when they swore allegiance to Muhammad just three years earlier were now reciting the Quran and fighting and dying to spread Islam to foreign lands.

Umar, the Second Caliph (634–644)

Muhammad once said, "Had Allah willed another prophet after me, it would have been Umar." Tall, strong, and very imposing, Umar ibn al-Khattab looked much younger than his fifty years, even though he was bald and had a thin beard. Rarely prone to self-doubt, Umar was hardworking, impatient, and brutally frank.

Umar was already thirty when he converted to Islam. As a teenager, he had excelled at wrestling, horseback riding, sword fighting, and firing a bow and arrow. In his twenties, he had been a prosperous grain merchant who sometimes traveled to Syria and Yemen by camel. He was one of the roughly twenty people in Mecca who could read and write but was also a forceful speaker who enjoyed the poetry of Arab tribesmen.

By all accounts, Umar's infamous temper was even worse before he embraced Islam. In a fit of anger, he once whipped a female slave simply because she was a Muslim. He used to drink occasionally but stopped cold after he converted (the Quran forbids drinking) and soon whipped drunkards himself.

When Mecca was still hostile to Islam, Umar was the first Muslim to openly prostrate himself in prayer at the Kaaba. Muhammad was so pleased by this act of courage that he gave Umar the nickname *Faruq*—one who distinguishes between truth and falsehood. It was Umar who had suggested adding the line "Prayer is better than sleep!" to the morning prayer call, and later, when he was caliph, it was also his idea to have separate prayers for men and women because Medina had grown in size and worshippers no longer knew one another. Umar also made stoning the punishment for adultery, although the drastic penalty is not mentioned in the Quran.

Umar was a stern husband and father and did not banter with women, as Muhammad had. Once, when he heard Muhammad's wives squabbling over some clothing, he walked into the prophet's compound to see what was the matter, which prompted the startled women to run in terror behind a curtain and Muhammad to howl with laughter. Umar shouted to the women, "Are you afraid of me and not of Allah's Messenger?" "Definitely," one of the wives replied from behind the curtain, "for you are much stricter than the Prophet."

Umar had six wives and three concubines, but he divorced one woman who would not accept Islam. He had nine sons and at least four daughters; the most famous was Hafsah, who became one of Muhammad's wives. Like her father, Hafsah was intelligent and literate and had a quick temper. Umar once told her that she would have to control her jealousy and resign herself to the fact that she was not as pretty as Aisha. (Hafsah and Aisha soon grew as close as sisters.)

Umar was even more severe on himself than he was on others. Determined to follow Muhammad's example of simple living, he ate bread made from unsifted flour and rarely consumed meat. He wore a waistcloth that had twelve patches, according to Muhammad's grandson Hasan, who did the counting. Umar could also humbly take the blunt criticism that he so often dished out, saying, "Allah's mercy be on those who bring me knowledge of my shortcomings."

One of Umar's first acts as caliph was to expel non-Muslims from the Arabian peninsula. When Muhammad was dying, one of the last things he said was, "Let there not be two religions in Arabia." Now Umar was fulfilling the Prophet's wish. The Muslims paid the Jews and the Christians a fair price for their land and gave them several years to leave. The Muslims tolerated Jews and Christians outside of Arabia for centuries, but the homeland was to be purely Muslim. Umar also decreed that no Arab could be a slave, a rule that Arabs have obeyed ever since.

Another of Umar's early deeds was to send more troops to Iraq, as the dying Abu Bakr had asked him to do. Unfortunately, in the fall of 634, the "Battle of the Bridge" on the Euphrates did not go well for the Muslims. Persian elephants trampled a number of Arab soldiers to death, but the Muslims could not retreat because an overly enthusiastic officer had cut a makeshift bridge of boats tied together that the Arabs had built across the river. "Victory or death!" he had shouted, hoping to inspire courage. Instead, the lack of a bridge caused panic, and four thousand soldiers either were cut down by the Persians or drowned in the fast-flowing Euphrates before the rest of the Muslim army could rebuild a bridge and retreat.

When Umar was told about the disaster, he took the news calmly. Realizing that Arabia was now vulnerable to Persian raids, he asked his generals for detailed maps and battle plans. To raise fresh troops, Umar permitted members of the recently apostate tribes to fight alongside longtime Muslims for the first time. He also warned his generals, "No land is good for Arabs unless it is good for camels. Find them a dry, healthy place, and do not let any river or sea come between them and me."

The next year the Muslims—reinforced by tribesmen, who were less afraid of elephants and more cautious about rivers—drove the Persians back to the Euphrates and began to occupy southern Iraq. They seized land owned by the Persian nobility and often gave it to the tenant farmers who had worked the land. They let ordinary farmers keep their plots as long as they paid taxes.

In 636, the Persians raised a new army. If they had kept it on the east side of the Euphrates, their empire might have lasted. But a willful twenty-year-old king named Yazdegerd III was determined to drive the Muslims from Iraq and ordered his enormous army west across the Euphrates. Umar wanted to lead a Muslim army against the Persian king himself but finally gave up the idea after older Muslims assured him that while a general could be replaced, a spiritual leader could not. Instead, Umar sent six thousand soldiers from Syria and four thousand from Medina.

The two giant armies met in the desert at Qadasiya, near a western tributary of the Euphrates, in April 637. This time, the Muslims knew more about elephants. They put flowing black robes on the humps of their camels, which spooked some of the elephants, and shot arrows into the eyes of others, causing them to turn and stampede the Persian troops.

Even without elephants, the Persians fought hard for three days. But on the third night, Arab tribesmen, without orders, continued the battle after dark. During the "Night of Fury," they slashed their way to the center of the Persian army, killed the commanding general, and then slew thousands more Persians as they tried to retreat. The fertile land between the Tigris and the Euphrates now belonged to the Arabs.

Back in Medina, Umar walked to the city's north gate at dawn each day to see whether any messenger had returned from battle. After seeing a young man on a camel one morning, Umar ran alongside him and asked him whether he had any news from Iraq. The courier did not recognize the caliph and gave him news of the victory without slowing down. Umar kept asking for details, panting as he tried to keep up with the camel. Finally, in the center of town, the people of Medina congratulated Umar, and the messenger apologized profusely. "It doesn't matter," Umar said. "Just tell me more."

The following spring the Muslims captured Ctesiphon, Persia's capital city on the east bank of the Tigris. The Arab tribesmen were astonished by the size of the many palaces, and they carried away vast amounts of gold, jewels, and carpets, then dutifully sent one-fifth of it all to Medina. When Umar saw the long caravans of plunder arriving from the north, he wept, for he knew that this immense wealth would cause many quarrels and much corruption later.

During three years of peace with Persia, Umar prohibited his troops from marching east of the Zagros mountains in western Iran. But in 641, Yazdegerd III raised a new army, and Umar told his generals to chase the Persians wherever they fled, no matter how many rivers they had to cross.

In 642, at Nahavand, in the mountains of western Iran, the Muslims defeated the Persians one last time. Killing tens of thousands of

Persians in battle and thousands more in flight, the Arabs wiped the Persian Empire from history. By 644, the Muslims held nearly all of what is now Iran. In later years, the Muslims advanced into Afghanistan and Azerbaijan as the Persian emperor Yazdegerd III fled from village to village. Finally, in 652, he was killed by local assassins. Persia would not have another king of its own until 1499, and he would be a Muslim. The once-thriving Zoroastrian religion dwindled rapidly in Iran and Iraq. Today, it is followed by less than one in a thousand Persians and by the small but wealthy Parsi communities in India and Britain.

In Syria, where Umar had made the brilliant general Khalid ibn al-Walid subordinate to Abu Ubeida, the two commanders continued to work as a team. In 635, the Muslims surrounded Damascus for six months but could not climb its well-guarded walls. Finally, on a night when the city was celebrating the birth of the Byzantine governor's son and many soldiers were drunk, some Syrian Christians who were tired of being discriminated against by the doctrinaire Byzantines helped some Muslim soldiers climb a wall unnoticed. Once the warriors were inside the city walls, the governor of Damascus immediately surrendered his city, narrowly avoiding having it sacked.

Umar chose Yazid ibn Abu Sufyan to be the governor of Syria, but when Yazid died in 639, Umar appointed Yazid's younger brother Muawiya to succeed him. Muawiya governed Syria effectively for twenty-two years before becoming caliph himself in 661.

The Byzantines responded to the loss of Damascus by raising a huge army, perhaps fifty thousand men, which marched down from the mountains of what is now Turkey in the spring of 636. General Khalid abandoned Damascus, returned the tribute that its people had paid, and retreated to the Yarmuk River, the gorge east of the Sea of Galilee where he had defeated the Byzantines two years earlier.

During the summer, the two armies engaged in light skirmishes. Arab women, who accompanied their tribesmen almost all the way to the battlefield, urged their menfolk on with verses like this:

> Daughters of Arabs fair are we,
> Advance—we'll give our kisses free,
> Our perfumed beds will ready be.
> But we'll desert you if you flee;
> Our love for braver men shall be.[1]

Finally, in August, a violent wind swept up behind the Arabs and whipped sand into the faces of the Byzantine soldiers. Khalid saw his opportunity and charged. "Paradise is before you," he shouted to his men, "Hell behind. Fight and you will live in gardens. Flee and you will burn in fire."

Blinded by stinging sand, thousands of Byzantines, including their commanding general, were massacred by Arabs wielding swords and lances. The few Byzantines who made it back to the Mediterranean boarded ships and left Syria and Palestine forever.

At first, Umar was elated by Khalid's victory, but after hearing that Khalid had taken a bath in wine, Umar sourly noted that Muslims were attributing their success to Khalid rather than to Allah. Before long, he charged Khalid with mishandling public funds, dismissed him from his command, and confiscated a quarter of his fortune. The remaining three-quarters were not enough. The flamboyant but now unemployed general had so many wives, concubines, and children that he could no longer pay his bills and died penniless in Syria only a few years later.

Perhaps Umar treated Khalid harshly out of jealousy of his youth and success, but it is more likely that he saw Khalid's military glory as a threat to his own religious authority and thus to the unity of the Muslims.

In Palestine, the Byzantine army was gone, but the walled Christian city of Jerusalem remained to be taken. When a Muslim army surrounded the holy town in 637, the Greek Orthodox patriarch Sophronius agreed to surrender the city if he could do so in person to the caliph himself. Umar agreed to make the long journey to Jerusalem immediately. The humble ruler was accompanied by only one teenage boy, and they took turns riding a camel and pulling the reins.

Umar first rode eight hundred miles to Dar'a, on what is today the border of Syria and Jordan, to settle some local disputes. Several generals rode south from the town to greet their caliph beforehand. Umar took one look at their silk robes and the decorations on their horses and angrily asked them, "Have you changed so much in two years to come to me dressed like this? I should dismiss you from the army right now!" The mortified generals quickly opened their robes to show Umar their chain mail underneath, which calmed the caliph somewhat.

When Umar finally reached the gates of Jerusalem in January 638, it was the teenager's turn to ride the camel and Umar's to pull the rein. The people of the holy city had waited for weeks to see their conqueror; now they were astonished to see a barefoot man in a sleeveless cloak of camel's hair leading a single camel that he was not even riding. Patriarch Sophronius was courteous to Umar, but when they reached the Church of the Holy Sepulchre, built on the site where Jesus was originally buried, Sophronius whispered to an aide, "Surely, this is the abomination of desolation spoken of by the Prophet Daniel."

At noon, the patriarch invited Umar to spread his prayer mat inside the church, but Umar declined. "We have promised to leave your churches alone," he explained, "but if I pray here, other Muslims will follow my example and will turn this church into a mosque." Umar prayed outside instead, and, as he had foreseen, a mosque was soon built on the spot where he had knelt.

Umar spent the winter in Jerusalem dividing Syria and Palestine into military districts and appointing tax collectors and judges. He also ordered that the Jewish Temple Mount be cleaned of the garbage that Christians had piled around it, and he helped to carry away some of the trash himself. Then, when spring came, he rode his camel back to Medina. Jerusalem remained a Muslim city for 461 years, until the Christian crusaders held it from 1099 to 1187 and from 1229 to 1244. Then it was Muslim again for another 723 years, until the Six-Day War in 1967.

Umar was deeply worried about the corrupting influence of his people's newfound wealth. To ensure that the Arabs would continue to be soldiers, he prohibited them from buying land or engaging in trade outside the Arabian peninsula. Instead, they would live apart from their conquered people in military camps where alcohol was prohibited. At first, these camps were just collections of tents where tribesmen left their wives and children before going into battle, but they quickly grew into big cities. In Iraq, the fortress of Basra eventually housed sixty thousand soldiers and their large families (Arab soldiers, rich with plunder, were taking many wives), while the garrison at Kufa housed forty thousand families.

Persian inspectors working for the Muslims carefully surveyed the fertile land near the Tigris and the Euphrates to determine the tax that non-Muslim farmers had to pay. From this money, Umar began to give pensions to soldiers and to the earliest Muslims, the "Companions of the Prophet." The amount of a pension was determined by how early a person had fought for Islam. Those who fought in the first battle of Badr were paid five thousand silver coins a year, while those who had merely fought in the recent battle at Yarmuk received only about four hundred coins.

Umar wanted the Arabs to be a warrior race, like the Spartans in ancient Greece, who also rarely did any farming. Under Umar's rule, this was possible. But later caliphs were not as strong as Umar, and during the long, dull months between battles, the soldiers in these fortress cities, having little to do, grew arrogant, disorderly, and finally insubordinate.

While Umar was caliph, however, discipline was tight. He personally whipped drunks in the streets of Medina, and when he heard that one of his sons had become drunk during a military campaign, he ordered that the young man be given the full punishment of eighty lashes. Tragically, his son was ill at the time and died from the blows.

Umar's severity was balanced by his accessibility. After prayers, he stayed at the mosque to listen to anyone who wanted to talk to him. At night, he took long walks, often incognito, to see how people felt and what they needed. Men and women felt free to criticize Umar. "I am your servant and you should question my actions," he told them.

One night Umar heard children crying and learned that they were hungry because their mother had no food to cook. Umar immediately fetched several sacks of flour and dates and carried them back to the woman's hut, then got down on all fours and played with the children while she cooked their first decent meal in days.

Umar expected his provincial governors to be equally accessible. He appointed a number of rich merchants from Mecca to high posts because they had both managerial skills and the knowledge of how to handle desert tribesmen. But he warned them not to live too well. Officials were not to ride large horses, wear fine cloth, eat white bread, and, most important, have doormen who could stop poor people from entering their houses. "I have appointed you not to rule over your people," Umar wrote to his new governors, "but to serve them." He also told his governors not to interfere with local customs if these customs did not interfere with the Quran.

Umar hired informers to watch his appointees, and he read their reports closely. When one official built a palace, Umar fired him and gave him a new job shepherding goats. If a governor could not account for a sudden increase in wealth, Umar sent a tax collector to confiscate a quarter or even half of the man's fortune. In Iraq, the governor of Kufa had so many petitioners that he built a fence around his house, but when Umar heard of this, he sent a deputy to remove the fence and burn it. "Do not build a fence to keep people out so they have to wait until you receive them," Umar wrote to the governor. Umar also created a separate judiciary of religious scholars. None of them had to answer to the caliph or his governors, and all of them believed that every Muslim, Arab and non-Arab alike, was equal before the law.

From Palestine to Persia, Muslim soldiers sent one-fifth of their plunder to the storehouses of Medina. Like Abu Bakr, Umar believed that public money should not be accumulated but spent as soon as it arrived, on pensions, weapons, and the poor. He had a rock-like faith that Allah would continue to keep the Muslims strong and the infidels paying. Prosperity was the reward for surrendering to God's will.

Umar paid for roads, bridges, reservoirs, police posts, and irrigation canals, but most important to him were the hundreds of new mosques and schools. Umar also sent men into the desert to teach tribesmen the Quran. The caliph made it compulsory for every Arab to learn at least a few verses of the holy book. Those who didn't were fined or whipped.

While Umar reigned, the Companions of the Prophet began to quote not only the Quran, which they believed to be the word of God, but also Muhammad's sayings (*hadith*). Some of them began to gather his sayings into a collection, but Umar was strict. No *hadith* was accepted by Umar and the other Companions until there was a consensus that Muhammad had actually said it.

Umar also adopted the Muslim lunar calendar. Twelve alternating months of 29 and 30 days total 354 days, so each year Muslim holidays arrive eleven days earlier on our solar calendar than they did the previous year. Umar may have chosen a lunar calendar to ensure that Muslim holidays would stay separate from pagan holidays, which often are related to specific seasons.

The Muslim calendar dates from the *hijrah*, Muhammad's emigration from Mecca to Medina, when Muslims first began to govern themselves. This was in 622, which is the Muslim year 1 AH (After Hijrah). The year AD 2000 began in the Muslim year 1420.

In 639 (18 AH), a Muslim general, Amr ibn al-As, led thirty-five hundred men on his own initiative to the border of Egypt, which still belonged to the Byzantines. Umar promptly sent Amr a letter, but, on a hunch, the general delayed opening it for a day until his army had crossed into Egypt. The letter said, "If this reaches you before you cross the border, return. If not, proceed and God be with you."

Amr captured the coastal city of Pelusium, near where the Suez Canal is today, then crossed the Nile in a daring raid south of Memphis in the spring of 640. Amr knew his army was in danger when it crossed the wide river, and he urged Umar to send him reinforcements. The caliph obliged and sent twelve thousand men, including one of his own sons. During the summer, the two armies surrounded a great Byzantine fortress called Babylon (not to be confused with the ancient city in Mesopotamia), near what is now the city of Cairo.

Outside the fortified cities, the Muslims found the countryside surprisingly easy to conquer because the Egyptian people welcomed liberation from the Byzantines. In the seventh century, most Egyptians were Coptic Christians, believing that Christ was entirely divine and in no way human, even though he had taken on a human body. Orthodox

Christians declared this "monophysite" belief to be a heresy, so Cyrus, the Greek Orthodox patriarch of Alexandria, imprisoned, burned, and pulled out the teeth of many Coptic priests and monks, greatly angering the Egyptian people.

The Muslim siege of Babylon had lasted five months when the Byzantine emperor Heraclius died and a violent conflict began over who would succeed him. The demoralized Byzantine soldiers were permitted by the Muslims to sail away after surrendering their city in April 641.

Suddenly, Alexandria, 120 miles away on the Mediterranean coast, was vulnerable. For nearly a thousand years, Alexandria had been one of the greatest cities in the world, home to Euclid, Eratosthenes, and Ptolemy. In the 640s, more than a million Greeks, Jews, Copts, Italians, and Africans lived in a city defended and supplied by Byzantine ships on one side and protected by high walls and guard towers on the other.

East of Alexandria was the Nile delta, but to the west was the Libyan Desert, a scorching wasteland where the seafaring Byzantines were impotent. Cyrus, the patriarch, knew that the Muslims could besiege his city for years and that supplies from the capital, Constantinople, would be scarce while the power struggle there continued. It seemed wiser to surrender the city on the best possible terms.

In November 641, Amr ibn al-As agreed to Cyrus's request that the Byzantines be given a year to evacuate Alexandria and be allowed to take their possessions with them. The Muslims also promised to protect the Christians and the Jews who remained.

When the Muslims took the city in 642, Amr wrote to Umar, "I have seized 4,000 villas with 4,000 baths; 40,000 tax-paying Jews; and 400 royal palaces." Umar read the letter without showing the slightest emotion. He merely invited the tired messenger who had delivered it to a simple meal of bread and dates.

In Egypt, the Muslims built a new garrison city near Babylon called Fustat, which was renamed al-Qahira (the Victorious) or Cairo in the 970s. The Arab soldiers took many Egyptian wives, and after several generations, the Egyptians were speaking Arabic.

Amr, the victorious general, now owned countless slaves, jewels, and herds of livestock, but Umar wanted to know how he had grown so rich so fast. Amr wrote to explain that he had increased his wealth through trading, but Umar replied, "I have had enough of dishonest officials and have sent an auditor to divide all that you have."

As Umar's personal representative examined and confiscated roughly half of the general's possessions, Amr complained, "An era when Umar treats us like this is certainly an evil age." Unmoved, the auditor replied,

"If it were not for this age of Umar that you hate, today you would be bending down at the feet of a goat back in Mecca, pleased if it was giving a lot of milk and disappointed if the milk was scarce."

Amr had to agree. "I beg you not to report what I have just said to Umar," he asked the official, who agreed to keep things confidential but later told the story after Umar had died. Meekly, the conqueror of Egypt submitted to the moral authority of a barefoot caliph seven hundred miles away and obediently allowed an unarmed auditor to carry off half of his wealth.

In Medina, a Persian slave named Abu Lulu Firoz complained to Umar that his master's share of his income, two silver coins a day, was too high. Umar asked Abu Lulu what his profession was, and the slave said that he was a carpenter and a blacksmith. "Your master's share is not excessive," Umar reasoned, "for as a carpenter you can earn enough to pay him and still have plenty for your own needs." The slave, angered by this response, walked away grumbling.

The next day Abu Lulu went to the morning prayer, pulled a dagger out of his cloak, and stabbed Umar six times. As horrified Muslims grabbed the assassin, he also stabbed and killed himself. When Umar was carried home, he asked who had attacked him. Told it was Abu Lulu, the dying caliph said, "Thanks to Allah he is not a Muslim." Umar also asked Aisha whether he could be buried at her home next to Muhammad, on the other side from Abu Bakr. Aisha replied that she had hoped to be buried there herself but added, "I prefer Umar there to myself."

Umar repeated his last words over and over: "I testify that there is but one God and Muhammad is His Messenger." He died the same day that he was stabbed, November 3 or 4, 644, and was probably sixty-one years old. In his will, Umar directed Muslims to fear Allah, give to the poor, and keep their promises to non-Muslims.

Before he died, Umar chose six men to pick the next caliph. He gave them three days to decide and said that they were to be locked in a house together while they deliberated. Umar required a majority to elect the new caliph and ordered that if anyone in the minority later claimed to be caliph, instead he should be executed. Finally, Umar said that his son Abdullah could take part in the discussions, but in no event was he to be chosen caliph.

The six men Umar selected were Ali, Muhammad's adopted son; Uthman ibn Affan, a rich merchant who was one of the earliest Muslims; Zubair, who had led the twelve thousand reinforcements into Egypt; Saad ibn abu Waqqas, who, along with Khalid, conquered

Iraq; Abdul Rahman, another early Muslim; and Talha, who was away from Medina and could not take part in the voting.

For two days, little was accomplished; the leading candidates seemed to be Ali and Uthman. On the third day, Abdul Rahman offered to withdraw his candidacy if the other four men would agree to accept his choice as caliph. Running out of time, the four leaders consented, and Abdul Rahman interviewed each of them separately. While everyone said that he would follow the principles of the Quran and the example of Muhammad, Uthman said that he would also follow the precedents of Abu Bakr and Umar, while Ali said that he did not regard the decisions of these two men as binding. Abdul Rahman decided that predictability was more important than independent thinking and proclaimed Uthman the third caliph of Islam.

Uthman was reliable, devout, and well liked but was a weaker man than the other four. Perhaps Abdul Rahman also chose Uthman because he had grown tired of living under Umar's strong hand. For ten years, Umar had kept the ambitions of thousands of proud Arabs subordinate to the good of the Muslim community. Uthman would have a much tougher time.

Umar's reign was a golden age of domestic harmony and foreign conquest. His fierce devotion to God, humble lifestyle, concern for the poor, and firm but fair administration served as both an example and a reproach to future, less virtuous caliphs—and helped to ensure that the many people his armies conquered would continue to be Muslim fourteen centuries later. Umar was not a general, but if conquests are measured by longevity rather than size, he may be the greatest conqueror the world has ever known.

Muslims recorded the sayings of Umar as well as Muhammad. Here are three of Umar's best:

- Allah's mercy be on those who bring me knowledge of my shortcomings.
- Penitence means not repeating sinful deeds.
- It is easier to abstain from sin than endure the agony of shame.[2]

3

Expansion, Civil War, and the Sunni-Shi'ite Split: Uthman and Ali (644–661)

FOR MORE THAN THIRTY YEARS Muhammad, Abu Bakr, and Umar had set a standard of spiritual and political leadership that was difficult to follow. No group of men and women could continue to produce leaders of that caliber, not even the early Muslims. During the next thirty-six years, each of the following caliphs lacked a quality that was vital to the preservation of Muslim unity.

Uthman (c. 576–656) was humble and devout but too weak to check the ambition of his relatives or maintain military discipline. His vacillation and nepotism sowed the seeds of civil war.

Ali (c. 600–661), the adopted son and son-in-law of Muhammad, was a strong warrior and a pious Muslim. But he was too cautious and legalistic and lacked the political skill needed to hold on to the power for which he had waited all his life. Most of his five years as caliph were plagued by civil war, as rivals constantly challenged his legitimacy.

Muawiya (c. 603–680) was firm, wise, and politically adept but not nearly as religious as his predecessors. He started a dynasty that lasted ninety years, but he changed Muslim society from an egalitarian theocracy to a more conventional empire.

Uthman, the Third Caliph (644–656)

"Even the angels are embarrassed when they pass by Uthman," Muhammad once said, a remark that testified to Uthman's kind heart and also to his naïveté. Elegant and easygoing, Uthman ibn Affan had been an old friend of Abu Bakr's and one of the richest cloth merchants in Mecca before he became the first man from the powerful Umayya family to convert to Islam. His uncle was furious. He tied Uthman to a post and beat him, but Uthman refused to renounce his new faith.

Uthman was not a brave fighter, but he bought fifty horses and almost a thousand camels to use in the earliest battles. When the Muslims arrived in Medina, he spent twenty thousand silver coins to buy a well so that they could have their own drinking water. He was also generous to the poor and often bought slaves to give them their freedom.

When he wasn't trading cloth, Uthman worked as a scribe for Muhammad. He had beautiful handwriting and wrote down parts of the Quran as they were being revealed. He knew much of the holy book by heart. The unusually handsome merchant married Muhammad's prettiest daughter, Ruqayyah, and when she died, the grief-stricken widower soon married one of her sisters, Umm Kulthum. The two wives bore him more than a dozen children.

Uthman was about sixty-eight and had a full beard when he became caliph in 644. His relatives hoped that the Umayya family might regain its place as the most powerful Arab clan, but other Muslims were appalled that a family that had fought Muhammad for twenty years now had one of their own as caliph.

In 646, the governor of Kufa, in Iraq, borrowed money from the public treasury but was unable to repay it. Uthman dismissed him from his post and appointed his half brother, a drunkard who scandalized Muslims by trying to lead public prayers while inebriated. Uthman fired him, too, and appointed a second relative, a sober young cousin who marched east and briefly captured Kabul in 651–652. Uthman chose yet another cousin, Muawiya, to be governor of Syria, reconfirming an appointment already made by Umar.

In Basra, rebellious troops demanded that Uthman send them a new governor. Instead of punishing them to maintain discipline, Uthman met their demand and chose still another cousin, this one just twenty-five years old. Members of the Umayya family now governed Kufa, Syria, and Basra.

Uthman saw nothing wrong with helping one's family and once even criticized Abu Bakr and Umar for not leaving more to their children than they did. In fairness to Uthman, the Umayyas were the best-educated family in Arabia. Even so, the benefits gained from the efficiency of their administration were far outweighed by the resentment that this family's dominance created.

In Egypt, Uthman dismissed Governor Amr ibn al-As, the general who had conquered the country, and replaced him with a foster brother, Abdallah ibn Sa'id, a man Muhammad had once wanted dead. Abdallah had been a scribe for Muhammad but had lost faith in Muhammad's divine inspiration.

Once, as a test, Abdallah altered a sentence while Muhammad was reciting a new verse of the Quran. Where Muhammad had recited, "Allah is knowing and hearing," Abdallah wrote down "Allah is knowing and wise." When Muhammad failed to notice the discrepancy, Abdallah stopped being a Muslim and moved back to Mecca, where the people were much amused by his story.

Years later, when the Muslims took Mecca, Abdallah was one of the few people Muhammad excluded from his general amnesty and thus was condemned to death. Uthman pleaded with Muhammad to spare his foster brother's life, but Muhammad, who was usually quick to forgive, stayed silent a very long time. Finally, he pardoned Abdallah, but later he scolded his followers for not having taken his silence as an opportunity to kill this man who had played a trick with the Quran.

Abdallah was allowed to become a Muslim again, and because he was unusually good at paperwork, a rare talent in the seventh century, he became one of Umar's leading tax collectors. Now, as Uthman's new governor of Egypt, he raised taxes and alienated the people.

In Alexandria, prominent citizens wrote to the Byzantine emperor and asked him to liberate their city. The emperor complied and sent hundreds of ships to the city's harbor in 645. Byzantine soldiers killed all of the Arabs since there were only a thousand of them, then fanned out to take the Nile delta.

Uthman asked his general, Amr ibn al-As, to be governor of Egypt again, and within a year Amr had reconquered both Alexandria and the Nile delta. But no sooner was his conquest complete than Uthman proposed that Amr share power with his brother Abdallah: Amr would command the army, while Abdallah would again collect the taxes. Amr refused, then explained, "I would be like a man who holds onto the horns of a cow while someone else milks her." After hearing this, Uthman dismissed Amr a second time and appointed Abdallah governor of Egypt once more.

The one place where few people were bothered by Uthman's nepotism was Syria. Syria had an unusually able governor, Muawiya, a cousin of Uthman's who did not convert to Islam until the Muslims took Mecca in 630. Despite his late start as a Muslim, Muawiya had served as a scribe for Muhammad and an army officer for Abu Bakr in Syria before he was appointed by Umar to succeed his older brother (who died in a plague) as governor of Syria in 639.

Muawiya managed to avoid implementing Umar's policy of building large military cities to keep the Arab soldiers separate from the people they had conquered. Instead, he made Damascus his capital, and most of the Arabs in Syria enjoyed living among civilians in a city full of gardens. Unlike Iraq, where intrigue was rife because tens of thousands of soldiers were crowded together with little to do, in Syria things stayed calm.

Muawiya worried that Syria's coastal cities were vulnerable to a Byzantine invasion. For five years, he had tried and failed to get Umar's approval to build a navy. For a desert warrior like Umar, a ship was no place for an Arab.

When Uthman became caliph, Muawiya tried again. He warned Uthman of the danger of an attack from the island of Cyprus and wrote that it was so close to Syria, "you can almost hear the barking of dogs."

Uthman granted Muawiya permission to build a navy, but it had to be a volunteer force—no Arab could be ordered to go to sea. Uthman also ensured that an attack would not be too risky by requiring Muawiya to take his favorite wife with him when he sailed from Syria.

The Muslims built two navies, one under the command of Muawiya in Syria and the other led by Abdallah in Egypt. Like their Byzantine counterparts, each Muslim ship had an upper deck crammed with swordsmen and two lower decks with fifty rowers each. In general, Arabs did the fighting, while Egyptians and Syrians did the rowing.

The two Muslim navies converged on Cyprus in 649. The practical Cypriots, who had already paid tribute to the Byzantines, stayed neutral by paying a second tribute to the Muslims. But four years later, when some Cypriots assisted a Byzantine naval raid, Muawiya invaded the island and stationed twelve thousand troops there permanently. He allowed most of the island, however, to remain neutral.

The climactic naval battle between the Muslims and the Byzantines took place in 655 off the southern coast of what is now Turkey, near the island of Rhodes. Arab soldiers tied each of their boats to a Byzantine vessel, then boarded the Byzantine ships and slaughtered the sailors in hand-to-hand combat. The Battle of the Masts, as the Arabs have called it, began a long era of Muslim naval supremacy. After this victory, the reconquest of Syria, Palestine, or Egypt by the

Byzantines was no longer possible. The eastern Mediterranean had become a Muslim sea.

Uthman's greatest achievement was his standardization of the Quran. When Zaid ibn Thabit finished the long work of collating the holy book's thousands of verses, Umar entrusted this definitive copy to his daughter Hafsah, who had been one of Muhammad's wives. Over the years, however, other versions of the Quran had appeared, so Uthman ordered new copies made of Hafsah's Quran and sent them to other cities in the empire.

Finally, in 651, Uthman ordered every other version of the Quran burned. The Companions of the Prophet approved, but the Quran reciters, who often had their own rendering of the holy book, were furious. Already angry over Uthman's nepotism, they now charged him with sacrilege, with burning the word of God.

The root of Uthman's troubles was that Arab tribesmen in the garrison cities of Iraq and Egypt did not like taking orders from governors who had neither helped Muhammad during his years of struggle nor led victorious armies during Umar's conquests. In Egypt, soldiers hated their governor because he was ruthless while collecting tax money and stingy in spending it. In Iraq, a complex dispute had become extremely bitter over which army veterans had the right to receive income from land taken from the Persian nobility. And in other parts of the empire, there was deep resentment each time yet another member of the Umayya family bought a large tract of land.

Open revolt broke out in 655 when a thousand soldiers prevented the governor of Kufa from returning to his city after a trip to Medina, charging that his sympathy lay with the Umayya rather than with the common people. Uthman appeased the rebels by dismissing the governor and installing in his place the man they wanted, Abu Musa.

In Egypt, the army sent a delegation to Uthman to complain about their governor, Abdallah, but Uthman merely wrote Abdallah a letter requesting him to improve his conduct. Abdallah's response was to arrest the delegation and execute its leader.

Nearly eighty, the tenderhearted Uthman was utterly bewildered by the volume of criticism he received. During a pilgrimage to Mecca, Amr ibn al-As, whom Uthman had twice fired as governor of Egypt, confronted the caliph directly. "You have subjected every Muslim to the Umayya family," Amr told him, "now either decide to be just or resign." "Allah is my defense," Uthman said meekly. Then he said that he would never use force against other Muslims.

As news of Uthman's promise not to use force spread, the rebellious troops in Iraq and Egypt became more brazen. In the spring of 656,

Kufa, Basra, and Fustat (Cairo) each sent a thousand soldiers to Medina to demand that Uthman reform his administration. Uthman's cousin, Muawiya, offered to send troops from Syria to protect him, but the caliph declined. "I do not want to be the first caliph to shed the blood of Muslims," he said.

When troops from Egypt and Iraq arrived outside the city, Uthman asked Ali to meet them. Ali criticized the soldiers for trying to change things by force rather than persuasion, but, siding with them, he also asked Uthman to dismiss Abdallah as governor, which Uthman agreed to do. In his place, Uthman chose the leader of the Egyptian insurgents, Muhammad ibn Abu Bakr, a son of the first caliph. This appointment greatly pleased the rebels, and they began to go home.

On the way back to Egypt, however, the soldiers encountered a messenger who carried a letter bearing Uthman's seal addressed to Abdallah, the governor of Egypt, asking him to kill the Egyptian troops. Furious, the soldiers turned around and marched to Medina immediately.

Confronted with the message, Uthman admitted that the seal was his but denied writing the letter. The rebels accepted his word, then asked that he turn over Marwan, his unpopular deputy, but Uthman refused to do so without proof linking Marwan to the evil letter. The frustrated soldiers angrily demanded that Uthman resign as caliph, but he would not leave an office that he believed Allah had entrusted to him.

Ali smelled a rat and asked the soldiers from Iraq what prompted them to return to Medina to meet their Egyptian colleagues, but no one gave an adequate reply. The truth of who wrote the letter to Abdallah will never be known, but most likely it was part of someone's plot to discredit Uthman and cause his downfall.

The mutineers surrounded Uthman's house for a month, preventing anyone from bringing in drinking water until Ali finally sent three goatskins full of water, which they let through. Ali had been Uthman's chief rival as a candidate for caliph twelve years earlier. Now, his role during this crisis was ambiguous and plainly showed how disgusted he was with Uthman's rule. On the one hand, Ali gave Uthman water and sent his sons Hasan and Hussein to guard the door to his home. But Ali and the other Companions of the Prophet never tried to rescue Uthman. They did not even criticize the rebels for surrounding the house; they simply stayed home the entire spring.

By mid-June, it was clear that Uthman could not be pressured into resigning. On his own initiative, Muawiya sent troops from Syria, and when they were just 120 miles away from Medina, the insurgents had to act. On June 17, 656, they fired a volley of arrows into Uthman's house. While the household defended the front door, Abu Bakr's son Muhammad and two others climbed over a wall in the back.

Uthman was reading the Quran when the three men entered his room. Muhammad ibn Abu Bakr grabbed Uthman by the beard, but the old caliph stayed calm and said softly, "Your father would hate what you are doing." Suddenly ashamed, ibn Abu Bakr let go of Uthman's beard and stepped back, but one of his lieutenants ran forward and swung an ax into the caliph's head. While Uthman's blood poured over his Quran, his wife tried to defend him but lost two (possibly three) of her fingers in the attempt. By this time, dozens of rebels had broken into the house, and some of them stabbed Uthman. Two days passed before Uthman's family could finally remove the dead caliph and bury him, at night, in his bloody clothes.

Medina was in anarchy. The Egyptian rebels led the public prayers, and the Umayya family fled to Damascus, taking Uthman's bloody shirt and his wife's severed fingers with them.

The Companions of the Prophet knew that if they did not elect another caliph quickly, the entire empire would fall apart. Ali, Muhammad's son-in-law, was the obvious candidate, supported both by the people of Medina and by the rebel soldiers. At Medina's main mosque, six days after Uthman died, the city's leading citizens took Ali by the hand and pledged their allegiance to him as Islam's fourth caliph.

Most Muslims are reluctant to criticize Uthman because he was so devout. He is considered one of the four "rightly guided" caliphs, a martyr, and a saint. Yet even the briefest look at his time as caliph shows that his leadership, however well-meaning, was deeply flawed.

Uthman was almost seventy when he began his twelve-year reign, and during his last years, he lacked the energy that a strong ruler needs. He allowed ambitious relatives to take advantage of his gentle nature, was too weak to impose discipline in the garrison cities, and lost the confidence of the majority of Muslims.

Uthman refused the protection of Muawiya's army because he did not want to be the first caliph to rule by force. He was willing to die rather than have Muslims kill other Muslims, but to no use. The Muslims were about to fight their first civil war.

Ali, the Fourth Caliph (656–661)

Shi'ite (also spelled Shia) Muslims think that Ali should have been caliph as soon as Muhammad died. "Muhammad is God's Messenger," they say, "and Ali is God's Executor." Shi'ites believe that God created a divine light, placed it inside Adam's backbone, passed it down the generations, and finally split it in two inside Abdul Muttalib, the grandfather of both Muhammad and Ali. One light entered Muhammad; the other, Ali.

More than 170 million Muslims are Shi'ites, including about 90 percent of the people of Iran, 62 percent of Iraq, 40 percent of Lebanon, 25 percent of Kuwait, 20 percent of Pakistan and Bangladesh, 15 percent of Afghanistan, and 9 percent of Saudi Arabia. While Sunni (Arabic for Orthodox) Muslims honor Abu Bakr, Umar, and Uthman as saints, Shi'ite (Partisan) Muslims see them as usurpers. They believe that Muhammad wanted Ali to be his successor, although non-Shi'ite Islamic scholars can find no evidence for this claim.

Around 605, five years before Muhammad began to preach, he decided to help a poorer cousin by adopting the man's five-year-old son, Ali. As a child, Ali ibn Abu Talib learned to read and write and sometimes worked as a scribe for Muhammad. He memorized thousands of verses of the Quran and knew exactly when and where each one had been revealed to the Prophet.

Unlike the first three caliphs, Ali was not a trader. He spent much of his youth tending livestock, digging wells, carrying water, and maintaining orchards. The manual labor made him strong, and he grew up to be one of the bravest and most skillful warriors in Arabia. His double-edged sword was called "the breaker of backbones" because Ali could slice right through the torsos of enemy soldiers. He won one-on-one fights against armed foes in several battles.

Around 624, Ali married Fatima, who was nineteen and was generally considered the most intelligent of Muhammad's daughters. Both Abu Bakr and Umar had wanted to marry her, but Muhammad knew that Ali and Fatima, who had grown up together, were in love. They had two daughters, Zaynab and Umm Kulthum, and two sons, Hasan and Hussein, both of whom are considered saints. (Another son died when he was a child.) Ali and Fatima never refused beggars who came to their door, even if they were short of food themselves.

In 632, after eight years of marriage, Fatima died from an illness only six months after the death of her father, Muhammad. Years later, as the Muslims grew rich, Ali married eight more wives, took several concubines, and fathered another twenty-six children. But Fatima held a special place in Muslim hearts. As the daughter of Muhammad and the mother of two saints, she is regarded by Muslims as "the embodiment of all that is divine in womanhood" and "the Queen of Paradise."

By the time Ali was thirty, it was clear to all that no one knew more about the Quran and about Muhammad's life and sayings than he did. When Abu Bakr was caliph, he asked Ali to draft letters and take charge of prisoners of war. Umar sought Ali's opinion on legal matters and also married one of Ali's daughters. Uthman, however, made little use of Ali's skills. Ali spent the twelve years of Uthman's reign giving talks on Islamic law and philosophy but, lacking more to do, slowed down in his middle age and perhaps lost some of his drive.

By all accounts, Ali was a forceful speaker, which undoubtedly made some of the rather pedantic material he taught easier to absorb. Faith, he said, is based on four pillars: forbearance, justice, struggle, and conviction. Forbearance is subdivided into devotion, fear of God, and righteousness; justice is divided into reason, learning, and charity.[1] Ali subdivided other virtues, too.

Ali was fifty-six and no longer a strong warrior when he became caliph in 656. He was short, bald, and plump and had a long white beard that contrasted sharply with his piercing black eyes.

Though often blunt, Ali was a compassionate man, dedicated to helping the needy. He once wrote to a governor in Egypt to "lighten the burden of the poor," explaining that money spent on the people "is an investment which they will return to you by generating prosperity in your land."[2]

Ali watched his governors closely to make sure that they did not spend public money on luxuries, and he was equally vigilant about his own expenses. Once, when a slave brought him some gold and silver spoons that had been part of an army's plunder, Ali exploded, "Do you want to throw me into hellfire?"

It was rare for Ali to be so angry. Usually, he was mild-mannered and perhaps a little too patient. Sometimes he was content to wait when events required him to act decisively.

As soon as Ali became caliph, most of the Companions of the Prophet urged him to restore discipline and punish Uthman's assassins. But many of Ali's supporters approved of Uthman's murder, including thousands of soldiers who gathered in Kufa and shouted, "We are all the assassins of Uthman."

Ali took a cautious, legal approach to the problem. "Let Uthman's sons go to court and present evidence against the assassins," he said, "and let the court decide." Of course, the revolt against Uthman had involved far more people than the handful of soldiers who actually stabbed him, but Ali did not feel that he had enough troops to challenge the mutineers in Egypt and Iraq. "These men are beyond our control," he said to a friend. "I will wait until Allah shows me a way out of this difficulty."

Yet if Ali had confronted the rebels the moment he became caliph, he would have enjoyed the support not only of Muawiya and his troops from Syria, but of moderates all over the empire who were horrified by Uthman's murder and wanted law and order restored. By doing nothing to punish Uthman's killers, Ali looked like a beneficiary of the assassination, a man who owed his power to murderers.

Ali swelled the number of his enemies by firing all of Uthman's governors, including Muawiya in Syria. Ali's friends advised him to leave Muawiya in office for a while, until he had the military strength to actually remove Muawiya. But Ali saw accommodation as a form of deceit. He wanted to renew Umar's tight control over the governors' finances and also to reestablish the independence of judges. Ali's nominee for governor of Syria, however, never got past the border. Muawiya, who had ruled Syria for fourteen years, refused to let the man in.

Ali asked for an oath of allegiance from Muawiya, but three months passed before Muawiya finally sent him a blank sheet. When Ali asked what this meant, the messenger told him that Muawiya had nailed Uthman's bloody shirt and his wife's severed fingers to the pulpit of the mosque in Damascus, and that thousands of warriors were ready to avenge the murder. It was clear that Muawiya could be ousted only by force.

Ali responded to this challenge by ordering soldiers to Syria, but many Companions of the Prophet were appalled that Ali was sending troops to fight Uthman's relatives in Syria, rather than his murderers in Iraq and Egypt. Ali seemed too willing to let power pass from the Companions in Medina to the rebellious soldiers in the garrison cities.

Zubair and Talha, two of Muhammad's oldest friends, decided to fight Ali. They were supported by Aisha, Muhammad's favorite wife, who had never forgiven Ali for advising the Prophet to divorce her after the episode of the lost necklace thirty years earlier.

Ali postponed his expedition to Syria and advanced toward the rebel force in Basra instead, collecting several thousand men along the way. Like Ali, Zubair was a cousin of Muhammad's. The two men had known each other all their lives, and neither really wanted to go to war. They began to negotiate, and this made the mutinous soldiers in Iraq fearful that they might finally be punished for Uthman's murder.

One night in December 656, rebel soldiers attacked both Ali and Zubair, and, as they had hoped, each blamed the other for treachery. For the first time, two Muslim armies slashed, stabbed, and drew blood from each other. The Arabs called it the Battle of the Camel because Aisha, middle-aged but still beautiful, rode her camel onto the battlefield and shouted encouragement to Zubair and Talha's warriors. But it was to no avail; it was a rout for Ali. Thousands died, including Zubair and Talha. As for Aisha, who was wounded by an arrow, Ali ordered that she be comfortably escorted back to Medina, where she gave many talks about Muhammad's life but never again participated in politics.

The following month, Ali moved Islam's capital from Medina to Kufa. Most of his supporters lived in this Iraqi city, and, unlike Medina, it was not vulnerable to a cutoff in grain shipments. Ali hoped to return to Medina when his power was secure, but, in fact, Medina was never a capital city again.

Ali's commanding general in Kufa was Malik al-Ashtar, a rebel who had led troops to Uthman's house just before they killed him. Ali added insult to injury when he reconfirmed Uthman's last-minute appointment of Muhammad ibn Abu Bakr as governor of Egypt. Ibn Abu Bakr was the man who had grabbed Uthman's beard before stepping back and letting his assistants kill him. Now Ali was rewarding the conspirator with control over an entire country.

Muawiya was outraged. He wrote to Ali demanding that he either "punish Uthman's assassins or accept the responsibility of an accomplice." As Uthman's first cousin, Muawiya had the right to demand vengeance. He could fight Ali without having to openly challenge Ali's right to be caliph. As a precaution, Muawiya made peace with the Byzantines and agreed to pay them a large annual tribute.

Ali raised an army of twenty or thirty thousand men and marched up the Euphrates River. He met Muawiya's equally large army in April 657 at Siffin, an old Roman town in northcentral Syria. Neither side was enthusiastic about killing other Muslims. For three months, skirmishes were light, even hesitant.

Ali's general, Malik al Ashtar, knew that if he lost this war, Muawiya would punish him as one of Uthman's murderers. Perhaps because of this extra motivation, he led a successful charge in July that killed thousands of Muawiya's Syrian supporters.

Amr ibn al-As, one of Muawiya's ablest generals, saved the Syrians from defeat. The man who had twice conquered Egypt and twice been dismissed as governor by Uthman was not fighting to avenge Uthman's murder but to be the governor of Egypt again. He shrewdly gambled that Muawiya would emerge triumphant.

Facing defeat, the wily Amr had more than five hundred of his soldiers put pages from the Quran on the tips of their swords and lances, then shout, "Let the Word of God decide!" Ali knew it was a trick, but his army, not wanting to kill other Muslims, took up the same cry, "Let the Word of God decide!" and urged Ali to submit to arbitration.

Ali's refusal to enforce military discipline by punishing Uthman's murderers a year earlier now came back to haunt him. His undisciplined army not only stopped fighting when it was on the verge of victory, but also loudly insisted that a former governor of Kufa, Abu Musa, be Ali's representative on the arbitration panel. Ali pointed out that Abu Musa had been neutral during the Battle of the Camel and asked his soldiers to choose someone more reliable instead. Ali was shouted down by the troops from Kufa, unable even to appoint his own arbitrator. Abu Musa, a simple soldier with no experience in politics, was grossly outmatched by Muawiya's representative, the sly conqueror of Egypt, Amr ibn al-As.

Accounts differ as to what the two arbitrators decided early in 658, but Ali rejected their verdict. Possibly, they agreed to bar both men from being caliph, which would have been a big victory for Muawiya since he had not yet claimed the office, while the very existence of the arbitration made a mockery of Ali's claim to supreme religious authority.

Some of Ali's supporters believed that it was a sin for Ali to agree to submit to arbitration, rather than allowing the battle to decide God's will. Called Kharajites, from the Arabic word for "leave," they rejected virtually all government and committed many acts of terrorism in Iraq. Ali had planned a second march to Syria to fight Muawiya again but had to postpone the campaign to fight the Kharajites instead. In the summer of 658, his troops easily massacred almost two thousand of the fanatics, but after the battle was over, his soldiers were tired of fighting other Muslims, and many deserted rather than march to Syria. Ali was forced once again to abandon his plans to attack Muawiya.

Muawiya, by contrast, sent Amr ibn al-As and six thousand troops to conquer Egypt a third time. Ali tried to recruit men to oppose them, but he had lost the capacity to inspire. War between Muslims also meant there would be no plunder from non-Muslims. As a result, no one stepped forward to fight for Ali.

Amr's troops conquered Egypt easily and captured Governor Muhammad ibn Abu Bakr, the rebel who had grabbed Uthman's beard moments before he was killed. Amr's troops taunted the governor, beheaded him, sewed his body into the skin of a dead donkey, and joyously threw the beast into a bonfire.

Muawiya's troops also made a quick raid to Mecca and Medina, showing everyone that Ali was too weak to defend the holy cities. Even Ali's brother switched sides to support Muawiya. Saint or not, the caliph had the scent of defeat.

In Jerusalem, in July 660, Muawiya's supporters formally declared him caliph, as tribal leaders throughout the western half of the

Muslim Empire gave him their oaths of allegiance. A truce existed between the two rival caliphs: Muawiya ruled Syria, Palestine, and Egypt, while Ali ruled Iraq, Iran, and Arabia.

Six months later, in January 661, three Kharajite terrorists tried to kill Ali, Muawiya, and Amr ibn al-As on the same day. One of them reached Muawiya but gave him only a slight cut. In Egypt, another assassin killed the wrong man because Amr was too sick to lead the prayers that morning, and a deputy took his place. When the murderer was brought before Amr, he said defiantly, "It was for you that my sword was intended." Amr smiled and replied, "You intended me to die, but Allah intended you."

In Kufa, the third conspirator, Abdul Rahman ibn Muljam, succeeded in slicing Ali's skull with a poisoned sword. It was the third assassination of a caliph in seventeen years. Ali lingered for a day and a half. He ordered his subordinates not to torture his assassin and to kill the man with just one sword stroke since that was all he had received. His last words to his oldest son, Hasan, included the warning that "the bad things you do that you are ashamed of are better to Allah than the good things you do that you feel vain about."

It was typical of Ali that his final concerns were with his son's character and his assassin's punishment, for Ali was always more interested in religion and law than he was in statecraft. As caliph, he could not make the tough but vital decision to imprison his most rebellious supporters because he did not have the ruthlessness that a ruler in ancient times needed.

Ali also showed that he lacked a skillful politician's ability to face reality when he fired Muawiya without first accumulating the power he needed to turn Muawiya out of office. Ali ignored a basic rule of politics: that it is better to postpone a battle you cannot win. Ali also revealed a surprising lack of objectivity when he appointed one of Uthman's murderers as governor of Egypt, and he displayed an unfortunate absence of personal magnetism when he could not lead his troops to victory at Siffin, where Muawiya's troops had put pages from the Quran on their lances.

Muslims consider Ali to be the last of the four "rightly guided" caliphs. When he died, Islam's theocratic republic came to an end. Today, his rule is seen by Sunni and Shi'ite Muslims alike as an unfortunate example of how a good and religious man can be defeated by the harsh realities of power politics; it is a lesson in life's injustices.

It is not certain where Ali is buried. Shi'ites claim that the internment took place outside Kufa in nearby Najaf, which today is one of Iraq's larger cities, partly because pilgrims have flocked there for thirteen centuries.

After Ali's assassination, the soldiers in Kufa pledged their allegiance to his eldest son, Hasan. Hasan closely resembled his grandfather, Muhammad, but lacked the Prophet's strength and will. Hasan was a lover, not a fighter, and he married and divorced ninety women in succession. Remarkably, nearly all of Hasan's ex-wives looked back on their brief marriages fondly.

Hasan wrote to Muawiya that he was willing to give up his claim to be caliph. Muawiya responded, "I admit that your blood relationship gives you a clearer title than I have to the high office. If I were sure of your ability to fulfill its duties I would unhesitatingly swear allegiance to you. Now then, ask what you like."[3]

Accompanying this note was a blank check signed by Muawiya. Hasan asked for, and received, a general amnesty for Ali's supporters, five million silver coins from Kufa's treasury, and the income from a district in Persia. In July 661, Hasan retired to a palace in Medina.

With Ali dead and Hasan reconciled, no one disputed Muawiya's claim to be caliph. Five years after Uthman was assassinated, the Umayya family was back in power. In the autumn, Muawiya went to Iraq in triumph to receive oaths of allegiance from the once-rebellious garrison cities. Even the soldiers who had fought against Muawiya still wanted the Muslims to be a single community, united and governed by one caliph.

Hasan enjoyed his palace and his wives for eight years. Occasionally, one of Ali's supporters told him that he should be ashamed of himself for not having fought Muawiya. But Hasan had no regrets about ending civil war. "Shame is better than hellfire," he said and added, "I saved the Muslim community from destruction."

In 669, one of Hasan's wives poisoned him to death. Ali's followers blamed the death on Muawiya, with no evidence to back their claim, and added Hasan to their list of saints and martyrs.

After the death of Ali and his sons, it took nearly a hundred years for Shi'ism to evolve into a major sect of Islam. Today, 12 percent of the world's Muslims are Shi'ites, and they revere Ali almost as deeply as they do Muhammad. Like Sunni Muslims, the 85 percent majority, Shi'ites believe that Muhammad is the Messenger of God and that the Quran is the word of God. But Shi'ite beliefs about Islam's past and future are very different. Except for Ali, Shi'ites believe that everyone in Islam's 1,292-year line of caliphs was a usurper. Instead, they claim, the true guardians of Muhammad's message, called imams, were Ali and his descendants (Ali being the first imam and Hasan the second), and they will mediate for mankind on Judgment Day.

Starting with Ali, Shi'ites believe that each imam has had a divine light inside him that has allowed him to know all things, including a secret name for God, hidden meanings in the Quran, and an infallible understanding of human affairs. Most Shi'ites think that there have been twelve imams: Ali and eleven of his descendants. Their faith is called "Twelver Shi'ism."

Twelver Shi'ites believe that the last *imam*, Muhammad al-Muntazar, disappeared as a child in 874. Since then, he has acted from the realm of the unseen, but someday he will return as a Messiah, or *Mahdi*, accompanied by Jesus, and will prepare the world for Judgment Day by restoring justice and equality. Until then, his views are interpreted in his absence by religious scholars. The most revered scholars have the title *ayatollah*, a word that means "the sign of God." Twelver Shi'ism has been Iran's state religion for five hundred years.

Ali is also remembered for his many sayings. Here are three of his best maxims:

- Beware of anger, for it begins in insanity and ends in remorse.

- Knowledge is better than wealth, for wealth has to be protected, but knowledge protects you.

- Some pray to seek rewards. This kind of prayer is from traders. Some pray out of fear of hellfire. This kind of prayer is from slaves. Those who think clearly pray to thank God for His blessings and mercy.[4]

4

The Beginning of Monarchy: Muawiya, the Fifth Caliph, His Son Yazid, and the Martyrdom of Hussein (661–683)

MUAWIYA IBN ABU SUFYAN was governor of Syria for twenty-two years before he became caliph in 661. Even his enemies conceded that he was an able ruler. His army was disciplined, his navy was strong, his Christian and Jewish subjects were loyal, and his finances were secure. Muawiya himself once described his method of governing: "If I have to use my sword, I will, but I never use my sword where my whip suffices, nor my whip where my voice is enough, nor my voice if I can use my money."[1]

Muawiya (pronounced mu-AH-we-ya) was as forceful a leader as Umar, but much less autocratic. He held frequent councils and pretended to be merely the first among equals. He preferred persuasion and flattery to command, and his use of bribes was legendary. Once, when an aide complained about the amount of money he spent, Muawiya replied, "War costs more!"

During his nineteen years as caliph, Muawiya transformed the Muslim Empire from an egalitarian theocracy into a hereditary dynasty, and for this reason he is criticized by many Muslim historians. But it is hard to see how the Muslims could have stayed united if Ali had lived longer, and it is impossible to look at Muawiya's career without admiring a good deal about the man.

Muawiya was a member of the wealthy Umayya family, which had fiercely opposed Muhammad until the year he entered Mecca. During the early battle of Badr, Muhammad's uncle Hamza killed Muawiya's grandfather in one-on-one combat. During the next battle, Muawiya's mother, Hind, avenged the killing of her father by hiring an expert javelin thrower to spear Hamza while he was in the middle of a sword fight. Then she exulted in her revenge by eating a piece of Hamza's liver.

Even by seventh-century standards, Hind's conduct was repellent, but Muhammad forgave her when he took Mecca and made her well-educated son Muawiya one of his scribes. Muawiya worked two years for Muhammad and impressed both Abu Bakr, who gave him troops to command in Syria in 632, and Umar, who appointed him governor of Syria seven years later.

Muawiya was almost sixty when he became caliph and had grown sufficiently plump that when he gave speeches, he had to sit down, which seemed much too regal to his enemies. In his youth, however, Muawiya had been a handsome man: tall, fair-skinned, and so imposing that Umar once prophetically called him "the Caesar of the Arabs."

As caliph, Muawiya encouraged people to speak freely and had the self-control to respond to insolence with humor. Once, when a tribal chief threatened to beat him with a stick if he didn't rule virtuously, Muawiya grinned and said, "Very well then, I will act virtuously." Another time, Muawiya asked a chief why he was silent during a discussion about his son. The tribesman replied, "I fear Allah if I lie, and you if I speak the truth." Muawiya praised his piety, listened to the chief's unfavorable opinion, and rewarded him with some money.

In the evening, Muawiya liked to hear poets and storytellers talk about the heroes of Arab history, but at dawn, he led the prayers at the central mosque in Damascus. Ancient Iraqi histories say that Muawiya was an unbeliever, but Syrian histories say he was a good Muslim.

Whether or not Muawiya was a pious Muslim, he was clearly tolerant of Christians, for many of his soldiers were Christian. They were loyal to Muawiya because they were free to worship as they pleased, which had not been true under the more rigid Greek Orthodox Byzantines. Because the Syrian army had so many Christians, its soldiers did not live apart from the people in garrison cities and therefore were better disciplined than soldiers in Iraq and Egypt were.

Since most Arabs were still illiterate, Muawiya employed many Christians as accountants and administrators. He also saw a Christian doctor, listened to a Christian poet at court, and married a beautiful Christian wife, Maysun. In Syria and Palestine, the Christians slowly learned Arabic even as they remained Christian, in contrast to Persia, where the people converted to Islam but kept their native language.

Christians and Jews had their own judges, just as no Muslim could be judged by a non-Muslim. Muawiya took care never to put a Christian in charge of anyone in Iraq or Persia and also appointed fewer relatives to office than Uthman had.

Unlike previous caliphs, Muawiya felt that a public treasury should have a lot of money on hand to meet unforeseen needs. But once a Muslim paid the annual 2.5 percent tax on his wealth, he was free to become as rich as possible. Muawiya may have introduced the world's first withholding tax, by deducting 2.5 percent from most pensions. He also appointed a tax collector in each province who was answerable to him, rather than to the local governor. Unlike Umar and Ali, Muawiya was tolerant of limited corruption and did not object if his governors amassed fortunes. Amr ibn al-As, the three-time conqueror of the Nile delta, did exactly that as governor of Egypt until he died in 663.

Muawiya's most talented and ruthless governor, Ziyad, ruled from Basra. Ziyad was the son of a prostitute, and his father was unknown, which meant that his very name was vague and humiliating: "Ziyad, the son of his father." As an army clerk, he had learned to speak Persian, so he was a useful secretary to several governors before Ali appointed him governor of Fars (South Persia) in 656.

Muawiya won Ziyad's loyalty in a novel way. Muawiya announced that his own father, Abu Sufyan, had slept with Ziyad's mother during the "Days of Ignorance" before the coming of Islam and was in fact the father of her child, Ziyad. Suddenly, Ziyad the bastard had both a prestigious name, Ziyad ibn Abu Sufyan, and a respected place in the Umayya clan, the world's most powerful family.

When Ziyad became governor of Basra in 664, he was determined to impose law and order in this long-rebellious garrison city. In his first speech, he warned, "Whoever breaks into a house, I will break into his heart. Whoever robs a grave, I will bury him alive in it."

With a massive force of four thousand policemen, bodyguards, and spies, Ziyad patrolled the streets, imposed a curfew, and jailed anyone who, if asked, refused to curse the memory of Ali. He also tightened finances by purging the dead from the lists of pensioners.

Muawiya was so pleased with Ziyad's work in Basra and southern Persia that in 670 he also made him governor of Kufa, a sprawling province that included Iraq, northern Persia, and eastern Arabia. In effect, Ziyad was Muawiya's viceroy for the eastern half of his empire.

In the west, Muawiya was "Commander of the Sea," *amir al-bahr*, from which we get our English word *admiral*. Like the ancient Phoenicians, he took the wood for his ships from the cedars of Lebanon. In 672, his navy captured the island of Rhodes. The Muslims sold the ruins of the Colossus of Rhodes, once one of the Seven Wonders of the World, to a scrap metal dealer, who needed fifty camels to take the mess away.

Muawiya's eldest son, Yazid, led a naval force that spent nearly seven years (674–680) trying to capture the Byzantine capital, Constantinople. The Byzantines successfully defended themselves with flamethrowers that spewed "Greek fire," a highly flammable liquid that burned on water and destroyed many Muslim ships.

If the Muslims had seized Constantinople in the 670s, they would probably have taken most of Europe, for the continent was still in the Dark Ages and completely defenseless. Instead, when the Muslims finally did conquer Constantinople in 1453, Europe was much stronger.

To the east, the Muslims conquered Kabul in 663 when an Arab bowman shot an elephant that collapsed right at the city's entrance. The beleaguered soldiers defending the city were unable to shut the gate, and Muslim soldiers stormed through.

In North Africa, Amr ibn al-As's nephew Uqba ibn Nafi conquered Tunisia in 670. Later, he rode westward to the Atlantic, but on the way home, he was ambushed by Berbers in 683. Twenty-five years passed before the Muslims reached the Atlantic again, but this time they secured their conquest, taking Morocco in 708 and Spain in 711.

As more of the Companions of the Prophet died of old age, the religious enthusiasm of many in the next generation of Muslims, who had never known Muhammad, declined. As one Muslim has written, "They no longer remembered the ecstasies derived in offering prayers." In Damascus and elsewhere, wealthy Muslims built lavish mansions with sculpted ceilings, mosaic floors, and large baths. In the evening, they wore silk, drank wine, and watched pretty girls dance to stirring music.

Muawiya's favorite wife, Maysun, was unimpressed by luxury. She missed the freedom of nomadic life and wrote a poem:

A flapping tent with a breeze that's cool
Delights me more than a palace high,
And more the cloak of simple wool
Than robes in which I've learned to sigh,

And more than the purr of a friendly cat
I love the watchdog's bark so mean;
And more than any blubber fat
I love a Bedouin young and lean.[2]

The overweight caliph divorced Maysun when he heard this poem but continued to designate their eldest son, Yazid, as his heir. Yazid fought well during the siege of Constantinople but had a frivolous side that made it difficult for people to take him seriously. Already plump in his mid-thirties, he preferred hunting to governing, and he assigned a slave to each of his hunting dogs. He kept a pet monkey constantly at his side and loved the company of singing girls. What was most scandalous for Orthodox Muslims was the fact that Yazid drank wine daily, although he does not seem to have become a drunkard.

Muawiya was anxious to prevent another civil war after his death and knew that the previous system of choosing caliphs by seeking a consensus among the old men in Medina would no longer work. Medina was too small and too far from the centers of the empire to govern the affairs of Muslims any longer. Muawiya proposed instead that his son Yazid be named heir apparent while Muawiya, his father, was still alive. This would ensure the smoothest possible transition after Muawiya died.

In Medina, the idea of making the caliph a hereditary monarch and the choice of a wine-drinker as heir were seen as blasphemous, but in Syria and Palestine, people liked having Syrian rule continue.

Muawiya personally went to Medina to try to persuade the sons of Abu Bakr, Umar, and Ali to support his son, but they told him that a caliph was not a king. In the end, it did not matter what the people of Medina thought. Muawiya lined up support for his son's succession by bribing one tribe after another in Syria, Egypt, Iraq, and Persia. They in turn sent delegations to Damascus asking that Yazid be the next caliph. Muawiya granted their request and formally named his son heir apparent. This was the beginning of the Umayyad dynasty, the first in Arab history. It lasted until 750, nearly a century.

With his son's succession as caliph assured, Muawiya died in April 680. He was about seventy-seven. On his deathbed, he warned Yazid that Ali's second son, Hussein, would try to become caliph but advised Yazid to "deal gently with him, because the Prophet's blood runs in his veins." Muawiya also asked that some of Muhammad's hair and nail clippings, which Muawiya had saved ever since he was Muhammad's scribe, be sprinkled on his eyes before he was buried. The ruler of Islam's vast empire hoped to be remembered as a Companion of the Prophet.

Yazid, the Sixth Caliph (680–683), and the Sunni-Shi'ite Split

Yazid succeeded his father as caliph, but, as Muawiya had foreseen, many Muslims wanted Ali's surviving son, Hussein, to be caliph instead. Unlike Yazid, Hussein was devout and had an air of command. In Kufa, the Iraqi city that had once been Ali's capital, many people wrote letters to Hussein begging him to come rule their city.

One friend cautioned Hussein that he should not leave Medina until the people of Kufa committed themselves to rebellion by driving out their governor. But Hussein was determined to challenge a caliph he despised; he ignored his colleague's advice and rode north to Kufa with his family and closest friends.

The governor of Kufa could not decide whether to support Yazid, the new caliph, or Hussein, the grandson of the Prophet. Yazid quickly dismissed him from his post and transferred young Ubaydallah, the ruthless Ziyad's son, to Kufa. As soon as Ubaydallah arrived, he beheaded Hussein's first cousin and spread a rumor that troops were arriving from Damascus. Within days, Kufa's people were cowed and its streets deserted.

Hussein and his small contingent of seventy-two men and their families bravely rode to Kufa anyway. At Karbala, twenty-five miles away, four thousand of Ubaydallah's troops surrounded Hussein's force and refused to let any of Hussein's troops fetch water from the nearby Euphrates. After several days, they also delivered a note from Ubaydallah demanding that Hussein swear allegiance to Yazid.

Hussein asked whether he could either go to Damascus to talk with Yazid or to a frontier to fight infidels, but both requests were denied. Finally, Hussein asked whether he could have a night to prepare for death, and this request was granted. He spent the night unsuccessfully urging his loyal men to leave, praying, and comforting his thirsty wives and children.

The next morning, October 10, 680, the women and children stayed in their tents as Hussein's men and horses went out to die. An hour passed; none of Ubaydallah's soldiers wanted to be the one to actually kill Hussein. Hussein called out to them, "Is not the grandson of the Prophet more worthy of your loyalty than the grandson of a prostitute?" One man, the commander of Ubaydallah's cavalry, deserted his troops and rode over to Hussein. He said that he preferred death and paradise to longer life and hellfire. The rest of his cavalry was unmoved.

Finally, Ubaydallah's archers fired hundreds of arrows. One landed in Hussein's jaw, but he managed to pull it out. Then a swordsman almost stabbed Hussein, but one of Hussein's sons ran out from his tent to fight with his father, and when the blow struck, it was the son who was stabbed instead. "You and I will soon be with the Apostle of Allah," Hussein comforted his son just seconds before a soldier knocked Hussein off his horse and onto the ground. Hussein, bruised, dazed, and knowing that he was about to die, asked God to "forgive the sins of my grandfather's people." A moment later, a soldier beheaded him. Within minutes, Ubaydallah's army cut off the heads of all seventy-three of Hussein's followers.

Ubaydallah's horsemen trampled Hussein's body until it was unrecognizable but took his head back to Kufa. There, while receiving the congratulations of his aides, Ubaydallah occasionally picked at Hussein's head with the tip of his sword until an old man shouted, "Stop that! Be gentle with that head, for with my own eyes I have seen the Prophet kiss those lips." Then the old man left the room, crying, "The Arabs have become slaves. After so much glory, today we are slaves."

Weeks later, when the heads of Hussein and his seventy-three followers were shown to Yazid in Damascus, the new caliph cursed Ubaydallah for not being merciful and sparing the lives of the Prophet's grandson and his men. He also ordered that the heads be returned to Karbala for a proper burial. But this was just for show. A few months later, Yazid appointed Ubaydallah governor of Basra as well as Kufa; so, like his father before him, Ubaydallah was viceroy of the eastern half of the empire.

After this tragedy, the people of Kufa and other parts of Iraq were deeply ashamed that they had urged Hussein to lead a revolt and then deserted him. As early as 684, some Iraqis began to revere Hussein as a saint who had stood up to tyranny, and over the next century, a growing number of Iraqis and Persians formed the Shi'ite branch of Islam. Shi'ites revere Hussein as the third imam (after Ali and Hasan) and all of the subsequent imams were direct descendants of Hussein.

Every year, in every town in Iran and southern Iraq, Shi'ites undergo a ten-day period of fasts and mourning during the first part of the lunar month of Muharram. For nine days, the story of Hussein's death is read aloud to tearful crowds, and each night shirtless men walk the streets, beating their chests and whipping their backs with chains as they sing hymns of grief to the martyred Hussein.

On the tenth day, Shi'ites reenact the battle of Karbala in an open field. After the battle, a procession of camels carries the (wooden) head of the dead Hussein back to town, along with seventy-two other grisly wooden heads, each painted pale green to suggest a rotting death. Throngs of people line the streets and wail as the camels pass by.

The brutality at Karbala horrified Arabs everywhere and pushed the people of Mecca and Medina into open rebellion in 682. The following year, Yazid's troops recaptured the holy cities, but not before a catapult hurled naphtha that burned the black cloth off the Kaaba, the stone cube toward which all Muslims pray. It was a perfect symbol for Shi'ites and other enemies of the Umayyad dynasty: the unbelieving, wine-drinking caliph had sent his army to burn the very center of Islam.

In what seemed to many Muslims to be retribution, Yazid died of an illness in 683, just weeks after the Kaaba burned.

Muawiya's Descendants and His Role in Muslim History

Yazid's lack of a suitable heir doomed the Muslims to another nine years of civil war, but in 692, the army of Muawiya's cousin Malik bombarded Mecca a second time and crushed the last challenge to Umayyad power.

During this second civil war, Malik built Jerusalem's Dome of the Rock, where Muslims believe that Muhammad left a footprint before ascending to heaven. Muawiya had begun the plans for the building, which was completed in 691.

Malik married Muawiya's granddaughter Atikah, an unusually intelligent and pretty woman who gave birth to four boys. Malik and his four sons ruled the Muslim world for fifty-eight years, from 685 to 743, and during that time, its vast reach spread from Spain to what is now Pakistan. When Malik's last son, Hisham, died in 743, the Umayyad dynasty fell just seven years later. The next royal house, the Abbasids, moved Islam's capital from Damascus to Baghdad. There they ruled for two hundred years before the Muslim world split into several competing empires.

The earliest accounts of Muawiya and the Umayyid kings were written two centuries after their fall by writers for the Abbasid family, which had overthrown the Umayyid monarchs. These historians distrusted Muawiya as a late convert to Islam and despised his son Yazid as the killer of Hussein. Even today, most Muslims take a dim view of Muawiya. While they concede his administrative ability, they think that when he chose his son Yazid to be his successor, he reduced the sacred office of caliph to that of a mere king, no better than the Persian emperor whom the Muslims had so recently overthrown. Muawiya's practical and secular statecraft, they believe, ended a golden age where saints ruled and everyone was equal.

Not until the beginning of the twentieth century did Western writers begin to question this hostile historical tradition. In part, this is because several of the things that scandalized many Muslims—drinking wine, wearing silk, listening to music—seem to Westerners to be merely some of the pleasures of civilized living. Indeed, one of the most attractive things about Muawiya is that he combined the accessibility and the unpretentiousness of the earliest Muslims with an urbane enjoyment of life's pleasures.

Muawiya's greatest achievement was ensuring the continued unity of the Muslims. Imposing a discipline in the garrison cities of Iraq and Egypt not seen since the days of Umar, he restored domestic peace and extended frontier conquests. When he died in 680, the Muslim Empire was both richer and more secure than it had been when he became caliph in 661.

The frequent criticism that Muawiya was not so much the Arabs' fifth caliph as he was their first king is quite true. But he was an excellent king, ruling ably from Tunisia to Afghanistan. Although his son Yazid was a disappointment, his great-grandchildren extended the empire still farther, from the Atlantic Ocean to the Indus River.

The Arabs' Marginal Role during the Next Thousand Years

The Umayyad dynasty created the greatest Arab state in history. After it fell in 750, the Arabs would never be so powerful again. The Abbasid dynasty made Baghdad its capital in 762 but drew its power from Persian and Turkish soldiers, rather than from Arab tribesmen.

Caliph al-Mamun, who ruled from 813 to 833, built a "House of Wisdom" where Muslim scholars translated hundreds of Greek works on medicine, astronomy, and mathematics. (They had no interest in Greek myths or plays, which they regarded as pagan.) Then, building on the Greeks' foundation, the Muslims made many advances of their own.

Avicenna (980–1037) wrote a medical encyclopedia that was used by doctors in the West, as well as in the Muslim world, until the 1600s. Ibn al-Haytham (965–1039) wrote the world's best work on optics until the time of Isaac Newton and, after observing the twilight, correctly determined that the air peters out about sixty miles up. Muslim scholars also created a new branch of mathematics: *al-jabr*, or algebra.

Despite the scholarship they sponsored, al-Mamun and his ineffectual successors were militarily weak and allowed Spain and North Africa to become independent in all but name. Persian mercenaries seized control of the Abbasid throne in 945. Power then passed to three groups of Turks: the Seljuks (1055–1243), the Mamluks (1250–1517), and the Ottomans (1453–1919).

For three quarters of a millennium (1000–1750) the Arabs' role in the Muslim world was marginal. Long before 1258, when the Mongols destroyed Baghdad, the largest and richest Arab city, Turkish had already replaced Arabic as the language of government, and Persian had replaced it as the language of culture. The Arabs could only resent the fact that they no longer controlled the great civilization they had once begun.

The Arabian peninsula became a backwater as the Arabs splintered into small tribes and tiny oasis-states that fought over pastureland whenever their neighbors received more rain than they did. Not until the eighteenth century—a thousand years after the fall of the Umayyad dynasty—did the tribesmen of Arabia unite once more.

PART TWO

THE FIRST AND SECOND SAUDI STATES (1744–1887)

I N THE HARSH ARABIAN DESERT, the great Muslim conquests of the seventh century were followed by a thousand years of disunity in which each oasis was an isolated fiefdom. Then, in the eighteenth century, a religious movement unified the Arabian people again.

The founder of this new sect was a scholarly preacher named Muhammad ibn Abdul Wahhab. He was appalled to see people chanting magic spells, hugging "sacred" palm trees, and kneeling before the tombs of saints. With a spade, he smashed one of the tombs. He called his movement against idol worship "The Call to the One True God." Critics dubbed ibn Abdul Wahhab's followers "Wahhabis," and this became the name by which the world knows them. (Today, although few Wahhabis are terrorists, many terrorists are Wahhabis.)

In 1744, ibn Abdul Wahhab joined forces with Muhammad ibn Saud, forming a religious and military alliance that has lasted more than 260 years. One oasis at a time, the new state conquered most of the Arabian peninsula until, by 1805, for the first time in a millennium, a caravan could travel safely from the Persian Gulf to the Red Sea.

The first Saudi state grew powerful enough to launch raids against the Ottoman Empire, but in 1818 the sultan exacted his revenge when an army with European artillery destroyed the Saudi capital.

A second Saudi state arose six years later, but it remained small and weak and fell in 1887. Yet the mere existence of this state meant that the Wahhabis had a home and a chance to become stronger in the future.

5

The Founder of Wahhabism: Muhammad ibn Abdul Wahhab (1703–1792)

THE DRAMATIC RISE in Muslim fundamentalism in the late twentieth century was encouraged by Saudi Arabia, which used its oil money to print books and build schools throughout the world to instill in new generations of students the Saudis' austere beliefs. Saudi Arabia is one of the most puritanical nations on Earth. Adulterers are stoned to death, habitual thieves sometimes have their hands cut off, and religious policemen make sure that women cover their hair and shopkeepers close their stores at prayer time. Yet it was not always so. For centuries, Arabian Islam had been lax. Adultery went unpunished, robbery was common, and few people prayed.

The man who changed this was Muhammad ibn Abdul Wahhab (1703–1792). In the eighteenth century, he began a religious awakening that some call a "Second Coming" of Islam. It swept across the Arabian Desert and had remarkable similarities to the original rise of Islam eleven hundred years earlier. The Wahhabi movement gave birth not only to the modern kingdom of Saudi Arabia but also to its strict brand of Islam.

Today, the majority of Saudi Arabia's citizens are Wahhabi Muslims, and the descendants of ibn Abdul Wahhab continue to control the government ministries in charge of mosques and law courts. Although only a minority of Wahhabis are extremists, Wahhabi-like beliefs are common among militant Muslim groups such as al-Qaeda, Egypt's Islamic Jihad, Afghanistan's Taliban, Palestine's Hamas, Algeria's Armed Islamic Group, and the fundamentalist Jamaat-i-Islami party in Pakistan. Some writers mistakenly compare Wahhabism to Nazism and say that it is America's next great enemy. In fact, al-Qaeda and other extremist organizations have been influenced much more by the Egyptian writer Sayyid Qutb (1906–1966) than they have been by the far more moderate ibn Abdul Wahhab, who, unlike Qutb, advocated violence only as a last resort.

Ibn Abdul Wahhab called his movement "the Call to the One True God." His followers refer to themselves as "People of Monotheism." Critics dubbed them "Wahhabis," as if their cause were a personal cult or a new religion. It was not a cult and not new, but the name stuck. Wahhabis, like Quakers, are known everywhere by a name first given to them in scorn.

Muhammad ibn Abdul Wahhab was born in 1703 in the oasis town of Uyaina, in central Arabia, far from the sea. While western Arabia was relatively cosmopolitan because of the many pilgrimages to the holy cities of Mecca and Medina, central Arabia was isolated, drought-stricken, and barely aware of the rest of the world. This poor and remote region, Najd (Arabic for "plateau"), was not worth conquering and was therefore free from outside influence.

Almost every oasis was ruled by a different sheikh. Most ruled arbitrarily and by tribal custom rather than Muslim law. Outside of town, bandits plagued desert trails, which aggravated the region's poverty. Despite the area's disunity, there was a regional feeling among the people, a sense of being Najdis, Central Arabians. There was also a growing weariness, at least among oasis-dwellers, with the endless raids and counterraids between towns. Ibn Abdul Wahhab's hometown of Uyaina, for example, fought a war nearly every three years.[1]

If there were enough days of rain—and no locusts—villagers in an oasis could grow dates, barley, and millet and trade them for the camels, sheep, and horses that the Bedouins tended in the desert. Farmers and Bedouins also bartered crops and livestock with traders from Yemen, Iraq, and Syria in return for swords, pots and pans, and coffee.

Few people in central Arabia were literate; almost no one read the Quran. The knowledge of Islam's basic tenets faded with each passing century until finally people no longer prayed toward Mecca or even knew what direction the city was in. Men and women forgot about the *zakat*, the tax to support the poor, but revived their belief in the "evil eye" and in Ghoul, an evil spirit that was said to rob graves and eat corpses.

Superstition grew rampant. Women hugged special palm trees in order to have children, Bedouins sacrificed camels to their ancestors, and generals consulted astrologers before going to battle. Some Arabs even prayed to the sun. Others knelt before the graves of Muslim saints and shouted out requests.

Muhammad ibn Abdul Wahhab was fortunate to come from a scholarly family. His grandfather was a leading judge who had written a book on the rituals involved with making a pilgrimage to Mecca. When he died, his son, Wahhab (ibn Abdul Wahhab's father), became a judge when he was only twenty. Wahhab was a forceful speaker and wrote several pamphlets explaining verses of the Quran. He was about fifty-five when his illustrious son Muhammad was born, for he had already been a judge for thirty-five years.

Little is known about Muhammad ibn Abdul Wahhab's youth, but it is clear that he was a quick study. Taught by his father, he memorized each chapter of the Quran before he was eleven and also read many of the *hadith*, the sayings and the deeds of Muhammad. He married soon after reaching puberty and made a pilgrimage to Mecca while still in his teens.

When the handsome young scholar was about twenty, he moved to Medina, where he was dismayed to see people praying to Muhammad in front of his tomb, something the Prophet had expressly forbidden. Ibn Abdul Wahhab studied in the city for a year or two, deeply influenced by a teacher from India who said that books can be spiritual weapons.

In Basra, in southern Iraq, ibn Abdul Wahhab studied Islamic law, more *hadith*, and works of Arabic literature. Because most people in southern Iraq were Shi'ite, the worship of saints at their tombs was common. To ibn Abdul Wahhab, this was polytheism, a violation of dozens of verses in the Quran and of the first of the Ten Commandments (which Muslims also heed), which says, "Thou shall have no other gods before me." He thought that the Shi'ites were corrupting Islam and felt compelled to speak out.

"To Allah alone is worship due," ibn Abdul Wahhab preached. "We walk in the light of a saint, imitating his example, but we pray only to Allah." His message was simple, but in Basra, it won him more enemies than friends, and soon he was banished from the city. He had hoped to continue his studies in Damascus but was robbed and had to return home instead.

His father had recently quarreled with a coarse new emir (prince) in Uyaina and was forced to leave the oasis even though he was eighty. He moved to a nearby town, Huraimila, and there father and son were reunited sometime after the year 1730. Although the elderly Wahhab agreed with his son's views on the evils of polytheism, he objected to his son preaching in public. In deference to his father, the dutiful son devoted the next decade to teaching and, more important, writing.

Ibn Abdul Wahhab wrote sixteen books and dozens of pamphlets. One book is about turning points in Muhammad's life. Another is a commentary on the Profession of Faith ("There is but one God. Muhammad is His Messenger") that starts every prayer call. A third book is a discussion of 131 issues on which Muhammad disagreed with the pre-Islamic Arabs who lived during the time that Muslims call *jahiliyah*, or "the Days of Ignorance." Ibn Abdul Wahhab saw his own era as a second *jahiliyah*, a new period of spiritual degradation.

Ibn Abdul Wahhab was influenced by a stern medieval scholar who also influences al-Qaeda today, Taqi al-Din ibn Taymiyah (1263–1328), a professor of Muslim law in Damascus. Ibn Taymiyah condemned both the use of Greek logic and the commentaries of his fellow clergymen as means for seeking truth. Instead, he urged people to read the Quran and the *hadith* themselves to discover God's truth firsthand, uncorrupted by later human opinions.

Ibn Taymiyah also denounced the tendency of many Sufis and Shi'ites to worship saints and kneel before their graves while asking them for blessings. "To call upon any being other than God, be he a prophet or a saint, living or dead, or to prostrate before him or before his grave, is polytheism," he wrote. Ibn Taymiyah particularly criticized those who prayed at Muhammad's tomb in Medina. In response, rival scholars put him in prison, where he died two years later.

One major difference between ibn Taymiyah and ibn Abdul Wahhab was in their view of *jihad*, or holy war. Ibn Taymiyah believed it was the duty of individual Muslims to "take the initiative" and fight an offensive *jihad* not only against infidels, but also against Muslim rulers who enforce tribal customs rather than Islamic law. By contrast, in his *Book of Jihad*, ibn Abdul Wahhab says that only a legitimate ruler, not an individual, can declare a holy war, and even then soldiers must take special care not to kill women, children, or the elderly.[2]

In the late 1730s, ibn Abdul Wahhab wrote his most important work, *The Book of Monotheism*. Written in a clear, simple style, more than 90 percent of the work consists of 341 different quotations from the Quran, the *hadith*, and the earliest and most established Muslim scholars.

On the very first page, ibn Abdul Wahhab quotes the Quran, "To every people we have sent an apostle saying: Worship Allah and turn away from idols." A few pages later, he quotes the Quran again to warn that polytheism is the worst sin of all, the one offense Allah will not pardon: "Allah will not forgive the union of other gods with Himself! But other than this He will forgive whom He pleaseth."[3]

Seven chapters in *The Book of Monotheism* warn that it is a sin to ask a saint or a spirit to plead with God on one's behalf on Judgment Day. Nor should one swear an oath by anyone other than Allah. Ibn Abdul Wahhab wrote that it is better "to swear by Allah while lying . . . than to swear by other than Him while speaking the truth."[4]

Ibn Abdul Wahhab did not publish *The Book of Monotheism* until his father died in 1740. He also started preaching again. He was a passionate, persuasive speaker who spoke from the heart and used ordinary language that anyone could understand—and he never once uttered a vulgar word. He also had a humble manner, which hid the fact that he possessed quiet courage. He took to heart ibn Taymiyah's observation that "the more you fear God, the less you fear anything else."

From the start, ibn Abdul Wahhab knew that he would never be able to persuade Arab tribesmen to give up their polytheistic customs unless his words were backed by force. Looking for political and military support, he wrote to sheikhs and emirs throughout Arabia about his mission to purify Islam. He found that Uthman ibn Mu'ammar, a new young emir in his hometown of Uyaina, was sympathetic.

"Fear Allah and he will make you king of all of Najd [Central Arabia]," ibn Abdul Wahhab told his new patron. A religious man, Uthman gave ibn Abdul Wahhab a palm grove and some cattle to ensure him an income, then Uthman cemented his alliance with his new teacher by arranging for his young aunt to become the scholar's second wife. Following the advice of his new relative, Uthman made the *sharia* (the Quran and the acts and the sayings of Muhammad) the law of the town.

As ibn Abdul Wahhab walked the streets of Uyaina, he saw that his neighbors continued to kneel before graves. "Mud cannot save you, neither can stone," he told them. "Pray to Allah and Allah alone." News of the fiery new preacher spread quickly, and people flocked to Uyaina from many nearby oases to hear ibn Abdul Wahhab lead the Friday prayers.

After a few months, ibn Abdul Wahhab asked some of his students to cut down certain palm trees that people were paying homage to. But one especially sacred tree still stood, where maidens and widows prayed for husbands and where young mothers prayed for children.

Ibn Abdul Wahhab announced in advance the date that he would personally chop down the tree. When the day came and a crowd gathered around the tree, he lifted his ax high and declared, "Truth has come. Falsehood shall cease to exist." These were the words Muhammad used when he smashed the 360 idols inside the Kaaba in Mecca.

The next target was a dome over the tomb of Zayd ibn al-Khattab, the brother of Umar, the second caliph. This time, ibn Abdul Wahhab arrived with the emir, Uthman, and a force of six hundred soldiers. The preacher took a spade and demolished the dome himself. Many people were sure that he was doomed, but as time passed and nothing happened, most of them concluded that ibn Abdul Wahhab was right, that the tomb was nothing but lifeless stone.

In 1743 or 1744, ibn Abdul Wahhab was faced with his most famous case. A devout woman admitted that she had committed adultery repeatedly and wanted to be punished in this life so that she might be spared an eternity in hell. She confessed four times, as is required if there are no witnesses, but ibn Abdul Wahhab was reluctant to order the traditional punishment.

He asked the woman whether the men had forced themselves upon her, but she vehemently denied this. He also asked her several questions to see whether she might be going mad, but she was quite sane. Finally, ibn Abdul Wahhab felt that the *hadith* on the subject gave him no choice, and he ordered that she be stoned to death.

The woman was carefully wrapped in several layers of clothing and put in a ditch that was deep enough to cover her up to her waist. Emir Uthman threw the first stone, ibn Abdul Wahhab threw the second, then many townsmen joined in. After the woman died, ibn Abdul Wahhab ordered that her body be washed and wrapped in a shroud and that a prayer be said at her burial.

The preacher became famous instantly. It was the first public stoning in Arabia in perhaps a century, and news of the event spread to every oasis in the desert. The eighteenth century was a period of sexual laxity in the Arabian peninsula, and many people who had engaged in illicit affairs reacted to the stoning with anger and fear.

In the region of Al-Hasa, on the shore of the Persian Gulf south of Kuwait, Shi'ite Muslims particularly despised ibn Abdul Wahhab and his teachings. Shi'ites were (and still are) a majority in this region, and like the Sufis, they revere their saints. The emir of Al-Hasa demanded that Uthman kill ibn Abdul Wahhab. Every year, the emir paid Uthman twelve hundred gold and silver pieces in return for the protection of his merchants when they traveled inland; now he threatened to end this payment.

Uthman asked ibn Abdul Wahhab to stage fewer public events, but the preacher sternly replied that if the emir feared Allah, he need not fear his enemies. Uthman decided that he would rather have twelve hundred coins and a friendly neighbor than no gold and a hostile one, and he reluctantly asked ibn Abdul Wahhab to leave Uyaina.

Ibn Abdul Wahhab had several followers in Ad Diriyah, an oasis town twenty miles away that today is just outside Riyadh, Saudi Arabia's capital. He moved in with one of them and began to teach, but the house soon became too crowded. Some of his students asked for help from a woman named Mudhi, who liked to help students and scholars. She was the wife of the town's ruler, Muhammad ibn Saud, whose obscure father founded the royal dynasty that still rules Saudi Arabia today.

The al-Saud family originally may have been part of a nomadic tribe that was known for breeding excellent camels. In 1446, the family acquired some land in Ad Diriyah, possibly because the villagers wanted to improve their stock of camels. In the 1710s, 270 years later, the emir of Ad Diriyah was banished for a reason unknown to us today, and the new emir was Saud ibn Muhammad ibn Miqrin, the founder of the Saudi dynasty. It was Saud's son, Muhammad ibn Saud, who welcomed ibn Abdul Wahhab to his oasis.

At first, the emir, who was a fierce warrior, was skeptical of the troublemaking scholar. But his wife, Mudhi, was deeply impressed by his sermons. "Allah has sent you a great gift," she told her husband. "Make him your ally." She was the first to see that her family could lead ibn Abdul Wahhab's movement to unify Arabia and that routine raiding could turn into holy war.

Ibn Abdul Wahhab Guides the First Saudi State (1744–1792)

The modern kingdom of Saudi Arabia officially began in 1932, but its true start took place in 1744, when Muhammad ibn Saud went to ibn Abdul Wahhab's cottage to welcome the famous preacher to his city. Ibn Abdul Wahhab thanked the Saudi monarch and told him that if he fought for the principles of Islam, his government would be a source of justice and his power would vastly increase. The emir agreed to an alliance with the preacher but asked for two conditions.

First, just as the people of Medina had asked Muhammad not to leave their city once he grew powerful, the Saudi monarch similarly asked ibn Abdul Wahhab not to move from Ad Diriyah. Second, the emir wanted to continue his tax on the harvest of dates when palm trees bore fruit.

Ibn Abdul Wahhab promised immediately never to move from Ad Diriyah but rejected the request to keep the tax. He assured the Saudi monarch that his plunder from holy war would far outweigh his revenue from the date harvest, and the emir agreed to repeal the tax. Overnight, this made ibn Abdul Wahhab popular with the people of Ad Diriyah.

The preacher and the Saudi monarch swore oaths that were similar to those that Muhammad and the people of Medina exchanged when the Prophet arrived in their city in 622. This included a promise by the emir to make the Islamic *sharia* the law of the oasis and to maintain a readiness to go to war for the principles of monotheism.

The emir provided ibn Abdul Wahhab with a house, a palm grove, and a grain field and regularly attended the preacher's classes and sermons. He consulted ibn Abdul Wahhab on every decision he ever made, and there is no record that the two men ever disagreed about anything. Muhammad ibn Saud sealed his alliance with ibn Abdul Wahhab by marrying his eldest son, Abd al-Aziz, to one of the preacher's daughters; the two families have continued to intermarry for more than 260 years. Almost everyone in Ad Diriyah willingly became a Wahhabi, but four families that objected to ibn Abdul Wahhab's teachings were asked to leave. Life in the oasis had an exciting new sense of purpose but also became brutally strict. Volunteer policemen made sure that shops were closed before prayers began and beat men if they did not appear at the mosque on time. The mosque was simple and unadorned, and the floor where everyone knelt to pray was made of gravel.

Believing that the harsher the punishment, the greater the deterrent, ibn Abdul Wahhab revived the ancient penalty for theft: amputation of the hand with a hatchet. Smoking tobacco was punished with forty lashes, drinking wine with eighty. The wearing of gold, jewels, and silk was forbidden as vain, while music and loud singing were banned because they interfered with prayer. Rosary beads were outlawed, but prayers at gravesites were still permitted as long as one did not ask the dead to intercede with Allah.

In the town of Ad Diriyah, ibn Abdul Wahhab was preacher, judge, and professor. He started a school to teach men to read and recite the verses of the Quran and the sayings of the *hadith*. He was a patient, precise teacher who was said to have a dry sense of humor. He also instructed his students on matters of etiquette, such as the best way to shake hands, embrace, laugh, and yawn. In all of his classes ibn Abdul Wahhab treated princes, merchants, and peasants as equals, as brothers in the Muslim faith.

Many of ibn Abdul Wahhab's former followers in Uyaina missed his moral leadership and moved to Ad Diriyah. They worked as manual laborers by day in order to be his students at night. Ibn Abdul Wahhab borrowed a great deal of money to feed and house his followers, and he was unable to pay his debts until he received the spoils from some military conquests years later.

As more and more promising young men moved from Uyaina to Ad Diriyah, the emir of Uyaina, Uthman, came to regret his decision to banish ibn Abdul Wahhab. He asked ibn Abdul Wahhab to return, but it was too late. The charismatic preacher had promised Muhammad ibn Saud that he would never move away from Ad Diriyah, and he kept his word.

Oddly enough, one of ibn Abdul Wahhab's most vehement opponents was his brother, Sulaiman ibn Abdul Wahhab, who wrote a book called *Divine Thunderbolts in Refutation of Wahhabism*. Sulaiman was appalled by his brother's intolerance of other branches of Islam and once accused him of adding a sixth pillar to the Muslim faith: "Anyone who doesn't follow me is not a Muslim."

In the desert, the Bedouins' feelings toward the Wahhabis were mixed. On the one hand, they loved the idea of joining the preacher in holy war because it gave them an opportunity to loot and plunder. On the other hand, the Bedouins hated the *zakat*, the annual 2.5 percent tax on wealth, but ibn Abdul Wahhab warned them that a refusal to pay the tax amounted to unbelief.

Every year, Muhammad ibn Saud sent armed teams of clerks and accountants into the desert to collect one-fortieth of a Bedouin's herd of camels or sheep as taxes. In town, they took one-fortieth of a merchant's capital, one-twentieth of an irrigated crop, and one-tenth of the crops on dry land.

When the Saudi monarch needed troops, he told each tribe and village how many men he wanted and where and when to meet. Each Wahhabi soldier brought his own weapons, barley flour, and water unless the campaign was going to last more than a month, in which case the emir would provide the food. Those who showed up late were fined or beaten.

During a battle or a raid, soldiers with camels rode in front and also brought up the rear. In between, infantrymen wielded swords, spears, javelins, shields, and a few flintlock rifles. Wahhabi soldiers were famous for their endurance. They could march two days without water, taking only dates and camel's milk as sustenance. Any army reckless enough to pursue the Wahhabis into the desert inevitably succumbed to thirst, hunger, and then a disastrous attack.

Wahhabi troops, fired up with religious fervor, were not disciplined fighters, but they were unusually brave because they were unafraid of death and martyrdom. Ironically, ibn Abdul Wahhab never wrote about martyrdom because he felt that virtue itself was important, not its reward. Fighting to reach paradise, he thought, was little better than fighting for money or glory.

Still, ibn Abdul Wahhab often spoke to soldiers before a battle. Polytheists should be given a chance to repent their sin, he said, but since they had failed to do so, it was better to kill them than to allow a schism in the Muslim community. It was also perfectly all right to confiscate their houses, tents, animals, fields, and palm groves.

Ibn Abdul Wahhab harshly criticized Christians and Jews for allowing polytheistic beliefs to corrupt their monotheism. Christians err, he said, in claiming that Jesus is the Son of God, while Jews err in asserting that they are a Chosen People. Ibn Abdul Wahhab never called for violence against Jews or Christians, however, and the Wahhabis allowed the few Jews who were still living in Arabia to worship without interference inside their homes (as long as they paid a tax) because they represented no threat to the unity of the Muslims.[5]

Although Wahhabi soldiers had no qualms about killing every man in a village, they always left women unmolested. After a successful raid, women from a defeated tribe sometimes rode with the Wahhabis in safety until they could find a new village with male relatives.

In *The Book of Marriage*, ibn Abdul Wahhab wrote that a father cannot force a daughter to marry against her will, and that a woman has the right to divorce a husband she detests. He also said that women have the right to an education and do not need to hide their faces in public if they have covered their hair. He also condemned marriage before puberty and wrote that if a man has sex with a servant or a slave, he is violating the bonds of his marriage. Despite the Wahhabis' reputation for extreme conservatism, Saudi women today can cite *The Book of Marriage* to support many of their calls for reform.[6]

When Wahhabi soldiers captured an oasis, Muhammad ibn Saud typically built a fortress and appointed a relative to rule the town. This gave rival branches of his family a stake in his rule and discouraged internal rebellion. He also sent Wahhabi missionaries to teach his new subjects that only Allah should be worshipped and that polytheism was deeply evil.

Ibn Abdul Wahhab taught classes in Muslim theology to prepare his students to spread the call to the One True God. Thousands of volunteers traveled to every oasis and Bedouin tribe in Arabia to attack polytheism, form alliances with emirs and sheikhs, and teach the illiterate how to read the Quran and the *hadith*. Like Muhammad, ibn Abdul Wahhab wrote letters to chiefs and scholars in every region of Arabia, explaining "the call" and asking them to join. He also wrote letters to prominent Muslims in Iraq, Syria, Yemen, and even India.

For a quarter of a century, Ad Diriyah's chief rival in central Arabia was the city of Riyadh, ruled by an extraordinarily cruel emir named Dahham ibn Dawwas. A sadist, Dahham once ordered a woman's mouth sewn shut, a man's teeth broken with a hammer, and another man to eat his own flesh.

Ad Diriyah and Riyadh fought thirty-six battles between 1746 and 1773, and roughly two thousand men died on each side. In one battle in 1764, when Dahham was joined by Bedouins from the south, the Wahhabis lost five hundred lives.

After this defeat, ibn Abdul Wahhab tried to comfort his monarch with a verse from the Quran: "We alternate these days of successes and reverses among men, that God may know those who have believed, and that He may take martyrs from among you."[7] He even said that men and women should praise adversity because it is a sin to doubt God's wisdom.[8] Still, the Saudi emir had never lost so many young men before, and it may have broken his spirit, for Muhammad ibn Saud died the following year.

His oldest son, Abd al-Aziz, became Ad Diriyah's new emir. Abd al-Aziz had led the army for fifteen years; he was a proven warrior who knew when to be patient. He was also ibn Abdul Wahhab's son-in-law. The preacher had personally tutored him and was pleased by his devotion to Islam. Like his father, Abd al-Aziz consulted with ibn Abdul Wahhab before making any decision, and there is no record of the two men ever disagreeing about anything.

By 1773, Riyadh was surrounded on every side by Wahhabis and their allies. Abd al-Aziz mounted a frontal assault on the city, and Dahham gave up and fled. After twenty-seven years, Ad Diriyah was at last the most powerful city in central Arabia.

Whenever ibn Abdul Wahhab had received spoils from previous military campaigns, he had always spent the money on his school and never kept a penny for himself. Now, because the city of Riyadh had been captured intact, there were so many spoils that the preacher finally felt free to pay off his personal debts.

At seventy, ibn Abdul Wahhab retired from the day-to-day administration of Ad Diriyah's affairs and finances. He still worked a full day on the things he loved: teaching, preaching, and writing. The emir, Abd al-Aziz, continued to follow his advice and out of deep respect gave him a title, *Sheikhul Islam*, Leader of Islam.

By 1781, the al-Saud family's territory extended outward from Ad Diriyah about one hundred miles in every direction. Along the perimeter, people in the oases constantly joined but also defected from the Wahhabis, as villagers and Bedouins were torn between their admiration for Wahhabi Islam and their ancient inclination to resist authority.

As Wahhabism spread, murder and theft decreased. Travel in central Arabia became safe for the first time since the seventh century, when Muhammad had also taught people to fear God's judgment. Ibn Abdul Wahhab had never forgotten what it was like to be robbed, and he encouraged Abd al-Aziz to hold each tribe collectively responsible for theft within its territory. The emir also forbade the Bedouins to collect any "protection money" from caravans that crossed the desert.

Because raiding decreased, farmers and shepherds no longer had to guard their fields and livestock at night. With crime down, domestic trade boomed, and Ad Diriyah became a thriving center of commerce. Despite the Wahhabi preference for simple living, the city prospered.

In the mid-1780s the Arabian peninsula suffered from a terrible drought, but because of the taxes the Wahhabis had received, they were able to feed thousands of people whose animals had died and whose crops had failed. They also stormed the city of al-Zilfi, where ibn Abdul Wahhab's brother Sulaiman had continued to denounce his famous sibling. Sulaiman was captured and taken to Ad Diriyah, where he was forbidden to write and preach but was otherwise allowed to live freely.

With central Arabia finally united, Abd al-Aziz and ibn Abdul Wahhab decided in 1788 that it was time to declare Saud, the oldest son of Abd al-Aziz and a grandson of ibn Abdul Wahhab, heir apparent in order to avoid any future struggle over succession. As chief judge and cleric, ibn Abdul Wahhab ordered the leaders of every oasis and Bedouin tribe under Wahhabi rule to swear allegiance to Saud as their future ruler.

At forty, Saud was an experienced general with a reputation so fierce that enemies often fled as soon as they heard he was coming.

Yet his manner was informal, and he always asked people to remain seated when he entered a room. He was handsome, with a deep voice, a long beard, and a mustache so thick that his four wives and half dozen Ethiopian concubines affectionately called him "Mustached Father."

After becoming heir apparent, Saud launched raids in every direction: Syria, Iraq, Oman, Yemen, and some oases near Mecca. In response, the sharif of Mecca, Ghalib, besieged a Wahhabi town without success. Saud then led raids to punish the western Bedouin tribes that had allied with Ghalib and took eleven thousand camels and a hundred thousand sheep. He also extended Wahhabi territory eastward to the Persian Gulf.

In 1789, ibn Abdul Wahhab became ill. The eighty-six-year-old preacher could leave his bedroom to attend Friday prayers only if he was supported by two disciples, yet each week he made the effort.

After three years of illness, Muhammad ibn Abdul Wahhab died in July 1792, just as the Industrial Revolution began in the West. We do not know how he would have used his formidable intellect to respond to the challenge that modern science poses to Islam and other faiths. For all his knowledge, ibn Abdul Wahhab remained blissfully ignorant of European civilization and its advances.

Thousands of people attended ibn Abdul Wahhab's funeral, but in accordance with his wishes, there was no marker on his grave. To his children, he left an orchard, a palm grove, a grain field, and a library with hundreds of books, a rarity in Arabia.

His oldest son, Husain, became the new judge and chief cleric of Ad Diriyah. His three younger sons and several grandsons started schools and wrote many books and essays about Islam and monotheism. Collectively, ibn Abdul Wahhab's descendants are known as *Al ash Shaykh*, the Family of the Sheikh. They are one of only four families with whom members of the House of Saud can marry. Today the family still runs two ministries: Justice and Islamic Endowments and Guidance, which pays the salaries of clerics at seventy-two thousand Sunni mosques.

In a chaotic region that had fragmented into hundreds of oasis-states, Muhammad ibn Abdul Wahhab forged a single nation based on the principles of Islam. He had both the courage to publicly oppose widespread superstitions and the eloquence to make his puritanical outlook appeal to ordinary tribesmen. A well-known Egyptian writer, Taha Husain, described Wahhabism as "A vigorous call towards the pure Islam, free from the contamination of polytheism and idolatry.

It is a call to the same Islam that the Prophet preached. . . . Had the movement not been suppressed [by modern weapons], it would have united the Arabs as in the first century of Islam."[9]

The Wahhabi movement has some resemblance to the Protestant Reformation. Just as Protestant clergymen rebelled against a corrupt papacy and began to strictly interpret the words of the Bible, so Wahhabi clerics have denounced the moral laxity of Islam under the Ottoman Empire—and later, in the modern world—and have strictly interpreted the words of the Quran.

Indeed, there are many parallels between the lives of ibn Abdul Wahhab and John Calvin, the stern Protestant cleric who ruled the city of Geneva from 1538 to 1564. (Arabia, of course, was a far more violent region than Switzerland.) Each man studied law and theology and considered his Scripture to be the word of God. Each wrote a concise, well-argued book that brought him fame while he was still young. And both clerics were invited to co-rule a small city.

Two hundred and seven years before ibn Abdul Wahhab made his pact with Muhammad ibn Saud in Ad Diriyah in 1744, John Calvin was invited by a council of twenty-five businessmen to help rule the city of Geneva, then a mere town of twenty thousand. Both men administered justice, taught students, wrote booklets, and gave advice to their co-rulers.

Both were also harsh disciplinarians. Each preacher insisted on death as the punishment for adultery, idolatry, and heresy, and each required that attendance at religious services be mandatory. Both men prohibited prayer beads, statues, loud singing, extravagant clothes, and the undue veneration of saints. (Calvin, however, did permit the drinking of wine in moderation.)

Most important, both clerics built schools so that as many of their faithful as possible could learn to read the word of God for themselves. Each man also instilled a sense of divine mission among his followers, which spurred them to work hard and accomplish more.

Finally, both preachers worked tirelessly to expand their influence. Long before the Wahhabis swept across Arabia, the Calvinists had spread their faith through Switzerland and Scotland in the sixteenth century and throughout much of colonial America in the seventeenth and eighteenth centuries. Yet with each passing decade, Protestants dropped the harshest parts of Calvin's creed, especially the doctrine that God predestined the damned to burn, including babies who died before they were baptized.

Wahhabism is two hundred years younger than Calvinism and may seem more comprehensible if it is compared to Protestant doctrines of the past, rather than to church beliefs today. The Wahhabis have had less time than Calvinists have had to let go of doctrines that conflict with the mercy of a loving God. But as the years pass in a new and technological millennium, it is possible and even likely that many Wahhabis will grow more tolerant and less xenophobic. Perhaps then Wahhabis will take pleasure not only in the clear, superstition-free purity of their own faith, but also in friendships with the followers of other monotheistic creeds.

6

Nineteenth-Century Saudi Arabia (1792–1887)

Aᴏ ᴛᴇʀ ᴛʜᴇ ᴅᴇᴀᴛʜ ᴏꜰ ɪʙɴ ᴀʙᴅᴜʟ ᴡᴀʜʜᴀʙ in 1792, Saud led his Wahhabi warriors on more raids, this time against oases near Mecca. The Wahhabis stopped pilgrims from traveling to the holy city if there were any prostitutes, beardless men, alcohol, hashish, musical instruments, or jewel-studded Qurans in the pilgrims' travel parties. They also stopped pilgrims from going to Medina to see Muhammad's tomb, which the Wahhabis regarded as an idol.

The sultan of the Ottoman Empire was enraged by the Wahhabi interference with pilgrimages and pressured Ghalib, the sharif of Mecca, into military action. But Mecca's paid soldiers were no match for the religiously inspired Wahhabis, especially in the heat of the desert. The Wahhabis thrashed Mecca's army in 1796 and again in 1798, which forced Ghalib to agree to allow the Wahhabis to come to Mecca as pilgrims themselves.

In 1800, Saud went to Mecca with his entire family and thousands of his subjects. He carried a bright green flag adorned with white letters that said: "There is but one God. Muhammad is His Messenger." Two centuries later, this is still the flag of Saudi Arabia.

In Mecca, few people were devout, and many did not hesitate to laugh or joke during a sermon. They were astounded to see the Wahhabis pray with such fervor.

Each year Saud grew bolder. He led raids into southern Iraq, defeated an army sent by Baghdad's pasha, and negotiated a truce. The truce was broken in 1801 when tribesmen loyal to the pasha plundered a Wahhabi-protected caravan.

The Wahhabis' revenge was fearful. At dawn one morning early in the spring of 1802, ten thousand Wahhabi soldiers riding six thousand camels sacked the Iraqi city of Karbala, where Hussein, the grandson of Muhammad and the leading Shi'ite martyr, is buried. Led by Saud, they demolished the massive golden dome and intricate glazed tiles above Hussein's tomb and carried away gold, jewels, and pearls that had decorated his grave for centuries.

In eight terrible hours, the Wahhabis killed more than two thousand people, including women, old men, and children—a savage departure from the usual Wahhabi practice. Plundering the whole city, the soldiers demolished the gravesites of dozens of Shi'ite saints and loaded hundreds of camels with sacks full of swords, guns, coins, lamps, vases, and carpets.

When Saud and his troops returned home to Ad Diriyah, his father, Abd al-Aziz, and the entire city turned out to congratulate them. The soldiers had destroyed Hussein's dome, the most evil idol of all because it was the center of the Shi'ite heresy. The rest of the world was horrified; to this day, the reputation of the Wahhabis has never fully recovered.

In the autumn of 1802, Saud and his troops committed another atrocity, killing hundreds of people, including children, in the town of Taif, just outside Mecca. They took control of some nearby mountain passes, leaving Mecca defenseless. Ghalib and his army fled to the Red Sea.

In contrast to their murderous sacks of Karbala and Taif, when the Wahhabis entered Mecca in April 1803 they behaved well and paid cash for food and necessities. During the next few weeks, they destroyed all of the saints' mausoleums and gravesite mosques in the city. They also banned prostitution near the Kaaba, the wearing of silk, any mention of the Turkish sultan during a public prayer, and smoking outside the home. The Wahhabis built a giant bonfire to burn water pipes and tobacco.

Six months later, in Ad Diriyah, a Shi'ite Muslim stabbed Abd al-Aziz to death during afternoon prayers. It is not certain whether the assassin was avenging the massacre of his children in Karbala the year before or was paid by the pasha of Baghdad, or both. In any case, the killer was overpowered, burned alive, and beheaded.

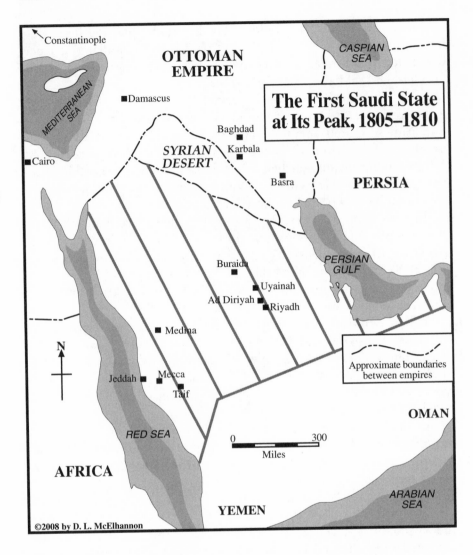

Constantinople

OTTOMAN
EMPIRE

CASPIAN
SEA

MEDITERRANEAN
SEA

■Damascus

The First Saudi State
at Its Peak, 1805–1810

Baghdad
■

SYRIAN
DESERT

Karbala
■

■Cairo

Basra
■

PERSIA

Buraida
■

PERSIAN
GULF

Uyainah
Ad Diriyah ■ ■
■Riyadh

N

Medina
■

Jeddah ■ ■ Mecca
Taif

Approximate boundaries
between empires

OMAN

RED SEA

0   300
Miles

AFRICA

YEMEN

ARABIAN
SEA

©2008 by D. L. McElhannon

Saud, who was now the emir, had accumulated a lot of plunder
and begun to live more luxuriously. His fortress was decorated with
gold, pearls, and Indian fabrics, and he lavishly entertained dozens of
guests a day. He owned hundreds of slaves and more than two thousand horses and mares. Within the privacy of his home, some of his
wives and concubines may also have worn jewelry and silk, in violation of Wahhabi law.

Saud returned to western Arabia in 1805 and took Medina
in the summer. He stripped the jewels and the gold plating from

Muhammad's tomb but otherwise left the large green dome that towers above his grave intact. This was because long ago, ibn Abdul Wahhab had written two letters saying that while he objected to prayers at Muhammad's tomb, he did not want to see the dome destroyed. But the Wahhabis demolished nearly every other dome in Medina.

With Wahhabis in control of Mecca and Medina, the number of pilgrims shrank dramatically. Their violent reputation discouraged other Muslims from making the trip. Incomes in Mecca and Medina plummeted, and many guides, food vendors, and camel tenders were forced to leave their homes and start new lives in Egypt or Syria.

The Wahhabi capture of Mecca and Medina was also a severe blow to the prestige of the Ottoman sultan, who as the caliph of Islam was supposed to be the protector of the Holy Places. Saud added insult to injury by ordering and sometimes leading raids on the outskirts of Baghdad in 1808, 1810, and 1812, and on villages south of Damascus in 1810. His clerics justified these raids by citing the fourteenth-century scholar ibn Taymiyah, who, unlike ibn Abdul Wahhab, had said that *jihad* against other Muslims was proper when a Muslim ruler did not follow *sharia* (Muslim) law. The sultan, the Wahhabis pointed out, wore silk and drank alcohol.

Saud may have hoped to repeat the conquests of the Caliph Umar in the 630s, when Arab tribesmen, inspired by their faith, conquered Iraq and Syria. But unlike the Persian and Byzantine empires, which the Arabs defeated in the 630s, the Ottoman Empire possessed European artillery, and the Wahhabis would soon discover that they could not defeat an army that had modern weapons.

The Fall of the First Saudi State

The Saudi emirate had reached a limit remarkably close to the boundaries of Saudi Arabia today. Had the Wahhabis confined their raids to the Arabian peninsula and paid even the slightest homage to the Turkish sultan, the first Saudi state that ibn Abdul Wahhab started with Saud's grandfather in 1745 might have continued indefinitely.

But the Wahhabis were completely unaware of the modern world and its technical progress, and, led by Saud, they overreached. Wahhabi soldiers could launch raids into Iraq and Syria, but they were incapable of conquering Baghdad or Damascus. They could not even take smaller towns if these were fortified. Saud's forays into Iraq and Syria, and his harassment of pilgrims on their way to Mecca, served only to antagonize the Ottoman sultan and his viceroy in Cairo, Muhammad Ali.

Muhammad Ali was a cunning Macedonian mercenary who had risen through the ranks of the Turkish army until, by 1805, he commanded all of the Ottoman troops in Egypt. Consolidating his power, he hired French officers to modernize his army and Greek shipbuilders to enlarge his navy.

In order to recapture Mecca and Medina and also take control of Yemen and its rich coffee trade, Muhammad Ali resolved to defeat the Wahhabis. In 1811, he put his eighteen-year-old son, Tusun, in charge of a force of eight thousand men. They sailed down the Red Sea and marched inland to meet the Wahhabis near Medina in December.

The attack was a disaster. Despite Tusun's bravery, he lost half of his men when the Wahhabis fired guns and arrows at them from both sides of a narrow mountain pass. "Come and fight us," the Wahhabis taunted the fleeing Ottoman soldiers. "Come and fight us, you pagans, you beard-shavers, you drunkards who have forgotten prayers."[1]

Tusun returned with a larger army in 1812. The troops encircled Medina, killed more than a thousand Wahhabi soldiers, and captured the city in November after a one-month siege. Mecca surrendered without a fight two months later. In Cairo there were fireworks, while in Istanbul cannons boomed to celebrate the fact that pilgrimages to Mecca and Medina could resume now that the holy cities were a part of the Ottoman Empire again. East of Mecca, however, Tusun lost seven hundred men as soon as he led his army into the open desert. The Wahhabis were still undefeated in their home terrain.

In the spring of 1814, Saud died of a fever at age sixty-six and was succeeded by his oldest son, Abdallah, a courageous fighter who nevertheless knew that his new kingdom was overextended. He negotiated a peace with Tusun in 1815. Abdallah gave up his claim to the holy cities and declared himself to be a vassal of the Turkish sultan. In return, Tusun recognized Abdallah as the ruler of central and eastern Arabia.

Tusun's father, Muhammad Ali, overruled his son and rejected the peace because he was determined to crush the Wahhabis and rule the Arabian peninsula himself. He relieved Tusun of command in 1816 and summoned his top aides and generals to his palace in Cairo to choose a successor. There, he showed them a large carpet with an apple in the middle. The apple represented the Wahhabi capital, Muhammad Ali said, and the carpet represented the inhospitable desert. The new commander's challenge was to seize the apple without setting foot on the carpet.

The tallest generals tried to reach for the apple, but the carpet was too big. Then Ibrahim, Muhammad Ali's second son, knelt down at the edge of the carpet and slowly rolled it up until he took the apple and gave it to his father. Ibrahim became the new military commander, and his strategy was to bribe the Bedouins in the outlying areas and slowly shrink the Wahhabis' territory, rather than fight a climactic battle in the desert.

When Ibrahim arrived in Arabia with his motley army of Albanians, Turks, and Libyans, he paid cash for the Bedouins' services and released the Bedouins from their obligation to pay the *zakat*, the Muslim tax on wealth. The Bedouins had always hated giving one-fortieth of their herds to tax collectors; now they cheerfully abandoned the Wahhabi cause. A grandson of ibn Abdul Wahhab, Sulayman ibn Abdallah, denounced Ibrahim's army and the turncoat Bedouins as infidels and said that *jihad* against them was justified.[2]

In contrast to the early Muslims, whose conquests stretched from Spain to India, the Wahhabis were defeated in their homeland by a well-organized Turkish army with modern arms. Ibrahim used howitzers and artillery to blast through fortresses and European doctors to treat disease and keep his soldiers healthy. Patiently capturing one oasis at a time, Ibrahim kept his supply lines open and constantly added fresh troops. By April 1818, seventy-six hundred of his men surrounded Ad Diriyah and began to shell the town. The siege lasted five months and killed thousands before the Wahhabis ran out of food. When Abdallah finally surrendered on September 11, 1818, the first Saudi state came to an end.

Bound in chains, a defiant Abdallah told Ibrahim, "You are great, your father is greater than you, and the Sultan is still greater than he; but Allah is by far greater than all of you. The war is over now, what Allah wished has come to happen. Your forces did not defeat us, but Allah alone is the Glorious and the Conqueror!"[3]

Muhammad Ali sent Abdallah to Istanbul, where the sultan had him beheaded. The Turks displayed Abdallah's head and body for three days, then threw them into the sea.

In Ad Diriyah, Ibrahim's soldiers, angry after a long, hot, and tedious siege, tortured and killed most of the city's princes and clerics but sent a few off to be executed in Cairo and Istanbul. Nine months later, before the Ottoman soldiers marched back to the Red Sea, they burned all of the city's buildings and cut down every palm tree. The people of Ad Diriyah had nothing to eat and either moved away or starved. The city never recovered. Today, the site is a ruin fifteen miles outside of Riyadh—a place where everyone can see that faith alone was not enough to defeat a modern army. It was a lesson the al-Saud family took to heart throughout the twentieth century, yet even today, it is a hard truth for many of the region's zealots to accept.

The Second Saudi State (1824–1887)

Although Ibrahim's soldiers killed almost every man and boy in the al-Saud family, one young man, Turki ibn Abdallah, a cousin of the beheaded ruler, managed to escape from Ad Diriyah. For three years, he hid among Bedouins in the southern desert before he returned to Ad Diriyah in 1821 and recaptured the city. Turki rebuilt only a few homes, however, before part of Ibrahim's army burned the town again. This time, the troops also plundered ibn Abdul Wahhab's library; they carted away hundreds of books and burned the rest.

Turki went into hiding for another two years. When Ibrahim's army finally left central Arabia completely, Turki returned with a small army. His soldiers surrounded the town of Riyadh, besieged it for several months, and finally took it in 1824. They were helped by the local people, who had remained Wahhabis and remembered the al-Saud fondly as a family that ruled according to the Quran.

Turki made Riyadh his new capital, appointed one of ibn Abdul Wahhab's grandsons chief cleric, and reintroduced the wealth tax. "God, who is great, tests the rich with the poor," he told his people at the beginning of his rule. "What he asks of you is easy . . . pay the *zakat.*"[4] Cautiously, Turki expanded his territory outward a few dozen miles and eastward to the Persian Gulf, but the second Saudi state was much smaller than the first.

In 1834, a cousin assassinated Turki, but the assassin was killed a month later by Turki's eldest son, Faisal. Faisal ruled just four years before Egyptian soldiers captured him and imprisoned him in Cairo in 1838. Egypt's ruler, Muhammad Ali, had broken his ties with the Ottomans, however, and soon realized that Faisal would be more useful to him in Riyadh, keeping Arabia free from the Turks, than he would be rotting in jail. Quietly, Faisal was allowed to "escape" from prison and return home in 1843.

In Cairo, Faisal learned that Turkey, Egypt, and especially Britain were far stronger than his small Wahhabi state. So while he consolidated his power over the oases of central Arabia, he also paid a small tribute to the Turkish sultan, left the holy cities alone, and never interfered with British commerce in the Persian Gulf. Faisal encouraged pearl diving in the Persian Gulf and sold Arabian horses to the British army in India. His twenty-two-year reign was peaceful and prosperous, a welcome period of calm in Saudi Arabia's troubled nineteenth century.

In 1865, Faisal suffered from an eye disease, went blind, and died. After his death, his two oldest sons, Abdallah and Saud, fought so hard for the throne that they lost their kingdom completely. Between 1871 and 1876, power changed hands seven times as the two brothers led Bedouins and villagers in raids against each other.

One by one, the disillusioned tribes and oasis-states of central Arabia refused to pay taxes to the al-Saud family and looked instead to a neighboring clan, the al-Rashid, to restore order. By 1884, the only city the al-Saud still ruled was their hometown, Riyadh, and its nearby oases.

Even so, the family continued to feud. To protect himself from insubordinate nephews, a desperate Abdallah asked for help from the al-Rashid family. The al-Rashid used Abdallah's request as an excuse to take Riyadh themselves in 1887, and this marked the end of the second Saudi state. The second kingdom had never been as powerful as the first, but it had served its purpose. It kept the Wahhabi movement alive, ready to influence Muslims again in the twentieth century—and in the twenty-first.

In 1890, Abdallah's youngest brother, Abd al-Rahman, began a rebellion against the al-Rashid clan that was crushed in 1891. The al-Saud family was forced to leave Riyadh and go into exile. At first they rode with Bedouins in the sand dunes on the edge of the vast, lifeless "Empty Quarter" in southern Arabia, but in 1893 they moved to Kuwait, where they were offered the protection and hospitality of the ruling al-Sabah family.

The one bright note for the al-Saud family during this difficult period was the birth of a son to Abd al-Rahman in 1876. The boy's full name was Abdul Aziz ibn Abd al-Rahman ibn Faisal al-Saud. A devout Wahhabi, Abdul Aziz was just seventeen when his vanquished family arrived in Kuwait, but nine years later, he founded the third Saudi state: modern Saudi Arabia.

PART THREE

THE CREATION OF MODERN SAUDI ARABIA: THE LIFE OF KING ABDUL AZIZ (1876–1953)

T HE MODERN KINGDOM OF SAUDI ARABIA owes its existence to the military courage and the political skill of one man: Abdul Aziz ibn Abd al-Rahman ibn Faisal al-Saud (1876–1953), known to Arabs as Abdul Aziz ("Servant of God, the Beloved") and to many Westerners as Ibn Saud. Abdul Aziz began with a daring early-morning raid on the town of Riyadh in 1902 and gradually conquered 80 percent of the Arabian peninsula—a vast desert the size of the United States east of the Mississippi River.

Unlike his ancestor Saud, whose raids into Ottoman Turkish territory led to the downfall of the first Saudi state in 1818, Abdul Aziz understood the importance of restraint. He never threatened the British protectorates on the Persian Gulf, and he waited until 1924 to conquer Mecca, when the British themselves had become disgusted with the holy city's king. Sir Percy Cox, Britain's longtime political resident in the region, once said that he never knew Abdul Aziz to make a wrong move.

Although Abdul Aziz possessed a deep knowledge of Islam and was a master at dealing with Arabia's fierce tribes, he knew little about the modern world or how to spend the oil money that rushed into his country after World War II. For forty years, Abdul Aziz ruled his kingdom skillfully as it slowly emerged from the Middle Ages, but the monarch's fifth decade as king proved to be one decade too long.

7

Exile and Return (1876–1902)

ABDUL AZIZ WAS BORN IN 1876 (some say 1880) in a mud-paneled palace in Riyadh. Although today Riyadh is a sprawling city of 4.5 million people, in 1876 it was a walled-in oasis with narrow winding streets, a few outdoor markets, and about a thousand mud-brick houses. The town was so isolated that only eight Europeans had ever been there. It was 550 sandy miles east of the Red Sea and 250 pathless miles west of the Persian Gulf.

Abdul Aziz's mother, Sarah al-Sudairi, was tall and unusually good at dealing with people. Though she was illiterate, she knew many verses of the Quran and also passed on to her son her love of Arab poetry. At seven, Abdul Aziz started the long process of memorizing the Quran. He began his day with a strict teacher an hour before the dawn prayer, and by the time he was eleven, he knew most of the holy book by heart and was also familiar with the lives of Muhammad and the first four caliphs.

Abdul Aziz much preferred the days when his father gave him lessons in warfare. Abd al-Rahman taught his son how to use a sword, shoot a rifle, and ride a horse both bareback and with a saddle, sometimes with only a half-ration of food and water. Abdul Aziz also enjoyed wrestling with his cousins and with African slave boys, who later grew up to become his most trusted bodyguards.

Although Abdul Aziz's nuclear family was happy, his extended family was bitterly divided by a feud between his uncle Abdallah and two cousins. Taking advantage of the al-Saud family's weakness, the army of a rival family, the al-Rashid, captured Riyadh in 1887, when Abdul Aziz was eleven. They installed a new governor, Salim, who ruled the city harshly.

Two years later, when Abdallah died, Abdul Aziz's father became the head of the family. In 1890, he tried to start a rebellion and sent secret messages to nearby towns. Salim, the governor, learned of the plot and asked to speak to every man in the al-Saud clan on the next feast day. Fearing a massacre, the men of the Saud family struck first. They ambushed the governor's guards, tied up Salim, and threw him down a well to die. Then they attacked the town's fortress and drove the remaining Rashid soldiers out of Riyadh. At fourteen, Abdul Aziz had fought in his first battle, but the victory lasted only a few weeks.

The al-Rashid warriors quickly returned with a larger army and camped just outside Riyadh. They cut down palm trees, destroyed irrigation channels, and poisoned wells with dead animals, yet still the town held out. Finally, when the al-Rashid clan killed hundreds of Saudi allies in a nearby oasis, Abd al-Rahman knew that Riyadh would soon fall, too.

On a cold night early in 1891, Abd al-Rahman gathered his family, bundled up his possessions, and silently led a train of camels away from the al-Rashid army. On one side of a camel, young Abdul Aziz hid inside a saddle bag. On the other side was his sister Nura, who remained his closest friend throughout his life. (As an adult, Abdul Aziz often identified himself proudly as "the brother of Nura.")

For more than a week, Abdul Aziz's family trudged toward the Persian Gulf and finally reached the island of Bahrain, where the emir agreed to house the women and the children. Because it was not safe for the men of the al-Saud family to stay in one place, Abdul Aziz, his father, and three younger brothers rode toward the broiling desert at the edge of the "Empty Quarter," a bone-dry wasteland the size of Texas, where the nomads of the Murra clan offered them protection.

The Murra were the most primitive tribe in Arabia. In knife fights, the men licked the blood off their daggers, and when making love, they entered their women from the rear, considering face-to-face intercourse indecent. Because the Murra were illiterate, they knew little about Islam. Abd al-Rahman regarded the tribesmen as pagans and hated living among them.

But Abdul Aziz, now fifteen, thrived. He tended camels by day and slept under the stars at night. He drank fresh camel's milk and ate dates, unleavened bread, and bits of lizard or, if a hunter was lucky, rabbit. The Murra ate camel meat only on feast days; the delicacy they prized most was raw camel's liver, dipped in salt and dripping with blood.

As Abdul Aziz rode the many miles between pastures, he came to appreciate the value of a female camel, which takes five years to mature, a sixth year to gestate, and a seventh to nurse its offspring. He learned how to read a camel's footprints, often as distinctive as a man's fingerprints, to determine what kind of caravan had passed and whether its camels were healthy or sick, hungry or thirsty, energetic or tired. He also examined the vegetation inside a camel's droppings to learn where the caravan had come from. And he took part in several raids on rival tribes. Under the nomads' strict code, attackers took only camels and weapons, never women or possessions.

Most important, Abdul Aziz absorbed the manners, the slang, and the humor of the Bedouin. For the rest of his life, he spoke Arabic with a Bedouin accent, and later, as king, he was completely at ease with tribal chiefs from every part of Arabia.

In 1893, the emir of Kuwait offered his protection to the al-Saud family, along with a small pension secretly paid for by the Ottoman Turks. The al-Rashid family had grown strong enough to become a threat both to Kuwait and to the Turks in Iraq. It therefore made sense for the emir to help the al-Saud family try to achieve its long-term goal of recapturing Riyadh.

Nineteenth-century Kuwait was a small city of yellow clay houses, with winding alleys that sloped down gently from the red sand of the desert to the calm, nearly green water of the Persian Gulf. Abd al-Rahman, his wife, five children, and some African servants moved into a three-room house with a courtyard. There was no bathroom or outhouse. Like their neighbors, the al-Saud clan bathed in the sea.

The Turkish pension did not last long. Young Abdul Aziz would have been too poor to marry were it not for the fact that a merchant who had once done business with the al-Saud family agreed to pay for the wedding. Abdul Aziz was eighteen when he married for the first time, but his bride became ill and died only six months later. Four years after that, he married a woman named Wadhba, and soon they had a son, Turki.

Kuwait (Arabic for "Little Fort") was Arabia's main port. In cafés by the sea, Abdul Aziz sipped coffee with boat builders and pearl divers and with sailors who took horses and dates to India and came back with ivory and spices. He met wealthy merchants who routinely traveled to Istanbul, Damascus, and Tehran, and he occasionally saw a modern British warship just offshore. Quickly, he learned that there was a wide world beyond Arabia.

Nevertheless, Abdul Aziz knew that his future lay inland. Often, he walked up a hill outside town and looked south toward Riyadh, three hundred miles away. He remembered the words of a favorite aunt: "You must revive the House of Saud and strive for the glory of Islam, leading the people toward the path of the Prophet."[1]

In Kuwait, Abdul Aziz's father arranged for his son to pursue an advanced study of Muslim law and theology. Abdul Aziz's teacher was a descendant of ibn Abdul Wahhab who had studied in Medina and Cairo before joining the al-Saud family in exile. Abdul Aziz studied hard, absorbed his lessons, and grew up to be a deeply religious Muslim. But his most valuable education in Kuwait came from a man his father despised: Mubarak ibn Subah al-Sabah, a ruthless prince who liked dancing girls, rarely prayed, and shot and killed his two brothers to become the city's new emir in 1896.

At first, the people of Kuwait were afraid of Mubarak, but soon the people saw that their new ruler was more generous, astute, and decisive than his brothers had been. Mubarak, fifty-nine, took a liking to Abdul Aziz, who at twenty was six feet, three inches tall, strikingly handsome, and powerfully built and had a trim beard, a magnetic personality, and a gentle, disarming smile.

Mubarak encouraged Abdul Aziz to attend his audiences. Each day, the ruler of Kuwait saw anyone who wished to see him. Later, in private, he told Abdul Aziz the reasons behind various decisions that he had made that day. It was a rare, firsthand look at the practical art of government, but Abdul Aziz had to conceal from his father his friendship with Mubarak.

In 1899, Mubarak signed a secret treaty with Great Britain. In return for British naval protection, Mubarak promised not to have dealings with any government without Britain's permission. The British regarded the Persian Gulf as vital to the security of their shipping lanes to India and made similar treaties with other small states on the Persian Gulf: Bahrain, Qatar, Abu Dhabi, and Dubai, and also with the larger domains of Oman and Yemen on the Indian Ocean. From an early age, Abdul Aziz understood that the Persian Gulf was a British-dominated sea.

In the winter of 1901, Mubarak launched a raid against al-Rashid family territory to the west. Simultaneously, Abdul Aziz led several dozen men south in a diversionary attack on his hometown, Riyadh. To his surprise, no one opposed him except at the fortress in the center of town, which he surrounded. The people of Riyadh had resented the al-Rashid family's harsh rule and were delighted to have someone from the al-Saud family lead them again. Unfortunately, the al-Rashid soldiers badly defeated Mubarak's army, which made Abdul Aziz's exposed position in Riyadh indefensible. The young warrior had to retreat to Kuwait but promised Riyadh's citizens that he would return soon.

Once Abdul Aziz knew that the people of Riyadh wanted him back, he was determined to lead a new expedition. After ten years in exile, the entire al-Saud family was restless, so in the fall of 1902, it was not hard for Abdul Aziz to assemble a force of about forty relatives, servants, adventurers, and slaves. (By custom, if a slave fought well, he won his freedom.) The men rode into the desert on some tired, mangy camels that Mubarak, who was dubious about the venture, had reluctantly given them. They carried nothing but rifles, swords, and daggers and ate only dates and unleavened bread.

Abdul Aziz's plan was to raid several villages near Riyadh, recruit some Bedouins who were interested in plunder, then attack Riyadh with a much larger army. The nomads, however, did not think much of Abdul Aziz's prospects and refused to join him. By December, Abdul Aziz commanded only sixty men, and his father sent him a letter from Kuwait asking him to come home.

Abdul Aziz told his men that he would rather die in battle in Riyadh than endure the humiliation of returning to Kuwait. He invited those who wished to die with him to stand to his right and those who wished to go home to stand to his left. All sixty of his men moved to the right, shouting, "To the death! Victory or death!"

With so small a force, Abdul Aziz had to take Riyadh by surprise. To achieve this, he first led his men to the edge of the Empty Quarter to stay out of sight and mislead the al-Rashid family into thinking that he had given up his dream of taking Riyadh. For fifty days, the warriors did nothing. Abdul Aziz worked hard to lift their spirits for the men became irritable from a lack of fighting, women, and shade.

Finally, in the second week of January 1902, Abdul Aziz's small army rode thirty miles a night to reach the outskirts of Riyadh in time for Eid al Fitr, the feast at the end of Ramadan, the month of fasting. On this night, January 14, the sky was lit only by the slimmest crescent moon.

On a plateau an hour and a half's walk from town, Abdul Aziz left his camels, his food, and twenty of his men. If they did not hear from him in twenty-four hours, he told them, they should return to Kuwait and tell his father that he had either died or been taken prisoner. The remaining forty men quietly walked to a grove of palm trees not far from the town walls.

Under the palms, Abdul Aziz divided his men again. He asked thirty-three of his men to wait and join him later, then picked six warriors to accompany him into Riyadh. The seven men stepped softly across a few hundred feet of vegetable gardens and irrigation ditches (an area that today is lit by giant Panasonic and Sanyo neon signs) and, using an old palm trunk as a scaling ladder, jumped over the town's wall and into the city.

Abdul Aziz and his cohorts entered the home of an old friend, climbed up to his roof, leaped across another roof, and broke into the house of the town's governor, Ajlan, a member of the al-Rashid family. Ajlan was not home because he spent his nights in the central fortress with his men and didn't see his wife until breakfast. The seven warriors gagged Ajlan's wife and her sister, sent for their thirty-three colleagues, and spent the rest of the night reciting the Quran and drinking the governor's coffee.

When the call to prayer began at the first light of dawn on January 15, the forty warriors knelt in several tight rows and prayed in the direction of Mecca. A few minutes later, when they heard the sound of the governor's horses, they grabbed their swords and rifles and waited a moment more. The instant the fortress gate opened, Abdul Aziz and his men charged out of the house toward Ajlan and his guards, shouting, *"Allahu Akbar!"* (God is Great!). Abdul Aziz seized Ajlan's legs and tackled the governor, but Ajlan kicked him in the groin and ran back inside a small door that was carved into the gate.

For a split second, the future of Arabia hung in the balance, but before Ajlan's men could close the door, Abdul Aziz's cousin, Abdallah ibn Jiluwi, leaped inside and killed the governor. The shock of Ajlan's death demoralized his guards, and when the Saudis killed several more of the governor's men, the rest surrendered.

By late morning, the people of Riyadh poured into the central mosque to swear their allegiance to the al-Saud family just before beginning the noon prayer. Losing only two men, Abdul Aziz had won a victory that earned the admiration of tribesmen throughout Arabia. His eleven years in exile were over. At twenty-six, Abdul Aziz's half-century as king was about to begin.

8

Expanding the Kingdom
(1902–1926)

I N 1902, ABDUL AZIZ held one town, Riyadh. By 1925, he ruled three-quarters of the Arabian peninsula. He financed and led an army of fierce religious warriors called the Ikhwan ("Brotherhood") but waited years before he let them take Mecca, to avoid antagonizing Britain. Abdul Aziz's capacity for restraint did not prevent him from seizing opportunities. He took Al-Hasa Province from the Ottoman Turks in just one night in 1913 but had no idea that he had just acquired a quarter of the world's oil.

After conquering Riyadh in 1902, Abdul Aziz sent a message to Kuwait inviting his entire family to join him. When his wife arrived, she proudly presented a new son, Saud, who by happy coincidence had been born on the same day that Abdul Aziz had captured the city. Yet only weeks later, Abdul Aziz took another wife, Tarfah, the daughter of Riyadh's chief judge and a direct descendant of ibn Abdul Wahhab. Abdul Aziz married her to assure the town's clergy that he was still a good Wahhabi, despite years of having lived in the more permissive city of Kuwait. After three years, Tarfah gave birth to Faisal, the future king.

Abdul Aziz formally handed over the city of Riyadh to his father, but Abd al-Rahman refused the offer to rule. He insisted that his son be king and gave him an ancient sword that had long been the symbol of leadership within the al-Saud family. Abdul Aziz remained a dutiful son, however, and consulted his father on matters of state almost daily until the old man died in 1928.

Abdul Aziz's first priority as ruler was to prepare for the battle that would come when the al-Rashid army returned to retake the city. Abdul Aziz personally led the effort to repair Riyadh's crumbling walls, working long days lifting buckets of mud up to masons at the top of the ramparts. He also borrowed money from the city's merchants to hire sharpshooters from Kuwait and gave them plenty of bullets.

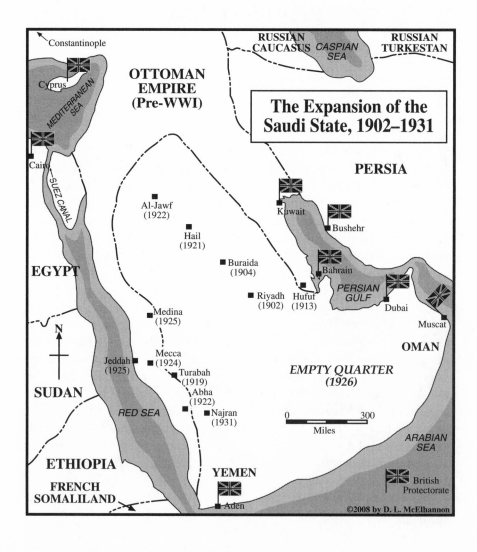

©2008 by D. L. McElhannon

Because each of Riyadh's four walls was more than two thousand feet long, the repairs took months. Abdul Aziz was lucky to have the time. Ibn Rashid, the leader of the rival family, did not take the Saudi conquest of Riyadh seriously. "The rabbit is in the hole," he said contemptuously, certain that he could recapture the town whenever he liked.

Ten months passed before ibn Rashid finally sent an army to Riyadh in November 1902. Only then did he discover that he had waited too long. The city was heavily fortified and could not be taken.

Ibn Rashid then sent a second army southeast to try to cut off Riyadh's supplies from the Persian Gulf. Abdul Aziz led two thousand warriors, including the marksmen, into the desert and ambushed the al-Rashid at Dilam, an oasis fifty-five miles from Riyadh. The riflemen achieved complete surprise. They fired at the al-Rashid for more than half an hour, killing dozens and wounding many more. The al-Rashid warriors retreated, not knowing that the Saudi fighters were almost out of ammunition. The al-Rashid family never threatened Riyadh again.

Early Conquests

Sometimes Abdul Aziz left his father in charge of Riyadh for a few days while he led his army to seize a nearby oasis. To relieve the boredom of the long camel rides, the young monarch brought along a cantor to recite the Quran. Often, when the cantor paused for breath, Abdul Aziz supplied the next verse.

Rather than wait to be conquered, it was more common for sheikhs and their tribesmen to come to Riyadh and swear allegiance to the al-Saud family. When they did, Abdul Aziz gave them money and fed them enormous helpings of mutton and rice (eaten by hand), followed by many cups of coffee. For special feasts, his chefs cooked entire camels in cauldrons eight feet high, stuffed the camels with boiled sheep, the sheep with chickens, and the chickens with eggs. As Abdul Aziz's kingdom expanded, his cooks fed hundreds and sometimes more than a thousand visitors a day.

The young monarch spent many evenings listening to tribal leaders and soon acquired an encyclopedic knowledge of the herds, the pastures, the feuds, and the loyalties of every tribe in central Arabia. By the summer of 1903, after eighteen months of raids and diplomacy, Abdul Aziz ruled a small empire extending out from Riyadh about a hundred miles in every direction.

Even the poorest Bedouin talked to Abdul Aziz as an equal; the Arabian people have always been egalitarian. The young king's manner with them was relaxed, frank, and unaffected. Abdul Aziz's clothes were always clean, unlike the clothing of many Bedouin. In the summer he wore linen; in the winter, some cloth beneath a coat of camel hair.

When Abdul Aziz spoke in public, he hit the ground with his riding stick to make a point. He spoke precisely, numbering his points, and peppered his speech with Bedouin proverbs and verses from the Quran. Sometimes he used his stick to beat a servant or a son. His temper was fierce but softened quickly. Often, he sent a gift to a servant whom he had beaten only hours earlier.

In moments of danger, Abdul Aziz remained calm. "Put your trust in God and do what you think is best," he once told a friend. Abdul Aziz had a deep faith that Islam was God's final revelation to mankind and the clearest path to human happiness, and that everything that happens is according to the will of Allah. Unlike many Wahhabis, he was not a fanatic and was willing to make friends with non-Muslims. Abdul Aziz had an unusual ability to assess a person's character, and as king, he was not afraid to do business with Christians.

In March 1904, Abdul Aziz captured Anaiza, an oasis more than halfway toward the al-Rashid capital of Hail. In an exultant letter to Mubarak, his old mentor in Kuwait, Abdul Aziz reported that his army lost only 2 men but killed 370 of the enemy, including a cousin of ibn Rashid's: "I struck him first on the leg and disabled him; quickly after that I struck at the neck; the head fell to one side, the blood spurted up like a fountain. [Upon] the third blow at the heart I saw the heart which was cut in two palpitate. . . . It was a joyous moment. I kissed the sword."[1]

The Ottoman Turks feared for the safety of a railroad they were building between Damascus and Medina, so the sultan ordered twenty-four hundred soldiers with six pieces of artillery into central Arabia. During the first battle, in July, Abdul Aziz was shot once in his hand and again in a leg as his Bedouin warriors fled in fear. They had never heard the boom of artillery before.

In August, Abdul Aziz's men harassed the Ottoman supply lines in Arabia, and soon the Turks were suffering from hunger, thirst, and disease. By September, they were so weak that the Saudis slaughtered them in hand-to-hand fighting, during which artillery was useless. Only a third of the Turks survived. The Saudis captured camels, sheep, a chest full of gold coins, and all six of the Turkish field guns, which none of the Saudis knew how to use.

Despite his victory, Abdul Aziz did not want to fight the Turks again. His father wrote submissive letters to the sultan, calling him "Our Lord the Great Caliph." He suggested that if the Turks left the Saudis alone, the Saudis would welcome Turkish troops as a buffer between Riyadh and Hail, the home of the al-Rashid family. The sultan accepted this offer, and in the spring of 1905, the Turks took control of the cities of Anaiza and Buraida. Their supply lines, however, were vulnerable to a cutoff any time that Abdul Aziz wanted.

A year later, when the al-Rashid chief died in a battle and Abdul Aziz no longer needed Turkish troops as a buffer against the weakened al-Rashid family, Abdul Aziz demanded that the Turks leave Anaiza and Buraida or suffer a loss of their supplies. By this time, the Turkish soldiers had grown to hate the isolation and the scorching heat of the Arabian Desert and happily left their fortresses for the greener city of Basra, in Iraq.

The first photograph of Abdul Aziz was taken four years later, in 1910, by a British army captain with a talent for languages named William Shakespear, a descendant of the great playwright and the first Englishman Abdul Aziz ever met. In this picture, the strong thirty-four-year-old king wears a checkered headdress and has a mustache, a trimmed beard, and an alert, slightly suspicious gaze. (Wahhabis permit photographs because cameras do not engrave images so much as preserve their reflections. Muhammad never forbade mirrors, so cameras are also acceptable.)

Abdul Aziz and Shakespear met a second time the following year, spent several weeks together, and greatly enjoyed each other's company. Shakespear wrote to his superiors that Abdul Aziz was "broadminded," had the support of his people, and "could probably be trusted."

Abdul Aziz had already developed a reputation for Solomon-like justice because of how well he handled the unusual case of a woman whose husband had been accidentally killed by a man who fell from a palm tree while picking dates. The woman demanded the date-picker's death (which by law was her right) and refused all offers of blood money. Abdul Aziz was silent for a long time, then said,

> It is your right to ask for this man's life. But it is my right, by Allah, to decide in what fashion he must die. . . . [The date picker] shall be tied to the foot of a palm tree. Then you yourself shall climb to the top of that palm tree and drop down on him from on high. Thus you may take his life as he took your husband's. . . . [long pause] Or perhaps you would prefer to take the blood money after all.[2]

Between 1906 and 1913, Abdul Aziz was unable to expand his domain. Although he ruled most of Najd (Arabic for "plateau"), which is what the Arabs call central Arabia, he was boxed in on four sides. To the north was the al-Rashid city of Hail. To the south was the lifeless Empty Quarter. To the east were the British protectorates of Kuwait and Qatar, and between them, the coastal province of Al-Hasa, which still belonged to the Turks.

To the west was the Hejaz, the region along the Red Sea that includes the holy cities of Mecca and Medina. (*Hejaz* is Arabic for "barrier" and refers to the steep hills that run parallel to the coast.) Since 1037, the ruler of the Hejaz had been a member of the Hashim family because the Hashemites were descendants of Muhammad. In the 1910s, the grand sharif of Mecca was a Turkish vassal named Husain; British diplomats described him as an arrogant man with a cold smile. Sometimes at night he personally beat his prisoners.

Before he became sharif in 1908, Husain had spent most of his life in cosmopolitan Istanbul. He despised the Wahhabis and looked down on Abdul Aziz as an ignorant Bedouin. Abdul Aziz, in turn, regarded Husain as a stooge for the decadent Turks.

A Typical Day

Abdul Aziz could not have afforded to pay tribute in any case. In the early 1910s, his entire treasury consisted of a few sacks of coins, while his expenses were immense. Every day, in a huge beige room lined on three sides with cushions of thick brocade, Abdul Aziz heard hundreds of petitioners and gave a present to each of them. To some, it was a sack of rice, a basket of dates, and a packet of coffee or tea. To others, with more status, it was a robe, a cloak, and three gold coins. Sometimes the young king joked that he felt "like a slaughtered camel, because anyone can take a cut from me." More often, he reminded his aides that "hoarded money does no one any good," and that "in peace I give all that I have, [but] in war I ask and my people give all that they have to me."[3]

Abdul Aziz's day began with the morning prayer at the first light of dawn. Afterward, he went back to bed for a sixth hour of sleep before eating a light breakfast of bread, honey, and curdled camel's milk. Work began around seven-thiry in the morning. He saw older relatives first and important visitors next, then dictated letters. In the middle of the morning, he hosted a general audience for anyone who cared to see him. Typically, about a hundred people showed up. Abdul Aziz answered each of their questions quickly, often in just a sentence or two. Most people needed help with personal problems, but a few asked political questions, as if they were at a press conference.

After the noon prayer, Abdul Aziz met with his closest advisers for almost an hour before stopping for a lunch of lamb or chicken with rice, some dates, and coffee spiced with cardamom. In the middle of the afternoon, he visited his wives. Around five, he liked to ride (after 1925, drive) into the desert in time for the sunset prayer. After a dinner of lamb and rice again, Abdul Aziz and his guests listened to a clergyman for thirty minutes before the king held a second and more informal audience for important visitors. Finally, before going to his harem for the night, he read a newspaper from Damascus if it had arrived that day and talked with his relatives, his scribes, and his children.

Abdul Aziz had more than seventy children. As an old man, he had trouble remembering the names of his youngest offspring, but when he was young, he was a loving and devoted father. His children were free to run anywhere in the palace, even to barge in on important meetings. In the late afternoon, when Abdul Aziz rode into the desert to pray, he often took one of his sons in the saddle with him and wrapped the boy's little fingers around the reins. By 1913, Abdul Aziz's oldest son, Turki, was already a teenager.

The Conquest of Al-Hasa (and Its Oil)

News came slowly to Riyadh, so it was only in 1913 that Abdul Aziz learned that the Ottoman Empire had lost Albania, Macedonia, and Kosovo in 1912. He knew at once that the Turks would be too distracted to defend Al-Hasa, the coastal province to his east, and seized his opportunity.

On a warm night in May, Abdul Aziz led three hundred warriors to the outskirts of the capital city of Hufuf, an oasis of gardens, orchards, and rice paddies that a British traveler once described as "an emerald in yellow sand." Using palm trees as scaling ladders, just as they had in Riyadh in 1902, Abdul Aziz and his men climbed over the town walls, then surrounded the central fortress.

The Turks had twelve hundred men inside, but Abdul Aziz was undeterred. In the morning, he told the Turkish commander that his men had placed mines under the fortress and that the Turks could either surrender and be given safe conduct to the island of Bahrain or die in an explosion. The Turks, already demoralized from the previous year's losses, decided not to call Abdul Aziz's bluff and gave up their arms: two machine guns, hundreds of rifles, and twelve pieces of artillery.

The merchants of Al-Hasa were delighted by the Saudi conquest because the province had grown increasingly lawless. Bedouin tribes charged caravans "protection money" every few miles because the timid Turks had rarely ventured away from their fortress to keep order.

Overnight, Abdul Aziz had not only doubled his territory but doubled his income. He charged customs duties of up to 8 percent in the small harbors on his new coastline and collected the annual *zakat* (2.5 percent tax) on the unusually sweet dates that the people of Al-Hasa picked in September and packed in boxes that were sold in Europe during the Christmas season.

But the province's most valuable prize stayed hidden for another quarter of a century. Under the sands of Al-Hasa, known today as the Eastern Province, lies all of Saudi Arabia's oil, a staggering one-fourth of the world's reserves. It could easily have belonged to another country. In the nineteenth century, Zionists briefly considered making Al-Hasa the Jewish homeland because the region is said to be the birthplace of Abraham. They decided on Palestine instead.

More significantly, had Abdul Aziz not taken Al-Hasa in 1913, the British would surely have sent troops there in 1914 when World War I began and Turkey allied itself with Germany.

Al-Hasa is two hundred miles from Riyadh, at least a week's camel ride. Abdul Aziz needed to choose a governor he trusted completely, a relative. He picked Abdallah ibn Jiluwi, the cousin who had saved the day in 1902 when he leaped into the fortress gate at Riyadh and killed the al-Rashid governor. The Jiluwi family continued to govern the province for seventy-two years, until 1985, and even today, it still governs the capital city, Hufuf.

Ibn Jiluwi was a fierce Wahhabi with a full black beard who often referred to the Shi'ites as "dogs." Unfortunately, almost half of the Eastern Province's people are Shi'ites, and although Abdul Aziz forbade his cousin from harming them, they have long been denied business opportunities, government posts, or even the right to worship outside their homes. Not until the 1940s, when U.S. oil companies hired thousands of workers, did Shi'ite Muslims in the Eastern Province have a real opportunity to improve their lives.

As for the Bedouins who were raiding caravans, ibn Jiluwi did not care whether they were Sunni or Shi'ite; he hunted them down mercilessly. Hundreds of thieves were beheaded and hundreds more lost one of their hands, until at last there was no theft in the province at all.

Once a townsman told a guard about a large sack of coffee lying on a street in Hufuf. Not knowing what to do, the guard took the man to see ibn Jiluwi. "How do you know it is coffee?" the governor asked. "Because I poked the sack with my toe," answered the townsman. "Take him outside and chop off his toe," ibn Jiluwi commanded the guard. "He knew the sack was not his and should not even have touched it."[4] (Today, amputation seldom takes place unless someone steals at a mosque or steals repeatedly.)

The Ikhwan

On his return from Al-Hasa, Abdul Aziz learned about a new religious movement that had just begun in Al-Artawiya, an oasis 160 miles northwest of Riyadh. Calling themselves Ikhwan, or "brothers," hundreds (and soon thousands) of Bedouin were giving up their nomadic ways for a new and much more interesting life of farming, religious instruction, and military training as holy warriors.

Abdul Aziz immediately recognized the Ikhwan as a twentieth-century revival of the Wahhabi movement and sent them missionaries and copies of the Quran, as well as seeds, agricultural tools, building materials, and bullets.

The young king saw a tremendous opportunity to solve two of his biggest military problems: the ease with which Bedouin nomads changed sides in the middle of a battle and the inability of the more dependable townsmen to leave their homes and fight for more than a few days. For a small price (Abdul Aziz did not have to feed or arm the Ikhwan, who already had their own farms and rifles), the king soon had the equivalent of a huge standing army that combined the rapid mobility of the Bedouin nomads with the reliability of the settled townsmen. Like all Wahhabi soldiers since the eighteenth century, the Ikhwan were loyal to the al-Saud family.

Within seven years of the movement's start, more than fifty Ikhwan settlements had sprung up, and Al-Artawiya was almost as large a city as Riyadh. More than 60,000 warriors were eager to become martyrs in a holy war, and by 1926 the number had grown to 150,000. With the exception of the British army and navy, the Ikhwan had become the most powerful military force in Arabia.

To describe the Ikhwan as extreme religious fanatics is an understatement. Many, when they saw a European, covered their faces to shield themselves from an infidel's stare. Others, in cities, stuffed their ears and nostrils with cloth to keep themselves from hearing or smelling anything evil. The Ikhwan prohibited singing, loud laughter, flower pots, and children's games as frivolous. They also prevented men from smoking tobacco and drinking coffee (because these were not known in Muhammad's time) and forbade women from wearing silk or shopping in a public market. The Ikhwan, wrote one British official in 1918, "live for the next world," but their asceticism came not only from their religious fervor but also from the long-standing resentment that the poorer Bedouin had always felt toward the richer townsmen.

An Alliance with Britain

Although the Ikhwan army was a bargain, it nevertheless added to Abdul Aziz's immense expenses. The king needed money and managed to get some from the British. On December 26, 1915, Abdul Aziz signed a treaty with Sir Percy Cox, Britain's political agent in the Persian Gulf. It was the beginning of a nearly century-long Saudi alliance with the West that continues to this day. Abdul Aziz promised never to attack the British protectorates (Kuwait, Bahrain, Qatar, Abu Dhabi, Dubai, and Muscat), while Britain recognized Abdul Aziz's sovereignty over Najd and Al-Hasa (central and eastern Arabia).

Abdul Aziz also agreed not to have any dealings with a foreign country without Britain's approval. Although this was an infringement on his sovereignty, his dealings with foreign governments were quite limited. Abdul Aziz knew that he could not rule long as Britain's enemy; it made much more sense to be Britain's friend. The following year, the British gave the desert king 4 machine guns; 4,000 rifles; 20,000 British pounds; and, most important, a monthly payment of 5,000 pounds (about $400,000 in today's money). For the next seven years, this subsidy was Abdul Aziz's largest source of income.

In November 1916, Abdul Aziz traveled to Basra, Iraq, to visit Sir Percy Cox, who was fluent in Arabic. It was the first time that Abdul Aziz had ever seen a large city, a fertile countryside, or an unveiled woman in public (Gertrude Bell, who served on Cox's staff). He rode in cars and trains for the first time and saw for himself how large, disciplined, and well equipped the British army was. He also saw his first airplane and an X-ray of the bones of his hand.

What may have impressed Abdul Aziz the most was a Sunday-morning church service that he attended on a British warship. He was surprised by the sincerity and the reverence of the worshippers, and when he returned home, he told his advisers that the British were more devout than many Muslims.

One thing Abdul Aziz discussed with Cox in Basra was his concern about "the Arab Revolt" against the Turks led by Colonel T. E. Lawrence, better known today as Lawrence of Arabia. Lawrence was Britain's liaison to Husain, the king of the Hejaz and the patriarch of the Hashemite family. Husain had been loyal to the Turkish sultan until the summer of 1916, when his warriors took the Turkish forts at Mecca and Jeddah and cut off the railroad that supplied the Ottoman fortress at Medina. The momentum of Husain's troops ground to a halt, however, until Lawrence revived the Hashemite army's fortunes with a new supply of weapons and a monthly subsidy of 100,000 pounds, twenty times the amount that the British gave Abdul Aziz.

Abdul Aziz was alarmed by Husain's sudden increase in power and particularly resented his claim to be "King of the Arabs." Abdul Aziz wanted to help Britain fight against the Turks, but not if it meant that Husain would be a threat to his kingdom. He wrote Husain a respectful letter asking for an acknowledgment of his sovereignty over central and eastern Arabia, but Husain contemptuously replied that Abdul Aziz must have been drunk to have written such a letter. This was a gross insult to an abstinent Wahhabi. Husain compounded the insult by returning Abdul Aziz's letter "so that you may reflect on what you have written."

As a result, Abdul Aziz stayed on the sidelines during World War I. He refused to help the "King of the Arabs," even when Husain's army, led by Lawrence, marched up the Jordan River and into Damascus in 1918.

Although many Arabs had helped Britain to defeat the Turks, World War I did not end happily for them. In a secret agreement made in 1916, two diplomats, Sir Mark Sykes of Britain and Georges Picot of France, carved up the territory that had once belonged to the Ottoman Empire. Syria and Lebanon would become mandates of France, a slice of northeastern Turkey would be ceded to Russia, and Palestine and Mesopotamia (soon to be renamed Iraq) would become mandates of Britain.

Mandates were a twentieth-century version of colonialism. The idea was for a less-developed country to be guided by a mandatory power until it was ready for independence. But the region covered by the Sykes-Picot Agreement was the most cosmopolitan part of the Muslim world. The area included the cities of Beirut, Jerusalem, Damascus, and Baghdad, each with thousands of middle-class Arab professionals who wanted independence immediately. When the secret treaty was made public by the Bolsheviks during the Russian Revolution in 1917, educated Arabs were furious but lacked the military strength to challenge their new masters.

It was Britain's policy in Palestine that upset the Arabs the most. In November 1917, Britain's foreign secretary, Arthur Balfour, published a letter that he had written to Lord Lionel Rothschild, the president of the British Zionist Federation, which stated, "His Majesty's Government view with favour the establishment in Palestine of a national home for the Jewish people . . . it being clearly understood that nothing shall be done which may prejudice the civil and religious rights of existing non-Jewish communities in Palestine."

The aim of this letter, known today as the Balfour Declaration, was to entice Jews in Britain and the United States into buying more war bonds. It is ironic that so momentous a document sprang from so small a purpose, but in 1917, Britain was fighting for its life.

At the time, Palestine had 800,000 people, 90 percent Arabs and 10 percent Jews. Today it has 10 million, 40 percent Arabs and 60 percent Jews. After World War I, the Palestinians protested a new wave of Jewish immigration, but the British were unmoved. As Balfour wrote privately in 1919:

> In Palestine, we do not propose even to go through the form of consulting the wishes of the present inhabitants of the country. . . . The Four Great Powers are committed to Zionism. And Zionism, be it right or wrong, good or bad, is rooted in agelong tradition, in present needs, in future hopes, of far profounder import than the prejudices of the 700,000 Arabs who now inhabit that ancient land.[5]

Abdul Aziz opposed Zionism all his life but, having neither a modern army nor a frontier with Palestine, was powerless to combat it.

In 1919, the first year after the war, the spread of influenza was a far more immediate concern. More than a thousand people in Riyadh, 10 percent of the city's population, died of the disease. They included Jauhara, Abdul Aziz's fourth and then favorite wife; Turki, his eldest, nineteen-year-old son; and four younger children. For the rest of his life, Abdul Aziz could not recall that terrible year without pausing to hold back grief.

Fortunately, Abdul Aziz's third son, Faisal, a frail and sickly boy, was out of the country. Only fourteen, the future king was on a diplomatic mission to Britain and France, the first member of the al-Saud family ever to travel west of Turkey. When he returned to Riyadh in 1920, he knew a little English and a lot more about the modern world than anyone else in the family. That was enough for him to become the kingdom's unofficial foreign minister, a post that became official in 1930 and that Faisal continued to hold until his assassination in 1975. (Faisal's son, Saud al-Faisal, succeeded his father as foreign minister and still holds this office today.)

Marriages Short and Long

During his lifetime, Abdul Aziz had forty-five sons, almost as many daughters, and hundreds of grandchildren. He obeyed Muslim law and never had more than four wives at a time (each with her own house and servants). But he divorced women often because there was no dishonor attached. On the contrary, it was an honor for a woman to marry a king, even if the marriage lasted only a few nights. Abdul Aziz's marriages helped to seal alliances with more than thirty tribes, which generally found his many marriages amusing.

Usually, Abdul Aziz had only three wives rather than four, so that if he saw a (veiled) woman and was struck by her eyes, voice, or ancestry, he was free to take her as his fourth wife. The king also had four concubines and four slave girls, and among them, the turnover was even faster. Occasionally, Abdul Aziz described the merits of a slave girl to a friend, then gave the girl to his friend with no thought as to the young woman's feelings.

"In my lifetime I have married seventy-five wives [including concubines]," Abdul Aziz told an Englishman in 1918, "and God willing, I am not done with wiving yet." By the end of his life, Abdul Aziz had married twenty-two legitimate wives and taken more than two hundred concubines, slave girls, and wives for just a night or two. About half of these women were virgins when he first slept with them.

Surprisingly, Abdul Aziz never ate meals with his wives. He also thought it was unbecoming for a woman to learn to read and write, although he did not forbid it. By all accounts, though, he was a gentle husband. Abdul Aziz married the woman who may have been his favorite wife, Hassa bint Ahmad al-Sudairi, around 1920. After five or six years, he divorced her briefly, and during that interval, she married Abdul Aziz's brother Muhammad. But Abdul Aziz missed Hassa and asked his brother to divorce her so that he could marry the young woman a second time. This time, the couple stayed married until Abdul Aziz died, more than twenty years later. Hassa bore the king eight sons and five daughters, including the late king, Fahad, and the current defense minister, Sultan, who is second in line to the throne.

Frontiers: Western, Northern, Iraqi

At the end of World War I, Husain, the king of the Hejaz, sent his son Abdullah with five thousand men to take Turabah, an oasis 120 miles east of Mecca, in a neutral area in between the kingdoms of Hussein and Abdul Aziz. Abdullah's men took the town with ease, plundered it, then made bold plans to ride northeast and conquer Riyadh.

The Ikhwan warriors were furious, and, with Abdul Aziz's approval, more than three thousand of them rode their camels to Turabah in less than a week. Each soldier carried only a rifle or a spear, a dagger, and just one bag of flour, some dates, and a skin full of water. They had practiced night attacks at home many times and looked forward to dying as martyrs.

Late in the evening of May 25, 1919, the Ikhwan divided into three groups and charged into Abdullah's camp from the north, the east, and the south. As they shot and slashed their way from one tent to the next, they spurred one another on by shouting, "The winds of paradise are blowing! Where are ye who seek it?" The attack was devastating. Abdullah escaped with only 150 of his men, most still in their nightclothes. Mecca and Medina were defenseless.

The British were shocked by the Wahhabi victory but were not yet ready to give up on King Husain, who had helped them fight the Turks so recently. When Abdul Aziz arrived in Turabah early in July with several thousand additional soldiers, a British telegram from Cairo was waiting for him. It ordered him to return to central Arabia and threatened to end his subsidy and take military action if he stayed put. To back up this threat, the British navy shipped six airplanes to the port of Jeddah, to bomb the Ikhwan army if necessary.

Abdul Aziz replied that he would be happy to restrain his soldiers if the British would hold back King Husain. He also suggested arbitration to determine a boundary. The British were impressed with his response, for it contrasted starkly with Husain's venom toward Abdul Aziz: "Let him go back to [exile in] Kuwait where he belongs. When he is in Kuwait again, I will consider arbitration!"[6]

With some difficulty, Abdul Aziz persuaded his Ikhwan warriors to leave Turabah and go home. He could afford to be patient. The ease of their victory left Abdul Aziz with no doubt that in just a few more years, the Hejaz and its holy cities would be his.

In March 1921, Winston Churchill, who had just become Britain's secretary of state for the colonies, met in Cairo with his top colonial administrators. The "Forty Thieves," as Churchill jokingly called them, renamed Mesopotamia "Iraq" and installed King Husain's son Feisal there as a puppet monarch. As for the "vacant lot" that existed west of Iraq and east of Palestine, Churchill and T. E. Lawrence talked late one night and created a new state, "Trans-Jordan," where they put another son of Husain, Abdullah, the losing general at Turabah, in charge as a second puppet king. (Iraq's monarchy ended in 1958 when the entire royal family was murdered in a military coup, but Jordan is still governed by a Hashemite king today.)

Abdul Aziz was appalled that he suddenly had frontiers with three hostile Hashemite kings in Iraq, Jordan, and the Hejaz. "The English have surrounded me with enemies," he complained to a friend.

In between central Arabia and Iraq is the city of Hail, which was still home to the al-Rashid family, although the clan was so torn by feuds and murders that it was finally ruled by a succession of teen-age boys. Abdul Aziz decided that he had better take Hail before the new kingdom of Iraq did, and he mobilized the Ikhwan in April. In May, they surrounded the city and began a siege. Ten thousand more troops arrived in August. By October, the city's deputy governor had decided that the town had suffered enough, and he opened its gates to the Saudis. Abdul Aziz was now the ruler of all of Arabia's interior between Yemen and Iraq.

After thirty-five years of war between the al-Saud and al-Rashid families, Abdul Aziz decided to show mercy. He invited the al-Rashid princes to join him in Riyadh as honored guests and brought their soldiers into his army as equals. He also married Fahada, the widow of an al-Rashid prince who had died in battle. Two years later they had a son, Abdullah, who in 2005 became the king of Saudi Arabia.

In July 1922, fifteen hundred Ikhwan warriors, emboldened by their conquest of Hail, rode farther north and attacked two towns less than twenty miles from Amman, the capital of Trans-Jordan, without any sanction from Abdul Aziz. As they plundered the towns and killed women and children, the British chased them back into the desert with airplanes and armored cars.

The majority of the Ikhwan had never seen machines before: now many died from a barrage of British machine-gun fire. Less than half of the men made it back home. When they arrived, an angry Abdul Aziz threw their commanders in jail for fighting without his authorization.

Abdul Aziz apologized to the British and agreed to Percy Cox's suggestion that they draw a border between his kingdom and Jordan, Iraq, and Kuwait. Borders were a new concept in Arabia. For centuries, nomads had been free to let their herds graze wherever there was rain. A king's territory was a matter of tribal loyalties, not lines on a map.

Negotiations began in November 1922 at Al-Uqair, a village on the Persian Gulf with a single mud-walled fortress. Conditions there were so primitive that Abdul Aziz set up tents for the British. Inside were chairs, tables, linen, silverware, bathtubs, cigars, and scotch. For Abdul Aziz, the duty to make his guests comfortable outweighed the Wahhabi prohibition against tobacco and alcohol.

For five full days, Abdul Aziz and an adviser to Iraq's King Feisal both made grandiose claims as to the other's territory. On the sixth day, an exasperated Percy Cox picked up a ruler and drew several straight red lines across a map of the desert, lines that still mark the border between Iraq and Saudi Arabia today.

The boundary between Arabia and Iraq was farther south than Abdul Aziz had expected, almost 150 miles south of the Euphrates River. By contrast, the Ottoman Turks had never bothered to exercise control more than three miles south of the Euphrates.

That evening Abdul Aziz, who could be an actor when he wanted to, came to Cox in tears. "My friend, you have deprived me of half my kingdom," he said. (In fact, the loss was about one-tenth of his realm.) "Better to take it all and let me go into retirement." Cox, primly wearing a bow tie and pinstriped pants even in the desert, took Abdul Aziz by the hand and replied, "My friend, I know exactly how you feel, and for this reason I have given you two-thirds of Kuwait."[7]

When the emir of Kuwait learned that the British had given his inland territory to the Saudis, he was furious, especially considering the hospitality that his family had given the Saudis when they were driven into exile in the 1890s. But Cox had made his decision, and there was no appeal. Cox also gave Abdul Aziz a large slice of eastern Jordan, placing Arabia's northwest frontier only 105 miles east of Jerusalem.

Finally, Cox drew a Connecticut-sized, diamond-shaped neutral zone at the eastern end of the border between Arabia and Iraq. There were water wells here and pastures when it rained, and Cox wanted nomads from both nations to be able to use them. He drew a second, Delaware-sized zone along the coast south of Kuwait. The Getty Oil Company discovered a major field there in 1953, and twelve years later, Saudi Arabia and Kuwait amicably divided the neutral zone.

For the first time in history, Arabian kingdoms had fixed borders. This would soon put an end to the ancient sport of desert raids, for a raid now had international consequences. But in the 1920s, the

Ikhwan had not yet accepted these invisible lines, and as the seasons passed, they felt increasingly confined inside them. "Since Abdul Aziz has ruled, no one has raided an enemy and taken so much as a chicken!" one Ikhwan complained. "Nothing to do but stay at home like women."[8]

In March 1923, the British announced that to cut costs, they would end their monthly subsidies to Arabia's rulers the following year. That summer, seeking new income, Abdul Aziz sold his first oil lease to Major Frank Holmes, an entrepreneur from New Zealand. In return for 2,000 pounds (about $10,000) in gold annually, Abdul Aziz gave Holmes the right to drill oil in eastern Arabia for seventy years.

Unfortunately, Holmes could not interest any oil companies in Arabia. The British had just drilled a well on the Iranian island of Qeshm, which geologists thought had similar underground formations to those in Arabia. But the well was a dry hole, which caused geologists to conclude that there was also no oil in Arabia. Two years later (and 4,000 pounds poorer), Holmes stopped paying the annual fee to Abdul Aziz and lost his rights to a quarter of the world's oil. He had been only ten years ahead of his time.

That same year, Abdul Aziz suffered a skin disease that infected his left eye. A surgeon from Bahrain rushed to Riyadh but arrived too late to save the eye, which closed permanently.

The Conquest of Mecca

Abdul Aziz's vision had been halved, but the size of his kingdom was about to double. On March 3, 1924, Kemal Ataturk, the leader who modernized Turkey after the Ottoman Empire fell, formally ended the caliphate. Beginning with Abu Bakr's acceptance of the title *khalifa* (successor) after Muhammad died in 632, this institution had lasted 1,292 years, although for centuries the caliph's leadership had been political, rather than spiritual. Since 1520, the Ottoman sultan had been caliph, but with the empire gone after World War I, there was no longer a sultan and therefore no longer a caliph. By abolishing the office, Ataturk was simply bowing to reality.

Two days after Ataturk's announcement, Husain, the king of the Hejaz and the sharif of Mecca, declared himself the new caliph. But a Muslim king could no more anoint himself caliph than a European king could make himself pope. Husain's proclamation was denounced throughout the Muslim world, and it particularly incensed the Ikhwan, who considered it sacrilege.

The Ikhwan were already angry that King Husain had forbidden them from making pilgrimages to Mecca—on the plausible ground that they would be a danger to less devout pilgrims. Still, Husain was hardly the pilgrims' champion. Everywhere in the Hejaz, travelers paid steep prices for food, lodging, guides, and even water. Hospitals were so bad that pilgrims stayed away even when they were dying. Worst of all was the fact that Husain made no attempt to stop local Bedouin from robbing pilgrims outright. Even royal visitors were not safe. One of the many victims of theft in 1923 was the mother of the ruler of Afghanistan.

In June 1924, Abdul Aziz summoned the leaders of Arabia's tribes, clergy, and Ikhwan to Riyadh and told them that it was time to cleanse Mecca and Medina of corruption. The clerics agreed that there were ample grounds for *jihad*, holy war, and the tribesmen and the Ikhwan were eager to fight.

This time Abdul Aziz did not have to fear the British. Their leverage over him had ended when they stopped his monthly subsidy. More important, the British themselves lost patience with Husain when he declared himself caliph and alienated India's seventy million Muslims, all of whom were British subjects.

Abdul Aziz waited more than two months for Mecca's pilgrim season to end, then sent three thousand Ikhwan soldiers across 470 miles of desert to the city of Taif, in the mountains above Mecca. The enemy army in Taif was led by Husain's son Ali, but on the night of September 4, the timid prince left Taif defenseless as he withdrew his troops first to Mecca and then to Jeddah. For the next three days, the Ikhwan plundered houses, smashed portraits and tombs, and killed more than three hundred men, women, and children. In Mecca, forty miles away, people panicked—a massacre was exactly what they expected from the fierce Wahhabis.

When Abdul Aziz heard the news of the slaughter in Taif, he wept with grief. He immediately sent orders forbidding another blood-bath and promised to execute any soldier who murdered unarmed civilians.

In Jeddah, the leading citizens urged Husain to abdicate in favor of his son Ali, in hopes that the Ikhwan might be willing to negotiate with them once Husain was no longer king. Since the Ikhwan army was at the outskirts of Mecca, Husain had no choice but to comply. He left on October 16, with his porters carrying 800,000 British pounds in gold, and sailed from Jeddah to become an exile in Cyprus.

The next day, as the people of Mecca hid inside their homes, two thousand Ikhwan entered the city. They smashed portraits, water pipes, musical instruments, and the domes that were built over the tombs of saints, but they did not kill anyone and they looted only the palaces of the royal family. Two or three days later, the men and the women of Mecca gingerly ventured back into the streets and resumed their normal lives.

Abdul Aziz, forty-eight years old, began his first pilgrimage to Mecca in mid-November. Before leaving Riyadh, he told a crowd, "I am a traveler to the Home of Revelation, to spread the Shariah [Muslim law] and enforce it."[9] After a three-week ride across the desert, he walked into the holy city bareheaded, wearing two lengths of white cloth like any other pilgrim. As he approached the Grand Mosque, he repeated over and over, as pilgrims do, "Oh, Allah! Here I am, at your call, to do your service!"

In Mecca, Abdul Aziz declined to live in a palace, preferring instead to sleep in a simple tent in the nearby hills. He also refused to let anyone in the city kneel before him and told everyone that he would rather shake hands. He appointed an eleven-member council of local merchants and noblemen to give him advice and allowed most of Mecca's officials to keep their jobs.

Abdul Aziz did replace the clergymen at Mecca's holiest mosques with his own Wahhabi imams. Soon there were strict rules about prayer. A merchant who failed to close his shop during prayer time was whipped, and if someone skipped prayers too often, he spent several nights in jail. In addition, drinking alcohol was punished by a month in prison, a second offense by two years in prison.

These laws and others prohibiting smoking, music, singing, eating during a fast, and the wearing of gold or silk were soon enforced by a new religious police force that Abdul Aziz created: the Society for the Advancement of Virtue and the Elimination of Sin. The purpose of the society was not only to enforce religious law (sometimes through beatings), but also, oddly enough, to tame the Ikhwan, to give them a structure for their previously wild, unrestrained fanaticism. Today, on the streets of Saudi Arabia, the religious police still enforce Muslim law.

Capturing Medina and Jeddah

In January 1925, more than five thousand Ikhwan surrounded the city of Jeddah, forty miles west of Mecca on the Red Sea, and began a long siege. *Jeddah* means "grandmother" in Arabic. The old city has a site where Eve is said to have been buried after she was expelled from the Garden of Eden. Jeddah was also where foreign diplomats lived because Mecca is forbidden to non-Muslims.

The Ikhwan stayed just out of range of Jeddah's artillery but shelled the town with artillery of its own. By springtime, there was so little food in the city that the poor were sifting through horse droppings to find kernels of undigested barley. Abdul Aziz could have taken Jeddah any time he chose to, but because of the presence of foreign diplomats, he did not want bloodshed and preferred to wait for the city to surrender.

For most of 1925, Abdul Aziz also besieged the city of Medina. The Ikhwan regarded Muhammad's tomb as just another idol to be smashed, and they fired on the city indiscriminately. Abdul Aziz ordered the shelling to be stopped immediately, and the tomb was unharmed. By autumn, when there was little to eat in Medina, the leaders of the city sent Abdul Aziz a message that they would be willing to surrender to a member of the al-Saud family but not to the Ikhwan. On December 6, Medina opened its gates to Abdul Aziz's fourth-oldest son, Muhammad, who brought hundreds of sacks of rice for the people to eat.

Muhammad kept the Ikhwan warriors in Medina under some restraint, but they still destroyed every tomb in the city except the Prophet's, and at his grave, soldiers prevented anyone from kneeling or from praying to the Prophet rather than directly to Allah.

Ten days after the fall of Medina, the citizens of Jeddah finally offered to surrender but only if the Ikhwan stayed out of their city. Abdul Aziz had never wanted the Ikhwan near foreign embassies to begin with and readily granted their request. On December 23, 1925, he personally accepted the city's surrender. For only the second time since the seventh century, an Arabian state stretched from the Persian Gulf to the Red Sea.

Denying the Ikhwan Power

The conquest of the Hejaz, the Red Sea region that includes Mecca, Medina, and Jeddah, was Abdul Aziz's greatest victory, but now he had to govern it. The two leading Ikhwan commanders, Faisal al-Dawish and ibn Bijad, suggested that they should become the governors of Mecca and Medina, but Abdul Aziz refused. He knew that western Arabia was a far more sophisticated place than central Arabia was. The cities of Mecca, Medina, and Jeddah had schools, newspapers, and regular contact with the outside world. They needed better leadership than the intolerant Ikhwan could provide.

Abdul Aziz decided that rather than incorporate the Hejaz into Najd, it would be better, at least for a few years, to govern the region separately. On January 8, 1926, just before the noon prayer, the *imam* of Mecca's Grand Mosque proclaimed Abdul Aziz "King of the Hejaz." The people of the holy city were relieved that their region would still have a separate identity, and they swore their allegiance.

A few months later, Abdul Aziz, the king of Najd and the Hejaz, appointed his eldest son, Saud, to be the viceroy of Najd, and his second son, Faisal, to be the viceroy of the Hejaz. In fact, Abdul Aziz would govern both regions himself. Faisal al-Dawish and ibn Bijad, the spurned commanders of the Ikhwan, had no choice but to return to their settlements and nurse their resentments. They had done a lot of fighting but felt they had reaped little reward.

9

Powerful but Poor (1926–1945)

HAVING CONQUERED MECCA, Medina, and Jeddah, Abdul Aziz imposed the Wahhabis' strict customs on the more relaxed people of these cities. He also made pilgrimages to Mecca cheaper, cleaner, and much safer than before. Although the king kept the Ikhwan warriors away from Jeddah and the holy cities, they soon began unauthorized and murderous raids into Iraq, which forced the Saudi army to attack them in 1929, killing hundreds.

In 1933, Abdul Aziz gave a lease to the Standard Oil Company of California (SOCAL, known today as Chevron) to drill for oil, but it took the company almost five years to find some, and by then, war made exports impossible. The Saudi kingdom remained poor throughout most of the 1940s.

Abdul Aziz stayed in western Arabia for two years after his conquest of the region. Governing the Hejaz personally, he insisted that tour guides be licensed and that there be fixed prices for lodging and for admissions to religious sites. He also greatly improved the region's sanitation, hospitals, and water supply, and he deported known prostitutes.

Most important, Abdul Aziz let the Bedouin know that their days of robbing pilgrims or asking them for "protection money" were over. One man who continued to steal from people was bound, handcuffed, and left to die in the sun. When another tribe robbed a caravan,

Abdul Aziz sent troops to its village and killed all two hundred of its men. Other thieves had their hands amputated in public squares.

Abdul Aziz believed that it was better to set a few terrifying examples of justice and end crime quickly rather than impose less severe punishments repeatedly, as Western nations do. "Once we have punished [the Bedouin] we shall not in the mercy of God have to do it again as long as we live."[1]

In 1925, only a few thousand pilgrims from India were brave enough to travel to Mecca, which was overrun with fierce Ikhwan warriors. Yet throughout their journey, they were safe and well-treated, and when they returned home, they spread the word that the Wahhabis had made the pilgrimage to Mecca much easier.

The next year, more than 126,000 Muslims visited Mecca, almost half from overseas. Each one paid the kingdom a fee of 5 pounds (about $260 in today's money), which all together was much more money than Abdul Aziz had ever had before.

The Ikhwan Become Lawless

In May 1927, after Abdul Aziz finally returned to Riyadh, he signed a seven-year treaty of friendship with Britain to replace the old pact of 1915. Britain recognized Abdul Aziz's new conquests and his "absolute independence" as a ruler, even in the realm of foreign affairs. In return, Abdul Aziz recognized Britain's special relationship with the Persian Gulf states and with the port of Aden in Yemen.

Abdul Aziz knew that there would be no more conquests; there was almost no place left in Arabia that was not protected by British arms. The Ikhwan warriors, however, were still burning to fight for their faith and saw the new treaty with Britain as literally a pact with the devil.

Sometimes the Ikhwan raided villages in Iraq, which to them was a sinful land of tomb-worshipping Shi'ites protected by English infidels. In one raid, witnessed in horror by Captain John Bagot Glubb, who later wrote superb books on Muslim history, Ikhwan soldiers yanked babies from the arms of their mothers and killed them if they were boys or, if they were girls, threw them back into the arms of their sobbing mothers. At Glubb's insistence, in September 1927, the British began to build a police post at a well called Busayyah, seventy-two miles from the Arabian border. The Ikhwan did not understand the distinction between the police and the military, and to them, the fort was an intolerable provocation.

On the night of November 5, Ikhwan warriors attacked the British post and killed eleven workmen. The British retaliated with several bombing runs deep inside Saudi territory, then rebuilt the fort with the protection of an army platoon and air force patrols. Abdul Aziz waffled. He knew the Ikhwan had become unruly but still wanted their support. He apologized to the British and assured them that the raid was unauthorized but also criticized them for building an armed post so close to the border.

The following year, Abdul Aziz called a conference in Riyadh of eight hundred leading warriors, clerics, and tribal sheikhs. Although some Ikhwan generals attended the meeting, the three most important commanders refused to come. They had already decided among themselves that they wanted to overthrow Abdul Aziz and govern his three regions, the Hejaz, Najd, and Al-Hasa—western, central, and eastern Arabia—separately.

Abdul Aziz opened the meeting by denouncing the murderous raids in Iraq that endangered a necessary friendship with Britain. The Ikhwan responded with criticisms of their own. Among their complaints were: (1) the treaty with Britain was evil; (2) the use of cars, telephones, radios, and other things not mentioned in the Quran was sorcery (although the Ikhwan never objected to the rifle); and (3) Shi'ites should not be tolerated—the Ikhwan should be free to enter Iraq and either convert them to Wahhabi Islam or kill them.

After listening to the Ikhwan, Abdul Aziz stunned the conference by offering to step down as king. "Choose anyone else in my family," he said, "and I will obey him." It was a masterful bluff because he knew that none of his relatives enjoyed enough support to replace him. As he anticipated, after a moment of shocked silence, the outcry was instant and deafening. "No, only you! We are loyal to you!"

With the complaints of the Ikhwan momentarily forgotten, Abdul Aziz asked each sheikh, cleric, and soldier to swear a new oath of allegiance to him. Everyone did, and this gave him the strength he needed for a showdown with the many Ikhwan who were still disloyal.

One month later, ibn Bijad, the Ikhwan commander who had wanted to be the governor of Medina, led three thousand warriors in another raid into Iraq. After hearing that some British aircraft were ahead, he turned his army south. He attacked an Arabian village instead, killing some unarmed Wahhabi merchants and stealing their camels. It was a fatal mistake, for it swung public opinion decisively against the Ikhwan. They had not fought infidels; they had robbed and murdered their fellow countrymen. Their lawlessness had to be stopped, even if it meant war.

Civil War

Abdul Aziz called for a double quota of men from the loyal tribes, which gave him a three-to-one numerical superiority over the Ikhwan. With money collected from pilgrims in Mecca, he paid each soldier three British pounds and bought fifteen hundred additional rifles from the British.

The two armies camped close to each other at Sabillah, a wheat field twenty-five miles west of Al-Artawiya, the largest Ikhwan settlement. Before the fighting began, Abdul Aziz talked for a day and a half with Faisal al-Dawish, the charismatic Ikhwan general who had wanted to be the governor of Mecca. Al-Dawish offered money to the Wahhabi merchants who had had their camels stolen, but Abdul Aziz replied, "It is not only a question of camels. The Ikhwan have also killed men and your chiefs must answer to the Shariah court and abide by its decision."[2]

When al-Dawish returned to his camp, he contemptuously referred to Abdul Aziz and his troops as "fat townsmen" who slept on soft mattresses and said they would be useless in battle.

The showdown took place on March 30, 1929. The Ikhwan held the high ground and had built a stone wall for their protection. But Abdul Aziz had kept secret the fact that he possessed a dozen machine guns. Now he ordered his gunners to hold their fire during the first part of the battle and wait until they could inflict maximum damage.

That moment came when Abdul Aziz's advance troops moved back to eat a late breakfast, and the Ikhwan mistakenly thought that they were retreating. When the Ikhwan warriors climbed over the stone walls to pursue them, the increasingly frustrated machine gunners restrained themselves for one or two minutes more, then let loose a barrage that killed hundreds of Ikhwan within seconds. The remaining Ikhwan were overrun by four columns of tribesmen, two of them led by Abdul Aziz's sons Saud and Muhammad. It was the first time the Ikhwan had ever lost a pitched battle and the last time an Arabian battle was fought on camels.

The next day Faisal al-Dawish was carried on a stretcher into Abdul Aziz's tent. He had been shot right through the stomach and was fighting for his life. Abdul Aziz remembered that al-Dawish had fought more battles for him than against him and decided to pardon the man. He hoped that his mercy toward al-Dawish would also entice the surrender of ibn Bijad, the commander who had led the raid on the Arabian village.

The lure worked. Within a week, ibn Bijad rode into Abdul Aziz's camp to ask the king whether he could take his remaining troops home. Instead, Abdul Aziz jailed him immediately. He also ordered the complete destruction of his settlement, the town of Ghotghot.

The Ikhwan were not yet finished. In the spring of 1929, while Abdul Aziz was in Mecca, an Ikhwan army rose up in rebellion, joined by Faisal al-Dawish, who had miraculously survived his bullet wound, and a fresh army of Ikhwan warriors. The Ikhwan poisoned many of the wells between Riyadh and Mecca, cutting off Abdul Aziz from his capital.

Abdul Aziz rounded up every car he could find in Mecca and Jeddah and led a convoy of several dozen Fords and Chevrolets east across the desert sand. Loyal tribesmen warned him of armies and contaminated wells ahead; Abdul Aziz had to take many detours to get home. The king was so new to automobiles that he did not even know that they had to be serviced. By sheer luck, most of the cars were still running when he finally reached Riyadh in July.

That summer and fall, Abdul Aziz attacked pockets of Ikhwan throughout Arabia. In the north, sharpshooters successfully prevented an Ikhwan army, led by al-Dawish's son, from reaching one well after another, until finally 450 men died of dehydration.

In the east, Abdul Aziz armed two reliable tribes with four thousand British rifles. He also sent them several cars mounted with machine guns operated by his sons Muhammad and Khalid. Together, the tribesmen and the machine-gunning princes drove al-Dawish and his men into Kuwait, where they surrendered to the British on January 10, 1930.

The British, who had no love for the Ikhwan, handed over al-Dawish to Abdul Aziz on condition that his life be spared. Al-Dawish asked Abdul Aziz for mercy again, but this time the king threw him in prison, where he mourned his dead son and died of throat cancer a year and a half later.

Arabia's civil war was finally over; Islamist fanatics would not reappear in the kingdom for fifty years. Abdul Aziz had been forced to kill his own soldiers because they had become homicidal religious militants who refused to accept life in the modern world or peaceful relations with the West. In the twenty-first century, Abdul Aziz's son, King Abdullah, made a similar choice to fight al-Qaeda.

The Minister of Finance

No one ever accused Abdul Aziz of governing with excessive bureaucracy. He had only ten or twelve clerks and typists, a few translators, and several dozen tax collectors to extract the annual *zakat*.

Abdul Aziz's closest aide was his political secretary, Yusuf Yassin, a Syrian who had fled the French colonialists and first came to Riyadh in 1923 as a teacher for the king's sons. He was an invaluable assistant during the conquest of Mecca the following year and always seemed to anticipate the king's thoughts and needs. In later years, he often went abroad to settle diplomatic disputes and sometimes came home with a new blond concubine for the king from the Caucasus or from his native Syria.

Abdul Aziz's most powerful adviser was his minister of finance, Abdullah Suleiman, for nothing could be funded without his sanction. A native of Najd, Suleiman had worked as a bookkeeper in Bombay before joining his uncle as one of the king's clerks. Hardworking and resourceful, he was instrumental in funneling pilgrim fees, customs duties, and the *zakat* to Riyadh and making sure that the king had plenty of gold and weapons. Suleiman always seemed to find money somewhere for the monarch's vast expenses, and when there was nothing left, he squeezed merchants for money in return for government contracts later.

When Suleiman was in Riyadh, he was the first person Abdul Aziz saw in the morning. He had the king's absolute confidence and was the only person at court who was free to make his own decisions without first checking with Abdul Aziz.

Radios and Schools

In 1930, Suleiman approved a contract with the Marconi Company to build a dozen shortwave radio stations in cities across Arabia and, more important, four mobile radio transmitters to accompany Abdul Aziz and his oldest sons on their travels through the desert. Wahhabi clerics objected to radios as the devil's work but were won over when Abdul Aziz let them hear friends in other cities recite verses from the Quran.

Later in the 1930s, when the British Broadcasting Corporation (BBC) began news broadcasts in Arabic, Abdul Aziz listened every evening. He was always interested in news from the outside world and questioned foreigners at length about their home countries. He also financed scholarships that enabled several hundred boys to attend prep schools in Syria and Egypt and a lucky few to study at universities in the United States and Europe.

Probably the kingdom's greatest problem was its severe shortage of primary and secondary schools. In the whole of Arabia, there were fewer than ten thousand elementary school students and five hundred high school students in the 1930s. It was hard to recruit foreigners to teach in Arabia and harder still for Wahhabi clerics to accept the need for foreign instruction.

In 1930, when the Directorate of Education proposed a curriculum for public schools, imams objected to teaching drawing because children would then know how to sketch human beings and make graven images. Imams also opposed instruction in foreign languages because it would enable students to read the scriptures of other religions. Finally, they objected to teaching geography because children would be told that the world was round, not flat. Abdul Aziz listened to the clerics and decided that students did not need classes in drawing, French, or German, but he insisted that they learn English and at least the geography of the Muslim world.

Schools cost money, as do cars, radios, and rifles. Abdul Aziz's income plummeted in 1931 because the Great Depression caused a 70 percent fall in the number of pilgrims going to Mecca. His debts rose to more than 300,000 British pounds ($1.5 million). For months at a time, he could no longer pay salaries, creditors, or, most humiliatingly, tribesmen who came to visit. To make ends meet, cooks pilfered rice and chauffeurs siphoned gasoline. "If anyone offered me a million pounds now," the anxious king told a friend, "he would be welcome to all the resources he wants in my country."

At fifty-five, Abdul Aziz had gained weight and had begun to wear glasses. His face was typically "sad" and "overcast," according to a British diplomat and an American entrepreneur keeping separate diaries, but both agreed that the slightest event or word could make the king's face "light up" with curiosity and excitement.

The Kingdom of Saudi Arabia

In September 1932, Abdul Aziz officially merged the dual monarchies of Najd and the Hejaz into one united country, the Kingdom of Saudi Arabia. It is the size of continental Europe west of Berlin and Venice and is the only country in the world named for a family.

The next year, Abdul Aziz formally chose Saud to be crown prince. The king knew that his second son, Faisal, who was both foreign minister and viceroy of the Hejaz, was much more hardworking and shrewd than his charming but lazy older brother. But the king was less concerned about the qualifications of his first heir than he was in establishing a secure pattern of succession for his dynasty.

The effect of Saud becoming crown prince was limited. Sometimes the king asked Saud to preside at banquets that he preferred not to attend himself; otherwise, he gave his son little to do. Faisal, by contrast, was five hundred miles away, governing an entire region.

First Lease to an Oil Company

The first man to envision Saudi Arabia as a modern country with cities, factories, highways, and airports was an American philanthropist, Charles Crane. He was a Quaker multimillionaire whose family had made a fortune manufacturing bathroom fixtures. Crane first became involved with the Middle East when he prepared a report on Syria and Palestine for President Woodrow Wilson. Ten years later, he helped Yemen build a harbor, a bridge, and some roads.

In 1931, he met Abdul Aziz in Jeddah and outlined his vision of a modern Arabia that he was certain could be paid for by minerals underground. Abdul Aziz did not believe it but listened politely and was pleased when Crane said that he would hire a geologist to explore the country. The king agreed to provide the technician with food, lodging, a car, and security.

Karl Twitchell arrived just two months later. He began by looking for water near Jeddah, a quest much dearer to Abdul Aziz's Bedouin heart than the search for oil, but none was found. The following year, the Standard Oil Company of California (SOCAL, known today as Chevron) discovered oil on the island of Bahrain, only twelve miles off the coast of Saudi Arabia.

Twitchell was sure that there must be oil on the mainland, too, and began to negotiate for an oil concession between SOCAL and the Saudis. Abdul Aziz was deeply skeptical that there was anything under the sand. He was far more interested in a lump sum up front that would help him pay his debts than he was in any future oil royalties.

Abdullah Suleiman, the king's finance minister, asked SOCAL for 100,000 British pounds in gold as an initial payment, but after three months of negotiation, he settled for an immediate payment of 30,000 pounds (about $1.8 million in today's money); 20,000 pounds ($1.2 million today) eighteen months later; and rent of 5,000 pounds ($300,000 today) per year. In addition, if oil were discovered in commercial quantities, SOCAL would pay the Saudis another 100,000 pounds ($6 million in current money).

In return, SOCAL won the exclusive rights to explore, drill, extract, and export oil from the eastern part of Saudi Arabia (where the oil is), for sixty years and to be exempt from Saudi taxes and customs duties.

"Put your trust in God and sign," Abdul Aziz told his finance minister on May 8, 1933. The king was pleased that the Americans had won the concession instead of the British. He had worried that if the British drilled wells in Saudi Arabia, they might start to influence his government. The Americans, wrote one of his aides, "would simply be after the money, a motive which the Arabs as born traders could readily appreciate."[3]

By August, 35,000 gold one-pound coins, representing the down payment and the first year's rent, finally arrived at Jeddah's one and only bank. Together, Abdullah Suleiman and a lawyer for SOCAL counted out the coins, one stack at a time.

In the fall, Twitchell and seven other geologists began to comb the desert in cars and on camels, accompanied by a dozen soldiers to protect them from hostile Ikhwan or larcenous Bedouin. Many people in the industry were highly doubtful about their chances, and at Shell, one director offered to drink all the oil that would ever be found in Saudi Arabia.

War with Yemen

In the spring of 1934, Abdul Aziz fought his last war, against Imam Yahya, the ruler of Yemen. Emboldened by promises of arms from Italian dictator Benito Mussolini, Yahya had taken two small towns across the Saudi Arabian border. Abdul Aziz proposed to create a neutral zone there and demanded a reply by April 5. When none came, his troops attacked.

Prince Saud and Prince Faisal led separate armies. Faisal had an easy time advancing down the Red Sea coast and captured the port of Al-Hudaydah in May. But Saud got bogged down in Yemen's rugged mountains, sometimes having to use ropes to lower cars down cliffs while under sniper fire.

Faisal wanted to march inland to Sana, Yemen's capital city, but Abdul Aziz offered Yahya a generous peace instead. In exchange for Yemen's recognition of the previous boundary and payment of 100,000 British pounds to reimburse the Saudis for the war's expense, Abdul Aziz ordered his armies to withdraw from Yemen.

One of the king's aides wept when he learned how much territory the king had given up, but Abdul Aziz knew that Yemen was a poor and violent country with almost as many people as his own kingdom. "You fool!" Abdul Aziz said to his adviser. "Where will I get the manpower to govern Yemen? Yemen can only be led by its own ruler!"[4]

Automobiles

By 1935, cars had fully replaced camels in the king's entourage. Since Abdul Aziz took even his files with him wherever he went, it was a relief not to have to balance a large wooden chest on top of a camel. During trips to Mecca in the late 1920s, when there were fewer cars, the king's wives and daughters rode in the back of a truck for five days. This may sound tedious, but in fact it was far more comfortable than riding a camel in the sun for three weeks. By 1935, however, each of Abdul Aziz's wives and grown daughters had her own car and (non-Saudi) driver.

When Abdul Aziz traveled from one region to another, it took a fleet of 250 cars to carry all of his soldiers, bodyguards, mechanics, clerks, cooks, and servants across the miles of sand. The mechanics were from India or Indonesia, while almost half of the king's bodyguards were black, the sons of slaves whom Abdul Aziz had known since childhood. Sometimes they rode on the running board of the king's custom-built Mercedes, their long red robes flapping in the wind.

Abdul Aziz especially enjoyed using cars to hunt gazelles with his relatives. Chasing the animals at top speed, they killed as many as two hundred on some days, until finally the gazelles retreated to the mountains, never to come down again.

The Late 1930s: Drilling for Oil, Anger at Jews in Palestine

Near the Persian Gulf, SOCAL drilled six oil wells in scorching 120-degree heat in 1935 and 1936. The first well produced only a hundred barrels (one barrel fills about two bathtubs) of oil a day, which was barely worth the expense of drilling. The second yielded thirty-eight hundred barrels, then "went wet" and produced only water. The third, fourth, fifth, and sixth wells were also either "wet" or dry hole "dusters."

The exploration for oil was proving more expensive than SOCAL executives had anticipated. They invited Texaco to split their costs and profits, and it was a good fit. SOCAL needed wider marketing and distribution, while Texaco needed new sources of oil. In 1936, they formed a new company, Caltex, establishing joint interests in a huge area from Egypt to Hawaii. (In 2000, Chevron and Texaco merged completely.) In Saudi Arabia, their operations were known as the California Arabian Standard Oil Company (CASOC), which was renamed eight years later as the Arabian American Oil Company, better known as Aramco.

The year 1936 was also when Palestine became more violent. Militant Palestinians who wanted to stop Jewish immigration attacked British troops, sometimes with weapons that Abdul Aziz had secretly shipped to them. Militant Jews who wanted even more immigration also attacked British troops.

The following year, a British commission recommended a partition of Palestine into Arab and Jewish states. Arab leaders unanimously rejected the plan. As Abdul Aziz explained to H. R. P. Dickson, who had replaced Percy Cox as Britain's political agent in Kuwait,

> I would prefer that my possessions and my children should cease to exist rather than that the Jews should establish a foothold in Palestine. . . . Our hatred for the Jews dates from God's condemnation for their persecution and rejection of Jesus and their rejection later of His Chosen Prophet Muhammad. . . . How would the people of Scotland like it if the English suddenly gave their country to the Jews?[5]

Nine hundred miles southeast of Palestine, the search for oil continued. Geologists drilled a seventh well in Dhahran that was also disappointing. But a decision to deepen the well to nearly five thousand feet beneath the surface paid off on March 4, 1938, when the well began to produce more than two thousand barrels of oil a day.

Within a year, in an area that once had only a few mud huts, there were many oil wells, acres of pipes and drilling equipment, and more than 350 tents and cabins, with showers, screen doors, and electric lights and fans. The engineers were American, and the manual workers were primarily Indians and Italians. Slowly, local Arabs also began to take these well-paying jobs because, unlike the Bedouin farther inland, they were not too proud to do manual labor.

At CASOC's request, Abdul Aziz enlarged the company's concession northward to the borders with Kuwait and Iraq. In return, CASOC agreed to pay the king $700,000 ($9 million in current money) immediately and another $500,000 if more oil was discovered and to quadruple its rent to $100,000 ($1.3 million today) per year.

In April 1939, Abdul Aziz went to see the new wells at Dhahran, then inspected the recently built port of Ras Tanura. On May 1, he opened a valve that let oil rush into an eight-thousand-ton tanker that would take the petroleum to a refinery in Bahrain.

Abdul Aziz's oil income grew nearly as large as his income from pilgrim fees, and the Americans were finding more oil every month. For the first time in years, Abdul Aziz had money to build not only a paved road from Mecca to Jeddah, connecting the holy city to the sea, but also a new mud-walled palace outside Riyadh for his expanding family. Most important, the king could pay his debts; the future looked bright.

World War II

Four months later, the Nazis invaded Poland and started World War II. Overnight, the growth in Saudi oil production stopped cold. Ships and industrial equipment were diverted to Europe, and U.S. engineers returned home to help their nation's war effort. The war also reduced the number of overseas pilgrims visiting Mecca to nearly zero. Suddenly, Abdul Aziz had almost no income.

Worse still, there was a severe drought during the winter of 1939 to 1940. The grass in the pastures failed to grow, sheep and camels died, and the Bedouin were hungry. As hard-pressed as the British were in their fight against Hitler in 1940, they did not let the Saudis starve. They assigned scarce ships to bring rice from India, flour from Egypt and Canada, and sacks of silver coins from banks in London. To keep Abdul Aziz solvent during this time of increased expenses, CASOC agreed to lend the king an advance of $3 million against postwar oil royalties.

The British also informed Abdul Aziz of an offer from Chaim Weizmann, soon to become Israel's first president, to give the king 20 million pounds ($1.3 billion in today's money) if he would allow Palestinian refugees to start new lives in his kingdom. Abdul Aziz, despite the drought, regarded the offer as a "bribe" and an insult, and he rebuked the official who had conveyed it: "Tell your government that Palestine is the land of my Prophet's Ascension. I will not give you a handful of its dust even if you were to offer me the wealth of the whole world."[6]

Some of Abdul Aziz's closest advisers, including the Syrian Yusef Yassin, openly favored the Nazis because of their enmity toward Jews, but Abdul Aziz had met several Nazi diplomats and did not trust them. He warned his aides, "Woe to the Arabs if Hitler wins!"

In the evening, when Abdul Aziz listened to BBC News, he cheered if there was a British victory. At first, there were few. On April 1, 1941, pro-Nazi Iraqi army officers overthrew Iraq's government and asked Abdul Aziz and other Arab leaders for their support. As tempting as it was for Abdul Aziz to support the expulsion of a Hashemite king he despised, he refused the request, saying that it would be an act of treachery against the British. Hitler himself sent Abdul Aziz a message promising him that if he attacked British bases in Jordan and the Persian Gulf, he could become king of all the Arabs. Instead, Abdul Aziz ordered his envoy to the Nazis to return home.

The British reoccupied Iraq in May and expelled the fascist Vichy French from Syria in July. They were the dominant power in the Middle East again but would not be preeminent in Saudi Arabia much longer.

During World War II, the United States produced 63 percent of the world's oil but saw its reserves shrink 3 percent each year. Saudi Arabia, by contrast, already had oil reserves equal to those of the United States. Thus, on February 18, 1943, President Franklin Roosevelt signed an executive order declaring that Saudi Arabia was "vital to the defense of the United States," which made the nation eligible for lend-lease aid. During the last two years of the war, the United States sent Saudi Arabia $33 million worth of food, industrial equipment, dollar deposits, and gold. The United States had unexpectedly replaced Britain as Saudi Arabia's chief ally.

In September 1943, two of Abdul Aziz's sons, Faisal and Khalid, visited Washington and dined with President Roosevelt at Blair House. Abdul Aziz himself was almost seventy, suffered from severe arthritis, and had difficulty walking.

By 1944, as the allies regained control of the sea, the United States shipped more materials to Saudi Arabia and also sent some Italian prisoners of war there to work as laborers. Joined by local Arabs, they built a refinery at Ras Tanura, a pipeline to Bahrain, and a U.S. air force base to protect them at Dhahran.

Saudi oil production increased 58 percent in 1944, and most of the oil was shipped to military bases in Italy and in the Pacific. In 1945, oil output almost tripled, as did Abdul Aziz's income. The king was growing old, but he would never have to worry about earning money again. The new problem would be managing it.

IO

The Influx of Oil Money
(1945–1953)

OR MORE THAN FORTY YEARS, King Abdul Aziz had generously given food, clothes, and money to his people without knowing where the next sack of coins was coming from. Now, when oil money poured in, the king was too old to understand the need for budgets and accounting procedures. As a result, almost half of the nation's income in the 1940s was misspent on palaces for hundreds of princes, while public education was completely neglected. A more positive development was the growth of the Arabian American Oil Company (Aramco). By 1949, it employed ten thousand Saudis. They worked long hours in scorching oil fields but received good salaries and excellent medical care. It was the beginning of a long friendship between the United States and Saudi Arabia.

The King Meets Roosevelt and Churchill

On February 12, 1945, Abdul Aziz drove to Jeddah and boarded the USS *Murphy*, the first U.S. Navy ship ever to dock in Saudi Arabia. To everyone's astonishment, the ship then sailed away. Rumors spread that the king had abdicated or been abducted, but his son Faisal assured the country that the king had planned this trip well in advance.

Abdul Aziz was about to meet President Franklin Roosevelt, who was on his way back from a summit with Winston Churchill and Joseph Stalin at Yalta, on the Soviet coast of the Black Sea. The talks would take place on Roosevelt's ship, the USS *Quincy*, in the Suez Canal. Total secrecy was required to prevent the ship from becoming a target for German bombers.

Abdul Aziz had assumed that he would have to feed the entire crew of the USS *Murphy* during the two-day voyage, just as he always fed everyone in his palace, so he arrived with a hundred sheep. The captain explained to the king that livestock were not allowed on U.S. warships, but the monarch refused to consider the idea of eating old, frozen meat. As a compromise, the captain allowed seven sheep aboard so that the Saudis could have fresh mutton.

The king's servants set up a tent, some carpets, and a wooden throne toward the front of the ship, and five times a day they used a compass to pray in the direction of Mecca. One evening the Saudis saw *The Fighting Lady*, a documentary about a U.S. aircraft carrier in the South Pacific. Abdul Aziz said it was a wonderful film, but, "I doubt whether my people should have moving pictures like this. . . . It would give them an appetite for entertainment which might distract them from their religious duties."[1]

Just before Abdul Aziz was hoisted aboard President Roosevelt's ship (his arthritis made him unable to walk the gangplank), he gave $40 to every member of the USS *Murphy*'s crew, a watch to each officer, and gold-plated daggers to the captain and the first mate.

On February 14, Roosevelt and Abdul Aziz conversed for an hour and a half, had lunch, and continued to talk another two hours. Roosevelt did not smoke in the Wahhabi king's presence, but during a break before lunch while going down an elevator, he pressed the emergency stop button and enjoyed two quick cigarettes before resuming his descent.

When Abdul Aziz admired Roosevelt's wheelchair, the president impulsively gave him his spare chair. It proved too small for the king, but later he had a bigger and stronger replica made and used it for the rest of his life.

Roosevelt spoke at length about the Nazi persecution of the Jews and the need to do something for them. Abdul Aziz suggested that the Jews be given the choicest lands in Germany. The president said that the Jews no longer wanted to live in Germany but in Palestine. The king argued that recompense for a crime should be made by the criminal, not by innocent bystanders, and that Palestine already had more than its share of Jewish refugees. Roosevelt later told a session of Congress that he had learned more about Palestine in five minutes with Abdul Aziz than in all the arguments and reports that he had ever received from his staff.

As a parting gift, the president gave the king a DC-3 aircraft, along with the services of its crew for a year. Because Roosevelt's ship had to rendezvous with a military convoy that was escorting him home, there was no time for the king to give the president a dinner. But Abdul Aziz insisted, before leaving the ship, that he at least brew some coffee for the president as a token of Arab hospitality.

After President Roosevelt returned to Washington, he sent Abdul Aziz a letter on April 5 that confirmed two promises he had made orally. First, he pledged not to do anything hostile to the Arabs, and second, he promised not to change U.S. policy toward Palestine without first consulting both Arabs and Jews. One week later, the president died suddenly of a cerebral hemorrhage, and his promises died with him.

It was only on the last day of the Yalta conference that Roosevelt had told the British prime minister, Winston Churchill, that he was meeting Abdul Aziz on his way home. Churchill quickly set up a conference with the Arabian king himself. Three days after Roosevelt sailed home, Abdul Aziz met Churchill at a slightly seedy lakeside hotel fifty miles south of Cairo.

Before beginning their three-hour lunch, Churchill smiled as he told the Wahhabi king, "If it is the religion of His Majesty to deprive himself of smoking and alcohol, I must point out that my rule of life prescribes as an absolutely sacred rite smoking cigars and also drinking alcohol before, after, and if need be during all meals and in the intervals between them."[2]

Though Abdul Aziz watched with equanimity as Churchill smoked and drank, their talks accomplished little. Churchill reminded the king that Britain had paid him subsidies for many years and now it needed Saudi help in Palestine. Abdul Aziz said that the objection to a Jewish state on Arab land was a matter of honor and beyond financial concerns.

After his conference with Churchill, Abdul Aziz sailed home. Arriving in Jeddah, he was greeted by cheering crowds. The people were proud that their king had met Roosevelt and Churchill on equal terms. They were also quickly becoming reconciled to Wahhabi rule. However dubious the people of the Hejaz had been when the Wahhabis conquered them in 1925, they began to realize that the immense oil wealth of eastern Arabia was theirs to share as well, and they no longer dreamed of breaking away from Saudi Arabia.

Bechtel and Aramco

Oil production increased sevenfold between 1944 and 1946, and by 1949, it tripled again. By then, Abdul Aziz was receiving more than $100 million a year, about two hundred times his income in 1925, the year he conquered the Hejaz.

In 1946, Abdul Aziz started to send Egypt's King Farouk a subsidy of almost $5 million a year, and in return, the Egyptians sent the Saudis thousands of teachers, technicians, and military advisers.

The U.S. presence in Saudi Arabia was even more striking than Egypt's. Aramco executives had urged Abdul Aziz to hire a trustworthy U.S. construction firm to build some public works. The king followed their advice, and during the next decade, the Bechtel Corporation built airports, roads, and electric power plants in Riyadh, Jeddah, and Dhahran; a highway between Mecca and Medina; and harbor facilities at Jeddah and Dammam.

Bechtel built the Trans-Arabian Pipeline (Tapline for short) connecting the country's oil wells to the Mediterranean Sea at Saida, Lebanon, and also built a railroad from Riyadh to Dhahran. Everyone but Abdul Aziz thought that the railroad was a waste of $70 million, but trains proved to be more efficient than trucks. Engineers had schedules to follow, while the Bedouins who drove trucks sometimes took detours to visit their friends.

Many Saudis worked as laborers on these projects. It was hard, monotonous work, but young men earned enough to pay for a wedding and buy a home.

Forty percent of the more than ten thousand Saudis who worked for Aramco were Shi'ite Muslims from the surrounding area, and half were under twenty. They were well fed, had good medical care, and were treated with respect.

The Americans at Aramco were determined to avoid the paternal attitude of British officials elsewhere in the Persian Gulf, whom they mocked as "lion-tamers" because they often carried swagger sticks. The Americans played baseball and soccer and watched movies with their Arab employees and let them pray as often as possible, although during workdays it was simply not practical to stop for every prayer call.

The Americans themselves lived in spacious compounds surrounded by barbed wire, in rows of well-kept bungalows with lawns, gardens, and communal swimming pools. As author Robert Lacey has observed, the compounds looked like small U.S. towns except that there were no churches or taverns.

Once an American reported a theft to the local Saudi police, then was shocked when the police chopped off the culprit's hand and was even more horrified when the amputee died of gangrene. After this, most Americans stopped reporting thefts, and larceny at the compounds increased because the fear of amputation was gone.

Aramco's profits were enormous, often providing an annual return on investment of more than 200 percent. With returns like that, Aramco wanted even more money to invest in drilling and refining so, in 1948, it sold 40 percent of its business to Standard Oil of New Jersey (known as Exxon today) and Mobil. At the time, Mobil thought that the price of buying into Aramco was too high, so it purchased only 10 percent of the company, allowing Exxon to buy 30 percent. Mobil would soon regret the penny-pinching that reduced its profits for the next thirty years.

The First Arab-Israeli War

In February 1947, the British announced their intention to end their mandate in Palestine. On May 29, the United Nations General Assembly voted to divide Palestine into Arab and Jewish states. Arabs quickly rejected the partition, and violence increased.

One year later, on May 14, 1948, as the last British soldiers left Palestine, Israel declared its existence. President Harry Truman announced America's recognition of the Jewish state the same day. The British army was no longer there to keep peace, and the new state of Israel was suddenly at war with Egypt, Jordan, Syria, Lebanon, and Iraq.

Iraq asked Abdul Aziz to stop selling oil to the United States. Alarmed, U.S. secretary of defense James Forrestal warned Americans that without access to Middle Eastern oil, "American car companies would have to design a four-cylinder car."

Abdul Aziz knew that Saudi Arabia could not survive without its oil revenues and thus had no leverage against the West. "Give me $30 million," he told Iraq's king, "and I'll join you." Abdul Aziz continued to sell oil to the United States and sent just one brigade of Saudi troops to fight as part of Egypt's army.

The 1948 war ended badly for the Palestinians. Not only did Israel capture new land, Palestinian territory ceased to exist: Egypt annexed the Gaza Strip, and, even worse, Jordan's King Abdullah, one of the Hashemite monarchs whom Abdul Aziz despised, annexed the region west of the Jordan River, the Delaware-size West Bank.

Financial Chaos, Uneducated Sons

Perhaps Abdul Aziz might have done more for the Palestinians if he had been younger, but he was in his seventies and his health was declining. Sometimes he dozed off during public audiences, and at night he needed to have his arthritic knees massaged before he could go to sleep. He took aphrodisiacs to counter a declining potency but fathered only one child in his final decade.

Abdul Aziz kept the same group of advisers that he had used since the late 1920s, and they, too, were growing old. Abdullah Suleiman, in particular, was completely out of his depth as minister of finance now that the nation's oil royalties were in the millions, rather than thousands, of dollars. He had never been one to delegate responsibility, and in his old age, Suleiman worked only an hour or two in the morning and drank the rest of the day. As a result, there were no audits of expenditures, no strategies for investing deposits, and no creation of reserves for emergencies. Sacks of coins lay about earning no interest, and royalties deposited in a bank in New York were commingled with Suleiman's own money.

Abdul Aziz did not mind. He once pointed to some sacks of gold and told a friend, "That's my financial system. I ask for money and it appears. What more do I need to know than that?"[3]

Part of the blame for this financial chaos lay with the Americans. They did not pressure Abdul Aziz to modernize his treasury until the very end of his life because they did not want to appear "colonial." In Kuwait, by contrast, the British were quick to insist that the country reform its finances, and the emir became the largest stockholder in many foreign corporations. Eventually, Kuwait would make almost as much money from its investments as it did from its oil.

Neither Abdul Aziz nor Abdullah Suleiman could say no to the hundreds of princes, including grandsons, nephews, and cousins, who wanted Cadillacs, diamonds for their many wives, shopping trips in Europe, and large palaces with swimming pools, servants, and expensive furniture. One man who built these mansions was terrorist Osama bin Laden's father, Muhammad Awadh bin Laden.

An illiterate dockworker from Yemen, Muhammad bin Laden earned a small real estate commission in Jeddah in the 1930s when he introduced a foreigner to a local landowner, then earned more money in the 1940s as a bricklayer for Aramco in Dhahran. He used his savings to buy secondhand construction equipment and slowly built a multibillion-dollar contracting company. He began by renovating old houses for Aramco, working alongside his men and earning a reputation for honesty and careful work. He bought bigger and

more modern machinery and won the royal family's favor by building palaces at below cost. The Saudi princes more than made up for
this loss by giving bin Laden lucrative contracts to pave a highway
between Jeddah and Medina, triple the size of the Prophet's Mosque
in Medina, and build a variety of hospitals, mosques, hotels, and more
highways. Soon, bin Laden–owned companies were making their
own bricks, concrete, doors, windows, scaffolding, and insulation.
Finally, the Saudi Binladin Group won the most prestigious contract
of all: the twenty-year renovation of the Grand Mosque in Mecca,
where every surface is covered with marble and a million people pray
simultaneously.[4]

In 1946, the Saudi government spent $10 million on cars and
chauffeurs for the royal family but only $750,000 on schools. It also
spent $21 million more than it received, which forced Suleiman to
ask Aramco for millions of dollars in loans against future oil royalties.
This cycle of borrowing against future earnings continued for another
decade as the royal family's size and demand for luxuries skyrocketed
even faster than its oil revenues. One has to wonder why Abdul Aziz
never restricted the number of princes who were entitled to palaces
or insisted that the rest of his family work for a living.

With so much money and so little accounting, corruption was
inevitable. Officials gave contracts to anyone who offered a large
enough bribe. Contractors in Saudi Arabia let middlemen take cuts
and charged prices five to ten times higher than the fee for similar
work in other countries. Knowing the prices were outrageous, princes
often refused to pay their debts when money ran short or paid just ten
to twenty cents on the dollar, which in fact was a fair payment.

The rise in oil revenues caused widespread inflation, and the
poor suffered. Inflation also led merchants to send their savings to
Switzerland or Lebanon, where their money could hold its value. In
addition, a surge in foreign imports destroyed the market for native
handicrafts because the mass-produced items were cheaper.

It was the rare Wahhabi cleric who criticized corruption or inflation. Some said that the mouths of the clerics were "stopped with
gold" because the government gave them millions of dollars to help
the poor and never asked for any accounting or reports.

Privately, many clerics thought it scandalous that several princes
drank whiskey in their palaces and that some had become drunkards.
In 1947, one prince, Nasir, gave a party with women present and served
some home-brewed alcohol that turned out to be poison. Seven of his
guests died, including a cousin whose death could not be covered up.

In front of most of his sons, Abdul Aziz took his camel stick and
beat Nasir unmercifully, crying, "Have things come to this? I would

have Judgment Day now! [Before things get worse]." He sentenced Nasir to death but commuted the sentence to life in prison and later, after several years, freed him.

In 1951, another prince, Mishairi, was refused a drink at a party in Jeddah when the British vice-consul told the prince that he had already had enough. Four days later, the prince returned to the vice-consul's house and killed him with a shotgun.

"Where is Mishairi's head?" Abdul Aziz shouted when he heard the awful news. The prince hid from his father for two weeks before he gave himself up. By then, Abdul Aziz was willing to offer the diplomat's widow a choice of blood money or the prince's execution. The widow initially favored execution but finally let her friends and fellow diplomats talk her into receiving $350,000 (about $2 million in today's money). Prince Mishairi went to prison but spent only two years there because of a general amnesty in 1953.

Abdul Aziz ordered a total ban on the importation of alcohol, even for foreigners. He never knew that despite his decree, some of his sons continued to import whiskey by the truckload. A few intrepid foreigners also made stills.

Abdul Aziz never bothered to educate his sons in any subjects other than Islam, desert skills, and horsemanship. Most of them were completely unprepared for the challenges of the modern world. Of the king's twenty-eight grown sons born before 1940, only one, Abdul Rahman, the current deputy minister of defense, had ever studied abroad. The king's second son, Faisal, and several like-minded princes understood the need for education and sent their children to an elite school in the mountain town of Taif, or to a new Princes' School inside the royal palace, both of which were free from clerical control.

In 1950, 95 percent of Saudi Arabians were still illiterate. Fewer than two thousand Saudi boys attended high school, with roughly a third going to prep schools in Egypt, Syria, and Lebanon. Even the number of boys in elementary school was barely twenty thousand, and almost 80 percent of their time was spent reading and memorizing the Quran. As for girls, there was no school for them in the entire country, and although several princesses were tutored privately, not one Saudi woman studied abroad.

Growing Oil Revenues

Educated or not, the Saudis continued to get richer. Oil production soared another 60 percent between 1949 and 1951, and during the rest of the 1950s, revenue grew a steady 6 percent each year. In 1951, just south of Kuwait, Aramco discovered what is still the world's largest offshore oil field, Safaniya, and inland from Dhahran also discovered what is still the world's largest land deposit, Ghawar, an oil field 150 miles long.

In 1948, Venezuela began to levy an income tax of 50 percent of the net profits earned by oil companies doing business there. Two years later, on December 27, 1950, Aramco signed a similar tax agreement with Saudi Arabia. The Saudis had justifiably argued that in the United States, oil companies pay both a royalty to the landowner and a tax to the government. The Saudis did not see why they should be penalized just because the landowner and the government in Saudi Arabia are one and the same. Despite the new tax, oil companies continued to make enormous profits because they bought oil from Aramco at a discounted price and then sold it at the market price.

In June 1951, the United States signed an agreement with Saudi Arabia promising to send the country tanks, gunboats, and modern aircraft, along with instructors to train Saudi commanders and pilots. In return, Saudi Arabia renewed America's right to maintain its air force base at Dhahran for another five years. Dhahran was now the largest U.S. air base between Germany and Japan and the closest base to many Soviet military installations.

In western Arabia the following year, Abdul Aziz authorized money to repair and enlarge the Prophet's Mosque in Medina, the building's first major improvement since the eighth century. In Mecca, he built the nation's first college to train teachers. Flush with oil money, the king also abolished the pilgrim tax to encourage more Muslims to make the pilgrimage to Mecca. More than two and a half million came in 2006.

Jeddah and Mecca had had hospitals since the 1920s. Now the king built a hospital in Riyadh. He also approved the construction of thirty-eight clinics in smaller towns and some mobile clinics to treat the Bedouins in the desert.

Declining Health

The monarch's own health was deteriorating fast. At seventy-five, he had become nearly blind in his one good eye and had grown too plump and stiff to get up from his wheelchair easily. His immobility depressed him, as did the death of his sister Nura. He talked in a hoarse whisper, without enthusiasm, and spent hours with his harem merely sipping coffee.

Abdul Aziz's advisers tried to conserve his strength by handling minor complaints before they reached him, but when the king heard about this, he was furious. In June 1952, he issued one of his last decrees: "Any complaint . . . shall be sent to us without any change. Those concerned shall not delay it or reveal its contents to the person complained of, whether he be a governor or a minister. . . . We inform all our subjects that we are always ready to receive any complaints."[5]

Abdul Aziz still thought like a local sheikh. He wanted to hear every complaint personally but also regarded the nation's oil wealth as his family's personal property. In 1951, 53 percent of the government's budget was allotted to "State Palaces, Princes and Royal Establishments." In 1952, after a system of fixed allowances was installed, this share of the budget was still an enormous 24 percent. The kingdom's debt grew to more than $150 million, a sum greater than a year's oil royalties.

Only at the very end of his life did Abdul Aziz make any attempt to modernize his government. In 1952, he created a central bank so that oil royalties would no longer have to be commingled with Abdullah Suleiman's personal accounts. The following year, he formed the Council of Ministers, a cabinet that had no power during the king's lifetime but proved important soon afterward.

In August 1953, an ailing Abdul Aziz flew to his palace in Taif in the mountains east of Mecca. Everyone sensed that he would die soon, and nearly all of his children, grandchildren, and cousins came to visit.

Abdul Aziz told his sons that he wanted his oldest son, Saud, to succeed him and his second son, Faisal, to be Saud's right-hand man. After Saud's death, however, Abdul Aziz did not want the throne to pass to one of Saud's sons but instead to one of Saud's brothers, to the "eldest able" among Abdul Aziz's many sons. Several times, the king asked Saud and Faisal to promise to work together. "Faisal, Saud is your brother," he whispered. "Saud, Faisal is your brother."

On November 9, 1953, Abdul Aziz died of a heart attack during a nap, with Faisal at his bedside. When Saud arrived, Faisal took a ring off one of his father's fingers, gave it to Saud, and proclaimed him king. All of the princes followed suit, except for the outspoken Muhammad, the third son, who did not think much of his oldest brother. Saud then gave the same ring back to Faisal and proclaimed him crown prince.

When news of Abdul Aziz's death was broadcast on the radio at noon, no one lowered any flags to half-mast. The Saudi flag contains a verse from the Quran—"There is but one God; Muhammad is

His Prophet"—and cannot be lowered for any man. By the end of the day, Abdul Aziz's body had been flown to Riyadh. There, in keeping with Wahhabi practice, the king was buried in an unmarked grave and his clothes were sold in the marketplace.

Abdul Aziz's Legacy

Although most Saudis revere Abdul Aziz, foreign opinions about him vary widely. One author called him "the greatest Arab of modern times"; another, "licentious and brutal." A third author said that Abdul Aziz did more for Islam than any other man in the twentieth century; a fourth said he created a "Bedouin police state."

What is clear is that Abdul Aziz single-handedly created a vast, unified kingdom in what had been a chaotic peninsula burdened by petty feuds and lawless raids. Critics charge that his Wahhabi followers were ignorant, xenophobic, and far less cultured than the people they conquered and whose conduct they then "policed" in Mecca and Medina. Yet without the unity that Abdul Aziz achieved, most of the Arabian peninsula would have suffered either continued fragmentation or, more likely, a carving up of the region by European powers that ruled through puppet sheikhs.

After Abdul Aziz took Riyadh in 1902, he spent twenty-four years expanding his kingdom, nineteen years ruling it in poverty, and eight years mismanaging its immense new wealth. Since his death in 1953, the kingdom has endured for another half century, a testament to the strength of the many tribal alliances he formed. Abdul Aziz has been harshly criticized for taking more than two hundred women into his household when the maximum number of wives a Muslim man can have is supposed to be four. Yet one benefit of these many marriages is that most of Arabia's major tribes have representation in the country's enormous royal family.

Without oil, Saudi Arabia might easily be as poor as Yemen, its neighbor to the south, where the income per person is less than half that in India and only one-twelfth that of Saudis. The Kingdom of Saudi Arabia controls one-fourth of the world's petroleum today because one night in 1913, Abdul Aziz led three hundred men into the town of Hufuf and captured twelve hundred already-demoralized Turkish soldiers. The Saudis see the oil as Allah's reward for their obedience, and despite the House of Saud's taste for luxury, obedience to Allah is still a big part of the family's and the nation's identity.

Abdul Aziz was a genuinely faithful Wahhabi who made use of Muslim zeal to conquer much of his kingdom, but he never became a zealot himself. He was open-minded enough to make friends with foreigners and use their inventions, and realistic enough to know the limits of his power. He understood what his ancestors and the Ikhwan did not, that religious fervor alone is no match for modern weapons.

The Arabia of Abdul Aziz's youth is so alien to us today that much of the king's life seems like an ancient tale. He was a big man—brave, bawdy, and generous—with many faults if we judge him by modern standards. Yet he was a wise ruler, shrewder than his subordinates or his rivals.

Abdul Aziz's biggest mistake was not to retire at seventy, appoint a first-rate cabinet of talented Saudis, and reserve to himself only the most important decisions. Instead, he delegated so little authority in his last years that even airline pilots needed his permission to take off. Given the age of his advisers and the inexperience of his sons, the king's reluctance to retire was understandable, but his gross misman-agement of hundreds of millions of dollars cost the nation a decade of progress and marred an otherwise remarkable career.

PART FOUR

OIL BRINGS POWER: THE LIFE OF KING FAISAL (1905–1975)

A<small>SK ANY SAUDI WHO WAS</small> their greatest king in the last fifty years, and the answer will almost certainly be "Faisal." No recent monarch has commanded as much respect within the royal family or among the general population.

Faisal ibn Abdul Aziz al-Saud was the king of Saudi Arabia for eleven years, from 1964 to 1975. Before that, he had been his father's foreign minister for twenty-three years and the power behind his brother's throne for five. He rescued Saudi Arabia from economic chaos in 1958 and 1959 and modernized the kingdom's economy (but not its politics) in the 1960s. In 1973, he led the Arab oil embargo that quadrupled prices and generated more than half a trillion dollars in revenues during the next decade. He also worked methodically to have Islam replace socialism as the Arabs' dominant ideology. Even as a young man, Faisal so impressed his father, Abdul Aziz, that the old king once said, "I only wish I had three Faisals."

II

The Young Prince and Foreign Minister (1905–1953)

WHEN FAISAL WAS BORN, birth certificates were unknown in Arabia. Accounts differ as to his date of birth, but the best estimate is that it was in 1905. In Arabic, his name means "sword." Faisal's mother, Tarfah, was Abdul Aziz's third wife and a descendant of ibn Abdul Wahhab. She died when Faisal was only seven, and the boy was brought up by her father, a strict religious teacher, in a home away from the royal palace.

Faisal had no brothers his own age to distract him from the work of memorizing the Quran and the sayings of Muhammad. He learned to speak a clearer, more classical Arabic than his siblings and was also good at composing poetry during long camel rides.

Faisal was tall, with large, piercing eyes. When he played with his sisters and cousins, he liked to shoot marbles, climb fruit trees, and use a sling to throw stones. Once, egged on by older boys, he jumped down a thirty-foot well.

An important part of Faisal's education was to learn to ride a horse, shoot a rifle, use a sword, and hunt with a falcon. Uncles and cousins taught him military tactics and strategy, along with the customs, the heritage, the blood feuds, and the grazing patterns of each

Bedouin tribe. Faisal also learned how to handle the proud warriors by watching his father, the unrivaled master of this art.

In 1917, when Faisal was twelve, Arthur Balfour, Britain's foreign secretary, announced that Britain would help to create a Jewish homeland in Palestine. Every Arab felt betrayed. It was Faisal's first introduction to foreign affairs and the beginning of a lifetime of opposition to Jewish settlement in the Middle East.

Two years later, Britain invited Abdul Aziz to London for diplomatic talks, but the monarch did not think it wise to leave his kingdom for such a long time. Turki, his oldest son, had just died of influenza, and the king was too cautious to send his second son, Saud. He dispatched Faisal instead. The frail and serious prince was only fourteen.

Faisal was accompanied by a Wahhabi merchant who spoke English, an older cousin who had grown up in Istanbul and spoke French, and several bodyguards. For most of their journey, they were also accompanied by one or more British army officers. Together, they took a paddle steamer from Bahrain to Bombay, then boarded an ocean liner that took them to Plymouth, England, on October 13, 1919.

The following morning, the Saudis were ordered out of their London hotel after their prayer call awakened everyone at 5:15 A.M. Because their next hotel did not serve food, the Saudis had to walk to a nearby restaurant every day through drizzling rain in their long wet robes. The *Times* reported the unusual sight and criticized the government for a lack of proper hospitality. Alerted and appalled by the article, King George V invited Faisal and his aides to Buckingham Palace.

Faisal met Queen Mary and her daughter, Princess Mary, and must have been astonished that a king would introduce his wife and daughter to strangers. He showed no undue emotion, however, and presented the king with a sword inlaid with gold and pearls.

The British showed Faisal a captured German submarine, a session of Parliament, telescopes at Greenwich Observatory, Cambridge University, an automobile plant in Wolseley, a gun factory in Birmingham, the shipyard at Belfast, and a steel mill (along with his first snowstorm) in Wales. When young Faisal was asked what he liked best, he answered that it was riding up and down the long escalator at the Piccadilly Circus underground station.

One subject that the British and the Saudis discussed was King Husain, the ruler of the Hejaz (Jeddah, Mecca, and Medina), whom the British supported and the Saudis loathed. Faisal's cousin promised not to take any military action against him for three years, a promise

King Abdul Aziz kept even though he was not there when the pledge was made.

In France, Faisal and his aides saw Verdun and several other World War I battlefields. It was just one year after the armistice, and the trenches, the barbed wire, and the shell holes made quite an impression, as did the ruins of nearby villages. Faisal was clearly moved. Years later, whenever he was asked about his military victories in Arabia, he would always dismiss them as "nothing much."

After two and a half months in Europe, Faisal and his companions sailed from Marseilles shortly after Christmas and arrived home six weeks later. His father was particularly pleased because King George V had written him a letter saying that he had enjoyed meeting Faisal and that he looked forward to a continued friendship between their two nations.

Faisal was unable to read the letter, but he had learned some spoken English and knew more about the outside world than anyone else in the royal family. The teenager became the country's unofficial foreign minister, a post that was made official in 1930 and that he held until his death in 1975.

Faisal had been home for only a few months when his father sent him to Asir, a poor and mountainous region on the coast of the Red Sea, south of Mecca and north of Yemen. (This area would be the home of eleven of the nineteen 9/11 hijackers.) The Idrisi family, which ruled Asir, had alienated their Wahhabi subjects by forming an alliance with Husain, the king of the Hejaz, who despised the Wahhabis as ignorant Bedouin.

With the support of four thousand rebellious Asiri tribesmen, Faisal and an older cousin led six thousand Ikhwan fighters into the heart of Asir. They took its capital without a fight, for by now most of the people of Asir felt that the time had come to unite with their fellow Wahhabis to the north.[1] Together, the Asiris and the Ikhwan routed an army sent by King Husain; Faisal then appointed some loyal aides to govern the province.

After returning home victorious, Faisal married Sultana, a younger sister of Hassa al-Sudairi, the woman who ultimately bore King Abdul Aziz seven sons. The newlyweds had a son of their own one year later.

In 1924, when Ikhwan warriors on their way to Mecca slaughtered three hundred people in Taif, Abdul Aziz sent Faisal to the front to make sure that the Ikhwan did not massacre anyone in Mecca—or in Jeddah, where many foreigners lived.

Faisal succeeded, although later there was one terrible incident. In the summer of 1926, some Egyptians arrived in Mecca with new black cloth to cover the Kaaba, the great stone at the center of the Grand Mosque. During their procession, an Egyptian soldier blew a bugle, which enraged the Ikhwan, who considered music sacrilegious. The Ikhwan threw stones at the Egyptians, prompting a frightened soldier to open fire and kill two dozen Ikhwan and nearby pilgrims.

Faisal heard the gunshots, galloped to the scene, arrested the Egyptian soldier, and beat back the Ikhwan troops with a cane to keep them from killing the rest of the Egyptians. The violence stopped, but Egypt severed its diplomatic relations with the Saudi kingdom for ten years.

That same summer, the king appointed Faisal's oldest brother, Saud, as viceroy of Najd and Faisal as viceroy of the Hejaz. At twenty-one, Faisal was not quite as tall as his father but had a regal bearing. Though his smile was kind, his eyes seemed mournful, and he had a curl in his upper lip that made him look cynical. Whether Faisal was distrustful of most men, no one could be sure, but no one ever doubted that his faith in God was as firm as a rock.

In the fall of 1926, Faisal made his second trip to Britain and negotiated a seven-year treaty of friendship that his father signed the following spring. Under this pact, Britain recognized the Saudis' conquest of the Hejaz two years earlier, while the Saudis acknowledged that the Persian Gulf states remained British protectorates.

As viceroy of the Hejaz, Faisal lived in Mecca, where he appointed six leading citizens of the region to advise him. Because only Muslims are allowed in Mecca and Medina, most foreign merchants and diplomats had to live in Jeddah. Faisal often drove there to meet with them. He studied English several hours a week in order to be less dependent on their spotty Arabic. Although later he spoke English only rarely, he understood it well and sometimes even corrected his translators.

Unlike most Saudis of his generation, Faisal read a great deal, was attentive to detail, and could work long hours at a desk six and even seven days a week. He also never lost his composure. When he spoke, he was tactful and precise, and when he listened, he was patient even with the most exasperating petitioner. "God has given us two ears and one tongue," he once said, "that we should listen twice as much as we talk."[2] Once Faisal wrote a poem in which the last line revealed the determination that may have been behind his self-control: "Deep within this humble soul burns an inward flame unseen."[3]

In 1932, Faisal went to Russia and saw factories, military academies, and an oil field on the Caspian Sea. He met Joseph Stalin and persuaded him to increase the number of Soviet Muslims who were allowed to make a pilgrimage to Mecca. The real purpose of his trip was to remind the British that if they did not continue to pay an annual subsidy to his father, there were other countries willing to bankroll him.

On the way home, Faisal stopped in Istanbul to see some relatives and settle a land dispute. There he met a beautiful and witty young woman named Effat al-Thunayan, a distant cousin of the al-Saud family who was well read and fluent in French. Faisal fell in love with Effat the moment he saw her, and he married her several months later when she and her mother visited Riyadh.

In marked contrast to his brothers, Faisal was monogamous for the rest of his life. Whether this was at Effat's insistence, Faisal's pleasure, or both, is unknown, but Faisal divorced one of his wives (another had died) and saw to it that a third, political marriage did not last long.

Faisal and Effat had five sons and at least an equal number of daughters. By the end of Faisal's reign, the Saudi people began to call Effat "Queen," a title never given before or since to any other woman in Saudi Arabia. Despite this honor, Effat never appeared on television or allowed herself to be photographed in public. In private, her husband and children took a few pictures, but to everyone else her beauty remained hidden.

Unlike many royal parents, Faisal and Effat did not spoil their children. Their sons endured Spartan conditions at a mud-walled but excellent school that Effat built in the mountains near Taif. She chose this remote location so that she could add modern subjects to the traditional Islamic curriculum without angering conservative clergymen in Riyadh.

With Faisal's approval, Effat hired some foreign women to tutor her daughters at their palace. Later, they received additional schooling in Switzerland. Faisal's sons went to Princeton, Cambridge, Georgetown, and two of Britain's top military academies, Sandhurst and Cranwell. By contrast, less than half a dozen of the 107 children of his older brother, Saud, even went to high school.

Faisal was a gentle father. On a typical night, when his work was finally done, he held a kind of family party at eleven o'clock. As his sons and daughters grew older, they discussed the issues of the day with their father and felt free to argue with him. One son, Saud al-Faisal, has been Saudi Arabia's foreign minister since 1975. Together, Faisal and his son Saud have held this office for three quarters of a century.

Early in 1939, Faisal and five other Arab foreign ministers sailed to London to discuss the problem of Palestine with the British.

They refused to consider partition or even to sit at the same table with Zionists. The British had to walk back and forth between conference rooms.

When the talks ended, the British announced that they would limit Jewish immigration to Palestine to an average of fifteen thousand people a year. Jews felt betrayed, for this number was far too small to accommodate the many victims of Nazi persecution. Arabs were also disappointed, for they wanted Jewish immigration to stop completely. Privately, however, the Arabs were satisfied enough with Britain's decision that they could stay neutral during World War II and leave British troops in Egypt and Palestine alone.

In the fall of 1943, Faisal flew to Washington in a propeller plane that required refueling stops in Ghana, Brazil, and Miami. He was accompanied by his favorite traveling companion, his younger brother Khalid, who later succeeded him as king.

In Washington, President Franklin Roosevelt had dinner with the two princes at Blair House. Already, Saudi Arabia's proven oil reserves were as large as those of the United States. Faisal and Khalid also met leading members of the cabinet and Congress. Afterward, the two princes spent six days in New York, where Faisal shocked the management of the Waldorf-Astoria Hotel by insisting that one of his black slaves eat with him in the whites-only Wedgwood Room.

The princes traveled west in a private railroad car paid for by U.S. oil executives and saw the Grand Canyon and a movie studio in Hollywood. In San Francisco, they met the top executives of the Standard Oil Company of California (Chevron) before returning east to visit an automobile factory in Detroit and a professor of Arab history, Philip Hitti, at Princeton University. By the time Faisal returned to Washington, he was speaking English well enough to discuss the building of an oil refinery in Saudi Arabia with Secretary of State Edward Stettinius.

In November, Faisal and Khalid flew to London, where they met the brave but tired crews of bombers and submarines. They saw neighborhoods that had been destroyed in the blitz and visited King George VI at Buckingham Palace. (Churchill had left for a summit in Cairo.) On the final leg of their long journey, the two princes met Charles de Gaulle, the commander of the Free French Forces, in Algiers.

After three months abroad, Faisal had seen enough of the Earth to know that Saudi Arabia could not stay isolated any longer. "We must join the modern world," he told the conservative sheikhs and clergymen, "whether we like it or not."

A year and a half later, Faisal returned to the United States to take part in the founding of the United Nations in April 1945. This time, he brought a half dozen of his brothers with him so that they could see the United States with their own eyes. While Faisal worked hard at the San Francisco conference—meeting diplomats and writing, practicing, and giving a well-received speech in English—his brothers went to nightclubs and particularly enjoyed an underwater restaurant where girls swam by the dining room windows.

In 1947, Faisal appeared again at the United Nations, now located in New York, and spoke passionately against the partition of Palestine. "If you want to be generous, then be generous out of what you possess," Faisal said. He urged that the West not treat Palestine "as if that country had no owners and as if her rightful inhabitants had no say in the matter."[4]

Secretary of State George Marshall had told Faisal that the United States would not vote for the partition of Palestine without first consulting Arab nations, and Faisal conveyed this assurance to his Arab allies. When President Harry Truman overruled Marshall and told his UN representative to vote in favor of the partition, Faisal felt personally betrayed. Adding insult to injury, Faisal was booed, shoved, and spat upon by Jewish demonstrators in New York.

Faisal returned home to Saudi Arabia determined to break diplomatic relations with the United States, but his father overruled him. Even when Israel declared its independence in 1948 and war broke out, the king continued to sell oil to the United States, saying that it was better to build up wealth and become stronger than to fight too soon with insufficient resources.

In the early 1950s, Abdul Aziz grew increasingly feeble and delegated more authority to his oldest son, Saud. By the summer of 1952, during the week of the pilgrimage to Mecca, the king was too weak to leave Riyadh and sent Saud instead. When the pilgrimage was over, Saud remained in the Hejaz for most of the autumn and reorganized Faisal's provincial government, strengthening the religious police and appointing his own men to important positions. Faisal did not challenge his older brother. A dutiful son, he accepted his father's wish that Saud be the next king. But Faisal was now the viceroy of the Hejaz in name only; his real power was limited to foreign affairs.

In August 1953, the king further increased Saud's power by giving him command of the army. Two months later, he picked Saud to be prime minister of the nation's first cabinet, the Council of Ministers.

It was the king's last decree. Abdul Aziz died on the morning of November 9, 1953. That afternoon, Saud fulfilled his father's wishes (and his brothers' expectations) by reappointing Faisal foreign minister and viceroy of the Hejaz and by giving him the new and more important titles of crown prince and deputy prime minister.

Despite the four offices that Saud conferred upon his brother, he wanted to rule by himself. At first, Saud completely ignored the Council of Ministers. He did not convene the new cabinet until March 1954, four months after his father's death, then treated it as if it were merely a ceremonial body. Eventually, he realized that a government costs money and that he needed Faisal's help with the financing.

The long struggle between the two brothers was about to begin.

12

The Struggle between
the Brothers
(1953–1964)

ABDUL AZIZ'S OLDEST SON, Saud, was king for eleven years, but he squandered so many millions of dollars on palaces, cars, shoddy construction projects, and foreign misadventures that the kingdom nearly went bankrupt, and a military coup became a real possibility. In 1958, Faisal took charge of the government and gradually restored both the kingdom's finances and its military security. During the next six years, as power seesawed between Saud and Faisal, their brothers made it clear that a Saudi king is not an absolute ruler—the House of Saud governs as a family.

When Saud succeeded his father in 1953, he was fifty-one years old. Tall and powerfully built, he looked much more like his father than Faisal did. He was open, friendly, and generous and loved being among the Bedouin. The tribesmen loved Saud, too, especially when he gave them handfuls of gold and silver coins, yet even they knew he was not as smart as his father. On seeing gold teeth when Saud smiled, even many Saudis felt that the nation's new king was almost as uncouth as a rustic tribal sheikh.

During public audiences, King Saud was indecisive, while in private he had difficulty following argument or listening to unpleasant advice. Unlike Faisal, Saud had little administrative experience. As viceroy of Najd, he had spent most of his life in his father's shadow in Riyadh, with nothing to do until his father finally gave him some responsibility when Saud was nearly fifty. Unaccustomed to real power, Saud was susceptible to flattery. He chose a chauffeur who supplied him with liquor and women to be director of the royal motor pool, then keeper of the king's appointments, and finally, to everyone's disgust, controller of the royal family's budget. Another close aide, Werner Otto Von Heuting, had recently been a Nazi diplomat.

Saud lacked energy as well as intelligence. He drank too much Cointreau and, on the advice of Swiss and German doctors, took many pills to lose weight and injections to increase sexual potency. The medications slowed him down, but they served their purpose. Saud had 107 children, about 35 more than his father had; he had trouble remembering their names.

Because Saud was warm and good-hearted, almost everyone in the royal family liked him. If he had shown any political and financial restraint as king, he might have been a well-loved monarch. But Saud insisted on treating the entire nation as if it were his (and his sons') personal property, and he needlessly antagonized nearly all of his brothers.

Saud's worst extravagance was Nasriyah Palace, outside Riyadh, the largest of ten palaces that Saud built across the country. As crown prince, Saud had already built a sprawling mansion near the capital city in the early 1950s that cost more than $11 million. But as soon as he became king, he had the mansion torn down and spent nearly $30 million ($200 million in today's money) replacing it with a thirteen-hundred-acre complex of huge pink palaces. Each palace was furnished with enormous Persian carpets, Chinese vases, and crystal chandeliers and was surrounded by luxuriant gardens, palm groves, fountains, and swimming pools (one was scented with Chanel No. 5). The complex was maintained by twenty-five hundred servants and mechanics, guarded by a thousand soldiers, and surrounded by a high pink wall seven miles long, with entrance gates the size of Paris's Arc de Triomphe. Altogether, the Nasriyah Palace used nearly as much water and electricity as all of the rest of Riyadh.

By contrast, Faisal's mansion was modest and tasteful and had no wall.

Saud Misrules the Kingdom (1953–1958)

For a while, there was plenty of money. Oil revenues soared in the early 1950s. By 1955, the government received twice as much money each day as it had earned during an entire year in the 1930s. But the king was not spending the money wisely. More than 320 princes were pampered with annual incomes of $30,000 ($200,000 in current money), and the brothers and the grown sons of Abdul Aziz received that much each *week*. Every prince wanted his own palace. The royal family's orgy of spending, which had been cut to 24 percent of the kingdom's expenses in 1952, climbed again to half of the national budget by 1956.

The government spent only 5 percent of its income on health care. In the whole of central Arabia, there were only 150 hospital beds. Only 6 percent of the budget was earmarked for education. Ninety-five percent of the adults in Saudi Arabia remained illiterate; only 8 percent of the nation's children went to school.

Saud built 350 elementary schools for boys, but in the 1950s, the number of high school students in the country was still well below five thousand. Princess Effat built the nation's first girls' school in Jeddah in 1956, although only fifteen girls attended in the first year because most fathers were reluctant to entrust their daughters to an unproven new venture.

Saud showed his complete lack of understanding of the need for education in 1955 when he let some clergymen talk him into banning all Saudis from studying abroad lest they acquire infidel beliefs. Fortunately, a year later, Saud rescinded the ban and even built the nation's first secular university in Riyadh in 1957.

In 1956, oil revenues fell 17 percent because of a worldwide oil glut. Saudi revenues would not reach their 1955 level again until 1961, but the king refused to cut spending. He even insisted that the government pay his personal debts of more than $12 million.

Early in his reign, Saud had appointed Faisal to be the prime minister of his cabinet, known as the Council of Ministers, but this was just for show and to keep Faisal in Riyadh where he could be watched. The government was really run by Saud's sons and friends, and despite Faisal's complaints, they continued to enrich their cronies with massive building contracts and refused to submit to a budget. Faisal did force the resignation of Abdullah Suleiman, the heavy-drinking minister of finance who had mismanaged the government's funds so badly during King Abdul Aziz's last years.

By the end of 1957, the government's debts exceeded a year and a half's oil revenues. Banks would no longer lend the kingdom money, and finally even Aramco refused to pay any more advances against oil royalties. Inflation soared as the Saudi currency, the riyal, fell to half of its former value. Many Saudis protected themselves by opening Swiss bank accounts or by buying real estate in Egypt or Lebanon, but the poor suffered greatly as the price of everything doubled.

As the government received less oil money, officials stopped paying employees and contractors for weeks at a time and sometimes pocketed the money even when they had sufficient funds. The government employees could do nothing, but the contractors left many buildings unfinished, although royal palaces were always completed.

As poor as Saud was at managing the economy, the royal family was equally alarmed by the fact that Saud was appointing his sons to powerful government posts for which they were not qualified. In 1956, Saud picked his oldest son, Fahd, to be minister of defense and his son Musaid to be commander of the Royal Guard.

The following year, he chose his son Khalid to form a new army made up of Bedouin tribesmen and descendants of the Ikhwan. The true purpose of this army, soon to be called the National Guard, was to prevent a coup by army officers, whose loyalty had been suspect ever since they were initially trained by Egyptian instructors with socialist leanings. To this day, it is the National Guard rather than the army that is stationed near big cities and oil fields, and its battalions are organized along tribal lines because tribesmen are the soldiers least likely to be influenced by foreign ideas.

Saud also appointed seven men who owed their careers to him as cabinet ministers, further depriving his brothers of any power. The new minister of public works was Muhammad Awadh bin Laden, who had a huge construction firm and, in January 1958, a newborn son, Osama.

In three and a half years, Saud had put his sons in command of the armed forces and his friends in charge of the bureaucracy. Faisal and the other brothers reluctantly concluded that Saud was trying to start a dynasty that would exclude them from power forever.

Although Faisal was prime minister of the cabinet, he did not assert his power. He remained a loyal brother and gave Saud plenty of time to show his incompetence to everyone. In June 1957, Faisal even left the country for eight months. He had his gallbladder removed in New York in July, read books and recuperated in August, met President Dwight Eisenhower and his top aides in September, and had a stomach tumor removed in October. He spent another month reading and recuperating but could easily have returned home by the end of November. Instead, he lingered in New York for a few more weeks, then spent the entire month of January 1958 in Egypt, meeting with President Gamal Abdel Nasser four times.

Faisal knew that his brothers had a tough choice to make, and his prolonged stay abroad was a way of pressuring them to make that choice. His brothers had to decide whether they wanted Saud or Faisal to lead them. They could no longer have both: Faisal did not want to be a part of Saud's inept government anymore.

Once Aramco stopped advancing money to the kingdom in the fall of 1957, the Saudis were forced to seek a loan from the International Monetary Fund, which insisted that the government impose a tight budget with deep cuts in the royal family's living expenses. The government complied in January 1958 with the first detailed budget in the history of the kingdom, and it infuriated the princes. They knew their incomes were being cut because of Saud's mismanagement. He alone was to blame. Faisal had not even been in the country since June.

When Faisal returned to Riyadh in February, it was not only Saud's mismanagement of the economy or his favoritism toward his sons that ultimately united all the princes against him. Saud had also severely damaged the kingdom's relations with Egypt.

To most Arabs, Egypt's president Gamal Abdel Nasser was a hero. Not only had he successfully defied the British and the French when he nationalized the Suez Canal in 1956, he had also excited Arabs everywhere with his dream of uniting all Arabs into one powerful confederation.

At first, Saud allied himself with the popular leader, sending him money and welcoming Egyptian teachers and military instructors into the kingdom. But when Nasser visited Dhahran and Riyadh in September 1956 and drew the largest and most enthusiastic crowds in Saudi history, crowds many times larger than the turnout for a mere king, Saud began to realize that Nasser was a threat to his monarchy. After all, Nasser had overthrown his own king in 1952, and now hundreds of Egyptian officers were training the Saudi army. To make matters worse, Radio Cairo's *Voice of the Arabs*, which had a vast audience in Saudi Arabia, gleefully broadcast news of the royal family's wild spending and womanizing and bluntly declared that the Saudi monarchy was an obstacle to progress.

When war broke out between Egypt and Israel in October 1956, Saud remained a loyal Arab ally. He let Egyptian planes use Saudi runways and ordered Aramco not to sell any oil to Britain or France,

Israel's allies in the war. Two months after the fighting stopped, however, Saud ended his friendship with Egypt and renewed his alliance with the United States.

In January 1957, Saud became the first Arabian king to visit the United States. In New York, Mayor Robert Wagner snubbed him, telling reporters that Saud "is a fellow who says that [in his country] slavery is legal, that in the Air Force you can't have any Jewish boys, and that a Catholic priest can't say mass."[1] In Washington, by contrast, President Eisenhower met Saud on the tarmac at National Airport, the first time the president had ever extended this courtesy to a foreign leader. Saud stayed next door to the president at Blair House, but some of Saud's aides were unimpressed with the restrained style of the old residence and expressed surprise that Eisenhower did not have enough money to buy a better guesthouse.

President Eisenhower was deeply concerned about the Soviet Union's shipments of weapons to Egypt. As a counterbalance, he agreed to send Saudi Arabia enough aircraft, ships, tanks, and artillery to double the size of its armed forces. The United States also agreed to send the Saudis instructors and technicians and secretly pledged that no Jews would be among them. In return, the Saudis renewed the lease of America's giant air force base at Dhahran for another five years.

Two months later, Saudi police arrested five Palestinians for plotting to blow up the king's palace with high explosives. Under questioning, they admitted to being led by an Egyptian military attaché. Nasser immediately sent his top aide, Anwar Sadat, to Riyadh to assure Saud that he had no knowledge of his envoy's plot, but Saud did not believe this for an instant. He deported hundreds of Egyptians and Palestinians and announced that in the future, Egypt would have to buy Saudi oil with U.S. dollars instead of Egyptian pounds.

Saud also hatched a plot of his own. Using a father-in-law as a go-between, he sent Syria's chief of intelligence, Abdul Hamid Serraj, three personal checks totaling 1.9 million British pounds (about $30 million today), as a down payment against the 20 million pounds that would be paid when the Syrians blew up President Nasser's plane as it approached Damascus.

Serraj double-crossed Saud and publicized the conspiracy at a press conference on March 5, 1958. He provided details of the plot and gave reporters copies of the three canceled checks, three telegrams, and a letter written on royal stationery. In Riyadh, no one denied the allegations. Days went by and the government stayed silent, causing even skeptical Saudis to decide that the accusations must be true.

Saud later wrote to Nasser that he had sent the Syrians money merely to help them fight communism, but he never produced any evidence to support this claim. Even if Saud had not planned a murder, he was still guilty of gross incompetence for allowing himself to be entrapped by a foreign intelligence chief.

For the royal family, this bungled plot was the last straw. Nasser was now openly calling for the monarchy's overthrow, and the princes were afraid that their army officers, who idolized the Egyptian leader, might take his advice and rise up against the king who had tried to kill their hero. It was not an idle fear. That summer a pro-Nasser army massacred the entire royal family in Iraq.

When Faisal returned home in February after eight months abroad, he went straight to the desert to talk to one Bedouin sheikh after another. A friend of the crown prince observed, "There are really two Faisals. The first is the intelligent man of the world, at ease in a London drawing room or a Washington conference. The second is a pure Bedouin, able to ride bareback, squat by a desert fire, dig barehanded into roast meat and rice and talk to the desert folk in their own dialect."[2]

The Bedouin sheikhs were the bedrock of Saud's support, and Faisal carefully explained to each of them why his older brother, their friend and benefactor, was unfit to govern.

After the disastrous press conference in Syria, Faisal could no longer pretend to be part of a government in which he obviously had no influence. On March 7, he resigned as both prime minister and foreign minister. It was his way of telling his brothers that time had run out. The Saudi monarchy was in danger, and the princes had to choose which brother they wanted to lead them.

When Prince Abdallah—the oldest prince, the brother of King Abdul Aziz—learned of Faisal's resignation, he immediately asked all the senior princes to come to his mansion for round-the-clock discussions. He also invited some top clergymen and tribal sheikhs, but Saud and Faisal stayed away. Saud retreated to his palace; Faisal remained in the desert.

After four days of talks, the princes, the sheikhs, and the clergymen were unanimous. Saud had to go. On March 22, a delegation of princes gave Saud a written ultimatum that if he wanted to continue as king, he had to surrender all of his power to Faisal. Faisal would become prime minister again, but this time Saud would not be able to interfere with the cabinet's decisions. Saud's sons could continue to serve as minister of defense and commander of the National Guard, but their uncle Faisal would be commander in chief of the Saudi armed forces. Saud himself would be just a figurehead but a rich one, with an income of more than $4 million a week in today's money.

Saud accepted these demands with almost no discussion. He knew that he had lost all of his support among his brothers and in the military. He may also have felt relief in letting go of responsibilities that he was so poorly equipped to handle. On March 31, 1958, he issued a royal decree giving Faisal "full responsibility . . . in domestic, external, and financial affairs."

Faisal Restores the Kingdom's Finances (1958–1960)

It seemed fitting that Faisal, who was about to force Saudi Arabia to balance its budget for the first time in its history, was himself underweight, while his older brother was corpulent. And while Saud owned a fleet of gold-plated Cadillacs, Faisal was content with a Chrysler New Yorker, which he often drove himself. *Time* magazine once described Faisal as "dour, ascetic and shrewd," yet his manners were gentle. He never shouted. A top aide said, "If he didn't like someone or something, he'd simply turn his face away and you could tell he'd reached his limit."[3]

Faisal's first priority was to see that government employees who had not been paid for weeks received enough money before the end of Ramadan to enable them to buy holiday gifts for their children. But when he opened the treasury's vault, he was shocked to find just 317 riyals, about $50. Osama bin Laden's father, Muhammad, lent the government enough money to meet its upcoming payrolls and interest payments, and Aramco, which had much more confidence in Faisal than it did in Saud, agreed to guarantee long-term loans of $92 million, enough to give Faisal some room to maneuver.

Faisal's second priority was to tighten control of the government. All revenues had to be collected by the ministry of finance—Faisal appointed himself finance minister—and no one could make a payment without the written approval of a cabinet official or a deputy. Faisal also halted all economic development projects until fiscal reforms were in place.

For the first time in history, Faisal separated spending for the royal family from the rest of the government's expenditures. The noble households still received an enormous 18 percent of the budget, but this was much less than what they had received the year before.

Faisal cut royal incomes, let palaces remain unfinished, and canceled the right of distant cousins to receive anything. He also banned the import of luxuries and all but the smallest cars for one year, then eased the restrictions gradually.

Faisal spent 12 percent of the budget on debt service in 1958, and 15 percent in 1959, by which time the budget was balanced. He spent Western currency to buy Saudi riyals, which stabilized the Saudi currency and stopped inflation. He also introduced paper money (backed by gold and Western currencies) to replace the nation's ancient gold coins.

While Faisal was imposing austerity, Saud spent most of 1959 on a yacht in the Mediterranean and at two German spas. Then he returned to Saudi Arabia and denounced Faisal for postponing the nation's economic development. He went to small villages and won Bedouin hearts by spending his own money to build mosques and water wells and by paying people's debts and medical expenses. In comparison, Faisal looked heartless and cheap.

Many princes were angry at Faisal for cutting their incomes so drastically. Faisal soothed their feelings by giving them tracts of desert outside the main cities. The transfers were off-budget because they did not cost money, and as the cities grew in size, the land came to be worth millions and sometimes billions of dollars.

On a typical day as prime minister, Faisal got up before dawn and knelt with his servants during prayer. He slept another hour, then had a breakfast of toast, honey, and cheese. Afterward, he held an audience, saw his advisers, and worked through papers. At noon, he prayed, then hosted lunch for as many as forty people. After lunch, Faisal always had an apple. He would peel, cut, and eat it, segment by segment, and it always took seven minutes. Never six and a half minutes, never seven and a half minutes, always seven.

Like his father, Faisal liked to get in his car at the end of the day and drive to the desert to pray at sunset. Some days, he prayed with friends whom he had known since childhood. On other days, he prayed alone, then sat in complete silence for half an hour.

After more meetings and dinner, Faisal visited one of his older sisters or met with other female relatives. Then he worked another two hours at this desk before joining his family at eleven. Often, Faisal and his children listened to the BBC, the Voice of America, or Radio Cairo, then began a lively discussion of current events.

By the middle of 1960, Faisal had successfully put Saudi Arabia's finances in order, but because so many building projects had been stopped, business was slow and unemployment was high. Many Saudis were tired of Faisal's austerity.

On August 8, 1960, Standard Oil of New Jersey (known today as Exxon) responded to a glut of cheap Russian oil by lowering the price of its Middle Eastern petroleum by ten cents a barrel. Within days, Texaco, Gulf, Mobil, Shell, BP (British Petroleum), and SOCAL (Chevron) followed suit. Faisal was furious that this decision had been made unilaterally in a corporate boardroom, and the shah of Iran shared his anger.

One month later, on September 9, the oil ministers of five nations met in Baghdad and formed a new organization: OPEC, the Organization of Petroleum Exporting Countries. The five founding members, Saudi Arabia, Iran, Iraq, Kuwait, and Venezuela, exported 80 percent of the world's oil, and today they still control 60 percent of the world's oil reserves.

OPEC demanded to be consulted before any future price changes, but for two years the oil companies refused to talk to OPEC, saying that they dealt with governments, not "outside organizations." Still, the five nations kept the promise they had made to one another in Baghdad: not to break ranks and accept better terms from an oil company if it would hurt the other four nations. Despite this solidarity, OPEC had little power in the 1960s because the supply of oil was greater than the demand. In the 1970s, when the situation reversed, OPEC would dominate the oil industry.

By November 1960, Saud was tired of being a figurehead and asked that Faisal not appoint any judges or governors without his consent. Faisal ignored the request. Then on December 19, Saud refused to sign the budget, charging that it lacked sufficient detail, a concern that had never troubled him before. That evening, Faisal wrote to Saud, "As I am unable to continue, I shall cease to use the powers vested in me as from tonight."

Saud Returns to Power (1960–1962)

Faisal probably thought that when Saud received his letter, he would back down, for Faisal had been careful not to use the word *resign*. Instead, Saud treated the note as if it were a resignation and resumed the duties of prime minister. The royal family, wanting an end to austerity, acquiesced in this countercoup. Many of the oldest brothers continued to favor Faisal, however, so Saud kept them out of the cabinet. He appointed his son Muhammad, the least incompetent of his children, as minister of defense, and Talal, the leader of a group of "liberal princes," as minister of finance.

The son of an Armenian concubine, Talal had lived in Lebanon for several years and had seen democracy work in an Arab country. He wanted Saudi Arabia to have a constitution and a national legislature with two-thirds of its members elected by the people. He proposed this idea to Faisal in 1960, but Faisal was not interested. "Our constitution is the Holy Quran," Faisal often said, adding that he was accessible to everyone. "If anyone feels wrongly treated, he has only himself to blame for not telling me. What higher democracy can there be?"[4]

Talal reluctantly concluded that Faisal, capable and conservative, was an obstacle to reform. He decided to support Saud instead, hoping that he could become a major influence on an uneducated king with so many weaknesses.

In fact, Saud had no more interest in democratic reform than Faisal did and quickly realized that Talal's presence in his cabinet was a liability. Talal irritated not only the more conservative princes with his calls for reform, but the clergy, too. When Talal tried to start a program of workmen's compensation for injuries, for example, Riyadh's top cleric ruled that the program was un-Islamic: an injured worker was entitled only to pay for the day of the injury. Because Saud needed the clergy's support, he canceled the compensation program, but clerics were annoyed that Talal was in the cabinet at all.

Talal particularly angered Saud when he opposed the king's attempts to bypass Faisal's financial controls. Although the Ministry of Finance continued to collect all of the government's money, officials at the ministry secretly diverted millions of dollars to Saud without entering it in the budget. Saud also took commissions on many government contracts.

At a press conference in August 1961, Talal said that the king was tending to his duties and "so far has been behaving himself." The disrespectful tone of the remark gave Saud the excuse he needed to fire Talal. Faisal was pleased by Talal's exit but wrote to Saud that he, too, was troubled by Saud's tendency to "treat the Kingdom as if it were your own estate."

Three months later, on November 15, 1961, Saud collapsed after vomiting blood. While unconscious, he was flown to the U.S. hospital for oil workers at Dhahran, where doctors found severe internal bleeding caused by an excessive intake of alcohol. As if to confirm the diagnosis, Saud's aides brought bottles of liquor to the king as soon as he regained consciousness, despite efforts by his nurses to prevent it.

Because Saud had liver complications, the doctors in Dhahran decided that they were not qualified to operate on the king and recommended a hospital in Boston. (They may also have been frightened by the prospect of losing a king on the operating table.) Just before Saud left the country on November 21, he signed a decree appointing Faisal as his regent. In turn, Faisal promised not to make changes in the cabinet while Saud was away.

After three months in the United States, Saud returned home on March 7, 1962, ready to take charge of the government. But the senior princes would not allow Saud to replace Faisal a second time. Firmly, they told Saud that Faisal would continue to govern the nation, although Saud's son Muhammad could still serve as minister of defense and his son Khalid could continue to command the National Guard. Saud went back to the United States for more medical treatment.

Faisal Back in Charge (1962–1964)

After fifteen frustrating months out of office, Faisal was back in power. He fired the oil minister, an admirer of Nasser, and replaced him with a young Harvard-educated lawyer named Ahmed Zaki Yamani. Yamani would remain Saudi Arabia's oil minister for twenty-four years. Faisal also ordered the government to begin to build schools for girls, but he appointed an unusually conservative cleric as minister of education in order to soften the opposition of the many men who were still opposed to this radical new idea.

Finally, to reduce Egypt's revolutionary influence on the kingdom, Faisal deported the army's last few Egyptian military advisers and set up a security service to watch Egyptian laborers and other expatriates. He also won the clergy's permission to make Radio Mecca more appealing to young people, so that fewer of them would listen to Radio Cairo.

Faisal's mistrust of Egypt was justified when three thousand Egyptian soldiers parachuted into Yemen on September 30, 1962, just four days after Yemen's army officers had launched a military coup and destroyed the royal palace. The speed of the Egyptians' arrival meant that Nasser had probably planned the assistance well in advance. On the radio, he gave a fiery speech predicting that Arab socialism would not only flourish in Yemen but would also destroy the antiquated monarchy in Saudi Arabia. For Nasser, Yemen was a stepping-stone to the Saudi oil fields, which he thought should belong to all the Arabs, not only to the Saudis. By March 1963, forty thousand Egyptian troops with Soviet weapons were fighting in northern Yemen, a force much too strong for the Saudi army to confront directly.

Yemen's new military leaders replaced Muslim law with civil law, but the majority of Yemen's people were hostile to this change. In the mountains, tribesmen fought for the religious young king Muhammad al-Badr, who had managed to escape from his palace before it was destroyed. The Saudis allowed him to assemble forty thousand troops on the Saudi side of the border and gave him guns, ammunition, and $2 million a month. In response, the Egyptian air force used its Russian-made propeller planes to bomb the young king's bases even though some of them were in Saudi border towns.

As frightening to the Saudis as the Egyptian invasion itself was the fact that less than a week later, four Saudi air force crews flew their planes to Egypt and turned them over to the Egyptian government. Shocked, Faisal immediately grounded the entire Saudi air force until security forces found and purged two dozen disloyal pilots.

Simultaneously, Talal and two other "liberal princes" suddenly appeared in Cairo, certain that the Saudi monarchy's days were numbered. The three men met Nasser, and Talal gave speeches on Egyptian radio denouncing the royal family for its "backwardness, underdevelopment, reactionary individuals, and tyranny."

While the Arabian peninsula was in turmoil, Faisal proceeded with a previously scheduled trip to Washington to meet President John Kennedy and warn him against improving U.S. relations with Nasser. Faisal asked Kennedy whether the United States would guarantee Saudi airspace, a request the president granted.

On October 31, just one week after Faisal returned home from the United States, he took complete unchallenged control of the government for the first time. With a hostile army only a few miles south of the kingdom's border, Faisal finally won the family's consent to dismiss Saud's two sons from the cabinet, along with six other ministers who were loyal to Saud.

Unlike Saud, who had angered his brothers by appointing his sons to key positions, Faisal kept harmony by balancing power between the royal family's maternal branches. He picked his brother Sultan to be minister of defense and, two months later, chose Abdullah, another brother by a different mother, to be commander of the National Guard. Today, forty-five years later, although Abdullah is king and Sultan is crown prince, both men still hold these key military posts.

On November 6, Faisal, only a week after gaining his new power, announced a ten-point plan for the country that included the

immediate abolition of slavery. Slavery had never been an issue that
Faisal felt strongly about; as foreign minister, he had resisted many
calls by the United Nations for its abolition. Yet by 1962, race relations had become a big issue in the United States, and Faisal understood that the United States could not ally itself with Saudi Arabia
much longer unless the kingdom abolished slavery.

Before Faisal went to see President Kennedy in October, he
had asked for permission from his brothers and from the nation's
top clergymen to promise President Kennedy an immediate end to
slavery. The clerics agreed reluctantly because slavery had existed
in Muhammad's time and was clearly sanctioned by the Quran.
However, it was never as central to life in Arabia as it had been to the
American South and therefore was far easier to abolish.

Less than 1 percent of Saudis were slaves. Most were of African
descent, and almost all of them worked as domestic servants, rather
than as field hands. Sometimes pilgrims sold themselves into slavery
after traveling to Mecca because they did not have enough money to
get home. Compensating slave owners did not cost the Saudi government much money. In the end, most slaves remained in their masters'
households as employees because few possessed the skills to work
elsewhere.

The abolition of slavery was the only part of the ten-point plan
that Faisal enacted immediately. Some promises, such as increased
economic development, welfare for the poor, and the introduction
of television, took several years to implement. Another pledge, the
creation of a consultative council to advise the king, was not fulfilled
until the 1990s.

Still another promise, "freedom of expression within the limits of
Islamic faith and public policy," was so vague as to be meaningless
and was quickly broken. In 1963, Faisal took control of the nation's
five newspapers and three magazines, fired everyone who supported
Nasser, and appointed new and much tamer editorial boards.

At a time when air force officers and even princes were rebelling against the royal family, Faisal wanted to shore up his support
among the urban middle class. His ten-point plan was an appeal to
their hopes, but as soon as the threat of Nasser's Pan-Arab socialism passed, the plan was quickly forgotten. Most middle-class Saudis
were loyal to the monarchy anyway because, as merchants, they never
cared for Nasser's socialism.

During the winter of 1962–1963, U.S. fighter jets occasionally
flew over Riyadh and Jeddah but stayed well north of Yemen's border and never attacked Egyptian positions. The purpose of the U.S.

patrols was to let Egyptian pilots know that whatever they were doing along the border, they had better not fly any farther north.

On January 1, 1963, Faisal declared a national emergency and imposed martial law. Although he disliked the limelight, he held large rallies in many cities and gave rousing and eloquent speeches about the war in Yemen. Quietly, he also used his police to arrest, jail, and, in a few instances, torture pro-Nasser army officers, oil workers attempting to strike, and members of the pro-Syrian Baath Party. The ordinary Saudi, however, was relieved to see that Faisal, in contrast to his brother Saud, relaxed the zeal of the religious police.

Faisal purged the officer corps of the National Guard of anyone who had been close to his brother Saud. He also removed all of Saud's sons from their government posts and moved two of the three battalions of Saud's Royal Guards from Riyadh to the border of Yemen, where they were absorbed into the regular army.

Faisal also reduced royal incomes another 20 percent, modernized the government's purchasing and payroll systems, encouraged investment by exempting foreign companies from income taxes for five years, and opened a dozen new engineering schools, including the College of Petroleum and Minerals in Dhahran.

In addition, Faisal renamed Saudi Arabia's provinces and created a new Northern Frontier Province near the border of Iraq.

Traditional Name	New Name
Najd	Central Province
The Hejaz	Western Province
Al-Hasa	Eastern Province
Asir	Southern Province

By 1963, Saudi Arabia was surrounded by radical regimes in Egypt, Yemen, Iraq, and Syria, each challenging the monarchy's legitimacy, but Faisal was slow to increase the size of his army and air force until he could be sure of their loyalty. Building up the National Guard and the security services came first.

Faisal's strategy in Yemen was not to risk his own small and unreliable army but to arm and finance Yemen's royalist army instead and draw Nasser into a quagmire. It worked. By 1965, fifteen thousand Egyptians had died in Yemen; many had been ambushed in the mountains. Away from the cities and the coast, the royalists were in full control. The war was a huge drain on Egypt's economy, while Faisal's oil revenues seemed limitless.

In Cairo, Talal and the other "liberal" princes were horrified when Yemen's rebel leaders urged the Saudi people to kill the royal family. The princes broke with Nasser, publicly declared that their previous criticism of the Saudi monarchy was "entirely wrong," and begged Faisal's forgiveness. Faisal let them return to Saudi Arabia, but they did not engage in politics again for forty years.

In the mid-1960s, many Saudis were beginning to travel abroad, and almost everyone listened to foreign radio stations. Exposure to new ideas caused many Saudis to question their traditional values and put the clergy on the defensive. Bowing to public opinion, the clergy grudgingly permitted smoking, record players, female radio announcers, film projectors at home, and the use of photographs in newspapers and magazines. They continued to outlaw cinemas and the imports of any statues, portraits, or Christian crosses.

The biggest social change of the 1960s was that girls began to go to school. In the 1950s, it had been common for college-educated Saudi men to marry similarly well-educated girls from Egypt, Syria, and Lebanon. The need for girls' schools in Saudi Arabia became more pressing as foreign girls consistently won the hearts of the best Saudi men. Even so, many Wahhabis resisted the idea of educating women.

The northern city of Buraida, well-known for being one of the most conservative towns in the country, sent a delegation to Faisal in 1963 to protest the building of a girls' school. "Is there one verse in the Quran that forbids teaching women to read?" Faisal asked them. "Am I forcing any of you to send your daughters to this school?"

Still angry, the people of Buraida rioted when the school year began. Faisal sent troops to restore order and insisted that the school stay open, even if no one in the city chose to attend. Almost no one did. During the school's first year, the only student was the daughter of the headmistress.

Resistance faded quickly when even small-town women saw that education improved a girl's marriage prospects. In 1960, only 2 percent of Saudi girls aged six to twelve went to elementary school. By 1975, the figure was 50 percent, although the number of teenage girls in high school was still well under 5 percent.

In Riyadh, Princess Effat founded a teachers college and a special school where adult women could learn to read, type, and speak a foreign language. Today, many women earn bachelor's and even graduate degrees, but education is still strictly segregated by gender. Male professors teach female students via closed-circuit television, and libraries keep separate "girls' hours."

Saud Fails to Regain Power (1963–1964)

Faisal once said, "Each time I dress a wound, another opens up elsewhere." While he was trying to run the country, Saud spent eleven months in Europe staying at clinics at Lausanne and Vienna and luxury hotels in Paris and Nice. Although he was sixty-one, he had a liver disease and a duodenal ulcer that caused him to walk with the stiffness of a man past eighty, yet Saud still led an entourage of 160 wives, children, and servants. They tipped bellboys $100 at a time ($600 in today's money), sent limousines to Lebanese restaurants to bring whole roasted sheep back to their suites, and ran up hotel bills of $50,000 ($300,000 in current money) a week.

In September 1963, Saud finally returned to Riyadh and within a week was seething over the loss of his power. As in 1960, he refused to sign the budget, but this time Faisal signed it instead. When Faisal and Saud were in a room together, Faisal treated his older brother with the utmost courtesy. He kissed Saud's hand, sat on the floor below him, knelt to put Saud's slippers on his feet, and never once raised his voice. In private, however, Faisal had developed such contempt for his brother that he refused even to speak his name, calling him simply "that man."

Pressed by his sons, who wanted their government jobs back, Saud wrote Faisal a letter on March 13, 1964, demanding that Faisal return his executive powers to him since his health had improved, and that he appoint two of his sons to cabinet posts. Saud's sons went to the desert to rally support for their father among the tribesmen, but the tribes stayed quiet.

Abdullah, the commander of the National Guard (who became king in 2005), was so angry at Saud that he wanted to overthrow the king and eject him from the country. Faisal, who almost never made a hasty decision, talked him out of it, insisting that the family's power struggle be resolved by constitutional means.

Faisal showed Saud's letter first to his brothers, who were unanimous that Saud remain a figurehead. Then Faisal took the letter to the kingdom's leading clergymen. On March 26, after more than a week of discussion, the clerics handed Saud a ruling that Faisal should keep his power, that Saud's personal bodyguards should be absorbed by the police and the army, and that his income should be cut considerably.

Saud rejected the clerics' ruling and defiantly ordered his eight hundred Royal Guards to surround and protect his palace. Abdullah promptly ordered the National Guard to encircle the Royal Guard.

The royal guardsmen, literally caught in the middle of a family dispute, hedged their bets by saluting Faisal each morning when his Chrysler sped past them on his way to work. After a few days, Faisal placed the commander of the Royal Guard, Saud's son Sultan, under house arrest, and within forty-eight hours, the rest of the Royal Guard swore their allegiance to Faisal.

On March 29, the clergy published a formal ruling that while Saud should remain king, Faisal should direct the nation's foreign and domestic affairs without any need for Saud's approval or signature. The next day, sixty-eight princes signed a document enforcing the ruling, and the cabinet transferred the control of Saud's guards to the army and to the police. It also cut his income in half, to $750,000 a week.

During the spring and the summer of 1964, tribesmen arrived in Riyadh from every part of the kingdom to swear allegiance to Faisal, a ceremony that Saud found humiliating because he still refused to be a figurehead. "I am not Queen Elizabeth!" he fumed.

Saud's Expulsion from the Kingdom (Autumn 1964)

In October 1964, Saud formally asked the clergy to reconsider the March 29 ruling that had freed Faisal from the need to obtain Saud's signature for the budget and other government documents. The unspoken question, which Saud did not realize that he had raised, was that if an Arabian king cannot be a mere figurehead, was Saud up to the job of being king?

Faisal's brothers were tired of facing a national crisis every few months. They thought they had resolved the family's power struggle once and for all in March. Now they realized that Saud had to go. He could no longer be king, not even as a figurehead.

Faisal began a weeklong trip through the desert, where he saw different tribal sheikhs every day. He knew that the decision to oust his older brother from the throne was not one that he could take part in and that it was best for him to stay away from Riyadh.

On the morning of October 29, two meetings took place. Sixty-five of the nation's leading clergymen met at the home of Riyadh's top cleric, Muhammad ibn Ibrahim, a descendant of ibn Abdul Wahhab. Across town, one hundred princes met at the Sahara Palace hotel. This informal group of princes, the *ahl al-hal wa'l-'aqd* (the

Committee That Binds and Loosens), was the most powerful body in Saudi Arabia, but since the eighteenth century, it had met only on rare occasions, when there was a division of opinion about who the next ruler should be. In 1964, it consisted of roughly thirty sons of King Abdul Aziz, about fifteen grandsons, several brothers, and forty-five nephews.

In the afternoon, the clerics joined the princes at the Sahara Palace. By then, everyone agreed that Faisal should be the country's new king. The final document, dethroning Saud and swearing an oath of allegiance to Faisal, was signed by sixty-eight princes and twelve clergymen. At this point, Faisal was only forty-five miles from Riyadh, and a delegation of princes and clerics drove into the desert to inform him that he was the country's new king. The moment they told him the news, the call to the prayer at sunset began. Without a word, Faisal went to pray. When he returned, he asked them, "What about the reigning king? In the house of Abdul Aziz we do not depose the king except after all attempts at persuasion have failed. Have you exhausted all means of persuasion?"[5] "Truly," they answered, "you are king."

That evening the same delegation went to Saud's palace to ask him to abdicate, but for three days, Saud refused. On November 2, 1964, the nation began to move ahead without him. The cabinet unanimously approved the October 29 proclamation and swore allegiance to the new king: Faisal. So did soldiers, provincial governors, and tribal sheikhs. The following day Muhammad, the third-oldest brother, who was known for his explosive temper, stormed into Saud's palace and told him that if he did not abdicate soon, his property would be confiscated and he would spend the rest of his life under house arrest. Saud had a final discussion with his sons, then gave up and signed a decree abdicating his throne.

The eleven years of struggle between Saud and Faisal were finally over. Saud had lost his throne because he had tried to rule an entire nation as if he were a tribal sheikh and the country were his personal possession. He was forty-two before the influx of oil money began to move his country out of the Middle Ages; his mind-set reflected the kingdom's long isolation from the world.

Oddly enough, the royal family emerged from the crisis stronger than ever because it had survived the century's most serious succession dispute with its unity intact. In the nineteenth century, family quarrels had led to the end of the second Saudi state. In the twentieth century, the al-Saud family showed that it had learned the lessons of its history by acting with near unanimity.

Saud's fifty-two sons took a month to come around, but in December, they swore their allegiance to King Faisal. As for Saud, Faisal insisted that when he left Riyadh, he be given full royal honors at the airport. Faisal himself bowed his head to him. As soon as Saud left, however, Faisal ordered workmen to tear down the seven-mile wall that surrounded Saud's massive palace. Today, part of the complex serves as guest quarters for foreign heads of state.

Saud spent most of his exile in Athens but did not go quietly into the sunset. In 1965, he tried to buy his own air force, perhaps to try to reconquer his kingdom. Secretly, he purchased twenty-three U.S. propeller planes—C-47s, B-26s, and DC-6s—from a variety of dealers and smuggled them as far as Portugal before the CIA learned of the plot and the Portuguese confiscated the aircraft.

A year later, in December 1966, Saud and an entourage of 130 people moved from Athens to the Nile Hilton in Cairo, taking with them three safes containing gold, jewelry, and cash worth more than $125 million ($650 million in current money). Soon, on Radio Cairo, Saud denounced Faisal as "an ally of colonialism," claimed that the CIA had helped Faisal to oust him, and called on the Saudi people to overthrow "the usurper."

The following April, Saud advanced from mischief to treason when he flew to Yemen and met rebel leaders who welcomed him as "the legitimate king of Saudi Arabia." Saud gave them $1 million ($5 million today) just as they were beginning a new bombing campaign against the southern Saudi towns of Jizan and Najran.

The Six-Day War of June 1967 put a quick end to Saud's troublemaking. Egypt, having lost its war with Israel, desperately needed Saudi money to rebuild its military and swiftly pulled its troops out of Yemen to get it. Nasser informed Saud that he was no longer welcome in Cairo, so the entourage of 130 returned to Athens.

That Saud was willing to give money to an army bombing his own people reveals the depth of the anger he felt toward his brothers. The fury may have consumed him. His liver and intestinal illnesses grew steadily worse, and he died in 1969. Faisal sent a plane to bring Saud's body back to Riyadh, where he was buried next to his father in an unmarked grave. Mercifully, Wahhabi custom forbids eulogies.

During his first week as king in November 1964, Faisal asked people to call him "Brother Faisal" instead of "Your Majesty." "I beg you to look upon me as both a brother and servant," he told his subjects, "Majesty is reserved to God alone." That same week, in an interview with a Beirut newspaper, he defended monarchy: "The important thing about a government is not what it is called but how it acts. There are corrupt republican regimes and sound monarchies and vice versa. . . . The quality of a government should be judged by its deeds and the integrity of its rulers, not by its name."[6]

The Eldest Able

Faisal waited four months before he chose a crown prince in March 1965. The new king passed over his next-oldest brother, Muhammad, because, although Muhammad was highly intelligent, he had a violent temper and no administrative experience. Muhammad did not appear to mind. He prized family unity above all other virtues, and if his brothers felt that he would not make a good king, that consensus was more important to him than his personal ambition. In Muhammad's place, Faisal chose Khalid, his good-natured younger brother, who had accompanied him on so many trips abroad when they were young.

Faisal and his younger brothers were unanimous that in the future, the "eldest able" among them must rule the kingdom. This is what the power struggle of the last eleven years had been all about. Saud was the eldest but had not been able. Faisal was the eldest able. After Faisal, although Muhammad was the eldest, it was the next-oldest brother, Khalid, who was the eldest able. Today, four decades later, this simple principle is still a fundamental rule of succession in Saudi Arabia.

13

The King in Full Control
(1964–1972)

KING AT LAST, Faisal built new schools, roads, hospitals, and power plants and financed troops in Yemen to fight the Egyptian army until Egypt finally withdrew from Yemen in 1967. In the early 1970s, Saudi Arabia and other OPEC nations began to increase the taxes and the royalties that Western oil companies had to pay. Faisal also organized Islamic summits and set up Islamic banks and charities to help poorer Muslim nations. By 1972, King Faisal was the most powerful man in both the Muslim world and the oil industry.

When Saud was king, Faisal had worked hard to keep the office of prime minister free from royal interference, but in 1964, now that Faisal himself was king, he served as his own prime minister. In November, his first month on the throne, Faisal appointed "technocrats"—Saudis who had graduated from foreign universities—to high positions in every nonreligious ministry. He encouraged young officials to speak freely at meetings and make their departments more professional, but he also supervised their work closely and ultimately gave them far less authority than he entrusted to his brothers and nephews. Once an official won Faisal's confidence, however, Faisal's support for him was permanent. In eleven years as king, Faisal replaced only two cabinet ministers.

Education, Development, and Television

In 1965, Faisal's government spent fifty times more money on education than Saud's government had during the first year of his reign. In the 1960s and the early 1970s, the number of boys in elementary school quadrupled, and the number of girls rose from a few hundred in 1960 to more than 214,000 in 1974. By then, half of the girls and three-quarters of the boys in Saudi Arabia were going to primary school. The children spent one-third of their time on Islamic and Arabic studies, but this was a significant change from the centuries-old tradition of simply memorizing the Quran.

While schools in the largest cities were reasonably good, English and science were taught poorly elsewhere. Many rural areas had no schools at all until the oil boom of the mid-1970s. As a result, the rate of illiteracy among people age ten and older, which was 95 percent in 1958, was still about 75 percent at the end of Faisal's reign in 1975. Equally disappointing, because there were too few middle schools and high schools, only one-third of the students who entered first grade in the mid-1960s were in middle school six years later, and only 6 percent went on to high school.

Even today, from age nine on, girls are required to wear veils, and classes are segregated by gender. In high schools and colleges, male teachers instruct female students via closed-circuit television. The majority of Saudi women never attend a university but marry at eighteen or nineteen. It is a young age to wed, but their grandmothers married at thirteen or fourteen.

Between 1960 and 1975, the number of Saudis studying at universities rose from fifteen hundred to thirty-one hundred. More than three-quarters of Saudi college students major in Islamic studies or the liberal arts, where classes are in Arabic. In the sciences and engineering, many courses are taught in English, but even science majors must take some required Islamic courses. A 1996 survey showed that 45 percent of the university-level teachers and instructors in Saudi Arabia were foreigners; the percentage is even higher among assistant professors and higher still among full professors.

The best college in Saudi Arabia is the former University of Petroleum and Minerals in Dhahran, renamed King Fahd University of Petroleum in the 1990s. Its faculty is largely American, with many professors coming from the Massachusetts Institute of Technology (MIT). During Faisal's reign, the student body grew from one hundred to one thousand, and it has tripled since then. Because the oil industry is the only means of advancement open to the 8 percent of the nation's people who are Shi'ite Muslims, whom many Saudis detest as polytheists, many young Shi'ites study especially hard. Admission to the competitive university is by merit alone; by 1981, half of the student body was Shi'ite.

The most conservative university in Saudi Arabia is the Islamic University of Medina, which has become a breeding ground for extreme fundamentalists. In 1966, the university's vice president, a blind cleric named Sheikh Abdulaziz ibn Baz, wrote an article that denounced the professors at Riyadh University for teaching students the "falsehood" that the Earth rotates and orbits the sun: "The Holy Quran, the Prophet's teaching, the majority of Islamic scientists and the actual fact all prove that the sun is running in its orbit, as Almighty God ordained, and that the earth is fixed and stable."[1]

Ibn Baz published his attack in two newspapers. When Faisal found out about it, he was furious and ordered the destruction of every unsold copy of both papers. It was too late. Egyptian newspapers gleefully picked up this story, which seemed to prove Nasser's claim that Saudi Arabia was a backward nation.

Ibn Baz did not change his mind about the cosmos until 1985, when the first Arab astronaut, Prince Sultan ibn Salman, returned home after a week aboard the space shuttle *Discovery*. The prince made a special trip to see ibn Baz to tell him that by watching the line that separates day and night, he had personally seen the Earth rotate. Despite the earlier embarrassment, ibn Baz eventually became the nation's leading cleric when King Fahad appointed him grand mufti (equivalent to chief justice) in 1993.

Faisal was fortunate that oil production quintupled during the first eight years of his reign, for this enabled government spending to quintuple as well. The king spent much of the extra money building the public works that were necessary for modernization, including more than eight thousand miles of highways. The roads connected many of the nation's cities for the first time, but driving was often chaotic because street signs and traffic lights were rare. The kingdom built international airports in Riyadh, Jeddah, and Dhahran; smaller airports in fifteen other cities; and the first of four treatment plants near Jeddah to desalinate seawater. It also erected power stations that doubled the electric wattage in cities, making air conditioning affordable for the middle class. Most rural areas, however, remained unwired and dark at night.

The kingdom opened more than thirty hospitals, three hundred rural health clinics (many on wheels), and dozens of orphanages, reform schools, and homes for the blind, deaf, and disabled. By 1967, medical care was free, but there was only one doctor and three nurses for every eight thousand people, and a lack of clean water kept dysentery and other intestinal diseases widespread.

Petromin, a publicly owned company, built the nation's first oil refinery, enabling the Saudis to make their own gasoline, diesel oil, jet fuel, and propane, as well as asphalt for the new highways. The company also built the country's first steel mill and its first fertilizer plant. To encourage the building of more factories, Faisal gave entrepreneurs tax breaks, free land, exemptions from import duties, and low rates for power and water. Many small businessmen started factories that made cement, pipes, bricks, plasterboard, soft drinks, and ice. Others set up construction firms or automobile repair shops with the help of the Saudi Industrial Development Fund, a new government agency that enabled entrepreneurs to almost double their starting capital.

Ordinary Saudis were happy to work as merchants, clerks, soldiers, guards, and drivers, but both the middle class and the Bedouin considered manual labor beneath them, and hardly any Saudi knew how to use or repair machinery. As a result, by 1968, 45 percent of the workforce in Saudi cities was foreign, to the dismay of the insular Wahhabi clergy. Almost half of these foreigners were uneducated laborers from Yemen; another 10 to 15 percent came from Pakistan and the Philippines. In addition, tens of thousands of teachers, engineers, and technicians arrived each year from Lebanon, Jordan, Palestine, the United States, Britain, and, after Nasser died in 1970, Egypt.

Industrial development did not help farmers, who still made up one-third of Saudi Arabia's population in the 1960s, or the Bedouin, who represented an additional 6 to 8 percent of the country's people. Saudi Arabia receives less than four inches of rainfall a year (half that of Phoenix) and has almost no rivers or streams. Without costly irrigation, only one-fifth of 1 percent of Saudi Arabia's land is moist enough to farm. Farms were small and limited to isolated oases and to the Red Sea coast north of Yemen. In the 1960s, a grove of date palms or a field of wheat or alfalfa was typically just two to five acres, while a patch of tomatoes or watermelons was even smaller. Some Saudi farmers did not even own the tiny plots they worked.

Faisal's Ministry of Agriculture set up five centers in different parts of the country where farmers could receive seeds, fertilizer, insecticides, and expert advice. The government also started the Bank for Agricultural Development in 1964 to give farmers no-interest loans to drill wells, purchase livestock, and buy farm vehicles and equipment.

Despite these opportunities, few farms had any machinery. As late as 1967, there were only 277 tractors in the entire kingdom. A tractor was simply too expensive for a farmer to buy when his plot of land was so small. As a result, the 40 percent of the Saudi people who farmed or herded livestock produced less than 9 percent of the nation's non-oil income, and the country continued to import half of its food. Until the oil boom of the mid-1970s made irrigation affordable, it was hard for a poor farmer with little water to compete against imported food from bigger, more fertile, and more efficient farms abroad.

In central Saudi Arabia, some homes did not have radios or televisions until the mid-1960s. While people in the western part of the country listened to Radio Cairo's *Voice of the Arabs* and people in the east tuned in to Radio Kuwait, the only civilian radio station in Saudi Arabia was Radio Mecca, with a signal so weak that no one outside Mecca or Jeddah could hear it. In some parts of the country, there was no radio reception at all.

This changed in 1963 when the government set up powerful radio transmitters in Riyadh and Jeddah that could be heard throughout the nation. Faisal shocked the clergy by allowing the stations to play songs by Umm Kalthoum, Fayrouz, and other female stars. When clergymen objected, Faisal pointed out that Muhammad himself had enjoyed the beautiful voice of a female poet, Al Khamsa.

In 1964, the government hired a U.S. television network, the National Broadcasting Company (NBC), to build four television stations in Riyadh, Jeddah, Medina, and Dammam. Transmissions began in Riyadh and Jeddah in July 1965. At first, all of the programming was religious: daily prayers, readings from the Quran, and theological discussions.

As Faisal had hoped, the Wahhabi clergy reluctantly decided that they could live with television, just as they had previously accepted record players and the viewing of films at home. The clergymen drew the line, however, at movie theaters, where men and women could sit together in the dark. Even today, there are no cinemas in Saudi Arabia.

After several weeks of religious programming, the new television stations began to broadcast entertainment: Egyptian films, Arab singers, cartoons, and dubbed episodes of *I Love Lucy*, *Gunsmoke*, and *Lassie*. Any reference to Christianity or Judaism was censored, as were scenes of Saudi women, alcoholic beverages, or the slightest display of affection. Even a cartoon sequence of Mickey Mouse giving a kiss to Minnie Mouse was carefully deleted.

As tame as Saudi television was, some people still objected to the broadcasts of "graven images." In September, one of Faisal's nephews, a playboy turned fundamentalist named Khalid ibn Musaid, led a group of armed militants in an attempt to destroy Riyadh's television station. Police arrived in time to confront them, and during the standoff, Faisal told the chief of security, "None of us is above the law. If the prince fires at you, then you must fire back."[2] Khalid did fire a gun at the officers, and the police chief killed him instantly.

In 1970, with the help of experts from Stanford University, Faisal's cabinet issued a five-year plan, the nation's first systematic approach to economic development. Under this plan, the first to use reliable statistics, the government allocated almost 60 percent of its budget to education, health, and infrastructure. Projects included the building of seventeen new piers to relieve the severe congestion at the seaports of Jeddah and Dammam and designs for two new ports, one at Jubail on the Persian Gulf and the other at Yanbu on the Red Sea. The government also built seven more airports and two thousand miles of new roads. Most important, it modernized the post office, which finally became dependable.

Because the Arabian-American Oil Company (Aramco) continued to find new oil deposits, production doubled between 1969 and 1972, causing the government's income to continue to skyrocket. For the first time, Saudi Arabia earned more money than its economy could absorb, given the country's constant shortage of skilled manpower. During 1971 and 1972, for lack of a better way to spend its money, the kingdom accumulated more than $4 billion in U.S. Treasury bonds and foreign currency deposits.

The government began to provide money and services, however unequally, to everyone in the kingdom. In the cities, schools and medical care were free, taxes were nonexistent, and government subsidies kept the prices of lamb, rice, flour, vegetable oil, milk, water, and electricity artificially low. In rural areas, the government offered farmers seeds and no-interest loans and gave the Bedouin the money to buy pickup trucks, water tankers, sewing machines, portable stoves, and television sets. It was hard for even the poorest Saudi to resent the royal family's wealth when everyone's life in Saudi Arabia was improving so rapidly.

As the lure of oil money drew more oasis dwellers and Bedouin into the cities, the power of the central government, which provided so many services, increased, while the influence of the tribal sheikhs, who were irrelevant in cities, weakened. The sheikhs still supported Faisal, but it was a measure of how much their power had declined that while Faisal met with tribal leaders almost every day during his first year as king, a decade later he saw them less than once a week.

Yemen, Israel, and Muslim Unity

When Faisal became king, sixty thousand Egyptian troops were fighting in Yemen, a force three times larger than Saudi Arabia's army of twenty thousand men. With such long borders to protect and so few men to defend them, Faisal concentrated on strengthening the nation's air force.

In December 1965, Saudi Arabia signed a contract with Britain to buy sixty-five jet fighters and bombers, an advanced radar system, and thousands of air-to-air missiles. The British also agreed to send a thousand instructors to train Saudi pilots and mechanics and promised to admit Saudi students into British military academies. In addition, the Saudis bought transport planes and surface-to-air missiles from the United States.

The enormous cost, $350 million, was just the beginning of a massive surge in arms spending. During the next five years, Saudi Arabia's defense budget grew seven times bigger as the Saudis bought tanks from the French; helicopters, supersonic fighters, and cargo planes from the Americans; and more jets, missiles, and radar systems from the British. By 1972, the Saudi Air Force had thirty-five hundred men and seventy-two aircraft ready for combat at any given time, but for seven years, Saudi Arabia had spent one-third of its oil royalties on the military. This money could have been used to build schools, clinics, roads, and wells.

Ironically, by the time Britain and the United States began to deliver their weapons, the threat in Yemen had subsided. By the end of 1966, it was obvious that Yemen's Egyptian-backed antiroyalist forces had neither the popular support nor the expertise in mountain fighting needed to win their nation's civil war. During the winter of 1966–1967, they resorted to terrorism, detonating more than a dozen bombs inside Saudi Arabia. Targets included an air force base, an oil pipeline, a U.S. military mission, a border post, and two royal palaces. The bombings ended when Saudi police arrested hundreds of Yemenis in February 1967, beheaded seventeen of their leaders in March, and deported thirty-five thousand Yemeni immigrants by April.

In May 1967, Nasser expelled forty-five hundred UN troops from Egypt's border with Israel, reoccupied the Gaza Strip, and closed the

Gulf of Aqaba to Israeli shipping. He was angered by an Israeli raid against Palestinian militants in the West Bank (which at that time belonged to Jordan), but his disproportionate response brought the region to the brink of war.

The Israelis did not wait to be attacked. Shortly before dawn on June 5, 1967, Israeli air force pilots flew out to sea, then turned 180 degrees and raced toward the airfields of Egypt, Jordan, and Syria at altitudes too low for radar to detect. In three hours, the Israelis destroyed all three air forces, then bombed and strafed the three nations' defenseless armies while Israeli tanks made rapid gains on the ground. In six days, Israel captured the Sinai peninsula, the West Bank of the Jordan River, including East Jerusalem, and the Golan Heights just forty miles southwest of Damascus.

At a giant rally in Riyadh on June 6, Faisal shouted, "To *jihad*, citizens! To *jihad*!" but the war ended before the Saudi brigade of three thousand troops that Faisal sent to Jordan could reach the front lines. Oil workers at Aramco went on strike for a week, and students at the University of Petroleum threw stones and wrecked several U.S. military residences.

To help his Arab neighbors, Faisal stopped selling oil to the United States for two months, but the action had no effect because there was a glut of oil and because neither Iran nor Venezuela joined the boycott. This prompted Faisal to form a new, smaller, and more politically cohesive group of oil exporters in 1968: OAPEC, the Organization of Arab Petroleum Exporting Countries.

Faisal was especially upset that the Israelis had captured East Jerusalem and, with it, Islam's third-holiest site, the Al-Aqsa Mosque, which includes the Dome of the Rock. From 1967 onward, the king often told guests that his greatest ambition was to pray there before he died—without the permission of Israeli soldiers. As for the Wailing Wall that surrounds the mosque, Faisal told an Egyptian newspaper that the Jews "have no historic right to it. Another wall can be built for them to weep against."[3]

Although Faisal always claimed to distinguish between Judaism and Zionism, no Jews could enter Saudi Arabia unless he personally approved their visa applications. He liked to point out that Karl Marx was a Jew, and for a time he accepted as authentic the distribution of the Tsarist Russian forgery *The Protocols of the Elders of Zion*, which in 1897 purported to outline a Zionist agenda to destroy Christianity and dominate the world. Copies of *The Protocols* appeared in most Saudi hotel rooms, along with the Quran.

Two and a half months after the June 1967 war, Nasser, Faisal, and other Arab leaders held a summit in Khartoum, the capital of Sudan. With Israeli soldiers on the east bank of the Suez Canal, Nasser's five-year war in Yemen seemed particularly foolish, and the Egyptian leader offered to withdraw his troops from Yemen in return for money to rebuild his army and air force.

The leaders of Saudi Arabia, Kuwait, and Libya together agreed to rearm Egypt and Jordan, with Saudi Arabia contributing $140 million annually, a hefty 15 percent of the kingdom's oil revenues in 1968. At a meeting on August 31, 1967, Faisal told Nasser that Saudi Arabia would send the money only after Nasser withdrew *all* of his forces from Yemen. Nasser promised to do this by the end of the year. In return, Faisal promised to stop financing Yemen's royalists.

Nasser's twin defeats in the Sinai and in Yemen in 1967 marked the end of his influence. The center of Arab power shifted decisively from Cairo to Riyadh, and the ideology uniting Arabs would soon shift from socialism back to Islam.

Despite years of Saudi aid, Yemen's royalists were unable to capture their capital city, Sana, when Egypt's troops left the country. With Saudi money and Egyptian troops no longer present in Yemen, a third force rose of tribal leaders who were antiroyal but otherwise traditionally Muslim. The country's civil war dragged on for two more years, but the tribal leaders were victorious in 1970. Faisal was satisfied with the outcome. The fact that a nearby king had been overthrown was not nearly as important to him as the fact that Nasser's forces had been driven from the Arabian peninsula forever.

No sooner had the Egyptians left northern Yemen than a new threat emerged in southern Yemen, after the British had decided to cut defense costs by abandoning their naval base in Aden in November 1967. To Faisal's alarm, the city was taken over by Marxists with Soviet weapons who, by 1969, had established the People's Democratic Republic of South Yemen. The Saudis did not have enough soldiers to overthrow the Marxist government, but Faisal did finance a small army of anticommunist Yemenis to encourage revolts and keep the pro-Soviet regime on the defensive. He also sent aid to North Yemen, still recovering from its civil war, to prevent it from being annexed by its southern neighbor.

From the beginning of his reign, Faisal had dreamed of a Muslim unity based on faith, rather than on socialism. In 1966, he visited eight Muslim nations with conservative governments—Jordan, Sudan, Pakistan, Turkey, Morocco, Guinea, Mali, and Tunisia—and hosted the leaders of Kuwait, Cameroon, Somalia, and Niger. He hoped to form a block of Muslim nations united against Zionism, communism, and Western imperialism.

Four years later, thirty-one countries formed the Islamic Conference, headquartered in Jeddah, to sponsor annual meetings of foreign ministers from every Muslim nation. During the next five years, these ministers established fifteen Arab and Islamic banks to distribute foreign aid from rich nations such as Saudi Arabia and Kuwait to poorer countries such as Palestine and Mali. The collective endowment of these fifteen charitable funds was over $10 billion, more than four times the size of the Ford Foundation then.

In 1971, Britain, in another move to cut costs, withdrew from the Persian Gulf and ended its long-standing treaties with Bahrain, Qatar, Abu Dhabi, Dubai, and five other coastal sheikhdoms. The British suggested that the nine states form a federation. Bahrain and Qatar declined, but the other seven principalities agreed. On December 2, 1971, with Faisal's good wishes, the seven sheikhdoms became the United Arab Emirates (UAE), a nation with about the size and population of South Carolina but with more than 8 percent of the world's oil reserves. (The United States has 2 percent.)

Islam in the UAE, Kuwait, and Qatar is less strict than it is in Saudi Arabia. In contrast to Riyadh, a tourist in Dubai can have a drink on Saturday night and go to church on Sunday morning.

When Faisal learned that Nasser had died of a heart attack on September 29, 1970, he went to a clinic in Geneva in order to have an excuse not to attend Nasser's funeral. Within months, however, Faisal developed a warm relationship with Nasser's successor, Anwar Sadat, an army general whom Faisal had known since the 1950s. Like Faisal, Sadat was a devout Muslim, and in private, Sadat admitted that both socialism and Egypt's alliance with the Soviet Union were mistakes.

Faisal visited Cairo in June 1971 and gave Sadat a check for 30 million British pounds ($84 million). He also invited the Egyptian teachers and technicians whom he had once expelled to return to their well-paying jobs in Saudi Arabia. In return, Sadat accepted Saudi Arabia's position that every nation it bordered, except Iraq, was within its sphere of influence.

Faisal helped to convince Sadat that U.S. diplomacy could be a much more effective means of persuading Israel to withdraw from the occupied territories than outdated Soviet weapons were but cautioned him that the United States would do nothing to help Egypt as long as it remained the host to sixteen thousand Soviet military advisers. Egyptian army officers were also wary of Soviet interference, so on July 18, 1972, Sadat stunned the world by giving every Soviet in Egypt one week to leave the country.

"Why has Sadat done me this favor?" Henry Kissinger asked when he learned of the expulsion. "Why didn't he demand all sorts of concessions first?" Sadat must have soon asked himself the same question, for Kissinger had to tell him that the United States could not possibly pressure Israel to withdraw from its new territories until after the presidential election in November. After that, of course, came the Watergate crisis, an even bigger distraction.

Faisal was shocked that the United States did not respond to Sadat's expulsion of the Soviets and soon joined Kuwait, Qatar, and the United Arab Emirates in increasing military aid to Egypt. In January 1973, Faisal also reluctantly agreed that it would be all right if Sadat spent this aid buying huge quantities of weapons again from Moscow. Faisal loathed the Soviet Union, but the struggle against Israel took priority.

Jailing Opponents

Faisal established a reputation for severity early in his reign when he ordered the beheading of twelve soldiers who had robbed buses filled with pilgrims near Medina. Saudi Arabia hosts Muslims from around the world, he said, and they need to know that their safety is the kingdom's number-one priority.

Faisal also ordered his police to arrest anyone who tried to organize oil workers or who spoke too highly of Nasser. Several hundred men were sent to jails that sometimes lacked beds or toilets, and there they read the Quran several hours a day.

By 1967, Faisal had also decided that the kingdom's official line of succession should not stop with Crown Prince Khalid but should include the next successor as well. He knew that Khalid, as charming as he was, preferred hunting in the desert with his falcons to the day-to-day work of running a government. When Khalid became king, he would need a strong second in command.

On October 17, Faisal picked his younger brother Fahad to be the nation's second deputy prime minister and second in line to the throne. Fahad was a Western-oriented prince with years of experience running the Education and Interior ministries.

Like his father, Faisal was able to choose the nation's next two kings. But while Abdul Aziz's desire for Faisal to succeed Saud was just a wish, Faisal's appointment of Fahad was public and in writing. It was the first time a king had officially chosen someone to be second in line to the throne, and for the rest of the twentieth century, the king also appointed a second deputy prime minister.

In the spring of 1969, several air force officers planned to shoot down Faisal's plane, bomb some royal palaces, and proclaim an Arabian republic. The leader of the attempted coup was the director of the air force academy at Dhahran, and he had the assistance of some Palestinian technicians and a rich merchant in Jeddah who opposed the Wahhabi domination of his region.

Saudi police learned of the plot on June 5 and arrested more than sixty air force officers and an equal number of civilians. Although Faisal did not let the conspiracy stop his long-term buildup of the air force, he grounded most of the air force for several weeks. The only pilots who stayed on duty were princes, and months passed before nonroyals were allowed to fly planes with bombs or missiles again.

The police made more arrests in 1970. They charged several hundred Shi'ites with being members of Iraq's Baath Party and arrested some students who had asked the United Nations to investigate the kingdom's detention of political prisoners. The police also began to screen foreigners seeking to enter the kingdom and watched them more closely after they arrived.

By the end of 1970, there was no opposition left in Saudi Arabia. Faisal's tough measures had done their work. In truth, public opinion was strongly behind the king and highly critical of his radical opponents. Ordinary Saudis loved living in a cradle-to-grave welfare state with no taxes and did not want it disrupted.

Even Western-educated Saudis, who resented the fact that the country had no elections and no criticism of the royal family, appreciated the enormous economic progress that the kingdom had made in a few short years. For most Saudis, the oil boom's business opportunities were much more important than the desire for political participation.

Taking Control of the Oil

In the 1950s and 1960s, the price of oil was set by seven corporations that together drilled almost two-thirds of the world's petroleum. Consumers know these companies today as Exxon, Mobil, Texaco, Gulf, Shell, BP (British Petroleum), and Chevron (formerly SOCAL). To keep the price of oil stable, the firms increased production when the demand for oil was high and decreased production when the demand was low.

During the 1960s, the price of oil hardly moved. Year after year, it was about $1.80 a barrel. The stability was deceptive. Throughout the world, especially in air-conditioned, car-dependent suburbs, people were burning less coal and more oil. In the United States, the share of energy consumption derived from coal fell from 50 percent in 1952 to just 20 percent in 1972. The price of oil stayed the same as long as it did because the Soviet Union needed money and created a glut by keeping its production high.

In 1960, the United States was nearly self-sufficient in petroleum, importing a little oil from Venezuela and less than 3 percent of its supply from the Middle East. By 1973, however, the United States had become the world's leading oil importer, buying more than 35 percent of its petroleum abroad and more than 10 percent of its oil from the Middle East. Western Europe and Japan were even more dependent on imported oil. In the early 1970s, these countries produced no oil of their own (the North Sea deposits had not yet been developed) and bought an astounding 85 percent of their oil from the Middle East.

When the Suez Canal closed after the 1967 war, the Europeans began to buy more oil from Libya and Algeria because North African crude needed only to be ferried across the Mediterranean. By contrast, oil from the Persian Gulf either had to be shipped all the way around Africa or else pumped through nine hundred miles of the Trans-Arabian Pipeline, a pipeline that was blown up by Palestinian Marxists in 1969 and ruptured by bulldozers in Jordan in 1970. By then, Western Europe was buying more than a quarter of its oil from Libya, a nation that had just overthrown its king in a coup led by an army colonel, Muammar Qaddafi, who was only twenty-seven.

One month after seizing power, Qaddafi demanded that oil companies pay 10 percent more taxes and an increased royalty of forty-four cents per barrel. Qaddafi said that Libya deserved these increases because its oil was much closer to European refineries than oil from the Persian Gulf was and therefore was cheaper to ship. Oil companies made more money selling Libyan crude, and Qaddafi wanted a share of this profit.

When the oil companies refused Libya's demands, Qaddafi ordered Occidental Petroleum to cut its production by 37 percent in June 1970. It was the first time in decades that a Middle Eastern nation had reduced its income as a way to pressure a company to change its royalty agreement. Libya, with few people to provide for, had enough cash reserves to pay for four years' worth of imports. Occidental, on the other hand, was a relatively small oil company with no wells in the Persian Gulf and was almost completely dependent on its Libyan production.

In September, Occidental agreed to a royalty increase of thirty cents per barrel and a tax hike of 16 percent. Within two weeks, three more small companies, Conoco, Marathon, and Amerada-Hess, signed similar agreements. Once Qaddafi was certain of a steady income, he told the larger oil companies to either pay more royalties and taxes or leave Libya. Chevron and Texaco gave in, and the other giant companies followed suit.

Faisal had met Qaddafi just a few months after the colonel had taken power and thought him rash and possibly mad. But he was pleased with what Qaddafi had achieved. Now, as the oil companies had feared, Saudi Arabia and the other Persian Gulf nations immediately demanded a 10 percent tax hike, which they quickly received, and, more alarmingly, a thirty-cent increase in their oil royalty per barrel. The Gulf nations wanted the same royalty as the Libyans, but, of course, the Libyans wanted a higher royalty because their oil was closer to Europe. A buyer's market favoring the oil companies had turned into a seller's market favoring the oil nations, and each country was trying to leapfrog a new royalty increase over a previous concession.

The oil nations wanted bigger royalties. The oil companies wanted price stability. These desires were not incompatible, so in February 1971, executives from fifteen oil companies met with representatives from the Organization of Petroleum Exporting Countries (OPEC) in Tehran. OPEC had eleven members now: seven Arab nations plus Iran, Venezuela, Nigeria, and Indonesia.

The oil companies and the OPEC nations signed the Tehran Agreement on February 14, 1971. The oil companies agreed (1) to pay host countries a tax of 55 percent (up from 50 percent) of the sale price of the oil they drilled, minus costs and royalties; (2) to increase the royalty they paid by thirty-five cents per barrel (in Saudi Arabia, this meant a 38 percent rise in income); and (3) to adjust the royalty for inflation with annual increases of 2.5 percent. In return, the Persian Gulf nations agreed not to leapfrog prices if the Mediterranean oil nations won slightly larger royalties at a conference one month later in Tripoli.

The Tehran Agreement was meant to last five years but endured just three. It was a turning point all the same. OPEC had formed a united front and seized control of the price of oil. The oil companies, divided among themselves, lost their power to set prices because it was easier and safer for them to pass a price increase on to their consumers (who paid, in this case, roughly two additional cents per gallon at the pump) than it was to risk the anger of an oil nation and suddenly lose a billion-dollar concession to a competitor.

The chief negotiator and strategist for OPEC was Saudi Arabia's minister of petroleum, Ahmed Zaki Yamani, the son of an Islamic scholar in Mecca. Forty years old, with law degrees from the University of Cairo and Harvard, the handsome, suave, and soft-spoken oil minister gradually become King Faisal's chief adviser. They were almost like father and son.

In 1957, Yamani opened Saudi Arabia's first law office when he returned home from his studies at Harvard. The following year, when Faisal took control of the government for the first time, Yamani wrote several newspaper articles that explained the legal issues involved. Faisal was impressed by the columns and asked Yamani to be his legal adviser. Four years later, in 1962, Faisal chose Yamani to be his minister of petroleum.

Yamani worked hard and acquired a deep knowledge of every aspect of the oil industry. He and Faisal agreed that what Saudi Arabia needed most was a large but reliable income. The price of oil should never rise so high as to make alternative fuels economical.

In 1963, Faisal's son, Saud al-Faisal, graduated from Princeton with a degree in economics. The king told Yamani that he wanted his son to work in the Petroleum Ministry but added firmly, "No favors." Saud's first job was as a common entry-level administrator, and his next position was midlevel. After eight years, when the king appointed his thirty-year-old son deputy minister of petroleum, Saud was thoroughly familiar with each division of the ministry. (In 1975, Saud became Saudi Arabia's foreign minister, a post he has held for three decades.)

Every now and then, Faisal rewarded Yamani by giving him land just outside one of the country's major cities. During the oil boom of the 1970s, when suburbs multiplied, his real estate was suddenly worth nearly half a billion dollars in today's money. Yamani was smart enough to sell most of his land before prices plummeted in 1976, and since then, he has enjoyed one of the largest nonroyal fortunes in the kingdom.

Although Yamani has homes in Riyadh, Jeddah, Mecca, and Beirut, he is as comfortable in Europe as he is in the Arab world. He loves French food, Wagner operas, and Savile Row suits and owns homes in London, suburban Surrey, Geneva, and Sardinia, where he keeps a huge 270-foot yacht.

Many princes resented Yamani, who was their equal not only in wealth but, more gallingly, in power. To soothe their feelings, Faisal formed a Supreme Petroleum Council to make policy recommendations and put his brother Fahad, the second deputy prime minister, in charge. But the council never had any power. When Fahad presented one of the council's first suggestions to the king, Faisal wanted to know whether the vote had been unanimous. "No," Fahad answered, the vote was four to one. "Who was the dissenting one?" Faisal asked. "Yamani," Fahad replied. Faisal paused for a moment and said, "Then we will do it Yamani's way."[4]

In January 1972, with Faisal's approval, Yamani took further advantage of the seller's market. Speaking for six Persian Gulf nations, he demanded that the oil companies sell them a minority share of their operations in the Gulf immediately and a 51 percent controlling interest after several years. The Gulf nations wanted only partial ownership because they still needed the technical expertise of the oil companies. They were willing to pay the oil companies a fair price for their equipment and installations but not for the oil reserves underground, which each country regarded as its own sovereign property.

At first, the oil companies rejected Yamani's demand, but they accepted the inevitable in February when Faisal sent a blunt statement to executives at Exxon, Texaco, Chevron, and Mobil that the sale of a stake in Aramco was not a matter for debate. The executives understood that unless they made a deal with Saudi Arabia and the other Gulf nations soon, other companies with no concessions in the Persian Gulf, such as France's Elf-Erap, Italy's ENI, and Belgium's Petrofina, would be happy to replace them. To protect their access to Saudi oil, the Aramco executives sent Yamani a letter on March 10 agreeing to sell 20 percent of their company.

After much negotiation, the General Agreement on Participation was signed in New York on October 5, 1972. The oil companies agreed to sell each OPEC member 25 percent of their stake in each country, followed by a transition period before they sold their majority ownership. In return, the OPEC nations agreed to take inflation (but not oil reserves) into account when they reimbursed the oil companies for their installations. To buy 25 percent of Aramco, the Saudis paid Exxon, Chevron, and Texaco $150 million each ($650 million each in today's money) and Mobil $50 million ($220 million today). The oil companies also agreed that by January 1, 1983, each member of OPEC would own 51 percent of its own national oil company. The oil nations and the oil companies were now partners.

At the end of 1972, King Faisal was the most powerful man in both the Muslim world and the oil industry, and along with the other Gulf monarchs, he was spending hundreds of millions of dollars arming Egypt and Jordan for a new conflict with Israel. Yet in the United

States, there was not the slightest inkling that 1973 would be a year of war, oil shortages, and economic turmoil. In the *New York Times*, there were just two articles about Saudi Arabia in 1970. In 1971, *U.S. News and World Report* did not mention the kingdom at all. And 1972's index to the *Congressional Record* contained 150 references to Israel but not one to Saudi Arabia.

The world was in for a surprise.

14

Oil as Political Power
(1973–1975)

I N 1973, THE WORLD STOPPED taking oil for granted. When the Yom Kippur War began in October, King Faisal led the Arab oil nations in cutting production to try to force the West to pressure Israel to withdraw from its occupied territory in Palestine. The Arabs also stopped exporting oil to the United States and the Netherlands. The panic these actions induced caused the price of oil to quadruple, leading to an unprecedented flow of money into Saudi Arabia and other Gulf nations.

"Oil and politics should not mix," King Faisal often told his advisers. In 1972, Zaki Yamani, his minister of petroleum, assured the public that Saudi Arabia "does not believe in the use of oil as a political instrument." But one year later, during the Yom Kippur War, Faisal reversed himself and cut oil exports sharply. The United States had ignored his many warnings about the need to pressure Israel to withdraw from the land it occupied in 1967, and the world's demand for oil had grown so fast that the Saudi kingdom was suddenly a major economic power.

The world's consumption of oil almost doubled between 1965 and 1973, and it was Saudi oil that met this increased demand. The kingdom's share of the world's oil exports had become an astonishing 21 percent.

At the beginning of 1973, Faisal and Egyptian president Anwar Sadat were frustrated that the United States had done nothing in response to Sadat's removal of Soviet troops from Egypt the previous July. In February, President Richard Nixon's national security adviser, Henry Kissinger, preoccupied with the Vietnam War, bluntly told Sadat that there was nothing the United States could do to help Egypt. Worse, the United States had agreed to sell Israel a new shipment of Phantom fighter jets. Sadat angrily and reluctantly concluded that the only way to get Israel to withdraw from the occupied territories was to start another war.

In the six years since the 1967 war, Saudi Arabia's alliance with the United States had become dangerous. Many Saudis worried that radical Palestinians might blow up key oil installations, cutting production—and royalties—for months.

Warnings Ignored

Yamani and his deputy oil minister, Faisal's son Saud, flew to Washington in April to tell Kissinger that Saudi Arabia would not increase its oil production again until the United States forced Israel to give up some of the occupied Arab land. Kissinger asked Yamani and Saud to keep the meeting secret, which made them suspect that he had no intention of acting on their warning. The two Saudis therefore decided to ignore their king's instruction not to talk to the press and leaked their meeting to the *Washington Post*.

It was the first time Saudi Arabia had ever publicly linked its flow of oil to America's support for Israel, but most U.S. officials did not take the threat of a production limit seriously. They overlooked the fact that Faisal's son had accompanied Yamani to Washington and chose instead to believe that Yamani's statement was just his own opinion, not Faisal's. "Yamani is getting above himself," said one U.S. official.

In May, Faisal met with directors of Exxon, Texaco, Chevron, and Mobil (the four owners of Aramco) and warned them that America's support for Israel was jeopardizing its interests in the Middle East. "You may lose everything," Faisal told them. "Time is running out." The king urged the executives to convey this message to the Nixon administration, but when they flew to Washington, a CIA official assured them that "Faisal is bluffing." Kissinger did not even see the oilmen.

In a report to stockholders in July, the chairman of Chevron wrote, "The United States should work more closely with the Arab governments. . . . There must be understanding on our part of the aspirations of the Arab people, and more positive support of their efforts toward peace in the Middle East."[1]

Mild as this statement was, it sparked a boycott of Chevron gasoline by supporters of Israel, who accused the company of "selling Jewish blood for Arab oil." Understandably, the boycott discouraged other oil companies from making similar public statements.

On August 23, Sadat flew to Riyadh to let Faisal know that the Soviet weapons that he had bought with the kingdom's money had been delivered and that war with Israel was imminent. During the meeting, Faisal may have promised Sadat that he would reduce oil exports to the West if events required it. One week later, on television, Faisal told an NBC News correspondent that "America's complete support for Zionism against the Arabs makes it extremely difficult for us to supply its petroleum needs."[2] The next day, the United Arab Emirates announced that it, too, would stop selling oil to the West if the struggle against Israel required it. Because Kuwait, Iraq, and Libya had already made similar announcements, it should have been clear to U.S. officials that the Arabs were not bluffing.

On September 1, Libyan leader Muammar Qaddafi announced that in thirty days, he would nationalize 51 percent of the oil companies in Libya, paying only minimal compensation. In response, the U.S. State Department urged wholesalers to boycott Libyan oil, and the oil companies threatened the buyers of Libyan crude with lawsuits.

In a press conference four days later, President Nixon warned Libya that "oil without a market . . . does not do a country much good," but the demand for oil was far too high to make the threat stick. The New England Petroleum Company, among other wholesalers, had a winter to prepare for and bought a large amount of the disputed Libyan oil at a discounted price. As the *New York Times* observed, President Nixon "had not yet grasped . . . that [today] the problem is not whether oil will find markets, but whether markets will find oil."[3]

The Yom Kippur War

At 2:05 p.m. on Saturday, October 6, 1973, which was that year's Yom Kippur, the Jewish Day of Atonement, four thousand Egyptian mortars, howitzers, and rocket launchers began to fire at Israeli troops along the east bank of the Suez Canal. Fifteen minutes later, eight thousand Egyptian soldiers crossed the canal in rubber motorboats, protected by a surprisingly strong force of 222 Soviet-built MiG supersonic fighter jets. Within an hour, the Egyptians had formed five beachheads on the Israeli side of the waterway. The Israelis had expected to defend themselves with napalm flamethrowers, but Egyptian commandos had quietly filled the flamethrowers' muzzles with cement the night before.

By midnight, eighty thousand Egyptian troops had crossed ten makeshift bridges to the east side of the canal, and by morning, they had surrounded Israel's command center and forced the rest of the Israeli army to retreat. Meanwhile, north of Israel, seven hundred Syrian tanks broke through the barbed wire at the 1967 cease-fire line and recaptured most of the Golan Heights.

On the first day of the war, Faisal sent President Nixon a message that the fighting could stop if the United States would agree to force Israel from its post-1967 land. Two days later, when Faisal had received no response, he sent Egypt $200 million to buy more arms. "The money we offer is much less than the lives you offer," Faisal said.

Arab newspapers said that it was time to use oil as a weapon, and the Palestine Liberation Organization called for a total freeze on oil exports. In Kuwait, oil workers threatened to strike unless the government cut its exports to the United States by 50 percent.

Faisal initially ignored the calls for an oil embargo but sent Syria an infantry brigade with armored cars and artillery. The brigade saw only one day's fighting in the Golan Heights and suffered nine casualties.

By October 12, after six days of fighting, the Israelis had pushed the Syrians back to the 1967 lines, but the Egyptians were still advancing east from the Suez Canal. Despite the war, it is doubtful whether President Nixon devoted more than a few minutes a day to the Middle East at this time. On October 10, Vice President Spiro Agnew resigned after pleading nolo contendere to charges of bribery and tax evasion, and two days later, a U.S. Court of Appeals ordered Nixon to turn over the Watergate tapes.

Kissinger, who was now secretary of state, had a freer hand than most presidential advisers do. At first, he kept arms shipments to Israel at a minimal level. He was actually pleased by the Egyptian advance because a lasting peace would be easier to achieve if the Israelis were less cocky and the Arabs no longer felt humiliated. On October 12, he called for a cease-fire, but Sadat rejected the proposal.

Sadat wanted to press his victory further, for each night the Soviet Union sent Egypt planeloads of new weapons. On October 12, sixty Soviet aircraft landed in Egypt and Syria, and the scale of this massive airlift changed Kissinger's mind about the need to arm Israel.

Kissinger wanted the Arabs to understand that Israel would withdraw from its occupied land only through diplomacy, that the Arabs would not be allowed to take territory with Soviet weapons. On October 13, at Kissinger's urging, President Nixon ordered a full-scale airlift of $2.2 billion worth of weapons to Israel. The Israelis themselves had requested only $850 million, but Nixon said, "If we are going to do it, let's do it big."

Two days later, the first of 550 planeloads of U.S. arms landed in Tel Aviv. It was the world's largest airlift since the U.S. supply of West Berlin in 1948–1949. The arrival of the giant C-130 cargo planes enabled Israeli generals to launch bolder offensives, confident that weapons in short supply would be replaced quickly.

On October 16, Israeli troops broke through Egyptian lines, crossed the Suez Canal, and occupied the western side. None of the Egyptian generals had the courage to inform Sadat of the bad news. Only when a Soviet official showed Sadat satellite photographs of the Israeli advance did the Egyptian president realize that it was time to negotiate a cease-fire. By this time, however, four Israeli tank brigades were approaching the city of Suez, while in Syria, Israeli troops had reached the suburbs of Damascus.

By coincidence, a meeting between the OPEC nations and the oil companies had been scheduled in Vienna for October 8, just two days after the Yom Kippur War began. The OPEC nations wanted to renegotiate the 1971 Tehran Agreement that called for an annual 2.5 percent increase in the price of oil to make up for inflation. In 1973, inflation was almost 8 percent a year, and President Nixon had devalued the dollar 10 percent, lowering oil royalties still further.

Led by Yamani, the OPEC oil ministers demanded a 70 percent rise in the price of oil, from $3.01 to $5.12 a barrel. The oil companies offered only a 25 percent increase, to $3.76 a barrel. On October 12, since the two sides were unable to agree on a price, further meetings were postponed indefinitely. It was the last time the oil companies played a role in setting the price of their product.

On October 16, the OPEC ministers met again in Kuwait and unilaterally fixed the price of oil at $5.12 a barrel, the first time the oil nations had set a price without negotiating with the oil companies. From now on, the price of petroleum would be a sovereign decision made exclusively by the oil exporters. The oil companies did not mind this new arrangement because a 70 percent rise in the price of oil increased their profits, too. They worried about the reaction of consumers back home but hoped that their loss of power over pricing would insulate them from blame for OPEC's enormous price increase.

Once the non-Arab oil ministers flew home, the Organization of Arab Petroleum Exporting Countries, OAPEC, met the next day in Kuwait. Yamani knew that Iraq wanted to nationalize everything the Americans owned in the Middle East and that other Arab nations also favored radical action. In response, he asked Faisal to approve a more moderate proposal: an immediate 5 percent cut in oil production, followed by an additional 5 percent cut each month until Israel withdrew from its post-1967 land. The advantage of this plan was that it would not cause the West any sudden harm and would also give the Western public some time to change its pro-Israel outlook. Faisal gave Yamani's plan his enthusiastic approval.

On October 17, all of the members of OAPEC (except the Iraqis, who walked out of the meeting) signed an agreement to cut oil production by 5 percent each month. To increase the measure's effectiveness, the oil ministers from four nations—Saudi Arabia, Kuwait, Algeria, and Qatar—agreed to cut the first month's output by 10 percent.

The Oil Embargo

On October 19, President Nixon formally asked Congress for $2.2 billion to finance the Pentagon's "air bridge" to Israel. Faisal had expected the United States to replace damaged Israeli weapons but warned Nixon that too much aid to Israel would make it impossible for Saudi Arabia to resist the anti-American tide of Arab public opinion. After months of similar Saudi warnings about the need for a more evenhanded U.S. policy in the Middle East, Faisal regarded Nixon's airlift, which was a gift to Israel, not a loan, as a personal insult.

The next day, October 20, 1973—the same day that President Nixon fired Attorney General Elliot Richardson in the Watergate crisis's "Saturday Night Massacre"—Saudi Arabia announced a total halt in oil exports to the United States. Algeria and Libya had already imposed an oil embargo, but to have Saudi Arabia join them meant that the United States would actually feel the shortfall. The Saudis ordered Aramco to reduce its production not only by the 10 percent announced on October 17, but by an additional 12 percent, the portion of Saudi oil that was shipped to the United States, a total cutback of 22 percent.

Kuwait, Qatar, and Bahrain joined the embargo the next day. The OAPEC countries also warned that any nation caught reshipping oil to the United States or Israel would be included in the embargo. Sea captains hauling Arab oil had to sign affidavits specifying the oil's destination and confirm the delivery of the petroleum by telex. As a precaution, the Arabs refused to send oil to ports such as Trinidad, Curaçao, and Singapore that routinely shipped oil to the United States.

The Netherlands, refusing to be intimidated by threats, sent oil to Israel and promptly became a target of the embargo. The Arabs also stopped shipping oil to Portugal because it had allowed the U.S. planes flying arms to Israel to refuel in the Azores.

Coming within four days of one another, the 70 percent price rise, the 10 percent production cutback, and the total oil embargo against the United States shocked the world. Journalists everywhere said that the Arabs had turned oil into a weapon, but Yamani disliked the use of this word. As he explained to biographer Jeffrey Robinson,

> Why do you refer to [the embargo] as the oil weapon? Why don't you think of it the way we did, as a political instrument? A weapon is used to hurt people. A political instrument is used to make a political point and hopefully effect political change.
>
> We did not believe in the use of oil as a weapon because we knew that this was not the best way for true cooperation with the West, notably the United States. But King Faisal saw American policies in the Middle East as being so very one-sided.[4]

On October 23, Israel and Egypt agreed to a cease-fire sponsored by the United Nations. Just hours later, however, Israel charged Egypt with violating the accord and resumed its counterattack. In less than a day, Israeli troops had surrounded Egypt's Third Army and reached the outskirts of the city of Suez. At this point, Soviet general secretary Leonid Brezhnev sent a note to President Nixon suggesting that the United States and the Soviet Union both send soldiers to the Middle East to keep the peace.

Secretary of State Henry Kissinger was deeply alarmed at the thought of Soviet troops stationed at the Suez Canal. Acting on behalf of President Nixon, whose time was consumed by the ever-escalating Watergate crisis, Kissinger put the entire U.S. military, including the nuclear forces, on a heightened state of alert, "Def Con 3," during the night of October 24–25. He also warned Israel against making any further advances, and the next day the Soviets withdrew their proposal for a joint force as Israel agreed to a second and permanent cease-fire. Syria accepted the cease-fire on October 29.

The nations of OAPEC, angry at Israel's victories and still hoping to influence events, met in Kuwait on November 4 and cut November's oil production by an attention-getting 25 percent instead of the 5 percent that had previously been agreed on. With oil at $5.12 a barrel, the OAPEC nations could still make more money than they did the previous year, even if they cut production by 40 percent.

Countries that the Arabs considered sympathetic to the Palestinian cause were assured of full supplies. These included all the Muslim nations, as well as India, Britain, France, and Spain. On November 6, representatives of the European Common Market issued a unanimous declaration on the need for Israel to withdraw from the land it had occupied in 1967. In response, OAPEC agreed to exempt Western Europe from the 5 percent cut in oil production that it planned for December.

Two days later, Secretary of State Kissinger took a break from his talks with the Egyptians and the Israelis to meet King Faisal. "Only WASPs can disembark here," Kissinger joked to reporters as his jet was about to land in Riyadh. Kissinger knew that Faisal did not trust Jews and later was not surprised when Faisal looked directly into his eyes and complained that "Jews are putting themselves into positions of authority around the world."

Kissinger told Faisal that the oil embargo was making Arabs unpopular in the United States and harder for him to be evenhanded. Faisal said that he could resume oil exports only when there was genuine progress toward an Israeli withdrawal, especially from Jerusalem, which Muslims consider their third-holiest city.

Two weeks later, on November 22, with no sign of the embargo ending, Kissinger told reporters that the United States would take economic "countermeasures" if the embargo continued "unreasonably or indefinitely." The next day, Yamani warned the United States and Europe that if they imposed sanctions, Saudi Arabia would cut its oil production by 80 percent.

The Arabs took a softer line on December 9 when OAPEC's oil ministers agreed to a Saudi proposal to link production increases to a timetable for Israeli withdrawal. This was a significant retreat from their insistence in October that the oil cutbacks would continue until Israel withdrew from all of the land it had captured in 1967. The Saudis also announced that they would postpone December's 5 percent cutback until January.

The Saudis eased their stance because their goal of making world opinion more sympathetic to the Arabs was succeeding. In November, the Europeans had called for Israeli withdrawals. In December, Japan urged Israel to acknowledge that it must eventually leave the occupied territories. It was the first time since World War II that the Japanese had broken ranks with the United States on a major foreign policy issue, but the Japanese had only fifty-nine days' worth of oil reserves and could not afford any more production cutbacks. On Christmas Eve, OAPEC increased its oil shipments to Japan to pre-embargo levels.

Reserves in Western Europe were not much bigger than they were in Japan, but Europe's situation was worse because the embargo against the Netherlands had disrupted oil deliveries throughout the region. The Dutch had exported almost 60 percent of the oil they refined to other European nations, and this oil was hard to replace because few ports besides Rotterdam were capable of handling supertankers. Even the countries that the Arabs considered friendly to the Palestinian cause, such as Britain and France, suffered oil shortfalls as high as 20 percent.

In December, most Western European nations had to adopt emergency measures that rationed heating oil, lowered speed limits, banned Sunday driving, and turned off neon lights.

In Britain, coal miners went on strike just when the nation was most short of fuel. To save energy, the prime minister, Edward Heath, put the nation on a three-day workweek and rotated blackouts at various times of the day and night. People rushed to buy candles and lanterns. Television stations ran ads for condoms, then stopped broadcasting at midnight. Faisal soon felt that the British had endured enough and began to send Britain an extra two hundred thousand barrels of oil a day to help restore it to its pre-embargo level of fuel consumption.

In the United States, the Nixon administration was afraid that there would not be enough heating oil for homes in the winter. To ensure an adequate supply, the government imposed price controls. Although the controls encouraged wholesalers to buy more heating oil, they also discouraged refiners from importing crude oil (which is refined into gasoline) because the price of oil had risen above the government's permitted sale price. For several weeks, there was no incentive for U.S. refiners to import oil.

By December on the East Coast, where imported oil was most common, a number of gas stations closed down. Signs said, "Sorry, No Gas." Adding to the winter's gloom, advertisers saved energy by turning off the neon lights in New York City's Times Square.

In the middle of this shortage, the major oil companies announced record profits. Exxon earned $2.45 billion in 1973, a 57 percent increase over the year before. Texaco's profits also went up 57 percent, Gulf's rose 79 percent, and Shell's 1973 profits were triple those of 1972. The oil companies were clearly benefiting from OPEC's higher prices.

The gasoline shortage grew worse in January and February 1974, as many people had to drive for miles to find gas stations that were open and had to wait on line for more than an hour when they did. To conserve gasoline, Congress reduced the speed limit on interstate highways to fifty-five miles per hour, and the Nixon administration ordered many gas stations to close on Sundays to discourage weekend driving.

America's shortage of gasoline finally ended when the Federal Energy Office, which had opposed price regulation in the first place, exempted imported oil from price controls on February 28. Things quickly returned to normal because the United States is much less dependent on Arab oil than Europe is, and because non-Arab oil exporters such as Iran, Nigeria, and Indonesia had negated much of the Arab embargo's impact when they increased their own oil production to make more money.

Still, the world scrambled for non-Arab petroleum. At an auction in Iran on December 16, several panic-stricken small U.S. oil companies offered the Iranians an astonishing $17.34 a barrel. In a time of shortage, it was not nearly as hard for an oil company to pass higher prices on to consumers as it would have been to have no oil to sell.

A Fourfold Price Increase

When the OPEC nations met in Tehran on December 22 and 23, the shah of Iran wanted to raise the price of oil to $14 a barrel, just a few dollars below the recent auction price. By contrast, Yamani, the Saudi oil minister, worried that a $14 price would throw the world's economy into a tailspin and proposed a price of $7.50 a barrel instead, which was still 46 percent more than the current price.

The two men compromised on a price of $11.65 a barrel, which ensured each nation a profit of $7 a barrel. It was more than double the previous price of $5.12 a barrel and almost four times higher than the $3.01 a barrel that had been the price of oil only ten weeks earlier. The speed and the size of the price rise shocked the world, but the OPEC nations believed that oil had long been an underpriced commodity, and that they were simply making up for lost time and revenue.

King Faisal, however, was worried about the damage the new price would do to the world's economy, and when Yamani returned home, the king criticized him for not insisting on a smaller increase. Yet it was Faisal's embargo that had driven the price of oil so high, and if Yamani had not compromised with Iran, OPEC might well have broken up. Faisal was lucky that his instinctive caution did not stop a once-in-a-lifetime opportunity for a lasting fourfold price increase.

The day after the OPEC session ended, the Arab oil ministers flew to Kuwait for a meeting of their own. The magnitude of the price increase that they had just agreed to in Tehran made them wary about confronting the West with further production cutbacks. The ministers also wanted to ease the energy crisis in Europe because the Europeans had already called for Israel to withdraw from the occupied territories.

The OAPEC ministers unanimously voted not only to cancel the 5 percent cutback scheduled for January 1974, but also to *increase* the level of oil production by an eighth, so that January's production would be only 15 percent less than September's. The rise in production was consistent with Faisal and Yamani's conception of the oil cutbacks as a flexible political tool that could be strengthened to apply pressure and relaxed to reward cooperation. The OAPEC ministers also voted to continue their total embargo against the United States and the Netherlands, a weapon far more blunt than the cutbacks.

The quadrupling of the price of oil in the fourth quarter of 1973 was the greatest challenge to the global economy since the Great Depression of the 1930s. The world paid the thirteen OPEC nations $66 billion more for oil in 1974 than in 1973, or $230 billion in today's money. The extra expense represented more than half of a normal year's economic growth; it was the biggest and fastest transfer of wealth in history.

The average annual rate of growth for industrial economies fell from 5 percent during the years just before 1973 to 2.5 percent during the years afterward. In Japan, the "oil shocku" lowered growth from 9 percent in 1973 to zero in 1974, while inflation rose from 1 percent to 24 percent. Italy also endured 24 percent inflation in 1974, and Britain, 18 percent.

Americans suffered 12 percent inflation in 1974, and almost a third of this increase was caused by the higher oil prices. Stock prices fell as the Dow Jones Industrial Average plunged to an anemic 550. Economists called the combination of stagnant growth and high inflation "stagflation," and it lingered until 1982. The U.S. Labor Department estimated that five hundred thousand Americans lost their jobs due to the Arab oil embargo, because of higher energy costs and because of the sudden decline in demand for large, gas-guzzling U.S. automobiles. Forty percent of these layoffs occurred in Michigan, the state hardest hit by the new recession.

Yet it was still cheaper to import oil than to find new oil in the United States. U.S. production fell even as geologists drilled deeper wells every year, and tar sands, shale oil, coal gas, and liquefied coal would not be economical unless the price of oil doubled yet again.

The nations hurt most by the price increases were the under-developed countries of Asia, Africa, and South America that had no oil of their own. They needed petroleum not only for their cars and trucks, but also to make fertilizer for their farmers. In 1970, these nations spent 1.2 percent of their gross domestic product for oil. Now it cost them 4.4 percent, three and a half times as much, which slowed down their economic growth considerably.

To help poor countries buy more oil, Saudi Arabia lent $1 billion to the International Monetary Fund and $750 million to the World Bank. It could afford the loans. The nation's oil revenues, which had already tripled between 1970 and 1973, quintupled again in 1974 as the country received a staggering windfall of almost $25 billion.

Even after increasing their budget for 1974 and giving hundreds of millions of dollars in military aid to Egypt, Syria, and Jordan, the Saudis still had a surplus at the end of the year of $6.75 billion, or $23 billion in current money.

Unlike the Kuwaitis, who liked to buy stock in Western corporations (they own, for example, about 10 percent of British Petroleum and 5 percent of Daimler-Chrysler), Faisal preferred to invest the country's surplus in U.S. Treasury bonds and short-term notes in pounds, yen, and deutsche marks. Saudi Arabia has ten times as many people as Kuwait does, and it needed to build ten times as many roads, schools, hospitals, and factories. Faisal wanted to start new development projects as soon as the economy could absorb the extra money, and he therefore kept the kingdom's surplus as liquid as possible.

The oil embargo gave Faisal enormous prestige. Muslims everywhere loved to watch the industrial nations grovel for oil. When Yamani traveled to Japan in January 1974, Emperor Hirohito invited him to the Imperial Palace, even though Yamani was a mere cabinet minister.

In February, the Islamic Conference held its second summit in Lahore, Pakistan. Leaders from almost forty countries attended, and the conference was televised throughout the Muslim world. During prayers, viewers could see that while the eyes of dictators such as Libya's Qaddafi and Syria's Assad darted about the hall even when they were kneeling, Faisal prayed with fervor for minutes at a time.

The Muslim nations also began to act as a diplomatic bloc. At their insistence, the United Nations gave observer status to the Palestine Liberation Organization, which allowed it to participate in UN debates.

The End of the Embargo

In January 1974, Secretary of State Henry Kissinger persuaded the Israelis to begin to withdraw twenty miles east of the Suez Canal. In February, he promised Faisal that the United States would sell the kingdom new jets, tanks, and ships that were much more sophisticated than those it had sold in the past.

Faisal was impressed with the U.S. offer of better arms, but it was not enough to end the oil embargo. On February 13, he met in Algiers with the presidents of Syria and Algeria, and together they announced that the embargo would continue until there was progress toward an Israeli withdrawal from Syrian land as well.

This happened on February 27, when Kissinger prodded Syria and Israel to start negotiating a slight Israeli pullback. Three weeks later, on March 18, 1974, the OAPEC ministers voted to suspend their oil embargo against the United States for two and a half months, until June 1, at which time they would decide whether or not to reimpose the cutoff.

Syria and Israel signed a disengagement agreement just in time, on May 31. Three days later, the OAPEC nations lifted their embargo against the United States permanently. They did the same for the Netherlands in July.

The Arab oil embargo did not achieve its stated aim. Israel was still in control of Jerusalem, the West Bank, the Sinai peninsula, and the Golan Heights. But Faisal understood that while the embargo had encouraged Europe and Asia to pressure Israel to withdraw from its post-1967 land, it had done nothing to reduce Israel's widespread support among the American people. Faisal ended the embargo as soon as Arab public opinion would allow it—in other words, as soon as the Israelis and the Syrians signed an agreement.

The embargo did not affect the outcome of the Yom Kippur War, but it had a deep influence on postwar diplomacy. The United States was no longer content merely to safeguard Israel; it also wanted a durable peace in the region. For the Arabs, this alone was a great improvement over 1967.

The embargo also had the unintended consequence of quadrupling the price of oil, which instantly transformed Saudi Arabia into a major economic power. During the next several years, the United States acknowledged the country's new importance by selling the kingdom almost as many advanced weapons as it sold to Iran and Israel.

As soon as the oil shortage ended, Americans bought big cars again, despite the fact that gasoline was 40 percent more expensive than it had been the year before. For the OPEC nations, the Americans' lack of any real attempt at conservation confirmed their belief that the price of oil had been far too low during the 1960s.

To keep Saudi oil flowing, the United States was determined to give the kingdom whatever it wanted, and what it wanted was a stronger military. During the 1974–1975 fiscal year, Saudi Arabia bought $2 billion worth of arms from the United States, including thirty F-5E fighter-bombers, air defense missiles to protect Mecca and Medina, base facilities for its fledgling navy, and dozens of patrol boats, escort ships, and minesweepers.

The Saudis hired 2,000 British instructors and technicians and paid France $900 million for 38 Mirage fighter-bombers, 250 tanks, 500 infantry carriers, and almost 1,000 antiaircraft guns and surface-to-air missiles. The Saudis also arranged a special shipment to France of 200,000 barrels of oil a day, bypassing the major oil companies.

On June 14, President Nixon flew to Saudi Arabia during his tour of the Middle East and met King Faisal briefly. Nixon wrote later that Faisal looked older than his sixty-nine years and saw Zionist conspiracies everywhere, even among the Palestinian terrorists.

Faisal gave a great banquet for Nixon and his advisers, not realizing that they were exhausted from so much traveling. After coffee, the president was about to get up and leave when Faisal reached out and grabbed an apple. Nixon and his tired advisers hid their impatience as Faisal slowly cut the fruit, one slice at a time. As was true in his youth, the king took precisely seven minutes to eat his apple.

A Modern Gold Rush

With oil four times more costly than before, Saudi Arabia was suddenly receiving $70 million ($230 million in today's money) *every day*. In uniform dollars, the kingdom received more money *every two hours* than it earned during the entire 1910s.

Hustlers hoping to get rich quick swarmed to Riyadh and Jeddah. Some had plans to build new factories. Others sold carpets, jewelry, or music cassettes or bought real estate in an overheated market where land prices rose daily. Car imports tripled, and ships had to wait in line for months to unload their cargo at the clogged ports of Jeddah and Jubail. Construction contractors with deadlines to meet hired helicopters to carry bags of cement, twenty at a time, from ship to building site.

Military contracts during the oil boom were riddled with commissions. By the end of 1975, Adnan Khashoggi had used his friendship with Prince Sultan, the kingdom's minister of defense, to earn $106 million in agent's fees from the Lockheed Corporation and another $55 million from European defense contractors.

Similarly, the Raytheon Company was ready to pay $75 million to Prince Abdallah al-Faisal, Faisal's son by his first wife, to secure a billion-dollar contract for military training. When Faisal learned that his son was Raytheon's agent, however, he immediately awarded the contract to the Vinnell Corporation instead. Soon, Vinnell sent a thousand Vietnam veterans to the kingdom to train soldiers in the National Guard.

Faisal was as worried by the flood of money pouring into his kingdom in the 1970s as Caliph Umar had been by the gold and the silver coming into Medina in the 630s. Like Umar, Faisal was afraid that easy money would corrode his people's virtue, but while Umar once shed tears when more gold arrived on camelback, Faisal became melancholy. Always reluctant to delegate responsibility, the king arrived at his office earlier in the morning, worked later in the evening, and took fewer weekends off than he did before. To his oldest son, he confessed, "I'm thinking of work all the time. I cannot relax. I can no longer feel life itself. I tell you, Abdallah, I can no longer tell the difference between what is cold and what is hot."[5]

Raising Taxes, Cutting Production

One of the many benefits of the kingdom's enormous increase in oil royalties was that a twenty-five-year-old border dispute between Saudi Arabia and Abu Dhabi (which joined the United Arab Emirates in 1971) over an oil field near the Buraimi oasis suddenly did not matter anymore. Both nations were earning more money than they could absorb and therefore were willing to compromise in July 1974. The UAE got the oil field, but in return it gave Saudi Arabia some coastline south of Qatar.

Earlier in 1974, Qatar and Kuwait had each bought 60 percent of their local oil companies, even though the 1972 Participation Agreement said that the oil companies would not sell a 51 percent majority stake to the OPEC nations until 1983. After the oil embargo, however, the OPEC nations wanted majority ownership sooner.

Once Qatar and Kuwait set the precedent for 60 percent ownership, Faisal found it impossible to resist. He ordered Exxon, Chevron, Texaco, and Mobil to sell the kingdom another 35 percent of Aramco so that Saudi Arabia could own 60 percent of the oil company.

Faisal renamed the company Saudi Aramco and told the four U.S. oil giants that he wanted to buy the remaining 40 percent of the company by 1980. He assured the four companies that the kingdom would continue to sell them large quantities of Saudi oil at a preferential rate below the market price.

In September, Faisal cut the kingdom's oil production to maintain the high price. Faisal was willing to lower the price of oil to help the world's economy, but he preferred that OPEC make this decision collectively. He did not want to antagonize other Arab leaders by acting unilaterally just before a summit of the Arab nations in Rabat, Morocco.

At the summit, which began on October 26, Arab leaders unanimously recognized the Palestine Liberation Organization (PLO) as the sole representative of the Palestinian people, ending Jordan's claim to the West Bank. In addition, the three nations with the most oil money, Saudi Arabia, Kuwait, and the United Arab Emirates, pledged a massive aid package for the nations bordering Israel. Over the next three years, they gave a total of $2.5 billion to Egypt, Syria, and the PLO. Faisal urged the PLO's leader, Yasir Arafat, to accept Israel's right to exist within its pre-1967 borders. He also sent $400 million to South Yemen in what proved to be a successful effort to get the Marxist state to reduce its ties to the Soviet Union.

Two weeks later, Yamani and the oil ministers of Qatar and the UAE cut the enormous profit margin that the oil companies had enjoyed in 1974 and increased their own profits instead. They raised their royalty rate from 12.5 percent to 20 percent, and their tax on oil company revenues from 55 percent to 85 percent. This reduced the profit that an oil company made on a barrel of oil from $3.70 to 78 cents, but this was still much higher than the 47 cents per barrel that oil companies had earned before the oil embargo.

The rest of OPEC adopted the new tax and royalty rates at a meeting on December 13 in Vienna. Because of the extra income these new levies generated, the oil ministers reduced the price of oil slightly, from $11.65 a barrel to $10.12. The OPEC nations felt that a 13 percent cut in the price of oil was more than enough because with annual inflation at 20 percent, the true price of oil had already fallen considerably. But after the fourfold price increase at the end of 1973, the 13 percent reduction was a much smaller cut than hard-pressed businessmen around the world had hoped for.

In an interview in *Business Week* in January 1975, Secretary of State Kissinger warned OPEC that the United States could not rule out the use of military force if it faced an "actual strangulation of the industrialized world." Although the remark angered the Arabs, America's new president, Gerald Ford, supported Kissinger and added that force would be used only as a last resort. During the same week as Ford and Kissinger's tough talk, however, the United States sold Saudi Arabia an additional sixty F-5E fighter jets for $750 million.

Because of the global recession, the world's demand for oil fell 12 percent in 1975. This would have created a glut and a steep price drop were it not for the fact that Saudi Arabia reduced its production that year by 40 percent, a reduction much larger than Iran's 19 percent cutback or Venezuela's 18 percent. With a population of only seven million people, Saudi Arabia could cut its revenues in half and still have more money than it needed. This gave the Saudis the freedom to pump as much or as little oil as they wished, and it made more sense to reduce production and enjoy a higher price per barrel than to increase production and make money from volume instead.

Allah's Will

At the end of 1974, *Time* magazine chose Faisal as its "Man of the Year." Reporters described him as "dour, ascetic, shrewd," and "deeply wrinkled."

Within days of *Time*'s cover story, Faisal had two dreams that filled him with foreboding. In the first, his grandmother told him that it was time for him to meet his mother, who had died when he was seven. In the second dream, his grandfather, his father, and his oldest brother, Turki (who died in 1919), forced him into a car and drove away. Faisal revealed his dreams to an aunt, then told her that he did not think he would live out the year.

Despite his two dreams, Faisal retained a lifelong contempt for security precautions. He believed that Allah determines the exact second when a man or a woman will die and thus felt that a small number of bodyguards was more than enough.

On March 25, 1975, Faisal arrived at work at 10:25 a.m. to meet Kuwait's new oil minister, Abdul Qasimi, who was waiting in a side room next to Faisal's office. Also in the room were Yamani and a young prince who wanted to see his uncle. When the door to the king's office opened at 10:32, the junior prince walked in with the two oil ministers, pulled a .38 pistol from under his robe, and fired six shots.

The first three bullets struck Faisal. The next three bullets hit the ceiling, for by this time a bodyguard had grabbed the shooter's hand. More guards arrived. Some of them pushed the prince onto a sofa, while others carried the king to an ambulance. It raced to Riyadh's Central Hospital.

Doctors gave Faisal a heart massage and a blood transfusion but could not save him. The first bullet had pierced Faisal's throat and ripped open his jugular vein. It was small consolation that the other two bullets did less damage, shattering an ear and grazing a temple.

At 2:12 p.m., a newscaster on Radio Riyadh held his tears back long enough to tell the nation that King Faisal had died, then broke down sobbing. An hour later, at 3:20 p.m., the station made a second announcement. The five most senior princes— Muhammad, Nasir, Saad, and Fahad, who were younger brothers of Faisal, and Abdullah ibn Abdul Rahman, the oldest surviving brother of Abdul Aziz—with the approval of the nation's top clerics, had chosen Khalid, Faisal's jovial younger brother who had accompanied him on many trips abroad, to be the nation's new king, and Fahad to be crown prince.

In the evening, the sons and the brothers of Abdul Aziz, the Saudi state's founder, swore an oath: "I give my loyalty to you, Khalid, in the name of God and in the name of His Prophet." Then the founder's nephews and grandsons swore the same oath. The next morning Khalid received this oath of loyalty from cabinet ministers, tribal chiefs, and the patriarchs of major families, and during the next few weeks, from large crowds in big cities.

Faisal's assassin was a twenty-seven-year-old nephew, Prince Faysal ibn Musaid. He was the younger brother of Khalid ibn Musaid, the Muslim fanatic who had died in a gun battle with King Faisal's police force in 1965 after trying to stop the nation's first television station from broadcasting "graven images." Apparently, the prince had nursed a decade-long desire to avenge the death of his older brother.

Prince Faysal had studied briefly at San Francisco State University and Berkeley before transferring to the University of Colorado at Boulder, where he was arrested in 1970 for conspiracy to sell LSD. King Faisal refused to interfere with the criminal proceedings against his nephew, but the U.S. State Department asked the Colorado judge to be lenient, and the judge gave the young man a suspended sentence. When the prince returned home to Saudi Arabia in 1971, King Faisal refused to let him leave the country again, and it is possible that this travel ban was an additional motive for the assassination.

King Faisal was buried the day after he died in an unmarked grave on the outskirts of Riyadh, close to the grave of his father. At a mosque nearby, heads of state from almost every Muslim nation attended his funeral. Surrounding the mosque were more than a hundred thousand grief-stricken Saudis, including women wearing white, the Muslim color of mourning. Many women were particularly saddened by Faisal's death because he had championed the cause of female education.

During the next two months, King Khalid personally interrogated the assassin several times and was finally satisfied that no foreigners had helped him. Doctors who questioned the prince decided that he was sane and therefore eligible for execution.

On June 18, in a plaza in front of the Ministry of Justice in Riyadh, twenty thousand people watched as the blindfolded prince knelt and placed his head on a chopping block. The executioner lifted his huge sword high and sliced through Faysal's neck in one swift stroke. Then he calmly picked up the severed head and placed it on top of a long pike, where it was displayed for fifteen minutes before medics removed the prince's head and body for a quick burial.

Faisal's Legacy

Abdul Aziz conquered and unified Saudi Arabia, but it was his son Faisal who turned it into a modern state. When Faisal first took power from his brother Saud in 1958, the country was despised by its neighbors and almost bankrupt. Seventeen years later, when Faisal died, the kingdom enjoyed unparalleled wealth and an influence that Arabs had not known for centuries.

As a young man, Faisal traveled to Europe and realized immediately that the kingdom needed to modernize, whether his people liked it or not. But as a religious man, he was determined to preserve Muslim values. As king, he let the clergy run the nation's schools and law courts, but he never allowed them to obstruct economic development, and he insisted that women be educated.

Faisal's cautious approach to modernization reflected centrist Saudi opinion. He won the respect of city dwellers and Bedouin, progressives and fundamentalists, businessmen and the poor.

"Revolutions can come from thrones as well as from conspirator's cellars," the king once said. Because oil royalties in 1975 were forty-five times higher in real purchasing power than they had been in 1958, Faisal could afford to build highways, ports, and power stations and give his people cradle-to-grave security: free schools and medical care, easy loans for homes and farm equipment, and heavily subsidized food and utilities.

Faisal saw anyone who wanted to speak to him, even illiterate Bedouin, but he was no democrat. He jailed dissidents, put his brothers in charge of the police and the military, and never fulfilled his 1962 promise of constitutional reform. Most Saudis, however, were too busy making money to care.

Faisal raised and lowered his kingdom's oil production adeptly enough to remain an ally of the United States, while simultaneously helping Egypt, Syria, and Jordan in their fight against Israel. Writing checks for hundreds of millions of dollars so that his Arab neighbors could buy more weapons and build more schools and mosques, he succeeded in turning the Arabs away from socialism and back to Islam.

Unlike the weaker kings who succeeded him, Faisal did not have to consult his brothers before making important decisions, although he usually did. His power was firm. No king would ever rule Saudi Arabia so forcefully again.

PART FIVE

MODERN SAUDI ARABIA
(1975–2001)

THE HISTORY OF SAUDI ARABIA in the first half of the twentieth century centers on one man, Abdul Aziz, the founder of the kingdom. Saudi history in the third quarter of the century also focuses on one man: Faisal, the monarch who turned the kingdom into a modern state. But in the century's final quarter, no single individual dominated the nation. Saudi Arabia had become too rich and too populous to be mastered by just one man again.

Three monarchs ruled Saudi Arabia during this period: Khalid (1975–1982), a genial caretaker; Fahad (1982–1996), a pro-Western but often indecisive king who let serious problems fester; and Abdullah (1996–present), a hardworking prince who became the kingdom's de facto ruler when Fahad suffered a second stroke in 1996, but who lacked full power while Fahad lingered.

The reigns of Khalid and Fahad and the regency of Abdullah include the oil boom and bust of the 1980s, the Persian Gulf War, the rise of militant fundamentalism in the 1990s, and the first of the kingdom's many economic reforms in the 2000s.

15

The Boom Years of King Khalid
(1975–1982)

DURING KHALID'S SEVEN YEARS AS KING, Saudi Arabia became one of the richest nations in the world. By 1981, Khalid's last full year as monarch, the kingdom's income soared to $300 million *a day*. There was enough money for everything: palaces for the royal family; free schools and medical care for the people; and new highways, seaports, refineries, and power plants for the economy. Although Khalid had virtually unlimited wealth at his disposal, he was not a strong monarch as Faisal had been. Warm, cheerful, and adored by his brothers and sisters, Khalid was more interested in hunting than in government. While not quite a figurehead, he delegated most of his authority to his younger brothers.

Khalid was tall, yet unimposing despite his mustache and goatee. Born in 1912, he spent his childhood memorizing the Quran and learning the ways of the desert. At seventeen, he fought Ikhwan warriors during the kingdom's brief civil war, and at twenty-two, he commanded troops in Yemen. In the 1930s, Khalid served as the Hejaz region's acting viceroy when Faisal was abroad or in Riyadh, and in the 1940s, he accompanied Faisal on a number of trips to the United States and Britain.

Khalid was a key backer of Faisal when Saud was king in the 1950s, and his popularity with desert tribesmen undercut Saud's main power base. In 1962, Faisal appointed Khalid as his deputy prime minister, and three years later, when Faisal was king, he chose Khalid to be crown prince. As the kingdom's second in command, Khalid presided over cabinet meetings and ceremonial functions that Faisal was either too busy or too far away to attend.

By all accounts, Khalid was kind, attentive, and devout. One American who knew him described him as "grandfatherly." Within the family he was an ideal mediator, while at weekly audiences he listened patiently to illiterate Bedouin.

Forming a New Government

Four days after Khalid became king at sixty-three on March 25, 1975, he chose a younger brother, Fahad, to be crown prince, and another brother, Abdullah (the current king), to be second deputy prime minister, second in line to the throne. To make these appointments possible, two older brothers, Nasir and Saad, publicly renounced their claims to the throne. Prince Nasir, the son of a Moroccan concubine, had not held a government position since 1947 and had supported King Saud in his power struggle against Faisal. Prince Saad had never held office at all.

In his first month as king, Khalid gave soldiers a raise, declared an amnesty for political prisoners, and relaxed censorship to allow criticism of his government's administration (but not of the royal family or its right to rule). He also appointed Faisal's son Saud as minister of state for foreign affairs. Saud was the first grandson of Abdul Aziz to join the cabinet and still serves as foreign minister today. Together, Saud and his father have been in charge of the kingdom's foreign affairs since 1930—three-quarters of a century.

Khalid himself had little interest in running the government. What he loved most was falconry. For weeks at a time, Khalid rode in the desert with tribesmen and admired his birds of prey as they soared to great heights and then suddenly swooped down on a small, unlucky animal. He loved the company of other hunters; he drank camel's milk with them in the morning and ate roasted meat with them in the evening.

In May, Khalid issued a royal decree that made Crown Prince Fahad responsible for the day-to-day management of the government. Fahad had been in charge of education under King Saud and of the police under King Faisal. He was the oldest of the seven sons of Abdul Aziz's favorite wife, Hassa bint Ahmad al-Sudairi.

The sons, commonly called "the Sudairi Seven," are the most powerful branch of the al-Saud family. Besides Fahad, they include Sultan, the minister of defense; Nayef, the minister of the interior (police); and Salman, the governor of Riyadh.

Fahad liked to have university graduates in the government, so in October he and Khalid appointed eighteen well-educated commoners to cabinet posts. Only eight princes were left among the twenty-six members of the new cabinet, although three men, the ministers of justice, higher education, and agriculture, were descendants of ibn Abdul Wahhab.

Khalid continued to make important decisions, especially if they affected a ministry that was not run by a Sudairi. But after he had heart surgery in Cleveland, Ohio, in October 1978 and then suffered a minor heart attack in February 1980, Fahad became the de facto ruler of the kingdom. When Khalid returned home after his operation in 1978, he had his private Boeing 747 equipped with sophisticated heart-monitoring devices that instantly sent data by satellite to his surgeons in Cleveland.

1975–1980: The Oil Boom Continues

In 1975, private contractors started work on $25 million worth of new projects a day ($110 million in current money). By 1979, this amount had *quadrupled*. They built roads, bridges, hospitals, government offices, universities, soccer stadiums, telephone exchanges, military bases, power plants, water desalination plants, more than fifteen hundred elementary schools, and thousands of high-rise apartments. The apartments were shoddily but quickly built for the more than one hundred thousand rural Saudis who were moving into cities every year. Often, entire extended families moved together into the same apartment complex, and the building would be named for the family living in it.

In 1965, the country was still two-thirds rural. By 1980, the kingdom was two-thirds urban. The nomadic Bedouin, who once made up three-fifths of the kingdom, were now just a little more than 5 percent of the population. For the Bedouin in cities, money replaced camels as the source of status, but honor came only when a man was generous to his poorer relatives.

Riyadh became a center of business, as well as government, and grew from a town of thirty thousand in 1945 to a metropolis of almost one million in 1980. A nationwide real estate boom turned hundreds of contractors and speculators into multimillionaires and later inspired the saying, "If you didn't become rich during the days of King Khalid, you will never be rich."

One of the lures of city life was that schools and medical care were free; gasoline, utilities, and food (including lamb, rice, milk, and sugar) were subsidized; government loans for housing charged no interest; and income, sales, and property taxes were nonexistent. There was also television at night. Although the government brought electric power to another four million of its citizens in the late 1970s, many remote oases still did not have televisions, refrigerators, or other conveniences.

Still, modernization was coming to rural areas, too. For the tens of thousands of families that herded sheep for a living, Datsun pickup trucks were faster and cheaper to ride than camels. True, a new Datsun cost four times more than a new camel, but with gasoline only twelve cents a gallon, it was cheaper and easier to fill a tank once a week than to feed a camel every day. The government also built high schools, clinics, power stations, and water-treatment plants in small towns and even in large villages.

Saudi imports of cars, television sets, cosmetics, food, bathroom fixtures, and countless other foreign products quadrupled between 1974 and 1977, and there were not enough docks to unload the ships in port. By 1976, two hundred ships in Jeddah and Dammam were waiting up to eight months to unload their cargo. The delays added 40 percent to the cost of imports and helped to sustain an inflation rate that was also nearly 40 percent. Adding to the cost of living were rising prices in the West and an exploding bureaucracy at home. The size of the government doubled between 1972 and 1980, as princes rewarded their tribal allies by putting another 150,000 people on the payroll. Eighty percent of these new bureaucrats did not have a high school education but merely made government more cumbersome.

With inflation rampant around the world, Iran wanted to raise oil prices again at an OPEC meeting in Doha, Qatar, in December 1976. But the Saudis and the United Arab Emirates did not want to deepen the global recession or encourage the West to look for alternative sources of fuel and therefore would agree only to a 5 percent price increase. Since inflation in most countries was still well over 10 percent a year, a price increase of just 5 percent amounted to a *decrease* in the true, inflation-adjusted price of oil of about 25 percent since the end of 1973. The rest of OPEC therefore insisted on a 10 percent increase, and for the first six months of 1977, there were two prices for oil, a world price and a slightly lower Saudi price.

By selling cheaper oil, the Saudis expanded their share of exports and showed the other OPEC nations that they could not defy the Saudis on issues of pricing. The Saudis and the United Arab Emirates did not press the matter, however, and raised their price another 5 percent in July 1977 to match OPEC's higher price. In return, the other OPEC nations agreed to a one-year price freeze at a meeting in Caracas in December 1977.

Unlike populous Iran, Saudi Arabia didn't need higher oil prices. The kingdom was already receiving far more revenue than it could absorb. To implement its second five-year plan from 1975 to 1980, the Saudi government spent a staggering $200 billion. Much of this money was devoted to easing the economy's bottlenecks. On the Persian Gulf, the government enlarged the existing port at Dammam and built a new port at Jubail, along with a steel mill, an aluminum mill, and a massive petrochemical complex. On the Red Sea, the government built new docks at Jeddah and another port and a giant petrochemical complex at Yanbu. The government also built more airports, highways, and oil pipelines.

Most of these structures were built by Western companies, with a Saudi prince or a prince's close friend often collecting a 5 percent commission for helping to close the deal. The Saudi people expect a prince to make money in business but resent it if he becomes too greedy. In 1977, in deference to this feeling, Khalid prohibited any Saudi from representing more than ten foreign companies. The effect of this order was to spread commissions around to many more princes and businessmen than before.

The physical work at the construction sites was also done by foreigners, as many Saudis considered manual labor beneath them. Until recently, a Saudi would drive a truck but not repair one or would own a shop but not clean it. Many Saudis feel entitled to their wealth, regarding it as a reward from God for being good Muslims, and they feel no sense of inferiority or concern that almost every item of technology that they use has to be imported. As Robert Lacey, the author of *The Kingdom*, has noted, "Does a duke feel inferior to his tailor because he cannot make a pair of trousers?"

In 1975, one-third of the kingdom's workers were foreign. By 1980, more than two million foreigners worked in Saudi Arabia, amounting to more than 60 percent of the workforce. Yemenis, Pakistanis, Bangladeshis, and Sri Lankans swept floors and did the hardest construction, dock, and factory work; Egyptians and Palestinians worked as teachers and civil servants; Filipino and Pakistani men ran grocery stores and repaired cars; and Sri Lankan and Filipina women cleaned houses and worked as nannies. In the 1970s, the number of South Asian and East Asian workers grew, while the number of Arab expatriates declined, because the Asians were cheaper to hire than Arabs and were much less dangerous politically. There were also more than a hundred thousand Westerners working as technicians, administrators, and teachers.

Unlike U.S. immigrants, foreigners in Saudi Arabia cannot become citizens or buy land, nor can their children, even if they are born and raised in the kingdom. What motivates foreigners to come to Saudi Arabia and work long hours is the chance to earn wages up to four times higher than they can earn in their native countries, assuming that they had a job in those countries at all. A foreigner who works several years in the kingdom can often support his or her family back home and still have enough money left to buy an air conditioner, a refrigerator, a color television set, a videocassette player, a sewing machine, and some jewelry. Once a worker returns home, he also usually buys something that will generate an income, such as a truck or a few acres of land. If he is a young man, this makes him attractive to young women.

Despite all the money that Saudi Arabia spent on palaces, welfare, weapons, and economic development in the mid-1970s, there was still enough money left to buy $133 billion worth of assets abroad, according to a 1978 report that the kingdom filed with the International Monetary Fund. Saudis invested about 60 percent of this money in the United States, making the kingdom the largest foreign investor in U.S. banks, treasury bonds, and real estate. By the end of 1981, the country's foreign assets had climbed to well over $150 billion, allowing it to earn more than $1 billion a month in interest and rent.

In 1978, the U.S. Congress approved President Jimmy Carter's request to sell Saudi Arabia sixty F-15 fighter jets over a five-year period. The sale was bitterly opposed by pro-Israeli congressmen but finally passed after the Saudis agreed not to deploy any of the jets at air force bases near Israel.

The Carter administration had hoped that the sale of the jets would encourage the Saudis to support the peace treaty that Israel and Egypt signed in March 1979, following the accord reached by Prime Minister Menachem Begin and President Anwar Sadat at Camp David, Maryland, in September 1978. Under this treaty, Israel agreed to return the Sinai peninsula to Egypt in return for Egypt's recognition of Israel's right to exist and establishment of diplomatic relations. Most Arabs saw Egypt's separate peace with Israel as a betrayal of the Palestinians; public opinion against the Camp David Accords was far too strong for the Saudi government to resist. Saudi Arabia joined fifteen other Arab nations in breaking diplomatic relations with Egypt and boycotting its products.

Crown Prince Fahad had approved of the peace treaty and wanted only minimal sanctions against Egypt, but he was overruled by King Khalid and Prince Abdullah, who wanted to join the Arab boycott of Egypt. After this defeat, Fahad took an extended vacation at his seaside palace in Marbella, Spain, where he also received treatment for ulcers and diabetes. He may have hoped that Khalid would grow tired of running the government and be more cautious about overruling him in the future. Instead, Khalid let Abdullah run the nation's cabinet meetings, which greatly solidified Abdullah's position as second in line to the throne. Finally, after two months, Fahad flew home to Riyadh and resumed running the government.

The Death of a Princess

The most whispered-about scandal of the 1970s involved an adulterous love affair between Mishaal bint Fahd al-Saud, a young princess, and Khalid Muhallal, the nephew of Saudi Arabia's ambassador to Lebanon. Mishaal was unhappily married to an older cousin and had little to do during the day but watch tapes of romantic American movies. One day she met young Khalid at a boutique, and apparently it was love at first sight. No one knows how they arranged to spend time together, but by July 1977, a servant who knew about their encounters feared for her own safety and demanded that the princess stop seeing the young man.

Instead, Mishaal faked her own drowning by leaving some clothes on the shore of the Red Sea. Then, after spending several days with Khalid in a seaside hotel, she dressed as a man, took a taxi to Jeddah's airport, and tried to leave the country with her lover. Mishaal's grandfather, Prince Muhammad, did not believe that she had drowned and alerted customs officials throughout the kingdom to watch for her. Police arrested Mishaal and Khalid at the airport, and under tribal law, Muhammad demanded a public execution to redeem his family's honor.

King Khalid, fearing publicity, suggested that Muhammad show mercy to the young couple, but Prince Muhammad (who had renounced his claim to the throne in 1965 so that his younger brother

Khalid could be next in line to Faisal) was known for his explosive temper and insisted that the adulterers die.

Two days after their arrest, Princess Mishaal and her lover were executed in a parking lot in Jeddah. Mishaal was blindfolded and made to kneel, then shot by a firing squad of six men. Young Khalid was beheaded by a relative, possibly Mishaal's husband. The relative was not a skilled swordsman and took five swipes before he finally cut off the young man's head. Later, when Muhammad was asked whether the two deaths were necessary, he said, "It was enough for me that they were in the same room together."

Unfortunately for the Saudis, who cherish their privacy, a British expatriate took pictures of the executions with a small camera hidden inside a pack of cigarettes. Later, a British television network broadcast a documentary, *Death of a Princess*, that so angered the Saudis that they expelled Britain's ambassador and canceled several multimillion-dollar contracts with British firms. The religious police also began to patrol bazaars, shopping malls, and any other place where men and women might happen to meet.

The Rise of Khomeini and the Second Energy Crisis

In the autumn of 1978, the Saudis increased their oil production from 7.2 million barrels a day to 10.4 million barrels a day. They did this to make up for the rapidly falling production in Iran, where striking oil workers had cut their nation's petroleum exports to one-fifth of their previous level.

The theocratic revolution that overthrew the shah of Iran in the winter of 1978–1979 was a response to corruption, inflation, police torture, and overly rapid modernization, but the initial unrest was sparked by a letter in a newspaper on January 7, 1978. The letter ridiculed Ruhollah Khomeini, a Shi'ite *ayatollah* who was a longtime opponent of the shah, and claimed (without any evidence) that he had written homosexual love poems as a young man. The next day there were demonstrations in the city of Qom, where Khomeini once lived, and soldiers loyal to the shah killed at least twenty protesters. After a forty-day mourning period, there were more Shi'ite demonstrations, more shootings by the shah's troops, and yet another forty-day mourning period. A cycle of protests began that one Shi'ite leader called "doing the 40–40."

The shah tried to soothe fundamentalist discontent by abolishing the Ministry of Women's Affairs, closing casinos, and purging members of the Bahai faith from his government, but anger against the shah rekindled on September 8 when soldiers killed hundreds of unarmed demonstrators in Tehran.

In October, strikes spread throughout Iran, including to its oil fields, and by November, Iran's exports had fallen from 4.5 million barrels of oil a day to less than 1 million barrels a day. By Christmas, exports had stopped altogether, and oil workers refused to give any petroleum to the police or the military. The army was already disintegrating, in any case; every day more than a thousand draftees deserted.

Finally, on January 16, 1979, the shah left his country for Egypt, never to return. Two weeks later, Khomeini, who had lived in exile in Iraq for thirteen years and in suburban Paris (near the home of Brigitte Bardot) for four months, flew to Tehran and immediately formed a new government. The Saudis were shocked that President Carter had not done more to help the shah and began to wonder whether the United States would defend their kingdom quickly enough in a crisis.

The Saudis hoped to have friendly relations with Iran, since their country was a theocracy, too. This hope was quickly dashed when Khomeini made repeated television and radio broadcasts that attacked the House of Saud as "pleasure-seeking mercenaries" unworthy of ruling the holy cities of Mecca and Medina. "How long must Satan rule in the House of God?" he asked. The effect of these broadcasts was to unite the Saudi people behind King Khalid. Liberals feared that Iran's strict brand of fundamentalism might spread to other Muslim nations, and religious conservatives despised Iran's Shi'ites as heretics.

In the West, the fall of the shah made some observers wonder whether Saudi Arabia's monarchy might be next, but they ignored five key differences between Iran and the Saudi kingdom. First, the al-Saud family is homegrown. It has ruled parts of Arabia for more than two centuries and was never propped up by foreigners as the shah had been in 1953. Second, any Saudi man can see his king at a public audience, where the king sits in an ordinary chair and listens to a subject's grievance carefully, while in Iran, the shah was imperious on his jeweled Peacock Throne.

Third, torture is the exception in Saudi Arabia's prisons but was common in Iran's. Fourth, Iran's Shi'ite clergymen were opposed to the shah and received their money from their congregations, while in

Saudi Arabia the Wahhabi clerics support the monarchy and receive government salaries. Finally, the shah had only a few dozen relatives, but anyone trying to overthrow the House of Saud would face more than fifteen thousand princes and princesses who have intermarried with almost every tribe in Arabia.

At the beginning of 1979, Iraq wanted to take advantage of the lack of Iranian oil production to raise the price of petroleum 25 percent. By contrast, Saudi Arabia, concerned about new oil fields in Alaska, Mexico, and the North Sea, wanted to freeze prices in order to discourage new exploration. As soon as the shah left Iran, however, the Saudis changed their mind and decided that good relations with Iraq were more important than moderately priced oil. On January 20, just four days after the shah arrived in Egypt, the Saudis cut their oil production by a hefty 2.3 million barrels a day, from 10.4 million barrels a day to just 8.1 million. Prices on the short-term "spot" market, which were always a little higher than the official OPEC price ($13.34 a barrel at the start of 1979), immediately surged from $16 a barrel to $25 a barrel.

At a meeting in Geneva on June 26, the OPEC nations raised the price of oil to $25.50 a barrel (including surcharges). In the past, Saudi Arabia had resisted price increases that might encourage the development of alternative fuels. But now that the kingdom was worried about its security, it let the price of oil rise 91 percent to please Iraq and Iran, both of which had much larger armies than Saudi Arabia's. Spot market prices climbed even higher and in June spiked briefly to $40 a barrel.

Despite the cuts in Iranian and Saudi production, there was still enough oil in 1979 to meet 95 percent of the world's normal demand for petroleum. But fears of a shortage led to stockpiling, and stockpiling caused a real shortage that sharply increased prices, especially in the spot market. For the first time, the spot market seemed to have more power to set the price of oil than OPEC did, and the OPEC nations repeatedly scrambled to catch up.

Before the rise of Khomeini, Japan had bought one-fifth of its oil from Iran. Afterward, when Iranian exports stopped, Japanese trading companies scavenged the world for oil and paid high prices anywhere they found some. To save energy, Japan's government even turned off all the neon lights in Tokyo's Ginza district. Israel and South Africa had also been dependent on Iranian oil (because no Arab country would sell to them) and were forced to buy petroleum in the increasingly expensive spot market.

British Petroleum was the company hardest hit by the Khomeini revolution. It had purchased 40 percent of Iran's oil exports in 1978. In 1979, with barely enough oil for its own refineries, it could no longer sell petroleum to smaller, independent oil companies. This forced the independents into the spot market to find oil for their customers. To make matters worse, Europe suffered an unusually cold winter in the first months of 1979, and this prompted European wholesalers to buy more oil than they needed in case the next winter was just as cold. In all, the world bought three million more barrels of oil a day than it needed in 1979, and this kept the high oil prices from falling back to their previous levels.

In the United States, a misguided government allocation system distributed gasoline according to past demand, rather than current needs, and caused widespread shortages in the Sun Belt cities and their fast-growing suburbs. For the second time in six years, U.S. drivers had to wait in long lines for gasoline. Many consumers stopped buying American gas guzzlers and instead bought high-mileage Japanese compacts, a trend that did severe harm to the automobile-based economy of Michigan and other parts of the industrial Midwest.

In July, as a gesture to the United States, Saudi Arabia raised its oil production to 9.5 million barrels a day, a move that kept oil prices stable during the summer. But fears of not having enough oil in the winter drove spot market prices up to $38 a barrel in October, and most OPEC nations followed the spot market by raising their total price to $28 a barrel, a price that Saudi Arabia adopted in January 1980.

At $28 a barrel, the price of oil was double what it had been a year earlier. Thanks to this increase, Saudi Arabia's oil revenues soared to $63 billion in 1979 ($400 million a day in today's money), almost 60 percent more than its income in 1978. The oil boom that began in 1973 was more robust than ever.

Twin Shocks: The Seizure of Mecca's Grand Mosque and Protests by Shi'ites

By the Muslim calendar, November 20, 1979, was the beginning of the year 1400 AH, the first day of a new century. At the Grand Mosque in Mecca, about thirty-five thousand people gathered in the predawn darkness for the start of the morning prayer. Near some pillars, several families stood by coffins to pray for relatives who had just died.

Suddenly, the "families" opened their coffins and pulled out hundreds of guns of varying quality: Soviet-made AK-47s smuggled in from Iraq, U.S. M-16s stolen from the Saudi National Guard, and British rifles from the nineteenth century that once belonged to the rebels' grandfathers. The armed men and several women and children quickly closed all of the mosque's forty-eight doors, posted snipers in the minarets, and seized the mosque's public address system.

The leader of the nearly three hundred rebels, Juhayman ibn Muhammad al-Utaibi, told the astonished crowd that a revolution had begun in Saudi Arabia, and he urged everyone to join him. He denounced the Saudi monarchy as un-Islamic and said that power should be based on one's devotion to Islam. He called for the Saudi princes to give a full accounting of their wealth and demanded that they break their diplomatic, military, and educational ties to non-Muslim countries. "Is it possible to declare *jihad* on unbelieving states while we maintain ambassadors in their territory?" he asked. "How can we preach Islam while we take Christians as professors?"[1] Juhayman also denounced television, alcohol, and the education of women and demanded that the Saudi government stop selling oil to the West and stop investing money abroad.

Juhayman and the majority of his followers had studied at the Islamic University of Medina, where many professors were fundamentalist Egyptians who had fled Nasser's regime because they were members of the militant Muslim Brotherhood. Most of the rebels also belonged to tribes that had supported the Ikhwan and rebelled against Saudi rule in 1929.

As a young man, Juhayman served in the National Guard and rose to the rank of corporal; he may have still had friends in the Guard who helped him to steal weapons. After leaving the military, he studied in Medina for two years, then preached in rural mosques and began to attract followers. In Kuwait, Juhayman published pamphlets that criticized the Saudi royal family. When he returned to the kingdom in 1978, he was arrested and imprisoned, but at the urging of Sheikh Abdulaziz ibn Baz (the senior cleric who still thought that the sun revolved around the earth), Juhayman was released on the condition that he promise to stay out of politics.

Juhayman's outlook was shared by many conservative Wahhabis, but he and his followers made two fatal mistakes that alienated both the Wahhabi clergy and the Saudi public. First, they seized the wrong target. The Grand Mosque that surrounds Mecca's Kaaba is the holiest site in Islam, and Muslims around the world regarded its seizure as sacrilege. Juhayman may have hoped that King Khalid would be in

Mecca to lead the first prayer of the new century, and perhaps he had planned to kidnap him, but Khalid was ill and never came. Khalid said later, "If he had attacked my palace, he might have met with more success."[2] Second, Juhayman puzzled everyone by declaring that his friend, a young theology student named Muhammad ibn Abdullah al-Qahtani, was the *Mahdi*, the Islamic equivalent of the messiah. To ordinary Saudis, this was just wacky.

At the end of his speech to the crowd, Juhayman and his supporters took two dozen people as hostages, then told everyone else to either declare their loyalty to al-Qahtani or leave, at which point all of the roughly thirty-five thousand worshippers fled the mosque as fast as they could.

Because violence at the Grand Mosque is forbidden, King Khalid needed a ruling from the Council of the Senior Clergy to authorize the use of force to retake the mosque. Surprisingly, it took the council four days to issue the ruling, which suggests that some of the Wahhabi clerics must have sympathized with Juhayman's reactionary agenda. While the clergymen deliberated, a mob in Pakistan decided that the Americans had planned the Grand Mosque's seizure, and they burned the U.S. embassy in Islamabad. When the senior clerics finally issued their ruling, they did not criticize any of Juhayman's statements but did call his seizure of the mosque "a crime and an act of atheism" and authorized the government to kill the rebels if they did not surrender.

When Saudi troops entered the mosque, Juhayman's men retreated downstairs to a maze of rooms beneath the complex, and the government had to fight them pillar by pillar because it did not want to destroy the holy site with bombs and grenades. At first, the army, the National Guard, the national police, and the local police each acted independently, without any coordination, but soon three men took charge: Prince Sultan, the minister of defense (and the current crown prince); Prince Turki al-Faisal, then the head of Saudi intelligence; and a hired French counterterrorism expert, Captain Paul Barril, who had quickly converted to Islam before he arrived in Mecca.

After eight days of intense fighting, Juhayman and about a hundred of his tired and hungry followers finally surrendered on December 3. A total of 117 of their colleagues had died in combat, including al-Qahtani, the professed *Mahdi*. The number of government troops and policemen killed in battle was even higher, 127, and a dozen hostages also died. King Khalid was appalled at how hard it had been for his troops to retake the mosque and soon formed an elite counterterrorism unit of twelve hundred men to face such internal challenges in the future.

The three dozen women and children among Juhayman's followers who survived the fighting were sent to religious schools for reeducation, but Juhayman and the sixty-two men captured with him were all sentenced to death. They were divided into eight groups and on January 9, 1980, several minutes after the morning prayer, were beheaded in public squares in eight different cities.

Although the seizure of the Grand Mosque proved to be an isolated incident, it seemed deeply ominous at the time because Iran's monarchy had fallen only ten months earlier. As a result, King Khalid took several measures. First, he raised the salaries of the clergy and began the construction of 241 new mosques. Second, he instructed the nation's clerics to give sermons that reminded the people that it is forbidden to rebel if a ruler governs according to Muslim law. Third, he replaced four regional governors with younger and better-educated men. In his speech, Juhayman had particularly criticized the governor of Mecca for gambling and financial corruption. Fourth, Khalid increased the size of the kingdom's 1980–1981 defense budget by almost 45 percent, to $20.9 billion.

Finally, in response to Wahhabi discontent, the government's social policies became more conservative. In March 1980, the Ministry of Education announced that Saudi women would no longer be allowed to go abroad to earn master's degrees or doctorates because too many women had returned home with "un-Islamic" ideas about how they should live. Two years later, the government also canceled scholarships for undergraduate women studying abroad, although women could still attend college overseas at their own expense. In Saudi universities, women continued to be barred from studying law, engineering, and petroleum geology.

The kingdom also closed video stores, prohibited mixed-gender beaches, banned women from appearing on television (they reappeared in 1984), and tightened the segregation of the sexes in the workplace. Women receptionists were replaced by men, and the careers open to women remained limited to education, health, and running small businesses.

The most noticeable change in Saudi Arabia in the early 1980s was the tightening of surveillance by the religious police. The men who make up the Society for the Advancement of Virtue and the Elimination of Sin are easily recognizable because of their bushy beards and short robes that reveal their ankles. They walk into restaurants and arrest couples who are not married, peer into car windows and detain a woman if she is alone with an unrelated male driver, and, in rare instances, enter a house and arrest the homeowner if he or she is drinking alcohol or holding a church service.

Few Saudis minded the extra scrutiny. The Saudis are a deeply conservative people, and most of them were quite happy with the kingdom's unique combination of puritanism and prosperity.

Among those who were unhappy with conditions in Saudi Arabia were the Shi'ites, who made up 9 percent of the kingdom's nonforeign population and almost 50 percent of the people in the oil-rich Eastern Province. On November 28, 1979, while the battle for Mecca's Grand Mosque was still raging, a large crowd of Shi'ites gathered in the city of Qatif, on the kingdom's east coast, for an Ashura procession. This is a festival where young men commemorate the martyrdom of Hussein, Muhammad's grandson, by whipping themselves as they march through the streets. Ashura processions were illegal in Saudi Arabia because Wahhabis regard the veneration of Hussein, who they concede was a saint, as polytheism. When local police tried to stop the march, young Shi'ites rioted.

Because Qatif is near many oil refineries and pipelines, the National Guard quickly sent twenty thousand troops to the city, and some of the guardsmen, who considered the Shi'ites to be heretics, fired on the demonstrators. The rioting spread to other towns and lasted three days; when it finally stopped, seventeen people were dead, hundreds were wounded, and several oil installations had been sabotaged.

The Shi'ites in Qatif had been fired up by radio broadcasts from Iran that claimed the unrest in Mecca was part of a larger uprising against the Saudi monarchy. With Shi'ite clerics in power in Iran, just across the Gulf, it was much harder for Shi'ites in Saudi Arabia to accept their second-class citizenship than it had been before. While it was true that half of Aramco's oil workers and many of its managers were Shi'ites who earned excellent wages, the majority of the kingdom's Shi'ites remained poor. This was especially unfair because 99 percent of Saudi Arabia's oil is in the Eastern Province, where 90 percent of the kingdom's Shi'ites live. Yet as the 1970s ended, most of the Eastern Province still lacked good roads, schools, hospitals, and sewers. The Saudi kingdom also barred Shi'ites from the military, from teaching, and from the upper and middle ranks of the government.

In December, Khalid sent Prince Ahmad, one of his youngest brothers, to the Eastern Province to listen to people's grievances and start some long-overdue public works. A few weeks after he arrived, however, violence erupted in Qatif again. On February 1, 1980, the first anniversary of Ayatollah Khomeini's return to Iran, thousands of young men marched through the streets shouting anti-Saudi slogans and carrying pictures of Khomeini. When the police arrived, the Shi'ites broke windows, burned cars, and destroyed several banks. Within hours, the National Guard surrounded Qatif with tanks. The guard cut off communications with the rest of the country for weeks and also killed fifteen Shi'ites as they restored order.

By autumn, the government had legalized Ashura processions, as long as the expressions of grief for the martyred Hussein were not overly exaggerated. In November, a week before the next procession, Crown Prince Fahad approved $240 million worth of construction projects in Qatif and, more important, freed several hundred Shi'ites who had been arrested the previous winter.

Because of this amnesty, the procession was peaceful. Five days later, King Khalid visited Qatif and authorized the expenditure of an additional $1 billion for new schools, clinics, highways, power stations, telephone exchanges, and water-treatment plants. It was the first time a Saudi king had ever visited the Shi'ite city.

Because Saudi officials understood that their oil fields were vulnerable if the people who lived near them were discontented, they made the economic development of the Eastern Province one of the highest priorities of the new five-year plan for 1980–1985. The government lent millions of dollars at low interest to Shi'ite businessmen to start new enterprises and vastly improved the province's administration by replacing Wahhabis who were bigoted against Shi'ites with young, university-educated technocrats. But even as money poured into the Eastern Province, Saudi policemen questioned thousands of young Shi'ite men and arrested several hundred, including anyone with books, pictures, or cassettes of Ayatollah Khomeini.

The government's policy of offering many carrots and a few sticks to the Shi'ites was highly effective. The overwhelming majority of Shi'ites were pleased to finally have a share of their nation's oil wealth. And because they were Arabs, not Persians, once they began to participate in Saudi Arabia's oil boom, they were no longer attracted to Iran's poorer and harsher theocracy.

Despite real progress in the 1980s, Shi'ites continued to be second-class citizens in Saudi Arabia. They were still denied any position of authority in the government, the military, and the judiciary or in schools and universities. They were not allowed to marry Sunni Muslims, build new mosques, create Shi'ite community centers, or teach religion. The government still hired Wahhabis to teach Islam to Shi'ite students and continued to print textbooks that described the Shi'ite faith in ways that Shi'ites found insulting. Most Shi'ite children learned to keep silent in class.

1980–1981: The Oil Boom Continues

When 1980 began, most nations in the Organization of Petroleum Exporting Countries were charging several dollars more for a barrel of oil than Saudi Arabia did. Zaki Yamani, the Saudi oil minister, feared that if these price discrepancies continued, OPEC would lose its unity and power. To keep OPEC strong, the Saudis tried to unify OPEC's oil prices, and therefore they raised the kingdom's production during 1980 and 1981 to ten million barrels a day, a level close to capacity. They hoped that the increased output would prevent other OPEC nations from raising their prices further.

Because Saudi Arabia's goal was price-unity and not price-reduction, it kept its own price high to try to close the gap between its price and that of other nations. Despite a global recession and the fact that most industrial nations had begun to use fuel more efficiently, the Saudis raised their price of oil to $28 a barrel in April 1980, and $32 a barrel in January 1981.

Other OPEC nations began to charge $36 a barrel in 1981, however, and Libya charged $41 a barrel. Then, in the spring of 1981, for the first time in years, the price of oil in the spot market fell below OPEC's official prices because non-OPEC nations such as Britain, Norway, and Canada decided to sell more oil by lowering their prices. It was an early sign of a coming surplus. Yamani himself warned that in 1982, "We will most likely encounter a big glut in the oil market. . . . The chances of a price collapse will be great."[3]

At a meeting in Geneva in May, the OPEC nations agreed to freeze their prices for the rest of the year. Only in October, to prevent a sharp fall in the price of oil, did the Saudis finally cut their production from 10 million barrels a day to 8.5 million barrels a day. In return, all of the OPEC nations, including Saudi Arabia, finally agreed to unify their price at $34 a barrel.

The combination of high production and high prices in 1980 and 1981 increased the world's supply of oil and decreased its demand, but the buyer's market this produced did not appear until 1982. During 1980 and 1981, the oil boom roared on. The same combination of high production and high prices that created a glut later also produced record revenues for Saudi Arabia in the present: $106 billion in 1980 and $116 billion in 1981, a two-year bonanza that averaged $26 million an *hour* in today's money.

As was true when the oil boom began in 1973, there was enough money for everything in the early 1980s: massive palaces, generous welfare programs, extensive economic development, huge foreign bank accounts, and a variety of sophisticated weapons. In 1980, Saudi Arabia signed a contract with France to buy $3.5 billion worth of warships, supply ships, and naval helicopters. In 1981, the U.S. Congress approved selling the kingdom sixty F-15 fighter jets and five jets with extraordinarily sophisticated radar, the Advanced Warning and Control Systems (AWACS), at a cost of $8.5 billion.

During the late 1970s and most of the 1980s, the U.S. Army Corps of Engineers also supervised $14 billion worth of construction in the kingdom, including the building of three giant army bases that the Saudis called "military cities": one near the border of Iraq, a second near Yemen, and a third near Jordan. A soldier may be isolated in the desert during his tour of duty, but when his tour is finished, the army rewards him with a plot of land and an interest-free loan to build a house.

The largest army base, King Khalid Military City, near Iraq, contains barracks for eighty thousand troops and runways long enough for B-52 bombers. The idea behind the base's vast size was that if Saudi Arabia ever needed the United States to defend it, everything would be ready.

The government also tried to create new industries. It offered foreigners who were willing to build factories ten-year tax holidays, duty-free imports, and subsidized land, water, and power. By 1984, there were more than twelve hundred industrial enterprises in the kingdom, most fairly small.

The need for liaisons between the government and foreign businesses was a tremendous opportunity for enterprising Saudis. During the oil boom, it was much easier to make money as a business agent than as a professional or a technician, so "going into business" became a more important goal for most students than learning a skill was. Even among engineering majors, a 1979 poll of three thousand college seniors revealed that 80 percent wanted a career in business, rather than in engineering.

Nearly every Saudi prospered in the early 1980s. If one includes the benefits of free education, health care, and subsidized food and utilities, the average Saudi family during this time made more than $100,000 a year in today's money. Unlike much of the Middle East, Saudi Arabia had never been colonized, but now it, too, succumbed to foreign influences: Sony, Panasonic, Nike, Dior, Cartier, Rolex, Mercedes-Benz, Toyota, McDonald's, Taco Bell, and more. Even the nomads prospered. On the outskirts of cities, the livestock pens behind the car dealerships disappeared because the Bedouin no longer swapped camels for their first pickup truck. Like consumers everywhere, they now traded in older vehicles for newer ones.

In any country, not only in Saudi Arabia, a by-product of prosperity can be boredom. Few women had jobs in Saudi Arabia, and many had servants. With little to do, it was common for wealthy women to spend many hours a day watching Egyptian soap operas on television and American movies on cassettes. One Japanese exporter claimed that Saudi Arabia had more VCRs per person than any other country in the world. A few women found solace in liquor or a home brew called *siddiqui* ("friend"). Among men, arrests for alcohol and drug offenses, which climbed steadily in the early 1970s, tripled during Khalid's reign, when even the unemployed had money.

Young Saudis also had a lot of free time. Many schools in Saudi Arabia are not that demanding, and literacy in the kingdom was still too recent—and newspapers and magazines too censored—for reading to be a widespread pastime. On some streets at night, cars full of teenage boys pulled up by the sides of cars full of teenage girls. The girls were fully veiled and driven by a chauffeur. If a girl saw a boy she liked, she wrote down her telephone number, wadded the paper into a ball, and threw it at him. The activity was called "numbering" and often resulted in long, flirtatious telephone calls.

The Start of the Iran-Iraq War

At dawn on September 22, 1980, Iraqi jets bombed several Iranian air bases and the oil refinery at Abadan, the largest refinery in the world. Minutes later, fifty thousand Iraqi soldiers crossed Iran's border and began a blitzkrieg toward Abadan and the port city of Khorramshahr. By November, they had taken the towns, but their success was short-lived. Iranian soldiers recaptured both cities a year later, then pushed Iraq's troops back across the border.

The man who started the war, Saddam Hussein, had dominated Iraq for half a decade, but when the war began, he had formally been the country's president for only fourteen months. Hussein knew that Iran's military was in chaos. Khomeini had fired too many capable pro-shah officers, and worse, the Iranian air force had lost its access to U.S. spare parts. Calling Khomeini "a shah dressed in religious clothes," Hussein hoped that a quick victory would increase his oil reserves and eliminate any possibility of Iran exporting its revolution to the 60 percent of Iraq's people who were Shi'ites.

Khomeini seized the opportunity the war provided to purge non-clerics from his government and execute more than fifteen hundred opponents on charges of "waging war against God." Calling Hussein a "dwarf Pharaoh" and his invasion "blasphemy against Islam," Khomeini launched air attacks that destroyed Iraq's oil-loading docks and a naval offensive that dropped mines in Iraq's only outlet to the Persian Gulf. In addition, Syria, wary of Iraq's troops just across its border, sided with Iran and shut Iraq's primary oil pipeline to the Mediterranean. This left Iraq with only one small pipeline through Turkey. Suddenly, Iraq's oil exports plunged to just one-fourth of their previous level.

The Saudis had no love for either Hussein or Khomeini, but they regarded Khomeini as the bigger danger because his fanaticism was a greater threat to the region's stability. Preventing an Iranian victory therefore became Saudi Arabia's top priority.

The kingdom's first concern was its own defense. At Crown Prince Fahad's request, President Jimmy Carter sent four advanced warning aircraft (AWACS) to patrol the border with Iraq and, pending congressional approval, which came a year later, allowed the kingdom to buy five AWACS of its own. In return, Saudi Arabia increased its oil production from an already-high 9.8 million barrels a day to a peak-capacity 10.2 million barrels a day, which prevented yet another increase in the price of oil.

Fearing that the Iran-Iraq War might spread to the kingdom's oil fields, Prince Abdullah sent two battalions of the National Guard to the city of Dhahran, on the Persian Gulf, and began to construct a permanent base there. Because Iran's navy was capable of blocking the Strait of Hormuz, which would cut off the Persian Gulf from the outside world, the kingdom also began to build a new Trans-Arabian pipeline across the Saudi desert. Completed in 1981 and expanded in 1985, it pumps up to 3.5 million barrels of oil a day westward from the Persian Gulf to the much less troubled Red Sea.

Finally, Saudi Arabia gave Iraq more than $3 billion a year in aid, loans, industrial equipment, and oil. During the war's eight years, Saudi Arabia's total aid to Iraq was a staggering $25.7 billion. Kuwait contributed an additional $14 billion.

By the mid-1980s, the war between Iran and Iraq had become a grisly stalemate. Iraq used much of the money it received from Saudi Arabia and Kuwait to buy weapons from the Soviet Union and France and regularly attacked Iran's oil installations with fighter bombers and long-range artillery. But Iran organized giant "human wave" attacks of hundreds of thousands of young men, with Khomeini telling them that "the purest joy in Islam is to kill and be killed for God."[4] Some men were so eager to become martyrs that they carried their own coffins with them. Others proudly wore gold-colored keys to heaven around their necks. Thousands of boys in their early teens died clearing minefields so that Iranian tanks, more scarce than human lives, could advance into Iraq, to the outskirts of Basra, Iraq's second-largest city.

For the next few years, neither Iran nor Iraq was a threat to Saudi Arabia. The long war between the two nations showed no sign of ending because one of Khomeini's conditions for a peace agreement was the removal of Saddam Hussein from office.

The Death of King Khalid

On June 13, 1982, King Khalid, at seventy, had a heart attack at his summer palace in Taif and died. His body was wrapped in plain brown cloth and flown to Riyadh, where his brothers carried him on a simple litter through streets lined with thousands of people. The king was buried before sunset, as required by Muslim law, in an unmarked grave in an unmarked cemetery.

Within minutes of Khalid's death, the government announced that "Royal family members, led by Prince Muhammad [the oldest living son of the nation's founder], have pledged themselves to Heir Apparent Fahad as King of the Country."[5] The announcement went on to say that King Fahad had nominated Prince Abdullah, the commander of the National Guard, as crown prince, and that the nomination had been approved by the senior princes. Several hours later, the government also declared that Fahad had appointed his full brother Prince Sultan (the minister of defense) as second deputy prime minister, second in line to the throne.

The speed of the announcement suggested that Fahad and his brothers had been concerned about Khalid's poor health for some time and had agreed on these appointments weeks and perhaps months in advance. For one thing, in order for the appointments of Abdullah and Sultan to be official, four older princes had to waive their claims to the throne. Princes Nasir and Saad had already stepped aside in 1975, when Fahad became crown prince, so their waiver this time was a mere formality. The third prince, Bandar, one year older than Sultan, was passed over because, like Saad, he had never held a government office. The fourth prince, Musaid, also a year older than Sultan, was skipped because his brothers considered him strange and because his second son, Faysal ibn Musaid, had assassinated King Faisal in 1975.

After three days of mourning, Fahad, the new king, received formal pledges of support from his brothers, nephews, and cousins; from tribal chiefs, top clerics, and generals; and, finally, from a crowd of tens of thousands of people in Riyadh's central square. In the Middle East's long history, few transfers of power have ever been as smooth.

Khalid's Legacy

Khalid was a caretaker king who continued Faisal's combination of rapid economic modernization and strict social conservatism. Although his government responded forcefully to the threats posed by religious fanatics in Mecca and Tehran, one of Khalid's main achievements was to preserve his family's unity.

Because Khalid governed only intermittently, his brothers grew more powerful. When Faisal ruled, a younger brother ran a government ministry at the king's pleasure. Under Khalid, these ministries became permanent fiefdoms, a key part of the al-Saud family's internal balance of power. More than twenty years after Khalid's death, the army and the air force are still controlled by Prince Sultan, the National Guard by Prince Abdullah, the Foreign Ministry by Prince Saud al-Faisal, the national police by Prince Nayef, and the Riyadh police by Prince Salman. (The Petroleum Ministry is always run by a commoner because if a prince controlled the nation's oil industry, it would make his branch of the family too powerful and would upset the royal family's equilibrium.)

The advantage of having a government with several clusters of power is that it makes the arbitrary one-man rule that is common in many other Middle Eastern countries impossible in Saudi Arabia. The disadvantage of having multiple power centers is that the number of people needed to make an important decision is considerable, and therefore so is the probability of indecision and delay. In the future, it would be harder for the royal family to make difficult decisions.

When Khalid was king, he did not have to make many tough decisions because the kingdom had so much money that there was seldom a need to prioritize. But a decade of high oil prices led to increased exploration, new fields, and a glut of new oil. When Khalid died, only a few people understood that the oil boom was over, that the seven fat years that marked Khalid's reign had come to an end, and that seven lean years, and more, would follow. As the nation's oil revenues plummeted, Saudi Arabia's new king, Fahad, would have many hard choices to make and, because of the growing need to consult his brothers, a more difficult time making them.

16

The Lean Years of King Fahad
(1982–1990)

FOR YEARS, THE SAUDIS had felt that their oil wealth was God's reward to them for being good Muslims, so when oil revenues plunged from $116 billion in 1981 to just $17 billion in 1986, they began to wonder if they were being punished for their recent materialism. During the 1970s, the Saudi government gave people free education and health care and subsidized food and utilities, but in the 1980s, oil revenues were no longer high enough to pay for these entitlements. Rather than levy taxes, which would cause people to want a say in how their money was spent, King Fahad preferred to draw on the country's foreign reserves, which shrank 70 percent during the 1980s. He also borrowed heavily from Saudi banks, running up more than $60 billion worth of domestic debt. Adding to Fahad's unpopularity was the fact that he was more pro-American than the rest of his brothers were, for most Saudis hated America's support of Israel. Fahad was vindicated, however, when the United States promptly came to the kingdom's defense after Iraq invaded Kuwait in 1990.

Although Fahad's name, which means "jaguar," is often spelled Fahd, it is a *two*-syllable name, pronounced FA-had. He was born either in 1921 or 1922, the eighth son of King Abdul Aziz and the oldest son of Hassa bint Ahmad al-Sudairi, the king's favorite wife. A grandson later described Hassa as "a combination of Mother Teresa and Margaret Thatcher. She was very pious, yet very strong-willed."[1] In her old age, Hassa insisted that her sons call her once a day, no matter how busy they were, and dine with her once a week if they were in Riyadh.

When Fahad was a child, he memorized the Quran and studied Arab history and culture at his father's palace with some of his brothers. He was also taught to shoot, ride, and live like a Bedouin, but he did not enjoy desert life nearly as much as Khalid did, and he much preferred watching his father hold public audiences in Riyadh. In his late teens, Fahad attended a religious school in Mecca, where he took advanced courses in Muslim law and history. Then he returned to Riyadh to become one of his father's closest advisers. The king once called his quick-witted son "a fox, not a jaguar."

As a young man, Fahad was among the handsomest of the princes. Tall and broad-shouldered, he had a sharp wit and a confident, magnetic smile. He looked a bit like Wolfman Jack, the famous American radio disc jockey, but had a far more regal posture and dignified manner. In his sixties, however, when Fahad had become king, he gained a great deal of weight. By 1990, he weighed three hundred pounds and suffered respiratory and back problems. He walked slowly, tired easily, spent most of his time in a wheelchair, and spoke to crowds while sitting down.

When Saudi Arabia fought Yemen in 1934, Fahad was too young to fight so he never acquired any military experience. His first trip abroad was to San Francisco, accompanying his brother Faisal at the signing of the United Nations Charter in 1945. On this trip and others, he learned to understand English but not speak it. After the war, when oil money rushed into the kingdom, Fahad often went to nightclubs in Beirut, where he gambled, watched belly dancers, ate big bowls of caviar, and also enjoyed other sensual pleasures. The gambling upset many Wahhabi clerics, who were mindful of Sura 5, verse 91, of the Quran, which says, "Satan sows hatred and strife among you, by wine and games of chance, and turns you aside from the remembrance of God, and from prayer: will ye not, therefore, abstain from them?"[2]

By 1950, King Abdul Aziz may have realized that Fahad did not have enough to do because he began to use his son as a trouble-shooter to ease his workload. Fahad proved to be a conscientious administrator who sometimes worked late into the night. When Abdul Aziz died in 1953, the new king, Saud, made Fahad his minister of education at a time when schools were almost nonexistent in the kingdom. Fahad's first priority was construction, and he built hundreds of elementary schools, high schools, and the nation's first secular university.

In 1962, when Faisal became prime minister, he appointed Fahad minister of the interior, in command of the nation's security police. Fahad modernized what was then a rustic force, and for the rest of the decade he arrested the supporters of Nasser, the Egyptian president, wherever he could find them. In 1967, Faisal picked Fahad to be second deputy prime minister—second in line to the throne, after Khalid—because by then, Fahad had more supervisory experience than anyone else in the family except for Faisal himself. Eight years later, when Khalid became king after Faisal's assassination, Fahad became crown prince.

Unlike Faisal, who lived simply, or Khalid, who preferred the desert, Fahad loved luxury. He was one of the richest men in the world—by 1990, his personal fortune was estimated to be much more than $10 billion. Fahad had seven palaces in Saudi Arabia and a hundred-room villa in Marbella, on Spain's Mediterranean coast, where the local merchants loved him because his entourage sometimes spent as much as $5 million a day. Fahad also owned palaces in Geneva, outside Paris, and in Antibes on the French Riviera, and he had a large mansion outside London.

A Greek tycoon who built ports in Saudi Arabia in exchange for cheap oil once gave Fahad a 495-foot yacht the size of a luxury liner. Fahad also owned a Boeing 747 staffed by eight pretty foreign stewardesses and fitted with chandeliers, a sauna, and gold bathroom fixtures. Even Fahad's toothbrushes were gold-plated.

Fahad often went to Monte Carlo, but his gambling days decreased in number after he and two younger brothers were photographed at a roulette table with several beautiful young women in 1974. As a crowd watched, they lost $6 million in one night. King Faisal ordered Fahad to come home immediately and was so furious that he seriously considered disinheriting him. A year later, after Faisal was assassinated and Fahad became crown prince, he and some of his brothers built palaces in Morocco, where they could indulge their whims far from Western photographers and disapproving Wahhabis.

The money that Fahad spent on luxurious living was dwarfed by the commissions his six sons received from government contracts. In 1977, his third son, Muhammad, collected more than $250 million for helping Philips-Ericsson win billions of dollars' worth of telecommunications contracts. Muhammad, a high-stakes gambler, has also received multimillion-dollar commissions from Bechtel; Brown and Root; and other U.S. construction firms and owns a dozen giant palaces around the world. Fahad's youngest son, Abdulaziz (nicknamed Azouzi), was only nine when his father became king, yet collected tens of millions of dollars in commissions even as a teenager and received $300 million as a present from his father in 1987, when he was fourteen. Today he is a billionaire and recently spent tens of millions of dollars building a restoration village outside Riyadh with full-scale replicas of early Mecca and Medina, the Alhambra, and other Muslim landmarks.

Since Fahad often spent months at a time at his palaces in Europe, many Saudis assumed, correctly or incorrectly, that he was fond of foreign women. As a result, while they honored the royal family, they had less respect for Fahad himself.

Because of his reputation as a libertine, Fahad had little ability to stand up to the clergy on social issues. Instead, while Fahad ruled, the religious police became more vigilant, the clergy increased the number of hours in school that students spent on religion, and the government sent missionaries and built many mosques and schools abroad. While Fahad was king, Saudi Arabia built more than fifteen hundred mosques and two thousand schools in non-Muslim countries and financed thousands of *madrassas*—schools that teach Islamic fundamentalism—in impoverished Muslim nations such as Pakistan, Sudan, and Indonesia.

Although Fahad was a charming, cheerful man and was kind to his wives, his chief character trait was his aversion to making tough decisions. As an aide once told a reporter, Fahad "felt his job was to develop the country, and he has done that. Now he's getting old and he does not like controversies."[3] Fahad's tendency to postpone decisions during international negotiations drove one frustrated U.S. diplomat to call him "the marshmallow monarch." To be fair, one reason that Fahad so often postponed decisions is that he hated the endless consultation with his brothers that was necessary for a decision to be final.

Fahad's First Months as King

Upon becoming king in June 1982, Fahad declared, "I am but one of you. Whatever troubles you, troubles me; whatever pleases you, pleases me." Fahad not only listened to people at public audiences, he also visited universities and took questions from the students. Less than three weeks after Fahad became king, however, a new law prohibited the publication of "anything that may harm the dignity of heads of state . . . or that may adversely affect relations with other countries."[4]

Fahad appointed several nephews, sons of his full brothers, as deputy governors and senior provincial officials, causing some people to grumble about the "Sudairi-ization" of the provincial governments. Three years later, in 1985, Fahad appointed his son Muhammad to be governor of the Eastern Province, ending seventy-two years of rule there by the Jiluwi family. (In 1902, it was Abdallah ibn Jiluwi who killed Riyadh's governor in hand-to-hand fighting, enabling his cousin Abdul Aziz to retake the city and resume the Saud family's rule of Riyadh. The Jiluwi still govern the Eastern Province's capital city, Hufuf.)

Fahad appointed another Sudairi nephew, Prince Bandar bin Sultan, to be the kingdom's ambassador to the United States in 1983. Bandar is an ex–air force pilot with a master's degree from the Johns Hopkins School of Advanced International Studies. His father has been minister of defense for more than forty years and became crown prince in 2005. Fahad's appointment of Bandar, a trusted nephew, allowed him to bypass the Foreign Ministry and deal with the United States directly. Bandar was the ambassador for twenty-two years, got to know everyone of importance in Washington, and became an especially close friend of the Bush family.

Fahad and his half-brother Abdullah, the National Guard commander who succeeded him as king, did not get along. Fahad was a playboy who often traveled to Europe, whereas Abdullah was devout and loved the desert. Fahad wanted closer ties to the United States; Abdullah wanted better relations with Arab nations. Fahad's children have made hundreds of millions of dollars in business commissions; Abdullah has barred his sons from engaging in what he feels is a corrupt practice.

When Khalid died, Fahad had no choice but to appoint Abdullah crown prince. Khalid had already chosen Abdullah to be second deputy prime minister, next in line to be crown prince. If Fahad had passed over Abdullah and appointed his full brother Sultan as crown prince instead, he would have infuriated not only the clergy, who preferred Abdullah, but everyone in the royal family who was not a Sudairi.

Fahad tried to reduce Abdullah's influence by asking him to resign as commander of the National Guard, explaining that a crown prince should not hold an additional post in the cabinet. But when Fahad was the crown prince in the 1970s, he was the de facto ruler of the nation because King Khalid hunted more than he governed.

Fahad, by contrast, was an active king, leaving Crown Prince Abdullah with little power beyond his command of the National Guard. Many people therefore worried that if Abdullah resigned as the Guard's commander, Fahad might appoint one of his full brothers to lead the National Guard instead. The Sudairi brothers would then control the army, the air force, the security police, *and* the National Guard and would have a complete monopoly of the kingdom's military power.

Abdullah, encouraged by the clergy, the rest of the royal family, and conservatives throughout the country, refused to resign his command of the National Guard. Fahad then ordered the kingdom's tribes to turn in their weapons to the security police. Because Abdullah was far more popular with the tribesmen than Fahad was, the tribesmen regarded the decree as a power grab by Fahad and refused to obey it. They even bought more weapons in case the security police tried to enforce Fahad's order. In the end, Fahad backed down and made no attempt to carry out his edict.

After a year as king, Fahad no longer challenged Abdullah's command of the National Guard. But the security police, run by Fahad's full brother Nayef, began to recruit in rural areas and among tribesmen who had just moved to the cities. The Sudairi brothers were trying to create a new set of loyalties among some of Abdullah's core supporters.

The End of the Oil Boom: The Fall in Price, Production, and Revenues

In 1982, the oil boom ended for a variety of reasons. First, the North Sea became a major oil field in the late 1970s, and by 1983, it was producing more petroleum than Algeria, Libya, and Nigeria combined. New fields were also developed in Mexico, Alaska, and Angola, and because the price of oil was so high, the Soviet Union increased its oil production, too. Second, persistent inflation, caused in large part by rising oil prices, led banks in the United States and Europe to increase interest rates to more than 20 percent. This brought on the world's deepest recession since the Great Depression of the 1930s, which in turn reduced the globe's demand for oil 12 percent between 1979 and 1983.

Third, high oil prices led to the use of more coal and nuclear power. While oil represented 53 percent of the world's energy use in 1975, it accounted for only 43 percent of its energy use in 1985.

Fourth, conservation measures, such as America's 1975 legislation to double the mileage of new cars to 27.5 miles per gallon by 1985, were very effective. By 1985, the United States was using oil one-third more efficiently than it had in 1973, and Japan was even more oil efficient.

Finally, the world's oil companies had accumulated large inventories of petroleum during the panic buying of 1979 and 1980. Now, in the early 1980s, they began a wave of selling that would soon be known as the Great Inventory Dump.

Together, the new oil fields, the deep recession, the increased use of coal, better gas mileage, and the unloading of inventories created an oil glut much larger than even the most far-sighted economists had predicted. The world's demand for expensive OPEC oil dropped from thirty-one million barrels a day in 1979 to just nineteen million barrels a day in 1982, a fall of 38 percent. This presented the OPEC countries with a cruel choice: they could cut their prices to increase their share of the market, or they could cut their production to maintain their high price of $33.80 a barrel.

They decided to cut production. At a meeting in March 1982, the OPEC nations set a total production limit of eighteen million barrels a day, with smaller individual ceilings set for each country. Saudi Arabia, however, would adjust its production level as needed to support the $33.80 price. As it happened, because the world's supply of oil was now so much greater than its demand, the Saudis had to cut their production 34 percent in 1982 to maintain their price, and revenues also fell 34 percent.

The OPEC nations met again in London in March 1983 and cut the price of oil 15 percent, to $28.75 a barrel. It was the first time OPEC had ever lowered its price, but it was too small a cut. To maintain even this price, the Saudis had to cut their oil production another 23 percent in 1983. In two years, 1981–1983, Saudi production fell by half, from 9.8 million barrels a day to 5 million barrels a day. The kingdom's revenues, which had been $116 billion in 1981, were only $42.8 billion in 1983. Things were no better in 1984. The price of oil remained $28.75 a barrel, but in order to maintain that price, the Saudis had to cut their production another 8 percent, and the year's revenues fell to $34.2 billion, less than 30 percent of what they had been in 1981.

The year 1983 was when Saudi Arabia began to face the new reality. Subsidies of education, medical care, food, and utilities, which had ballooned to one-seventh of the kingdom's budget, were cut 19 percent. People had to pay 70 percent more for electricity, and the price of gasoline and car registrations went up, too. The government also reduced the annual bonuses it paid to its 250,000 employees. Altogether, the government cut its 1983–1984 budget by a painful 20 percent, but this did not begin to make up for its decline in revenues. A decade of accumulating an enormous surplus of foreign currency was now followed by a decade of deficit spending.

Many building projects were canceled or postponed, including airports, oil refineries, port facilities, and hundreds of small factories. By 1985, the number of new construction projects was less than half of the number started in 1983, a decline so steep that one-third of the kingdom's construction contractors were now suddenly in danger of bankruptcy.

Adding to the oil glut was a 1984 trade where Saudi Arabia received ten Boeing 747s for its national airline, Saudia, in return for 34.5 million barrels of oil. The kingdom's oil minister, Zaki Yamani, strongly objected to the barter deal because pumping that much extra oil would increase the glut and decrease the price. But Fahad felt that he was getting free jets for oil that would otherwise have remained in the ground. Adding to the arrangement's appeal was the fact that some of Fahad's relatives—at least three brothers-in-law, two nephews, and his youngest son, Azouzi—together earned a commission of roughly $100 million.

Defense in the Early 1980s

In May 1981, six monarchs—the leaders of Saudi Arabia, Kuwait, Bahrain, Qatar, Oman, and the United Arab Emirates—met in Abu Dhabi and formed the Gulf Cooperation Council (GCC), an organization for economic cooperation. The GCC nations formed a free-trade zone for locally made products, let their citizens travel freely from one sheikhdom to another, and allowed people to own homes and businesses in one another's cities. The GCC countries also coordinated their electric power networks and worked together to build roads and bridges, including the sixteen-mile-long causeway between Saudi Arabia and the island of Bahrain.

In 1982, the GCC became a military alliance as well. Five states formed a rapid-deployment unit called the Peninsula Shield Force. (Kuwait joined in 1986.) The force is too small to be anything more than a symbolic presence. Wary allies, the six monarchies continue to buy billions of dollars' worth of weapons without making the slightest effort to coordinate their purchases.

In 1983, the U.S. Army established its Central Command, a much larger rapid-deployment force created especially for operations in the Middle East. It would later be led by such well-known generals as Norman Schwarzkopf and Tommy Franks. The new corps was the result of a declaration by President Jimmy Carter on January 23, 1980, that the Persian Gulf was of "vital interest" to the United States, and that an attack there would "be repelled by any means necessary, including military force."

Despite falling revenues, Saudi Arabia spent more than $20 billion on defense each year from 1982 to 1985. Much of this money was used to buy massive amounts of ammunition, spare parts, and electronic equipment for the air force. Saudi pilots learned how to use the advanced warning and control (AWACS) radar technology that the kingdom bought from the United States in 1981, and by 1983, the Saudis had created an air defense identification zone known as the "Fahad Line" off the shore of the Persian Gulf.

The zone was put to good use in June 1984. When two Iranian F-4 fighters flew into Saudi airspace, two Saudi F-15s that were keyed into the new AWACS technology immediately shot down the Iranian jets.

Osama bin Laden and the War in Afghanistan

To help Iraq fight Iran, Saudi Arabia sent Iraq money and oil. To help Afghanistan fight the Soviet Union, the kingdom sent money and "volunteers." On Christmas Eve 1979, eighty-five thousand Soviet troops invaded Afghanistan to keep a new communist government from falling, but despite their use of helicopters, bombs, and land mines, the Soviets could hold only the cities. At night, in the countryside, farmers and nomads joined together to fight the foreign, atheist invader. They called themselves *mujahadeen*, fighters of the holy war.

In 1980, President Carter's national security adviser, Zbigniew Brzezinski, promised Saudi Arabia that the United States would match Arab contributions to the Afghan resistance dollar for dollar. It was a promise the Reagan administration renewed in 1981 and kept. Every month for the rest of the 1980s, an average of $100 million was sent to help the Afghans fight the Soviets. Half of the money came from the United States, about a quarter ($300 million a year) from the Saudis, and the rest came from rich Gulf states such as Kuwait, Qatar, and the United Arab Emirates. In accordance with the strong preference of both the Saudi government and Pakistan's dictator, General Zia ul-Haq, almost all of this money went to fundamentalist army officers who were sympathetic to Wahhabism, rather than to any of the more moderate Afghan militias that also fought the Soviets.

The war was brutal. One million Afghans died. Another five million people, one-third of the country, fled their homes for refugee camps in Pakistan and Iran. Despite the carnage, Afghanistan became a magnet for idealistic young Arabs who wanted to fight the Soviet atheists, just as in the 1930s, many educated young Europeans went to Spain to fight the Fascists.

The roughly twenty-five thousand "Afghan Arabs" made up about 10 percent of Afghanistan's fighting force. More than a third of them were Saudis; most of the rest were from Yemen, Algeria, and Egypt. The majority of them came to Afghanistan out of a strong sense of religious duty. (Cynics say that a few may also have decided that they preferred a martyr's harem in paradise to an arranged, earthbound marriage.)

Saudia, the national airline, offered a 75 percent discount to anyone who flew to Peshawar, Pakistan, a large city of fruit canneries and drug smugglers on the Afghan border, to help the Afghan resistance. Even high school students joined the war effort for a few weeks, as if it were a summer camp, and hoped to return for a longer time when they finished school. Rich men also enjoyed several weeks of adventure, then gave their jeeps and machine guns to the Afghan fighters who had been their guides. Most of the Saudis, however, were committed young men who were willing to spend years of their lives in cold mountain trenches.

The most infamous of the Saudi fighters was Osama bin Laden. In 1980, right after the Soviet invasion, bin Laden, then twenty-two, flew to Pakistan to meet Afghan leaders. Then he returned to Saudi Arabia to urge his friends to give money to the *mujahadeen* and his relatives to send construction equipment. Bin Laden forwarded millions of dollars to the Afghans to help them buy guns and medical equipment, and he shipped hundreds of bulldozers and dump trucks to help the Afghans build roads, trenches, supply depots, and hydro-electric-powered tunnels, some of which bin Laden designed himself. He also sent explosives, which he had learned how to use, along with bulldozers, while working for his father's construction company during his college years.

Bin Laden's mother, a beautiful young Syrian woman named Alia Ghanem, was only fourteen when she married Muhammad bin Laden.

They divorced just two years later, and she remarried when Osama was about four. Osama (which means "Lion") grew up in Jeddah with three younger stepbrothers and a young stepsister in a home that was only moderately religious. He liked to watch Westerns on television, including the TV series *Bonanza*, and loved to ride horses on a family farm outside the city and hike in the snowy mountains of Turkey.

Bin Laden's father, who over the course of his life had twenty-two wives (four at a time), twenty-five sons, and twenty-nine daughters, died in a plane crash in 1967 when Osama, his eighteenth son, was only nine. Still, the religious man, who had refurbished the Grand Mosque in Mecca, the Prophet's Mosque in Medina, and the Al-Aqsa Mosque in Jerusalem, was a formative influence on the boy. Bin Laden once told a Pakistani reporter, "My father was very keen that one of his sons should fight against the enemies of Islam. So I am the one son who is acting according to the wishes of his father."[5]

When bin Laden's father died, Osama's share of his father's company was worth over $5 million, but by the time he actually received his inheritance at age thirty-one, at the end of the 1980s, its value had grown to roughly $20 million ($35 million in today's money). As a teenager, bin Laden drove a gray Mercedes 280 S, often at high speeds. At seventeen, he married a tall, shy, and beautiful fourteen-year-old Syrian cousin, Najwa, and together they had eleven of his nineteen children. Bin Laden seems to have been a loving and attentive father.

In high school, bin Laden took afterschool classes in the Quran and the *hadith* (the sayings of Muhammad) from a charismatic Syrian gym teacher who was a militant Muslim. Bin Laden soon grew a small beard, played soccer in long pants, refused to play cards, and stopped watching television, except for the news. He also prayed five times a day and fasted on Mondays and Thursdays, as Muhammad had sometimes done.

Tall, quiet, and reserved, bin Laden spent three years studying economics, management, and civil engineering at King Abdul Aziz University in Jeddah before he dropped out of college to work full time for his family's construction company. He is the only bin Laden brother never to have studied in Lebanon or the West and the only brother who enjoyed manual labor, often working in the hot sun beside Pakistani and Filipino laborers.

Bin Laden took courses in religion from Abdullah Azzam, the Palestinian professor who would later cofound Hamas, the Palestinian resistance (most say "terrorist") group. Azzam believed that holy war was every Muslim's most important duty, and that Muslims needed to reconquer every territory they had ever lost, including Palestine, Kashmir, the southern Philippines, and even southern Spain. His guiding principle was "*Jihad* and the rifle alone: no negotiations, no conferences, and no dialogue." When the Soviets invaded Afghanistan, Azzam traveled all over the world, at bin Laden's expense, to recruit men for the war. "One hour in the battle line for Allah," he told students, "is better than sixty years of prayer."[6] (In 1989, Azzam and two of his sons were killed by a car bomb outside a mosque in Peshawar. No one knows who set it off.)

Inspired by Azzam, bin Laden moved to Peshawar in 1984 and opened a home, "the House of the Supporters," where unmarried recruits could stay before they went into battle. If the recruits were married and brought their families with them, bin Laden paid them $300 a month, more than enough to live comfortably in Pakistan. Bin Laden also supplied the *mujahadeen* with four-wheel-drive pickup trucks that were specially equipped with mine detectors and antitank missiles.

One prominent new arrival in Peshawar was Ayman al-Zawahiri, an Egyptian surgeon and a member of the militant Muslim Brotherhood who had just served three years in prison for activity related to Anwar Sadat's assassination. During his first year in Afghanistan, Zawahiri operated on wounded soldiers. He also became close friends with Osama bin Laden and, in time, the number-two man in al-Qaeda.

In 1986, bin Laden built a fortress of caves and training camps called "the Lion's Den" high above an Afghan village called Jaji. In April 1987, more than a hundred specially trained Soviet troops spent three weeks firing mortar shells and napalm bombs at the fortress. Bin Laden and about two-thirds of the fifty Arabs who had been fighting in the caves managed to break free and retreat, destroying their camp before they left to keep it from falling to the Soviets. The battle was widely seen as a victory for the Arabs because they had immobilized a much larger and vastly superior force for almost a month.

The Afghan Arabs deeply admired bin Laden's courage, quiet eloquence, gentle manners, and total commitment to Islam. As one volunteer explained, "He was a hero to us because he was always on the front line. He not only gave his money, he also gave himself. He came down from his palace [in Saudi Arabia] to live with the Afghan peasants and the Arab fighters. He cooked with them, ate with them, dug trenches with them. That was bin Laden's way."[7] Peter Bergen, an author who interviewed the al-Qaeda leader in 1997, said that

" 'love' is not too strong a word for the feelings of those who surround bin Laden."[8]

Custodian of the Two Holy Mosques

While Osama bin Laden was fighting the Soviets, his older brothers ran the family's huge construction business. In 1985, King Fahad authorized $11.2 billion for some highly prestigious construction projects that were either completed or supervised by the Saudi Binladen Group. These projects included:

- Doubling the size of Mecca's Grand Mosque, allowing one million people to circle the Kaaba

- Enlarging the Prophet's Mosque in Medina to ten times its former size, enabling five hundred thousand people to pray there at one time

- Expanding the airport in Jeddah and the tent cities in Mecca and Medina so that more Muslims could make the pilgrimage to the two holy cities

- Restoring the Al-Aqsa Mosque and the Dome of the Rock in Jerusalem

King Fahad, proud of his family's role in making the pilgrimages to Mecca and Medina easier, cheaper, and safer for Muslims around the world, announced on October 27, 1986, that he wanted a new and more humble title. "I want to replace 'His Majesty' by something I adore and am honored to carry, and that is 'Custodian of the Two Holy Mosques.' " The Arabic word that Fahad used is also translated as "Servant," but in English-language publications the Saudi government preferred the word *Custodian*.

The Mid-1980s: Rock-Bottom Oil Production, Prices, and Revenues

In the mid-1980s, the world's supply of petroleum exceeded its demand by several million barrels a day because energy conservation was rising, and the North Sea oil fields were producing. If the OPEC nations wanted to keep the price of oil at $27 a barrel, they would have to honor the production ceilings that they had agreed to in previous meetings.

Instead, most of the OPEC nations routinely cheated by pumping more oil than their ceilings allowed. To try to stop the cheating, OPEC hired an accounting firm in 1984 to investigate the violations. Each country promised the accountants access to every oil installation and document, but when the investigations actually began, several countries never even gave the accountants a visa. The cheating continued.

To prevent the price of oil from collapsing, Saudi Arabia cut its production several times to keep the supply of oil in line with the demand. In 1981, the kingdom had pumped more than 10 million barrels of oil a day. By 1984, its production had fallen to 5 million barrels a day, and during one month in the summer of 1985, it plunged to just 2.2 million barrels a day, less than the North Sea oil production of Britain. Oil was still $27 a barrel, but Saudi revenues in 1985 were just one-fifth of what they were in 1981 because the kingdom had lost its share of the market to many competitors—to the Soviet Union, which sold as much oil as it could at this high price; to Britain and Norway, the North Sea producers; and to the OPEC nations that cheated by exceeding their ceilings.

Zaki Yamani, the Saudi oil minister, repeatedly warned the other OPEC nations that if they continued to ignore their ceilings, Saudi Arabia would be forced to abandon its sacrificial role as OPEC's swing producer and would flood the market with Saudi oil. This would cause a price collapse, but since Saudi revenues had already fallen 80 percent since 1981, they could not fall much further.

Yamani's threat to stop supporting the $27 price had no effect; the other OPEC nations continued to exceed their ceilings. Because Iran was at war, it had no interest in the price of oil next year or even next month. It needed to sell as much oil as it could *now*. Indonesia and Nigeria had vast populations many times larger than Saudi Arabia's and were desperate for cash to meet their people's most basic needs. Britain was not a member of OPEC and had never agreed to a production ceiling; Margaret Thatcher, the prime minister, strongly believed that a free market, not OPEC, should set the price of oil.

In January 1986, Saudi Arabia finally made good on its threat and increased its oil production 50 percent, to about five million barrels a day. What probably triggered this decision was Iran's invasion of the Faw peninsula, Iraq's only outlet to the sea. If Iran were not stopped, Iraq would become landlocked. The Saudis hoped not only that their long-threatened increase in oil production would let them regain their market share, but also that the resulting fall in price would devastate Iran's economy and its ability to maintain a large army.

Yamani had warned King Fahad that the kingdom's extra production would make the price of oil fall to $20 a barrel and possibly to $15 a barrel. But to the Saudis' dismay, the price nose-dived to $13 a barrel in February and to only $9 a barrel by November. This was partly because President Reagan and Margaret Thatcher saw a chance to break OPEC and encouraged Western producers to pump as much oil as they could.

The increase in Saudi Arabia's oil production could not make up for this steep fall in price, so the kingdom's revenues plunged 30 percent in 1986, to only $17 billion, less than one-sixth of the nation's revenue in 1981. Fortunately, Saudi Arabia had foreign reserves to draw on. By contrast, Iran, with no such cushion, slowly ran out of money and, very soon, weapons.

The fall in the price of oil also had an enormous effect on the Soviet Union. The Soviets were almost as dependent on oil revenue as the Arabs were, and the Soviet Union had prospered greatly in the 1970s when the price of oil was high. Now, with the price in 1986 only one-third as high as it had been in 1985, the Soviet economy, already frayed, began to collapse. It is probable that this steep drop in price was even more instrumental in ending the Cold War than the Reagan administration's purchases of advanced weapons were.

By the time OPEC met in Geneva in August 1986, most oil exporters had been seriously hurt by the falling price and were finally ready to honor their production ceilings. They proposed new and lower ceilings and that Saudi Arabia once again become the swing producer. "Not on your life," Yamani said. "We all swing together or not at all." Saudi Arabia would no longer cut production to reduce the supply of oil but would have a production ceiling of its own.

Yamani also insisted that if the new ceilings were going to work, at least some of the *non*-OPEC nations would also have to cut their production. Chastened by the falling price, the Soviet Union and Mexico promised small cuts, and Norway pledged that an increase already in the works would be its last.

Yamani knew that the fall in the price of oil was hurting everyone, yet he felt that patience would pay off. But Yamani did not have to govern the kingdom while revenues fell. King Fahad did. Not only did the kingdom's revenues decline 80 percent between 1981 and 1986, its population grew 36 percent during the same period. By 1986, Fahad did not know where the money to finance the 1986–1987 budget would come from. In March, with tears in his eyes, the king announced on television that there would be no official budget that year. As had been true when his father, Abdul Aziz, was king, the government would improvise its finances, one month at a time.

Fahad was mortified by the kingdom's budgetary troubles and blamed them on Yamani's strategy of letting the price of oil fall in order to regain market share. The king also began to feel pressure from the United States because, ironically, even the United States felt that the price of oil had fallen too low. At $30 a barrel, America's domestic oil industry had boomed. Geologists explored new fields in Alaska and Texas, tar sands in Alberta and Colorado, and offshore deposits in the Gulf of Mexico. At $9 a barrel, none of these ventures was profitable. The U.S. oil industry was shutting down, but the U.S. government was not prepared to be 100 percent dependent on imported oil.

In April 1986, Vice President George Bush flew to Riyadh to warn Yamani and several other Saudi ministers that if the price of oil stayed this low, Congress would place a tariff on imported oil. Bush did not mention this when he met King Fahad the next evening, and later the Reagan administration assured Arab nations that it was opposed to a tariff. But the message had been delivered: the price of oil needed to rise.

In the United States, a consensus emerged among politicians and businessmen that the best price of oil would range between $15 and $18 a barrel, roughly the price of oil in 1978 just before the second energy crisis. Within this range, oil would be low enough to boost economic growth, but just high enough to let America's domestic oil industry survive.

King Fahad, of course, preferred that oil be $18 a barrel, rather than $15 a barrel. In October, before OPEC's next meeting in Geneva, he instructed Yamani to ask for both the $18 price and the increased production level that Saudi Arabia had maintained during the previous year. Yamani tried to tell the king that this was not possible, that there was a tradeoff between price and production, but Fahad was insistent. Finally, Yamani said that he would distribute a statement asking for both increased production and the $18 price with the king's signature, but that he could not issue it in the name of the Petroleum Ministry.

One week later, on October 29, after two more conversations with the king, Yamani was fired. The announcement was made on television, and no one had told Yamani beforehand. King Fahad had never liked his oil minister but had kept him in the cabinet for eleven years after Faisal's assassination because of his enormous talent. In September, Fahad had complained to one of his ministers, "Instead of Yamani coming to me with oil policy, trying to convince me and let me say yes, I have to go to him, to try to convince him, and he says no."[9]

Zaki Yamani had been Saudi Arabia's oil minister for twenty-four years, from 1962 to 1986. He was the driving force behind OPEC, and although the cartel hurt the world's economy, it brought tremendous wealth to his own country. Yamani also knew that if the price of oil climbed too high, it would lead to energy conservation, new fields, and a large glut, and for many years he tried to keep the price from rising too quickly. What he wanted most was for OPEC to keep its control over the price of oil, but this could happen only if every nation respected its production ceiling. When discipline loosened, OPEC lost its power and the market reasserted its control over the price of oil.

One of Yamani's many admirers was James Schlesinger, secretary of defense under President Richard Nixon and President Gerald Ford, and secretary of energy under President Jimmy Carter. "He was the smart one," Schlesinger said. "Why did the cartel weaken? Because the cartel overshot its goals, over the protest of one Zaki Yamani. Prices would never have been $35 a barrel if he'd had his way."[10]

Fahad appointed Hisham Nazer to be the kingdom's new minister of petroleum. Nazer was a UCLA graduate who had been the minister of planning. At Nazer's first OPEC meeting in Geneva in December, the member nations agreed on a "reference price" of $18 a barrel. In fact, as Yamani had tried to tell Fahad, the price fluctuated between $15 and $18 a barrel, and because the OPEC nations were now obeying their quotas, it stayed within this $15 to $18 range for the rest of the 1980s.

Cutting Back

Oil revenues stayed low throughout the mid- and late 1980s; no one thought that the glut would last so long. Mercifully, King Fahad's government did not have to cut its budget as fast as its income had fallen because it could draw on the massive foreign reserves it had accumulated in the 1970s. Even so, Saudi Arabia cut its budget in half between 1983 and 1987, yet by 1990, the government had still spent $120 billion more than it had earned and had used up three-quarters of its foreign exchange reserves.

Money was tight, but the government did not cut education and health-care benefits. Instead, it cut the defense budget to half of its 1983 level, although the amount spent on high-tech weapons remained the same as before. The government canceled or postponed many construction projects, including oil refineries, power grids, and desalination plants. It also delayed payments to many creditors. At one point, the kingdom owed South Korean contractors $4 billion and French contractors another billion. With money scarce, the economy shrank in half between 1981 and 1986. (It is a testament to Saudi stability that there was no political turmoil during this period.) Many office buildings stayed empty despite steep cuts in rent, and hundreds of construction firms and other businesses went bankrupt.

Many desperate contractors freed themselves from having to pay interest on their loans by suing for debt relief in *sharia* (Islamic) courts, claiming that interest is un-Islamic. The courts usually agreed with the contractors because Muhammad had specifically forbidden interest, once calling it a sin equal to incest with one's mother or to committing adultery thirty-six times. To sidestep this prohibition, Muslim banks have charged "commissions," "service charges," and "bookkeeping fees," but often a *sharia* court deducts these costs from the amount that a borrower has to pay. Partly because of these lawsuits, Saudi banks lost a great deal of money in the 1980s, and four banks needed government help to keep from going bankrupt.

Today Saudi banks rarely lend money except to the government and to a few wealthy and highly reliable borrowers. Until the clergy resolves the question of the role of interest in a modern economy, few Saudis will be able to borrow money from anyone outside their own families.

Almost every government ministry announced a hiring freeze in the 1980s. As unemployment grew, the government also pressured universities to tighten admissions and flunk more students to reduce the number of graduates looking for jobs.

Many women graduated from Saudi universities, but only 5 percent of adult women had jobs in the late 1980s. The percentage today is still only 7 percent. Work for women is restricted to fields where they can be separate from men, typically in education, health, beauty salons, and all-female banks. The country's economic troubles led many people to call for a loosening of these restrictions, but fundamentalists strongly objected to such a change. Still, many Saudi husbands who used to regard it as a point of honor that their wives not work now encouraged their wives to do so because an extra income allows a family to maintain its standard of living during hard times.

New Oil Deposits and Markets

Amid the economic gloom of the 1980s, there was also a striking find. In 1988, geologists discovered two gigantic new Saudi oil fields that together contained eighty-five *billion* barrels of oil, an amount equal in size to Iran's reserves or to four times the reserves of the United States. One field is 117 miles south of Riyadh; the other is in Dilam, a suburb just 29 miles south of the capital. Together, the two fields increased the nation's proven oil reserves by 50 percent, enough to keep the kingdom at peak production for another quarter of a century.

That year, 1988, was also when Exxon, Chevron, Texaco, and Mobil finally sold their remaining 40 percent share of Saudi Aramco to the Saudi government. The Saudis had bought 25 percent of the company in 1972 and another 35 percent in 1974. The amount that the kingdom paid the oil companies for the final 40 percent of Saudi Aramco is secret, but in 1972, the parties agreed that the Saudis would pay for all of Aramco's installations plus inflation, although not for the kingdom's vast oil reserves, which the Saudis understandably felt that they already owned.

Exxon, Chevron, Texaco, and Mobil continue to provide Saudi Aramco with "substantial technical and managerial services" and are paid a sliding fee for their work, based on the number of barrels of oil produced. However much or little the oil companies earn from this new arrangement, they can hardly complain. During Aramco's first fifty years, the four corporations collectively made well over $100 billion.

One of Saudi Aramco's first actions as a 100 percent Saudi-owned company was to pay Texaco $812 million in August 1988 for a 50 percent share of Star Enterprises, a subsidiary that owns fourteen hundred gas stations in the eastern and southern United States and franchises at least ten thousand more. The purchase guaranteed Saudi Arabia a market for six hundred thousand barrels of Saudi oil a day—insurance against a future oil glut like the one in 1986 and 1987 when the United States imported almost no Saudi oil at all.

Agriculture

Until about 1970, 50 percent of Saudi Arabia's adults farmed or herded livestock, yet contributed only 1 percent to the nation's gross domestic product. Saudi officials were determined to make agriculture more productive, for they also worried that someday the West might counter an oil embargo with a food embargo. One of the chief goals of Saudi Arabia's fourth five-year plan (1985–1990) was to reduce the kingdom's dependence on imported food, and between 1986 and 1990, the government succeeded in tripling the amount of farmland.

As was true in King Faisal's time, the government paid farmers for half and sometimes all of the costs of seeds, pesticides, animal feed, and veterinary services, plus equipment for pumping, spraying, and milking cows. It also gave farmers long-term, no-interest loans to buy land and, in the case of wheat farmers, gave them free land.

The government hoped that by making farming more attractive, it might slow the large migration of rural Saudis into cities, but often a farmer who received the government's help lived in a city and hired foreigners to work the land. Still, by the early 1990s, Saudi Arabia was self-sufficient in some kinds of food and was exporting wheat, eggs, fish, poultry, tomatoes, watermelons, dairy products, and, as always, dates. The kingdom also created a food-processing industry and produced its own pipes, irrigation pumps, and fertilizer. Even so, the kingdom still imported 65 percent of its food.

The government bought crops at subsidized prices. It paid wheat farmers a price five times higher than that of imported wheat. The government sold this wheat at a loss to foreign buyers and, more often, simply gave the wheat away as foreign aid.

The most wasteful thing about Saudi wheat farming is the amount of water it uses, because it takes more than a ton of water to grow a pound of wheat. Only 8 percent of the water that Saudis consume each year is for industry and home use, and most of this comes from rainwater captured by dams or from expensive desalinization plants. By contrast, until the government finally began to gradually reduce its subsidies to wheat farmers in 2008, water used in agriculture accounted for 91 percent of the kingdom's consumption, and nearly all of it came from aquifers, giant underground lakes that are not renewable. Every year, the level of these aquifers sinks another few meters, and farmers have to drill that much deeper to find water. Already, many farmers have to build water-cooling towers, because when water at great depths first comes to the surface, it is much too hot to use. If the kingdom's wheat farming is not cut back substantially, as is planned in the 2010s, the aquifers will disappear in seventy-five years.

Foreign and Saudi Workers

Although the 1980s was a decade of economic decline in Saudi Arabia, foreigners continued to make up more than a quarter of the population and 60 percent of the workforce. By the end of the decade, there were four million expatriates in the kingdom from all over the world, especially from Yemen, Egypt, India, and Pakistan. Nearly all of them worked for private employers. Many worked in factories or on construction sites, but a third of the foreigners had jobs as chauffeurs, housekeepers, and cooks. The goal of most expatriates, who often live five or six to a room, is to make money as quickly as possible and then go home. Only 3 percent of foreign workers stay in the kingdom more than six years.

Even Saudi employers prefer to hire foreigners. Not only are foreigners much cheaper to hire than Saudis are, but often they also have better skills, work harder, and take orders more easily than Saudis do. Laws dating to 1954 require that half of a firm's workforce be Saudi, but this impractical requirement has never been enforced. About three-fourths of the Saudis who work do so for the government, which makes up an enormous one-third of the workforce. Sometimes the government hires three Saudis for a single job, then hires a foreigner to do the work, said Anthony Cordesman, a highly respected military analyst who is a tough critic but nevertheless a friend of the House of Saud.

Many Saudi bureaucrats arrive for work late and leave early because they have family businesses that take precedence over their government jobs. They can do this because the law makes it difficult to fire a Saudi. Even when two Saudia airline mechanics were negligent and caused a plane crash, it still took the government two years to fire them. "Given the low work ethic and productivity of most Saudis," Cordesman said, "the only incentive to hire a [Saudi] national is usually that he is the son of a friend or a relative or the employer must meet some quota."[11]

Because few employers hire more Saudis than they have to, unemployment has grown so high that today almost a third of young Saudi men are without work. This is a more likely threat to the kingdom's stability than a foreign invasion. Fortunately, the scarcity of work has changed Saudi thinking. In the 1970s, an ex-Bedouin who just moved to the city might have taken offense at an employer's directions, and in the 1980s, a young college graduate might have been too spoiled by wealth to work hard. Today, if a Saudi man is lucky enough to have a job, he is much more willing than his father was to do whatever his employer requires. The skills of young Saudi men remain limited, but their work ethic is improving.

The Abuse of Housemaids

The foreign workers in Saudi Arabia with the hardest lives have been the domestic servants of sexually abusive employers. Although most servants in the kingdom are treated well, until 2004 more than a thousand young women a year from impoverished Asian nations such as Indonesia, Sri Lanka, or the Philippines arrived at Saudi homes only to discover that their employers or the employers' sons wanted sex. Young women in this predicament were unable to leave the country because their employers had their passports, and a few were even beaten if they dared to leave the house. If a woman was lucky, she escaped to her country's embassy and lived in a hostel for several months until her employer finally agreed to return her passport and let her fly home unpaid.

In 1988, the president of the Philippines, Corazon Aquino, was so outraged by the repeated abuse of Filipino women that she banned single women from working in Saudi Arabia. When King Fahad learned of this restriction, he took it as an insult and refused to grant visas to any Filipinos, male or female, who wanted to work in the kingdom. After several months, Aquino had to back down because too many Filipino families needed the money that a relative working in Saudi Arabia can earn.

By 1989, hundreds of thousands of Filipinos were working in Saudi Arabia again, and an unlucky fraction still endured the unwanted advances of an employer or his son. To discourage sexual abuse, Saudi Arabia began to require housemaids to be at least forty years old, but the regulation was never enforced, and no sexually aggressive homeowner was punished until 2002. A minority of Saudi men continued to sexually harass their servants until the Ministry of Labor finally began to crack down on the abuse in 2004.

King Fahad was said to be insulted by President Aquino's 1988 prohibition of single women working in Saudi Arabia, but, apparently, the bad publicity bothered him more than the abuses themselves did. One woman suggested that if the violation of Asian girls had truly disturbed the king, a single public flogging of a sexual predator would probably have put an end to 90 percent of the problem.

Education

A 1988 survey in the Eastern Province revealed that while 81 percent of women fifty-five years or older were illiterate and only 3 percent had a fifth-grade education or better, education had dramatically improved for their daughters. Among women thirty-five or younger, 23 percent had a university degree, 68 percent had graduated from high school, and no one was illiterate. Across the country, 45 percent of the 2.5 million children in school in 1990 were women, as were half of the 130,000 Saudis in colleges and universities.

Educational facilities for Saudi women were often inferior and became more so after the budget cuts of the 1980s. Male students enjoyed smaller classes, longer library hours, and more teachers with advanced degrees and had slightly fewer religion courses in their curriculum. Still, most girls were happy to have a reason to get out of the house and consistently did better than boys on standardized tests.

Education is not compulsory in Saudi Arabia, and dropout rates were high. One-third of Saudi children did not graduate from high school. Many boys in rural areas left school if they had a paying job, as did many women if they married young.

The number of students in college tripled in the 1980s, and the number of engineering colleges grew from five to forty-two. Yet the number of Saudis studying overseas declined from 12,500 in 1985 to only 3,554 in 1990. Because of budget cuts and growing conservatism, the government no longer paid for a student's education abroad if the same courses were available at home, and women were no longer given money to study abroad unless they were accompanied by a husband or a father.

The rise in unemployment greatly improved the Saudi attitude toward manual labor. As part of its third five-year plan (1980–1985), the government built vocational schools to teach carpentry, plumbing, welding, electrical work, automobile mechanics, refrigerator repair, and architectural drawing. Not only did the government pay for room, board, and tuition, it also paid a student a salary during training and, after an apprenticeship, gave him a $59,000 interest-free loan to help him start a business. Despite these incentives, few young Saudis were interested in a career in manual labor in the early 1980s. Even the school for air traffic controllers had more teachers than students.

Attitudes changed in the late 1980s, when oil fell to $9 a barrel and unemployment climbed to 30 percent. The country's twenty-six vocational training centers, which required only a fifth-grade education, began to fill up, as did the eight technical institutes that required only a high school diploma. By 1993, there were almost eighty thousand vocational and technical students in Saudi Arabia, about the same as the number of young men studying at colleges and universities.

Marriage

The 1988 survey in the Eastern Province that showed how illiteracy had declined among women also highlighted some striking changes in the way young Saudi women marry and live. The study revealed that most Saudi women marry between the ages of sixteen and twenty-five, while their grandmothers had married at thirteen or fourteen. Forty-five percent of current marriages were arranged, 36 percent were "semi-arranged," and 19 percent, not arranged at all. Thirty-one percent of the young women had married their first cousins, and 23 percent had married second cousins, although the percentage of college-educated women who marry cousins is slightly lower. The percentage of women who marry their cousins is much lower in most other Arab nations but is equally high in Kuwait and Pakistan.

Ten percent of young Saudi women were married to men with two or more wives, but for their grandmothers, this percentage was 61 percent. Finally, young wives today are much more likely to have their own homes. Only 6 percent of young Saudi couples lived with their in-laws, but 68 percent of their grandmothers had.

The Tanker War

In January 1986, Iran sent tens of thousands of troops into Iraq and captured much of Iraq's twenty-five-mile-long Faw peninsula within a month. For a brief period, it seemed as if Iran might win the war. Iraq's only outlet to the sea was cut, and the Iranians were only forty-five miles from Basra, Iraq's second-largest city. With no allies, however, and with the price of oil falling, Iran did not have enough money to buy the tanks and the artillery it needed to advance its lines. The fighting literally bogged down in the marshes of the Faw peninsula, where eventually twenty-five thousand Iranians and fifteen thousand Iraqis lost their lives.

Iraq fired artillery at nearby oil refineries and missiles at distant cities, but it could not expel Khomeini's troops from its territory. In July, Iraq tried a different strategy: firing missiles at oil tankers sailing to and from Iran. Iran responded by attacking Kuwaiti tankers that were carrying oil to Iraq. The Tanker War had begun. During the next two years, Iran and Iraq damaged more than three hundred oil tankers from two dozen nations, although they sank only a few.

In November, Kuwait asked the United States to protect its shipping. President Reagan hesitated at first, so, as a precaution, Kuwait also asked for protection from the Soviet Union. The prospect of Soviet ships fighting in the Persian Gulf greatly alarmed the Reagan administration, and in March 1987, the United States offered to protect Kuwait's ships without any help from the Soviets, and Kuwait agreed.

As an Arab nation, Saudi Arabia was careful not to seem too close to the United States, but it had welcomed a U.S. naval presence "over the horizon"—outside the Persian Gulf—in Oman, Kenya, and the island of Diego Garcia in the Indian Ocean. In public, Saudi Arabia criticized Kuwait's request for U.S. protection, but in private, the pro-American Fahad was pleased by the added security the U.S. Navy would provide. The United States already had AWACS aircraft in Dhahran and a small navy base in Bahrain, which Bahrain now allowed it to upgrade. The U.S. Navy also built large platforms just off the Saudi and Kuwaiti coasts as maintenance stations for its warships.

By July 1987, Kuwait had put U.S. flags on eleven of its oil tankers, making them eligible for escorts by the U.S. Navy. The United States sent thirty ships to the Gulf: aircraft carriers, battleships, frigates, and minesweepers, manned by thirty thousand sailors. Britain, France, and Italy contributed ships, too. It was the largest flotilla since the Vietnam War, and it kept Iran from expanding its war into Kuwait or Saudi Arabia. Iraq continued to receive money from Saudi Arabia and Kuwait and weapons from the Soviet Union and France, and this tipped the war in Iraq's favor.

Carnage in Mecca

On July 31, 1987, 402 people died during a riot in Mecca, including 275 Iranians and 127 people from many other nations. Accounts as to what happened differ widely.

What is undisputed is that in the summer of 1987, Iran's war against Iraq was going badly, and in desperation the Iranians decided to make trouble during the *hajj*, the pilgrimage to Mecca, with the vague hope of overthrowing the House of Saud. Khomeini sent more than 150,000 pilgrims to Mecca that summer, including his wife, Khadija, with specific instructions to engage in marches and demonstrations. On July 31, the crowd surged through the streets of Mecca carrying posters of Khomeini and banners that said, "Victory Is Made by Waves of Martyrs." Saudi law banned demonstrations near the Grand Mosque, and as the crowd approached the holy site, it was met by Saudi riot police.

The Iranians charge that the Saudi police simply opened fire, killing 402 people and wounding more than a thousand. The Saudis claim that the police were trying to stop an unruly mob from seizing the Grand Mosque and from trampling innocent people.

In Tehran the next day, thousands of people ransacked the Saudi embassy as Khomeini vowed to avenge the deaths of the pilgrims by overthrowing the Saudi government. "We will export our . . . Islamic teachings to enslaved nations," he declared.

Before next year's *hajj* began, Saudi Arabia set a quota for the number of pilgrims it would allow into the kingdom: 1 for every 1,000 people in a given country. This quota allowed an ample number of people to come from every nation, including 45,000 from Iran. But Khomeini wanted to send 150,000 pilgrims again, and when the Saudis refused, he announced a boycott of the *hajj* and banned any Iranian from making the pilgrimage. Surprisingly, he said that an Iranian's political duty not to go to Mecca took precedence over his religious duty to make the journey.

The carnage in Mecca turned Arab public opinion decisively against Iran. Arabs were outraged that Khomeini's supporters would corrupt the *hajj* to engage in a tawdry political demonstration. In Saudi Arabia, the tragedy ended any possibility that the kingdom might become neutral later in the war, and it greatly increased the public's support for King Fahad's massive aid to Iraq.

Buying Missiles from China and Jets from Britain

In 1988, Communist China delivered fifty long-range CSS-2 surface-to-surface missiles to Saudi Arabia, a type of missile that the Chinese themselves use to carry nuclear warheads. The $3 billion arms deal was made in secret in 1986 and became public only when the missiles arrived in the kingdom. The purchase included a dozen mobile launchpads and a team of Chinese technicians to operate and maintain the missiles.

Although the missiles could be modified to carry nuclear, biological, or chemical weapons, both Saudi Arabia and China have assured the United States that the missiles' warheads are conventional. There has been no evidence to lead anyone to doubt this. The missiles have a range of 1,650 miles and can hit targets in Iran, Iraq, and Yemen. All three nations had already purchased medium-range missiles themselves, so Saudi Arabia felt the need to buy its own missiles to deter them. The Saudi missiles can also reach Israel, and Israel has publicly reserved the right to destroy the kingdom's missile bases if it ever feels sufficiently threatened. The United States has warned Israel never to take such a step.

As long as Saudi Arabia's missiles are conventional, their effectiveness is limited. They have no more destructive power than a single fighter jet and are accurate only to within two miles. This means that while the missiles can destroy a block or two of a city, the target is essentially random. For the Saudis, it is enough that the Iranians know that Saudi missiles can hit some part of Tehran.

The U.S. Congress did not like the idea of an Arab country buying nuclear missiles, even if the nation was an ally and the warheads were conventional. It therefore refused to approve a pending sale of F-15 fighter jets to the kingdom, which prompted the Saudis to buy weapons from Great Britain instead. In a huge, ten-year, $20 billion arms contract, perhaps the largest arms deal in history, the Saudis bought squadrons of fighter-bombers, helicopters and training planes, a fleet of minesweepers, and the services of hundreds of technicians and instructors. The British also began the construction of two giant new air force bases. Even today, the Saudis account for about 75 percent of Britain's weapons exports.

The End of the Iran-Iraq War

By 1988, Iran's peasants and factory workers were refusing to send any more of their sons to suicide on the battlefield. On February 29, Tehran was hit by 17 Iraqi Scud missiles, followed by another 120 in March. One-fourth of the city's people fled to stay with relatives in smaller towns, but some provincial cities were hit, too. On April 18, Iraq retook the Faw peninsula, and on the same day, U.S. planes destroyed two Iranian oil platforms in retaliation for an Iranian naval mine that had damaged a U.S. frigate.

A week later, King Fahad, emboldened by the U.S. presence and the Iraqi advance, broke off diplomatic relations with Iran and announced that if any Iranian ship or plane entered Saudi territory, the kingdom would respond with force, possibly including the use of its Chinese missiles. Fahad's tough stance was in marked contrast to his reluctance to fight Iran three years earlier.

In June, Iraq, using satellite photos supplied by the CIA and its own stocks of poison gas, finally succeeded in pushing Iran's soldiers back across the border. The troops of both nations were now in almost the same position they had been when the war began eight years earlier. In mid-July, Iran's top clerics (but not Khomeini) met one night to review the situation. The Iranian theocracy was running out of soldiers, weapons, and money, and, unlike Iraq, it had no allies.

Iran had no chance of winning the war, and if it did not accept the UN cease-fire soon, it would start to lose large tracts of land and oil to Saddam Hussein.

After long discussions, the clerics agreed on the need to end the war as soon as possible, but their unanimity was irrelevant unless Khomeini concurred. Reluctantly, he did. On July 18, 1988, Iran announced its willingness to accept a UN cease-fire. After a month of negotiating, the war finally stopped on August 20. In Tehran, the people danced in the streets for days, but Khomeini, in his address to the nation, was somber:

> Taking this decision was more deadly than drinking hemlock. I submitted myself to God's will and drank this drink for His satisfaction. To me, it would have been more bearable to accept death and martyrdom. . . . God willing, we will empty our hearts' anguish at the appropriate time by taking revenge on the Al Saud and America.[12]

More than 190,000 Iranians and 200,000 Iraqis died in the war, and an additional 250,000 Iranians and 300,000 Iraqis were seriously wounded. The Iran-Iraq conflict saw more trench warfare than any other conflict since World War I, but as was true on Europe's western front, neither side's troops ever moved more than a few miles, despite all the slaughter.

Khomeini died just ten months after the war ended, on June 4, 1989. Millions of people from all over Iran poured into Tehran to see his body, but in Saudi Arabia, across the Persian Gulf, a relieved government did not even send a note of condolence.

With Iran no longer a threat, Saudi Arabia had a new problem: Iraq. A huge, well-equipped, and battle-hardened army of one million men lay idle just north of the kingdom's border, led by a reckless and ruthless dictator. Since 1985, Saddam Hussein's Iraq had been the world's largest purchaser of weapons. Now it was one of the world's biggest debtors. Iraq owed Saudi Arabia $26 billion, Kuwait $14 billion, the Soviet Union $9 billion, France $4 billion, Japan $3 billion, China $1.5 billion, and Poland $1 billion, and it owed $15 billion more to many other nations. Unfortunately, because Iraq and Iran were selling oil again, the price of oil fell to $15 a barrel, so Iraq's revenues in 1989 were only $15 billion, barely enough to run a nation of seventeen million people, much less pay any debts.

The Saudis quickly realized that Iraq would never be able to pay its $26 billion debt to the kingdom and adjusted their books accordingly. Kuwait, by contrast, continued to raise the issue of debt with Iraqi officials.

The "Afghan Arabs" Return to
a Poorer Saudi Arabia

In February 1989, Mikhail Gorbachev decided that it was time to withdraw his nation's troops from Afghanistan. Thirteen thousand Soviet soldiers had died there, and thousands more had lost legs to land mines. The "Afghan Arabs" had only a marginal role in defeating the Soviets. The key factors in the *mujahadeen* victory were the perseverance of the Afghans themselves and the U.S. hand-held "Stinger" missiles that made it possible for the *mujahadeen* to shoot down Soviet helicopters.

That was not how many Arabs saw it. They believed that they would have won a victory even without the Stinger missiles because Allah was on their side. They had defeated the Soviet Union just as their heroes, the early Muslims, had vanquished the Persian Empire in the seventh century. Their next task, they believed, was to fight the other great infidel empire, the United States of America, just as the Companions of the Prophet had fought the Byzantines, the western infidels of their day. In the words of Osama bin Laden, "the myth of the superpower was destroyed not only in my mind but also in the minds of all Muslims."

In August 1988, bin Laden founded an organization of Arab veterans called al-Qaeda ("the base"). This base was not a training center, since his followers were returning from Afghanistan and Pakistan to homes throughout the Muslim world, but a database—a complex network of secret contacts, many addresses (at first physical, later electronic), and large stashes of explosives and cash. Only a few months later, bin Laden had to leave Pakistan because he had given briefcases full of money to four political opponents of Pakistan's first female prime minister, Benazir Bhutto. Bhutto let bin Laden know that he was no longer welcome in Pakistan, and bin Laden, thirty-two, returned to Saudi Arabia.

The ten thousand or so Saudi veterans of the Afghan war came back to a much poorer country than the one they had left in the early 1980s. Not only was the kingdom's economy just half the size it had been in 1981, its population had grown 50 percent, from ten million to fifteen million people. In other words, instead of two people sharing a large pie, three people had to share a smaller pie. Income per person in 1989 was only one-third of what it had been in 1981.

The people hurt most by Saudi Arabia's declining economy were the underemployed peasants and ex-Bedouin who had just recently moved to the cities. Unlike their fathers, many of these men could read, and they were keenly aware of the corruption and the inequality rampant in a monarchy with five thousand princes. At mosques, they listened to fiery preachers who, without having to say so, condemned the lavish lifestyle of the royal family by emphasizing the humility and plain living of Muhammad, Abu Bakr, and Umar.

In Afghanistan, the Saudi veterans had been respected warriors who handled explosives and machine guns. In the kingdom, they were just unemployed young men. But in contrast to other jobless Saudis, the "Afghan Arabs" had a network of war-tested friendships, and together they turned their critical eyes toward their own government.

Prelude to the Gulf War

In spite of everything, the first half of 1990 was a calm time in Saudi Arabia. The Soviets were out of Afghanistan, the Iranians were out of Iraq, and with oil only $15 a barrel, the Western drive to conserve energy, find new deposits, and use alternative fuels had petered out. The industrial nations were importing more oil from the Persian Gulf than ever before. Even the merger of North and South Yemen on May 21, which troubled the Saudis because Yemen now had a population as big as the kingdom's, was not a cause for too much worry. With no oil, Yemen was simply too poor to ever be much of a military threat.

In June, Saddam Hussein became more bellicose. He asked each of the Arab members of OPEC to give him $10 billion as payment for Iraq's services in fighting Iran. The money would have enabled Iraq to pay its debts, but, not surprisingly, this unusual request was refused. Hussein also renewed a territorial claim to two sparsely populated Kuwaiti islands off Iraq's war-torn Faw peninsula: Warbah, about half the size of Manhattan, and Bubiyan, about the size of the rest of New York City.

On July 16, Iraq lodged a more serious charge when it accused Kuwait of illegally tapping into Iraq's Rumaila oil field just north of its border with Kuwait and demanded $2.4 billion as payment for the stolen oil. On July 20, King Fahad telephoned both Saddam Hussein and Kuwait's Sheikh Jabir al-Ahmad as-Sabah to try to get them to settle their growing differences, but the next day Hussein sent thirty thousand troops to the border of Kuwait, to join another forty thousand Iraqi soldiers who were already there.

On July 23 and 24, Egypt's president Hosni Mubarak flew to Iraq and Kuwait to try to mediate the dispute. In private, Mubarak thought that Hussein was "psychotic," but he succeeded in getting the two nations to agree to talks in Jeddah the following week. Before the talks even began, Hussein sent another thirty thousand men southward. He now had three hundred tanks and a hundred thousand troops poised along Kuwait's border. Hussein had promised both King Fahad and President Mubarak, however, that he was not planning an invasion.

When the talks started on August 1, Kuwait's crown prince, Sa'ad al-Abdallah as-Sabah, made major concessions. Kuwait was willing to lease Warbah island, pay part of Iraq's $2.4 billion claim for siphoned oil, and, most important, forgive all of Iraq's $14 billion debt. But Hussein's deputy, Izzat Ibrahim, insisted on Bubiyan island as well and demanded billions of dollars more from Kuwait as "compensation" for fighting Iran. He then ended the talks and flew back to Baghdad. The Gulf War began the next day.

The Invasion of Kuwait

At 2:00 a.m. on August 2, 1990, more than a hundred thousand Iraqi troops crossed the border to invade Kuwait. Iraq's elite Republican Guard, its less-disciplined regular army, and its brutal security police entered Kuwait in tanks, armored personnel carriers, and ordinary buses. Within one hour, they were advancing southward down the six-lane highway to Kuwait City. Within five hours, they had conquered the capital.

Iraq has 11 percent of the world's oil; Kuwait, 9 percent. For a few months, Saddam Hussein controlled 20 percent of the Earth's petroleum. Had he been allowed to keep Kuwait, he would have had more than enough money to re-equip his army and start another war, probably against Iran, which, unlike Saudi Arabia, had no allies to protect it. Iran was a war-weary nation with 9 percent of the world's oil. If Hussein had won a second war against Iran, he would have controlled 29 percent of the globe's petroleum, more than Saudi Arabia.

Hussein claimed that Kuwait had once been Iraq's nineteenth province and that the British had drawn Iraq's borders in 1922 with the express purpose of denying it Kuwait's oil. Both arguments were absurd. Kuwait was founded in 1756, 164 years before Iraq came into being—and in 1922, when Iraq's southern border was drawn, no one knew that there was any oil in Kuwait.

Hussein assumed that the world would accept his conquest of Kuwait. It had been only fifteen years since the United States had left Vietnam and only seven since it had left Lebanon. Hussein did not think that the United States had the will or the staying power to pursue another bloody conflict. "Yours is a country which cannot accept ten thousand deaths in one battle," Hussein told U.S. ambassador April Glaspie just one week before the invasion. But Hussein failed to foresee that the world's condemnation of his invasion would be almost unanimous, and that a weakened Soviet Union (it would fall just one year later) would actually join the West in votes at the United Nations.

Incredibly, Saudi television did not broadcast news of the invasion for several days. By then, the Saudi people knew all about it from watching CNN and listening to the BBC. They never really trusted their own government's news again. By 1994, there were almost three hundred thousand satellite dishes in the kingdom, and many Saudis received their news from MBC (Middle East Broadcasting Center), a private Saudi network that is based in London and is therefore much freer than the government-controlled media.

On August 3, at Kuwait's request, the Arab foreign ministers met for talks in Cairo. But the Arabs' wars had always been against Israel, not against each other, and this crisis was too new for the leaders to come to any immediate agreement. By contrast, the United Nations acted swiftly. On the same day as the invasion, the Security Council adopted Resolution 660, which demanded "an immediate and unconditional" Iraqi withdrawal from Kuwait and threatened "sanctions and military action if compliance was not forthcoming." Three days later, Security Council Resolution 661 called on all of the world's nations to stop trade with Iraq, except for medical or humanitarian purposes.

On August 5, President George H. W. Bush declared that the invasion of Kuwait "will not stand." In a speech to Congress a month later, he explained that "We cannot permit a resource so vital to be dominated by one so ruthless." On August 6, Bush sent his secretary of defense, Dick Cheney, and General Norman Schwarzkopf to Jeddah to meet King Fahad. They showed the king satellite photos of Iraqi tanks just eight-tenths of a mile from the Saudi border and told the king that without a large U.S. force, there was nothing to stop Saddam Hussein from advancing south another twenty-five miles and conquering some of the kingdom's largest oil fields. Cheney also reassured Fahad, "We will seek no permanent bases. And when you ask us to go home, we will leave."[13]

Crown Prince Abdullah loathed the very thought of infidel troops, including unveiled women, desecrating the home of Islam, although he understood the need for a U.S. presence. Abdullah urged Fahad not to invite U.S. soldiers to the kingdom without first taking a little time to develop a broad consensus for the action. But the king replied, "The Kuwaitis did not rush into a decision, and today they are all guests in our hotels!"[14] He then requested that U.S. troops come to the kingdom as a strictly temporary measure, and by August 8, a brigade of the 82nd Airborne Division and two squadrons of F-15 fighter jets had already arrived.

The indecisive king had just made the biggest decision of his life.

King Abdul Aziz, the founder of modern Saudi Arabia (seated left), and President Franklin D. Roosevelt (seated right) aboard the USS *Quincy* near the Suez Canal, February 14, 1945.

King Abdul Aziz (left) and Sir Percy Cox (right) at Uqair in 1920.

King Abdul Aziz at seventy-three, four years before his death.

King Saud at the United Nations, January 29, 1957.

King Faisal listens to President Lyndon Johnson at the White House, June 21, 1966.

Khalid, king of Saudi Arabia,
1975–1982.

Fahad (aka Fahd), king of
Saudi Arabia, 1982–2005.

King Abdullah, when he was crown prince, speaking to the United Nations General Assembly, September 6, 2001.

Prince Nayef, minister of the interior since 1975, in February 2005.

Prince Saud Al-Faisal, minister of foreign affairs since 1975, speaking to the United Nations General Assembly in 2003.

Well #7, Saudi Arabia's first
successful oil well, in 1938.

An oil refinery near Dhahran in 1956.

Mecca's Grand Mosque at night.

Pilgrims at Mecca's Grand Mosque, home of the Kaaba.

One corner of the Prophet's Mosque in Medina.

The town of Qatif, north of Dhahran, in the early 1950s.

An alley in the town of Qatif in the early 1950s.

Riyadh in 1950.

Riyadh in 2004.

A residential area in Jubail, Saudi Arabia's most industrial city.

17

The Persian Gulf War
(1990–1991)

IN THE AUTUMN OF 1990, 695,000 soldiers from the United States, Europe, and fourteen Muslim countries arrived in Saudi Arabia to enforce a demand by the UN Security Council that Iraq withdraw from Kuwait. Most Saudis were grateful for the global effort, but many disliked having non-Muslim soldiers on their home soil. Saudi pilots flew 7,018 missions (more than Britain) during the coalition's five-week bombing of Iraq in 1991 and lost only three planes. Then, while a quarter of a million U.S. and French troops attacked Iraq itself, a shoreline force of Saudis, Kuwaitis, and U.S. Marines took just four days to liberate Kuwait. After the war, to enforce "no-fly" zones and to deter Iraq from another attack, the Saudis allowed the United States and Britain to keep jets in the kingdom permanently. This angered many clerics, who thought that the Arabian peninsula should be a region for Muslims only.

When Saddam Hussein invaded Kuwait on August 2, 1990, he also sent 130,000 soldiers and 1,200 tanks to the Saudi border. It would take the United States more than a month to assemble enough troops to oppose this force, and during this time, the Saudis were nervous. Iraq's ill-trained but giant army of more than one million troops was at least fifteen times bigger than Saudi Arabia's better-trained but much smaller force.

The first U.S. troops to arrive in the kingdom were fighter pilots and paratroopers from the 82nd Airborne Division. They slept in tents and ate Saudi food (typically, lamb and rice) because their own huts and prepackaged meals had not yet arrived. Initially too few in number to fight the Iraqis successfully, the soldiers jokingly called themselves "speed bumps."

Quickly, reinforcements arrived by sea. Thousands of marines left Diego Garcia, the U.S. base in the Indian Ocean, on ships that carried weapons, equipment, and food for just such military emergencies. The 24th Mechanized Infantry Division sailed from Savannah, Georgia, with troops, tanks, helicopters, spare parts, food, and enormous amounts of water so that soldiers could work in the Arabian Desert's 120-degree heat. It was the largest movement of U.S. troops since the Vietnam War.

The officer in charge of the U.S. effort was General Norman Schwarzkopf, a big, decisive man known for his bear hugs, explosive temper, and broad knowledge of Muslim culture. (When he was a boy, he had lived in Iran, where his father helped to modernize the shah's police force.) Schwarzkopf's first order enforced Saudi law and banned the possession of pornography or any other sexually explicit material, including "body-building magazines, swimsuit editions of periodicals, lingerie or underwear advertisements and catalogues." He also banned alcohol, and there were far fewer disciplinary problems than in previous wars.

On August 9, King Fahad promised the Saudi people that the U.S. presence in Saudi Arabia was strictly temporary, while Iraq falsely claimed that U.S. troops were marching toward Mecca. Four days later, the kingdom's Council of the Senior Clergy issued a *fatwa* (legal ruling) that approved of inviting Christian and Jewish soldiers to a Muslim country if they could help a Muslim army.

Egypt sent troops to the kingdom on August 11, and Syria and Oman followed soon afterward. At sea, the U.S. Navy blockaded the coasts of Iraq and Kuwait to enforce UN Security Council Resolution 661, which established a global boycott of Iraq's oil exports.

In a speech on August 14, President George H. W. Bush called for "the immediate, complete, and unconditional withdrawal of all Iraqi forces from Kuwait." Two weeks later, the U.S. Congress approved Bush's request to send Saudi Arabia 24 F-15 fighter jets and 160 M-1 tanks. In response, Saddam Hussein said that thousands of U.S. troops "will go home shrouded in body bags."

In August, the price of oil soared from $18 to $30 a barrel, but in September, OPEC allowed Saudi Arabia to make up for the loss of petroleum from Iraq and Kuwait by pumping an additional three million barrels of oil a day and also let the United Arab Emirates pump an extra half million barrels a day. This calmed the oil markets and kept the price of oil from climbing higher.

By September, President Bush had called up two hundred thousand members of the Army Reserves and the National Guard, and four U.S. aircraft carriers were speeding toward the Arabian peninsula, accompanied by dozens of submarines and battleships armed with cruise missiles. Huge ships and cargo planes arrived each day carrying thousands of troops and tons of weapons, spare parts, and food. It was a great help that Saudi Arabia had modern ports, six-lane highways, and military and civilian airports with long runways. By the end of the month, enough U.S. troops and equipment had arrived to make Saudi Arabia's oil fields and coastal cities reasonably secure.

Initially, Saudi Arabia's armed forces had 58,000 men, 350 combat aircraft, and 1,200 tanks and armored vehicles. But several thousand more men volunteered for duty, including many Shi'ites, who were allowed into the army for the first time.

The commander of the kingdom's forces was Prince Khalid ibn Sultan, a lieutenant general who was the oldest son of Prince Sultan, the minister of defense. Khalid had graduated from Sandhurst, the British military academy, and earned a master's degree in political science from Auburn University in Alabama. King Fahad had put Khalid in charge of the kingdom's air defenses in 1986, and four years later, when Iraq invaded Kuwait, he was given the command of all of the kingdom's forces. Like General Schwarzkopf, Prince Khalid is big, burly, energetic, and decisive, and by all accounts, the two became fast friends and coordinated their efforts smoothly.

While Prince Khalid assembled a "Joint Arab Task Force" that included troops from Egypt, Kuwait, Syria, Morocco, Oman, Qatar, and the United Arab Emirates, General Schwarzkopf supervised the buildup of a thirty-three-nation coalition of soldiers and airmen from France, Germany, Italy, Britain, Canada, Australia, Turkey, Pakistan, and two dozen smaller nations. By November, more than sixteen hundred U.S. and eight hundred European warplanes had landed in Saudi Arabia, including U.S. F-15, French Mirage, and British Tornado F3 fighters. More than 240,000 U.S. troops had also arrived in the kingdom, but this was enough to defend only Saudi Arabia—"Operation Desert Shield"—and not enough for the liberation of Kuwait, which would soon be called "Operation Desert Storm."

General Schwarzkopf told Secretary of Defense Dick Cheney and Joint Chiefs of Staff chairman Colin Powell that the best time to fight an offensive war against Iraq was in January and February, before the holy month of Ramadan (which fell in March in 1991) and before the scorching heat of April and May. To begin a war in January, President Bush had to decide by early November whether to send 250,000 more troops to Saudi Arabia.

Many Americans were asking why U.S. soldiers should have to die for oil or to protect Kuwait's monarchy. President Bush was reluctant to call the growing conflict a war for oil, but, in fact, oil was the prime issue. Bush, King Fahad, and many European leaders were determined to prevent Saddam Hussein from gaining control of 20 percent of the world's petroleum. It was bad enough that he controlled 11 percent of the Earth's oil even without occupying Kuwait.

On November 8, with King Fahad's approval, President Bush announced his plan to double the number of U.S. soldiers in Saudi Arabia to more than 540,000. Two weeks later, he flew to Saudi Arabia to meet King Fahad, and together, Bush and Fahad repeated their demand for Iraq's "unconditional" withdrawal from Kuwait. They also hoped that the sheer size of their coalition army (760,000 troops by year's end) might make war unnecessary if it convinced Saddam Hussein to yield to world opinion. On November 29, the UN Security Council passed Resolution 678, which demanded that Iraq leave Kuwait by January 15, 1991, or face war.

The Reaction of the Saudi People

Many Saudis wondered how their government could have spent $200 billion on defense during the 1970s and 1980s and ended up with an armed force of only sixty-seven thousand men at the start of this war. "When a few Iraqi troops came along, we had to call on thirty nations to defend us," one Saudi intellectual complained. Another said, "The real 'Guardian of the Two Holy Places' was the U.S. army, not King Fahad."

The arrival of foreign troops was particularly humiliating because there were not supposed to be any infidels in the kingdom. "Let there not be two religions in Arabia," Muhammad had said on his deathbed in 632. Two years later, Umar, the second caliph, put his plea into effect and expelled Jews and Christians from Arabia, although they were paid a fair price for their land and given several years to leave. Centuries later, when foreign oil workers arrived in the 1940s, some Saudis saw their presence as a desecration, but most Saudis felt that their stay was acceptable because their purpose was merely commercial.

Soldiers, however, were a political force, and many Saudis saw the presence of Christian and Jewish soldiers as a violation of Caliph Umar's ancient edict. Some clerics inflamed passions with outright lies, claiming, for example, that Jewish women in the U.S. army had left "their menstrual rags at the base of the *kaaba*."[1] In fact, U.S. troops were always more than five hundred miles away from Mecca.

A more serious challenge to royal authority came from the millions of audiocassettes of the sermons of "the Awakening Sheikhs": Salman al-Awda and Safar al-Hawali. Al-Awda, a professor of law and theology in Riyadh, denounced the senior princes for inviting infidel soldiers to the Arabian peninsula and said that the royal family "believed in President Bush more than it believed in God."

Al-Hawali, who taught theology in Mecca, said in September, "If Iraq has occupied Kuwait, then America has occupied Saudi Arabia. The real enemy is not Iraq. It is the West. . . . While Iraq is the enemy of the hour, America and the West are the enemies of Judgment Day."[2]

Al-Hawali echoed al-Awda's criticism of the royal family: "You do not say 'God will protect us,' you say 'America will protect us.' America has become your God."[3] At the end of *Kissinger's Promise*, a book about Western designs on Arab oil, al-Hawali wrote, "The Crusader invasion of the Arabian peninsula has already undermined the honor . . . of every Muslim."[4] Other, less articulate, clerics repeated these charges in mosques throughout the country.

The Saudi people deeply disliked having so many Western troops in their kingdom, but a large majority supported the royal family's decision to invite them because they saw the Iraqi threat to their nation as the greater evil. The support intensified when refugees from Kuwait described widespread rapes and looting, and when a nationwide convention of 350 clerics in September ruled that it was permissible to ask non-Muslims for help in a holy war.

It also helped that 95 percent of the Western troops were in the Eastern Province, where people were used to the presence of foreign oil workers. In Riyadh, U.S. and European troops were kept on bases far from the city's center, and relatively few Saudis saw them.

The Saudis were determined that Western troops respect Muslim law and customs and not act as wildly as they had in Vietnam. Detailed negotiations about the troops' conduct took place between General Schwarzkopf and Prince Khalid in Riyadh, and in Washington between Colin Powell and his longtime racquetball partner, Prince Bandar bin Sultan, Saudi Arabia's ambassador to the United States.

Together, the four men came up with many compromises. Soldiers could wear crucifixes and Stars of David inside their shirts and blouses but not outside, and they could read Bibles on base but not off base. Ambulances had to replace their red crosses with red crescents. Radio stations could play Christmas melodies, but not Christmas lyrics, and when religious policemen tried to censor incoming Christmas cards, General Schwarzkopf gave them access to the hundreds of tons of mail that arrived each day. The policemen, seeing the enormous amount of work involved, gave up immediately.

Women could drive on base but not off base, and when they were off base, they had to wear hats and cover their arms and legs but not their faces. At first, the Saudis asked whether the female soldiers could just stay home, but both Schwarzkopf and Powell insisted that Western public opinion would not allow troops to fight and die for a country where their women were not welcome.

The Saudis also tried to ban Jewish worship services. Powell was aghast. "They can die defending your country, but they can't pray in it?" he asked Prince Bandar.[5]

"Colin, be reasonable," Bandar replied. "It will be reported on CNN. What will our people think?"[6] The two friends eventually agreed that on Saturdays and holidays, helicopters would fly devout Jewish troops to services on nearby ships.

Christians, by contrast, could worship on Saudi soil in "private gatherings" as long as they were not filmed or publicized. Television reporters such as Katie Couric begged General Schwarzkopf for permission to videotape just *one* service somewhere, but the general was adamant. Not one would be filmed. Even a Thanksgiving service that President and Mrs. Bush attended, which was televised, took place on a U.S. ship offshore.

General Schwarzkopf also banned female entertainers from U.S. bases, so Bob Hope had to leave his troupe of young dancers and actresses behind. In nearby Bahrain, however, the Pointer Sisters gave several concerts for more than ten thousand enthusiastic U.S. and European soldiers.

The Saudi government, for its part, ordered its religious police to keep a low profile during the war and specifically instructed them not to bother Western female soldiers or reporters. For a few brief months, Saudi women could also relax a little and show a wrist, an ankle, or even a wisp of hair without fear of harassment.

On November 6, 1990, forty-seven women in fourteen cars met at a parking lot at a supermarket in Riyadh and dismissed their chauffeurs. Then, in broad daylight, they drove their convoy of automobiles through the center of the city until both the religious and the secular police began to stop them, one car at a time. As the religious policemen surrounded some of the cars, screaming, "Whores!" at the top of their lungs, the calmer secular policemen took the women to their central station for questioning.

The women drivers came from prominent families, had university degrees, and possessed U.S. and European driver's licenses. They told the policemen that chauffeurs were expensive, often consuming 20 percent of a family's income, that Muhammad's wives had ridden camels, that Kuwaiti women who fled Iraq's invasion had driven their cars into Saudi Arabia in August, and that the king was currently allowing American women to drive trucks on military bases only a few miles away. Nevertheless, the police did not release the women until their husbands or fathers had signed statements pledging that their wives or daughters would never drive again and that they would not speak about their protest to anyone.

One woman, however, had invited a *New York Times* reporter to the convoy, so, despite the promises to be silent, the event became world news immediately. Leaflets in Arabic the next day called the women "Communists" and "promoters of vice and lust," called their male relatives "pimps," and listed each woman's name, profession, and telephone number. "Do what you think is appropriate!" the leaflets said menacingly. Many women received hostile telephone calls for months.

Just hours after the pamphlets appeared, twenty thousand fundamentalists gathered at Riyadh's central square to protest what the "whores" had done. Giving women the right to drive, they said, would lead to secret meetings between unrelated men and women and then to the removal of veils. The angry men refused to leave the square until they were asked to do so by Sheikh Abdulaziz ibn Baz, the blind cleric who had not rescinded his ruling that the sun orbits the Earth until 1985.

One week later, Prince Nayef, the minister of the interior, turned custom into law. A new ruling, approved by the senior clergy, made it illegal for women to drive in Saudi Arabia, even though the Quran says nothing about driving, and driving is legal in every other Muslim country.

Ironically, King Fahad had seriously considered measures to make it easier for women to drive but now had to abandon them in the face of conservative fury. At a time when the king desperately needed the clergy's approval of the arrival of more than six hundred thousand non-Muslim troops, the last thing he needed was a conflict over women's rights. The women drivers who were public employees, including several university professors, were fired and not hired back for a year. One well-educated woman, a relative of one of the drivers, said, "I thought the time was right. Now the cause has been set back ten years."[7]

Troop Buildups and Diplomacy in the Final Weeks before the War

As 1990 ended, the coalition's force against Iraq consisted of 541,000 Americans (including 35,000 women); 45,000 Britons; 14,000 Frenchmen; and more than 8,000 troops from twenty-two other non-Muslim nations. In addition, a Joint Arab Task Force included 67,000 Saudis; 36,000 Egyptians; 19,000 Syrians; 10,000 Kuwaitis; 6,000 Omanis; 5,000 Pakistanis; 4,000 troops from the United Arab Emirates; 2,500 Qataris; and more than 5,000 troops from seven other Muslim countries. General John Yeosock, the commander of the U.S. ground forces, thought that the Saudi National Guard was "the most professional and disciplined" of the Middle Eastern forces.

Iraq's army was ill-equipped but larger in size: more than a million men, and 623,000 of them were stationed in Kuwait or on the Saudi border. Approximately 175,000 troops were in the well-trained Republican Guard, a well-paid and politically loyal force hardened by eight years of war with Iran. Only a fraction of these troops, however, were stationed in Kuwait. Of the rest, 130,000 were behind the front lines, near Basra, and another 30,000 to 40,000 were near Baghdad. Iraq also had an enormous number of tanks—about 5,500—and 800 aircraft, 160 helicopters, 3,200 pieces of artillery, and 350 surface-to-air missiles.

To protect themselves, the Iraqis laid minefields, tank traps, and razor wire along 175 miles of Kuwait's southern border with Saudi Arabia and then laid some farther inland along 40 miles of Iraq's border with Saudi Arabia. An allied assault would require careful planning.

In a final attempt to avoid war, U.S. secretary of state James Baker met with Iraqi foreign minister Tariq Aziz in Geneva on January 9, 1991, for six hours of talks. Afterward, Secretary Baker said that Iraq had shown "no flexibility" on the need to withdraw from Kuwait. In Washington, Prince Bandar bin Sultan, Saudi Arabia's ambassador, had warned President Bush, "To you, sending Baker is goodwill. To Saddam, it suggests you're chicken."[8]

On January 12, three days after the talks, the U.S. Congress gave President Bush the authority to fight Iraq. Many Democrats, with memories of the Vietnam War and its fifty-eight thousand U.S. dead still fresh, opposed the Gulf War because they were afraid that thousands more Americans might die or be seriously injured. "Are we really ready for another generation of amputees, paraplegics, and burn victims?" Senator John Kerry asked, opposing the war. Large demonstrations against the war also took place in Western Europe. Nevertheless, the vote for war passed the House of Representatives 250 to 183 and passed the Senate by a much smaller margin, 52 to 47.

To the Saudis, one of the biggest shocks of the Gulf War was that the United States proved to be a more loyal friend to the kingdom than many Arab nations were. Yemen's cabinet ignored the UN resolutions and called the war against Iraq "a flagrant challenge to the declared will of the world." Libya, Algeria, Sudan, and the Palestine Liberation Organization also sided with Iraq. Perhaps the biggest surprise was that Jordan, normally a U.S. ally, also backed Iraq. King Hussein had little choice. The majority of his people were Palestinian and vehemently anti-American.

One of the reasons that many Arabs supported Iraq was resentment of the Gulf states' oil wealth. Kuwait has one of the highest incomes per person in the world, and an ordinary enlisted man in Kuwait earns a higher salary than even a general in an Arab country with no oil. In Yemen, a typical family earns just 8 percent of what a family earns in Saudi Arabia and 4 percent of what a family earns in Kuwait. As Saudi Arabia's current minister of labor, Ghazi al-Gosaibi, explained in his book *The Gulf Crisis*, the Saudis and the Kuwaitis discovered "that money does not buy friends and frequently buys enemies."

As war approached, the Saudi government retaliated against Iraq's new friends by changing its labor code. Suddenly, a worker from Yemen had to either find an employer who was willing to be his legal sponsor or leave the country. About half of the 1.5 million Yemenis in the kingdom were forced to return home. Saudi Arabia also expelled most of the workers from Jordan, Palestine, and the Sudan. Saudi businesses replaced their lost workers with more politically docile laborers from the Indian subcontinent and the Philippines, who now make up about 60 percent of the kingdom's foreign workforce.

The Saudi economy was hard hit by the Gulf War. Although oil revenues doubled in 1990 and 1991 because of rising prices and increased production, the $25 billion gain was more than offset by the huge cost of housing the foreign armies, building up the kingdom's own forces, and reimbursing the allied nations for their military services. The total cost of the war to the Saudi government was about $65 billion, which included payments of $16.8 billion to the United States, $1.6 billion each to Egypt and Syria, and smaller amounts to other allied nations.

To pay for all this, the kingdom incurred debts of more than $40 billion. The war not only depleted the country's foreign reserves, it forced the kingdom to borrow $4.5 billion from foreign banks. This particularly upset the fundamentalists who had objected to Western troops in the first place because now the kingdom had to pay interest, which Muhammad had forbidden, to infidel banks. It also became clear that the $26 billion that Saudi Arabia had lent to Iraq during its eight-year war with Iran would never be repaid and had to be written off as a bad debt. By 1994, when Saudi Arabia's oil revenues returned to prewar levels, the country was nearly bankrupt.

The Air War

The Gulf War, also known as "Operation Desert Storm," began on January 17, 1991, at 2:40 a.m. when twelve U.S. special-operations helicopters swooped into Iraq just thirty feet above the sand and destroyed two early-warning radar installations. Then eight F-15 fighter-bombers streaked in where there was no radar and destroyed an air-defense command center, effectively blinding Iraq along this part of the Saudi border. Now hundreds of jets flew into Iraq and destroyed more radar sites. They were followed by dozens of cruise missiles and more waves of bombers and cruise missiles as the attacks continued hour after hour.

In Baghdad, a fleet of F-117 Stealth fighters, invisible to radar, bombed the city's telephone exchange, power plants, and air defenses, as well as Saddam Hussein's lakeside palace. Stymied, the Iraqi anti-aircraft gunners fired their shells at random, which made for an impressive sight on CNN (it was prime time in the United States) but did almost no damage to U.S. aircraft.

Elsewhere in Iraq, British Tornadoes destroyed many air fields, and U.S., French, and Italian warplanes obliterated dozens of missile sites, especially in western Iraq, where Scuds were aimed at Israeli cities. A Saudi pilot, Captain Aved Shamrani, was in one of the war's only dogfights when he shot down two Iraqi Mirage fighter jets trying to attack allied ships. Saudi television jubilantly reported Captain Shamrani's feat and soothed religious sensibilities by referring to the coalition troops as "Arab, Muslim, and other friendly forces."

By noon on January 18, the allies had flown 850 missions and lost only two aircraft. Iraq was no longer a threat to the Saudi oil installations. The price of oil, which had climbed to $40 a barrel when the war began, now fell to only $20 a barrel. This was almost as low as the price had been before Iraq's invasion of Kuwait in August.

After two weeks, the allies had flown 30,000 missions and lost only 18 of their 4,065 aircraft. Iraq's sky belonged to the allies; not one Iraqi airplane or helicopter dared to take off. Over the war's six weeks, the Saudi Air Force flew 7,018 missions (more than Britain) and lost only 3 of its 351 combat aircraft.

Altogether, the coalition dropped ninety-six thousand tons of explosives on Iraq and its forces in Kuwait, a destructive force equal to about seven Hiroshima bombs or two hundred 9/11s. Most residential areas, however, suffered little damage. The horrific bombing had a specific purpose: to weaken Iraq's resistance to the ground forces that were poised to liberate Kuwait.

On ships in the Persian Gulf, 17,000 U.S. Marines engaged in exercises designed to deceive the Iraqis into expecting an amphibious landing on the shores of Kuwait. Instead, General Schwarzkopf planned an end run around Iraq's defenses—moving a huge army of 117,000 men; 28,000 vehicles; 1,000 helicopters; and 36 million gallons of fuel and water westward across 530 miles of desert. The U.S. army's fast-moving 18th Airborne Corps and France's swift 6th Division regrouped at a point 200 miles west-northwest of westernmost Kuwait, from which they could lunge inside Iraq to an area where Iraq had no defenses at all—the middle of the desert—and split Iraq in two. Then the U.S. Army's Seventh Corps, with 140,000 men, could attack the Republican Guard divisions in southern Iraq and cut them off from their supply lines to the north.

Schwarzkopf knew he could not move such enormous armies in secret until Iraq's air force and radar facilities had been totally destroyed. But after just one day of bombing, Iraq's military was blind, and Schwarzkopf ordered nearly a quarter of his army deep into the Arabian Desert. Most soldiers rode in armored personnel carriers up the "Tapline," an old road built for an oil pipeline no longer in use, as hundreds of trucks covered with camouflage netting carried food, weapons, spare parts, and ammunition. Most of the truck drivers were Pakistanis, Bangladeshis, and Filipinos who raced to their destinations each day in order to arrive in time for evening videos of American

professional wrestling, which they adored. At one point, the convoy
of men and matériel was 120 miles long.

At three in the morning on January 18, twenty-four hours after
the air war had begun, Iraq fired seven Scud missiles at Tel Aviv
and, one hour later, an eighth missile at Dhahran, the center of
Saudi Arabia's oil industry. The Scud was an obsolete Soviet missile
designed to propel a nuclear warhead 190 miles. It was never meant to
be accurate, since accuracy hardly mattered when a missile carried an
atomic bomb. Iraqi engineers extended the Scud's range to 300 miles,
but the conventional bombs inside Iraq's Scuds were small, and the
missiles tended to miss their target by 2 to 3 miles. The Scuds' targets
were therefore virtually random.

The Scud over Dhahran was intercepted by a U.S. Patriot missile,
an antiaircraft weapon the Raytheon Company had just redesigned to
intercept incoming missiles. It had never been used in battle before,
and its success in intercepting Scuds would prove to be mixed. The
Israelis did not have any Patriot missiles at the beginning of the war,
and the seven Scuds that fell on Tel Aviv damaged several homes.

By striking Israel, Saddam Hussein hoped to spur young Arabs
to overthrow those governments allied with the United States. But
while the Palestinians rejoiced in the attacks, most Arabs elsewhere
were quiet. Hussein had also considered launching chemical weapons against Israel, but attaching gas canisters to a missile is tricky and
proved to be beyond Iraq's capabilities.

After two days of war, coalition planes destroyed thirty-six fixed
Scud launchers and ten mobile ones. The camouflaged mobile
launchers were hard to find because they were no bigger than a gasoline truck and could drive away from a site just six minutes after a firing. On the war's third day, two more Scuds hit Tel Aviv.

Israel wanted to retaliate and send hundreds of bombers and
helicopters into western Iraq, but President Bush dissuaded Prime
Minister Yitzhak Shamir from doing so by convincing him that an
Israeli raid would break up the international coalition against Iraq.

For several days, however, more than seven hundred flights a day
were devoted to the hunt for Scuds. Every suspected launch site and
storage bunker in western Iraq was bombed, and U.S. A-10 attack
jets streaked up and down the region's roads and canyons in hopes of
sighting and obliterating the hard-to-find mobile launchers.

On January 21, the fifth night of the war, six Iraqi Scuds raced
toward Riyadh just after midnight. Radar picked up the Scuds when
they were still three minutes away, and sirens blared all over the
city. None of the six missiles landed anywhere near the center of
the city, and no one was killed or hurt.

The missiles did create a great deal of fear. During the next few days, one-sixth of Riyadh's people loaded up their cars and drove more than five hundred miles west on jammed highways to stay with friends or relatives in Jeddah, Mecca, and other cities well out of the range of Scuds. In the Eastern Province, which borders Kuwait, more than half of the people made a similar exodus.[9]

The Scuds that fell on Riyadh and Dhahran temporarily silenced the fundamentalist preachers who had thundered against the presence of U.S. troops, and the Saudi people rallied behind King Fahad and gave the war effort their full support.

Iraq launched 88 Scud missiles during the war: 44 at Saudi Arabia (20 at Riyadh, 14 at Dhahran, and 10 elsewhere), 40 at Israel, 3 at Bahrain, and 1 at Qatar. Iraq fired 35 of these Scuds during the first week of the war, 18 Scuds during the second, and then, as more launchers were destroyed, just 1 Scud a day.[10] On February 25, however, one of the last Scuds of the war hit a U.S. army barracks in Dhahran, killing twenty-eight U.S. troops and wounding ninety-eight. This one missile accounted for a fifth of the Gulf War's U.S. combat deaths.

In addition to indiscriminately firing Scuds at cities, Saddam Hussein deliberately released more than four million barrels of Kuwait's oil into the Persian Gulf on January 25, an act that most of the world immediately condemned as "eco-terrorism." Fortunately, the giant spill did little lasting damage.

On January 29, in another inexplicable move, Iraq sent a division with four hundred tanks and armored personnel carriers into Saudi Arabian territory and took the coastal oil-refining town of Ras al-Khafji. Prince Khalid led eight battalions against the Iraqi troops: six Saudi, one from Qatar, and one battalion of U.S. Marines. In two days of heavy fighting, the biggest battle in modern Saudi Arabia's history, thirty-six Saudis died. But the coalition forces killed or captured more than three fourths of Iraq's division as allied helicopters repeatedly fired on retreating tanks. Perhaps Saddam Hussein attacked the town of Ras al-Khafji to make the war seem less one-sided, but the annihilation of his division by Saudi forces was a great boost to Saudi morale and pride.

The Ground War

After thirty-eight days of coalition bombing, the ground war to liberate Kuwait began at four o'clock in the morning on February 24, 1991. U.S. Marines, riding in tanks and wearing suits to protect them from chemical weapons, crossed the border into southern Kuwait, raced through minefields that had been cleared by weeks of massive bombing, and shelled and destroyed Iraq's first line of defenses.

They were quickly followed by the Joint Arab Task Force, which had split into three units. One force, led by Prince Khalid, advanced in tandem with the marines and sped north along Kuwait's shoreline highway. A second force, primarily Egyptians, moved north more slowly into Kuwait's interior. Finally, in the rear, the Saudi National Guard became a mobile reserve unit, sending extra troops where needed. A separate British force also helped to liberate Kuwait's interior.

As the marines, the Saudis, and other Muslim armies advanced up Kuwait's coast, thousands of Iraqi soldiers jumped out of their trenches, waved white flags, and surrendered. The allied bombing had cut them off from their supplies, and in the last few days, U.S. planes had dropped millions of leaflets in Arabic that told the Iraqis how to surrender: "1) Remove the magazine from your weapon. 2) Sling your weapon over your left shoulder, muzzle down. 3) Have both arms raised above your head. . . . IF YOU DO THIS, YOU WILL NOT DIE."

By the end of the ground war's first day, the allied armies had taken more than thirteen thousand Iraqi prisoners at a cost of only eight dead and twenty-seven wounded. On the second and third days, the Saudis and the U.S. Marines faced a few pockets of resistance but continued north toward Kuwait City as allied aircraft pounded Iraq's fleeing tanks.

As the Iraqis retreated, however, they set fire to more than six hundred oil wells. The flames consumed six million barrels of oil a day, and in much of Kuwait, smoke reduced visibility to less than a hundred feet. It took a special team of "hell-fighters" from Houston, Texas, eight months to put out all the fires. One hell-fighter, Coots-Matthews, said that the Iraqis "couldn't fight worth a s——t, but they sure knew how to blow up wells."

While the marines and the Saudis fought in Kuwait, the U.S. 82nd Airborne Division and the French Army's 6th Division raced deep into the Iraqi desert and seized an Iraqi air force base on the second day of the ground war. This enabled them to protect the other allied armies from any counterattack from central Iraq. Simultaneously, the U.S. 101st Airborne Division launched the largest helicopter attack of the twentieth century. Three hundred Apaches, Cobras, Black Hawks, Hueys, and Chinooks, some piloted by women, transported an entire brigade, with Humvees, howitzers, and huge tanks of fuel, deep inside Iraq. There, overnight, U.S. soldiers built a new air base within striking distance of Highway 8, southern Iraq's main artery.

The U.S. Army's 24th Mechanized Infantry Division, led by General Barry McCaffrey (who would later become the government's "Anti-Drug Czar"), also moved into Iraq—sixty miles in one night—and reached Highway 8 the next day. Then the division sped south along the main road to Basra, cutting off both supplies from the north and the possibility of an Iraqi retreat from the south. The surprise was total. "Never once did we attack an enemy force that saw us coming," McCaffrey recalled. "They were looking the wrong way."

Finally, the twelve hundred tanks of the U.S. Army's Seventh Corps also rolled through the Iraqi desert, and as they approached the outskirts of Basra on February 27, the fourth day of the ground war, they pounded two divisions of the Republican Guard. That same day, U.S. Marines and the Joint Arab Task Force reached Kuwait City, where, at General Schwarzkopf's insistence, the first troops to enter the city were Kuwaitis.

With Kuwait liberated, President Bush declared a temporary cease-fire the next morning, February 28. Later that day, Iraq delivered a letter to the United Nations confirming its willingness to comply with the cease-fire, although the precise conditions were not specified until U.S., Saudi, and Iraqi generals met three days later.

During the Persian Gulf War, 246 soldiers died fighting for the coalition. They included 148 Americans (35 from friendly fire), 47 Saudis, 25 Britons, 12 Egyptians, and 10 soldiers from the United Arab Emirates. Another 151 Americans died from illnesses and accidents, as did about 100 servicemen from other nations.

The 894 allied wounded included 467 Americans, 220 Saudis, and 207 others—surprisingly few for an army of 760,000. One large army hospital in Riyadh never had more than 76 patients. The staff soon put plywood on some of their gurneys and turned them into ping pong tables, and the surgeons, with little to do, removed moles.

Not one Kuwaiti soldier died in combat, but an estimated 5,000 Kuwaitis were killed during Iraq's invasion and seven-month occupation. As for the Iraqis, no one knows how many died. The best estimate is 20,000 to 30,000 soldiers and 2,000 to 3,000 civilians. The total number of deaths during the Gulf War is therefore probably about 25,000 to 35,000, with as many as another 100,000 Iraqis wounded.

The Aftermath

Iraq lost at least 3,700 tanks, 2,400 armored vehicles, 2,600 pieces of artillery, 104 airplanes, and 19 helicopters, a rout that rendered almost two-thirds of Iraq's sixty-six army divisions impotent. In addition, damage to roads, bridges, power stations, sewage plants, and so on, was greater than $50 billion.

The war cost the U.S. taxpayer $50 billion, too, but unlike Iraq, the United States was reimbursed by its allies. Saudi Arabia paid the United States $12.8 billion and $4 billion more in goods and services; Kuwait paid the United States $13.5 billion; Japan sent $9 billion; Germany, $5.5 billion; and the United Arab Emirates, $2 billion.

Kuwait, like Iraq, also suffered at least $50 billion in war damage. Iraqi troops set more than six hundred oil wells on fire, mined Kuwait's harbor and beaches, sabotaged oil installations and utilities, and looted homes, stores, restaurants, and museums. By the time Iraq's soldiers left Kuwait on February 27, the country had no water, electricity, and telephone service, and, worst of all, no police.

When the Kuwaitis first returned home, some of them immediately killed anyone they thought had collaborated with the Iraqis, without so much as a hearing. Only when Kuwait's crown prince, Sheikh Sa'ad Abdullah al-Salim as-Sabah, threatened to hang the vigilantes did the violence stop.

For the U.S. troops that did not go home immediately, helping Kuwait to restore its harbor, police force, and utilities was one of their top priorities, along with blowing up Iraq's ammunition dumps, sending POWs back to Iraq, and helping the Saudis to build an enormous refugee camp for more than fifty thousand homeless Iraqis.

With Iraq so weak, the temptation for the allied armies to advance to Baghdad and oust Saddam Hussein was strong. But as President Bush and Brent Scowcroft, his national security adviser, explained in their 1998 book *A World Transformed,*

> We would have been forced to occupy Baghdad and, in effect, rule Iraq. . . . There was no viable "exit strategy.". . .
>
> Occupying Iraq, thus unilaterally exceeding the United Nations mandate, would have destroyed the precedent of international response to aggression that we had hoped to establish. Had we gone the invasion route, the United States could conceivably still be an occupying power in a bitterly hostile land.[11]

President Bush, King Fahad, and John Major, the British prime minister, along with other coalition leaders, also assumed that some Iraqi generals would soon do their work for them and overthrow Saddam Hussein in a military coup. After all, few leaders who lose a war stay in power. But everyone underestimated the iron grip that Hussein and his Baath Party had on Iraq.

On March 3, about twenty generals and colonels from the allied and Iraqi armies met at Safwan, an Iraqi town occupied by the allies, to discuss the details of the cease-fire. The principal negotiators for the coalition were General Schwarzkopf and Prince Khalid, and for Iraq, Lieutenant General Sultan Hasim Ahmad, the Iraqi army's deputy chief of staff. In a brisk two-hour meeting, the Iraqis quickly agreed to a cease-fire line, to return three thousand hostages that they had taken from Kuwait, and to give the Kuwaitis the location of every mine and booby trap they had laid. Both sides also agreed to return their prisoners of war immediately. The coalition had captured more than seventy-one thousand Iraqis; the Iraqis had taken only forty-one allies.

Later, in a formal United Nations peace agreement that Iraq signed on April 6, Iraq agreed to destroy its chemical and biological weapons and its medium- and long-range missiles and to accept visits by inspectors to verify their absence. The Iraqis also agreed to a UN peacekeeping force on Kuwait's border and to pay Kuwait reparations, which were later set at $15.9 billion.

At the end of the meeting at Safwan, Lieutenant General Ahmad had a request: "We would like to fly helicopters to carry officials of our government to areas where roads and bridges are out. This has nothing to do with the front line. This is inside Iraq."[12]

Schwarzkopf agreed. "I will instruct the Air Force not to shoot at any helicopters flying over the territory of Iraq where our troops are not located."[13]

"That seemed like a reasonable request," Schwarzkopf later told television interviewer David Frost, but he added, "I think I was suckered because I think they intended—right then, when they asked that question—to use those helicopters against the insurrections that were going on."[14]

In fairness to General Schwarzkopf, the revolts against Saddam Hussein's rule had not yet started at the time he met the Iraqi generals. But only six days later, on March 9, the Shi'ites in southern Iraq began a violent uprising against Hussein's tyranny, and the Kurds in the north started another revolt just one week later. Schwarzkopf is no doubt correct that General Ahmad was anticipating the revolts when he asked whether Iraq could use its helicopters.

The Shi'ite rebellion deeply worried the Saudis. An independent Shi'ite state on Saudi Arabia's northern border would seek military aid from its Shi'ite neighbor, Iran, which Saudi Arabia had just spent $26 billion trying to contain in the 1980s. Worse, an Arabic-speaking Shi'ite state could destabilize Saudi Arabia's oil-rich Eastern Province, where Shi'ites, 40 percent of the people, live as second-class citizens.

The Saudis told President Bush that as awful as Saddam Hussein was, they preferred a single Iraq under his rule to a splintered Iraq where the Shi'ites were independent. Turkey also expressed similar fears to Bush about an independent Kurdish state.

Faced with pleas from two of America's closest allies and his own reluctance to occupy Baghdad, President Bush did nothing as Saddam Hussein ruthlessly killed Shi'ite and Kurdish rebels in the second half of March. Iraq's helicopters fired guns and missiles that killed thousands of people, but far worse were Iraq's eighteen hundred remaining tanks and six hundred pieces of artillery, which killed tens of thousands.

By early April, more than 250,000 Shi'ites had fled Iraq for the safety of Iran, and more than half a million Kurds had left their homes for the treeless mountains of eastern Turkey. The Kurds had little food and water and no shelter, and many of the oldest and the youngest died. Fortunately, television news covered the Kurds' suffering in vivid detail and aroused the world's conscience.

On April 11, President Bush announced a large international relief effort to feed and house the Kurds and, more important, sent ten thousand troops to northern Iraq to carve out a territory where the Kurds could be safe from Saddam Hussein's murderous troops. In May and June, when northern Iraq became safe again, the Kurds returned home. U.S. troops left northern Iraq on July 13, with the condition that no Iraqi aircraft could fly north of the 36th parallel of latitude, where most of the Kurds live. To enforce this "no-fly zone," the United States, Britain, and France sent fighter jets and advanced radar equipment to a nearby air force base in Turkey.

One week before General Schwarzkopf returned to the United States, on April 20, the Saudis gave him the Order of King Abdul Aziz, the first time they had ever given the award to a foreigner. Presenting the decoration, Prince Khalid said, "The American troops who came to Saudi Arabia . . . did indeed respect the values of the host nation. . . . I have often said that if the world is to have a superpower, thank God it is the United States."[15]

Ironically, King Fahad fired Prince Khalid from his post as commander of the armed forces just five months later because Khalid had demanded to be promoted to chief of staff. This position, however, is traditionally given to a commoner so as not to alter the balance of power between factions of the royal family, and the king did not want to disturb this arrangement. A civilian again, Khalid bought *Al-Hayat* (Life), one of the best and most reliable newspapers in the Arab world. It is based in London and is therefore uncensored, although it rarely criticizes the royal family. In 2001, Prince Khalid rejoined the government as an assistant minister of defense in order to ease the workload of his father, who by then was seventy-seven. In the future, when command finally passes to the grandsons of Abdul Aziz, the war hero Khalid may be one of the leading candidates to share power.

After the war, the United States asked Saudi Arabia whether it could establish a U.S. air force base on its soil, under U.S. control, flying the American flag. The Saudis refused, explaining that the U.S. air base would cause them endless trouble with fundamentalists. They did, however, let the United States use an air force base the Americans had built in Dhahran forty years ago in an unofficial capacity and as a place to store spare parts and maintenance equipment for airplanes and tanks in case a U.S. force suddenly needed to return to Saudi Arabia again.

By January 1992, 504,000 U.S. soldiers had returned home, and most of the 37,000 who remained in the kingdom were there as instructors and technicians, rather than as combat troops. By late spring, less than 10,000 U.S. troops remained in the kingdom, but their presence still aroused intense hostility.

As time passed, it became clear that Saddam Hussein was going to remain in power. Neither his defeat in Kuwait nor the continuing UN boycott of his oil exports had been enough to oust him. As a result, in the summer of 1992, King Fahad invited the U.S. and British air forces to return to the kingdom, without a formal agreement, to establish a second "no-fly zone" over southern Iraq. In September, the United States and Britain officially prohibited Iraq from flying any aircraft south of the 32nd parallel of latitude, where most of Iraq's Shi'ites live. They did this not only to protect the Shi'ites, but to try to weaken Saddam Hussein's regime further. Saudi Arabia also agreed, informally, to let the United States and Britain keep combat aircraft in the kingdom permanently and to support them with refueling tankers, air defense patrols, and AWACS radar.

In making this decision, King Fahad and his brothers let the militant clerics know that they could not hinder the kingdom's pursuit of national security. Iraq, even after its defeat, still had an army five times larger than Saudi Arabia's, and so did Iran. Whether the clergy liked it or not, Saudi Arabia still needed the West's military support to survive.

Yet even the royal family felt that they should not rely on Western troops alone. Although the Saudis protect their oil fields with thirty thousand elite troops and constant air force surveillance, they looked at what Kuwait had just endured and decided that they needed a stronger deterrent against a foreign attack.

Starting in 1992, according to author Gerald Posner, the Saudis began to attach powerful remote-controlled explosives to many of their oil wells, pipelines, pumping stations, refineries, and computer consoles. The purpose of this "scorched earth" capability is to prevent an invader from ever using Saudi oil. Posner, citing an Israeli intelligence file and an unnamed European oil-construction executive, also said that many of the explosives are packed with shards of radioactive metal, possibly strontium 90. These dirty bombs, strategically placed and disguised, can contaminate not only the country's oil facilities, but also much of the kingdom's underground, yet-to-be-pumped oil, potentially making up to an eighth of the world's oil unusable for years.[16] Posner's claims, however, have been met with skepticism by many journalists and members of the intelligence community.

18

The Rise of Militant
Fundamentalism
(1991–1996)

D URING THE 1990s, fiery clerics, dissidents in London, and
Osama bin Laden all charged that the royal family was
betraying Islam by continuing its long alliance with the
West. In Riyadh in 1995 and Al-Khobar in 1996, car bombs killed
twenty-four Americans—the first attempts by terrorists to end the
fifty-year friendship between the United States and Saudi Arabia.

Although most of the pressure for change in Saudi Arabia in the
1990s came from conservative clerics, the decade's first call for reform
was a petition signed by liberals. Forty-three businessmen, professors,
and ex-cabinet ministers submitted their "Secular Petition," as it was
soon called, in the hope that the Gulf War might bring greater freedom. The document, addressed to King Fahad, was deeply respectful in tone. Its goal, it said, was the preservation of "the noble Royal
family . . . the axis of unity and the just rule that serves the country."

The 1990 petition called for ten reforms, including freedom of
the press, the equality of royals and commoners before the law, and
a greater role for women in public life. The document's most urgent

request was for an assembly, appointed by the king, of "competent, learned and fair-minded people" from every region of the kingdom, "to study, develop and approve laws and regulations."[1] In 1991, King Fahad agreed to this request, but it took almost three years before the first Majlis al-Shura (Consultative Council) finally convened.

In response to the Secular Petition, fifty-two conservative clerics and professors signed a "Religious Petition" in February 1991. This document was then posted at mosques throughout the kingdom, and by May, more than four hundred clerics had signed it. Like the Secular Petition, the Religious Petition called for a national assembly and for the equality of royals and commoners before the law. But while the liberals had asked for a free press, the conservatives wanted the media to be "purified" of anything that was not "serving Islam," including Lebanese magazines showing unveiled movie stars and video stores that quietly but openly sold pornography.

The clerics demanded the repeal of commercial laws that were not in accordance with the *sharia* (the Quran and the sayings and the deeds of Muhammad), including laws that allowed banks to charge interest. They also called for "the development of military industries," so that one day the kingdom could end its "illegitimate alliances" with infidel nations.[2]

With more than four hundred signers, it was impossible to keep the Religious Petition secret, and within days, an Egyptian newspaper printed it in full. The Saudi government, which tolerated petitions as long as they were private, responded to the publicity with intimidation. Policemen visited the homes of many of the people who had signed the petition to question them and forbid them from teaching and preaching. The Justice Ministry issued a new law making it illegal to publicize a petition, and the Council of the Senior Clergy denounced the four hundred clerics for leaking their petition to the press.

Emboldened by the conservative clergy and free from the need for restraint during the Gulf War, the religious police—the Society for the Advancement of Virtue and the Elimination of Sin—increased its patrols in the summer and the fall of 1991 and harassed more women than ever before, including foreigners. Western women in the kingdom had always dressed conservatively, but now they, too, began to wear the Saudi *abaya* (full veil). For the first time, the religious police also raided upper-class homes and homes in the city of Jeddah. In one raid, the *mutaween* arrested one of the king's translators for attending a mixed-gender party where alcohol was served. The unfortunate linguist was sentenced to ten months in prison.

Salman al-Awda and Safar al-Hawali, the two "Awakening Sheikhs" who had opposed the presence of U.S. troops in the kingdom, had stopped criticizing the royal family after Iraq launched Scud missiles at Riyadh and Dhahran in January 1991. Instead, in hundreds of thousands of tape cassettes, Al-Awda called for a boycott of U.S. consumer goods and for the expulsion of the kingdom's one million Shi'ites. On other cassettes, Al-Hawali attacked the Jews for corrupting the Middle East "through drugs, immorality, filthy films and filthy magazines" and said that God would torment them until the end of time. "Hitler was a part of this promise," al-Hawali said, "and the [Palestine] liberation and *jihad* movements are a part of this promise as well."[3]

Another preacher, Ayed al-Qarni, rereleased a cassette called *America as I Saw It*, which criticized the royal family for allying itself with a United States "overrun" by homosexuals, children out of wedlock, and "beasts who fornicate" outside of marriage. On another cassette, a cleric who remained anonymous called the United States "the atheistic enemy of Islam" and said that "no allegiance is owed to the royal princes unless they follow Muslim law." One cleric even called for the execution of nonreligious Muslims.

The King Creates an Unelected Legislature

In a televised speech on November 15, 1991, King Fahad responded to the secular and religious petitions and agreed to reform the government—to strengthen legal protections, reorganize provincial governments, and appoint a national consultative council to advise him. The details of these reforms were spelled out three and a half months later in a series of royal decrees on March 1, 1992.

The first decree, the Basic Law of Government, is still in force today. Article 5(b) states that the nation is a monarchy. "The rulers of the country shall be from among the sons of the founder, King Abdul Aziz . . . and their descendants. . . . The most upright among them shall receive allegiance according to the Holy Quran and the Sunnah."

The Quran, in fact, does not demand allegiance to a king or an upright man or discuss any kind of government at all. But the clause was a bombshell when it became public. From now on, at least theoretically, if the royal family agrees that a grandson of Abdul Aziz is more upright than his uncles are, he can leapfrog over them and become crown prince or even king. The law was in place to transfer power to a new generation of princes.

The Basic Law says nothing about the rights of women, and Article 39 prohibits the press from publishing "anything that might lead to internal rifts or struggle." But the decree did expand the rights of the Saudi people slightly. Several articles declare that no one shall be arrested, imprisoned, or have his or her mail read or telephone tapped except according to law. Obviously, the government can still arrest anyone it wants; the articles were aimed not at the ordinary police but at the religious police. Article 37, for example, says, "Dwellings shall be sacrosanct . . . and may not be searched except under the circumstances laid down by law." In other words, the religious police need genuine cause to search a home. They still raided homes after the Basic Law was published but far fewer than before. King Fahad also put some moderate clerics in charge of the religious police. They recruited slightly better educated men to the force and ordered both rookie and experienced *mutaween* to try to be less rude.

King Fahad's second set of decrees, the Law of the Provinces, standardized regional government. Until then, local government had been completely dependent on whether a ruling prince was broad-minded or narrow, hard-working or lazy, honest or corrupt. Now, under the new law, each governor would have to consult a council of local citizens appointed jointly by the governor and the minister of the interior.

The Saudi system is hardly democratic, but it is not quite as authoritarian as it appears. An ordinary Saudi can easily see a tribal sheikh, and the sheikh can easily see a governor. An aggrieved citizen can also see a governor at a public audience. For a nation with no right to free speech, there is a surprising amount of communication from the bottom of society upward.

Article 40 of the Basic Law set up the most important of King Fahad's 1992 reforms, the Majlis al-Shura, or Consultative Council. The Shura is an unelected body appointed by the king and has only advisory power, but it is nevertheless playing an increasing role in Saudi government and may become an elected parliament in the future.

King Fahad was no democrat. Just two weeks after announcing his reforms, he said that democracy "does not suit this region or our people." He waited more than a year before he appointed the Shura's members in August 1993, and the council did not have its first working session until January 1, 1994.

The powers of the first Consultative Council were limited; some contemptuously called it a "Poodle Parliament." Its members could propose new laws or changes to old laws only if these were related to an issue that the king had brought before them. And while council members could question cabinet ministers and comment on government reports, they had no power over the government's budget.

A majority of the men (there are no women) in the Consultative Council are academics and former government officials with graduate degrees from Western universities. The Shura also contains many businessmen, engineers, retired army and police officers, and even a few token Shi'ites. Surprisingly, Islamic clerics and scholars make up less than a fifth of the body.

In 1995, King Fahad gave the Consultative Council the right to examine the budget, although its powers remained strictly advisory. By the end of the 1990s, however, Crown Prince Abdullah was following almost all of its recommendations, and in 2003, the Shura was given the important right to examine an issue without a prior request from the king.

While researching this book, I had the pleasure of meeting more than a dozen members of the Shura. Every one of them seemed intelligent, broad-minded, and public-spirited. For better and for worse, Saudi Arabia's Consultative Council is comparable to legislatures from our own past such as Virginia's House of Burgesses. Like the House of Burgesses, the Shura's power is limited by a king, but it benefits from the fact that its members are chosen for their learning, rather than for their ability to raise campaign money.

"If we go for elections now," said Prince Abdulaziz ibn Salman, a nephew of the king, "we would get a parliament of fundamentalist clergy and Bedouin groups."[4] Abdullah Uthaimin, a historian of the kingdom and a member of the Shura, agreed. "Reforms that lead to democracy step by step," he told me, "are better than reforms that jump right in." Dr. Uthaimin looks forward to a time when "half the Shura will be chosen by the king and the other half will be elected by the public. The half that get elected may not be such nice people, but they will have more respect than the appointees and they will strengthen the Shura."

Budget Cuts and Arms Buying in the Early and Mid-1990s

Because the price of oil declined slowly from $20 to just $16 a barrel between 1992 and 1995, there was no economic growth in Saudi Arabia during this period and only 1.5 percent growth in 1996. Income per person had not grown since 1988 and was only half of what it had been at the peak of the oil boom in 1981.

Government spending, however, rose 38 percent between 1991 and 1993. This was partly because of an increase in arms buying after the Gulf War, but also because King Fahad took steps to reduce public discontent. To please the clergy, the government built more than a thousand new mosques and hired seventy-three hundred clerics to lead prayers. To please businessmen, the government made it easier to get loans to start new enterprises.

By 1994, the deficit swelled to more than $9.2 billion. The government froze hiring, delayed hundreds of construction contracts, and abandoned plans to double the size of its army. It also doubled the price of gasoline to fifty cents a gallon. The austerity budgets cut spending by 20 percent and reduced the deficit to $7.3 billion in 1995 and $5.1 billion in 1996.

The hiring freeze was long overdue. For years, the number of public employees had risen an average of 7 percent a year, twice the rate of the kingdom's population growth. By 1995, there were more than six hundred thousand Saudis working for the government, and few contributed much to the nation's productivity. The real purpose of many government jobs was simply to give young Saudis something to do because the number of college graduates in the kingdom doubled every seven years.

In rural areas, the austerity budgets reduced the number of loans for farms and factories by a third and slashed wheat and barley subsidies to one-sixth of their previous levels because wheat was cheaper to import than to grow. Raising wheat also depleted aquifers and made the soil more salty and less fertile. By 1996, Saudi farmers grew less than one-third of the wheat they had grown in 1992, but government subsidies continued to make Saudi Arabia self-sufficient in dairy products and potatoes and almost self-sufficient in chicken, fruit, and vegetables.

Most farmhands in Saudi Arabia are foreigners, as are most housekeepers, construction workers, cab drivers, and chauffeurs. By 1995, expatriates made up 30 percent of the population and 60 percent of the workforce. Most of them worked six and sometimes seven days a week with no overtime, yet still earned two to four times as much as they would have received back home in India, Bangladesh, or the Philippines.

Even during a time of austerity, the royal family did not reduce military spending. Iran was hostile, Yemen was envious, and Saddam Hussein still ruled Iraq. Saudi Arabia shares a 500-mile border with Iraq and a 900-mile border with Yemen and also guards 1,500 miles of coastline.

Saudi Arabia spent more than $260 billion (in today's dollars) on defense in the 1990s, about 30 percent of each year's budget. The kingdom spent $70 billion (in current dollars) on weapons from abroad, including almost $25 billion worth of U.S. arms between 1991 and 1996. These included F-15 fighter jets; laser-guided bombs; Apache helicopters; M-1 tanks; Bradley fighting vehicles; Patriot, Stinger, TOW, and Hawk missiles; and several upgrades of the AWACS air defense system.

The biggest purchase of the period, which began in 1992 and cost $9 billion (in 1992 dollars), was the procurement of seventy-two F-15 fighter jets from the McDonnell-Douglas Corporation. The F-15, which made an impressive debut during the Persian Gulf War, can carry 160 bombs and twelve tons of missiles. The Saudis also spent $7 billion buying forty-eight Tornado fighters from the British in 1993. In all, 90 percent of Saudi Arabia's arms imports during the mid-1990s came from the United States and Britain.

Almost a third of the money for arms purchases goes to supplies, maintenance, and training. It takes eighty men to service an F-15, and another dozen to maintain the missiles. Because most Saudi soldiers have only a mediocre high school education, the great majority of the kingdom's aircraft technicians are foreign.

In 1994, Saudi Arabia signed a four-year, $819 million contract with the Vinnell Corporation for its twelve hundred employees to train, maintain, and modernize the Saudi National Guard. From 1990 to 1998, the Vinnell Corporation was owned by the Carlyle Group, a Washington-based holding company. One of the Carlyle Group's partners is James Baker, who served as secretary of state under President George H. W. Bush. A small percentage of the company was owned by the bin Laden family until they sold their interest shortly after September 11, 2001. In 1995, former president George H. W. Bush himself joined the firm as a senior adviser, and occasionally he flew to Saudi Arabia to meet potential investors in a Carlyle project. Bush also received two large contributions from Prince Bandar bin Sultan, one to Bush's presidential library in Texas, and the other to a campaign against illiteracy run by his wife, Barbara. Prince Bandar also endowed a chair in Middle Eastern Studies at the University of Arkansas when Bill Clinton became president.

Although Saudi Arabia has spent hundreds of billions of dollars on defense and has trained many superb pilots, it is doubtful whether the kingdom has a big enough army or national guard to defend its oil fields from a prolonged foreign attack. It is also questionable how long the kingdom's aircraft could fly without foreign maintenance. Throughout the 1990s, the Saudis, whether they liked it or not, continued to be dependent on the United States and Britain for their security.

1993: A Compromise with Shi'ites, a New Grand Mufti

Saudi Arabia's Shi'ites, who make up 9 percent of the kingdom's population and almost 50 percent of the people in the oil-rich Eastern Province, have long been second-class citizens. The kingdom bars them from building new mosques, discriminates against them in university admissions, and denies them good jobs in government, the military, and schools and universities. There are no Shi'ite generals, mayors, police chiefs, or college presidents. During the Gulf War, many Shi'ites had hoped that the arrival of Western troops would lead to more religious freedom, but in 1992, none of King Fahad's reforms promised the Shi'ites more liberty or greater tolerance.

In the summer of 1993, however, the king released about forty Shi'ite activists from prison, then met some of them personally in October to reach an informal agreement. The king returned passports to three thousand politically suspect Shi'ites, increased university admissions for Shi'ite men and women, and let dozens of Shi'ite activists who lived in exile come back home safely. In return, the exiles stopped publishing their anti-Saudi newsletter.

Both the king and the Shi'ites agreed that it was best not to publicize the agreement, for fear of angering the many Wahhabi clerics who still regarded the Shi'ites as polytheists. Most Shi'ites understand that they are better off under the royal family than they would be if Wahhabi fundamentalists took power instead. Thus, of the kingdom's million and a half Shi'ite citizens, probably fewer than a thousand are militantly opposed to the al-Saud family's rule.

Another action King Fahad took to win popular support in 1993 was to appoint Sheikh Abdulaziz ibn Baz as the kingdom's grand mufti, or supreme religious leader. Traditionally, this post had always been held by a descendant of ibn Abdul Wahhab, but when the last grand mufti died in 1969, King Faisal let the post stay vacant in order to give himself more freedom to maneuver on religious issues.

King Fahad wanted to limit the impact of the militants' petitions, tape-recorded sermons, and *fatwas* (religious rulings). With ibn Baz as grand mufti, his rulings would have more legal authority than any other *fatwas* in the kingdom, and ibn Baz strongly believed that it was better to obey a flawed but good government than to kill innocent people in order to form a new government with only slightly fewer flaws.

Ibn Baz became blind from an eye infection at age twenty in 1932, when the Saudis had no access to modern medical care. After World

War II, he wrote a *fatwa* objecting to the use of non-Muslims as oil workers because "the presence of infidels, male or female, poses a danger to Muslims, their beliefs, their morality, and their children's education." After reading the *fatwa*, King Abdul Aziz summoned ibn Baz before him, reminded him that Muhammad had hired foreign workers, and ordered him to withdraw his ruling. Ibn Baz did so but told his fellow clerics that he still believed in his *fatwa*. When Abdul Aziz heard about this insubordination, he jailed ibn Baz but released him after a second conversation in which the king explained to him that public dissent can undermine a kingdom's stability. Fortunately for ibn Baz, his brief time in prison gave him a reputation for independence, and this enabled him to be an intermediary between radical clerics and the government.

In addition to his 1966 ruling that the sun goes around the Earth, the blind cleric wrote a number of other quirky *fatwas*. He banned praying behind a man who is wearing pants instead of a *thobe*, for example, because the sight of the outline of a man's rear end is not appropriate during prayer. And in 1977, he declared, "If a woman wants to leave the house of her husband, she is to tell him of her destination, and he authorizes her to leave, provided no harm is done . . . [because] he is better aware of her interests."[5]

As late as 1993, the same year he became grand mufti, ibn Baz cautioned Saudi parents against sending their sons to non-Muslim countries to vacation or study. Young men overseas might doubt their faith, he warned, and do wild things such as attend parties with women. People who want to travel, he wrote, should visit Mecca and Medina instead.

It is a measure of just how reactionary many of Saudi Arabia's clerics are that King Fahad chose ibn Baz to be the grand mufti in order to *reduce* the fundamentalists' growing influence.

Dissent by Fax, E-Mail, and Satellite TV

On May 3, 1993, six scholars announced the formation of Saudi Arabia's first organization devoted to public protest, the Committee for the Defense of Legitimate Rights (CDLR). Its mission was to restore the Saudi people's "legitimate rights"—not democratic rights, but rights under the *sharia*, Muslim law, which, it said, includes "the people's right to express their opinions freely." The CDLR said nothing about women and accused the kingdom's Shi'ite minority of "apostasy," an offense that is traditionally punishable by death.

Nevertheless, the organization's leader, Muhammad al-Masari, a cheerful professor of physics with a trim black beard, in an interview with BBC Television criticized Saudi Arabia's repression and described the CDLR as if it were a Western human rights organization.

A week later, Saudi Arabia's Council of the Senior Clergy asked the government to ban the CDLR as an un-Islamic organization since "*sharia* courts are widespread and no one is prevented from raising a grievance in these courts." The next day, Saudi police closed the CDLR's offices and arrested the organization's founders and thirty-two of its supporters. The police released twenty-nine of the men as soon as they surrendered their passports and signed a statement promising not to criticize the government or to telephone or fax anyone outside the kingdom.

Al-Masari remained in prison. During his first two months in jail, the police sometimes beat the soles of his feet with a cane, a common torture in the Middle East called *fallaqa*. Amnesty International adopted al-Masari as a "prisoner of conscience," and the publicity that resulted persuaded the Saudis to free him in November, after six months in prison. Two other founders of the CDLR spent four years in prison.

Not long after his release, al-Masari outsmarted the policemen who constantly followed him by trading places with a look-alike during a hospital visit. Then, with a false passport, he flew to a small town in the south, where he was met by a guide who led him by foot across the desert into Yemen.

In April 1994, al-Masari, now in London, announced the rebirth of the CDLR. He set up a Web site, a toll-free international phone number, and a room full of fax machines that could send a thousand faxes a day to Saudi Arabia. In one fax, al-Masari wrote, "Our leaders imprison preachers, torture them and prevent them from saying the word of truth. Our leaders have mismanaged our economic resources and stolen our wealth."[6]

In other faxes, al-Masari compared the royal family to a "mafia" and the senior princes to "dinosaurs" who "should die out." He also called the senior clergy "paid accomplices" of the royal family.[7]

Al-Masari called for free speech, free assembly, elections, and a more equal distribution of wealth in the kingdom. (More than fifty princes are billionaires, according to al-Masari.) He also wrote about lax morals and financial corruption within the royal family in a series of faxes called "Prince of the Month."

The worst of these princes, al-Masari wrote, would "ask" to buy a commoner's land, store, or restaurant at well below the market price.

The unlucky businessman had little choice but to agree to the sale, afraid that if he refused to sell, the police might arrest him on a trumped-up charge. Al-Masari also wrote that Abdul Aziz, the youngest son of King Fahad, won a large government contract for AT&T even though Philips-Ericsson, the European telecommunications giant, had submitted a bid to do more work for less than half the money.

Al-Masari's faxes and e-mails infuriated the royal family, and the security police briefly imprisoned more than fifteen of his relatives. A court also sentenced a young man to five years in jail just for possessing some CDLR leaflets. The Council of the Senior Clergy, led by ibn Baz, condemned the CDLR's faxes as "seditious" and warned the Saudi people "not to read them."

At first, many young Saudis defied the government and the clerics and eagerly read al-Masari's e-mails and faxes and forwarded them to friends. But gradually, al-Masari lost his credibility among young Saudis for two reasons. First, he issued a *takfir* (excommunication) against any Muslim who obeyed the laws of the Saudi kingdom, which alienated all but the most extreme militants. Second, too many of his reports about the royal family were based on nothing but hearsay so, before long, even his most credible charges were received with skepticism.

The Saudi government demanded that Britain deport al-Masari, but Britain resisted this plea until November 1995, when al-Masari announced his support for the bombing of the National Guard building in Riyadh. The British immediately began proceedings to deport him to Dominica, an island in the Caribbean with few communications facilities. Eventually, a judge ruled that al-Masari could remain in Britain, but by then, al-Masari owed more than $300,000 in legal fees and had to declare bankruptcy. Donations to the CDLR went to al-Masari's creditors instead and then quickly stopped altogether.

As this book goes to press, al-Masari still lives in London but writes more about Islam and less about Saudi Arabia. The CDLR has been replaced by another organization, the Movement for Islamic Reform in Arabia (MIRA), led by Saad al-Faqih, an activist who once worked for al-Masari. For years, MIRA sent e-mails to Saudis that advocated the nonviolent overthrow of the royal family and the election of an Islamist government. Then, in 2003, al-Faqih briefly hosted *Reform TV*, a satellite broadcast that for the first time beamed direct criticism of the royal family into Saudi living rooms. For three hours a day, al-Faqih answered telephone calls about politics and religion, but in August, his program suddenly vanished. Possibly, the royal family paid the European network that had aired the program more money to just stop the transmissions. Al-Faqih switched to radio and today still broadcasts a phone-in talk show to an unknown number of Saudis every evening.

Jailing Clerics

When the CDLR had just formed in 1993, the "Awakening Sheikhs," Salman al-Awda and Safar al-Hawali, showed caution and stayed quiet for a few months. In 1994, however, they began to criticize the royal family again for not applying Islamic law strictly enough. They knew they were inviting arrest. To shield al-Awda from the police, several hundred of his young followers surrounded his home in the ultraconservative city of Buraida, where in the 1960s people had rioted to try to prevent the opening of a girls' school.

Many of al-Awda's guards were barely out of their teens. Like other young men across the kingdom, they had joined militant groups in high school, going on weekend picnics and summer camping trips where fiery young clerics urged them to build a new society based on the caliphate of the early Muslims. "They teach you that you're the only good Muslims, the others are not," said Abdullah Thabet, a fiction writer who used to be a militant. Thabet said he enjoyed the feeling of superiority the clerics gave him but added, "If there were girls in our high school, I would never have joined those groups."[8]

On September 13, 1994, more than a thousand royal bodyguards and antiriot police surrounded al-Awda's followers in Buraida. Al-Awda chose not to resist. "I don't think it's a good idea to fight," he said, "everyone has a machine gun. No need to shed blood."[9] Police arrested al-Hawali the same week, and because neither cleric would sign a statement promising to stop preaching, both spent the next five years in prison.

The day after al-Awda's arrest, thousands of clerics, professors, and devout young men gathered outside his mosque in Buraida to protest his imprisonment. Police arrested 155 of the demonstrators for "actions that undermined national security" but released 130 of them within six weeks.

Encouraged by faxes from the CDLR, hundreds of militants gathered at mosques in Riyadh, Jeddah, and Buraida during the next few months to protest the arrests of al-Awda, al-Hawali, and other clerics. The police, who had greatly increased their surveillance of mosques and preachers, made more arrests, and by the summer of 1995, there were more than four hundred political prisoners in the kingdom, about double the usual number. Newspapers began to print articles in favor of religious moderation, and antigovernment tape cassettes, which used to be sold everywhere, now had to be bought in secret.

Osama bin Laden in Saudi Arabia and Sudan

When the Soviets finally left Afghanistan in 1989, after a decade of fighting, Osama bin Laden decided that it was time to go home. But soon after his arrival, the Saudi police confiscated his passport and said that he could travel abroad only if Prince Nayef, the minister of the interior, approved of the trip. Bin Laden had given money to rebels fighting the Marxist government in South Yemen, and the Saudis were afraid that they might derail negotiations for the unification of North and South Yemen that had begun when geologists discovered oil along their border.

The following year, when Iraq invaded Kuwait and King Fahad invited U.S. troops to defend the kingdom, bin Laden was furious. Speaking at schools and homes in Jeddah, he denounced America's desecration of Arabia's holy soil and its support for Israel and called for a boycott of U.S. products. The presence of U.S. troops was unnecessary, he insisted, because an army of a hundred thousand dedicated Muslim guerrillas could defeat Iraq without Western help.

Bin Laden proposed to lead fifteen thousand veterans of the Afghan War himself and asked for an audience with King Fahad. Because of his years of hard work in Afghanistan, he succeeded in getting a meeting with Prince Sultan, the minister of defense (and now crown prince). Bin Laden showed the prince maps, diagrams, and detailed plans typed in Arabic, but Sultan pointed out that Saddam Hussein had more than fifty-five hundred tanks and asked, "What will you do when he lobs the missiles at you with biological and chemical weapons? There are no caves in Kuwait to hide in."

"We will fight them with faith," bin Laden answered.[10]

The meeting ended amicably, but bin Laden concluded that the Saudi government had become an apostate regime and a puppet of the United States, while Prince Sultan wondered whether bin Laden's mind had become "disturbed."[11]

Even after the Gulf War began, bin Laden continued to denounce the royal princes for making the United States "their master." Bin Laden's siblings tried but failed to stop their brother from preaching, so for several months the Saudi police confined bin Laden to the city of Jeddah. Then, late in 1991, they allowed him to leave the country.

Bin Laden chose Sudan to be his new base of operations. At the time, the country was ruled by Hassan al-Turabi, who had made his desperately poor country a haven for Algerian and Chechen guerrillas, Egyptian jihadists, Hamas, and even the notorious Venezuelan terrorist Carlos the Jackal. Al-Turabi allowed bin Laden to live in the Sudan, too, on condition that bin Laden invest in his country.

Exactly how much money bin Laden had when he arrived in the Sudan in a chartered jet with his four wives and seventeen children is a mystery. When his father died, bin Laden's share of the estate was $20 million, but during the 1970s and the 1980s, the money he controlled grew considerably, not only because of successful investments but also because he received large donations from Saudi, Kuwaiti, and United Arab Emirates businessmen who were sympathetic to the Afghan cause. In the 1990s, bin Laden may have invested nearly $50 million in the Sudan.

Bin Laden's ventures in the Sudan included an Islamic bank; a trading firm that grew and exported sesame, white corn, and sunflowers (bin Laden greatly enjoyed being a farmer); and the construction of a highway called "the Challenge" that connected Khartoum, the capital, with a port on the Red Sea almost five hundred miles to the northeast. The government paid for this highway by giving bin Laden more than a million acres of farmland. Bin Laden also built several buildings in Khartoum and started a bakery, a salt mine, a soup factory, a leather tannery, a cattle-breeding company, and firms that imported insecticides and bicycles. He spent several hours a day tending to these enterprises and had a nine-room office in Khartoum with a receptionist and some secretaries.

Although bin Laden hired about four hundred Sudanese men at $200 a month, a very high salary in that poor country, he entrusted most of his businesses to veterans whom he had known in Afghanistan. More of these veterans arrived in Sudan in 1993, when Pakistan's prime minister, Benazir Bhutto, who did not trust them, let them know that they were no longer welcome in Pakistan. Bin Laden sent money for 480 veterans to fly to Khartoum, where some of them began to manage bin Laden's businesses and others formed a personal bodyguard.

When bin Laden was not running his businesses, he took his sons on picnics along the Nile, rode horses with Hassan al-Turabi's sons, and spoke at a mosque on Fridays, before the noon prayer, about the continued need for holy war. He also set up three al-Qaeda training camps in northern Sudan and gave money and camels to opponents of Egyptian president Hosni Mubarak to help them smuggle weapons and printing presses into Egypt. Later, some of these Egyptians tried to assassinate Mubarak while he was on a state visit to Ethiopia. One CIA analyst called bin Laden "the Ford Foundation of Sunni Islamic terrorism" because he received many proposals for *jihad* and funded the ones he thought best.

In December 1992, President George H. W. Bush sent twenty-five thousand U.S. troops to Somalia, a few hundred miles east of Sudan, to protect food deliveries and prevent more than a hundred thousand people from starving to death. Bin Laden did not believe that famine relief was America's prime motive. Instead, he saw the U.S. action as a first step toward regime change in Sudan. Bin Laden promptly sent money (and a few men) to train and finance Somali guerrillas, and in October 1993, these Somalis used rocket-propelled grenades to shoot down two U.S. Black Hawk helicopters, killing eighteen U.S. Army Rangers. Television viewers saw a crowd of jubilant Somalis dragging American bodies through the streets of Mogadishu, the capital, which caused many Americans to wonder why U.S. troops were there at all.

With the threat of mass starvation gone, President Bill Clinton withdrew the U.S. troops from Somalia. Unfortunately, because bin Laden did not understand that America's reason for going to Somalia was humanitarian, not political, he saw the withdrawal as a sign of softness. "Our brothers in Somalia . . . saw the weakness, frailty, and cowardice of U.S. troops," bin Laden told a reporter. "Only eighteen U.S. troops were killed. Nevertheless, they fled."[12]

The debacle in Somalia made Western leaders much more careful about sending troops to Africa again, yet only six months later, Rwanda endured suffering far worse than Somalia's. A suspicious plane crash that killed Rwanda's president led the Hutu tribe to massacre eight hundred thousand Tutsis, largely with machetes. Western leaders, overly cautious, did not send troops to Rwanda until it was too late. By then, Rwanda had suffered the worst genocide since the Cambodian tragedy of the 1970s.

Osama bin Laden never killed a Tutsi himself, but he made the humanitarian mission in Somalia needlessly lethal in 1993 and therefore bears much of the blame for the timidity of the global effort to stop the massacre in Rwanda just months later. Bin Laden is directly responsible for almost 3,000 deaths on September 11, 2001, but he is indirectly responsible for more than 250 times that number of deaths in Rwanda in 1994.

As soon as the Committee for the Defense of Legitimate Rights was formed in 1993, bin Laden formed his own organization, the Advice and Reform Committee (ARC). The ARC published pamphlets that called for the abolition of the Saudi state, typically with a picture of bin Laden on the cover.

During the winter of 1993–1994, Prince Turki al-Faisal, then the director of Saudi intelligence (and later the ambassador to the United States), sent at least seven delegations of bin Laden's friends and relatives to the Sudan. They begged bin Laden to come home, renounce violence and apologize to King Fahad, be forgiven, and resume the life of a multimillionaire. Prince Turki, who had worked with bin Laden in Afghanistan, hoped that he was just a confused young man whose wealth had allowed him to be more rebellious than most. Turki even sent bin Laden's mother to Khartoum to try to talk sense to her errant son, but bin Laden felt that he could not return to Saudi Arabia as long as U.S. troops were in the kingdom.

Finally, in February 1994, bin Laden's oldest brother, Bakr, who led the family's multibillion-dollar construction conglomerate, issued a statement to the Saudi press expressing "regrets, denunciation and condemnation of all acts that Osama bin Laden may have committed, which we do not condone and which we reject."[13]

The Saudi government waited a month to see whether the bin Laden family's statement had any effect on Osama, then froze his Saudi assets and stripped him of his citizenship on March 5 "because of his irresponsible behavior that contradicts the interests of Saudi Arabia and harms sisterly countries." By this action, the government cut bin Laden off from his family's income, which made financing his Sudanese businesses much more difficult and ensured that he could never return to Saudi Arabia to finance militants at home. In April, when a Saudi official came to bin Laden's home to confiscate his passport, bin Laden threw it at him, saying, "Take it!"[14]

A few months later, several men fired machine guns into the mosque where bin Laden usually prayed and into his office at home. No one knows who was behind the unsuccessful attacks, but some analysts think the gunmen may have been Egyptian agents seeking revenge for the attempted assassination of President Hosni Mubarak during his visit to Ethiopia.

Bin Laden increased his security but continued to finance terrorists and print anti-Saudi pamphlets. On August 3, 1995, he published an open letter to King Fahad. The ten-page document criticized the king for his lack of commitment to Wahhabism, his squandering of oil money on palaces and other luxuries, his arrest of clerics such as al-Awda and al-Hawali, and especially his military dependence on non-Muslims, "the Crusaders and the Jews, who are profaning the Holy Places."[15]

Bin Laden told the king that "the source of the [nation's] disease" was "you, your defense minister, and your interior minister," that is, Fahad and two of his full brothers, Sultan and Nayef. (He did not criticize Abdullah, who is known to be more devout than the three Sudairi princes.) Bin Laden concluded, "We have proven that your regime is un-Islamic. It is mired in corruption and applies non-Islamic laws to . . . commercial law. It has also failed in the areas of the economy and defense. Thus, you should resign."[16]

Bin Laden cited King Saud's abdication of the throne in 1964 as a precedent and added that King Saud "was ten times less corrupt than you."[17]

Oil Prices and Installations in the Mid-1990s

Despite the kingdom's austerity budget in 1994, many government ministries were slow to cut spending. They were full of men who had held their jobs for fifteen or even twenty-five years and had trouble adjusting to new realities. King Fahad decided to make changes. In the summer of 1995, he replaced 173 top officials with younger men, including half of the cabinet. For the first time, a majority of the ministers had postgraduate degrees from Western universities.

The king also appointed a new minister of petroleum, Ali ibn Ibrahim al-Naimi, the chairman of Saudi Aramco. Al-Naimi was still the minister of petroleum as this book went to press. Under his leadership, OPEC made small cuts in oil production in 1995 and 1996, enough to make the price rise to $21 a barrel and improve the kingdom's economy. Oil revenues were $8 billion higher in 1996 than they had been in 1995, and they remained just as high in 1997. The government used this extra money to soften many of its budget cuts in 1996 and 1997 and to reduce its deficits, too.

Geologists found seven new oil fields in Saudi Arabia in the first half of the 1990s and increased the production at fourteen more, including the giant Safaniya field off the shore of the Persian Gulf. By 1994, more than a third of Saudi Arabia's oil production came from offshore rigs. In the Empty Quarter, fourteen hundred oil workers lived in trailers and drilled more than a hundred new wells that started to produce five hundred thousand barrels a day in 1998.

The government also began $20 billion worth of projects to enlarge and modernize its refineries and petrochemical complexes. The products they make include gasoline, jet fuel, diesel oil, fuel oil, kerosene, ammonia, naphtha, asphalt, ethylene, propylene, and liquid petroleum gas. Sixty percent of these products are sold to buyers from China, Japan, and other nations in East Asia.

The Spread of Satellite Television

During the Gulf War, Saudi television news was so bad that more than ten thousand people bought satellite dishes so that they could watch CNN and the BBC. By 1994, there were more than 150,000 satellite receivers in the kingdom, which greatly alarmed both the clergy and the government. The new Arab Radio and Television Network (ART), for example, was soon broadcasting talk shows on divorce, drug use, and premarital sex, while the Orbit Network began to show Western movies and episodes of *Seinfeld*. On the Saudi government's channel, by contrast, women could not sing or dance or appear at all during the month of Ramadan. An actor and an actress on television could not be in a room together if the door was closed, and no drama could show a crime being committed.

Afraid of the effect of foreign television on Saudi culture, the ministry of the interior outlawed the import, the sale, and the possession of satellite dishes and receivers on June 27 and gave dealers just one month to export their inventory. The fine for putting up a receiver was $27,000, yet still the number grew. People built water tanks on their roofs to hide their dishes, and by 1996, more than three hundred thousand Saudi families watched television from all over the world, about one-seventh of the kingdom, not counting foreign workers.

Although only the most prosperous Saudis enjoyed satellite TV in the mid-1990s, almost everyone had a videocassette recorder. By 1996, there were nearly eight million VCRs in the kingdom. Saudis might criticize the growing influence of Egyptian and American movies, but they watched them all the same. Hundreds of thousands of Saudis also had fax machines and cellular phones; try as the government might, Saudi Arabia was no longer a closed society.

In Qatar, a Connecticut-sized peninsula in the Persian Gulf with 14 percent of the world's natural gas, changes came quickly after Crown Prince Hamad ath-Thani overthrew his reactionary father on June 27, 1995, and began a series of reforms. Hamad gave women the vote and allowed the press to be free, and in 1996, Al Jazeera, today the most well known Arab news network, began to broadcast. (*Al Jazeera* is the Arabic word for "the peninsula.") Many of Saudi Arabia's officials and clerics deeply resent Qatar's reforms and Al Jazeera's critical coverage of their country, but some of the more senior Saudi princes see Qatar as a stimulus for helpful change in the kingdom.[18]

Women in the Mid-1990s

In a poll taken at the peak of the oil boom in 1980, more than two-thirds of young Saudi men said they would not marry a woman with a college education, and almost 80 percent did not want their wives to work. By 1995, when incomes were much lower, it was acceptable and even welcome for an educated woman to contribute to a family's income. Women still made up only 6 percent of the Saudi labor force, and the few who did work were still strictly segregated from men. Most worked in women's schools, at women's banks, and in hospitals, where female patients see female doctors and nurses. A wealthy female Saudi engineer offered to build an all-woman factory in 1996 to make parts for high-tech electronics equipment, but she failed to get the government permits she needed, despite the enthusiasm of some officials. The problem was not the all-female assembly line, but the impossibility of doing business without male intermediaries.

Yet by 1996, for the first time in Saudi history, a majority of adult women could read and write. Literacy was still the exception among the elderly, but it was the rule among the young. More women than men were graduating from high school, and at universities the percentage of women students climbed to 46 percent. Because in rural areas women still marry in their late teens, only about half of the kingdom's young women actually finished high school in 1995, and only one-seventh went to universities.

Saudi women in the 1990s continued to have an astonishing average of six children each, causing the kingdom's population to more than double from seven million in 1974, at the beginning of the oil boom, to eighteen million by 1994. Despite this enormous increase, the Council of the Senior Clergy forced the government to withdraw from a United Nations Population and Development Conference in Cairo in September 1994 because it was "an insult to Islam." The council objected to the conference's calls to make contraceptives and reproductive health-care information more available and to raise the minimum age for marriage. The clerics also objected to the conference's call for equality between men and women because "equality is against God's law [the *sharia*] and against the law of nature."[19]

Another example of how different Saudi mores are from those of most of the rest of the world took place that same summer, when a neighbor saw a Filipino servant named Maria deliver breakfast to her family's driver at dawn. In Saudi Arabia, a woman who is alone with a man she is not related to can be charged with prostitution, and in this case the unfortunate servant was sentenced to two hundred lashes and ten months in prison. She served six months and suffered the full caning before she was finally deported to the Philippines. (Some foreign observers say that while policemen in Saudi Arabia are a bit more lenient than are policemen elsewhere in the Middle East, the judges in the kingdom are the harshest in the Muslim world.)

Money for Afghanistan

In 1992, when the Soviet Union agreed to stop supporting the Afghan government and the United States agreed to stop aiding the Afghan rebels, Afghanistan quickly descended into anarchy as warlords and ethnic armies competed for power. In Kabul, artillery duels were fought between neighborhoods that no longer had electricity, and in rural areas, crumbling roads made food supplies unreliable and malnourishment and disease common.

The head of Saudi intelligence, Prince Turki al-Faisal, tried and failed to get Afghanistan's warring factions to work together. Then, in 1994, a new force swept through Afghanistan, the Taliban. At first, the black-turbaned Taliban, whose name means "religious students," won wide acclaim for rescuing girls near Kandahar from gang rape and hanging the rapists. The Taliban then raised $250,000, bought some pickup trucks and machine guns, and took over downtown Kandahar. "For the Quran's sake, put down your weapons," they told warlords when they entered a town. If the warlords refused, the Taliban killed them. By the end of 1995, the Taliban had taken control of all of southern and western Afghanistan. In 1996, they moved east and took Kabul in September.

The initial attitude of city dwellers toward the Taliban was relief that order had finally replaced chaos. Living more devoutly seemed a small price to pay for safe streets. But the Taliban were not just strict Muslims, they were followers of Deobandism, an austere branch of Islam that began in Deoband, India, in the nineteenth century.

Deobandis believe that good Muslims should live just as Muhammad and his companions did in the seventh century, and they are deeply suspicious of anything modern.

Deobandism flourished in the religious schools of Pakistan, called *madrassas*, where many young Afghan men acquired an education when they fled the Soviets in the 1980s. Because Pakistan is a country where the rich do not pay taxes, there are not enough public schools. To fill the void, religious groups have started their own schools, where students memorize the entire Quran by chanting its verses over and over again. By the 1980s, there were more than twenty-five hundred *madrassas* in Pakistan. Today there are roughly fifteen thousand *madrassas*, with more than a million students, and the Pakistani government is urging the schools to teach nonreligious subjects, too.[20] Tuition and board remain free, an arrangement that makes the students unusually devoted to their teachers.

Many graduates of the *madrassas* later fought for the Taliban or for the Muslims in Kashmir. (Members of al-Qaeda, however, usually have a high school diploma, and a majority have spent some time in college.) At the Haqqania School near Peshawar, eight future ministers of the Taliban government absorbed the Deobandi sect's rigidly antimodern outlook as they memorized verse after verse of the Quran. More than 60 percent of Pakistan's *madrassas* are Deobandi, and until the autumn of 2001, many of them received money directly from the Saudi and Pakistani governments or from Wahhabi and Pakistani charities.

When the Deobandi-indoctrinated Taliban took over Kabul and other Afghan cities in 1995 and 1996, they outlawed television, VCRs, audio cassettes, music, singing, dancing, fashion magazines, cigarettes, alcohol, kites, and marbles. They even banned using toothbrushes and being clean-shaven because Muhammad had grown a full beard and cleaned his teeth with a root. In soccer stadiums, the Taliban whipped drunkards, amputated the hands of thieves, and let the families of murder victims machine-gun the killers of their loved ones.

The Taliban's most oppressive laws dealt with women. Women could not work, teach, or even go to school. They had to stay home all day except to buy food and could go to a market only if they wore a *burqa* from head to toe. Unfortunately, because of the recent war against the Soviets, there were fifty thousand widows in Kabul alone, many with six, eight, and even ten children. Thousands of these widows had no brothers to support them, and now, because they could not work, many were reduced to begging in the streets.

Incredibly, Saudi officials and clerics liked what they saw. The Taliban reminded them of their own pre-oil past, of the early Wahhabis in the eighteenth century and the Ikhwan warriors in the 1910s and the 1920s. Saudi intelligence officers gave the Taliban money, vehicles, and tankers of gasoline to help them take Kabul. Saudi religious policemen helped the Taliban to create a religious police force of their own and gave them money to build police stations and buy patrol cars.

Osama bin Laden admired the Taliban, too, because they tried to live like his heroes, the early Muslims. Thus, when the Sudanese government bowed to Western pressure and expelled bin Laden from the Sudan in 1996, he picked Afghanistan to be his new home.

The Bombing of the Saudi National Guard Building

At eleven thirty in the morning on November 13, 1995, four men in Riyadh drove a pickup truck to the front of a three-story building, set a timer connected to about two hundred pounds of explosives, and sped away in a different car.

The bomb, the first one ever detonated in a Saudi city, ripped away the front of the Saudi National Guard building, where U.S. employees of the Vinnell Corporation regularly trained Saudi guardsmen how to use and maintain high-tech weapons. The bomb killed five Americans and two citizens of India and wounded thirty-seven Americans and twenty-three others. No Saudis were killed or injured because the bomb had been timed to explode during the midday prayer, when Saudi guardsmen left their building to pray at a nearby mosque. The United States immediately sent nineteen FBI agents to Riyadh to investigate the bombing, but the Saudis ignored them because they did not want foreigners meddling in matters of internal security.

Six months later, on April 22, 1996, the four men who had detonated the bomb suddenly appeared on Saudi television with no advance notice and confessed their crime. The public was shocked to see that the young men were not foreigners or intellectuals but ordinary Saudis from the heart of the kingdom. Three had fought in Afghanistan in the 1980s, and one had fought in Bosnia in the 1990s. After returning to the kingdom, they worked at menial jobs such as selling fruit and vegetables on the street, and none had any prospect of a career. The four men said that the presence of U.S. troops in the kingdom had driven them to violence, and that they had been influenced by the pamphlets of Osama bin Laden and Muhammad al-Masari, the founder of the CDLR.

Five weeks later, on May 31, as a crowd roared its approval, an executioner with a long curved sword cut off the heads of the four terrorists in Riyadh's central square. The Saudis never gave the FBI agents a chance to talk to them before the prisoners died.

Fahad's Two Strokes, Abdullah's New Authority

Shortly after the bombing in November 1995, King Fahad suffered a severe stroke. He survived but was much weaker. Overweight, arthritic, and diabetic, the king had long been in bad health. Now he could no longer work because often he forgot where he was and why he was there. After several weeks of intense discussions among the senior and midlevel princes, the royal family announced on January 1, 1996, that King Fahad had written a letter to Crown Prince Abdullah asking him to manage the government while Fahad recuperated. Abdullah accepted the new responsibility, wished his brother a speedy recovery, and flew to Oman to attend a summit of the Gulf monarchs.

Prince Sultan, who is the king's full brother and next in line to the throne after Abdullah, publicly described Fahad's illness as only a "slight ailment." This may have been simply courtesy and typical Saudi understatement, but some people wondered whether Sultan was also cautioning Abdullah not to assume too much power during Fahad's recuperation. Prince Sultan, the minister of defense; Prince Nayef, the minister of the interior; and Prince Salman, the governor of Riyadh, were all full brothers of King Fahad, and they did not want Abdullah—whose mother was not even Saudi, but Syrian—to take power any sooner than necessary. Together, they made sure that Fahad received the best medical care in the world.

On February 21, after six weeks of rest, King Fahad sent Prince Abdullah a second letter that said, "I have finished my recuperative period," and he formally resumed his powers as king. He remained confined to a wheelchair and continued to suffer from dementia, but sometimes he was lucid enough to open a cabinet meeting, appear briefly at a royal reception, or lead prayers at a mosque.

Although Fahad was still king, Abdullah continued to be the nation's day-to-day ruler, and this worried many princes. Some were afraid that Abdullah might reduce their stipends. Even the roughly three thousand *great*-grandsons of King Abdul Aziz, for example, received incomes of $225,000 a year. Other princes were afraid that Abdullah might limit their "consultant's fees" for business deals, and they, too, wanted Fahad to live as long as possible. For example, Fahad's youngest and most indulged son, Abdulaziz, is said to have received a fee of more than $200 million from AT&T for securing the company a $4 billion government contract, while his brother Muhammad received an equally large fee from Philips-Ericsson. Prince Sultan, the minister of defense, is also known for the huge commissions that he and his sons receive from Western arms manufacturers, and the Ibrahim family, the brothers of Fahad's youngest wife, Jawhara, have also collected large fees for international arms deals.

Still other princes feared Abdullah because they had bought government land at bargain prices or borrowed money from banks that they never paid back, and they knew that Abdullah detests such corruption. "You can't believe how corrupt some of my family is," Abdullah once told a foreign visitor. But changing business-as-usual without a king's signature is difficult, and as long as Fahad stayed alive, Abdullah's power to cut his fellow princes' incomes was limited.

Fundamentalists, by contrast, were delighted with Abdullah's increased power. Although Abdullah is not a fundamentalist himself, he is quite devout. He prays five times a day, does not drink, refuses to let his sons take business commissions, and vacations in the Arab world rather than in Europe. He has also been an effective commander of the National Guard, spending less money to modernize it than Prince Sultan spent to modernize the army and the air force. Abdullah is popular with the desert tribes, too, in part because he speaks like a Bedouin, having spent much of his childhood in the desert.

King Fahad suffered a second stroke late in 1996 that further weakened his body and mind. Afterward, more often than not, Fahad could no longer recognize his closest relatives, not even Jawhara, his fourth and favorite wife. The king's illness gave Jawhara and her son Abdulaziz tremendous power, for they decided who could see the king and who could not and when and how many documents could be presented for his slow and barely legible signature. The government made no announcement about the king's second stroke, but the stroke ended any hope that his wife, sons, and full brothers might have had that Fahad would one day recover from his illness and relieve Abdullah of his duties.

The Bombing of the U.S. Military Apartment Towers at Al-Khobar

Just before ten at night on June 25, 1996, several men in a getaway car, possibly a white Chevrolet Caprice, sped away from the Khobar Towers, a U.S. military housing complex in the city of Al-Khobar, near the U.S. air force base in Dhahran. A few minutes later, a fuel truck packed with more than five thousand pounds of explosives burst into an enormous fireball. The blast caused one of the apartment towers to collapse, killing 19 U.S. servicemen and wounding 373 other Americans. It was the worst act of foreign terrorism against the United States since the 1983 bombing in Beirut that killed 241 U.S. Marines, and it ended the feeling of complete safety that Americans had always enjoyed in Saudi Arabia.

The explosion at Al-Khobar was more powerful than the 1995 blast in Oklahoma City. It left a crater thirty-five feet deep, blew out windows a mile away, and was felt even twelve miles offshore on the island of Bahrain.

The United States had fortified the towers to withstand several hundred pounds of explosives, but this bomb had ten times that amount. "I have great respect for the people who did this," Osama bin Laden told CNN a year later. "What they did is a big honor that I missed participating in."[21]

Ironically, the bin Laden family won the contract to rebuild the Khobar Towers, but the U.S. military had no intention of moving back into the buildings. It was clear that operating a U.S. air force base in a populated Muslim area had become too dangerous, so the Saudis agreed to let the United States move its air base to a new location in Al Kharj, seventy miles southeast of Riyadh. The new base was secure because it was in the middle of the desert, and no one could approach it undetected.

As the investigation of the bombing began, there was a severe clash of law enforcement cultures between the FBI and the Saudi police. To the FBI agents, many Saudis seemed perversely silent and guarded. To the Saudis, the FBI agents were useless because they did not speak Arabic and arrogant because they appeared to have no sense that the bombing was a crime with Saudi suspects on Saudi soil. As Anthony Cordesman has written, "The Saudi investigators often seemed unable to open their mouths, while the FBI investigators seemed unable to keep them shut and avoid posturing for the press and Congress."[22]

The Saudi police did let FBI agents trained in forensics examine the bomb site, but they did not allow FBI agents to interrogate suspects. At first, the Saudis thought that Osama bin Laden was behind the bombing. They briefly detained more than six hundred veterans of the Afghan war and did not want the FBI to know how many of these militants came from prominent, educated Saudi families. The Saudis also did not want Christians to interrogate Muslims.

After a year passed without any solid leads, FBI director Louis Freeh flew to Riyadh to try to jump-start the investigation. But Prince Nayef, the minister of the interior, was jealous of the kingdom's sovereignty and made a point of being out of town that week, staying on his yacht in the Red Sea. After several more visits to Saudi Arabia (and a dispute with U.S. national security adviser Samuel Berger over pressing for and sharing information with the Saudis), an exasperated Freeh met with former president George H. W. Bush, whom the Saudis still revered for his tough stand during the Gulf War. Freeh asked Bush whether he could persuade the Saudis to be more cooperative with the FBI, and finally, more than two years after the Khobar bombing, the Saudis agreed to let Arabic-speaking FBI agents monitor the Saudi interrogations behind mirrored glass.

United States and Saudi law enforcement officers concluded that the Khobar Towers were destroyed by Saudi Shi'ites who belonged to a branch of Hezbollah ("the Party of God"), an Iranian-financed organization that has a militia in Lebanon. Although investigators heard testimony that some of Iran's security agents had trained and financed the Khobar bombers in an attempt to drive U.S. forces from the region, direct evidence of aid by a specific Iranian official or agency was lacking, and the Iranian government denied any involvement in the bombing. Without direct evidence, both the Saudis and the Clinton administration were reluctant to punish Iran with air strikes and inflame the region.

By 1998, the election of the relatively moderate Muhammad Khatami as Iran's president and the need for Saudi Arabia and Iran to work together to raise oil prices caused the United States and Saudi Arabia to try to thaw their long-frosty relations with Iran. The investigation of the Khobar explosion continued, but it was no longer an urgent priority. Because nineteen Americans had died, however, there are still strong feelings about the bombing.

On June 21, 2001, at the request of U.S. attorney general John Ashcroft, a federal grand jury in Alexandria, Virginia, indicted thirteen Saudi militants and a Lebanese chemist, all members of Hezbollah, for murder, conspiracy to use a weapon of mass destruction, and other crimes.

(The indictment did not name any Iranians.) It was unusual for the United States to indict foreigners for crimes committed abroad but was necessary, Ashcroft explained, to avoid having the statute of limitations for the noncapital crimes expire on the fifth anniversary of the bombing, June 25.

The United States has no extradition treaty with Saudi Arabia, and Prince Nayef has said, "The trials [of the bombers] must take place before Saudi judicial authorities. . . . No other entity has the right to try or investigate any crimes occurring on Saudi lands."[23]

Six of the fourteen suspects were arrested in Saudi Arabia soon after the bombing and remain in jail there, but eight others quickly left the kingdom with false passports and are still at large, and two of them, the alleged leaders of the conspiracy, live freely in Iran. Even if all fourteen suspects were extradited to the United States, however, it is questionable whether the evidence against them is beyond a reasonable doubt. The majority of the murderers remain unpunished.

On December 22, 2006, after a trial that Iran's government refused to take part in, a U.S. District Court judge in Washington, D.C., ruled that several officials in Iran's army and its intelligence agency helped to plan and finance the Khobar bombing. The justice entered a default judgment, allowing fifty-five relatives of the victims to try to collect $253 million in damages from the Iranian government. In practice, Iran's foreign assets will be extremely difficult for the victims' kin to attach because most courts around the world are reluctant to enforce default judgments that can be overturned later if they are contested. Still, the relatives were grateful for the verdict.

King Fahad's Legacy

During the fourteen years in which King Fahad was a functioning monarch, 1982 through 1995, Saudi Arabia suffered economic decline, runaway population growth, and increasingly militant fundamentalism. Despite his relatively modern outlook, Fahad did little to improve the lives of women, make the press freer, reduce the Saudis' dependence on oil and foreign labor, or make his own relatives less corrupt. Unlike his older brother, Faisal, who could overrule the clergy's objections to the introduction of girls' schools and television because he was known to be pious, Fahad had a playboy past that haunted him. It kept him from being able to challenge the clergy on vital issues such as encouraging women to work, taming the religious police, and beginning at least a discussion of the need for contraception.

Even Fahad's boldest action, inviting Western troops to protect the kingdom after Iraq's invasion of Kuwait in 1990, was a mixed success. He never explained to the Saudi people why the nation needed both foreign troops during the Gulf War and foreign aircraft afterward to enforce the "no-fly" zones. As a result, the rise in militant fundamentalism was more powerful than it needed to be. Stoking the militants' discontent further was the fact that King Fahad had no reputation for piety, and that in 1986, only four years before the Gulf War, he had begun to call himself the Custodian of the Two Holy Mosques. This title rang so false during the war that it heightened the embarrassment that the Saudi people felt at needing Western troops to defend their kingdom.

But militant fundamentalism did not grow stronger in the 1990s only because the presence of foreign troops was humiliating. It was aggravated by a high rate of unemployment, especially among young men, a problem made worse because the kingdom's population has doubled every twenty-five years. No job means no income, and therefore no wife and no sons. The feelings this condition produces—inadequacy, frustration, rage—are a greater threat to the kingdom's stability than is an unlikely foreign invasion. It is not clear whether King Fahad fully understood his country's social and economic problems. If he did, he did not appreciate their urgency.

19

Abdullah Begins Reform, bin Laden Steps Up Terror (1996–August 2001)

AFTER KING FAHAD suffered his second stroke in 1996, Crown Prince Abdullah became the nation's de facto ruler. Because he was both more devout and more reform-minded than Fahad, he also became more popular than his predecessor. Under his leadership, although unemployment remained high, the press and the universities became freer, the Internet arrived, and satellite television became universal. Saudi Arabia also enacted new laws to make it easier for foreigners to invest in the kingdom.

Osama bin Laden moved from Sudan to Afghanistan in 1996. In February 1998, only a few months after he was settled, he publicly declared that killing Americans was "an individual duty for every Muslim." Six months later, on August 7, followers of bin Laden simultaneously blew up two U.S. embassies in Kenya and Tanzania, killing 224 people and injuring nearly 5,000. The former Saudi had begun a new era of mass terror.

Background and Character of Abdullah

Abdullah (the name means "Servant of God") has dark brown eyes and a slight stutter, a speech defect more than compensated for by a ramrod-straight posture that makes him seem taller than his six feet two inches. A coal-black goatee makes him look even more imposing.

By all accounts, Abdullah gets along well with everyone. He speaks frankly but is eager to hear what other people have to say, whether they are illiterate Bedouin or Western-educated professors. Even Abraham Foxman, the national director of the [Jewish] Anti-Defamation League, was pleasantly surprised during a trip to Saudi Arabia by Abdullah's willingness to listen carefully and ask questions. Foreigners have also observed that Abdullah's aides and household servants seem relaxed, and his great-grandchildren enjoy playing with him.

Abdullah was born in 1923 (some say 1924), the thirteenth son among King Abdul Aziz's more than seventy children. He was already an adult when oil money first began to change the kingdom, and he spent much of his childhood in the desert learning about horses, camels, and tribal histories and traditions. He liked the scorching days and the starry nights of the desert better than his half-brothers Fahad and Sultan did, and today, while many of his brothers vacation in Europe, Abdullah prefers to relax in the Arabian heartland. He often went hunting with tribal leaders until, as regent and then king, he became too busy. He also liked to hunt in Morocco and built a large library in Casablanca in gratitude for Moroccan hospitality.

Abdullah was a fine horseman, having raced Arabian horses when he was young and bred them in later years. His sons own horses, too—thoroughbreds that compete against each other at the King Abdul Aziz Racetrack in Riyadh. When Abdullah was younger, he loved to play polo with his sons.

Abdullah's chefs cook French and Middle Eastern feasts daily for his many guests, but the monarch himself eats sparingly and sometimes is content with just the traditional desert meal of dates and camel's milk. When he was younger, he smoked occasionally but never in public.

Opinions differ about Abdullah's intellect. Some say that he is uneducated, uses poor grammar, and is one of the worst speakers in the Arab world. Others agree that his education is limited but say that he reads widely and watches a half dozen TV news channels at a time. Saudis and foreigners both agree that he is a shrewd and hardworking politician. One prominent recent U.S. official told me, "Everyone respects him. Presidents Bush and Clinton, the heads of the FBI and CIA, everybody."

When Abdullah's father defeated the al-Rashid clan in 1921 and took the northern city of Hail, he treated the vanquished family well and brought their soldiers into his own army as equals. The king also married Fahada, the widow of an al-Rashid prince who had died in battle. Fahada, of Syrian descent, was Abdul Aziz's eighth wife, and they had two daughters and one son, Abdullah.

With no full brothers to play with, Abdullah spent time with his maternal uncles in the northern desert where Saudi Arabia borders Iraq and Jordan. When he was a child, he memorized many chapters of the Quran and learned about Muslim history from local scholars.

By the time Abdullah was ten, the Saudi kingdom had already reached its present boundaries so he never had to fight in a military campaign. Because Abdullah's slight stutter kept his father from giving him a government post, Abdullah did not become commander of the National Guard until he was thirty-eight. What he did before that is a mystery. I have asked many Saudis what Abdullah did in his twenties and thirties, and no seems to know. One political science professor explained, "Our leaders don't run for office, so we don't have to know these things."

The best guess is that as a young man, Abdullah spent a lot of time watching his father hold public audiences, reading books and magazines his friends bought in Beirut and Cairo, and training for (and winning) horse races. Abdullah also acted as a liaison between his father and the northern tribes and took some advanced courses in religion when he lived in Mecca, where for a while he helped his older brother Faisal govern the region.

In 1956, Abdullah and six of his younger brothers wrote a letter to King Saud that sharply criticized his excessive spending. Two years later, they helped to convince their older and more powerful brothers that the time had come for Faisal to replace Saud as prime minister.

In Beirut in 1962, Talal, a left-wing prince, criticized Saudi Arabia's lack of freedom and called for a constitutional monarchy with communal farms and state-owned industries. Three days later, Prince Abdullah sent a written reply to the press on behalf of the royal family:

> Talal knows full well that Saudi Arabia has a constitution inspired by God and not drawn up by man. . . . All laws and regulations in Saudi Arabia are inspired by the Quran, and Saudi Arabia is proud to have such a constitution. . . . Our understanding of democracy . . . removes all obstacles between the head of state and the humblest person in the land. Anyone can secure an audience with the King.[1]

In January 1963, Faisal appointed Abdullah to be commander of the National Guard, the second-most powerful post in the cabinet after the defense minister. Abdullah holds this post today, more than forty years later, even while serving as king.

The Saudis had learned an important lesson in the 1950s when Gamal Abdel Nasser overthrew Egypt's King Farouk: An army can be dangerous to a monarchy because well-educated officers often have revolutionary antimonarchist ideas. The government therefore created a new force, the National Guard, in 1956 as a check on the army. It gave modern weapons to eighteen thousand Bedouin who were loyal to the royal family and stationed the tribesmen near cities and oil fields because the guard's true purpose was to combat internal, not external, threats.

King Faisal chose Abdullah to lead the National Guard because of Abdullah's deep knowledge of the desert tribes and his loyalty during the long struggle to limit King Saud's power. Abdullah quickly enlarged the guard to thirty thousand men, hired British soldiers to train and modernize the force, and purged the officer corps of King Saud's supporters,

The British instructors started from scratch. In the 1960s, few Bedouin had more than a fourth-grade education, yet they were proud men who did not like taking orders. Slowly, with tact and patience, the British taught the guardsmen how to use their weapons and maintain their equipment. (This included, at first, pointing out the difference between a dishwasher and a washing machine.)

In 1969, the National Guard helped stop an attempt by air force officers to bomb the king's palace and create a republic, which proved that it was the most reliable of the armed forces.

Abdullah paid $77 million ($300 million in today's money) to the Vinnell Corporation in 1974 to arrange for more than a thousand Vietnam veterans (including some CIA agents) to train his guardsmen in missile firing, infantry tactics, and the maintenance of weapons and vehicles. The U.S. officers set rigorous standards for the Saudis and also ordered a new line of MREs (meals ready to eat) with no pork.

To increase the number and the quality of recruits, Abdullah raised the guardsmen's salaries, provided free housing, and built two huge hospitals and many smaller clinics that treat not only the guardsmen and their wives and children, but also their extended families. Unlike other princes, Abdullah refused to let his sons negotiate any of the military or hospital contracts. In fact, to avoid any conflict of interest, Abdullah makes his personal investments outside, not inside, Saudi Arabia.

Foreign analysts have estimated that the National Guard spends its money 30 percent more efficiently than the army does. This is not only because the Guard's contracts have fewer "consulting fees" and other commissions but also because promotions in the guard are more merit-based than they are in the army. Also, the National Guard buys simpler missiles and vehicles requiring fewer foreign technicians than the army's weapons require.

When the Persian Gulf War began, Abdullah's years of effort paid off. Nearly all of the full-time National Guardsmen were high school graduates, and the guard's three mechanized brigades could move thousands of men hundreds of miles in just a few hours, a mobility the army did not share.

In 1975, after Faisal was assassinated, the new king, Khalid, consulted with his brothers and chose Abdullah to be second deputy prime minister. Despite its lackluster name, this was the third-most powerful post in the kingdom, next in line to the throne after the crown prince. Considering that Abdullah had never had a network of full brothers behind him, his rise within the royal family was a tribute to his political abilities. Now, as the third-ranking prince in Saudi Arabia, he began to take official trips abroad. He met President Gerald Ford in Washington, D.C., in 1976 and visited many Arab countries.

In 1979, Abdullah and most other Arabs were outraged that Egypt's president Anwar Sadat had made a separate peace with Israel in return for the Sinai peninsula. Fahad, who ran the government while King Khalid was ill, did not want Saudi Arabia to join an Arab boycott of Egyptian goods, but Abdullah strongly favored the boycott, and from his sickbed, King Khalid sided with Abdullah. Fahad, angry at being overruled, left the country in a huff to vacation in Spain for several weeks, and during his absence, Abdullah ran the government well and solidified his reputation as a worthy successor to the throne.

Three years later, Khalid died, Fahad became king, and Abdullah became crown prince. Abdullah appeared in public more often than before and hired a speech therapist to help him overcome his stutter.

Before the Persian Gulf War, Abdullah had been wary of the kingdom's alliance with the United States because of America's support for Israel, but during the war, he was deeply impressed that the United States had kept its promise to Saudi Arabia and had driven

Iraq from Kuwait. "I have heard some in the U.S. Congress suspect that I am anti-American," Abdullah told the publisher of *Gulf Wire* in February 2001. "We have a saying in Arabic that 'a friend is someone who will be straightforward with you.' Yes, I do criticize America because it is in America's interest for its friends to be critical. I don't criticize to be unfriendly."[2]

Abdullah has four wives, fourteen sons, and twenty daughters. Sometimes he hosts a reunion for his extended family at Taif or another resort city. Three wives are of long standing; the fourth slot has been for brief political marriages to maintain alliances with various tribes. The number of these short marriages has greatly decreased, however, as Abdullah has grown older.

Abdullah's oldest son, Khalid, commands the National Guard in Mecca and has a British university degree. Abdullah's second-oldest son, Mitab, is a lieutenant general who went to Britain's Sandhurst Military Academy in the mid-1960s and is now the third-ranking commander of the National Guard. Like his father, Mitab is well liked by both tribal leaders and foreign military advisers, and in the future, should a Sudairi brother such as Sultan or Salman become king, the new monarch might have to appoint Mitab as commander of the National Guard in order to balance the power of the royal family's factions.

Abdullah's sixth son, Turki, graduated from the Saudi air force academy and now commands a squadron of F-15s. Two other sons, Faisal and Abdulaziz, work as advisers to Abdullah, and several other sons are businessmen. Unlike Fahad's sons, none of Abdullah's children have used their connections to acquire large fortunes. They are rich enough to own racehorses, but their father has not allowed them to be really wealthy.

After praying at dawn, Abdullah sleeps another several hours. Then, after a half day of seeing princes, clerics, businessmen, diplomats, professors, and subordinates, he has lunch and naps after the midafternoon prayer. After the sunset prayer, Abdullah sees more people in the evening. In the cool of the night, he reads and signs documents in his wood-paneled office and, in the summer, plays with his grandchildren and great-grandchildren in the shallow end of his swimming pool, for during the hot summers, children are often up at night and asleep during the day. Abdullah and his family also take walks and play *boules*, an Arab game of ball tossing similar to Italy's boccie.

Author Steve Coll has described Abdullah's compound in Riyadh as resembling a midsize U.S. college in Florida or California, with white marble mansions, well-watered lawns, and luxuriant groves of palm trees. Abdullah also has a farm outside the city where he keeps 150 Arabian stallions. If he needs to think particularly carefully before making a decision, however, he may take his luxurious private bus farther into the desert and set up camp for a while. Once a week, if he has time, he flies to Jeddah, often with several brothers, and boards his yacht in the Red Sea. He also meets weekly with the Council of the Senior Clergy and other prominent clerics. Because Abdullah is more devout than Fahad was, radical preachers have been much less critical of him than they were of the former king.

On Wednesday afternoons, if Abdullah is in Riyadh, he holds an audience for any man who wants to see him. Some people need money. Others want to graze their sheep on royal land. Others just need advice. Like all Saudi kings and princes who hold audiences, Abdullah sits in an ordinary chair and often shakes hands with his petitioners.

Abdullah's First Year as de Facto Ruler

After strokes in 1995 and 1996, King Fahad was incapacitated both mentally and physically, but like Britain's King George III in his last years, Fahad was occasionally lucid. Sometimes he appeared on television, sitting in a wheelchair, shaking hands with a dignitary, but often even a handshake was beyond his capacity. Yet as long as Fahad lived, Abdullah lacked full power, even though he clearly ran the government's day-to-day affairs.

Abdullah made some important, incremental reforms. He upset many relatives by cutting the income of thousands of less-senior princes to a still-comfortable $10,000 a month, by requiring competitive bidding for government contracts, and by insisting that princes pay for airline tickets, utilities, and other perks that had once been free. Despite the cutbacks, Abdullah's overall support within the royal family grew. King Faisal's sons, including Saud al-Faisal, the foreign minister, are particularly staunch allies of Abdullah. Indeed, unlike Fahad, Abdullah regularly seeks Saud's advice. Abdullah and Saud al-Faisal both favor an opening of the political process but feel that the result will be chaos if it comes too quickly.

Abdullah appointed thirty new members to the Consultative Council in 1997, increasing its size from sixty men to ninety. As before, the men he appointed were well educated: 62 percent had master's degrees or PhDs from Western universities. Sometimes Abdullah attended a session of the council. Usually, he listened rather than spoke, but his presence signaled that he cared about public opinion. In 1999, the government allowed women to attend the council's sessions, as long as they sat in the balcony, segregated from men.

By the mid-1990s, 28 percent of the people who lived in Saudi Arabia were foreign. The number was even higher in cities: 35 percent in Riyadh, 43 percent in Mecca, and 51 percent in Jeddah. Because three-fourths of the Saudis in the labor force work for the government, foreigners accounted for an alarming 85 percent of the employees in private companies with ten workers or more.[3]

Since 1995, more than 50 percent of the expatriates have been from South and Southeast Asia: India, Pakistan, Bangladesh, Nepal, Sri Lanka, Indonesia, and the Philippines. Not only is it cheap to hire Asians, they also have no interest in Arabian politics. Their inability to speak Arabic, however, occasionally leads to abuses, especially in rural areas. Some Saudis give uneducated foreigners lower wages than they were promised back home; others prevent them from getting exit visas until they drop claims for unpaid salary.

Despite the fact that most foreigners work up to twelve hours a day for low pay, the Saudis have misgivings about them. Expatriates sent home $5 billion in 1985, $11.2 billion in 1990, and $16.6 billion in 1995—money that left Saudi Arabia forever.

To reduce this outflow, Abdullah offered an amnesty to illegal immigrants in the summer of 1997. Foreigners who were willing to go home could leave without an exit visa, no questions asked, and illegal workers who wanted to stay could do so if they could find a Saudi employer who was willing to sponsor them. By October, when the amnesty ended, three hundred thousand immigrants had obtained work permits and five hundred thousand went home. The government then deported more than six hundred thousand illegal immigrants over the next five years.

The legalization of many immigrants and the repatriation of others led to an improvement in Saudi working conditions, according to a human rights report by the U.S. State Department. With fewer illegal workers in the kingdom, the competition for jobs eased, and the pay for some jobs rose. There have been fewer instances of employers withholding many months' wages or paying wages lower than promised, and in 2004, the government stopped granting work visas to employment agencies that were guilty of such practices.

While Saudis welcomed the improvement in working conditions, what really pleased them was the fact that the amount of money that foreigners sent home finally stopped increasing and in fact declined almost 20 percent between 1997 and 2000 and has hardly risen since.

Osama bin Laden's Move from Sudan to Afghanistan

Although no evidence connects Osama bin Laden to the unsuccessful attempt to kill Egyptian president Hosni Mubarak in Ethiopia on June 26, 1995, when a rocket-propelled grenade launcher malfunctioned, from that day forward, bin Laden's days in Sudan were numbered. After Sudan refused to send Egypt three men connected with the shooting, the United Nations Security Council voted to boycott Sudan's products, causing the country's already weak currency to plummet in value.

Sudan's president, Omar Bashir, finally understood that there were consequences to harboring militants. He expelled the Egyptian radicals behind the assassination attempt and realized that Sudan would never receive Western or Saudi investment as long as bin Laden was living in Khartoum. Bashir told bin Laden that he had to leave the country, and both U.S. and Sudanese officials tried to find another country that was willing to accept him.

The United States did not take bin Laden because in 1996 he had not yet killed any Americans, and prosecutors would have been unable to indict him. Anthony Lake, President Bill Clinton's national security adviser, still wanted bin Laden to leave Sudan as soon as possible, thinking that bin Laden would be weakened if he had to keep moving. Indeed, bin Laden probably lost more than $35 million in investments when he left Khartoum.

President Bashir offered to give bin Laden to the Saudis if they promised not to arrest him, but the Saudis did not want bin Laden back in the kingdom under any circumstances. They did not want him on the streets organizing militants or in jail becoming a martyr. For similar reasons, Egypt, Jordan, and Yemen also refused to accept bin Laden.

Bin Laden contacted Afghan friends in Jalalabad, where he had once lived, and they said they would be honored to welcome a veteran of their long war against the Soviets. On May 18, 1996, on a chartered jet, bin Laden; three wives; fifteen of his nineteen children, including one who is mentally impaired; his closest followers; and his most trusted bodyguards flew from Khartoum to Jalalabad to begin a new life in Afghanistan. One of bin Laden's wives, unwilling to live in Afghanistan, asked for and received a divorce and returned to live in Saudi Arabia with a son and two daughters. Bin Laden's oldest son, Abdullah, also left Sudan at this time and today runs an advertising and marketing company in Jeddah.

Dozens more militants arrived on later flights. One of them, Khalid Sheikh Muhammad, spent less than three months in Afghanistan before he presented bin Laden with a plan to crash jets into New York's World Trade Center, although bin Laden did not begin to finance the plan for another two and a half years.

When bin Laden arrived in Afghanistan, he was friendly with many factions at first, but within four months, the Taliban swept through eastern Afghanistan and took both Jalalabad and Kabul. Their leader, Mullah Muhammad Omar, invited bin Laden to move to his hometown, Kandahar, probably in order to keep an eye on him. Bin Laden quickly built a new training camp in the desert outside the city and endeared himself to the impoverished Taliban by paying for the building of mosques, trucks, irrigation channels, and a large dam.

Bin Laden had already built several camps in Afghanistan to train fighters bound for Chechnya and Kashmir. Training them served bin Laden's purposes, too, because it allowed him to run his own camps, free from Taliban control.

Bin Laden soon found that he had much more freedom in Afghanistan than he had ever had in Sudan. Members of al-Qaeda could enter and leave Afghanistan without visas or border searches, and they could import vehicles, weapons, and bags of cash with no questions asked. The machine guns his followers used were mostly Russian and Chinese AK-47s but also included Israeli Uzis and American M-16s. The militants learned how to use dynamite, hand grenades, mortars, shoulder-fired rockets, and C3 and C4 explosives. Some nights they watched Hollywood action movies, partly to relax, but also to gain tips.

Bin Laden's mountain quarters were rustic, with walls made of mud and tree branches, rather than boards or cement. Even with fireplaces and space heaters, it was a struggle to stay warm when winter temperatures dropped to minus fifteen degrees Fahrenheit. Still, his office had a fax machine, a Macintosh computer, and hundreds of books about Islam and Islamic history. At home, he also had many books on horses. There was no girls' school at the compound, so bin Laden taught math and science to his two teenage daughters.

Abdul Bari Atwan, a newspaper editor who once visited bin Laden in Afghanistan, said, "You feel a sadness in him—which he did not express—that he was not martyred when he was fighting the Soviet army. . . . You feel like he's saying: Why am I alive?"[4]

If bin Laden was sometimes melancholy, it did not prevent his followers from being devoted to him—a rich man who had given up his luxuries to fight for the Muslim faith. By 1998, according to Saudi intelligence estimates, al-Qaeda had more than two thousand members. By 2001, according to U.S. estimates, more than ten thousand militants had received training at bin Laden's Afghan camps. A Pakistani report said that the five countries that had produced the most militants were Egypt, Saudi Arabia, Yemen, Algeria, and Jordan.[5]

Despite the fact that the Taliban was harboring someone who wanted to overthrow the Saudi monarchy, relations between Saudi Arabia and Afghanistan were good. The Saudis gave the Taliban $100 million in aid in 1997 and seemed relieved just to have bin Laden out of the way in distant mountains. Two midlevel Saudi princes were so pleased with bin Laden's training of Chechen and Kashmiri guerrillas, according to an unconfirmed U.S. intelligence report, that they sent him money despite his anti-Saudi views.

Bin Laden's 1996 "Declaration of War" against the Americans in Saudi Arabia

On August 23, 1996, when Osama bin Laden had been in Afghanistan for only three months, he faxed a ten-thousand-word essay, "A Declaration of War against the Americans Occupying the Land of the Two Holy Places," to several Arabic newspapers in London. In his "Declaration," bin Laden said that the Saudi monarchy had forfeited its right to exist because it had replaced Muslim law with civil law, had raised and lowered oil production "to suit the American economy," had rejected clerics' petitions, and, worst of all, had allowed the "American crusader forces" to occupy "the Land of the Two Holy Places." (Bin Laden never legitimizes the Saudi monarchy by calling his native land "Saudi Arabia.")

Bin Laden then said that except for a belief in God, "there is no more important duty than pushing the American enemy out of the holy land." He called on Saudi consumers to boycott U.S. goods and asked Saudi soldiers to give militants "information, materials and arms."[6] Finally, bin Laden promised young men that if they die for the Islamic cause, they will be "wedded to seventy-two of the beautiful ones of Paradise," and he warned Americans that "nothing between us needs to be explained, there is only killing and neck smiting."[7]

Although bin Laden's essay contains many religious turns of phrase that are alien to the Western ear, his Arabic, according to

Princeton professor Bernard Lewis and University of California—
Berkeley professor Geoffrey Nunberg, is eloquent and precise. Bin
Laden makes many references to the Quran and to Muslim history,
but selectively. Toward the end of his "Declaration," for example, he
quotes Sura 9, verse 5, of the Quran: "Slay the idolaters wherever you
find them." Yet he neglects to include the end even of that verse: "but
if they shall convert, and observe prayer, and pay the obligatory alms,
then let them go their way, for God is Gracious, Merciful."[8]

One common error that many Western journalists have made
since September 11, 2001, is to ascribe the violence of bin Laden and
al-Qaeda to Wahhabism, the Saudi form of Islam. I myself made this
mistake when I began this book. While it is true that the Wahhabis
have a violent past and that many Wahhabi clerics are vehemently
anti-Western, only a small minority of militant Wahhabi clerics advocate violence. The few who do ignore both the works of ibn Abdul
Wahhab, the eighteenth-century founder of Wahhabism who believed
that only a sovereign ruler can declare a *jihad*, and the modern rulings
of the Saudi [Wahhabi] Council of the Senior Clergy.

Unlike Osama bin Laden, ibn Abdul Wahhab repeatedly warned
soldiers not to kill women, children, or the elderly and never lured
young men into martyrdom by describing the pleasures of paradise.
He spent most of his time teaching and applying Islam to daily problems, whereas bin Laden has never written about the possibility of
educating non-Muslims or offered any vision of life beyond *jihad*.[9]

The mind-set of Osama bin Laden and al-Qaeda does not come
so much from Wahhabism, which is more than 260 years old, as
from the far more recent books and essays of the Egyptian Muslim
Brotherhood's vivid and widely read writer Sayyid Qutb.

Sayyid Qutb, the Muslim Brotherhood, and the Ideology of *Jihad*

Whether one measures a writer's influence by the number of his readers or by the extent to which he or she has spurred those readers to
change the way they live, Sayyid Qutb (1906–1966) is unquestionably
one of the twentieth century's most important authors. Although the
"father of Islamic radicalism" would have hated the comparison, Qutb
is comparable in global influence to Karl Marx. Both men had wide
interests, a lively writing style, a mistrust of money-controlled
democracies, and a belief that a determined elite can seize power and
change the world.

While Marx contemptuously dismissed religion as "the opiate of the people," Qutb (pronounced KUH-tub) spent most of his adult life writing about Islam. During his eleven years in Egyptian prisons in the 1950s and the 1960s, Qutb wrote *In the Shade of the Quran*, a huge, thirty-volume commentary on the 114 chapters of the Quran. Although the books are extremely anti-Western, they are beautifully written in a simple, modern style. *In the Shade of the Quran* has been translated into a dozen languages, and millions of devout Muslims read from it daily in homes and mosques throughout the world. To date, only a few of the volumes have been translated into English.

Qutb's most influential book, *Milestones*, also translated as *Signposts*, was published in 1964. A few years later, Iran's Ayatollah Sayyed Ali Khamenei, who succeeded Khomeini as his nation's supreme leader in 1989, translated much of the book into Persian. In 1977, Osama bin Laden read *Milestones*, then began to read the thirty volumes of *In the Shade of the Quran*. Ayman al-Zawahiri, al-Qaeda's second in command, read *Milestones*, too. In a memoir called *Knights under the Prophet's Banner*, published in December 2001, al-Zawahiri defended the killing of Western civilians and said, "Sayyid Qutb's call . . . to acknowledge God's sole authority was the spark that ignited the Islamic Revolution against the enemies of Islam."[10]

The son of a minor landowner in a village on the Nile, Sayyid Qutb had pleased his devout mother by memorizing the Quran by age eleven. Later, his family moved to a suburb of Cairo so that Qutb and his brother could get a better education. By 1933, Qutb had acquired a bachelor's degree in education and a thorough knowledge of Islamic history and theology. At first, as a young teacher and an inspector of schools, Qutb was primarily interested in literature. He wrote a book of poetry, *The Unknown Shore*, and two autobiographical novels, *An Egyptian Childhood* and *Thorns*, the latter about a broken engagement. (Qutb never married.) He was also a critic and was an early champion of Naguib Mahfouz, who in 1988 would win the Nobel Prize in literature.

In 1948, Qutb wrote his first major work of theology, *Social Justice in Islam*. After a long discussion of economics, he concluded that the real struggle in the modern world was not between capitalism and communism, but between Western materialism and Islam. Although it is fine for a Muslim to study science at a Western school, Qutb wrote, he should learn about human origins and human nature only from other Muslims.

Like most Egyptians, Qutb deeply resented the British presence in his country, which had steadily increased since the British first began to run the Suez Canal in 1882. A new organization, the Muslim Brotherhood, was formed in 1928 when six men pledged to follow a hardworking young teacher and writer, Hassan al-Banna (1906–1949). "The Muslims . . . are no more than hirelings belonging to the foreigners," the founders declared, and they offered "our blood, our lives, our faith and our honor" to make Egypt strong again.[11]

In newspapers and books, al-Banna condemned Britain's "economic occupation" of Egypt, where the "luxurious homes of foreigners" overlook the "miserable homes of their workers." In one essay, "Between Yesterday and Today," al-Banna condemned the European colonialists who brought "their half-naked women into these regions, together with their liquors, their theaters and their dance halls." He predicted that "the day must come when the castles of this materialistic civilization will fall upon the heads of their inhabitants."[12]

Each year, the Muslim Brotherhood grew in power as it started schools, newspapers, magazines, health clinics, and, occasionally, armed underground cells. The Brotherhood's motto is "God is our objective; the Quran is our constitution; the Prophet is our leader; struggle is our way; and death for the sake of God is our highest aspiration."[13]

In December 1948, members of the Muslim Brotherhood assassinated the Egyptian prime minister, Nuqrashi Pasha, along with his chief of police and minister of the interior. Two months later, the police took revenge by shooting and killing al-Banna as he was getting into a taxi.

Qutb, who joined the Brotherhood two years later, was in the United States at the time, studying briefly in Washington, D.C., before getting a master's degree at Colorado's State College of Education, known today as the University of Northern Colorado. One professor who taught writing there was James Michener.

Unlike most foreign students, Qutb hated the United States. He wrote that it is a place where "a man is valued according to the size of his bank balance." Before he even arrived in New York, he was shocked by the advances of a tipsy woman aboard his ship. In Washington, he undoubtedly encountered racism, for in the 1940s Washington was still a segregated Southern city and Qutb was dark-skinned. He was also short, frail, soft-featured, and high-strung, but photographs in his later years show a proud, determined face.

The University of Northern Colorado is in Greeley, a pungent meat packing town in the high plains, between Denver and Cheyenne. In 1949, Greeley had no bars or liquor stores, yet Qutb still found the town lewd and decadent. He called jazz "music that the savage bushmen created to satisfy their primitive desires."[14] He was also appalled by church dances. In *Islam and the Problems of Civilization*, Qutb wrote that after a weeknight service, young men and women moved to a "dance hall" within the church, where,

> every young man took the hand of a young woman. And these were young men and young women who had just been singing their hymns! Red and blue lights, with only a few white lamps, illuminated the dance floor. The room became a confusion of feet and legs, arms twisted around hips, lips met lips, chests pressed together. The whole atmosphere was one of romance . . . [as the minister] picked out a famous song called "But Baby, It's Cold Outside."[15]

Qutb could have stayed in the United States to earn a PhD but decided to return to Egypt instead in August 1950. His trip to the United States had strengthened his belief that the materialism of the West was soulless and destructive and that Islam could not look to the West for renewal. Qutb was also angered by the pro-Israeli slant of U.S. newspaper articles and radio broadcasts and by what he saw as America's contemptuous attitude toward the uprooted Palestinians. (Years later, in his comments on chapter 5 of the Quran, Qutb condemned Karl Marx's "materialism" and Sigmund Freud's "permissiveness" and wrote, "most evil theories which try to destroy all values and all that is sacred to mankind are advocated by Jews.")

When Qutb returned to Egypt, he joined the Muslim Brotherhood and quickly became the editor of its magazine. In July 1952, Lieutenant Colonel Gamal Abdel Nasser visited Qutb at his home just four days before he overthrew the corrupt King Farouk, an action that the Muslim Brotherhood supported. By then, the Brotherhood had two thousand chapters and half a million members in cities and villages throughout Egypt. In 1954, however, the Muslim Brotherhood criticized Nasser for failing to make Egypt's constitution more Islamic and for signing a treaty that allowed Britain to continue to run the Suez Canal. A few members of the Brotherhood tried to assassinate Nasser while he was giving a speech in Alexandria on October 26, 1954. As millions of Egyptians listened to the speech on the radio, gunmen fired eight shots at the Egyptian leader but missed.

Nasser immediately imprisoned fifty thousand members of the Muslim Brotherhood, including Qutb. A panel of three judges that included Anwar al-Sadat, who would succeed Nasser in 1970, sentenced Qutb to fifteen years in jail for conspiring to overthrow the government. For six or seven months, prison guards beat Qutb constantly as he cried in pain over and over again, "God is great!" and "All praise is for God alone!" Nasser offered Qutb his freedom and a cabinet post as minister of education if he would only ask for a pardon, but Qutb said, "I cannot bow down pleading for mercy before injustice and error."[16] Finally, in the summer of 1955, the beatings stopped and officials moved Qutb to the prison hospital and gave him a desk and a quiet place to write. During the next seven years, Qutb wrote most of the thirty volumes of *In the Shade of the Quran*.

In 1964, during a visit to Cairo, the president of Iraq, Abdul Salam Aref, asked Nasser to free Qutb as a goodwill gesture, and Nasser did. During Qutb's seven brief months of freedom, he published his short but most influential book, *Milestones*, also known as *Signposts*, which he had worked on for years. But in 1965, the Egyptian police discovered that secret cells of the Muslim Brotherhood were planning to assassinate officials and blow up roads, bridges, and power stations. Nasser promptly jailed twenty thousand Muslim Brothers (and seven hundred Sisters), including, once again, Qutb. Qutb defended the Muslim Brotherhood's possession of weapons as necessary to avoid another repressive government purge like the one in 1954, but Nasser's judges were unmoved and sentenced Qutb and two other men to death.

As crowds gathered to protest Qutb's imminent execution, Nasser sent Sadat to see Qutb in prison. Once again, Nasser offered Qutb his freedom and the post of minister of education if Qutb would simply ask for a pardon. "Write the words," Qutb's sister begged her stubborn brother. But Qutb shook his head and said, "My words will be stronger if they kill me."[17] A few weeks later, on August 29, 1966, Qutb was hanged or, as his supporters prefer, "martyred."

During the government's two purges in 1954 and 1966, thousands of Muslim Brothers fled to Saudi Arabia. They were devout and well educated and arrived at a time when Saudi Arabia desperately needed teachers. Soon, Muslim Brothers were teaching in almost every high school and college in the kingdom, and they were especially numerous at the new Islamic University of Medina. Some Brothers found jobs at Saudi charities such as the Muslim World League and the World Assembly of Muslim Youth, and soon both of these organizations were publishing Qutb's books and essays. The Muslim Brothers became a major force in Saudi Arabia's intellectual life. Some formed friendships with princes; others grew rich during the oil boom and sent money to militants in Egypt, Palestine, and other Muslim countries.

Sayyid Qutb's brother, Muhammad, remained in Egyptian jails until 1972, when President Anwar Sadat freed many Muslim Brothers as he backed away from Nasser's socialism. Muhammad Qutb immediately moved to Saudi Arabia and became a professor of Islamic studies at King Abdul Aziz University in Jeddah. Osama bin Laden was a student there in the late 1970s and went to his lectures. Qutb also taught at Umm al-Qura University in Mecca in the 1980s, where he supervised the doctoral thesis of Safar al-Hawali, one of the "Awakening Sheikhs" who objected so strongly to the presence of U.S. troops in Saudi Arabia during the Persian Gulf War.

In addition to teaching and writing, Muhammad Qutb edited his brother's work and published the definitive editions of *Milestones, In the Shade of the Quran,* and other works, for by then several presses had published inaccurate versions of his brother's books. An author himself, Muhammad Qutb disagreed with some of his brother's most violent statements, yet it was Muhammad, in books such as *Ignorance in the Twenty-First Century,* who first used the inflammatory word *Crusader* as a substitute for *Christian* or *Western.*

Sayyid Qutb's Ideas

Sayyid Qutb started his multivolume work *In the Shade of the Quran* with the observation that because the Quran is God's specific instruction on how men should live, "To live 'in the shade of the Quran' . . . gives meaning to life and makes it worth living."[18]

Qutb's argument in this book for the existence of God and God's justice is unusually succinct:

> The very nature of the universe rules out any possibility of its formation by chance, for no chance could result in such perfect and absolute harmony on such an immeasurable scale. . . . It is inconceivable that . . . evil and tyranny can get away without retribution. . . . Such an assumption is, in its very essence, contrary to the fact of the elaborate planning so apparent everywhere in the universe.[19]

People do not have to be Muslims, Qutb said. One is "free to embrace any faith one likes."[20] In chapter 4 of *Milestones,* Qutb explained, "Islam does not force people to accept its belief, but it wants to provide a free environment in which they will have the choice of beliefs. What it wants is to abolish those oppressive political systems under which people are prevented from expressing their freedom to choose whatever beliefs they want."[21]

Qutb wrote in the next chapter, however, that "all the societies existing in the world today are ignorant," including communist nations; the "idolatrous" regions of India, Japan, and Africa; and "all Jewish and Christian societies."[22]

In the first volume of *In the Shade of the Quran*, Qutb was more specific: "Humanity today is living in a large brothel! One has only to take a glance at its press, films, fashion shows, beauty contests, ballrooms, wine bars, and broadcasting stations! Or observe its mad lust for naked flesh, provocative postures, and sick suggestive statements in literature, the arts and the mass media!"[23]

Qutb made similar accusations in *Milestones*: "Look . . . at this behavior, like animals, which you call 'free mixing of the sexes,' at this vulgarity which you call 'emancipation of women,'" where a woman uses "her ability on material productivity rather than in the training of human beings."[24]

In such a "rubbish heap," Qutb said, no one is free to choose a faith because everyone's mind is too clouded by sin. Muslims therefore have "a God-given right to step forward and take control of the political authority."[25] Once in power, a Muslim ruler's only duty is to enforce the *sharia* (the Quran and the sayings and the deeds of Muhammad), and the citizen's duty of obedience is contingent on the ruler's faithful performance of this trust. By contrast, when parliaments pass laws that are not part of the *sharia*, they are "usurping the right which belongs to God alone."[26]

Nations rise and fall according to their virtue, Qutb said. The Arabs' power declined because "Allah deserted them whenever they deserted Him."[27] Now, Qutb said at the beginning of *Milestones*, "It is essential that a community arrange its affairs according to [Islam] and show it to the world. . . . I have written *Milestones* for this vanguard."[28]

Whether Qutb consciously or unconsciously borrowed the term *vanguard* from Lenin, who often used this word, is unknown, but in the first videotape that Osama bin Laden recorded after 9/11, bin Laden said, "God has blessed a group of vanguard Muslims, the forefront of Islam, to destroy America."[29]

In the last volume of *In the Shade of the Quran*, Qutb said that Muslims are engaged in "an everlasting struggle to lead humanity to the submission of everything in human life to Allah alone."[30] And in *Milestones*, Qutb charged that "those who say that Islamic *jihad* is merely for the defense of the 'homeland of Islam' diminish the greatness of the Islamic way of life and consider it to be less important than their 'homeland.'"[31] "Divine authority," Qutb said, must "be carried throughout the earth."[32] Even as early as 1948, in *Social Justice in Islam*, Qutb wrote, "We in the Islamic world . . . have a view of life higher than any possessed by Europe, America or Russia. . . . Our place, then, is not at the back of the caravan but in front, holding the reins."[33]

Bin Laden's February 1998 Announcement of War and August's African Embassy Bombings

On February 23, 1998, at his camp in Khost, Afghanistan, Osama bin Laden dictated a two-page statement by satellite phone to an Arabic newspaper in London, *Al-Quds al-Arabi*. His new organization, the World Islamic Front, was declaring a "*Jihad* against Jews and Crusaders" because

> Since God laid down the Arabian peninsula, created its desert, and surrounded it with seas, no calamity has ever befallen it like these Crusader hosts that have spread in it like locusts. . . . For more than seven years the United States has occupied the lands of Islam in the holiest of territories, Arabia, plundering its riches, overwhelming its rulers, humiliating its people.[34]

Bin Laden and the four other men who signed this document also denounced the "devastation inflicted on the Iraqi people by the Crusader-Zionist alliance" and the Jewish "occupation of Jerusalem and murder of Muslims" before concluding, "In compliance with God's order, we issue the following ruling to all Muslims: To kill the Americans and their allies—civilians and military—is an individual duty for every Muslim who can do it in any country in which it is possible to do it."[35]

The "*Jihad* against Jews and Crusaders" was the first attempt by anyone to justify the killing of U.S. civilians. Bin Laden said that U.S. citizens are legitimate targets because they vote in elections and therefore are responsible for their government's policies. But as Princeton's Bernard Lewis has written, the declaration is "a grotesque travesty of the nature of Islam and even of its doctrine of jihad. . . . At no point do the basic texts of Islam enjoin terrorism and murder. At no point do they even consider the random slaughter of uninvolved bystanders."[36]

According to Nasser al-Bahri, a Saudi who knew Osama bin Laden in Afghanistan, bin Laden said again and again, "We must carry out painful attacks on the United States until it becomes like an agitated bull, and when the bull comes to our region he won't be familiar with the land, but we will."[37]

The most prominent of bin Laden's cosigners was a radical Egyptian surgeon, Ayman al-Zawahiri, who after thirty years of fighting and failing to overthrow Egypt's government, "the near enemy," decided to begin merging his organization, the Islamic Jihad, with bin Laden's al-Qaeda in order to fight Egypt's backer, the United States, "the far enemy." Al-Zawahiri, who wrote the statement's first draft, spent three years being tortured in Egypt's prisons before he was released in 1984. He became a close friend and a political mentor to bin Laden in the Pakistani city of Peshawar, and in the early 1990s, bin Laden gave money to the Islamic Jihad when both men lived in Sudan. After the merger, Al-Zawahiri became al-Qaeda's second in command and began to encourage the use of suicide bombers.

Less than six months after the declaration, al-Qaeda committed the most deadly act of terrorism of the 1990s. At 10:35 a.m. on August 7, 1998—eight years to the day after King Fahad had invited U.S. troops to come to Saudi Arabia—a young Saudi militant drove an old and dented brown Toyota pickup truck packed with about two thousand pounds of explosives into a parking lot behind the U.S. embassy in Nairobi, Kenya. The blast ripped away the rear of the embassy and killed twelve Americans and thirty-seven Kenyan employees. It also caused a building next door to collapse, killing more Africans, including many students at a secretarial college. Flying shards of glass, steel, and cement shot like bullets in every direction, killing dozens of pedestrians and blinding more than 150. In all, the Nairobi explosion killed 12 Americans and 201 Africans, including many Muslims, and wounded more than 4,500 people.

Just nine minutes later, a second truck driven by an Egyptian militant four hundred miles to the south exploded outside the U.S. embassy in Dar es Salaam, Tanzania. Fortunately, a water truck happened to be in between the suicide bomber and the embassy, and although pieces of the truck flew thirty feet into the air, the water absorbed much of the explosion's impact. Eleven people were killed by the second blast, all of them Africans, and eighty-five people were wounded.

Within an hour, a fax from Baku, Azerbaijan, a largely Muslim city on the Caspian Sea, arrived at *Al-Quds al-Arabi*, the London newspaper, announcing that the bombs at the embassies had been detonated by the Islamic Army for the Liberation of the Holy Places (Mecca and Medina).

Investigators quickly learned that there had been many faxes and satellite phone calls between Afghanistan and Nairobi, but because the bombings killed eighteen Africans for every American, bin Laden never took credit for them. In an interview with an African newspaper, however, bin Laden defended the explosions:

> Imagine it was my own children taken hostage, and that guarded by this human shield, Islam's enemies started to massacre Muslims.

I would not hesitate, I would kill the assassins even if to do that I had to kill my own children with my own hands. So one evil will have averted an even greater evil. Sometimes, alas, the death of innocents is unavoidable. Islam allows that.[38]

Two weeks after the blast, the CIA told President Clinton that many terrorists were about to meet at an al-Qaeda training camp at Zawhar Kili in the mountains of Afghanistan, and that bin Laden himself might come. On August 20, Clinton ordered the U.S. Navy to fire sixty-six cruise missiles at two camps, with each missile costing almost $1 million. The nighttime launches of Operation Infinite Reach killed six al-Qaeda militants but no leaders, and they destroyed dozens of mud-brick dwellings. Unfortunately, bin Laden did not go to either camp that day. Worse, the missiles enhanced bin Laden's status among radical Muslims, for the United States had taken its best shot at him and missed.

U.S. ships also fired thirteen cruise missiles at the Al Shifa pharmaceutical factory in Khartoum, Sudan. A soil sample that the CIA had obtained near the factory contained a chemical called EMPTA, a key ingredient of VX, a nerve agent so deadly that just one drop on the skin is lethal. By itself, the ingredient had no commercial use, and the manager of the drug factory lived in bin Laden's old compound. To President Clinton, this was sufficient evidence for a strike because he was always worried that Muslim terrorists might obtain chemical or biological weapons.

Whether the Sudanese factory was really making chemical weapons or "just ibuprofen for headaches," as the plant's owner told the *Washington Post*, may never be known. No other samples of EMPTA were ever found.

The cruise missiles were fired at the height of the Monica Lewinsky scandal, just three days after President Clinton had admitted his affair to the nation. Some commentators suggested that Clinton had launched the cruise missiles to distract the American public from his failings. Radio host Rush Limbaugh, for example, asked how many innocent people had died because Clinton bombed "an aspirin factory." (The answer, whatever the factory was making, is one: a night watchman.) Three weeks later, after Special Prosecutor Kenneth Starr released his near-pornographic report on the president's affair with Ms. Lewinsky, a second attack against Osama bin Laden became politically impossible.

President Clinton did offer a $5 million reward for bin Laden's capture and formed a task force of dozens of Treasury agents to investigate bin Laden's finances. He asked the leader of the bin Laden family, bin Laden's older brother, Bakr bin Laden, for his cooperation in the investigation, and Bakr agreed. The bin Laden family allowed FBI and Treasury agents to look at the records of hundreds of bank accounts, including secret accounts at Swiss banks. This is one of the main reasons the FBI cleared several planeloads of bin Ladens to leave the United States during the first few days after 9/11. Federal agents had already spent three years investigating the family.

Strained Relations with the Taliban

By the end of 1997, the Taliban controlled 85 percent of Afghanistan and had boxed the Northern Alliance into a single valley on the country's northern border. The leader of the Taliban is Mullah Muhammad Omar Akhund. More commonly known simply as Mullah Omar, he is a tall, illiterate soldier with a big black beard who lost one eye fighting the Soviets in 1989 and is not known to have ever watched a movie or a television show with his other one. The only subjects he has ever studied are Islam and Arabic, and he has learned many chapters of the Quran by heart.

Only three countries, all Muslim, had diplomatic relations with the Taliban: Pakistan, the United Arab Emirates, and Saudi Arabia. That was fine with Mullah Omar. He had never met an infidel or even been seen by one, and he had no wish to meet one now. Prince Turki al-Faisal, the director of Saudi intelligence in the 1980s and the 1990s, subsequently defended Saudi Arabia's recognition of the Taliban in 1997, saying, "The Taliban had not yet created any controversy." In fact, by 1997, the Taliban had already begun to confine women to their homes, but they had not yet massacred five thousand Shi'ites in the city of Mazar-i-Sharif (and taken four hundred women to be concubines), and Osama bin Laden had not yet begun his bombings of embassies, ships, skyscrapers, and trains. Prince Turki also said that the Taliban promised him that they would not allow bin Laden to harm Saudi interests.

In June 1998, several months after bin Laden's declaration of war against Americans and their allies, Prince Turki flew to Kandahar in southern Afghanistan and asked Mullah Omar to hand over bin Laden to Saudi agents. Omar said that he had a duty of hospitality to bin Laden and suggested instead that the Taliban and Saudi Arabia jointly appoint a commission of religious scholars to judge bin Laden's conduct according to Islamic law. After the meeting, the Saudis, to win the Taliban's favor, sent the Taliban four hundred pickup trucks.

In September, a month after the African embassy bombings and the retaliatory cruise missiles, Prince Turki flew back to Kandahar and again asked Mullah Omar to turn over Osama bin Laden. By then, however, bin Laden had pledged his personal loyalty to Mullah Omar, and the mullah did not want to give bin Laden up. "Why are you persecuting and harassing this courageous, valiant Muslim?" Omar asked Turki angrily. "Why don't you put your hands in ours and let us go together and liberate the Arabian peninsula from the infidel [U.S.] soldiers?"[39]

Now Prince Turki grew angry, for Omar's use of the word *liberate* was an insult to the al-Saud family. "What you are doing today is going to bring great harm not just to you but to Afghanistan," Turki predicted as he walked out of the meeting.[40] Several days later, Saudi Arabia recalled its ambassador and broke off relations with the Taliban. But a Saudi charity, the International Islamic Relief Organization, continued to give the Taliban about $10 million a year, stopping only after 9/11. A Saudi government audit in 2000 also showed that during the 1990s, depositors at the National Commercial Bank, the kingdom's largest, had sent bin Laden $3 million.

When a truck bomb exploded outside Mullah Omar's house in 1999, killing some of his relatives, Osama bin Laden built Omar a luxurious new compound with high walls and a bright blue mosque. By then, the close friendship between the Taliban and bin Laden had made many officials in the Clinton administration willing to launch missiles against the Taliban as well as against al-Qaeda. But National Security Adviser Sandy Berger thought that another round of inaccurately aimed missiles would only further enhance bin Laden's status among militant Muslims. In the first half of 2000, bin Laden was known to have killed only twelve Americans, and that was simply not enough to go to war.

Bin Laden inspected training camps, visited friends and subordinates, and preached at mosques but was a difficult target because he varied his routes and because all of his bodyguards were Arabs he had known for years. Bin Laden never told an Afghan (who might be susceptible to bribery) of his plans.

In October 2000, bin Laden was known to often be at a camp called Tarnak, near Kandahar, but there were also more than a hundred women and children at the camp. "It was almost like he was daring me to kill them," Clinton told *Newsweek* in 2002.[41] It was also just too close to the presidential election in November. In December, the Clinton administration persuaded the United Nations Security Council to pass Resolution 1333, which declared Afghanistan to be a sponsor of terrorism and banned all arms sales to the country.

Unfortunately, the UN embargo was ignored by Pakistan's Inter-Services Intelligence (ISI). It had long supported the Taliban because it wanted a reliable Muslim government in Afghanistan that would never form an alliance with India. Despite Resolution 1333, the ISI continued to send the Taliban oil, money, and weapons.

Pakistan's ISI and Saudi Arabia's International Islamic Relief Organization were not the only groups giving money to the Taliban. Incredibly, the Bush administration gave the Taliban money, too. In May 2001 (just one month after Taliban soldiers destroyed the two giant fifteen-hundred-year-old statues of Buddha carved into the cliffs at Bamiyan, which they considered to be idols), Secretary of State Colin Powell announced that the United States was giving the Taliban $43 million to help it enforce its ban on growing opium. In a blistering column, Robert Scheer of the *Los Angeles Times* wrote, "Enslave your girls and women, harbor anti-U.S. terrorists, destroy every vestige of civilization in your homeland, and the Bush administration will embrace you. All that matters is that you line up as an ally in the drug war, the only international cause this nation still takes seriously."[42]

1997–1999: Lower Oil Prices, Lower Revenues

During the autumn of 1997 and the winter of 1998, the price of oil fell from $23 to $13 a barrel, and by the end of 1998, it was less than $10 a barrel, the lowest price, allowing for inflation, since the early 1970s. The government's oil revenues were $20.5 billion lower in 1998 than in 1997, forcing officials to make many painful cuts in spending.

The events that caused the fall in the price of oil began in Venezuela, accelerated in Thailand, and also involved Iraq. In the mid-1990s, Venezuela began to increase its oil sales to the United States by pumping more than three million barrels of oil a day, 30 percent more than its OPEC quota. It surpassed Saudi Arabia as America's number-one source of imported oil.

To win back its U.S. market, Saudi Arabia pressured OPEC to raise its production quotas in November, allowing the kingdom to pump one million more barrels of oil a day. But during the same month, a currency crisis in Thailand spread to other countries and plunged the whole of East Asia into a severe recession. A mild winter in the United States and Europe in 1998 further reduced the world's demand for fuel, and Iraq also started to pump 400,000 barrels of oil a day under the United Nations' Oil for Food Program.

Suddenly, there was a huge glut of oil, and the price fell by half. An OPEC cutback of 450,000 barrels a day in June 1998 kept the price from falling further but failed to spark a recovery; prices stayed low through most of 1999. Saudi Arabia's economy shrank 11 percent in 1998 and was stagnant in 1999, and the average living standard at the end of the 1990s was no higher than it had been at the beginning of the decade. Some Saudi families experienced poverty for the first time in decades.

Oil revenues fell 37 percent in 1998, but the kingdom cut spending only 16 percent because the price drop came without warning. Still, the government canceled many plans for new housing, roads, sewers, and power plants; delayed payments for existing construction; and increased the price of utilities, including gasoline (from sixty cents to ninety cents a gallon). The government did not cut health and pension entitlements, education spending, or subsidies that let people use water at 5 percent of its cost.

To pay for this continued spending, the Saudi government ran deficits of $12.3 billion in 1998 and $9.1 billion in 1999 as the kingdom's debt to domestic banks climbed to 119 percent of its gross domestic product, a dangerously high level.

In a speech in December 1998, Abdullah discussed the government's huge deficits and warned, "The days of affluence are over and they will never come back. . . . We must all get used to a different way of life which does not stand on total dependence on the state. . . . Governments can no longer afford to give their citizens everything on a silver platter."[43]

In 1999, the cash-starved Saudi government surprised everyone and cut the defense budget almost 25 percent. The kingdom also imported 70 percent fewer weapons in the late 1990s than it had in the early 1990s and spent much less on their maintenance. The cuts were possible because Iraq was impotent after the Gulf War and Iran was still exhausted after its eight-year war with Iraq.

Even with a reduced budget, Saudi Arabia still spent more than 11 percent of its gross domestic product on defense and security, a percentage higher even than Israel's lofty 9 percent. Among the kingdom's largest expenditures were new army, navy, and air force bases near its border with Yemen; a variety of warships from France; and new U.S. computer systems to improve Saudi air defenses.

The kingdom also spent hundreds of millions of dollars upgrading missiles and radar installations and on new software and parts for its F-15 jet fighters. By 2000, some of Saudi Arabia's F-15s were eighteen years old; its F-5 jets were even older. Saudi Arabia had spent tens of billions of dollars to make its twenty-thousand-man air force the best in the Middle East but would soon need to spend billions of dollars more just to replace its aging fighters.

It was not only oil prices that collapsed in 1997 and 1998. Petrochemical prices fell, too, typically 25 to 35 percent. As a result, profits earned by the Saudi Basic Industries Corporation (SABIC) were less than half of what they had been the previous year.

SABIC is the world's third-largest corporate producer of petrochemicals—plastics, resins, fertilizers, chemicals, and industrial gases—and the largest non-oil industrial company in the Middle East. Together, its three plants in Jeddah, Yanbu, and Jubail make about 10 percent of the world's petrochemicals, employ more than ten thousand Saudis, and account for a majority of Saudi Arabia's non oil exports.

Although SABIC is run as if it were a private corporation, the government owns 70 percent of the company. The firm began in 1976 as a government holding company for jointly owned ventures with foreign oil companies, but during the 1980s, the Saudis bought the foreign shares and began to pay fees for the foreigners' technical services instead. In 1987, SABIC began to sell shares to the public, and by the mid-1990s, investors owned 30 percent of the company. In 1996, the government announced a long-term goal to sell an additional 45 percent of SABIC to the public, but a decade later, this sale has yet to take place.

In 1997, the Saudi government signed a $2 billion contract with Fluor Daniel to double the size of SABIC's petrochemical complex at Yanbu, on the Red Sea. Completed in 2001, the Yanbu plant is the world's largest manufacturer of polyethylene, a plastic widely used in packaging and insulation. SABIC also has a chemical research and development center in Houston, Texas, a sign that it is changing from a regional Saudi company into a multinational corporation.

SABIC has become a huge, world-class, and highly profitable company in just one generation, but it has done little to ease the kingdom's ongoing problem of high unemployment, for it employs less than half of 1 percent of the Saudis in the labor force. In fact, the Saudi oil, gas, and petrochemical industries combined account for 95 percent of the country's exports, yet employ less than 5 percent of working Saudis.

Star Enterprises, jointly owned by Saudi Aramco and Texaco, owned 1,400 gas stations in the eastern and southern United States by the 1990s, and franchised another 10,000. In 1998, it grew even bigger when it merged with a subsidiary of Shell Oil. The new company,

Motiva Enterprises, owns more than 2,000 Texaco and Shell stations in the eastern and southern United States and franchises 13,000 more. Saudi Arabia owns 32.5 percent of the company, which also owns four U.S. refineries that convert more than 800,000 barrels of oil a day into gasoline.

Saudi Aramco modernized its oil refinery at Ras Tanura, on the Persian Gulf, in 1998 and its refinery at Rabigh, on the Red Sea, in 2001. Together, the two facilities load about an eighth of the world's daily supply of crude oil onto supertankers and refine what's left into enough gasoline to meet all of the kingdom's needs.

At the end of the 1990s, Saudi Aramco had no plans to increase its oil production capacity beyond 10.5 million barrels a day or its actual production beyond 8–9 million barrels a day. This gave Saudi Arabia a surplus capacity of about 2 million barrels a day, enough to make it the world's "swing producer," the country that could often (but not always) move the price of oil in any direction it chose. Saudi Arabia could not only lower its oil production to raise the price, it could also raise its production to lower the price because, unlike other oil-exporting nations, it almost never pumped at its full capacity.

1998–1999: Abdullah Meets Foreign Leaders, Encourages Women, and Allows More Debate

In August 1998, King Fahad underwent surgery three times—to heal an inflamed colon, remove a gallbladder, and fix complications following its removal. In the autumn, the royal family formally made Abdullah the king's regent, and in a reciprocal move, Abdullah appointed Fahad's youngest son, Abdulaziz, as cabinet minister without portfolio, in other words, troubleshooter. Despite the rivalry between the Sudairi brothers and the rest of the royal family, Abdullah and Abdulaziz get along well, and Abdulaziz often had his infirm father sign a document when Abdullah felt that his own signature as crown prince was insufficient.

In September, as King Fahad recovered physically but not mentally, Abdullah began a series of long-planned state visits around the globe. Abdullah had rarely traveled outside the Arab world but now felt the need to meet the leaders of key nations such as the United States, Britain, China, Japan, and Pakistan.

On his trip, Abdullah saw that women make up 51 percent of the labor force in East Asia. In Saudi Arabia, by contrast, the percentage of Saudi women in the workforce was (and still is) only 6 percent.

Although women in the kingdom own more than twenty thousand businesses and dominate the fields of teaching and medicine, most women do not work because they are forbidden to have male clients, supervise male workers, or work with male officials. Educated women cannot take a job that requires even a minimal amount of travel, and uneducated women cannot compete with foreigners who work for low wages.

In speeches in November 1998 and April 1999, Abdullah said that the kingdom needed women's "full participation" and that "talent is not a male monopoly." The speeches sparked a national debate in the press about women's issues and also a suggestion by some officials that women over thirty-five be permitted to drive between 7:00 a.m. and 7:00 p.m. if they have a husband's written permission. Abdullah's favorite wife, Hissah, and two of his daughters, Adela and Sita, have openly supported a woman's right to drive. Allowing women to drive would free many families from the enormous expense of hiring chauffeurs, but most of the clergy remained against the idea, including the blind grand mufti, Sheikh Abdulaziz ibn Baz, who said, "Women driving leads to . . . mixing with men . . . [and] promiscuity that overruns a society."[44]

Although Saudi women became free to study architecture, engineering, and geology in 2003, they still cannot work, travel, buy real estate, or even open a bank account without the written permission of a father, a husband, or another male guardian. In practice, most husbands and fathers are happy to grant their wives' and daughters' requests to work, travel, or buy property, but it can still be humiliating to ask for permissions that are unnecessary anywhere else in the world. Some husbands and fathers are too conservative to allow their wives to work or their daughters to study abroad, and in these cases, a woman cannot appeal her patriarch's decision. In other instances, even a sympathetic male relative—a widow's brother, for example— can be hundreds of miles away.

Nearly all Saudi women, both rich and poor, agree that the kingdom's worst injustice is that after a divorce the husband gets custody of boys seven and older and girls nine and older. *Sharia* courts also rarely enforce an ex-wife's right to collect alimony from her husband. A quarter of Saudi marriages end in divorce today; the rate is more than 35 percent in Riyadh and Mecca and almost 60 percent in more cosmopolitan Jeddah. By the 1990s, many marriage contracts made divorce automatic if a husband refused to let his wife continue her studies or if he took a second wife. These contracts protect young women who have not yet had children and older women whose children have already grown, but in between, a young mother who does not want to lose custody of her children has little protection.

Advances have occurred in some areas. By 1999, there were slightly more women in Saudi universities than men, and they usually earned better grades. When the century ended, only a third of the kingdom's women were illiterate and nearly all of these were middle aged or elderly. Among young women, illiteracy is rare.

One reason progress is slow for Saudi women is that in Saudi society, one can only advocate change within a religious framework. Women control almost 40 percent of Saudi real estate and bank deposits, for example, because Muhammad's first wife, Khadija, was a businesswoman. Working within this confine, many Saudi women have majored in Islamic studies so that they can determine which of society's rules come from the Quran (which they believe to be God's word) and which constraints are merely old traditions that can be discarded. Today, feminists, influenced by Egyptian writers, can be found in almost every high school and university in the kingdom, but they are *Muslim* feminists and politically centrist. Most women understand that while the kingdom limits their freedom, an Islamic republic would probably be much less sympathetic to their concerns.

Being good Muslims, most Saudi women do not mind wearing the *abaya*, the full black veil that covers all but their eyes. It lets a woman see without being seen and greatly reduces the chances of male attention or harassment. The *abaya* also allows a poor woman to avoid the need to dress like a rich woman. To the Saudis, a Western woman who reveals her thighs and cleavage has made herself a plaything of lustful men. In fact, some Saudi women claim that Western and Saudi women both dress with men in mind, one group arousing men's desires and the other dampening them.

By the end of the 1990s, Abdullah had the support of reformers on the left, clerics on the right, and his own family in the middle. Secure in his power, he began to encourage open debate on many subjects. Journalists became free to criticize the government's policies, though not its legitimacy, and in social gatherings, people said whatever they liked about Abdullah or any other prince without fear of being overheard and reported. It was still forbidden to teach courses on Darwin, Marx, or Freud, but in other classes, professors could discuss their theories with impunity.

A clear sign that the kingdom was becoming freer came in June 1999, when the government released from prison Salman al-Awda and Safar al-Hawali, the "Awakening Sheikhs" who had opposed the presence of U.S. troops on Saudi soil. After serving five years, the two men were forbidden to travel abroad but were allowed to resume their criticisms of the kingdom's long alliance with the West, although their articles and speeches were less strident than before.

1999–2000: Oil Prices Rebound

For years, Iran's *ayatollahs* ridiculed the Saudi princes as corrupt puppets of the United States, but when the price of oil plunged in the fall of 1997, the two nations had a common interest in pushing the price back up. In December, Abdullah attended an Islamic conference in Tehran and had two private talks with Iran's newly elected president, Muhammad Khatami, on the price of oil. Two months later, Iran's former president, Hashemi Rafsanjani, flew to Saudi Arabia for talks with Prince Abdullah.

By 1999, the Saudi-Iranian thaw produced concrete results. Because Iran is poorer than Saudi Arabia, it had often ignored its OPEC production quota and pumped more oil than the organization permitted. Instead of retaliating by pumping more oil itself, Saudi Arabia persuaded Kuwait and the United Arab Emirates to help the Saudis absorb the production cuts that Iran had ignored. At an OPEC meeting in March 1999, each of the three nations agreed to cut its oil production 7.3 percent, and Saudi Arabia cut its own an additional 150,000 barrels a day. Iran's new quota was set at 3.9 million barrels a day, up from 3.6 million. In return, Iran promised to honor this quota and to obey all future OPEC agreements. The March 1999 cuts took several months to have an effect, but the price of oil, which had averaged only $12.70 a barrel in 1998, rose to $25 a barrel by the end of 1999.

When the price of oil briefly sank to just $10 a barrel early in 1999, all of the OPEC nations finally understood that they had to stop cheating on their quotas. Saudi Arabia, which rarely cheated, set an example by limiting its production to 7.44 million barrels a day, well below the quota of 8 million barrels a day that it had long sought. Venezuela responded to the Saudi initiative by giving up its goal of 3 million barrels a day, and Iran began to abide by its new quota of 3.9 million barrels a day. Even non-OPEC nations, such as Mexico, Russia, Norway, and Oman, promised not to take advantage of OPEC's cuts by increasing their own production.

While the oil-exporting nations maintained discipline, Asia's economy began to recover and the West's technology-led economies boomed. The increased demand and reduced supply for petroleum caused the price of oil to rise to $18 a barrel in April, $25 a barrel in December, and $37 a barrel in the summer of 2000. Saudi oil revenues, which had shrunk to $34.2 billion in 1998, rose to $43.9 billion in 1999 and soared to $75.2 billion in 2000, their highest level since the 1980s.

Oil revenues account for more than 70 percent of the kingdom's budget, so, to avoid wide fluctuations, the Saudis suggested that OPEC try to stabilize the price of oil. The Saudis suggested a price range of $20 to $25 a barrel. Under their plan, if the price of oil exceeded $25 for twenty trading days, OPEC would automatically boost its production five hundred thousand barrels a day to try to bring the price down. Similarly, if the price fell below $20 a barrel for ten trading days, OPEC would automatically cut its production to push the price back up. The other OPEC countries, facing the same budgetary uncertainties as the Saudis, agreed to the plan, but Venezuela asked for a price band of $22 to $28 a barrel, and the rest of the nations agreed to this at a March 2000 meeting. OPEC also agreed to increase its production by 1.45 million barrels a day. Oil exporters were now flush with cash and did not want to harm the global economy or encourage a search for alternative fuels.

For three years, before growing Chinese demand pushed the price of oil even higher, the $22 to $28 price band worked remarkably well. The price of oil stayed within this range, despite strikes in Venezuela, breakdowns in Nigeria, terrorism in New York and Washington, and war in Iraq.

In 2000, the demand for oil was so strong that the OPEC nations increased their production in March, June, September, and November. By December, the Saudis' flow was a voluminous 8.67 million barrels a day, and still the price of oil stayed at or above $28 a barrel throughout the summer and the autumn.

The rise in the price of oil enabled the kingdom to post a surplus of $12 billion in 2000, which eased its fiscal problems considerably. The government increased its reserves of foreign currencies to more than $20 billion and paid off a fifth of its debts to domestic banks. Less sensibly, the kingdom also resumed its subsidies to wheat farmers, further depleting its aquifers but making Saudi Arabia an exporter of grain again.

In 2001, global demand slackened as the dot-com boom came to an end, so OPEC cut production in February, April, and September. The average price of oil in 2001 remained an ample $25 per barrel, and Saudi oil revenues for the year were still a hefty $63.1 billion. This enabled the kingdom to reduce its deficit in 2001 to a manageable $6.7 billion.

To keep it from growing larger, the cabinet decided in December to ban the creation of new government jobs. This was a major departure from previous years, when the government routinely funded thousands of new positions for princes to dispense as patronage.

New Mufti, Lingering Bigotry

In May 1999, Saudi Arabia's leading cleric, Grand Mufti Abdulaziz ibn Baz, died. Abdullah quickly chose the deputy mufti, Abdul Aziz ibn Abdullah al-Sheikh, to be ibn Baz's successor. Since ibn Baz had been so reactionary, he had been well situated to defend the royal family against attacks by militant clerics. The new mufti, although he was a descendant of ibn Abdul Wahhab, the founder of Wahhabism, would need time to gain the stature of his predecessor.

Because Muhammad on his deathbed said, "Let there not be two religions in Arabia," there is no religious freedom in Saudi Arabia today. On Sundays, foreign Christians throughout the kingdom, especially Filipinos, meet in private homes to worship in secret. Several times a year, the religious police raid one of these houses and detain the priest, but unless he has tried to convert a Muslim, he is released within a day or two.

More serious is the continuing discrimination against Shi'ites, whom the Wahhabis regard as polytheists. On April 23, 2000, religious policeman stormed a Shi'ite mosque in Najran, a city near Yemen, arrested a Shi'ite teacher, and charged him with sorcery. The unfortunate teacher spent twenty months in jail and endured an unbelievable three thousand lashes, an average of thirty-five lashes a week. Another instance of bigotry in the same city took place when four Shi'ite high school students were arrested in December for beating a Wahhabi schoolteacher who had insulted their faith in class. The boys were sentenced to terms ranging from one to four years in prison and five hundred to eight hundred lashes; the teacher went unpunished.

The Plot against Los Angeles Airport and the Attack on the USS *Cole*

Fears of U.S. intelligence officials that al-Qaeda might plan an attack on the night of the new millennium were confirmed on December 5, 1999, when police in Jordan raided a house and found seventy-one plastic containers of nitric and sulfuric acid, enough material to make sixteen tons of TNT. The purpose of the explosives, militants soon confessed, was to blow up the Radisson Hotel in Amman, Jordan, where Americans were planning a lively New Year's Eve party.

That same month, Diane Dean, a U.S. Customs officer at the ferry terminal in Port Angeles, Washington, saw an Arab man waiting to drive a Chrysler off the ferryboat. Suspicious because the man was sweating as if it were August rather than December, Ms. Dean opened his trunk and found it packed with ingredients used to make explosives. Ahmed Ressam, an Algerian militant whose Canadian passport had made him useful to al-Qaeda, tried to get off the ferry by hijacking another car, but customs officials quickly captured him. Soon, Ressam confessed that he had planned to blow up a terminal at Los Angeles Airport on New Year's Day 2000. Al-Qaeda had given him $12,000 and detailed instructions on how to build a bomb. Five years later, after a long investigation and trial, a U.S. district court convicted Ressam of attempted murder and sentenced him to twenty-two years in prison.

On the morning of October 12, 2000, al-Qaeda struck again, this time successfully. In Aden (Arabic for "Eden"), Yemen's main port, three men steered a small fiberglass boat stuffed with plastic explosives alongside the USS *Cole*, a missile-launching destroyer, and blew a hole in its hull forty feet wide. The blast and the flames killed seventeen U.S. sailors waiting in line for lunch and severely burned or wounded thirty-nine more. Ironically, the USS *Cole* had fired Tomahawk cruise missiles at one of bin Laden's camps in Afghanistan in 1998. The $1 billion ship had a computerized radar system that could track more than a hundred airplanes, ships, and missiles simultaneously, but it could not detect a nearby fiberglass skiff until it was too late. Investigators said later that if the three bombers had struck a more vulnerable part of the vessel, they could have sunk the ship and killed all 294 of its crew. As it was, repairs cost $250 million.

The bombing of the USS *Cole* took place just three weeks before the 2000 U.S. presidential election, at a time when President Clinton was trying to get the Palestinians to agree to an Israeli peace plan, and another missile attack on Afghanistan or any other Muslim country might have derailed the talks. Instead, Clinton simply ordered that U.S. ships along the Arabian coast move out of ports and into open waters. By the time the FBI and the CIA agreed that al-Qaeda had bombed the USS *Cole*, George W. Bush had been elected president. A forceful response to the ship's bombing would have to wait for his administration, although, in fact, it never came.

A Yemeni, Fahad al-Qusaa, was supposed to videotape the explosion from an apartment overlooking Aden's harbor, but he over-slept because he had not set his pager properly. The footage would have been used in an al-Qaeda recruitment video, but even without the pictures, bin Laden praised the bombing and read a poem he wrote commemorating "young men who stood up for holy war and destroyed a destroyer."

Yemen's government put six conspirators on trial in 2004. After appeals, the court's sentences ranged from five to fifteen years in jail. All six men were members of al-Qaeda, and both the fiberglass boat and the money to pay for the explosives originally came from Saudi Arabia. In 2006, one of the terrorists who organized the attack, Jamal Ahmed al-Badawi, tunneled his way out of prison, along with twenty-two other militants, almost certainly with the help of sympathetic Yemeni guards. Since then, four of these militants have been killed and eleven have been recaptured, including al-Badawi. Another ring-leader of the USS *Cole* bombing, Khaled al-Mihdhar, a Saudi, became a hijacker on United Flight 175, the second plane to crash into the World Trade Center.

An End in Sight for Torture, but Not Flogging, and a New Penal Code

Torture in Saudi Arabia is rarer than in other Middle Eastern countries, but it nevertheless exists. Because Saudi police do not have the sophisticated forensic units that Western law enforcement agencies have, they use confessions to obtain criminal convictions much more often than Western police do and sometimes use torture to secure them. As is true throughout the Middle East, the most common form of abuse is *falaqah*, the beating of the soles of a prisoner's shackled feet with a stick or a cable. A two-hour beating can make a victim crawl for weeks.

Like many governments, the Saudi state includes people who inflict torture and people who condemn it. In 1997, the kingdom signed a United Nations Convention Against Torture with the understanding that the treaty would not be used to contradict *sharia* law, which sanctions both amputation and flogging, and which Saudis therefore refuse to regard as torture. Amputation in Saudi Arabia is rare, occurring on average about four times a year, and generally is used only for theft in a mosque or a repeated act of armed robbery. Foreigners who have lived in the kingdom for twenty years or more are virtually unanimous in saying that they have never seen anyone with an amputated hand.

By contrast, floggings of up to a hundred lashes are common throughout the Middle East, but in Saudi Arabia, criminals can receive sentences of several hundred lashes (administered over several sessions) and, on rare occasions, thousands of lashes. A man using a cane to inflict a punishment is expected to move only his wrist and forearm, not his upper arm. By tradition, he should also have a Quran under his armpit as he gives the lashing. Even if these rules are followed, a flogging is very painful. One woman, a married Filipina named Nieves who was misled into signing a confession (in Arabic) to prostitution in 1992, told Amnesty International what it was like to receive sixty lashes with a hard stick: "I thought it would be fast but no, it was done one at a time. . . . He really takes his time before striking. I started counting and when it reached forty I thought I could not make it. . . . I prayed so hard. . . . I could not explain the pain I experienced."[45]

In 2000, the Saudi government established bureaus within the Ministry of Justice and the Ministry of the Interior to investigate accusations of torture, but to date, no policeman has been charged with misconduct. The kingdom barred organizations such as Human Rights Watch and Amnesty International from inspecting most of its jails, but in October 2000, on a visit to the United Nations in New York, Abdullah invited investigators from the United Nations Commission on Human Rights to visit Saudi Arabia and examine its courts and prisons. "Human rights, as we Muslims understand the concept, is an inalienable gift of the Creator," Abdullah said, "and no one has the right to deny this gift to anyone."[46]

The inspection by the UN special rapporteur did not take place until October 2002, but he was free to go where he liked, and he praised the many improvements Saudi Arabia had made in its penal code and prison conditions. Although a few jails are still broiling dungeons with no fans, mattresses, or toilet seats, most prisons in Saudi Arabia, while hardly pleasant, provide ventilation, decent food, proper toilets, family visits, and daily exercise. Saudi prisoners are also much less violent than U.S. inmates are.

The ultimate criminal sanction, of course, is execution. In an average year, about sixty people are executed in Saudi Arabia, about two and a half times the number put to death in Texas and South Carolina, which together have about the same population as the kingdom. Men are beheaded; women are shot by a firing squad. Typically, half are executed for drug dealing, a third for murder, and the remainder for rape or aggravated cases of armed robbery.

In a typical year, dozens of the prisoners waiting to be executed are teenagers. (In November 2005, the number of minors on death row was 126.) The United Nations Convention on the Rights of the Child prohibits the killing of criminals for offenses committed before age eighteen, and in 1998, Saudi Arabia ratified those parts of the convention that do not conflict with *sharia* law. *Sharia* law also forbids the execution of minors, but many Islamic judges continue to order the beheading of young criminals as soon as they reach adulthood.

For decades, a lawyer in Saudi Arabia could not attend his client's trial but could only give advice beforehand. This changed in November 2001, when the Saudi cabinet adopted a new 225-article code of criminal procedure that specifically gives defendants the right to a lawyer and lawyers the right to present arguments in court. Poor Saudis and non-Western foreigners do not benefit from this, however, because the kingdom has no public defenders, not even in capital cases. Trials are decided by judges, rather than by jurors, and are usually closed to the public. Judges are appointed by the king or by his minister of justice. Most are extremely conservative Wahhabi religious scholars, and once appointed, they are independent of the government. Many judges, for example, ignore the new criminal code and still refuse to let lawyers into their courtrooms. Often, the sentences of the judges are very harsh, especially if the defendants are Shi'ites, whom the Wahhabis often regard as heretics.

The new criminal code requires a policeman to question a prisoner within twenty-four hours of his or her arrest and then either to indict or release him within five days. The minister of the interior (Prince Nayef), however, can still sign an order to imprison anyone indefinitely for any reason.

The new code also bans the use of torture to extract confessions. As soon as the code became effective in May 2002, the city of Jeddah, the kingdom's second largest, set up a hotline so that people could phone in any complaints they had about abuse by police officers. Although no policeman has been disciplined yet for using excessive force, the mere existence of the hotline undoubtedly deters some who might otherwise be prone to sadism.

Even before these recent reforms were enacted, no one ever "disappeared" in Saudi Arabia, as so many thousands have in Iraq, Syria, and Russia. Amnesty International, no friend of the kingdom, said that there are only one to two hundred political prisoners in Saudi Arabia, and that their imprisonment is public knowledge. The police release most political prisoners quickly if they sign a statement promising to refrain from political activity, but the courageous few who refuse to sign such a document may stay in prison several years. The U.S. State Department, in a conservative estimate, said that the number of political prisoners in Saudi Arabia is fewer than sixty.

More People Than Jobs

Because most Saudis think birth control is un-Islamic, they have one of the highest birth rates in the world. By 2000, Saudi Arabia had 21.5 million people, double its population in 1980. In 1980, however, the kingdom was at the peak of an oil boom, and Saudis enjoyed a U.S.-style income per person of almost $20,000 a year. In 2000, with the price of oil lower and the population higher, Saudi per capita income was only $8,600 per person, while America's had risen to $35,000.

In the twenty-first century, Saudis make less than half of the income enjoyed by their neighbors in less-populated Kuwait, Qatar, and the United Arab Emirates, although even this amount is three times higher than the average income in the rest of the Arab world and twelve times higher than the average income in crowded, oil-dry Yemen.

In the early 1980s, when money was no object, the average Saudi mother had eight children. In 2000, with incomes down by half, the average Saudi woman still had five children. Today, 60 percent of the Saudi people are age twenty-three or younger, and because nearly all of them will have children themselves, there will be at least forty million people in the kingdom by 2030, even if the Saudi birthrate declines.

Already, almost half a million Saudis reach adulthood each year. While thousands of Saudi women become teachers, doctors, and bankers, more than 90 percent stay home after they leave school and simply take care of younger siblings until they marry and start new families of their own. As for men, there are twice as many becoming adults each year as there are new jobs, and many of these jobs involve work that Saudis will not do, such as slaughtering chickens or cleaning hotel rooms. Other jobs require skills that few Saudis have because only one-sixth of Saudi university students major in technical subjects such as architecture or engineering.

In the first years of the new millennium, more than one-quarter of Saudi men ages twenty to twenty-four were unemployed, and even among those who were twenty-five to twenty-nine, 10 percent were still jobless. Without a job, a young man cannot marry, and because there is almost no premarital sex in Saudi Arabia, many young men have been celibate for years. Some have become angry militants.

Many more have started to take jobs that their parents would never have considered, such as catering at banquets, clerking at a hotel, or working in a store or a factory.

Most young Saudis understand that they have to work harder than their parents did in the 1970s and early 1980s, so foreign complaints that the Saudis are not hardworking are declining. The real problem is that it is cheaper to hire a foreign worker than a Saudi in nearly every field. A Saudi just out of college may make $3,000 a month, while an expatriate with years of experience will cost the same company only $1,500 a month. Even an illiterate Saudi, on average, makes slightly more than an Indian, a Pakistani, or a Filipino with two years of college.

It also takes more time to fire a Saudi if he proves unsatisfactory, so companies are understandably cautious about hiring a Saudi in the first place. As a result, while 86 percent of those working for the government in 1998 were Saudi, more than 80 percent of the people working for private companies were foreigners.

New Laws to Encourage Investment

Saudi Arabia needs more foreign investment not only to create more jobs for its young people, but also to balance an economy that is much too dependent on oil and petrochemicals. Unfortunately, to start a business before the year 2000, it often took foreigners six months to fill out more than a hundred forms from at least a dozen government ministries. By contrast, a businessman in the United Arab Emirates could frequently start a company with a single telephone call.

With Abdullah's strong encouragement, the government instituted many commercial reforms in 2000, 2001, and 2002 to make the kingdom an easier place to do business. The most important reform was the Foreign Direct Investment Code of 2000, which permitted foreigners to own 100 percent of a business in Saudi Arabia, instead of just 49 percent, and reduced the tax on corporate profits from 45 percent to 30 percent. (In 2004, the tax was further reduced to only 20 percent.) It also allowed foreign companies to send profits home, to buy land (but not in Mecca or Medina), and to apply for loans from the Saudi Industrial Development Fund. Foreigners are still not allowed to start companies in sensitive areas such as oil exploration, nursing, the media, or weapons manufacturing.

To make foreign investment easier, the government created the Saudi Arabian General Investment Authority (SAGIA). Designed to be a "one stop shop" for foreign businessmen, SAGIA deals with sixteen cabinet ministries and takes only thirty days to approve an application to start a new business or to give detailed reasons for rejecting it.

During its first four years, SAGIA was led by Prince Abdullah bin Faisal bin Turki, the engineer who supervised the construction of the industrial cities of Yanbu and Jubail. He is highly regarded by both foreigners and Saudis and is nonchalant about his royal status. "In this country there are more princes than taxi drivers," he told me one night, "and at midnight a taxi driver is a lot more important than a prince." Through his efforts, many government officials have repealed regulations that had become an obstacle to doing business. By 2004, SAGIA had issued more than sixteen hundred licenses to foreign-owned ventures.

Another important reform was the creation of a duty-free market, effective January 1, 2003, among the six states belonging to the Gulf Cooperation Council (GCC): Saudi Arabia, Kuwait, Bahrain, Qatar, Oman, and the United Arab Emirates. Tariffs for items from outside the GCC states were reduced to 5 percent, a change that required some painful cost-cutting in the Saudi furniture, cement, steel, and detergent industries, which until then had enjoyed a highly protective 20 percent tariff.

In the spring of 2001, the kingdom published accounting guidelines on what Saudi companies needed to do to make their finances transparent because the lack of transparency had long been a bar to foreign investment. Within two years, many of these guidelines became binding regulations. In August, the government also announced that foreign companies were no longer required to have a Saudi agent to do business in the kingdom. This promised major savings for foreign firms because agents had often received a 5 percent commission on every transaction.

The Internet and Satellite Television

Although thousands of Saudis began to use the Internet via phone lines to Bahrain and the United Arab Emirates as early as 1995, local access did not begin in the kingdom until January 1999. By 2001, there were about 250,000 subscribers, usually with another two or three people sharing the same account. A large majority of the kingdom's subscribers were women. Some joined chat rooms; others used the Internet to plan parties, seek advice about family matters, or ask religious questions. (Sometimes a bold woman e-mailed or text-messaged her cell phone number to a man, then the two of them could stand at a shopping mall and see each other while they talked to each other on their cell phones.)

Web sites also proliferated, despite the fact that except for China, Saudi Arabia censors more Web sites than any other country. By 2001, it had blocked more than two hundred thousand sites devoted to pornography, swimsuits, lingerie, bombs, drugs, alcohol, gambling, Zionism, women's rights, gay and lesbian rights, abortion, religions other than Islam, criticism of the royal family, and a variety of sites devoted to comedy, with the blocked pornography sites being by far the most numerous. Saudi students have nevertheless found it not so difficult to bypass the blocks.

Even in Mecca, Internet cafes began to appear in 2000, drawing several complaints about "virtual colonialism." In May of the same year, Abdullah launched a $1.3 billion program to provide schools with computers and access to the Internet, and by 2003, more than half of the Saudi people had such access. Despite the deep misgivings that the rulers of the kingdom have about the content of the World Wide Web, most of them want their grandchildren to make use of this tool in a fast-changing world.

In addition to censoring the Internet, the Saudi government removes lingerie ads from foreign newspapers, critical articles from foreign magazines, and any reference to sex, alcohol, pork, or religions other than Islam on Saudi television. But the influence of Saudi television has greatly diminished in the last few years. By 2000, there were millions of VCRs and more than a million satellite dishes in the kingdom, and a government study that year showed that with so many channels and movies to choose from, the Saudis spent at least 50 percent more time watching television, VCRs, and DVDs than Americans and Europeans did, largely because women rarely leave their homes at night.[47] By 2003, according to a Zogby poll, more than 80 percent of the Saudis had access to satellite television.

Four of the most popular Arab satellite networks are owned by Saudis. The Middle East Broadcasting Center (MBC) in Dubai, with fifty million viewers, is owned by Walid al-Ibrahim, a brother of Princess Jawhara, King Fahad's favorite wife. The Arab Radio and Television Network (ART) in Cairo is owned by Saleh Kamel, another Saudi billionaire. The ORBIT network in Bahrain is owned by investors led by Prince Khalid al-Abdul Rahman, and the Lebanese Broadcasting Corporation (LBC-SAT) is 49 percent owned by Prince Alwaleed bin Talal, a nephew of King Abdullah.

Prince Alwaleed, worth more than $20 billion, is one the world's ten richest men, according to *Forbes* magazine. He earned his first billion dollars by age thirty-four through a series of land and construction deals in Riyadh and by turning several failing Saudi banks around. Today he owns 3.6 percent of Citigroup, the world's largest bank outside of Japan; 6 percent of Rupert Murdoch's News Corporation; three Arab music channels geared to different age groups; 22 percent of the Four Seasons Hotels; 1 percent (or nearly 1 percent) of Hewlett-Packard, Apple Computer, Compaq Computer, AOL Time Warner, Motorola, and Kodak; and more than $50 million worth of stock each in Ford, PepsiCo, Disney, and Proctor and Gamble. Recently, Prince Alwaleed also gave $20 million each to the Louvre Museum, Georgetown University, and Harvard.

While most young Saudis watch Arabic-language films, dramas, concerts, and music videos, some also watch HBO and MTV on English-language channels. A few Saudis are even starting to say "Hi" instead of "Salaam-o-alaikum." The impact of satellite television is especially profound on Saudi women because millions of them watch soap operas produced in Beirut and Cairo, with female characters who are good Muslims even though they drive cars, work with men, and run their own businesses. Once I asked a Saudi book collector whether he thought satellite television would change the way Saudi women will live in the future, and he said, "It will change everything."

Watching the Palestinians Suffer, Sending the Palestinians Money

When the first Palestinian *intifada*, or uprising, took place in the late 1980s, young Palestinians threw stones at Israeli soldiers. The second *intifada*, which started in 2000, involved suicide bombers and killed nearly a thousand people. By then, the high hopes generated by the 1993 Oslo Accords had vanished when Palestine Liberation Organization (PLO) chairman Yasir Arafat rejected Ehud Barak's offer to return the Gaza Strip and 95 percent of the West Bank (but few settlements near Jerusalem) to Palestinian control.

The second *intifada* began on September 29, 2000, the day after Ariel Sharon walked to the sensitive area where both the Al-Aqsa Mosque and the Jewish Temple Mount are located. Whether the violent reaction that followed was a spontaneous burst of anger at Sharon and his hard-line Likud Party or was orchestrated by Arafat in hopes

of winning a better deal at the next peace conference is open to question. Perhaps both theories are correct; they are not contradictory.

However the uprising began, during the next four years, from
September 2000 to August 2005, 151 Palestinian suicide bombers
killed 515 Israeli adults and children and wounded almost 3,500.[48] In
response, Israeli soldiers entered hundreds of neighborhoods in Gaza
and the West Bank that they suspected of harboring terrorists and
killed more than 3,000 Palestinians.

Many suicide bombers were encouraged and trained by an organization called Hamas (Arabic for "Never"). Article 13 in its charter
states, "There is no solution to the Palestinian problem except by
holy war. . . . International conferences are a waste of time."[49] The
stridency of this charter did not stop Abdullah from paying a visit to
Hamas's founder, Sheikh Ahmad Yasin, when Yasin was undergoing
tests at a hospital in Riyadh in 1998. Later, after Yasin was killed by
an Israeli missile, his successor, Abdulaziz al-Rantisi, defended the use
of suicide bombers: "Hamas . . . lacks F-16s, Apaches, tanks and missiles, and so we use any means that we have. It is not just for paradise,
or the virgins, but because we are under occupation and are weak."[50]

When a Palestinian became the first suicide bomber (outside of
Sri Lanka) on April 6, 1994, almost every Palestinian and Saudi disapproved of both the suicide and the random murder of innocent
people. But by 2001, as Israel's response to the second *intifada* grew
harsher, Arab public opinion changed, and people honored the bombers as "martyrs" and "freedom fighters."

Important issues such as why the peace talks broke down and
whether Arafat was responsible were overshadowed by the bloodshed that was broadcast into Arab homes every day by Al Jazeera and
other Arab networks. Several million Saudis and more than forty million other Arabs watch Al Jazeera's news reports daily, although Saudi
businesses refuse to advertise on the network because it gives air time
to opponents of the Saudi monarchy.

The killing of Palestinians affected the Saudi people more deeply
than did Iraq's invasion of Kuwait in 1991 because the videos from
Palestine were so vivid, while there were almost no tapes of Iraqis
looting Kuwait City. A Zogby poll showed that 87 percent of the
Saudis strongly disapproved of U.S. aid to Israel, and in 2001, they
began spontaneous boycotts of Coca-Cola and other U.S. products.
Crown Prince Abdullah shared his people's feelings and was perplexed
and angry that the United States, in his view, continually opposed its
own national interest by supporting Israel. He also knew that the
kingdom's friendship with the United States no longer seemed defen-
sible to the Saudi public.

On October 9, 2000, the royal family started a fund to support "the Jerusalem *intifada*," and King Fahad, although incapacitated, donated $8 million. Within days, a series of telethons raised $40 million from the Saudi public, and the kingdom's foreign minister, Saud al-Faisal, said, "Saudi Arabia will never accept any place other than Jerusalem as the capital of the Palestinian state."[51] By the spring of 2002, Saudi government and private funds had raised a staggering $2.61 billion for Palestinian causes, according to the Saudi embassy, with most of this money going to projects for economic development.

The most controversial Saudi donations were made to the families of the suicide bombers, beginning in June 2001. At first, the royal fund sent checks of 10,000 Saudi riyals ($2,667) to the bombers' families, but after seven months, the charity doubled this figure to $5,333. The fund also sent $5,333 if a Palestinian fighter became handicapped; $4,000 if he had a less serious injury; and $2,667 if he spent time in an Israeli prison. It also paid for the education of a "martyr's sons."

That the family of Abdel Rahman Hamad, whose bomb killed twenty-three teenagers in a Tel Aviv discotheque on June 1, 2001, should receive any money at all understandably infuriated many people in Israel and the West. The Saudis, however, denied that they were financing suicide bombing and said instead that they were merely "putting food on tables, medicine in cabinets, and children in school." No evidence exists that any Saudi official or fund ever helped a Palestinian to blow himself up, and on April 21, 2001, the kingdom's top cleric, Grand Mufti Abdul Aziz al-Sheikh, said that Islam prohibits suicide bombing. His opinion was widely condemned in the rest of the Arab world.

A Friendship at the Breaking Point

After President Bill Clinton had spent so much time in 2000 trying to mediate an agreement between Israel and Palestine, only to see Yasir Arafat reject the Israeli proposal with no counteroffer of his own, America's new president, George W. Bush, was determined not to waste any more time on the inflexible Palestinian leader. Because Israel's reprisals against the *intifada* were killing three times as many people as the *intifada* itself did, Bush's desire to stay out of the conflict looked to the Arabs like a full-blown tilt toward Israel. Among ordinary Saudis, America's refusal to restrain Israel's military was creating more hostility toward the United States than years of militants' sermons had.

Many Saudis thought that the United States applied a double standard in the Middle East: bombing Iraq every time one of its planes entered a "no fly zone" but ignoring what the Saudis saw as Israel's noncompliance with UN resolutions demanding its withdrawal from the West Bank. The Saudis also continued to resent the presence of U.S. troops in their country, and many wondered whether the United States was exaggerating the military threat posed by Saddam Hussein in order to keep its troops in the kingdom.

In May 2001, Abdullah publicly declined an invitation from President Bush to visit the White House, a snub that was widely approved by both the Saudis and other Arabs. "Don't they [Americans] see what is happening to Palestinian children, women, the elderly—the humiliation, the hunger?" Abdullah asked a reporter for the *Financial Times*.[52]

On June 5, after signing a free trade agreement with Syria, Abdullah returned to the kingdom and said,

> Israeli bullets have assassinated old men, women and even tod-
> dlers. . . . But tomorrow—God willing—will be ours, and every drop
> of Arab blood that has been spilled on our Arab land will be paid
> for by those who spilled it. . . . Violence only breeds violence. . . .
> We call upon the United States, Europe and the whole world to meet
> their historic commitments towards the peace process.[53]

Three weeks later, George H. W. Bush, the president's father, telephoned Abdullah to tell him that his son had "his heart in the right place" and would "do the right thing."[54]

But later that summer, on August 23, Abdullah was horrified when he saw television pictures of an Israeli soldier trying to keep an elderly Palestinian woman down on the ground by putting his boot on her head. The next day, when President Bush said, "The Israelis will not negotiate under a terrorist threat, simple as that," Abdullah "just went bananas," a Saudi official told the *Washington Post*.

Abdullah asked his ambassador to the United States, Prince Bandar bin Sultan, who was at his estate in Aspen, Colorado (later appraised by a local realtor at $135 million), to return to Washington to deliver an angry letter to the White House. Three days later, on August 27, Prince Bandar gave Condoleezza Rice, President Bush's national security adviser, a blistering twenty-five-page complaint about America's indifference to the suffering of the Palestinians. Prince Bandar, who was so close to the Bushes that they affection-ately called him "Bandar Bush," told Rice, "This is the hardest mes-sage I've ever had to deliver."

Abdullah particularly criticized Israel's practice of destroying the homes of the families of suicide bombers and asked how Americans would feel if the U.S. army had destroyed the homes of relatives of Timothy McVeigh, who killed 168 people in Oklahoma City in 1995. The letter concluded that after half a century of friendship, it was time for the United States and Saudi Arabia to end their alliance and go their separate ways. "From now on we will protect our national interests, regardless of where America's interests lie in the region."[55]

The letter shocked President Bush and his advisers, and within thirty-six hours, the president sent Abdullah a conciliatory two-page reply that included an explicit statement of support for a Palestinian state:

> I reject people who say when you kill a Palestinian, it is defense; when a Palestinian kills an Israeli, it's a terrorist act. . . .
>
> I am troubled and feel deeply the suffering of ordinary Palestinians in their day to day life and I want such tragedies and sufferings to end. I firmly believe that the Palestinian people have a right to self-determination and to live peacefully and securely in their own state in their own homeland.[56]

Abdullah was so pleased with President Bush's reply that he personally showed it to the leaders of Egypt, Syria, and Jordan. It was the first time that a U.S. president had supported a Palestinian state in writing. On September 7, Ambassador Bandar returned to the White House to tell everyone how happy he was that the long friendship between the United States and Saudi Arabia would continue. "You scared the s——t out of everybody," Secretary of State Colin Powell told his old racquetball partner. "I don't give a damn," Bandar replied, "we scared ourselves."[57]

The Saudis wanted President Bush to make his support for a Palestinian state public, which Bush agreed to do, although he did not promise to work with Yasir Arafat. There were many details to discuss about how to announce this new policy, so the president invited Prince Bandar to come back to the White House the following week, after Secretary of State Powell returned from a trip to Peru. The date of the Saudi ambassador's appointment was September 13, 2001.

Planning the September 11 Attacks

It is common knowledge that fifteen of the nineteen suicide-hijackers on September 11, 2001, were Saudi. Fourteen of these Saudis were "muscle men," college dropouts whose sole task was to storm the planes' cockpits and keep them secure. Eleven of the fourteen muscle men were from two southwestern provinces where unemployment is particularly high: Asir and Al-Baha (which was carved out of Asir in the 1960s).

Unlike the people of Jeddah to the north or Yemen to the south, the people of Asir are fervent Wahhabis. According to a leading historian of the region, Dr. Muhammad al-Zulfa, when the Ottoman Empire ruled the area from 1872 to 1919, the Asiris deeply resented the Turks, who seemed morally lax, and fought them constantly, trying to preserve what the Asiris regarded as their more devout and virtuous way of life. Osama bin Laden has written poems in praise of this struggle, appealing to the Asiris' pride, although the great majority condemn bin Laden's indiscriminate violence.[58]

Only one Saudi hijacker was a pilot; the other pilots were from Egypt, Lebanon, and the United Arab Emirates. The Saudi was a last-minute replacement because the pilot who was originally intended for the job, a Yemeni militant named Ramzi bin al-Shibh, could not get a visa to come to the United States. The Yemeni had already sent a deposit to a flight school in Venice, Florida, but the State Department denied him a visa because, as a bachelor, his ties to his home seemed weak, meaning that there was a risk he might overstay his visa and not go home.

The Saudi pilot who replaced him, Hani Hanjour, flew American Airlines Flight 77 into the Pentagon, a target that bin Laden chose when the preparations for the 9/11 attack began in earnest in 1999. Hanjour was from Taif, a mountain resort near Mecca, and was deeply religious even as a teenager. He studied English at the University of Arizona in 1991 and returned to Arizona in 1997 to study aviation and earn a private pilot's license. He took more courses to try to become a commercial pilot, then flew home to Saudi Arabia in 1999 in hopes of finishing his training there. Unfortunately, the Saudi civil aviation school rejected Hanjour, and soon he joined al-Qaeda instead and flew to Afghanistan in the spring of 2000.

In December, Hanjour returned to the United States and spent several months training on a Boeing 737 simulator at the Pan Am International Flight Academy in Mesa, Arizona. He was not a good student and, unlike the other 9/11 pilots, never earned a commercial pilot's license.

In April, Hanjour moved to Falls Church, Virginia, a suburb of Washington, to live near several other Saudis, and in May, he flew a private plane north of New York City along the Hudson River. In July, he flew from Fairfield, New Jersey, to Gaithersburg, Maryland, enjoying aerial views of the White House, the Capitol Building, and the Pentagon. The other fourteen Saudi hijackers knew nothing about airplanes. As former CIA director George Tenet has speculated, they "probably were told little more than that they were headed for a suicide mission in the United States."[59]

Al-Qaeda never pressured its members to become martyrs. A new recruit simply filled out a form, and one question asked whether he would be willing to participate in a suicide mission. If he answered yes, he was asked to swear an oath to affirm this. According to the man who planned the 9/11 attacks, Khalid Sheikh Mohammed, who was captured in Pakistan in 2003, people from Saudi Arabia and Yemen answered yes to the suicide question more often than other recruits did, and of the two nationalities, it was much easier for Saudis to obtain U.S. visas.

Al-Qaeda gave its recruits basic training in military discipline and in the use of weapons and explosives. Instructors particularly looked for men who showed patience because terror missions often require years of planning and months of waiting for a go-ahead. After the Saudi muscle men finished their training, they flew back to Saudi Arabia to apply for U.S. visas, then returned to Afghanistan for additional instruction on how to storm a cockpit and overpower an air marshal. Instructors even gave the musclemen sheep to kill to get them used to cutting throats. When the extra training was complete, the musclemen flew to Karachi, then to Dubai, and finally, with new Saudi passports, to Newark, Miami, or Los Angeles. By the middle of July 2001, all nineteen of the 9/11 hijackers had arrived in the United States.

Most of the men lived in suburban Miami. They opened bank accounts and mail boxes, rented cars and apartments, took classes in English and street fighting, worked out at gyms, and used prepaid calling cards at phone booths, rather than risk detection on a cell phone. As FBI director Robert Mueller later said to Congress, "They came lawfully. They lived lawfully. They trained lawfully."

Money for the hijackers came from al-Qaeda operatives in the United Arab Emirates. They used Western Union and other money exchanges there to wire more than $400,000 to Muhammad Atta and others in 1999, 2000, and 2001. Atta in turn sent back almost $35,000 of unused money in the last three days before 9/11.

On August 1, four of the Saudi muscle men flew first class from Boston to San Francisco to familiarize themselves with a Boeing jet. Movie actor James Woods, whose films include *Nixon*, *The Onion Field*, and *Casino*, was in the first-class section, too. He was so troubled by the Saudis' secretive behavior that he told the jet's copilot that he was afraid the four men might hijack the plane. "I'm very much aware," Woods added, "of how serious it is to say the word 'hijack' on an American aircraft."[60]

In the last week of August 2001, the hijackers bought their plane tickets for the September 11 flights. Bin Laden and Khalid Sheikh Mohammed had chosen September, rather than August, as the month for the attack because if they succeeded in destroying the Capitol Building, Congress would be in session.

On September 10, the day before the attacks, two hijackers watched a pay-per-view porn film in their Portland, Maine, motel room, while a third hijacker in Newark went to a topless bar with "Jersey Style table dancing."[61] Whether or not these three men were anticipating the pleasures of paradise, a fourth hijacker clearly was: Abdulaziz al-Omari, one of the men who accompanied Muhammad Atta on American Airlines Flight 11, the first of the two planes to crash into the World Trade Center. Unlike most of the hijackers, who were single, al-Omari was married and had a baby daughter. Yet in a notebook, part of which was released by the FBI, al-Omari wrote, "The houris [virgins] are calling you: 'Come, O friend of Allah,' and they are wearing their finest clothes. And if Allah grants one of you a victim's throat to slit, then carry out the sacrifice. . . . Don't argue, just listen and obey."[62]

Al-Omari may have copied this passage to give himself courage on the day of the mission, but the words are not those of a man thinking of his wife.

In the summer of 2001, many U.S. intelligence experts were deeply worried about the possibility of terrorist attacks on American soil or against U.S. buildings abroad. In June, bin Laden himself told a Saudi television reporter in Afghanistan, Bakr Atiani, that attacks against the United States would come "within the next several weeks."[63] Also worrisome were excerpts from dozens of phone calls made by suspected terrorists, calls that the CIA and the National Security Agency had intercepted. Many of the militants hinted that multiple strikes against the United States were imminent, and some used sports metaphors: "The Olympics are coming." "The score will be 200 to nothing."[64]

PART SIX

SAUDI ARABIA
SINCE 9/11

THREE TRAGEDIES made the Saudis realize that religious extremism had become a big problem in their kingdom: the attacks of September 11, 2001; a fire in Mecca on March 11, 2002, that killed fifteen schoolgirls because religious policemen refused to let firemen rescue the unveiled women; and bombings in Riyadh on May 12, 2003. In the fight against terror, the Saudi government has killed or captured more than a thousand Saudi terrorists, fired more than thirteen hundred militant clerics, shut down charities that had become fronts for al-Qaeda, and replaced many textbooks that encouraged hostility toward Christians and Jews. The government has also given the press more freedom, sponsored national dialogues on controversial issues, and in 2005, at the municipal level, held the kingdom's first nationwide elections.

Equally important are the government's many economic reforms, fortuitously coinciding with a surge in oil income. With Abdullah's encouragement, the government paid off most of its debts, signed several international commercial treaties, and joined the World Trade Organization. Saudi Arabia became an easier and more transparent place for foreigners to do business, and its petrochemical industry began to attract massive international investment.

On August 1, 2005, King Fahad died after nine years of mental and physical incapacitation. Abdullah became Saudi Arabia's new king at a time of great optimism. Despite continuing problems of gender segregation, high unemployment, and regional turmoil, the kingdom is booming economically and is unmistakably becoming a freer place to live.

20

Fighting Terror,
Fostering Reform
(2001–2007)

O N SEPTEMBER 11, 2001, before anyone knew who the
hijackers were, many Saudis had two reactions to the day's
attacks: first, "Now the Americans know how we feel when
we watch our brothers, the Palestinians, die," and also, "I might hate
someone's guts, but I don't condone his murder."[1]

At the official level, Saudi Arabia's response to the attacks was
exemplary. Crown Prince Abdullah said, "Arabs and Muslims stand
aloof from such acts that no sane and God-believing individual would
commit."[2] The country's leading cleric, Grand Mufti Abdul Aziz
al-Sheikh, said, "Hijacking planes, terrorizing innocent people and
shedding blood . . . cannot be tolerated by Islam, which views them as
gross crimes and sinful acts."[3]

Even the radical preacher Safar al-Hawali, one of the "Awakening
Sheikhs" who objected to the presence of U.S. troops on Saudi soil,
condemned the 9/11 attacks as a "sinful deviation" from peaceful
proselytizing.

The crown prince ordered the immediate shipment of nine
million barrels of oil to the United States to keep the price of oil from
soaring in a nervous market. The United States returned the favor by

helping 302 Saudis, including 22 members of the bin Laden family, leave the United States on sixty-one flights between September 13 and 24, with six planes chartered especially for the exodus. Many people, including Michael Moore in his film *Fahrenheit 911*, have asked why the bin Ladens and other Saudis were allowed to leave the United States so quickly, ignoring the obvious explanation of concern for the Saudis' safety. In *The 9/11 Report*, the National Commission on Terrorist Attacks (also known as the 9/11 Commission) concluded: (1) No flights took place before the reopening of national airspace on September 13; (2) neither President Bush nor Vice President Cheney was involved or even consulted in the decision to let the Saudis leave the country; and (3) FBI agents checked each Saudi against several government agency databases, interviewed every passenger they wanted to talk with, and were satisfied that none of these Saudis had any links to terrorism.[4]

The FBI had begun a massive investigation of the bin Laden family after the African embassy bombings in 1998, and the bin Ladens had fully cooperated with the probe. By 2001, the investigation was in its fourth year, and the bin Ladens living in the United States had been vetted. "I say baloney to any inference we red-carpeted any of this entourage," one FBI official wrote in an internal memo.[5]

One Saudi about whom there were questions was Prince Ahmed bin Salman, a nephew of King Fahad who owned racehorses, including War Emblem, the winner of both the Kentucky Derby and the Preakness in 2002. Shortly after 9/11, a captured al-Qaeda leader, Abu Zubaydah, told U.S. interrogators that Prince Ahmed had advance knowledge of the approximate day (but not the sites) of the 9/11 attacks, although no one has ever come up with a shred of evidence to support this charge. Then on July 22, 2002, the prince died of a heart attack. Some say it was not a coincidence; he was only forty-three. His death is much less mysterious, however, if one considers that he was obese and that his older brother, Prince Fahd, had died of a heart attack the year before at forty-six.

Initial Denial after 9/11

As shocking as 9/11 was, the Saudis were even more stunned a few days later when they learned that fifteen of the nineteen hijackers were Saudi. As the kingdom's foreign minister, Prince Saud al-Faisal, said, "I couldn't believe that something like this could happen from the hands of a Saudi. This is why you had a period of denial. People refused to accept that this was the Saudis' doing. Imagine if you have children, wake up one day, and find that one of your sons is a mass murderer."[6]

Prince Alwaleed bin Talal, who owns more than $10 billion in stock in New York–based corporations such as Citigroup, Rupert Murdoch's News Corporation, and AOL Time Warner, gave New York's mayor Rudolph Giuliani a $10 million check for the victims' families on October 11. While offering no direct words of apology for the attack by his countrymen, he said to the press,

> We have come here today to offer our condolences to the people of New York, to condemn terrorism and to donate $10 million to the Twin Towers Fund.
>
> However . . . the United States of America should re-examine its policies in the Middle East and adopt a more balanced stance toward the Palestinian cause. . . . Our Palestinian brethren continue to be slaughtered at the hands of the Israelis while the world turns the other cheek.[7]

Mayor Giuliani was outraged that Prince Alwaleed implied that there could be a political justification for the murder of so many civilians and returned the check immediately. In Saudi Arabia, however, people praised the prince's statement as something that Americans needed to hear.

Not until a year after September 11 did Crown Prince Abdullah, in an open letter to President Bush, acknowledge that most of the hijackers were Saudi: "Mr. President, we in Saudi Arabia feel an especially great pain at the realization that a number of young Saudi citizens . . . allowed themselves to be used as a tool to do great harm . . . to the historic and strong relationship between the American people and the people of Saudi Arabia. . . . Nothing can ever justify the shedding of innocent blood."[8]

By then, the kingdom had paid for more than fifteen hundred television commercials in the United States that condemned the 9/11 attacks and reminded viewers of America's sixty-year friendship with Saudi Arabia. The Saudi police had also questioned more than 2,000 Muslim militants, arrested 250, and indicted 90 for having ties to al-Qaeda. The police shared the information they obtained with the FBI and the CIA, although they did not let FBI agents question the hijackers' families. The Saudis kept their cooperation with these U.S. agencies secret, however, because much of the public still refused to believe that any Saudis were behind 9/11.

For a while, Saudis ignored even overwhelming evidence such as the videotape that U.S. soldiers found in an Afghan home in December

2001 in which Osama bin Laden said, "As regards the towers, we assumed . . . if the plane hits the building here [he gestured with one hand perpendicular to the other] the portion of the building above will collapse. This was the most we could hope for."[9]

Most Saudis could not believe that a handful of college dropouts, mostly from the mountains of Asir, could have successfully executed such a devastating raid. Nor did even one Saudi newspaper print an article about who the hijackers were or why they chose to become murderers.

A vile rumor spread throughout the Muslim world that Israel had attacked the World Trade Center on September 11, and that four thousand Jews who had worked in the Twin Towers did not show up for work that morning. As late as 2004, a former deputy mayor of Riyadh asked me during a dinner at his home whether I were sure that the Israelis had not been behind 9/11, since the United States responded to the attack by going to war against Muslim countries. I answered him by discussing the "smoking gun" video of Osama bin Laden, of which he seemed only dimly aware, and reminded him that hundreds of Jews had died on 9/11. He then asked, "Aren't the Israelis ruthless enough to kill several hundred of their own if they need to?" I pointed out that an Israeli strike against the United States would have been improbable and unbelievably reckless: if even the slightest evidence of such an attack had become public, it would have destroyed the U.S.–Israeli alliance forever. Only then did this retired city official reluctantly accept the hard fact that Saudi militants were responsible for 9/11.

My host's views were not unusual. Prince Nayef, the minister of the interior, told reporters in December 2001 that the fifteen Saudi hijackers "did not have the capability to act in such a professional way." A year later, on November 29, 2002, Prince Nayef still denied that Saudis were responsible for 9/11. Talking to a reporter for a Kuwaiti newspaper, *Al-Siyasa*, Nayef said, "Who benefited from the events of 9/11? I think they [the Zionists] are behind these events. . . . It is impossible that nineteen youths, including fifteen Saudis, carried out the operation of September 11 . . . since their action was against Islam."[10]

As outrageous as this statement is, Prince Nayef was in the mainstream of Arabian public opinion. A Gallup poll of 790 Kuwaitis in January 2002 showed that 89 percent of the country did not believe that Arabs had carried out the 9/11 attacks, and a poll of Saudis would almost surely have yielded a similar result.

Because few Saudis in the winter of 2001–2002 believed that Osama bin Laden was behind 9/11, they did not think that the Taliban should have to hand bin Laden over to the Americans and therefore did not approve of the war that the United States and its NATO allies began in Afghanistan on October 7, 2001. Following public opinion, the Saudi government refused to allow U.S. troops and planes heading to Afghanistan to stop in the kingdom. The defense minister, Prince Sultan, said, "We do not accept the presence in our country of a single soldier at war with Muslims," apparently forgetting Saudi Arabia's alliance with the United States and Europe against Iraq during the Persian Gulf War just ten years earlier.[11]

The United States sent its soldiers and jets to al-Udeid Air Force Base in Qatar instead, but the Saudis did, quietly, allow U.S. generals and technicians to oversee the Afghan war from the computerized U.S. command center at Prince Sultan Air Force Base in the desert south of Riyadh. With U.S. help, the Northern Alliance, an Afghan army opposed to the Taliban, took Kabul on November 12 and Kandahar, the home city of the Taliban, on December 6.

More than 600 Saudi militants took up arms for al-Qaeda. The United States and its NATO allies killed at least 45 of them and captured 240. The United States sent 136 of the Saudis, along with 218 Afghans, 107 Yemenis, and 298 other Muslims—a total of 759 men—to an aluminum-roofed prison at its navy base at Guantanamo Bay, in easternmost Cuba. It is the one place where inmates are not subject to the jurisdiction of any foreign tribunal or U.S. state court but instead are under the U.S. federal government's sole control. In September 2006, the CIA transferred another 14 men to Guantanamo, including 2 Saudi members of al-Qaeda. Previously, they had been in the prisons of unknown U.S. allies.

To date, the United States has permitted only defense attorneys, officials of the Red Cross, and journalists to visit Guantanamo, although in June 2007 the United States let a delegation of Saudi scholars, clerics, and psychologists see the Saudi prisoners. While fewer than 20 of the 773 inmates have had a trial, almost 40 percent remain imprisoned more than six years after 9/11. Twenty-six inmates at Guantanamo have tried to commit suicide, and on June 9, 2006, three men—two Saudis and a prisoner from Yemen—succeeded in taking their lives, according to U.S. officials, by tying bedsheets into a noose. A third Saudi committed suicide the following May.

By March 2008, the United States had sent 125 of its Saudi prisoners back to Saudi Arabia, and the Saudi government had freed sixty-one of the returned detainees. Only thirteen Saudis remained at Guantanamo.

Despite the direct link between Afghanistan and 9/11, most Saudis considered the U.S. action in Afghanistan in 2001 to be a war against innocent Muslims. In 2002, the Saudi people began a spontaneous, phone text–driven boycott of U.S. goods that caused U.S. exports to the kingdom to fall 30 percent that year, and sales of obviously American products such as Coca-Cola, McDonald's hamburgers, and Marlboro cigarettes to fall more than 50 percent. The boycott did little to hurt the U.S. companies themselves because they are not dependent on the Saudi market, but it did great harm to local Saudis who were franchise owners or distributors of U.S. goods.

Changing Charities, Sermons, and Schoolbooks

In the first year after 9/11, a majority of Saudis rejected accusations that their kingdom's charities, clerics, and schools were encouraging extremism. The most notorious criticism of the kingdom was made in a briefing at the Pentagon on July 10, 2002, for Donald Rumsfeld, Henry Kissinger, Newt Gingrich, Dan Quayle, two former defense secretaries, and two retired naval chiefs of staff. The lecturer, Lawrence Muraweic, an analyst for the Rand Corporation, said that Saudi Arabia was the "kernel of evil" in the world today, financing "every level of the terror chain." He also said that if the Saudis did not stop this funding immediately, the United States should seize their oil fields.[12]

Immediately after the briefing, Secretary of State Colin Powell telephoned the Saudi foreign minister, Prince Saud al-Faisal, to reassure him that Muraweic's views were not shared by the Bush administration, Defense Secretary Rumsfeld, or others in the group he spoke to. Several months later, in a speech in Brussels, Prince Saud alluded to the briefing when he said "It is folly [for Saudis and Westerners] to accuse each other of being the root of all evil."[13]

Even the Saudis who acknowledged the guilt of the fifteen Saudi hijackers still wanted to believe that these individuals were no more representative of their nation than Timothy McVeigh, who killed 168 people in the 1995 Oklahoma City bombing, was representative of the United States. But slowly, as Western criticisms of Saudi charities, clerics, and schools increased, the Saudis had to admit that many of the critics' accusations were true. Soon, the Saudi government took significant steps to make their charities more responsible, their clerics less militant, and their schools more tolerant.

Charities

According to Jean-Charles Brisard, an expert on terrorist financing, more than 240 Saudi charities annually give an amount greater than $3 billion to a variety of causes, and until recently they sent about

15 percent of this money abroad.[14] Out of this total, several tens of millions of dollars may have inadvertently gone to al-Qaeda in the years before 9/11. A few Saudis knowingly gave money to the organization, just as a few Irish-Americans used to take up collections for the Irish Republican Army in the 1970s and the 1980s. For the most part, however, money went to al-Qaeda out of carelessness and a lack of auditing, rather than from a desire to fund terrorism.

The U.S. 9/11 Commission found "no evidence that the Saudi government as an institution or senior Saudi officials individually" gave money to al-Qaeda but said instead that al-Qaeda "took advantage of Islam's strong calls for charitable giving . . .[which] was both essential to the culture and subject to very limited oversight."[15]

Zakat, the obligation to give one-fortieth of one's income-producing *assets* (not just income) to charity each year, is one of the five pillars of the Muslim faith. Wealthy Saudis, Kuwaitis, and citizens of the United Arab Emirates have typically been much more concerned about whether they were giving enough of their money away than about how their money was spent. Until recently, Arabs also considered it rude, a diminishment of the charitable act, to monitor a donation closely.

A good example of a gift going awry occurred when Princess Haifa al-Faisal sent $15,000 to Osama Bassnan in 1998 and 1999 to pay for medical care for his wife, only to discover after 9/11 that Bassnan and another Saudi, Omar al-Bayoumi, had helped two 9/11 hijackers pay their first month's rent for an apartment in San Diego in January 2000. Princess Haifa is King Faisal's daughter and the wife of Saudi Arabia's longtime ambassador to the United States, Prince Bandar bin Sultan, so no one has accused her of knowingly assisting the 9/11 hijackers. Still, the princess was mortified.

The gift became even more embarrassing in 2003 when a nine-hundred-page congressional report alleged that al-Bayoumi was a Saudi intelligence agent, although, after helping the hijackers with a month's rent, al-Bayoumi did not give them any more money during the final year and a half before 9/11. The details of al-Bayoumi's work are not fully known because President George W. Bush classified and removed twenty-eight pages from the congressional report, ostensibly to protect CIA sources.

In Saudi Arabia, even when a donor or a government agency wants to trace a gift, it can be difficult to do. Saudi Arabia has no income tax, so, until the last few years, financial records were lax if there were records at all. Many payments, even large ones, are still made in cash. Most wealthy Saudis also have foreign bank accounts that are beyond the reach of the government.

Just how much money went from Saudi charities to al-Qaeda will never be known. Western investigations after 9/11 showed that several Saudi charities were often fronts for al-Qaeda, including Benevolence International, the Muwafaq Foundation, the al-Wafa Humanitarian Organization, several divisions of the International Islamic Relief Organization, and a dozen foreign branches of the Al Haramain ("the Call") Islamic Foundation, which in Saudi Arabia was as reputable a charity as the United Way is in the United States.

In addition, a search by NATO policemen immediately following 9/11 of the Sarajevo office of the Saudi High Commission for Aid to Bosnia, a charity run by Prince Salman, the governor of Riyadh, found photographs of U.S. government buildings, maps of U.S. cities, and files with information on crop-dusting planes—proving that the fund had been infiltrated by al-Qaeda sympathizers who were in the initial stages of planning a biological or chemical attack.

It took several months for the Saudi people to fully understand that many of their charities had been manipulated by extremists, but by 2002, the evidence was impossible to ignore. In March, the Saudi government helped the United States freeze the assets of the Bosnian and Somali branches of Al Haramain. During the next few months, the Saudis froze $5.7 million in forty-one bank accounts belonging to men on a U.S. list of suspected terrorists.

The Saudis also cooperated with a global effort to shut down dozens of charities and sham companies run by Osama bin Laden and other suspected members of al-Qaeda, and they gave the FBI and European police forces information about suspicious Saudi bank accounts in Switzerland, Liechtenstein, Luxembourg, and Sweden. In an unprecedented move, the Saudis also allowed fifteen agents of the FBI and the Internal Revenue Service to open a bureau in Riyadh.

Equally important, the Saudi government ordered the removal of tens of thousands of donation boxes from mosques, supermarkets, and shopping malls, although full compliance with this order took several years.

At first, the Saudis thought that they could solve the problem of wrongful donations by a simple order: in March 2002, the government required all Saudi charities to notify the Ministry of Foreign Affairs before sending any money abroad. By the end of 2003, however, after closing more than a dozen foreign branches of Al Haramain and other charities, the government concluded that mere notification was insufficient. In January 2004, Abdullah issued a royal decree, signed by the ailing King Fahad, ordering all Saudi charities to completely stop their work abroad. The government merged all the foreign assets of all of the kingdom's charities and formed a new and more carefully run entity called the Saudi National Commission for Relief and Charity Work Abroad. Donations abroad can be made only through this organization, and unlike its predecessors, it is adopting modern, rigorous accounting procedures.

In February, the Saudi police created a Financial Intelligence Unit to enforce the laws against terrorist financing and money laundering that the cabinet had approved six months earlier. The penalties for these crimes range up to fifteen years in prison, and banks must keep records of all of their transactions for ten years.

The Saudi Arabian Monetary Authority issued "Rules Combating Money Laundering and Terrorist Financing" in May 2002. Charities must consolidate their finances into a single account, and only two people authorized by a charity's board can write checks on this account. Checks cannot be made to "Cash" but must be designated "For Deposit Only" into a specific beneficiary's account. No ATM or credit card withdrawals can be made from a charitable account, and no charitable funds can be transferred overseas.

In September 2001, Saudi Arabia's charities were completely unregulated. By the spring of 2004, the kingdom had some of the strictest rules for charitable giving in the world. The government took a further step in April 2006 when it banned students from collecting money for charity inside school buildings.

Clerics

After 9/11, many Westerners asked how the fifteen Saudi hijackers could have turned into such murderous fanatics, and some wondered whether the extremism of many of Saudi Arabia's clerics was not partly to blame. Certain Saudi clerics, for example, have issued *fatwas* (rulings) that forbid Muslims not only from becoming friends with non-Muslims, but even from smiling at them. Other clerics routinely end their sermons with prayers such as "O God, please destroy the Jews, the infidels and all who support them."[16] In the neighborhood where I lived in Riyadh, one cleric sometimes prayed for God "to shorten the lives of Jews and Christians, and break America up into fifty states that fight wars with each other."

Only a month after 9/11, a cleric at one of Mecca's largest mosques, Sheikh Wajdi al-Ghazawi, said that it is "permissible according to Islamic law to terrify the cowards, the hypocrites, the secularists. . . . The meaning of the word 'terror' that is used by the media . . . is *jihad* for the sake of Allah [which] is the peak of Islam."[17]

Some clerics spew hate on television. On a talk show on the Al Jazeera network on January 22, 2002, only three months after 9/11, Abdallah al-Haddal, an employee of the Saudi Ministry of Islamic Affairs, called the September 11 attacks a "Jewish deception" and the Jews themselves "the brothers of apes and pigs . . . [who] murdered the prophets and the messengers . . . and are the worms of the entire world." "Bin Laden defended the oppressed," al-Haddal added, "we warn the U.S. and advise her to get rid of the Jews."[18]

Just a few days later, a partial transcript of this broadcast appeared on www.memri.org, the Web site of the Middle East Media Research Institute. Founded by Israelis soon after 9/11, the purpose of MEMRI is to translate a cross-section of television broadcasts and newspaper columns from every Arab country. Arab clerics on television today hate the fact that the Israelis are watching them, and often, though not always, this has made them soften their language.

A Saudi Web site called *al Minbar* (the Pulpit), at www.alminbar .com, contains thousands of sermons for Muslim preachers to use around the world. The majority of the sermons are nonpolitical, but many say that Jews "have sold their faith and their souls to Satan." Other sermons say that "Muslims must educate their children to hate" non-Muslims, and that "women's rights are a Western ploy to destroy Islam."[19]

Al Minbar averages three thousand hits a day, according to its executive director in Mecca, Wajdi al-Ghazzawi, and receives an even higher number of hits on Wednesdays and Thursdays, when clerics are preparing their Friday sermons.

Abdullah, a devout monarch, reportedly feels that many of the kingdom's clerics have betrayed the nation by allowing such appalling militancy to spread so widely. On November 14, 2001, he called a meeting of the nation's leading clergymen (including three descendants of ibn Abdul Wahhab) and asked them to "act with moderation and examine every word you say."

Saudi Arabia has no separation of mosque and state. The Ministry of Islamic Affairs maintains more than seventy-two thousand Sunni mosques and pays the salaries of the *imams*, so the government can exert considerable pressure on the clergy. On December 7, 2001, the minister of Islamic affairs sent a letter to all of the nation's clerics, reminding them that mosques are places for prayer and spiritual guidance, not for political activism. In a second letter, the deputy minister specifically warned preachers not to give anti-Jewish or anti-Christian sermons.

The Ministry of Islamic Affairs also ordered more than fifteen hundred militant clerics to attend classes taught by moderate clerics for several weeks. The moderates went through many chapters of the Quran verse by verse to show the militants that many of their beliefs lacked a proper Quranic foundation. Then, in the final class, they asked the militant clerics for a commitment to be less extreme in the future. The government has held similar classes for more than 3,200 militants in prison and more than 1,500 of them have been released after renouncing their former beliefs. Only a dozen of them have been arrested again. The government also hires moderate clerics to go online and engage young militants in chat rooms.

About thirteen hundred clerics were not reeducated but were simply dismissed from their posts and forbidden to preach. Most of these men had refused to attend the classes taught by the moderate clergymen, and many, perhaps several hundred, were about to retire anyway. In some mosques, however, when a preacher stopped his fiery rants against the West, the crowds stopped coming. At others, clerics reluctantly called for tolerance in a deliberately dull monotone.

Classes can change the minds of only those clerics whose minds are somewhat open to begin with. Thousands of Saudi clerics are still militant, and some continue to appear on television. On May 20, 2004, on Saudi TV-1, Dr. Ahmad bin Abdul Latif, a professor of religion at Um al-Qura University, was asked whether it was permissible to pray for the deaths of Jews and Christians. He replied, "The prayer that Allah will annihilate them is permitted. . . . But if it is possible, people should pray that Allah guides them. . . . We should not pray only for their annihilation."[20]

Textbooks

After 9/11, many Western writers criticized Saudi schools for using textbooks that encouraged intolerance. A fifth-grade text, for example, *The One God and the Sayings of His Prophet*, published by the government in 1999, asks students to check "yes" or "no" to the following questions:

"The Islamic religion is the road to heaven."
"Other religions bestow eternal damnation on their adherents."[21]

A seventh-grade textbook warns, "We have to be careful of infidels, and we can ask Allah in our prayers to destroy them."[22] *Explanations*, a book for ninth and tenth graders published by the Saudi Ministry of Education in 2000, says, "It is allowed to demolish, burn and destroy the bastions of the unbeliever."[23] Another textbook for the same age group says that it is permissible to visit a non-Muslim country, provided that "the stay includes hidden hostility toward and hatred of the infidels."[24] A tenth-grade text even cites the notorious czarist Russian forgery *The Protocols of the Elders of Zion* to bolster its argument that the Jews seek "control over the world."[25]

From first grade through high school, religious courses make up a third of the Saudi student's curriculum, a fact that does much to explain why so few Saudis acquire advanced technological skills. Students spend thousands of hours studying the Quran and its rules of conduct, Muhammad's life and sayings, and the dangers of polytheism but spend no time at all on the beliefs of Shi'ites, Sufis, or trends in modern Islam. (Many Saudis at U.S. colleges have taken introductory classes on Islam to try to lighten their coursework, only to discover how little about Islam they actually knew.) Many of Saudi Arabia's history textbooks say that God gave the kingdom a "unique . . . responsibility in leading humanity to Islam,"[26] and only 1.5 percent of the material in the kingdom's history textbooks covers events outside the Muslim world.[27] Newspaper columnist Khaled al-Dakhil said that this omission shows a "lack of faith in Islam and its ability to coexist with other belief systems."[28]

In 2002, Professor Eleanor Doumato, a specialist on women in the Middle East, read two dozen Saudi textbooks and found that the ones on the Quran and the life of Muhammad were rarely hostile to non-Muslims, but that other textbooks on the dangers of polytheism were frequently and aggressively hostile not only to Jews and Christians, but to Shi'ite and other non-Wahhabi Muslims as well.[29]

Saudi Arabia's foreign minister, Prince Saud al-Faisal, came to a similar conclusion. After hearing so many complaints from the West, he ordered a review of the nation's textbooks in February 2002 and determined, as he told *60 Minutes*'s Lesley Stahl six months later, that "Ten percent of what we found was questionable. Five percent was actually abhorrent to us." He promised to delete the offending passages.

With Abdullah's encouragement, the Ministry of Education appointed fourteen men, half of them religious scholars, to make the necessary changes in the kingdom's textbooks and curriculum guides. Starting with thirty-two textbooks in 2003, the editors of new editions had to remove any passage that "directly or indirectly promotes enmity, hostility, and hatred." For example, a sentence in a fourth-grade text that once said, "Give love and support to the sincere, and dislike and hostility to the infidels," now reads, "Give love through Allah, and do not be unfair to infidels."[30] Replacing all the deficient textbooks in the kingdom's more than thirty thousand schools has been a slow and haphazard process, however, and until early 2008, many of the objectionable texts were still in use.

Many clerics and government officials object to these changes, and some teachers refuse to use the new textbooks. "If five or eight percent of our curriculum has to be changed, then eighty or ninety percent of the content of the American media has to be changed [too]," a deputy minister of education told *New York Times* columnist Maureen Dowd.[31] Saleh al-Fawzan, who wrote a tenth-grade textbook called *Monotheism*, has called his Saudi critics "parrots" for "repeating what our enemies say about Islam."[32] Fundamentalist cleric Nasser al-Omar asked, "Did we interfere in the American curriculum . . . [though] American social affairs are abundant with flaws?"[33] Some clerics also wondered, if these textbooks are so bad, why there was not a wave of terrorism when the books were first written. "The curriculum is not to blame, since we have had it for over thirty years," said one cleric, Sheikh Mohammed al-Fifi. "The problem is with some of the teachers."[34]

In December 2003, 156 Islamic judges and professors of religion signed a petition that condemned the changes in textbooks and the curriculum as "submission to the demands of the enemy . . . the Zionist rulers of America" and an "attack on the sovereignty of the nation."[35]

Abdullah received this petition politely, but he did not stop the government's push for new textbooks and curriculum guides. In September 2004, his minister of education, Muhammad Ahmad al-Rashid, warned school officials that extremism "will be uprooted from the educational system."[36] "Watch your teachers," Abdullah told the same audience, "we want [them] to serve Islam and the homeland, not terrorism."[37]

In February 2005, however, at the urging of conservatives, Abdullah dismissed al-Rashid from his post as minister of education and replaced him with Abdullah ibn Salih al-Ubaid, a staunch conservative who recently led the World Muslim League, a major religious charity. After three years of limited reform, conservatives have resumed their traditional control of the kingdom's schools, although the government is continuing its drive to replace intolerant textbooks with new editions, and in 2008 began posting all of its textbooks online. "It's a long, ongoing process," Saudi Arabia's former director of intelligence, Prince Turki al-Faisal, told me, "but the decision to remove all these texts, these objectionable materials, has been taken, and there is no going back."[38]

A Deadly Fire Leads to a Freer Press

Six months after 9/11, the Saudis became much more willing to look at their society critically, and it happened because of a deadly fire. At eight o'clock in the morning on March 11, 2002, on a potholed street outside Mecca, a girl smoking in a hallway of the Thirty-First Girls' Middle School suddenly saw a teacher coming and threw her still-lit cigarette into a pile of trash. A fire quickly spread to a staircase and caused panic as 835 girls tried to flee the overcrowded school, which had been built for just 300 students. The dilapidated old building had no fire extinguishers, no fire escapes, and only one exit, and because it was a girls' school, this exit was locked and the windows were barred to prevent any commingling of the sexes. The male guard who had the door's only key had wandered off to run an errand, and as the smoke grew thicker, hundreds of girls pressed against the door, shouting, "Break the lock!"

Within minutes, seventeen fire engines responded to the alarms, but the firefighters were met by half a dozen religious policemen who refused to let them into the burning school because the girls were not wearing their *abayas* (veils and head scarves) and therefore were insufficiently dressed to mingle with men. "We told them that the situation was dangerous and it was not the time to discuss religious issues," a fireman told the *Arab News*, "but they refused [to leave] and started shouting at us."[39] The religious police even hit some of the girls to keep them from fleeing the schoolyard, until finally some civil police dragged the leader of the *mutaween* away, broke open the school door, and let the firemen put out the flames. By this time, fifteen girls had been crushed or trampled to death, and another fifty-two girls were injured.

The editor of Mecca's newspaper, *Al Nadwa* (The Forum), published eyewitness accounts and editorials about the tragedy without first informing the Ministry of Information, and across the kingdom other newspapers followed suit. Saudis everywhere were outraged by the mindless rigidity of the religious police. "The Girls Were Killed by Pure Negligence," a headline insisted in *Okaz*, Jeddah's leading daily. Another newspaper, which had never before dared to criticize the religious police (officially called the Society for the Advancement of Virtue and the Elimination of Sin), allowed one of its columnists to demand the abolition of "the Society for the Advancement of Death and the Elimination of Life."

For the first time in Saudi history, the press forced the resignation of a high official, Dr. Ali al-Murshid, the director of the General Presidency for Girls' Education. The long-bearded cleric had insensitively called the fire "God's Will." Abdullah, by contrast, said "The deaths were unacceptable, the work of negligent, incompetent and careless officials."[40] Less than two weeks later, he abolished the Girls' Presidency completely, citing its gross neglect of safety, and transferred the responsibility for girls' schooling to the Ministry of Education. The government announced its decision as if it were a minor administrative matter, but newspapers trumpeted the story with eight-column headlines.

Girls' schools would no longer be run by clerics. From now on, both boys' and girls' schools would be run by the same government agency. The time that girls spend studying Islam was reduced slightly, and in 2004, girls as well as boys began to study English in the sixth grade. (By 2015, the government hopes to begin English-language instruction in the fourth grade.) There is still no physical education for girls, because many Saudis believe that girls should not disrobe outside their homes, not even in a locker room. Partly for this reason and also because of the prevalence of fast food, a growing number of Saudi women are overweight, according to two studies.[41]

As crown prince, Abdullah had the power to reform education, but the religious police answered to a much more conservative prince, Nayef, the minister of the interior. For weeks after the Mecca fire, newspapers demanded an investigation and even the abolition of the religious police, until finally Prince Nayef, who also controls the Ministry of Information, summoned the nation's editors in chief and ordered them to stop their editorials. Not one religious policeman in Mecca was punished because Nayef felt that it was the school's lack of safety precautions that killed the girls, not the zealousness of the religious police. Nayef did, however, open a new training center in November to try to make the *mutaween* more professional. Today, religious policemen continue to scold boys for flirting and girls for showing a bit of their hair, and they continue to confiscate "provocative" items such as Barbie dolls and cards celebrating Valentine's Day, which to them is a decadent pagan holiday that glorifies premarital love.

Although criticism of the religious police again became taboo, along with critiques of the royal family and Wahhabism, the Saudi press was still free to cover many social issues, including women's rights, school curricula, immigration, unemployment, poverty, drug abuse, and crime. A new newspaper, *Al Watan* (The Nation), with a logo on its front page of an arrow crossing a red line, ran articles criticizing schoolteachers who create a "culture of death" by encouraging their students to fight in foreign wars. The articles were significant because *Al Watan* is owned by Prince Khalid, the governor of Mecca

Province and a son of King Faisal. Similarly, in the newspaper *Okaz*, a columnist criticized "the ideology of dividing society into believers and non-believers" and denounced "the culture of violence that has infiltrated religious education."[42]

A long-running television comedy, *Tash Ma Tash* ("Does It Splash?"), became much sharper and began to make fun of many of the absurdities of Saudi life—for instance, the fact that even in an emergency, a policeman cannot enter a home to help a woman unless one of her male relatives is present. Hugely popular in Saudi Arabia and often denounced by conservative clerics, the show has also made fun of the rote memorization that is common in high school religion classes.

Newspapers hired more female reporters and columnists after the Mecca fire. Some complained about the scarcity of public transportation in a nation where half of the adults are forbidden to drive. Others argued that gender segregation comes from tradition, not from Islam. When Muhammad was alive, they pointed out, women spoke to men in public, sold goods in the marketplace, and went to mosques to hear sermons, none of which is permissible in Saudi Arabia today.

Saudi Arabia's best newspapers are edited in London before they are printed in the kingdom and therefore can be much more critical of the Saudi government than papers edited at home, but even they do not criticize the royal family or Wahhabi Islam. In 2002, however, one of these papers, *Asharq Al-Awsat* (The Middle East), began to translate articles and columns from the *New York Times*, the *Washington Post*, and the *Los Angeles Times*. In addition, *Newsweek* began to print an Arabic edition in 2000, CNN started an Arabic Web site in 2002, and both the BBC and France 24 launched Arabic-language TV news channels. Today, even Saudis who cannot speak or read English have daily access to a variety of non-Muslim views.

Before 9/11, foreign journalists rarely received visas to enter the kingdom and, when they did, were often watched closely by the Ministry of Information. After 9/11, there were so many negative articles about Saudi Arabia in the West that the government began to encourage foreign journalists to visit and travel unsupervised, to see for themselves that most Saudis are peaceful and that the kingdom is not the "kernel of evil" that some writers who have never been to the country claim it to be.

While the Saudi press is much freer today than it was several years ago, thanks in large part to the tragic school fire, it remains only half-free. A 1963 law still on the books forbids any criticism of the government, and the Ministry of Information appoints and often removes editors in chief. The editors the government chooses almost never have experience as investigative reporters and often are reluctant to risk their well-paying jobs to push the limits of their newspaper's freedom. The Ministry of Information also has the power to suspend an aggressive reporter from his job for weeks, months, and, in rare cases, indefinitely.

As a result, Saudi newspapers seldom discuss government corruption and never do so if a prince is involved. A story about sewage overflowing in the streets of Jeddah, for example, was not reported in any depth because it involved bad decisions made by the region's governor, a prince who is a nephew of the king. Similarly, petitions to the king are not mentioned in Saudi newspapers, even when a demand for an elected parliament is signed by hundreds of professors and clerics. Because the number of investigative reports is small, the Saudis are only beginning to trust their newspapers, and, to date, only two of them, *Al Riyadh* and *Okaz*, have more than a hundred thousand Saudi readers.

Prelude to America's War in Iraq: Saudis Stay Aloof

During most of 2002, the royal family was undecided about whether to let the United States use Saudi bases for warfare in Iraq. The Saudi public was strongly against helping the United States. In February, just weeks after President Bush called Iraq "an axis of evil," only 16 percent of the Saudis had a favorable opinion of the United States, according to a *USA Today* poll. The many broadcasts of Israelis bombing Palestinian towns and bulldozing Palestinian homes had taken their toll. When the United States finally invaded Iraq in March 2003, the number of Saudis who looked at the United States favorably fell to only 3 percent (although the number slowly climbed to 40 percent by December 2007, according to polls by the Center for Public Opinion).

Most Saudis felt that Iraq's people were too unruly for a democracy to succeed there, and that war could ultimately lead to a breakup of the country. The Saudi stereotype of Iraq is that it can be governed only by ruthless tyrants such as Ziyad in the seventh century (see chapter 4) and Saddam Hussein in the twentieth. Most Saudis therefore felt that America's true reason for going to war in Iraq had little to do with democracy and a great deal to do with oil.

In 2002, although the Saudis liked the idea of toppling Saddam Hussein, they were also afraid that a Shi'ite-led democracy in Iraq might embolden their own Shi'ite minority and destabilize the oil-rich Eastern Province, where Shi'ites are 45 percent of the population. The Saudis strongly advised the United States against going to war in Iraq and tried to prevent the war by urging Iraq's generals to overthrow Saddam Hussein, thus maintaining Sunni supremacy.

As the Saudis waffled on the question of the use of their bases, the United States strengthened its military facilities in Kuwait, home to twelve thousand U.S. servicemen; Bahrain, the headquarters of the U.S. Navy's Fifth Fleet; and Oman, a country at the eastern tip of the Arabian peninsula where thousands of U.S. special forces conduct some of their training.

In September, Saudi Arabia's foreign minister, Prince Saud al-Faisal, finally announced that the United States could send combat forces to Saudi Arabia only if the war in Iraq were authorized by the United Nations Security Council. With France, Russia, and China each having a veto, this was an uncertain prospect.

By then, however, the United States had negotiated the right to use military bases in Qatar, including the enormous Al Ubeid Air Force Base in Doha, the capital of this emirate. Qatar (pronounced "gutter") is a Connecticut-sized, thumb-shaped peninsula that juts northward into the Persian Gulf from Saudi Arabia's east coast. It has one-eighth of the world's natural gas and is famous as the home of the Al Jazeera television news network. Like the Saudis, the people of Qatar are Wahhabi Muslims but are much less strict in outlook than Saudi Wahhabis. Women in Qatar can drive and do not have to wear full veils. Hotels in the capital city, Doha, serve alcohol to non-Muslims.

Al Ubeid Air Force Base has giant hangars, a runway three miles long, and barracks for ten thousand men. It was clearly built with the needs of the U.S. Air Force in mind because in 1996, when the base was completed, Qatar's own tiny air force had only twelve planes.

To prepare for war in Iraq, the United States began to send thousands of troops to the Middle East in the fall of 2002, many to Kuwait, on Iraq's southern border. Unlike the Saudis, the people of Kuwait had vivid memories of Iraqi troops killing and looting during the Persian Gulf War just eleven years earlier and were immensely pleased by the prospect of finally overthrowing Saddam Hussein. By December, the United States had more than fifty thousand troops in the region.

On November 8, the United Nations Security Council unanimously passed Resolution 1441, which required Iraq to admit UN and International Atomic Energy Agency inspectors into the country to look for nuclear, biological, and chemical weapons. It threatened military force if Iraq were in "material breach" of the resolution, but such action would require another vote of the Security Council. Alone, UN Resolution 1441 was not enough to persuade the Saudis to allow U.S. troops and planes to use their bases.

How the Saudis Quietly Helped the United States in Iraq

Quietly, the Saudi government did assist the United States, its long-time ally, in four important ways. First, the Saudis allowed U.S. combat planes to fly over their airspace. (They may also have let some U.S. special forces maneuver along their border with Iraq.) Second, the Saudis sent thirty-three hundred troops to Kuwait to help protect Kuwait from a possible attack by Iraq, freeing more U.S. troops for the invasion.

Third, to make up for the imminent loss of Iraqi petroleum, the Saudis increased their oil production when the war began, from 8.4 million to 9.5 million barrels a day, and Kuwait and the United Arab Emirates also raised their combined output by half a million barrels a day. The extra petroleum not only kept the price of oil from soaring during the first few days of the war, it actually made the price fall from $37 a barrel to $26 a barrel.

Fourth and most important, the Saudis allowed U.S. generals and technicians to direct the war in Iraq from a computerized U.S.-built command-and-control center at Prince Sultan Air Base, deep in the central Arabian desert. The U.S. originally used its Combined Aerospace Operations Center to enforce the "no-fly" zone in southern Iraq and later used the center to direct the war in Afghanistan in 2001. The center was set in an enormous underground bunker that soldiers called "the Cave." There, three thousand computers received a constant stream of data from spy satellites, reconnaissance drones, airborne radar, ground troop radio reports, and other intelligence sources to give General Tommy Franks and his aides a real-time view of the war, which influenced their choice of targets during successive waves of bombing.

Once the United States and Britain began Operation Iraqi Freedom on March 19, 2003, the soldiers in "the Cave" tried to pick military targets that were away from populated neighborhoods, but with massive bombing came the unavoidable killing of innocents. The Arab press focused almost completely on Iraqi civilian deaths. Arab satellite channels called the Iraqi conflict "America's War on

Children." Saudi newspapers put graphic pictures of dead boys and girls on their front pages for two weeks until the Ministry of Information, knowing that the Saudi people were seething, ordered the newspapers to soften their coverage.

The Saudi government denied that Americans at Prince Sultan Air Base had anything to do with choosing targets in Iraq. This denial had plausibility because in 2002, when the Saudis had advised the United States against going to war in Iraq, the Americans had built a second command-and-control center in Qatar. By the time the war in Iraq began, the Qatar center was operational so the Saudis claimed that the United States was choosing its Iraqi targets in Qatar, when in fact the Qatar center was overseeing the U.S. war in Afghanistan.

By April 9, U.S. troops controlled most of Baghdad, and in the city's central square a large crowd pulled down a giant statue of Saddam Hussein. Three weeks later, off the coast of San Diego, President Bush landed on an aircraft carrier, the USS *Lincoln*, decorated with a giant banner that said "Mission Accomplished." The president told the ship's seamen that the combat in Iraq was almost over. But as everyone knows, the real struggle was just beginning.

The Saudis and Iraq's Insurgency

Many Saudi clerics are wary of Iraqi democracy. They do not object to democracy itself, but they are fearful that once a Shi'ite majority begins to rule Iraq, it will not be long before the Shi'ites in Saudi Arabia (about 9 percent of the kingdom) will demand full political and religious equality with the Sunnis. To many Saudis, the Shi'ites are polytheists who pray to saints instead of to God alone. For them to have power in Iran and Iraq is bad enough, but for them to have power in Saudi Arabia, even if it is just local influence in the Eastern Province, is anathema. As a result, many clerics approve of the Iraqi insurgency that has killed and wounded more than thirty thousand U.S. soldiers, and a few have even encouraged young Saudis to join the *jihad*.

When the war in Iraq began in 2003, several hundred young Saudi men, heeding the call to *jihad*, were suddenly missing. Foreign fighters, many of whom are members of al-Qaeda, make up less than 2 percent of Iraq's insurgency but account for nearly 90 percent of its suicide bombers. Just over 40 percent of these foreign insurgents are Saudi. Most of the rest come from Libya, Algeria, Yemen, Morocco, and Tunisia.[43] Some Saudi journalists worry that these insurgents will become "addicted to fighting," like the Arabs in Afghanistan, and will return home determined to fight some more.

Considering that there are hundreds of thousands of militant Muslims in Saudi Arabia, the number of Saudis who have actually left the kingdom to fight in Iraq is surprisingly small, roughly a thousand. Although many of the kingdom's clerics have praised the Iraqi insurgency, and a few have even given young Saudis money and bus tickets to make their way to Iraq's Syrian border, most Saudi clergymen say that the insurgency is an Iraqi struggle, not a Saudi *jihad*. In Saudi Arabia, only the king and the Council of the Senior Clergy have the authority to declare a *jihad*. In the absence of such a call, most clerics say, young Saudis should avoid violence.[44]

Saudi border guards patrol a 6-mile wide, 560-mile-long "no man's land" on the harsh desert border between Saudi Arabia and Iraq, with a 20-foot-high earthen wall, body-heat detection equipment, long fences topped with razor wire, and many night-vision cameras. From 2005 through the first half of 2007, guards arrested between a hundred and two hundred Iraqis a month trying to smuggle heroin, hashish, guns, bombs, and dynamite into Saudi Arabia and about ten Saudis a month trying to join the Iraqi insurgents. Every month, border guards have confiscated hundreds of pounds of explosives and thousands of guns. Because security at the border is tight, Saudi Sunnis who are determined to join Iraq's insurgency usually go to Syria instead.

As for Iraq's insurgents, many Saudi clerics have urged them on. In November 2004, twenty-six Saudi professors of religion, including the "Awakening Sheikhs," Salman al-Awda and Safar al-Hawali, signed a *fatwa* called "An Open Sermon to the Militant Iraqi People." It said that in Iraq, no formal call to *jihad* is necessary because the Iraqi insurgency is a defensive *jihad* against U.S. occupiers. It is therefore the duty of every young man in Iraq to fight the Americans if he can and the task of the rest of the Iraqi people to give the insurgents their support. The insurgents have a duty to avoid killing civilians, journalists, and humanitarian workers, the clerics said, while the Iraqi people are duty-bound not to help the Americans in any way.

Although the *fatwa* did not ask the Saudis to join the Iraqi *jihad*, and Salman al-Awda has repeatedly said that it was written only for the Iraqis, many Saudis nevertheless interpreted the *fatwa* as an implicit call to Muslim men everywhere to join the Iraqi *jihad*. One Saudi insurgent who was captured and then interviewed on Iraqi television said, "I hadn't thought of coming to Iraq until I read the communiqué of the twenty-six clerics."[45]

Many Saudis denounced the clerics' November *fatwa*. Prince Bandar bin Sultan, Saudi Arabia's ambassador to the United States, said, "These individuals do not represent the Saudi government nor the Council of the Senior Clergy, both of whom have repeatedly condemned terrorism." Newspaper columns and editorials condemned the twenty-six clerics for encouraging murder, kidnapping, and suicide. A columnist for *Okaz*, for example, said that the clerics failed to understand that the Iraqi insurgency is a war of "booby-trapped cars and roadside bombs against pedestrians—children, women and the elderly—what is going on in Iraq today is madness."[46]

Six weeks after the *fatwa*, on December 21, a twenty-year-old Saudi medical student, who may or may not have been influenced by the clerics' ruling, blew himself up in a U.S. military dining hall in Mosul and killed twenty-two Americans.

After Thirteen Years, the United States Withdraws Its Troops from Saudi Arabia

When the Persian Gulf War ended in 1991, no one foresaw that U.S. troops and planes would have to stay in Saudi Arabia to enforce the "no fly" zone in southern Iraq, where Saddam Hussein's air force was forbidden to fly. By 2003, U.S. troops had been stationed in the kingdom for nearly thirteen years.

The presence of U.S. troops in Islam's homeland was Osama bin Laden's number-one complaint against the royal family, and in the 1990s, it fueled the rise of militant fundamentalism. In the twenty-first century, neither the United States nor Saudi Arabia wanted the troops to remain in the kingdom much longer, but after 9/11, it was impossible to remove the troops without appearing to appease Osama bin Laden.

The war in Iraq changed this. With Saddam Hussein overthrown, the reason for the U.S. force in Saudi Arabia—to enforce the southern "no-fly" zone—no longer existed. And having conquered Iraq in just three weeks, the United States could now withdraw its forces from Saudi Arabia looking strong, rather than weak. Thus on April 29, 2003, U.S. secretary of defense Donald Rumsfeld and Prince Sultan, the Saudi defense minister, met at Prince Sultan Air Base in the heart of the Arabian desert and announced the imminent withdrawal of ten thousand U.S. troops and two hundred U.S. aircraft from the kingdom. The United States also decided to close the Combined Aerospace Operations Center—the Cave—with its three thousand computers.

By September, only five hundred U.S. soldiers remained in Saudi Arabia, mostly instructors staying behind to train the Saudi National Guard. And the new U.S. operations center in Qatar took over all of the command activities formerly performed at the Cave.

The U.S. military presence is gone from the kingdom, and so is the threat from Saddam Hussein. For the first time in decades, Saudi Arabia is strong enough to protect itself against most foreseeable threats. The kingdom has roughly 200,000 men in the military today, including about 75,000 in the army; 75,000 in the national guard (which includes at least 25,000 men protecting the kingdom's oil installations); 20,000 in the air force; and 20,000 in the navy and the coast guard. This sounds like a big force until one considers that Iran's military has more than 450,000 men. At present, however, most of Iran's army is ill-equipped and poorly trained; Saudi Arabia spends six times more on its military than Iran does. But thanks to the dramatic rise in the price of oil since 2003, Iran has much more money to spend on arms than before, and Saudi Arabia, which already spends about 9 percent of its gross domestic product on defense, may soon have to spend even more.

In the first years of the new century, the biggest challenge for Saudi generals was to maintain readiness in an era of austerity budgets. The fall in the price of oil from 1997 to 1999 led to drastic cutbacks in arms purchases. From 2001 to 2004, Saudi Arabia's weapons imports totaled $19 billion, 47 percent less than its imports between 1997 and 2000.

Abdullah had long been wary of expensive arms purchases for their own sake. He declined to increase the number of tanks between 1995 and 2003 and let the air force mothball its twenty-year-old fleet of F-5 fighter jets without immediately ordering replacements. Saudi Arabia still had 256 relatively modern Tornado and F-15 fighter jets, while Iran had only 156 fighters, and many of these were F-4s, jets even older than the F-5s the kingdom had just grounded.

After 9/11, because the U.S. press was so critical of Saudi Arabia, many Saudis began to wonder whether the United States would really deliver advanced weaponry to the kingdom in a time of crisis. The Saudis therefore began to buy more arms from France, China, and recently, Russia, especially ships, helicopters, missiles, and refueling aircraft, and fewer weapons from the United States. The kingdom does, however, have several ongoing multibillion-dollar contracts with U.S. firms to maintain air defense systems, F-15s, AWACS radar planes, Apache and Black Hawk helicopters, Abrams tanks, and Bradley fighting vehicles. Saudi Arabia is also buying $2.9 billion worth of battle tanks and tank improvements from General Dynamics, and there are detailed plans for U.S. firms to sell the Saudis satellite-guided "smart" bombs.

In September 2007, the kingdom's defense minister, Crown Prince Sultan, signed a U.S. $8.9 billion contract to buy seventy-two Eurofighter Typhoon warplanes from Britain, along with a multitude of spare parts, for delivery between 2009 and 2012 at a cost of about U.S. $122.5 million per jet. An equal amount will be spent on maintenance. It is Britain's largest export contract, providing jobs for nine thousand defense workers in Britain and fifteen thousand Saudis at an assembly-and-maintenance plant to be built in Taif. The new Typhoons will replace some of the kingdom's older Tornado fighters, but other Tornadoes will be refurbished and upgraded.[47] Several years ago, to start the negotiations for the fighter jet contract, Britain's largest defense contractor, BAE Systems, gave a peacock-blue Rolls-Royce to one of Crown Prince Sultan's daughters and treated a group of fifty princes, princesses, and friends to an all-expenses-paid trip to Hawaii.[48]

Al-Qaeda's 2003 Bombings: A Major Political Blunder

The Saudi people suffered three shocks before most of them finally stopped denying that religious extremism had become a big problem in the kingdom: the 9/11 attacks, the Mecca girls' school fire, and "5/12."

Half an hour before midnight, on May 12, 2003, three groups of Saudi terrorists sprayed gunfire at three Western housing compounds in Riyadh, then drove bomb-filled pickup trucks into each complex. The simultaneous explosions, so characteristic of al-Qaeda, ripped out three apartment walls and killed 36 people, including 9 Americans and 7 Saudis (along with the 9 Saudi suicide bombers). The blasts wounded 144 people, including 40 Americans. One building the terrorists destroyed was a high school for British children. Another complex housed 70 U.S. employees of the Vinnell Corporation, the firm that has trained soldiers of the Saudi National Guard for decades, but 50 of the 70 Vinnell employees were out in the desert on a training mission. The explosions took place just a few hours before U.S. secretary of state Colin Powell arrived in Riyadh to ask the Saudis for more help in the fight against terrorism.

The 5/12 incident was the first time that Saudi civilians had died from acts of terrorism. The explosions came just two weeks after the

United States had announced the withdrawal of its troops from the kingdom, troops whose presence had been al-Qaeda's number-one complaint against the Saudi monarchy. That al-Qaeda would proceed with terrorism led most Saudis to believe that the organization's true goal was the departure of *all* foreigners from the kingdom, even though this would cause enormous economic harm.

In a televised speech the day after the bombings, Crown Prince Abdullah, visibly shaken, called the acts "a devil's sting" and the terrorists "murderers with total disregard for any Islamic and human values . . . no different from vicious animals." He continued, "We specifically warn anyone who tries to justify these crimes in the name of religion. We say that anyone who tries to do so will be considered a full partner to the terrorists and will share their fate."[49]

In April, a month before the attacks, U.S. intelligence officials had warned the Saudis that al-Qaeda was in the final stage of a plan to attack a Western facility in the kingdom, probably a housing compound. They asked the Saudis to assign more guards to the residences. Even more frustrating, police in Riyadh had raided a house full of terrorists on May 6 but failed to surround the home before the gun battle began and thus allowed about twenty terrorists to escape.

After the 5/12 bombings, the police set up checkpoints at every major hotel, office building, and foreign compound. No one could drive in without first having his car's hood and trunk searched, and even then, a driver had to zigzag slowly through a maze of concrete barriers under the watchful eyes of policemen in armored jeeps with mounted machine guns. Only a few years earlier, a foreigner in Saudi Arabia never had to lock a door. Now checkpoints are a permanent part of life in the kingdom.

Despite the extra security, many Westerners left Saudi Arabia in 2003 and 2004 or sent their wives and children home. Before 9/11, there were 50,000 Americans and 35,000 Britons in the kingdom. By the middle of 2004, a year after 5/12, there were only 27,000 Americans and 25,000 Britons remaining. The American School in Riyadh, which once had 2,400 high school students, soon had just 800 pupils, and only about half of them were Western.

The police put up posters and bought newspaper advertisements with the faces of the nineteen most-wanted al-Qaeda militants. They urged citizens to call a special phone number (990) if they had information about the wanted men and offered a million Saudi riyals ($270,000) for information leading to the arrest of a suspect and 5 million riyals ($1,350,000) if the information led to the arrest of a group of suspects. It was a sharp break with the past, when the Saudis rarely admitted having any problem with internal security.

"Al-Qaeda made a huge mistake attacking Saudi Arabia," said one member of the kingdom's Consultative Council, because "now the government has declared a holy war on these terrorists."[50] During the next eight months, according to U.S. ambassador J. Cofer Black, a State Department specialist in counterterrorism, the Saudis arrested more than six hundred suspected terrorists and began to share more information with the FBI and the CIA. The Saudi police also stormed a half dozen al-Qaeda hideouts in 2003, often after hours-long shoot-outs that left a total of eleven policemen and sixteen militants dead. The police found many tons of explosive chemicals, homemade bombs, rocket-propelled grenades, high-powered rifles, and other weapons.

The 5/12 bombings changed the thinking of the Saudi people. A newspaper quoted a Saudi who lived at one of the compounds:

> For the first time in my life I realized what the word "terrorism" means. . . . I saw the flesh of innocent people who had been killed as they slept. . . . I heard the cries and moaning of the injured whose only fault was that they happened to be there at that particular moment. I saw the door and windows of my own house being blown away and glass flying everywhere. I saw the burned bodies of two small children still hugging each other. . . .
>
> I realized our need to wake up from a long sleep and confront the causes and conditions that allowed such a terrible thing to happen.[51]

In an article later that summer, a moderate cleric, Iassim al-Shamri, attacked the militant clergymen who encourage such bombing: "These gentlemen sit in air-conditioned rooms and drink iced mango juice and issue *fatwas* for indiscriminate killing. We never see any of them or their children sent on suicide missions."[52]

A Zogby poll of six hundred Saudis early in 2004 showed that 99 percent of them condemned the 5/12 bombings, confirming that al-Qaeda had committed a major political blunder. A year later, however, a huge government-commissioned poll of fifteen thousand Saudis revealed that 49 percent of the Saudis liked bin Laden's statements (probably because he calls many of the Saudi princes corrupt, something that journalists in the kingdom cannot do). Still, only 4.7 percent of the Saudis wanted bin Laden to have political power. As French professor Gilles Kepel has written, the al-Qaeda terrorists hoped that their "sheer audacity . . . would spur the masses into a general upheaval," but they "had no patience for the slow building of a [political] movement."[53]

Immediately after the 5/12 bombings, a columnist for *Al Watan*, Abdul Qadir Tash, wrote, "The time has come for us to admit the bitter truth—the phenomenon of violence and terror has a domestic dimension."[54] The newspaper also published a cartoon showing two men: one wearing a belt of explosives; the other, a cleric wearing a belt of *fatwas*. The caption read, "A terrorist. And the one who issues *fatwas* inciting terrorism is a terrorist, too."[55]

Conservative clerics were most offended by a column in *Al Watan* that attacked the teachings of Ibn Taymiyah (1263–1328), the medieval scholar who deeply influenced the early Wahhabis. Ibn Taymiyah, who had wanted to expel the Mongols from Syria, wrote that if a Muslim ruler will not proclaim *jihad* against infidels, it is the clergy's duty to do so, and in a holy war it is permissible for Muslims to kill other Muslims if the action is necessary to defeat the infidels.

The columnist, Khaled Al-Ghanami, wrote that Ibn Taymiyah's words "are a mistake and a true disaster that lead to anarchy . . . because anyone who thinks himself a cleric will try to remove anything he considers vice. . . . To speak candidly, today it is with Ibn Taymiyah himself that we have a problem."[56]

Four days later, a leading cleric called for a boycott of *Al Watan* (The Idol), and the following day Prince Nayef fired the newspaper's editor in chief, Jamal Khashoggi. Conservatives saw the column as a direct attack on the 260-year-old alliance between Wahhabi clerics and the royal family.

Another story that led to a dismissal was a fantasy written for the newspaper *Okaz* on July 1, 2003, by columnist Hussein Shobokshi. Shobokshi imagined a future time when his daughter, a lawyer, could pick him up at the airport and drive him to his office. In the car, she talks about who she will vote for in an election the next day, while on the radio the kingdom's finance minister presents a detailed national budget for a parliament's approval. Shobokshi was widely criticized by religious conservatives who hated the idea of women driving and voting. He even received some death threats. Crown Prince Abdullah wrote to Shobokshi to tell him that he liked the article, but a few weeks later Prince Nayef ordered *Okaz* to stop printing Shobokshi's columns.

In *Al Riyadh*, the columnist Mansour al-Nogaidan suggested that the Wahhabis' mistrust of Westerners was "a source of terrorist thinking." The minister of information promptly banned al-Nogaidan from writing any more columns, and an Islamic judge found him guilty of slander and sentenced him to seventy-five lashes, a sentence that was suspended on appeal.

During the summer and fall of 2003, the Saudi police killed more than twenty suspected al-Qaeda terrorists and arrested a hundred others.

Despite this effort, another bomb exploded in Riyadh at midnight on the night of November 8. With help from accomplices firing machine guns from a nearby cliff, a suicide bomber drove a van past the main gate of the al-Muhayya housing compound, then triggered a blast that killed 17 people, including 5 children, and wounded 122 more, of whom 36 were children.

Saudi terrorists have often targeted housing compounds because inside their high walls, Western men and women swim and drink liquor together, ignoring Muslim law. But al-Muhayya was a compound for Egyptians, Lebanese, and Saudis. Not one Westerner was killed by the car bomb, and of the 122 people injured, only 4 were American. Al-Qaeda had done nothing but kill and injure many Arabs, and nearly a third of the victims were children. Across the kingdom, even the most militant Saudis were outraged by this act of terrorism.

By the end of November, the police had killed or captured 14 of the 19 most-wanted terrorists, and on December 6, they published a new list of 26 terrorists, including the 5 from the old list who were still at large, and put up thousands of new posters. During the autumn of 2003 and winter of 2004, the police arrested another three dozen militants and confiscated more than 50,000 pounds of explosives, 300 explosive belts, and 300 rocket-propelled grenades.

Later in the winter, Raid Qusti, a columnist for the *Arab News*, wrote, "Our war against terror is really a war against an ideology. . . . The first step . . . is to teach that those who differ with our opinions, even when it comes to religious matters, are not our enemies. Differences of opinion are signs of a healthy society."[57]

In the spring of 2004, Dr. Haifa Jamal al-Lail, the dean of Effat Women's College, summed up the feelings of many Saudis about terrorism when she told a group of Americans, "We are fighting al-Qaeda in our country every day. . . . It is not a clash of civilizations, it is a battle between those who are civilized and those who are not."[58]

Killing and Capturing Saudi Terrorists

Acts of terror in Saudi Arabia were typically isolated events separated by periods of calm that lasted at least six months or, more often, several years. Then in 2004, the pace of terror suddenly picked up. Learning a lesson from the anger that followed the bombing of the Arab housing compound in November, Saudi terrorists struck only Western or Saudi government targets in the spring of 2004 as they tried to destabilize the Saudi economy by targeting foreign workers. The first strike came only six weeks after the al-Qaeda bombings of four trains in Madrid on March 11 that killed 191 people—and would have killed thousands more if the trains, each just a few minutes late, had arrived at the central station on time.

Saudi terrorists launched nine attacks in the kingdom in the spring of 2004, killing 38 and wounding almost 200:

- On April 21, a suicide bomber driving a Chevrolet Blazer destroyed the headquarters of the Riyadh police, killing 5 and wounding 148. Only six days before this blast, the U.S. State Department had recommended that all nonessential U.S. citizens leave Saudi Arabia because of the increased threat of terrorism. The move was widely criticized by Americans and Saudis alike because, as one Saudi official explained, "the State Department is asking Americans to do what the terrorists want them to do."[59]

- On May 1, four teenage Saudis in Yanbu, an industrial city on the Red Sea, put on coast guard uniforms and used stolen employee passes to enter the grounds of ABB Lummus, a Swiss engineering company, then stormed the office with machine guns and killed two Americans, two Britons, an Australian, and a Saudi. The teenagers, a pair of brothers and their cousins, tied one of the dead bodies to the back of a Toyota Land Cruiser and dragged it through the streets of Yanbu for two miles, shouting, "*Jihad, jihad!*" as they also fired bullets into a McDonald's and a Holiday Inn. (No one was injured.) After a seven-mile chase, Saudi policemen finally killed the young terrorists, but not before a dozen officers were wounded by gunfire. Abdullah's first instinct was to blame Israel. On television the next day, he said, "It is not 100 percent, but 95 percent [clear] that the Zionist hands are behind what happened."[60] There was not a shred of evidence to support his statement, and Abdullah never mentioned the possibility of an Israeli conspiracy again.

- On May 22 in Riyadh, two people in a Honda opened fire and killed Jonathan Hermann Bengler, a German chef who worked for Saudia Airlines, as he was leaving a bank. The killers were never caught.

- On May 29, in the year's bloodiest attack, four men in army uniforms in Al-Khobar, a city on the Persian Gulf, launched two early-morning attacks on the offices of two small oil companies and then attacked the Oasis Resort, a luxurious complex of houses, two European restaurants, and an apartment building. The terrorists asked the apartment building residents for identification to see whether they were Muslim, then herded forty-one Christians and Hindus to the top floor as hostages. Not until dawn the next morning could Saudi special forces land a helicopter on the roof of the apartment building and rescue the hostages. By then, the terrorists had killed twenty-two people: thirteen Asians (including eight Indians), three Saudis, a ten-year-old Egyptian boy who burned to death when a car exploded during a gunfight, and five Westerners, including a Swede and an Italian who had their throats slit.

Somehow, during the rescue, three of the four terrorists drove away, causing many Saudis to wonder how they could have escaped from a walled compound surrounded by police. Either some of the policemen sympathized with the terrorists' goal of ridding the country of foreigners or, much more likely, they made a deal with the terrorists to secure the release of the remaining hostages. A year later, the MBC satellite television network broadcast a miniseries about this attack called *The Beautiful Virgins*. It was the first Arab drama to show fundamentalist Muslims as villains, and it has been followed by another antiterrorist series called *Deviants*.

- On June 1, militants in a GMC Yukon opened fire on several vehicles carrying U.S. soldiers on a highway south of Riyadh. No one was hurt, and no one was caught.

- On June 6 in Riyadh, militants in cars shot and killed Simon Cumbers, a BBC cameraman, and critically wounded Frank Gardner, a BBC correspondent. The two men were filming the home of a terrorist who had been killed in a shootout six months earlier. The terrorist's house was in the Suwaidi district of Riyadh, the poor area featured in the 2007 film *The Kingdom* that is known both for crime and religious conservatism. (Many barbers there refuse to give shaves because Muhammad had a beard.) Fifteen of the Saudi government's twenty-six most-wanted terrorists either grew up in Suwaidi or had recently moved there. Some of the district's neighborhoods are so rough that even the police do not go there at night.

- On June 8, just two days later, three terrorists killed an American, Robert Jacobs, in the garage at his home in Riyadh. Jacobs worked for the Vinnell Corporation, the same company that lost seven employees in the 5/12 bombings. A video of Jacobs's murder later appeared on the Internet; Jacobs's last words were "No, no, please!"

- On June 12, terrorists shot and killed another American in Riyadh, Kenneth Scroggs, in his driveway. Scroggs worked for a Saudi company that made electronic components for computerized warfare systems.

- That same day, June 12, members of "Al-Qaeda in the Arabian Peninsula," dressed as policemen, set up a phony checkpoint near Riyadh's airport, and stopped the car of Paul Johnson Jr., an American. Johnson worked on the targeting systems of Apache helicopters, the helicopters that the Israelis use to fire missiles. The terrorists anaesthetized Johnson, pulled him out of his car, dragged him into another vehicle, and, several hours later, released a video of him, blindfolded, on the Internet. In this video, the leader of the terrorists, Abdulaziz al-Muqrin, wearing a black ski mask, demanded that the Saudi government release hundreds of al-Qaeda prisoners within seventy-two hours, "or else we will sacrifice his [Johnson's] blood to God in revenge for our Muslim brothers who have been liberally killed everywhere."[61]

Al-Muqrin, after leaving high school at seventeen, had fought in Afghanistan, Algeria, Bosnia, and Ethiopia. Despite his lack of schooling, he often posted knowledgeable, well-written articles about terrorism on the Internet. At twenty-eight, he was captured by the Ethiopian police, and they turned him over to the Saudis. A court sentenced him to four years in prison for recruiting and training terrorists, but the government released him after two years because he had memorized the Quran, a common way for Saudi prisoners to shorten their sentences.

After al-Muqrin threatened to kill Johnson, fifteen thousand Saudi policemen set up checkpoints throughout Riyadh and its suburbs and searched more than twelve hundred homes, farms, and caves. At times, they sealed off entire neighborhoods. Helping the police, to no avail, were U.S.-supplied drones and Saudi Air Force helicopters that flew above the desert with heat-detecting technology. On June 18, Al-Qaeda in the Arabian Peninsula posted pictures on the Internet of a bloody knife and Johnson's severed head lying on top of the rest of his body. "The infidel got his fair treatment," the Web site said. "Let him taste something of what Muslims have long tasted from Apache helicopter fire and missiles."[62]

Even militant Saudis were revolted by the photographs. A columnist in *Asharq Al-Awsat* wrote, "If all those who hate Arabs and Muslims . . . had gathered in order to create the best way to malign us, even they wouldn't have done what a group of sickos did when they cut off the head of an innocent person in the name of Islam and transmitted this image by satellites to be seen around the world!"[63]

The Saudi police found that 99 percent of the terrorists they had captured had joined al-Qaeda before the 5/12 bombings.[64] Since then, public support for al-Qaeda has been negligible.

I lived in Riyadh in 2004 and was struck by the change in the attitude of the Americans and the Britons who had lived in the kingdom for twenty years or more. At first, they told me not to worry about terrorism. "You are so much more likely to die from a car wreck here than from terrorism," a pharmaceutical wholesaler told me. And as I saw drivers make left turns from the right lane and right turns from the left lane, I knew he was right. Even when terrorists killed twenty-two people in the apartment building in Al-Khobar and news channels showed a staircase drenched in blood, longtime residents in the kingdom still took the violence in stride.

But during the week of June 6–12, when terrorists struck four times in seven days, even the veteran expatriates were spooked. The gunning down of the two Americans at home and the German chef in the street was especially scary because, unlike a bombing, which requires months of assembly and planning, a shooting can be done on a whim. By mid-June, many Americans and Europeans started to send their families home (or to Dubai), bought tinted windows for their cars, and began to take different routes to work each day. Others decided to look less Western. Some stopped wearing ties, and a few even grew mustaches and beards.

Then, as suddenly as it started, the wave of terrorism subsided. On June 18, only hours after Paul Johnson was beheaded, Saudi policemen killed al-Muqrin and three other al-Qaeda leaders when they tried to shoot their way past a roadblock. One of the dead militants had terrorized the Oasis Resort in Al-Khobar in May. Another had helped to shoot Robert Jacobs in his garage the previous week. Five policemen died in the shootout, but at the scene, the police found information that led to the storming of another al-Qaeda hideout and the capture of twelve terrorists just hours later, including one of the planners of the bombing of the USS *Cole*. The police also confiscated an arsenal of weapons and $38,000 in cash. Two days later, in another raid, the police killed two more members of al-Qaeda, found Paul Johnson's head in a freezer, and seized another cache of weapons, including ten grenade launchers, twenty-two machine guns, and a surface-to-air missile.

Al-Qaeda in the Arabian Peninsula did not recover from these blows, and terrorism in Saudi Arabia became rare again. Drive-by shooters killed three Europeans later in the summer, and on December 6, 2004, four terrorists died in an unsuccessful attempt to storm the U.S. consulate in Jeddah, killing five Asians in the process. Osama bin Laden praised the attack in an audiotape several days later. After declaring "all who help this [Saudi] regime . . . are no longer Muslims," bin Laden called for Crown Prince Abdullah's death because "rebelling against an apostate ruler . . . is obligatory." He also said, "If some Muslims are killed during the operations of the holy warriors, we pray for Allah's mercy upon them. This is to be considered accidental manslaughter, and we ask Allah to forgive us for it, and we bear responsibility for it."[65]

Despite bin Laden's encouragement, terrorism in Saudi Arabia declined greatly. While terrorists killed more than ninety civilians and forty policemen in 2003 and 2004, only five people died from terrorism in 2005, seven in 2006, and just four in 2007, although the police did raid several al-Qaeda hideouts and arrested more than four hundred Saudi militants that year.

Since May 2003, the Saudi police have spent hundreds of millions of dollars creating SWAT teams in every region of the kingdom. They have raided dozens of hideouts, killed more than 150 militants, captured at least one thousand more, and detained and questioned more than 3,000 young men who were thought to be sympathetic to al-Qaeda. By June 2005, the police had killed or captured 25 of its 26 most-wanted terrorists and issued a new list of 36 most-wanted terrorists. By February 2006, the police had killed or captured 14 of these three dozen men, and another 21 had fled the country, mostly to Iraq. The government also arrested most of the roughly 150 militants whose names have appeared on al-Qaeda Web sites.

Al-Qaeda in the Arabian Peninsula is weak because the Saudi police have the support of the public and therefore have many more informants and leads than U.S. soldiers have in Iraq. In China, Mao Zedong once said that guerrilla fighters must move among the people as fish swim through water, but al-Qaeda never had that kind of support in Saudi Arabia, particularly after the 5/12 bombings. There has always been a neighbor willing to call the police to report something suspicious. In fact, one Saudi counterterrorism specialist said that 90 percent of his intelligence comes from "disgusted neighbors."[66]

In a televised speech after the 5/12 bombings, Abdullah vowed to take "decisive action" against not only the terrorists themselves, but "the theology that fuels them." Across the kingdom, hundreds of prominent clerics, both moderate and militant, condemned the 5/12 bombings. Three clergymen praised the attacks, and police arrested them immediately. Six months later, after the November 8, 2003, bombing, each of the three clerics agreed to retract his statement on national television in return for his freedom. One of them seemed truly remorseful about having advocated violence, and another specifically called his fiery words "a mistake." The third cleric's apology seemed grudging, but the government freed him anyway.

In June 2004, when terrorists were killing someone every few days, the kingdom's most famous militant clerics, Safar al-Hawali and Salman al-Awda, the "Awakening Sheikhs" who had objected to U.S. troops in the kingdom, published a joint statement strongly condemning terrorism, with quotes from the Quran to support their arguments.

The government also began to broadcast hundreds of TV public service announcements that showed graphic pictures of terrorism's victims, along with weeping mothers. The Saudi definition of terrorism, however, does not include suicide bombings by the Palestinians, whom the Saudis see as freedom fighters trying to get their land back. There are still clerics on Saudi television such as Ayed al-Qarni, who said that in Palestine, "throats must be slit and skulls must be shattered. This is the path to victory."[67]

Petitions Expose a Rift among the Princes

Although there is no freedom of religion in Saudi Arabia and only a limited freedom of the press, the right to petition in the kingdom is absolute because the Quran commands rulers to seek advice. In 2003, the royal family received six major petitions, each signed by at least a hundred people asking for more freedom. One petition, signed by 300 women, asked for new laws that would allow women to work in a wider variety of occupations, keep custody of their children after a divorce, and conduct business in public without a chaperone. Another document, signed by 450 Shi'ites, asked for a declaration by the government that the Shi'ite faith is an acceptable branch of Islam.

In a partial response to this petition, the government in 2005 allowed Shi'ites to publish their own religious books and build their own mosques and elementary schools, although on side streets, not on main boulevards. In the city of Qatif, in the Eastern Province, the government let Shi'ite men openly mourn the martyrdom of Hussein, Muhammad's grandson, for one day during the holiday of Ashura by marching in the streets while beating their heads and chests with chains or whips. In other cities, however, religious policemen continue to ban such processions as heresy. In 2005, only 5 of the Saudi government's top 550 officials were Shi'ites, and 4 were in the Majlis al-Shura, the national advisory council.[68] To date, no city with a Shi'ite majority has a university of its own.

Two of the most significant petitions of 2003 were given to the royal family at the beginning and end of the year. In January, the "Vision for the Present and Future of the Nation" was signed by 104 professors, writers, businessmen, and retired officials, including both liberals and conservatives. Although the petition began and ended with pledges of loyalty to the royal family and never once used the words *democracy* or *parliament*, the document forcefully called for absolute freedom of speech, assembly, and association; equal rights for women; elections for legislatures with authority over the budget; an end to religious discrimination; amnesty for nonviolent political prisoners; and the promotion of "national dialogues" on important social issues. In essence, the petition asked the royal family to begin moving toward a constitutional monarchy.

Not a word about this petition appeared in any of Saudi Arabia's newspapers, which never discuss the fundamental structure of the Saudi government. But on January 20, 2003, Abdullah met about forty of the petition's signers and told them, "Your demands are indeed my demands. . . . But we need time. Be patient, and rest assured that we are working on this."[69] The signatories left the meeting elated.

By the end of the year, however, many people began to wonder how much time the royal family needed, and around December 1, 116 men signed a new petition that repeated the demands of January's "Vision," with two differences. First, the petition was addressed to Crown Prince Abdullah *and* the people of Saudi Arabia. Previously, petitions were supposed to be a private matter between the petitioners and the ruler. Second, the document asked that the government become a constitutional monarchy within three years, with a constitution approved by a vote of the people.

In the first week of January 2004, the minister of the interior, Prince Nayef, summoned about twenty of the signers of this document to his office and asked them to promise not to sign any more petitions. They refused, and Muhammad Sa'id Tayyib, an elderly lawyer from Jeddah, told the prince, "If you want to stay two hundred years or more, you must change to constitutional monarchy, . . . otherwise the ceiling will fall on all of us." In response, Prince Nayef angrily accused the group of trying to dismantle the royal government and turn the princes into "figureheads."[70] Even Abdullah gave a speech that called the request for a written constitution an "arbitrary demand" that threatened "to destroy national unity."[71]

A few weeks after the meeting with Prince Nayef, several of the petition's signers and some other activists met at a hotel in Riyadh to discuss what to do next to promote constitutional reform. To Nayef and many other princes, this was an illegal assembly and perhaps even the beginning of a political party. The Saudis cannot arrest someone merely for signing a petition, but in mid-March, the police arrested twelve of the men who had attended the meeting for making "statements that do not serve national unity or the cohesion of society."[72] The police also detained a lawyer who criticized the arrests.

Within days, the police released ten of the thirteen men when they signed a promise not to present any more petitions or talk to the media. But three men, a poet, a human rights activist, and a political science professor, refused to make this promise and remained in prison. A few weeks later, some reformers met with Prince Nayef to ask for the release of their three friends. Nayef refused and bluntly told the men to stay out of politics. "You're playing a game that's not yours," he said. "You're getting into the business of the state, in which you don't belong."[73]

After the arrests in March, there were no more petitions in 2004, and newspapers stopped running articles about the need for reforms such as a more independent judiciary and a more detailed national budget. On May 15, after a trial that was closed to the public, a Saudi court found the professor, the activist, and the poet guilty of sedition and sentenced them to six, seven, and nine years in prison, respectively.

In June, in a speech in Cairo, U.S. secretary of state Condoleezza Rice called the three men "brave citizens" and said that dissent "should not be a crime in any country." The next day, a Saudi court agreed to hear an appeal of the case, but on July 24, it upheld both the verdict and the long prison sentences.

One week later, King Fahad died and Abdullah became the country's new king. For the first time, Abdullah could overrule Nayef's decisions, and on August 8, after just one week on the throne, Abdullah freed the three dissidents, although they still lack their passports. (Abdullah also pardoned a chemistry teacher who had been sentenced to three years in prison and 750 lashes for praising Judaism and Christianity in class.) The pardons were signals from the new king that Saudi Arabia's reforms would continue. They also let Prince Nayef know that he was now subordinate to Abdullah, even within his own fiefdom of internal security.

National Dialogues on Key Issues

One request of the January 2003 "Vision" petition that Abdullah granted right away was to organize national dialogues between people on opposite sides of important social issues. The first "National Meeting for Intellectual Dialogue" was a gathering of more than fifty religious leaders in Riyadh in June 2003. After four days of debate, the clerics published a statement that said that only a legitimate ruler can declare a *jihad*, and that clergymen must explain the rules of *jihad* to young people in order to prevent them from starting a *jihad* illegally.

Abdullah, in his opening message to the gathering, urged all Saudis to "respect the opinions of others." The statement seemed bland enough, but in fact Abdullah's advocacy of pluralism was a signal to Wahhabi militants that they must learn to become more tolerant. (Three years later, in a speech in June 2006, Abdullah was more specific when he told Wahhabis in Buraida, the kingdom's most conservative city, that calling liberal opponents "hypocrites" or "secular" was divisive and harmful to national unity.[74])

What was most remarkable about the first national dialogue was that many of the clerics the government invited were not Wahhabis at all. Delegates included Shi'ite, Sufi, Ismaili, and Malakite Muslims. For this reason, Safar al-Hawali, one of the Awakening Sheikhs, declined to attend, and his refusal to meet "deviant" Muslims was applauded by many conservative clerics. By contrast, the other Awakening Sheikh, Salman al-Awda, not only attended the conference, but even gave a Shi'ite leader a ride in his car.

A second national dialogue took place in Mecca at the end of December and included businessmen, militant clerics, signers of the reform petitions, and ten women who participated via closed-circuit television. The sixty delegates recommended elections for both national and regional consultative councils, the establishment of trade unions, and greater public control of the budget. Abdullah met the delegates and praised their work but made no promises about their recommendations.

A third national dialogue on women's issues was held in Medina in June 2004 and had more conservatives than reformers as delegates, yet even this conference recommended that the government give women the right to work and study without a man's permission, create new courts with female judges to deal with women's issues, and build a nationwide public transportation system because women cannot drive. (The kingdom's largest cities have only a few bus lines, and their schedules are unreliable.) Afterward, Abdullah met with the female delegates and promised to consider their recommendations. By meeting these women, Abdullah let everyone know that he approves of women working outside the home.

A fourth national dialogue on the problems of young people took place in Dammam in December 2004, and a fifth dialogue on relations with foreigners and their societies, televised live, convened in Abha in December 2005. A sixth national dialogue on education, including the issue of how Saudi schools can adequately prepare students for the job market—a topic specifically chosen by King Abdullah—was held in Sakaka in November 2006. It recommended that more of the high school curriculum be devoted to scientific and technical subjects. A seventh dialogue, on employers and employment, took place in several cities in April 2008. The government plans to continue holding dialogues on sensitive subjects annually. By revealing the kingdom's deep divisions of opinion, the sessions make the royal family seem moderate and middle of the road.

Abdullah instituted a particularly important reform on November 29, 2003, when he gave individual members of the Majlis al-Shura, the national consultative council, the right to propose legislation. Previously, only the king or his regent had this right, and members of the council merely responded to his questions. In 2002, Abdullah gave council members the right to ask cabinet officials questions about their policies, but the Shura still has no role in defense, security, or the formation of the budget.

In 2004, Abdullah increased the number of people in the Shura to 150, and some of its sessions began to be televised. More than 40 percent of its members have PhDs from U.S. universities, and Abdullah has continued to follow almost all of the council's recommendations.

Local Elections Bring More Hope Than Change

On October 13, 2003, Abdullah ordered several government agencies to prepare to hold elections, in roughly a year's time, for half of the seats on the 178 municipal consultative councils across the country. These would be the first nationwide elections in the history of the kingdom. As a *New York Times* editorial pointed out, the strictly advisory local councils "are far removed from issues like corruption, unemployment, women's rights and constitutional issues," although they do have the power to audit municipal budgets and prioritize local projects.[75] The real significance of the government's announcement was that it would hold elections at all, because many conservative Muslims do not believe in the rule of man but only in the *sharia*, the law of God.

Abdullah and many other Saudis think that local elections are the safest way to begin to teach the Saudi people about democracy. By contrast, they believe that an immediate election for a powerful national parliament would lead to bitter and possibly violent battles between militant fundamentalists and Western-oriented reformers. Abdullah and other cautious Saudis particularly want to avoid the experience of Algeria, where a disputed national election in 1991 led to a civil war and the deaths of more than 150,000 people. They would like to nurture a democracy gradually instead. "The steps have to come slowly so the society can accept it," said the mayor of Riyadh, Prince Abdul Aziz al-Mugrin, an appointee of the king, "but there is no going back."[76] Al-Mugrin has also said that he will personally recommend that women vote in the next set of municipal elections in 2009.

In the 2005 elections, all Saudi men who were twenty-one and older could vote unless they were currently serving in the military; the royal family did not want soldiers politicized. Television advertisements were forbidden; instead, candidates placed ads in newspapers, on billboards, and on the Internet. They also put up huge tents where voters could meet them and get something to eat, and in the Eastern Province, several candidates even had debates. Some of the nominees promised to improve parks and provide parking spaces for the handicapped. Others pledged to create community centers where people could get all of their government paperwork done in one building.

Before the campaign, only 25 percent of Riyadh's men registered to vote. After a lifetime without any say in the government, the initial attitude of most Saudis was skepticism. But once Saudis elsewhere read and heard about the first campaigns in Riyadh, interest in the elections increased, and in the rest of the kingdom, about 50 percent of the men registered to vote.

In most of the country, the winners were conservative but not reactionary professors who had been endorsed by leading clerics. In the words of one op-ed writer for the *Arab News*: "The citizens of Riyadh chose well and wisely. They ignored the rich and powerful who thought that pouring millions into advertising campaigns, parties and speeches would be enough. On election day, those who won were the ones who knew their neighborhoods well and worked hard on charities and social and community work before elections were even on the horizon."[77]

Even the kingdom's militant clerics welcomed the municipal elections as a first step toward greater democracy. There was no opposition to this relatively new way of electing Muslim leaders, probably because the Islamists know that they outnumber the reformers and therefore see democracy as a way to make the government more conservative. The elections familiarized the Saudis with the mechanics of voter registration, campaigning, poll watching, and vote counting, and since the vote, some council members have held town meetings to answer questions from their constituents. In general, however, while the new councils have rubber-stamped some budgets in 2006 and 2007, they have been completely powerless and may not have had any effect on municipal government at all.

Elsewhere in the Arabian peninsula, Qatar has been holding elections for its municipal councils since 1998 and Oman since 2003. While many Arab parliaments are shams, Kuwait, a monarchy, has an elected national parliament with real power, including the power to remove cabinet ministers.

In Saudi Arabia, Abdullah seems to understand that monarchy and democracy can be compatible. On April 14, 2005, a week before the third round of elections for the council seats, Abdullah asked a reporter from the French newspaper Le Monde, "How old is democracy in your country? And how long did it take to reach its present stage? We too will get there by the grace of God. . . . We are working on implementing true democracy, the democracy we want and wish for. I hope that can be achieved in the next twenty years."[78]

Similarly, Saud al-Faisal, the kingdom's foreign minister, has said that he looks forward to a time when the people will elect two-thirds of the members of the national legislature, the Majlis al-Shura.[79]

Although the kingdom's new election laws do not bar women from voting or running for office, in an announcement to the press on October 10, 2004, Prince Nayef, the minister of the interior, said, "I think that women's participation is out of the question." Officially, the government's reason for denying women the chance to vote was that there was not enough time to set up women's-only registration centers and polling booths. This was absurd, but the secular nature of this excuse pleased Saudi women immensely because no one was citing Islam as a reason for women not voting.

The government chose to be cautious in 2005. First, establish the principle of elections. Then let women vote. Barring a major change in the kingdom's political climate, almost everyone expects that Saudi women will vote for the first time in 2009. "We are not moving back," Prince Turki al-Faisal, Saudi Arabia's newly appointed ambassador to the United States, told PBS television interviewer Charlie Rose in February 2006. "In three years' time universal suffrage will be the standard."[80] When I interviewed Prince Turki three months later, however, he cautiously added that the approval of the Council of the Senior Clergy will be needed, but the prince was optimistic that the clerics will approve of women's suffrage.[81]

Elsewhere in the Gulf, women gained the right to vote and run for office in Bahrain in 2002 and in Oman and Qatar in 2003, and all three of these nations had female cabinet members by 2004. In Kuwait, women won the right to vote in 2005.

Saudi women did win a victory in June 2004 when the cabinet declared that a woman no longer needed the permission of a male guardian to obtain a business license. The purpose of this decree was to make it easier for Saudi women to work because, while women comprise 53 percent of the kingdom's high school graduates and 58 percent of its college graduates and own or partly own more than twenty-two thousand businesses, only 6 percent of Saudi women of working age actually have jobs. In 2006, the cabinet also repealed a regulation that had required businesswomen to hire male representatives, although today most Saudi men would still rather deal with a woman's *wakeel* (male representative) than with the female entrepreneur herself.

Women Attend the Jeddah Economic Forum

A group of Saudi businessmen, businesswomen, and foreign leaders met in Jeddah on January 17–19, 2004, to discuss the kingdom's need for economic and social changes. Former U.S. president Bill Clinton spoke and drew loud applause when he said that the Prophet Muhammad would have allowed his wives to drive if cars had existed in the 600s. Thurayya Arrayed, a female economist working for Aramco, told men on a panel, "even if you don't want your own daughter to drive, don't stop others." And Crown Prince Abdullah's daughter, Princess Adela, said that it is important that women actively participate in the nation's economy.

In 2000, women could not attend the Jeddah conference at all. In 2001, they had to sit in the balcony, were forbidden to speak, and could submit questions only in writing. Now, while a screen still separated the women in the audience from the men, a few brave women walked around the screen to talk to some of the men. In addition, for the first time in Saudi history, female speakers talked to men directly from the podium, rather than through closed-circuit television.

The forum's most notable speech was given by financier Lubna Olayan, the kingdom's richest businesswoman, and was broadcast live on ART, the Saudi-owned satellite network. Olayan criticized the widespread Saudi belief that it was possible to advance technologically without changing socially. "If we want progress in Saudi Arabia," Olayan said, "we have no choice but to embrace change."[82]

Unfortunately, while Olayan was giving her speech, her headscarf gradually slid back, revealing more and more of her hair, and she never readjusted it. *Asharq Al-Awsat* put a picture of Olayan and her hair on the front page, and *Okaz* ran a photograph of a group of twenty-seven women at the conference who covered their hair but not their faces (which is legal but bold).

Conservative clerics were outraged both by Olayan's hair and by the women who walked around the screen. Mecca's grand mufti, Abdul Aziz al-Sheikh (a descendant of ibn Abdul Wahhab), denounced "the obscene scenes of female wantonness at the Jiddah Economic Forum," where women did not "wear the *hijab* [headscarf] ordered by God."[83] The mufti also said, "I severely condemn this matter and warn of grave consequences. I am pained by such shameful behavior in [Saudi Arabia]. Allowing women to mix with men is the root of every evil and catastrophe . . . a reason for greater decadence and adultery."[84]

Significantly, the grand mufti did not question the need for the annual forum itself; even conservative clerics like economic growth. For conservatives, the issue is the rate of women's progress, not the trend itself. Two years later, at the 2006 forum, six hundred women still sat separately behind a screen, but in the press center in the back of the hall, male and female Saudi journalists worked and laughed together.[85]

Wife Beating and Other Family Issues

Three months after the Jeddah Economic Forum, another woman as famous as Lubna Olayan—Rania al-Baz, a young television personality—also made the front pages when her husband nearly beat her to death. The husband, an unsuccessful singer, had beaten her several times before, but al-Baz had never filed for a divorce for fear of losing custody of her children. This time, after her husband had repeatedly slammed her face into a marble floor at their luxurious home in Jeddah, he put her in a car and dumped her at the entrance to a hospital. A hospital worker took a photo with her cell phone, and the next morning the whole country saw al-Baz's bloody, bruised, and swollen face. Within weeks, one court granted al-Baz a divorce and sole custody of her two children, and another court found her husband guilty of aggravated assault and sentenced him to three hundred lashes and six months in prison. After the man served half of his sentence, however, al-Baz forgave her husband, which under Saudi law allowed him to go free.

Al-Baz suffered a broken nose and thirteen fractures, and she broke a taboo by giving interviews to reporters and allowing photographers to take pictures. In the past, Saudi women had endured beatings in silence because they did not want to tarnish their family's reputation and make it harder for their children to marry. Now there was suddenly a flood of newspaper articles about domestic abuse, and battered Saudi wives filed more than five hundred lawsuits. One study by a pediatrics professor at King Saud University found that 12 percent of Saudi children are beaten at least occasionally by parents or relatives. Another study by pediatricians in Jeddah found that this figure rises to 45 percent if beatings by school bullies are included.[86]

Even before al-Baz was beaten, a new law required hospital workers to report suspicious injuries to the police. The next year, in October 2005, the city of Mecca opened the kingdom's first center for victims of abuse, a place where 150 women and children can have temporary shelter if they need it. Within two years, there were women's centers in eight more cities, and the government also built special clinics for rape victims in Riyadh and Jeddah.

Recently, some hospitals and community centers have offered wife-beaters counseling. At first, most abusive husbands deeply resent any outside interference in what they consider a private matter, one Riyadh social worker, Samiha Hayder, told me. But in time, she said, about 60 percent of the husbands can be persuaded to stop their beatings.

These men may be lucky. Many husbands stop abusing their wives only after they themselves have been beaten by their wives' brothers and cousins. Saudi hospitals treat as many injured husbands as they do battered wives.

One interview that Rania al-Baz gave was to producers from the *Oprah Winfrey Show*. She had thought that her piece was about battered women around the world, but when the show aired on April 25, 2005, it was a general look at "Women across the Globe" that included happy women making chocolate in Belgium and bathing in hot springs in Iceland. Al-Baz's segment made no mention of the outrage the Saudi public had felt toward her husband or the fact that he had gone to prison.

The one-sidedness of the piece embarrassed al-Baz and made her feel that she had been victimized a second time.[87]

One controversy where Saudi Arabia deserves the bad publicity it has received involves dozens of children who were born in the United States to American mothers who later divorced their Saudi husbands. The Saudi fathers have violated U.S. court orders that awarded custody of the children to the mother and have taken their children to Saudi Arabia to raise them. They refuse to let their children return to the United States, even though the children are U.S. citizens. (Under Saudi law, no woman or child, even an American, can leave the country unless a husband or a father approves.) In many cases, Saudi fathers have married their half-American daughters to other Saudis because once a girl has a child, she rarely wants to go to the United States, knowing that it means leaving her baby behind.

In September 2002, Prince Saud al-Faisal, the kingdom's foreign minister, announced that any adult American woman who wishes to leave Saudi Arabia can do so even without the permission of her male guardian. He did not say anything about half-American children, however, or address the fact that most girls in this situation marry before they reach adulthood.

Prince Saud has also said that Saudi Arabia does not recognize U.S. child custody laws. Although the foreign minister is one of the most enlightened men in the kingdom (he once said, "Nowhere in the Quran does it say that women are not allowed to drive cars, have the right to vote, or choose their career"), on this issue he uncharacteristically misses the point.[88] The United States is not asking the Saudi people to follow U.S. law. It asks only that Saudis living in the United States obey U.S. laws. American, not Saudi, law applies here because the Saudi husbands chose to live, marry, and have children in the United States. They then illegally abducted American children.

A Wider Choice of Careers, a Limited Choice of Husbands

"We girls are suffocating inside the four walls," one girl wrote to the *Arab News*. "What do we do to pass our time? Watch TV, read books. Listen to music and surf the Internet."[89] Seeking alternatives, almost 80 percent of Saudi women say that it is acceptable for women to work outside the home, according to a 2005 Zogby poll, and surprisingly, more than half of the men polled agreed.[90] Yet only a small minority of Saudi women work or consider themselves feminists.

Most Saudi women object to the Western word *liberation* and instead quote writer Juhayer al-Musa'ed, who said that Muslim women need to free themselves not from men, but *with* men. "It's less about changing legislation than changing attitudes," one woman told an Irish reporter.[91]

A Saudi woman cannot work without the written approval of her father or husband, and even then, she can deal with male supervisors and clients only by e-mail, telephone, or fax. To get a telephone or a fax line of her own, she must provide a second letter from her male guardian. Even a Saudi woman who owns her own business must usually hire a male manager if any of her clients are men. Not surprisingly, although more women than men graduate from Saudi high schools and colleges, Saudi women still make up only 6 percent of the kingdom's workforce, about one-eighth of the comparable percentage in East Asia. Among Saudi women who work, 85 percent have careers in education, health care, or government because gender segregation makes work in the private sector impractical, except in beauty salons and clothing stores.

A few women have made spectacular strides. In November 2004, Captain Hanadi Hindi became Saudi Arabia's first licensed female jet pilot, an ironic achievement since she is not permitted to drive a car. Captain Hindi, who learned to fly in Jordan, is a pilot for Prince Alwaleed bin Talal, the financier who is worth more than $20 billion. Prince Alwaleed also hired the kingdom's first female racing jockey, Alia al-Howaite.

In December 2005, Dr. Nahed Taher became the first Saudi woman to chair a large investment bank, Gulf One, which, although it is headquartered in Bahrain, primarily serves Saudi investors. In that same month, thousands of businessmen in Jeddah elected two women to the board of directors of their city's chamber of commerce, and a national society of five thousand engineers, 99.6 percent male, elected a woman to serve as one of the society's ten directors. A few weeks later, in February 2006, the foreign minister, Prince Saudi al-Faisal, announced that he planned to appoint five women to top diplomatic posts.

Most women, of course, need more ordinary jobs. To reduce the kingdom's dependence on foreign labor, the government allocated $2.4 billion for technical colleges and training institutes in 2006, including schools where women can learn to be beauticians, tailors, caterers, nutritionists, decorators, marketers, photographers, jewelry makers, and Web designers. A new regulation in 2005 gave women four weeks of maternity leave before childbirth and six weeks afterward. It also required businesses with fifty or more employees to provide day-care centers for all working mothers with children under age six, although in 2007 this provision had yet to be enforced.

The government's most unusual initiative is the planning of an all-female industrial city near Jeddah, where companies from China and Malaysia will train twenty thousand women to work in more than eighty factories. That Saudi women no longer look down on factory work became clear in 2003, when fifteen hundred women applied for jobs at a high-tech dairy farm outside Riyadh. Two all-female factories that produce light fixtures also began to operate near Riyadh.

While career choices for Saudi women are expanding, the opportunity for a woman to meet a man outside her family is almost nonexistent, as the Saudis continue to maintain the world's strictest gender segregation. Restaurants, offices, and even homes have separate sections for men and women. In places where the sexes do mix, such as hospitals, supermarkets, and shopping malls, it is nevertheless taboo to talk with anyone of the opposite sex unless that person is a relative or a fellow employee of the establishment.

Sometimes Saudi women can meet suitable Saudi men (they are prohibited from marrying foreigners) in other nations in the Gulf. In Kuwait, Bahrain, Qatar, and the United Arab Emirates, women work, drive, and study with men. Some women in the Gulf States wear tight-fitting *abayas* that highlight their figures, clothing that is banned in Saudi Arabia. Even in the kingdom, however, more women are wearing *abayas* embroidered or beaded with colorful stripes, floral and paisley patterns, butterflies, peacocks, and even Hello Kitty logos.

In Jeddah, a few sophisticated young Saudi men and women sip drinks at the Java Lounge, a co-ed, no-alcohol nightclub that so far has avoided being shut down by the religious police because the ground floor is for men only and the second floor has a partition that the staff can put up at a moment's notice.

The overwhelming majority of young Saudis, of course, have no access to the opposite sex and are completely dependent on their relatives to introduce them to suitable young men or women. Sometimes two mothers arrange for their children to meet, and lightning strikes. More often, it seems safer or more comfortable to marry a cousin rather than a stranger. Forty-five percent of the marriages in the Arab world are between cousins. In Saudi Arabia, the figure is 55 percent, and along the kingdom's southern border with Yemen, it is almost 70 percent.[92] Inbreeding leads to a higher incidence of genetic disorders such as deafness, sickle cell anemia, and spinal muscular atrophy and also to blood diseases such as hemoglobin deficiency and diabetes.

The worst drawback of limiting a woman's contact with men is that it increases the chances of an unhappy marriage. One woman I talked with, a hospital worker, married a cousin who became abusive. She married him when she graduated from high school because she had only two cousins near her own age, and she was afraid that the other cousin would be worse.

Despite gender segregation, most Saudi women are quick to tell you that they are reasonably happy. "We are not as miserable and submissive as you think," a social worker told me, trying to dispel the common Western stereotype of Saudi women, "and we often have the final say in the house." Compared to other Arabs, Saudi women are rich and well educated, and marrying a cousin often works out fine. One elegant homemaker, Monera, told me that when she turned eighteen, she received proposals from four slightly older cousins. She chose her favorite, and they have been happily married for more than thirty years.

Medieval Judges, Promising Legal Reforms

Saudi Arabia's police departments are run by Prince Nayef, who once dismissed recent calls for reform as "useless barking." His domain, the Ministry of the Interior, employs more than two hundred thousand uniformed officers, electronically listens to hundreds of telephone conversations, and occasionally detains people for weeks without letting them see a relative or a lawyer. Usually, however, the Saudi police either release or indict a prisoner within days of his arrest. And beatings, while still common, are declining.

Much worse than the police, from the standpoint of human rights, are *sharia* (Islamic) judges who preside over family and criminal cases. The minister of Islamic affairs appoints the judges, but once in office, they are independent of the ministry and are free to ignore pleas for mercy, a public trial, or even impartiality.

Islamic judges continue to order about a half dozen amputations for robbery each year, and typically, the amputees are non-Saudis from Asia or Africa. Amputations are not the only medieval relics in the kingdom's legal system. In August 2005, a judge in Mecca affirmed a sentence of eight thousand lashes for a woman who had kidnapped a child, but a lengthy appeal is still pending. In December, a *sharia* judge in Dammam ruled that a citizen of India, Puthan Noushad, should have his right eye gouged out because Noushad had struck a Saudi in the eye with a jumper cable while defending himself in a fight that the Saudi had started when he could not get a refund for the cable. A month later, however, the Saudi who lost his eye agreed to accept money in lieu of the judge's sentence.

The most notorious example of an inhumane judgment occurred on November 13, 2007, when the General Court of the city of Qatif sentenced a twenty-year-old Shi'ite woman, who had been gang-raped at knifepoint by seven men, to two hundred lashes and six months in jail because prior to the rapes she had been in a car with a young man who was not her relative. The verdict was widely condemned in Saudi Arabia and around the world, and on December 17, King Abdullah pardoned "the Qatif girl," as the unidentified woman has become known to the Saudi public.

Executions in Saudi Arabia numbered thirty-two in 2004, eighty-six in 2005, thirty-eight in 2006, and almost a hundred in the first half of 2007. More than half of the men beheaded (executions of women are rare) are drug dealers, so the spikes in executions in 2005 and 2007 suggest that there has been a rise in drug trafficking. The most popular drugs in Saudi Arabia are hashish, speed, and heroin, and one poor neighborhood in Jeddah, Kerantina, is so dangerous that at night the police are absent and drug dealers sell their wares openly.

In an effort to reduce the kingdom's small but growing drug problem, the Saudi cabinet passed an unusually enlightened law in July 2005 offering amnesty and complete confidentiality to drug addicts who are willing to undergo medical treatment.

Between 1996 and 2000, Saudi Arabia signed four UN treaties to ensure the rights of the child (1996), an end to racism (1997), an end to torture (1997), and an end to discrimination against women (2000). The Saudis signed these four documents with the reservation that they cannot supercede the *sharia* (the Quran and the sayings and the deeds of Muhammad); nevertheless, the treaties are clearly a major step toward legal reform.

In March 2004, the government asked thirty-one men and ten women, most of them professors, to form the National Society for Human Rights (NSHR). Their first assignment was to visit prisons across the country, talk to inmates, and submit a detailed report of their findings to the minister of the interior, Prince Nayef, and to the director of the prison system. The contents of this report have remained secret, but the society did say that while conditions at most prisons are good, the prisons are also badly overcrowded. Eighty percent of the kingdom's prisoners are foreigners, the NHSR reported, and some have waited many months and even years for their trials. While the Ministry of Justice's response to the report has been slow, the ministry has promised to create faster-moving courts so that no prisoner will have to wait more than six months for a trial. The NSHR is also planning to produce some television commercials to educate the Saudi public about human rights and several short films to inform expatriates, especially housekeepers, about their rights under Saudi law.

By 2007, the NSHR had opened offices in Riyadh, Jeddah, Dammam, and Jizan and had received more than eighty-five hundred complaints of government and employer injustice and prison and domestic abuse. Some human rights activists question whether the NSHR can be independent of the Ministry of the Interior because the organization prefers to negotiate quietly with government agencies, rather than file lawsuits. But the day-to-day effectiveness of the NSHR may not be as important as the existence of the society itself. Wardens, guards, and police interrogators are more likely to refrain from violence knowing that forty-one officials working for Prince Nayef can investigate them at any time.

On May 21, 2007, the NSHR published its first annual report on human rights in the kingdom. Praising recent progress but detailing the need for more reform, the NSHR called for more freedom of expression, search and arrest warrants, investigations of beatings, and rights for women, religious minorities, and foreign workers. The sixty-seven-page document also called for an end to the sponsorship system for foreign workers and for the creation of a supreme court with the power to declare laws unconstitutional if they conflict with human rights treaties that Saudi Arabia has signed. The report was front-page news in Saudi newspapers, and King Abdullah not only praised the report but established a ten-man supreme court (and new commercial, labor, and family courts) five months later.

The king has also created a second organization, the Human Rights Commission, that, unlike the National Society for Human Rights, can *publicize* the violations of human rights that it encounters. This commission, which did not begin work until 2007, can inspect prisons without any official permission or advance notice and can question officials and demand information from any government agency.

Most important, the Human Rights Commission bypasses the Ministry of the Interior and reports directly to Abdullah, which could make it difficult for the ministry to postpone a reform or cover up a violation. The commission is also seeking to codify some of the sentences that are currently left to the discretion of Islamic judges, which would go a long way toward eliminating many of the kingdom's most inhumane punishments.

The very existence of the two commissions may also change the public's view of what law enforcement agencies should and should not do.

More Books, More Schools, More Students Abroad

The Saudis spend many millions of dollars translating and publishing the Quran, the sayings of Muhammad, and scholarly works on Islam into other languages, yet there is no comparable effort to translate foreign books into Arabic. The 2002 United Nations *Arab Human Development Report* says that fewer than 350 books a year are translated into Arabic, less than one-fifth the number of books translated annually into Greek. In most countries, only 5 percent of published books are religious in nature, but in the Arab world, the number is 17 percent, and in Saudi Arabia, it is even higher.

"The best books have to be smuggled in," wrote one young Saudi blogger. Until recently, the three novels in Turki al-Hamad's trilogy, *Adama*, *Shumaisi*, and *Karadib*, were banned in Saudi Arabia because the main character hires a prostitute, joins an underground political organization, and makes fun of some well-known religious books. A fourth book by al-Hamid, *Reeh al-Jannah*, a novel about the 9/11 hijackers, continues to be forbidden. Even *The Insane Asylum*, a gentle satire by Ghazi al-Gosaibi, the current minister of labor, has been banned because it pokes fun at the Saudi government.

Another novel, *A Heart from Banqalan*, about a wife in King Saud's harem a generation ago, is also prohibited. Written by her son Prince Saif al-Islam ibn Saud, the book was published in Beirut in 2004 but disappeared from Lebanon's bookstores almost immediately because of either pressure or bribery from the Saudi royal family.[93]

Many works of Western literature are never translated into Arabic at all. Not surprisingly, with so many Arabic novels banned and foreign books untranslated, a recent survey of high school students in Riyadh found that fewer than one in six read for pleasure. The kingdom's roughly 250 public libraries are far too few for a nation of twenty-six million people, but in 2005, they at least began to set aside hours for female readers.

The government may have turned a corner in February 2006 when it eased its censorship and allowed the Ministry of Education to sponsor Riyadh's first International Book Fair. At least 500 Saudi and foreign publishers exhibited more than 150,000 books in Arabic, including the Bible, the trilogy by Turki al-Hamad, dozens of other previously banned books, and nearly a hundred contemporary Saudi novels on social issues such as divorce, teenage alienation, and the impact of satellite television. One book, *The Girls of Riyadh*, by Rajaa al-Sanea, about four wealthy female Saudi university students and their search for love, caused a particular stir when some conservative scholars filed a lawsuit against the author, a young female dentist, for "slandering" Saudi society. The case was dismissed. Today, more than five thousand books a year are published in Saudi Arabia, the third-highest number in the Arab world, after Egypt and Lebanon. Publishers at the book fair also exhibited more than a hundred thousand books in English, French, German, and other foreign languages.

Not everybody was happy with the fair. When a female poet and a female novelist had a book signing, a dozen religious policemen arrived, ordered the women to cover their faces (they had already covered their hair), and loudly demanded that the fair's organizers put up a partition to separate the men in the audience from the women.

"Why are you harassing her?" someone asked. "She is a poet signing a book. What's wrong with that?"

"Mind your own business, woman," replied a *mutaween*.

The poet explained to the religious policeman that she was wearing an *abaya* and covering her hair, and that many Muslim scholars say that a woman does not have to cover her face.

"You're wrong," one of the *mutaween* shouted. "Covering your face is a must."

Another *mutaween* yelled, "If you were an educated woman, you wouldn't be sitting in front of men showing your face."

At last, the religious policemen left the room, threatening to put an end to the book signing, although in fact it continued without further incident.[94] At a similar fair in Jeddah that autumn, the sponsors forbade book signings, but authors held signings again at Riyadh's Book Fair in 2007. One of the most talked about books at this fair was *The Others*, by Sada al-Haize (a pseudonym), about the daily lives of lesbians in Saudi Arabia. More than a quarter of a million people attended the 2007 fair, with at least half of them women.

Saudi Arabia devotes more than 25 percent of its budget, an amount greater than $25 billion a year, to education and technical training. "Education is the basis of all progress," Abdullah told a reporter from the newspaper *Asharq Al-Awsat*.[95] The government is currently building more than twenty-seven hundred new primary and secondary schools, equipped with computers and modern laboratories; eighteen large technical and vocational training centers; and six new universities in the cities of Jizan, Hail, al-Jawf, Tabuk, Abha, and Baha. It is also constructing a medical school in Dammam and a new engineering college in Riyadh that will be partly staffed by teachers from the Boeing Corporation. A foundation run by the children of King Faisal has built Alfaisal University, a private college in Riyadh that by 2009 will offer advanced English-language courses in science, engineering, medicine, and business administration. Eventually, its founders hope, the college will become a great technical university. It has already signed an agreement with the Massachusetts Institute of Technology to do joint research in biotechnology.

Although the student-teacher ratio in Saudi Arabia is only fourteen to one, one of the lowest in the world, the Saudi educational system has many deficiencies. Few teachers encourage their students to ask questions in class, and almost none ask students for their opinions. One Saudi woman told me that during her first months as a freshman at Boston University, she was completely flustered and tongue-tied whenever a professor asked for her opinion during a class discussion.

Learning in Saudi Arabia is mostly a matter of repetition and memorization. "Our educational system is sterile," said Prince Khalid al-Faisal, the governor of Mecca, "our children don't know how to engage in dialogue, but [only] to obey blindly."[96]

One-third of the Saudi high school curriculum is devoted to Islam, which leaves insufficient time to teach other subjects. Many college freshmen find that they have to take remedial courses in math and science, and a study by one newspaper found that only 9 percent of Saudi high school graduates are proficient in English. Many of the rest struggle when they go to college because much of the coursework in medicine, engineering, and other technical subjects is in English. About a third of Saudi college students avoid technical subjects and foreign languages altogether by majoring in Islamic studies, earning degrees that are not taken seriously by scholars elsewhere, even in the Muslim world. At present, only two Saudi universities are highly regarded by foreigners: King Saud University in Riyadh and the University of Petroleum and Minerals in Dhahran.

A highly respected women's prep school in Jeddah, Effat Women's College, became the kingdom's first private women's college in August 1999, just months before the death of the school's founder, Queen Effat, King Faisal's widow. All classes at the college are in English, and in 2005, the college began a program with Duke University in which Duke sends Effat several professors each semester to teach women computer sciences and electrical engineering, and Effat sends Duke several women with bachelor's degrees in engineering to do graduate work. Effat has worked with Cisco Systems to offer women a variety of new courses in computer routing and networking.

The government is merging six public women's colleges in Riyadh into one large all-female university, and it has similar plans for women's colleges in other cities. It is also building an all-female research center in Riyadh where women with master's degrees and doctorates in the sciences will use biotechnology to improve crop yields and nanotechnology to enhance petrochemical production.

Before 9/11, more than five thousand young Saudis studied at U.S. colleges every year. Visa procedures for Saudis were so lax before 9/11 that some of the hijackers did not even answer all of the questions on their application forms. Since then, procedures have been tightened considerably. An applicant is fingerprinted (ten fingers, not just one), photographed without a headdress or *abaya*, and finally, after delays of four to five months, interviewed in Riyadh by a visa security officer from the U.S. Department of Homeland Security, who often wants details about the applicant's prior trips to other Muslim countries. "The whole thing made me feel like a criminal," said one young math teacher who had hoped to earn his PhD at the University of Indiana but finally went to the University of Manchester in Britain.

In 2003, wary U.S. officials even denied visas to half of the Muslims who had won Fulbright scholarships that year. More common than denial, however, is delay. Many students have had to postpone their American studies for a semester or even a year while waiting for an interview at the U.S. embassy.

Not surprisingly, the number of Saudi students in U.S. schools fell to just 25 percent of their pre-9/11 levels during the 2003–2004 school year. Thousands of Saudis simply gave up their dream of studying in the United States and applied to schools in Canada, Britain, Australia, and New Zealand instead. Americans and Saudis both worried whether this trend might harm U.S.-Saudi relations in the future. Currently, more than two-thirds of the men in Saudi Arabia's cabinet have graduate degrees from the United States, and the goodwill this creates is incalculable. Saudis studying abroad are "the future leaders of our country," said Yusof Rafie, Saudi Aramco's senior vice president for industrial relations. "I don't want to lose the American heritage."[97]

By the spring of 2005, the number of Saudis studying in the United States had almost returned to pre-9/11 levels, but it still takes nearly half a year for a student to get a visa. With a backlog of thousands of applications, Saudis usually have to wait more than three months before they can get an appointment for an interview with a Homeland Security officer. One reason the backlog is so large is that the United States has closed its consulate in Jeddah because it is too close to busy streets and therefore too vulnerable to terrorists. As a result, thousands of visa applications that used to be handled there now have to be processed at the U.S. embassy in Riyadh.

At his ranch in Crawford, Texas, in April 2005, President Bush assured Crown Prince Abdullah that he understood the need for the United States to ease its visa procedures. The State Department soon helped things considerably when it began to triple the number of student visas it issued and made them valid for four years instead of only one.

Shortly after this summit, Abdullah started a scholarship program to send more than twenty-five thousand students abroad. More than 70 percent of them are undergraduates or students of English as a second language. More than fifteen thousand are going to the United States, mostly to state universities, but more than five thousand Saudis are attending universities in Britain, which often issues visas in only one day. More than twenty-five hundred Saudis are studying in Canada, and another several thousand are in East Asia studying science, computers, and engineering at universities in Malaysia, South Korea, China, and Singapore, as well as Australia. The Ministry of Higher Education gives each student a full four-year scholarship, typically worth $31,000 a year, and also helps with visa applications by providing foreign governments with recommendation letters and bank guarantees.

About fifteen hundred of the Saudis at U.S. universities are women, and almost half of them are in programs for master's degrees. Most of these women are married, studying in the United States at the same time as their husbands.

In a few years, there will be more Westerners teaching in Saudi Arabia. A German-Saudi business school will open in the city of Sudair in 2008, and several universities in Texas are helping the Saudis start a new college, Prince Muhammad ibn Fahd University, with classes taught only in English. The Saudis are also seriously considering letting some British universities open branches in the kingdom.

The presence of Western professors in the kingdom might spur Saudi universities to become more lively. At present, no Saudi university offers a course in Western or Asian religion or literature, and student committees, which are dominated by Muslim militants, prevent any performances of Western music or theater. Even at prestigious

King Saud University, conservative Muslim professors and students succeeded in closing the school's theater department in 2000. But the true purpose of a university is to open minds, not only to teach technical skills. If Islam is to have a prominent role in the world's multicultural future, Muslims must not shun other cultures but must learn from them with enthusiasm.

More Cell Phones and Use of the Internet

By the spring of 2006, almost every Saudi adult, the majority of Saudi teenagers, and more than half of the kingdom's foreign workers each had a cell phone. The number of subscribers doubled between 2003 and 2006, to more than 14.5 million.

Seventy percent of the kingdom's cell phone towers belong to Saudi Telecom, a giant government company that privatized itself in 1998 in order to become more efficient, then sold 30 percent of its shares to the Saudi public in 2002 to raise the money it needed to provide more cell phone service. At the beginning of 2005, the government allowed a second firm, Ettihad Etisalat, jointly owned by Saudi and United Arab Emirates investors, to compete for cell phone subscribers. Within two years, it set up the Mobily phone service and acquired 6.5 million customers.

When the Saudi government awarded this license to Ettihad Etisalat, many people were surprised that the company did not have a single Saudi prince as an investor. In a big departure from previous practice, the Saudi government published all six of the final bids for the telecommunications license so that everyone could see that at $3.25 billion, Ettihad Etisalat was truly the highest bidder. (The second-highest bidder was a South African company, MTN, at $2.94 billion.) The government plans to allow a third company to begin competing for cell phone users late in 2008.

With more than fourteen million cell phones in use, the Saudis talk freely because they know that today, even if the government wanted to, it could not possibly monitor more than the tiniest fraction of the nation's telephone conversations.

Sixty-three percent of the Saudi people had access to the Internet by the summer of 2003, according to a Zogby poll, up from 13 percent in 2001. The only Saudis who do not have Internet access today are those who just don't want it.

A government agency, the Communication and Information Technology Commission (CITC), censors thousands of Web sites. Ninety percent of the blocked sites are pornographic; the rest are devoted to gambling, al-Qaeda, religions other than Sunni Islam, dirty jokes, homosexuality, and sites such as megaproxy.com that allow one to bypass government censors. The blocked sites make up about 2 to 3 percent of the World Wide Web, but many Saudis have become experts at hacking into the forbidden sites or reopening them under new names. Some of the more than one thousand Saudi bloggers openly call the censors "jackasses," but while the government blocks sites where people talk too freely about sex or religion, it generally censors political opinions only when someone questions the royal family's legitimacy or directly criticizes a high official.

In June 2004, the IBM Corporation rated Saudi Arabia forty-fifth in "e-readiness" among the world's sixty largest economies, but since then, the government has moved the kingdom farther into the digital age. In July 2005, a government agency sold one million personal computers to lower-middle-class Saudis at subsidized prices, so today there is a computer for every two Saudis. In January 2006, the government awarded large contracts to Cisco Systems, Lucent Technologies, and Alcatel to build more than 250,000 new digital subscriber lines (DSLs) in order to create a broadband network accessible to three-fourths of the kingdom's people by January 2007. Three months later, several women Saudi investors started a joint venture with a German software company to create a new Arabic-language search engine called *Sawafi* ("Sandstorm") to challenge Google. The government also hired the Intel Corporation in 2007 to begin training fifty thousand teachers how to use information technology in the classroom.

Satellite Television Brings the World to Saudi Homes

The spread of satellite television has been dramatic. By 2005, 91 percent of Saudi Arabians watched satellite television regularly, and already there were 150 Arabic-language channels. By 2008 there were 370.

More than 60 percent of Saudis watch Western networks, too, especially the Disney Channel. In 2003, Saudi children spent an average of 3.1 hours a day watching cartoons, television shows, music videos, and movies, according to a survey by Merlin, a consumer research firm, and the programming choices available today are even wider.

Teenagers and young adults enjoy a show called *Star Academy*, a clone of *American Idol* where millions of young Arabs who have never voted in a political election vote by telephone for their favorite singer. Saudis who understand English also watch satellite broadcasts of suggestive shows such as *Friends* and *Sex and the City*. The majority who do not understand a foreign language are more likely to watch Egyptian and Lebanese soap operas, but even these Saudis watch many Western movies and police shows with Arabic subtitles.

A quiz show called *Who Will Win a Million?* was the Arab world's number-one show for several years. *Al Shamshoon*, a remake of *The Simpsons*, where Omar Shamshoon goes to a coffeehouse instead of a bar, began broadcasts on the MBC (Middle East Broadcasting Center) network in October 2005.

Music videos are especially popular. Although many Saudis have access to MTV, most prefer Arab music channels, including three owned by Alwaleed bin Talal, the Saudi prince worth more than $20 billion. Rotana Clip, a channel aimed at Arabs in their teens and twenties, is extremely popular because it allows viewers to display text messages on the TV screen. Rotana One is geared to twenty-five- to forty-five-year-olds, and Rotana Classic plays Arab golden oldies. Their music videos show little or no skin beyond the face and the hands. Most of the singers are Egyptian and Lebanese; the people of the Gulf agree that they are the region's best performers. MTV itself launched an Arab music channel, MTV Arabia, in Dubai in November 2007.

Prince Alwaleed will soon launch two more channels devoted to movies, and in 2006, he produced a movie himself: Saudi Arabia's first feature film, *How's It Going?* The comedy is about the admiration a secular young Saudi feels for his fundamentalist cousin's pretty sister, and the sister's struggle to pursue a career despite her family's conservatism.

Ironically, *How's It Going?* was shown in every Gulf state but Saudi Arabia because the kingdom still has no movie theaters. The Saudis had to be content with pay-per-view broadcasts on Showtime Arabia. Many Saudi clerics fear that cinemas would allow young men and women to mingle in the dark, although Salman al-Awda, one of the Awakening Sheikhs who opposed the presence of U.S. troops in the kingdom, said, "Movies are a huge industry in the West which often targets Islam, so if setting up a film industry will do justice to Islam, this is a good demand and a good thing."[98]

In Jeddah, several commercial real estate developers have already built movie theaters in their shopping malls in anticipation of the day when theaters will be legal, although at present this still seems a number of years off. In November 2005, however, the government allowed Riyadh's InterContinental Hotel to show cartoons at night to women and children in a twelve-hundred-seat theater during the

Eid al Fitr holiday season. It was the kingdom's first public movie screening in decades, although many outdoor cafes for men routinely show movies on large flat-screen TVs.

The associate producer of *How's It Going?* Haifa al-Mansur caused a huge controversy in 2005 when she released a documentary, *Women with No Shadow*, that starred a reform-minded cleric who says that Islam does not require a woman to cover her face but only to dress modestly. Al-Mansur also began hosting a newsmagazine show called *A Woman and More*, which is devoted to the struggles of Saudi women for more rights, on the Lebanese LBC network in April 2007.

Just fifteen years ago, before the arrival of the satellite dish, the only news broadcasts available to the Arabs were "iron curtain"–style shows of leaders cutting ribbons and greeting foreign dignitaries. Today, this is still the main fare of the Saudi government's original news channel, although its coverage of prayer services in Mecca can be quite moving.

In 2003, the government launched a second news channel that soon had female anchors who not only report the news with their faces uncovered, but even interview men. When a Saudi cleric said on a Lebanese talk show in March 2007 that it is forbidden for women to show their faces on television, Saudi newscaster Buthayna Nasser replied,

> Sir, when I appear on TV, and when I claim my right to play a role in this professional field, I demand that my face, which constitutes my identity, be seen. . . . Why is it that there is always a male voice deciding how I should behave? . . . I know what I am doing and I know how to maintain my honor. . . .
>
> You, who frighten people with Hell, have brought [young Muslims] a hell upon earth. You have banned books of various intellectual streams. You've prevented the mind from operating, thinking, comparing and choosing, even though it is the same mind the Creator gave people in order to choose between Paradise and Hell.[99]

As this excerpt makes clear, Arabs today have access to a wide variety of political and religious opinions. By far the most influential Arab channel is Al Jazeera (The Peninsula), which has been broadcasting from Qatar since 1996. Al Jazeera's highly professional Muslim reporters showed graphic videos of the Palestinian *intifada* in 2000, the U.S. bombing of Afghanistan in 2001, and the U.S. invasion of Iraq in 2003, often from vantage points that were unavailable to Western reporters. As a result, Al Jazeera's audience grew rapidly, and today it numbers more than forty million viewers.

Al Jazeera irritates the U.S. government because it has called the Americans in Iraq "occupiers" and the Palestinian suicide bombers "martyrs." It has also angered the Saudi government because it broadcasts audiotapes of Osama bin Laden, gives airtime to Israeli officials, and, worst of all, has invited opponents of the Saudi monarchy to appear as guests on its talk shows. Ironically, while much of the advertising on Al Jazeera is aimed at the Saudi public, which economically is the biggest market in the Middle East, Saudi businesses refuse to buy advertising time on the network because of the guests who question the Saudi royal family's legitimacy. Until Qatar's government, seeking Saudi support against a resurgent Iran, finally ordered Al Jazeera in September 2007 to soften its coverage of Saudi Arabia, the Saudi government did not even let Al Jazeera reporters into the kingdom.

To challenge Al Jazeera, a group of Saudi, Kuwaiti, and Lebanese investors, led by Walid al-Ibrahim, a brother-in-law of King Fahad, launched a new and less strident news network, Al Arabiya, in 2003. The network's purpose, al-Ibrahim said, was to be a more responsible "CNN to Al Jazeera's Fox News." Although Al Arabiya's ratings in the Arab world are well below those of Al Jazeera, one-third of Arab viewers watch Al Arabiya at least twice a week, and in Iraq and Saudi Arabia, the audiences that watch the two news networks are about even in size.

Al Arabiya is based in Dubai, which in 2001 built "Media City," an office park where television networks, news magazines, and software companies are free to broadcast, print, or e-mail anything they like other than pornography and blasphemy. While most of Al Arabiya's news reporting is excellent—its coverage of the war in Iraq is far more balanced than Al Jazeera's—the network rarely criticizes the Saudi government because its biggest investors are Saudi. Recently, the BBC and France 24 have started Arabic-language television news channels, seeking to be more critical than Al Arabiya and more balanced than Al Jazeera.

With names like *No Limits*, *More Than One Opinion*, *The Opposite Direction*, and *Open Dialogue*, the talk shows on Al Jazeera are even more influential than its newscasts. Guests are chosen to oppose one another, and viewers are invited to call and join in. On one show, a conservative cleric was so upset by a Jordanian feminist's interpretation of the Quran that he stormed off the set. On another show in 2000, an Iraqi caller denounced Saddam Hussein. In 2004, after broadcasting a videotape by al-Qaeda's second in command, Ayman al-Zawahiri, Al Jazeera invited four moderate clerics to refute al-Zawahiri's video, one point at a time.[100]

Never before have so many different political and even religious points of view been presented to the Arab public. As Marc Lynch, a professor at Williams College and an expert on Al Jazeera, has written, "In the short term, the station may well have strengthened anti-American sentiment in the region. But in a longer view, Al Jazeera and its Arab competitors are creating perhaps the most essential underpinning of liberal democracy: a free and open critical public space, independent of the state, where citizens can speak their piece and expect to be heard."[101]

Foreigners: Two-Thirds of the Workforce

In May 2004, Saudi Arabia's energetic new minister of labor, Ghazi al-Gosaibi, shocked the nation when he announced that 8.8 million foreigners lived in the kingdom, about 2 million more than previous estimates. Foreigners today comprise one-third of the kingdom's people, two-thirds of its workforce, and more than 85 percent of the employees in the private sector.

More than half of the kingdom's foreigners, about 4.7 million people, come from South Asia: India, Bangladesh, Pakistan, Sri Lanka, and Nepal. Another 1.2 million are from the Philippines, and more than 600,000 are from Indonesia. In all, about 6.5 million of the kingdom's 9 million foreigners come from South and Southeast Asia. They are far less likely to stay in the kingdom or engage in political activity than are the 2 million immigrants from Egypt, Yemen, Palestine, and other Arab nations. Americans and Europeans make up only about 1 percent of the workforce.

Often, five or six South Asians share a room with just a concrete floor, one small window, and no air conditioning. They live either at their boss's work site or in small but crowded slums that Saudis sometimes call "Little Delhis." Egyptians and Syrians typically work as clerks and teachers. Immigrants from Asia and Yemen often toil twelve hours a day or more as construction workers, farm hands, chauffeurs, taxi drivers, and fruit and vegetable sellers or, if they have skills, as plumbers, welders, carpenters, and electricians.

Most of the kingdom's foreigners make only several hundred dollars a month, live on half of that, and send the other half to their families. Even the small amount they send, however, is often double what they can make back home. To come to Saudi Arabia, though, immigrants must often sell land or jewelry to raise $1,500 for a recruiter and another $1,000 for plane tickets and visa fees. They must also arrive with about three months' savings because many employers withhold the first three months' pay from their workers to prevent them from quitting to take other jobs. They are paid the first three months' wages only when their two- or three-year employment contracts expire.

Foreigners lose money in other ways, too. A young Nigerian with a radiant smile who works as a security guard in an office building told me that he was once involved in a six-car accident. No one was injured, but because he was the only foreigner in the pile-up, the police concluded that he was mainly at fault and needed to pay $4,000 in damages—a year and a half's savings. The Nigerian's only choice was to pay the money or return home.

More than half of Saudi families have a maid or a nanny, usually from Indonesia, Sri Lanka, Nepal, or the Philippines. For years, they earned only $100 to $200 a month, but in 2007, the Philippine, Indian, Indonesian, and Sri Lankan governments asked for and secured a gradual doubling of the wage to $200 to 400 a month, with at least one day off every ten days and a month off every two years. Most Saudis treat their servants well but with less courtesy than most Westerners use. Rather than saying, "Come here, please," for example, a Saudi is likely to say only, "Come!"

With roughly two million nannies and maids in the kingdom, horror stories are inevitable. Some young women have been locked in their rooms and even beaten by cruel employers. In August 2007, two Indonesian maids were killed when seven of their Saudi employers accused them of witchcraft and beat them to death. The seven Saudis were arrested and await trail.

Dozens of Sri Lankan maids flee their employers' homes each month to seek help from their embassy, and the numbers are similar for Filipinas and Indonesians. Usually, these women live in special shelters for several months until the paperwork allowing them to return home is complete. In 2004, six Indonesian maids committed suicide, possibly because they had been raped.

In contrast to the Saudi government's indifference to the abuse of housekeepers in the past, in May 2004, the Ministry of Labor began to keep a list of families that harassed their employees. After a first offense, the head of household must sign a written promise to stop such conduct. After a second offense, the family can no longer hire foreign servants (and there are no Saudi servants). Within a year, the Ministry of Labor banned hundreds of Saudis from hiring foreigners, although it is too soon to tell whether the new system has truly succeeded in reducing the abuse of Asian maids.

The Ministry of Labor created a Department for the Protection of Domestic Workers in August 2005 and threatened criminal prosecution against those who continued to abuse their servants. It also enacted a new law that requires Saudi employers to sign written contracts with their workers and guarantees foreign laborers one day off a week and three weeks of vacation a year, a period that most workers use to fly home to visit their families. The law does not apply to domestic servants, which is why the Ministry of Labor negotiated separate agreements with Indonesia, India, the Philippines, and Sri Lanka.

In August 2006, the Ministry of Health announced that by 2008, a group of private companies will offer health insurance to every foreigner in the kingdom, and that Saudis wishing to hire foreigners will have to provide such insurance.

Other parts of the Saudi government are much less conscientious about helping foreign workers. The Ministry of Justice, for example, has no program to translate court proceedings from Arabic into English, Hindi, Bengali, or any other foreign language, and if a worker sues his employer, he is usually suspended from his job without pay until the case is decided. In effect, the Saudi judicial system is closed to foreign workers.

The educational system is closed to immigrants, too. Children of temporary foreign workers are not permitted to go to Saudi public schools because the Saudis want these workers to go home after several years, not to stay and raise families. The lack of public schooling for foreign children has not stopped tens of thousands of workers from Yemen from bringing children with them anyway, because the boys and the girls can make extra money selling packets of tissues or bubble gum on the streets or by begging.

In addition, tens of thousands of people from Chad and other African nations never returned home after making pilgrimages to Mecca but stayed in Jeddah to work as laborers and cleaning women. Many of these Africans have had children in Jeddah, and today roughly fifty thousand young people have residency permits that classify them as citizens of Chad, even though they have never been to their parents' homeland. Most of these boys and girls attend Saudi public schools, but some have been refused admission.

The number of foreign workers in the kingdom vastly exceeds the number of unemployed Saudis, so for decades the government has tried, unsuccessfully, to make more of the labor force Saudi. With some success, the Ministry of Labor has required workforces in commercial and industrial companies to be 20 percent Saudi, and 10 percent Saudi in construction and maintenance firms. The airline and banking industries have exceeded the government's goals and have labor forces today that are more than 70 percent Saudi. The all-important oil industry is more than 85 percent Saudi. The travel industry hopes to be 70 percent Saudi by 2009, and utilities, real estate firms, and insurance agencies are not far behind. Comparable Saudization is also taking place in schools and stores. Nearly ten thousand Saudis also drive taxis today, but unlike foreign taxi drivers, most Saudis own their cabs.

If a job is administrative or clerical, Saudis are willing to do it. Few Saudis do blue-collar work, however, except in the oil industry, where workers average more than $50,000 in salaries and benefits, although even here, many of the fieldworkers are Shi'ites, not Sunnis. As unemployment persists, some Saudis are becoming butchers, bakers, and grocers. In grocery stores, however, the Saudis work as cashiers, while Indians and Pakistanis still do the bagging. Few Saudis work in restaurants or on construction sites, for these jobs are some of the lowest paying in the kingdom.

In 2004, the government enacted a new law that Saudi women had long wanted, a requirement that only Saudi women can work selling items of personal feminine clothing such as bras and panties. It had always been embarrassing for Saudi women to buy these items from Indian and Pakistani men, and Saudi women were relieved that they would no longer have to do this.

Unfortunately, the government postponed the law's implementation because male shop owners complained about the impracticality of keeping their male and female employees separate. More than a hundred conservative clerics and businessmen also signed an online petition that said it was wrong for the government to dictate that only women can do a job when "a woman who frequently leaves her home unnecessarily is an indecent woman." In response, several women journalists charged that many shop owners were using religious arguments to mask their real objection to the new law, that it costs a lot more to hire a Saudi woman than a foreign man, and her workweek is several hours shorter.[102]

In theory, every Saudi wants more Saudis in the workforce. In practice, many Saudi employers resist the government's mandates. "Saudization is a painful process because people have become accustomed to cheap and obedient foreign labor," said labor minister Ghazi al-Gosaibi.[103] Foreigners usually make only a third as much as Saudis with the same qualifications do, and they are much easier to fire. As a result, employers often change job descriptions to make skilled labor look like menial work, which is exempt from Saudization laws, or to make the temporary hiring of a Saudi look permanent. The Ministry of Labor has rarely punished small or medium-size employers for providing such misinformation.

More People, More Unemployment

In 1980, there were eight million Saudi citizens. By 2007, the number had doubled to eighteen million, and if current trends continue, there will be thirty million Saudis by 2030. One half of the Saudis today are nineteen and younger. Saudis who work support an average of five dependents each.

Because Saudi Arabia's population soared in the 1980s and the 1990s while the price of oil plummeted, the average Saudi income in 2000, allowing for inflation, was only a third of what it had been at the height of the oil boom twenty years earlier. By the twenty-first century, it was not only foreigners who lived in "Little Delhis"; there were pockets of Saudi poverty, too. On live television in November 2002, Abdullah visited a Saudi slum on the outskirts of Riyadh and talked to the residents. The next day, front pages showed a photograph of an unkempt old man pointing his finger in Abdullah's face, which enhanced Abdullah's reputation as a man who listens to the poor. Several days later, Abdullah took $533 million from that year's budget surplus to build more than ten thousand homes for the poor, a program that he made six times larger in 2006. Abdullah also loosened the eligibility for welfare so that almost four hundred thousand Saudi families (about 7 percent of the population) could receive payments.

If the kingdom's population keeps doubling every twenty-five years, these efforts will not be nearly enough. If trends persist, by 2020, the kingdom will need to build more than two million new houses and apartments, two thousand new clinics, and ten thousand new schools at a cost of hundreds of billions of dollars.

As late as 2003, only 20 percent of the kingdom's young married couples used any form of contraception, and Saudi women were still bearing an average of four children.[104] Author and defense analyst Anthony Cordesman has emphasized in many books and reports that even a booming economy cannot raise a nation's standard of living unless there is also a fall in its birthrate. Saudi Arabia, he warned, "must either reduce its population growth or breed itself into poverty."[105] "Strong leadership is needed to persuade the Wahhabi [clergy] that voluntary population control is necessary," Cordesman said, and the "virtual conspiracy of silence on the subject of population growth and demographics is pure intellectual cowardice."[106]

Almost 30 percent of Saudi men in their early twenties are unemployed, and nearly 10 percent are still jobless in their late twenties.

In a survey the government commissioned in 2003, 79 percent of the Saudi people said that unemployment was the kingdom's number-one problem. By contrast, only 10 percent said that it was religious extremism, and just 1 percent said that it was terrorism.[107] These results were confirmed in a 2005 Zogby poll that found that "expanding employment opportunities" was the issue Saudis cared about the most. Some young men watch television all day and snack on fast food; obesity and diabetes are growing afflictions in the kingdom.

Many men seek positions in the army or the national guard, but often there are twenty applicants for each opening. To create more jobs, the government lent $1 billion to nine thousand small businesses in 2005 because small businesses create many more jobs per dollar than large firms do.

The challenge of creating enough jobs for the coming new generation of Saudis is enormous. Leaving aside women, whose problems were discussed earlier in this chapter, more than 250,000 Saudi men reach adulthood every year, and their skills are limited. More than 20 percent of Saudi men do not finish high school, and only a third go to college. Of those who do pursue higher education, less than 10 percent earn degrees in scientific or technical fields; together, they represent just 3 percent of the Saudis who look for work each year. Until the new oil boom started in 2003, there were jobs for only about half of the Saudis who left school annually, and an additional hundred thousand young men joined the ranks of the unemployed each year. Fortunately, the boom has eased this situation, but many Saudis fear that as soon as it ends, the number of jobless youths could soar even higher.

In the aftermath of 9/11 and 5/12, Saudi officials understand that unemployment is a matter of national security, not only economics, because young men without jobs are more likely to become violent. They also know that the government cannot get much bigger, and that the oil, gas, and petrochemical industries combined employ less than 5 percent of the Saudi workforce.

Only the private sector can create the new jobs that the kingdom so desperately needs, and businesses can expand only if there is more foreign investment. Abdullah has taken many measures to create the business climate that foreign investors require, and he understands that reform today is not only good business, it is a political and social necessity.

The Cumulative Power of Small Reforms

Saudi Arabia may not have an elected parliament or let women work with men, but in the last few years, the press has become freer, petitions have grown bolder, cities elect advisers, women have more job opportunities, human rights commissions take complaints, forums discuss controversial issues, and ordinary people enjoy cell phones, the Internet, and satellite television.

"The kingdom is moving on the path to reform step by step, without rushing," Abdullah said on a trip to China in January 2006.[108] Although talking about issues is not the same thing as participating in decision making, the many small reforms have nevertheless created a big shift in the kingdom's political climate, and most Saudis are pleased with the change.

Western-oriented liberals in the kingdom admit that they are heavily outnumbered by Islamic fundamentalists, and they know that change in Saudi Arabia can come only so fast. Abdullah "is trying very hard to push the envelope," one of his advisers told *Middle East Online*, but "a leader can only be a few meters ahead of his people."[109]

Reformers understand that having a national election immediately would lead to a fierce struggle among interest groups that could easily result in an Islamist victory and an abrupt end to social and economic reforms. They are thus content to move slowly. Their hope is that when national elections do come, after more advances in human rights, press freedom, budget transparency, and the rule of law, the elections will more likely be both peaceful and significant, with people voting for a Majlis al-Shura that has genuine legislative power.

In the meantime, the royal family does a good job of reflecting the will of the people in its mediation between liberals and religious conservatives because ordinary Saudis do not want either group to be too dominant. While almost no one in Saudi Arabia today questions the royal family's right to rule, many people do wish that Abdullah would democratize the kingdom a little faster. In 2003, for example, both liberals and Islamic conservatives petitioned Abdullah to start forming a constitutional monarchy. "We should not deny the credit Abdullah deserves," a young Saudi blogger wrote me. "The thing is we don't have much time. Abdullah is old."

Perhaps because the United States began its existence in 1776 by declaring its independence from a king, Americans today remain deeply suspicious of monarchs who are not subject to a constitution. More than two-thirds of Americans have an unfavorable view of Saudi Arabia, according to a Gallup poll taken early in 2004. As Prince Turki al-Faisal, the kingdom's ambassador to the United States, conceded to PBS's Charlie Rose in February 2006, "While relations on the official [executive branch] level have never been better, we have a long way to go with the American people and with Congress."[110]

U.S.-Saudi relations would be much smoother if more Americans were willing to judge the Saudis by their actions *since* 9/11, rather than before 9/11. Before 9/11, the Saudis were careless about what their textbooks said and where their charity money went. But as the U.S. 9/11 Commission made clear in its report, no one in the royal family or the Saudi government had anything to do with 9/11 or had the slightest idea that it was about to happen. In other words, the Saudis did not know where their carelessness was leading.

Since the 9/11 and 5/12 bombings, with Abdullah's full encouragement, the Saudi government has tightened charitable giving, fired militant clerics, rewritten xenophobic textbooks, cooperated with U.S. law enforcement agencies, and killed and captured hundreds of terrorists. One can argue that the Saudis could do more to fight terrorism in one instance or another, but for authors of books and articles about Saudi Arabia to have titles such as *Hatred's Kingdom* and *Princes of Darkness* is deeply unfair to this country, which for all its faults is indisputably a U.S. ally making real social progress.

The kingdom's critics are correct when they say that two of Saudi Arabia's biggest problems are its lack of a manufacturing base to rely on when its oil runs out and the related issue of chronic unemployment. During the 1980s and the 1990s, the government's failure to address these fundamental problems helped to accelerate the growth of Muslim extremism. But in the 2000s, a dramatic rise in the price of petroleum has led to a new oil boom and, with it, an extraordinary opportunity for business-minded Saudis to make the sweeping changes needed to solve the kingdom's long-term problems.

21

A New Oil Boom,
a New Business Climate
(2003–)

A T THE BEGINNING OF 2002, the price of oil was $18 a barrel and Saudi Arabia's oil revenues were less than $4 billion a month. In 2003, when a new oil boom began, the price climbed to $30 a barrel, and in 2006, it soared past $60, rising to $78.40 a barrel in July when Israel and Hezbollah fought their one-month war. Oil revenues in 2006 averaged nearly $4 billion a *week*, almost four times what they were in 2002. The income of ordinary Saudis nearly doubled between 2002 and 2006, and the stock market more than tripled. Saudi Arabia's long, twenty-year economic slump was over.

On August 1, 2005, in the middle of this new boom, King Fahad died of pneumonia and Crown Prince Abdullah became Saudi Arabia's sixth king. In contrast to Khalid, the easygoing king who led Saudi Arabia during its first oil boom in the late 1970s, Abdullah is more farsighted, keenly aware that the new boom is temporary because in the long run, the price of oil and the size of the kingdom's oil revenues are cyclical: fat years will eventually be followed by lean ones.

Saudi Arabia's great challenge is to make its private sector strong enough to generate new jobs and investments on its own, so that the nation will be less vulnerable to swings in the price of oil. To this end, King Abdullah and his ministers have taken hundreds of steps to make it easier to do business in Saudi Arabia in order to integrate the kingdom into the world economy. "We cannot remain rigid while the world around us is changing," Abdullah told his consultative council in April 2006.

Propelling the New Oil Boom: Chinese Demand

Three-quarters of the world's oil is used for transportation, but in the mid-1980s, when the first oil boom ended, almost no one in China had a car. As late as 1993, when China had already begun to industrialize, there were still only eight million cars, trucks, and buses in the People's Republic of China. Even then, China's domestic oil production was no longer enough for its needs, and it began to import petroleum for the first time in thirty years. Within a decade, it was importing almost 45 percent of its oil.

By 2004, as more Chinese families bought cars of their own, the number of vehicles in China had tripled to nearly 29 million: 20 million cars and 9 million trucks and buses. China surpassed Japan as the world's second-largest oil importer, after the United States, and spent more money importing petroleum than it did on all of its other imports combined. Yet China's demand for oil will only grow higher because it still has just one passenger car for every forty people, a level equal to that of the United States in 1915. By 2025, if growth trends continue, China will have more than 150 million cars, slightly surpassing the number that the United States has today.

To fuel its cars and factories, China imported five times more oil in 2004 than it did in 1996, and its oil imports are expected to double again by 2025. Between 2002 and 2007, China's oil consumption rose fifty percent, from 4.9 million barrels a day to more than 7.5 million barrels a day. In other words, China needed at least 2.6 million more barrels of oil a day in 2007 than it did in 2002, an amount greater than Iraq's maximum daily output. Because no one has found new oil deposits even close to this size in recent years, China's increasing demand for petroleum has pushed the price of oil upward.

More than half of China's oil imports come from the Middle East. Seventeen percent came from Saudi Arabia between 2005 and 2007; another 24 percent came from Iran, Oman, and Sudan. Because China is completely dependent on oil from the Middle East, it cannot seriously threaten Taiwan, for the U.S. Navy could respond to Chinese aggression by preventing oil tankers from sailing to China.

The Chinese dislike being dependent on a handful of countries, so in recent years they have spent tens of billions of dollars acquiring oil leases and holdings in Angola, Azerbaijan, Canada, Indonesia, Iran, Iraq, Kazakhstan, Kenya, Nigeria, Sudan, and Venezuela. China therefore occasionally lends its diplomatic support to some dreadful governments. For example, until 2007, it blocked any UN action in Sudan, which sends nearly 80 percent of its oil exports to China, even though for four years Sudanese Arab militias had massacred more than 250,000 blacks in Darfur province and driven 2 million more from their homes. "We don't care about internal issues like genocide," a top Chinese official once told an aide to Condoleezza Rice, "we only care about the oil."[1]

More Reasons the Price of Oil Increased

From 1983 to 2002, when the price of oil was low, the incentive for oil companies to look for new deposits was weak. Corporations merged, cut costs, and spent less than half as much money on exploration as they had when prices were high. As a result, when the world's demand for oil sometimes exceeded eighty-four million barrels a day in 2004, there were no big new discoveries of oil to match the rise in consumption and slow the increase in price, as there had been in the 1970s when geologists discovered oil in Mexico, the North Sea, and Alaska's North Slope.

In addition, the United States failed to enact any serious automobile fuel-efficiency measures until 2007 and therefore used 25 percent more oil in 2005 that it did in 1985. The United States consumes more than twenty-one million barrels of oil a day, an amount equal to that of China, Japan, India, Germany, Britain, and Russia *combined*, and at least 60 percent of this oil must be imported.

The United States also has 176 fewer oil refineries today than it had in 1976, the last time a company built one in the United States. This is partly because twenty years of low oil prices made it harder to run a refinery profitably, but it is also because local "Not in My Backyard" citizens' movements were especially powerful when they opposed the construction of oil refineries. Today America's refineries operate at 95 percent of their capacity, which means that a disruption of any kind can cause a shortage of gasoline, as happened in 2005 when Hurricane Katrina damaged four refineries along the Gulf of Mexico and regular gasoline suddenly cost more than $3 a gallon.

In Iraq, hundreds of attacks by Sunni insurgents on the nation's oil facilities caused the nation's production of crude oil to fall from a prewar level of 2.5 million barrels a day to a postinvasion level of only 1.7 to 2.1 million barrels a day until Iraq's oil production finally returned to its prewar level when the attacks declined in 2007. Nigeria has also lost about 500,000 barrels a day, nearly 25 percent of its production, because of attacks on offshore oil platforms and the kidnapping of foreign oil workers by the Movement for the Emancipation of the Niger Delta (MEND). Even Russia pumps no more oil per day than it did in 1991, because it is still recovering from the disrepair that accompanied the fall of communism. Iran also pumps 700,000 fewer barrels of oil per day than it did before its revolution in 1979, and Venezuela pumps 700,000 fewer barrels of oil a day than it did before a crippling strike in 2002 that caused many of its wells to be shut down permanently.

Britain's oil production has fallen, too, as the deposits off Scotland's North Sea coast have become depleted. In 2003, Britain had to import oil for the first time since the 1970s. Indonesia, an oil exporter since the 1930s, also had to begin importing oil at this time. This was partly because of the lack of skill of its national oil company, Pertamina, in developing new fields, but mostly because its 240 million motorcycle-riding people use an enormous amount of gasoline and kerosene.

Elsewhere in Asia, countries with almost no oil are importing more petroleum than ever as their economies boom. Japan and South Korea together still use more oil than China. By 2010, India will have more than forty-five million cars and will consume more oil than Germany. Even the Middle East's consumption of oil is rising about 3 to 5 percent a year, as air-conditioning becomes nearly universal.

By 2004, with Asia's demand for petroleum soaring, every oil-producing nation except Saudi Arabia was pumping as much oil as it could, and even Saudi Arabia pumped a near-record 9.5 million barrels a day. The kingdom's vaunted spare capacity of 1.5 million barrels a day was less than 2 percent of global demand, a margin far too small for the comfort of the world's oil buyers. They knew that if trouble occurred in even one country—UN sanctions against Iran, more violence in Nigeria, renewed strikes in Venezuela—Saudi Arabia would no longer have enough oil to make up for the loss. It was therefore better to buy more oil now even though it was expensive, buyers concluded, than risk suffering from a shortage later when the price of oil might be even higher.

Wall Street also caused the price of oil to rise. Hedge funds specializing in energy, pension funds diversifying into commodities, and individual financial speculators put twenty times more money into oil futures in 2007 than they did in 2001. This made the oil market much more volatile than before as it reacted to daily and even hourly news with much stronger swings upward and downward than in previous years.

A final factor that sends the price of oil up is the "fear premium," which the *Economist* has said adds $7 to $15 per barrel to the cost of petroleum. Three families, the al-Saud, the al-Sabah, and the al-Nahayan—the royal houses of Saudi Arabia, Kuwait, and Abu Dhabi in the United Arab Emirates—control 43 percent of the world's oil reserves, and al-Qaeda would like to overthrow all of them because each one is an ally of the West. Each nation has unique vulnerabilities but also massive security. Saudi Arabia, for example, has more than thirty pumping stations, ten thousand miles of pipelines, and twenty miles of port facilities on the Persian Gulf that are susceptible to terrorism, but it also has nearly thirty thousand troops guarding these facilities and helicopter and fighter jets that maintain round-the-clock surveillance.

On February 24, 2006, three terrorists died while trying to attack Saudi Arabia's huge oil facility at Abqaiq, twenty-five miles inland from the Persian Gulf, with cars full of explosives.

The terrorists damaged only a minor pipeline and had no effect on Abqaiq's oil production because, like other petroleum facilities in Saudi Arabia, Abqaiq has redundant pumps, pipelines, gas-oil separators, and desulfurization towers. But even the failed attack at Abqaiq caused the price of oil that day to jump 4 precent, to $62 a barrel.

Has Saudi—and World—Oil Production Peaked?

In 1956, a geologist who worked for Shell Oil, M. King Hubbert, predicted that America's oil production would peak in 1970, then decline. When U.S. production did peak in 1970, as predicted, many geologists began to wonder when the world's production might decline. The world's production of oil today is still growing but not as fast as its demand. The last year when people found more oil than they consumed was 1987; the world now consumes two barrels of oil for every one it discovers. In non-OPEC nations, oil production may already have peaked, although it has not yet declined. The world's demand for oil, however, is still increasing up to 2 percent a year.

A recent and alarming book that has sparked a lot discussion in the oil industry is *Twilight in the Desert* (2005), by Matthew Simmons, an investment banker who specializes in oil. After reading more than two hundred technical papers by petroleum engineers on the details and the difficulties of Saudi oil production, Simmons concluded that Saudi production is at or near its peak and is likely to decline just as the world's demand for oil is accelerating.

Simmons pointed out that 60 percent of the kingdom's production comes from three giant old fields—Ghawar, Abqaiq, and Safaniya—that have been producing oil for more than fifty years. All three fields need more water injections to keep their well pressure high, a clear sign that the oil fields are aging and approaching their peak output. The Saudis dismiss these claims and insist that they have enough oil to produce fifteen million barrels a day (60 to 80 percent more than current output) for more than fifty years. But Simmons said that if the Saudis want to prove that he is mistaken, "they should issue field-by-field production reports and reserve data and have it audited. It would then take anybody less than a week to say, 'Gosh, Matt is totally wrong.'"[2]

Ghawar, a 174-mile-long stretch of interconnected fields southwest of Abqaiq, has accounted for about 60 percent of the kingdom's oil production since it first began pumping in 1951. This one field still produces almost five million barrels of oil a day, more than half of the kingdom's total production and more than the amount produced in Iraq and Kuwait combined. But the depth of the boundary between Ghawar's oil and its water varies by as much as 815 feet, and geologists do not know the reason for this perplexing tilt. Because of this puzzle and other unknowns, Simmons said that Saudi Aramco's prediction that it can continue to use water injections to keep oil at Ghawar flowing for another fifty years is merely "boastful optimism rather than knowledgeable understanding."[3] And if Ghawar's production does fall, it is doubtful whether enough new exploration in Saudi Arabia could make up for this loss.

Abqaiq, which for many years was the kingdom's second-largest field, has been pumping since 1946. It is less than a fourth the size of Ghawar and suffers from declining well pressure, corrosion from years of water injection, and wells that increasingly produce more water and less oil. These are classic signs that an oil field is becoming depleted, but Saudi Aramco officials insist that the Abqaiq field can produce half a million barrels a day for one more decade. Finally, at Safaniya, the kingdom's largest offshore field, the wells are also pumping more water and less oil than before, with some wells nearing a 50–50 split.

Simmons does not claim that Saudi Arabia will run out of oil, only that its production will decline to a lower level, just as production in the United States has since 1970. But he does worry that once the

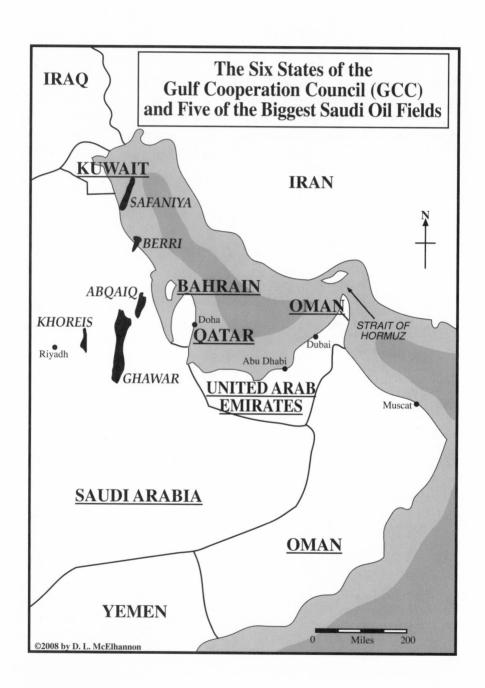

The Six States of the
Gulf Cooperation Council (GCC)
and Five of the Biggest Saudi Oil Fields

IRAQ

KUWAIT

SAFANIYA

BERRI

IRAN

N

ABQAIQ

BAHRAIN

KHOREIS

OMAN

Doha

STRAIT OF HORMUZ

Riyadh

QATAR

Dubai

Abu Dhabi

GHAWAR

UNITED ARAB EMIRATES

Muscat

SAUDI ARABIA

OMAN

YEMEN

©2008 by D. L. McElhannon

0   Miles   200

472

production at these older Saudi fields starts to decline, the drop-off will be steep. The average oil field yields only 25 percent of its petroleum during the second half of its producing life, and a field's output typically falls by half within ten years after its production has peaked. Saudi experts say that because Ghawar is a series of interconnected fields, they will not deplete at the same time, so that when Ghawar finally does peak, its decline will be gradual.

How much oil does Saudi Arabia still have? In 2007, the government's estimate of the nation's proven reserves was 261.2 billion barrels, a quarter of the world's total and enough to sustain the kingdom's present rate of production for seventy-five years. But Saudi Arabia's estimate of its reserves has not changed since 1988, a time when the estimates of oil reserves in the Middle East were suspect.

Until Saudi Arabia bought 60 percent of Aramco from Exxon, Chevron, Texaco, and Mobil in 1974 (it bought the remaining 40 percent in 1980), the oil company's estimates of the kingdom's reserves were subject to oversight by the U.S. Securities and Exchange Commission (SEC). The estimates were therefore supported by specific information about individual oil fields, and the estimates went up and down from year to year. After 1974, the Saudi-run company was no longer subject to SEC regulation, and the Saudis regarded their oil field data as a state secret. Other OPEC nations also bought or nationalized their oil facilities in the 1970s and became equally secretive.

Although Saudi Aramco stopped providing field-by-field breakdowns of its oil reserves, it nevertheless increased its estimate of the kingdom's total proven reserves from 100 billion barrels to 150 billion barrels in 1979, then increased the estimate again to 163 billion barrels in 1982. In the 1980s, Kuwait also raised its estimate of its proven reserves from 65 to 90 billion barrels (on flimsy evidence, according to *Petroleum Intelligence Weekly*), while Iran raised its estimate from 58 to 100 billion barrels. Reserves in the United Arab Emirates leaped from 58 to 93 billion barrels in the 1980s, and, under Saddam Hussein, Iraq increased its proven reserves from 31 to 100 billion barrels of oil. Finally, in 1988, Saudi Arabia raised its estimate of proven reserves a third time to 260 billion barrels, an amount that has not changed for two decades.[4]

In the 1980s, each of the OPEC nations was angling for a bigger OPEC production quota so that it could pump more oil, and many of these countries probably tried to gain more stature by moving some of their "probable reserves" of oil into the category of "proven reserves." In fairness to their governments, oil production since the 1980s has justified the increased estimates. But no one can seriously argue that the proven Saudi oil reserves increased 50 percent in 1979, stayed about the same for nine years, increased 62 percent in 1988, and then stayed the same for another two decades. Clearly, there is a huge need for more transparent reserve estimates, with supporting evidence based on field-by-field data. If, for example, the 1988 increase in Saudi Arabia's proven reserves was unjustified, the kingdom might have only 160 billion barrels of oil instead of 260 billion.

If the world's consumption of oil continues to grow 2 percent a year, and if the production at existing fields declines 2 to 3 percent a year, then geologists must find almost four million new barrels of oil a day each year just to keep up with the world's increasing demand. "That's like a whole new Saudi Arabia every couple of years," said Sadad al-Husseini, who was Saudi Aramco's director of exploration and production before he retired in 2004. "It can't be done indefinitely. It's not sustainable."[5]

The danger is that if the demand for oil exceeds the supply for even a short time, the price of oil could easily climb to $200 a barrel and the price of gasoline could reach $6 a gallon. The suburban way of life, with two-car garages, hourlong commutes, and frequent trips to shopping centers, athletic events, and friends' houses, could suddenly become very expensive.

Many people vigorously disagree with Simmons and other doomsayers. On October 14, 2005, King Abdullah told Barbara Walters that "Saudi Arabia's reserves are sufficient to provide supplies for longer than sixty or seventy years." Only three weeks earlier, his oil minister, Ali al-Naimi, assured the Eighteenth World Petroleum Congress in Johannesburg that Saudi Arabia could easily add another 200 billion barrels of recoverable oil to its current estimate of 260 billion barrels of proven reserves. "Give us the customers and we will pump more oil," he told the conference.[6]

Executives at Saudi Aramco, whose techniques of oil field management are widely admired by Western experts, insist that their estimate of 260 billion barrels of proven reserves is conservative, based on the standards set by the Society of Petroleum Engineers, and does not include another 108 billion barrels of "probable" reserves. And Western engineers with decades of experience in the kingdom's oil fields generally agree with the Saudi government's assurances that the kingdom can continue to pump 10 million barrels a day or more for another fifty years.

The older fields, the Saudis claim, are depleting at a rate of only 1 to 4 percent a year, compared with 4 to 10 percent elsewhere in the world, and because of new, improved methods of water injection, the percentage of water that is pumped from the wells at Ghawar is actually lower than it was in 1999. The Saudis have successfully used new steam-injection techniques that vastly increase the amount of oil that can be recovered when the crude is "heavy" and sludgelike. This alone could raise the kingdom's proven reserves by tens of billions of barrels. The Saudis also point out that the kingdom's long border with Iraq is still largely unexplored. Finally, the Saudis say, because Simmons's research is based mainly on technical papers, he described many problems that Saudi Aramco has already solved and therefore was much too pessimistic.[7]

As for the global supply of petroleum, Daniel Yergin, one of the world's leading experts on oil, is not worried. The Pulitzer Prize–winning author of *The Prize: The Epic Quest for Oil* has said that new sources of oil such as tar sands; ethanol derived from corn, grass, and sugarcane; and gas-to-liquids (diesel fuel made from natural gas) are all economical now that oil is more than $40 a barrel, so "the very definition of oil is changing."[8]

Yergin also said that the Society of Petroleum Engineers' "1978 System" of measuring "proven" reserves is outdated because it does not include enough of the oil in tar sands or in deposits that lie under thousands of feet of water. Indeed, if "probable reserves" are added to "proven reserves," then, according to Professor Peter Odell of Rotterdam's Erasmus University, geologists have discovered more than fifteen hundred billion barrels of oil since 1971, while the world has consumed less than a thousand billion barrels during this period. Odell has said that the world is "running into oil," not out of it.[9]

Many experts are optimistic that high prices will spur oil companies to pay for better exploration technology that will lead to more oil production. But Simmons has warned, "Advanced technologies, particularly extended reach, multilateral horizontal wells and hydraulic fracturing, are essentially turbo-charged super-straws designed to suck out the recoverable oil faster—not miracle drugs that prolong field life and recover [more] oil-in-place."[10]

Technology has increased the percentage of recoverable oil, currently about 35 percent of a reservoir, but the rate has gone up slowly, only a few percentage points a decade.

The two most likely places where a lot more oil will be found in the near future are underwater and in tar sands. New technology has made it possible to drill ten thousand feet under a seabed for the same price, allowing for inflation, that it cost to drill just a hundred feet under a seabed in the 1960s. Today, only 3 percent of the world's oil comes from seabeds under a thousand or more feet of water, but marine geologists have only begun to explore the world's oceans. If the price of oil stays above $30 a barrel, the percentage of the world's oil extracted from deep water is likely to increase considerably.

An even more promising source of oil is the vast expanse of tar sands in Alberta, in Western Canada. Over 1.7 *trillion* barrels of oil are locked inside the dirt there, but the process of extracting and burning the natural gas from the same deposits in order to create the heat that is needed to separate the oil from the dirt is expensive and is not economical unless oil is selling for $40 a barrel or more. In 2004, the year that the price of oil finally reached this level, the Canadian government announced that 255 billion barrels of oil are recoverable from its tar sands. In other words, there is as much recoverable oil in the tar sands of Alberta as there is in Saudi Arabia; it just costs more to extract. Venezuela also has 1.7 trillion barrels of oil locked in tar sands north of the Orinoco River and claims that 235 billion barrels of this oil is recoverable. Geologists are skeptical of this large estimate, but the amount of oil that is recoverable is still massive.

Will Saudi Arabia's oil production peak soon? The only people who know for sure are geologists and officials working for the kingdom's oil ministry, and they are not sharing any field-by-field data. Occasionally, they issue confident statements about the kingdom's reserves and its ability to pump plenty of oil for another half century, but even if they are mistaken, and Saudi Arabia's production falls in half, the kingdom would still be the largest oil producer in the Middle East.

Will the world's oil production peak soon? It is unlikely. There is plenty of oil to be found underwater, in tar sands, and in remote regions, especially Siberia, that geologists have not yet explored with current technology. It is therefore much too soon to predict the end of the oil-fueled suburban lifestyle.

Unfortunately, even if geologists do succeed in finding the equivalent of a new Saudi Arabia every three or four years, the demand for oil is likely to keep pace with these new discoveries because the number of cars around the world is growing rapidly. The need for more gasoline will keep the price of oil high, and this will encourage more production of the newer kinds of oil from tar sands, corn, sugarcane, natural gas, and deep water. "We might be running low on $20 [a barrel] oil," said Harvard economist Kenneth Rogoff, "but for $60 we have adequate oil supplies for decades to come."[11]

The Price of Oil Inched Up in 2003 . . .

The $22 to $28 price band that the OPEC nations had agreed to in March 2000, to try to create some price stability, worked well for three years. When the price of oil climbed above $28 for twenty trading days, the OPEC nations pumped five hundred thousand extra barrels of oil a day to drive the price back down. When the price fell below $22 for ten trading days, the OPEC nations cut their production by five hundred thousand barrels a day to push the price back up. The price stayed comfortably within this range as the world's economy gradually recovered from the dot-com bust of 2000, for the recovery made the glut of oil disappear.

In 2003, however, China's demand for oil was 10 percent higher than it had been in 2002, so the price of oil often climbed above $28 a barrel. The OPEC nations responded each time by pumping more oil, and by the end of the year Saudi Arabia was producing a voluminous 8.4 million barrels a day. Because of the world's growing demand, the price of oil stayed high despite OPEC's extra production.

Just before the United States invaded Iraq in March 2003, market jitters pushed the price of oil to $37 a barrel. Once the war began, however, Saudi Arabia made up for the loss of Iraq's oil by boosting its production to a near-capacity 9.5 million barrels a day, and the other OPEC nations also raised their output to maximum levels. The flood of new oil briefly brought the price down to $25 a barrel, prompting the OPEC nations to cut their production slightly in April. By June, the price of oil rose to $30 a barrel again, and except for a brief dip in September, which caused OPEC to cut its production to pre–Iraq War levels, the price of oil stayed between $28 and $31 a barrel for most of the rest of the year, inching up to $32.50 a barrel just before the year ended.

Saudi oil revenues in 2002 were $64 billion, and the government ran a budget deficit of $7 billion. But the rise in the price of oil pushed revenues up to $82 billion in 2003, and the Saudi government suddenly had extra money to spend. It rescinded some painful budget cuts and still posted a surplus of $9.6 billion. As the new oil wealth spread throughout the kingdom, personal income rose 9 percent in 2003, a welcome increase after a decade of stagnation.

. . . And Skyrocketed from 2004 Onward

At the beginning of 2004, the OPEC nations did not expect the price increases of 2003 to last, so in February they cut their production 10 percent to try to keep the price of oil from falling. (The new Saudi output was 7.6 million barrels a day.) Instead, China's demand for oil rose 16 percent in 2004, an increase that by itself was equal to almost half of Iraq's daily output. India's demand that year also increased 11 percent. By April, the price of oil climbed to $40 a barrel, and in the United States, regular gasoline soared to $2 a gallon. OPEC rescinded its February cuts, and Saudi Arabia was soon pumping at a near-capacity 9.2 million barrels a day.

The April 2004 production increase came too late to calm nervous traders. The world's demand for oil had already passed 82 million barrels a day, and many buyers decided that it was better to pay more and have a secure supply of oil than to wait for a better price and risk having no oil at all. By October, with war in Iraq and violence in Nigeria, oil reached $55 a barrel before the tight, demand-driven market finally loosened a bit, causing the price of oil to fall to $40 in December.

As buyers accumulated inventories, the OPEC countries, which were pumping at maximum levels, began to worry that they might be creating a glut. At an OPEC meeting in December, Saudi Arabia agreed to cut its daily production by 500,000 barrels, to 8.7 million barrels a day, while the rest of OPEC agreed to share a second cut of another 500,000 barrels a day. OPEC was not trying to push the price of oil up to $55 a barrel but was defending the $35 to $40 range, where the price was currently fluctuating. The Saudi oil minister, Ali al-Naimi, defended the new price range in January 2005. "The world is not suffering," he said, "from where prices are today."

The purpose of OPEC's December production cuts was merely to preserve the price gains of 2004, but because demand was strong, the price of oil soared even higher. It reached $50 a barrel at the end of January 2005, and $58 a barrel in April. In June, the OPEC nations rescinded their December cuts and resumed pumping at maximum levels for the rest of 2005. The Saudis also began to operate two relatively small new oil fields, Qatif and Abu Sa'fah, to boost their country's maximum capacity to 11 million barrels a day, almost three times the output of Iran, the Middle East's second-largest oil producer.

Saudi Arabia pumped almost 9.5 million barrels of oil a day in 2005 and during the winter of 2006 and a hefty 9.1 to 9.3 million barrels a day during the spring and the summer of 2006. Unfortunately, global demand in 2005 approached 86 million barrels a day, driving oil to $60 a barrel in July and almost $71 in August, when Hurricane Katrina damaged four refineries in Louisiana and a third of the drilling platforms in the Gulf of Mexico. The price of oil had quadrupled in just three and a half years, and in the United States, regular gasoline began to cost $3 a gallon.

When Israel and Hezbollah went to war in July 2006, the price of oil soared to $78.40 a barrel as traders also worried about the coming hurricane season and the possibility of UN sanctions against Iran.

In the autumn, however, with a cease-fire in Lebanon and no hurricanes or UN sanctions, the price of oil fell to $57 a barrel in October as relieved buyers enjoyed large inventories.

In response to this 27 percent price drop, the OPEC nations held emergency meetings in Doha, Qatar, in October 2006 and in Abuja, Nigeria, in December. To keep the price of oil above $50 a barrel, they agreed to reduce their oil production 4.3 percent on November 1 and 2 percent more on February 1, 2007—OPEC's first production cuts in almost two years.

Saudi Arabia dutifully cut its daily oil production by 380,000 barrels in the last two months of 2006 and another 158,000 barrels in February 2007 but still pumped at a robust clip of 8.6 million barrels of oil a day, a volume it maintained through the spring and summer of 2007. Other OPEC nations, however, skirted their agreements and cut their oil production by less than half of the amount they promised. Still, the price of oil nearly always stayed between $55 and $75 a barrel during the spring and summer of 2007, until a fear of hurricanes, winter shortages, increased Chinese demand, the falling dollar, and a Turkish invasion of Kurdish Iraq caused the price of oil to climb to $83 a barrel in September.

Until then, the price of oil had been low enough not to harm the world's economy. To try to keep the price from soaring higher, the OPEC nations agreed to increase their production 2 percent, starting November 1. Saudi Arabia's new quota was 8.9 million barrels a day, although soon it actually pumped 9.2 million barrels daily. But the price of oil continued to climb, and in mid-April 2008 it set an all-time, inflation-adjusted record of $115 a barrel as pension and hedge fund investors sought refuge from a falling U.S. dollar.

The Money Pours In

Although the Saudis were delighted to receive $82 billion in oil revenues in 2003, they cautiously planned their 2004 budget on the assumption that 2004's revenues would shrink to what they had been in 2002: $64 billion. Instead, the price of oil stayed above $40 a barrel most of the year, so 2004's revenues soared to $110 billion, more than three times what they had been in 1998.

The government gave a bonus of two months' pay to every soldier and policeman in the kingdom, doubled the number of vocational training centers, and increased the number and the size of its loans to businessmen, contractors, and homebuyers. It spent $14 billion more than it had planned in 2004 and still posted an enormous $27 billion surplus.

The same thing happened the following year. The government cautiously planned its 2005 budget on the assumption that revenues would return to their 2003 level of $82 billion. Instead, oil exports in 2005 leaped to $161 billion—$441 million a *day*—almost double what they had been just two years earlier. Oil revenues in 2006 climbed another 18 percent, to more than $190 billion, almost $22 million an *hour*—and to over $210 billion in 2007.

The government increased social security payments in 2005 and using money from its 2006 budget, too, it began to build more than 2,600 schools, 80 hospitals, and 250 clinics, and disbursed $10 billion for new roads, bridges, street lights, power plants, sewage systems, housing projects, and desalinization plants. The government spent 22 percent more than it had planned in 2005 and still posted an unheard-of surplus of $58 billion. In 2006, when the budget surplus was $77.5 billion, the government cut the cost of regular gasoline in the kingdom from 96 cents a gallon to just 64 cents a gallon.

During 2007, the Saudi government forecast a balanced budget using an extremely conservative estimate of the price of oil, $35 to $40 a barrel, yet still spent more than $118 billion, more money than it had ever spent before. Because in 2007 the average price of oil was about $70 a barrel, almost double this estimate, the year's surplus was an enormous $48 billion. (The budget for 2008 is based on an equally conservative estimate of $45 for a barrel of oil, so 2008's surplus is likely to be just as high.)

From the Persian Gulf to the Red Sea, contractors have built new homes, office buildings, and shopping malls. National income per person (that is, gross domestic product [GDP] per capita) rose from $8,728 in 2002 to $13,575 in 2005, about the same as income in Hungary. If foreign laborers are excluded, however, the per capita income of Saudi citizens in 2005 was about the same as that of South Koreans, roughly $20,000 a year. This was still well below the income that many Saudis enjoyed in 1980 at the peak of the previous oil boom, but few Saudis complained because it was more money than most of them had seen in twenty years. It also may not be a coincidence that there was almost no terrorism in Saudi Arabia during the boom years of 2005 and 2006. "You have a young and growing population," said Mohammed al-Sheikh, a top lawyer in Riyadh, "but I don't think they are as angry as they used to be."[12]

One of the most important and necessary things the Saudi government did with the enormous amount of money it has received since 2003 was to reduce the large debt that it owed to domestic banks. The government paid these banks $5.3 billion in 2003, $46 billion in 2004, $37 billion in 2005, and $28 billion in 2006, reducing the size of its public debt from a dangerously high 93 percent of GDP (that is, eleven months' national income) at the beginning of 2003 to a much more manageable 19 percent of GDP (two months' national income) by the end of 2007.

In the United States and Europe, people feel that the high price of oil will last forever, but in the Middle East, where the memory of the low prices in the 1980s and the 1990s is still vivid, few people think the high prices will last. The government has therefore spent money less lavishly than it did in the 1970s and has concentrated on debt reduction and the replenishment of foreign assets, which can act as a cushion in hard times. The kingdom's central bank increased its foreign assets by $33 billion in 2004, $65 billion in 2005, and another $63 billion in 2006. By the fall of 2007, the central bank had accumulated $250 billion in assets abroad, more than five times the total it had in 2002 and enough to buy more than three years' worth of imports in an emergency.

Nearly three-quarters of the kingdom's foreign assets—more than $165 billion—are in foreign securities, mostly U.S. Treasury bonds. At the end of 2006, the kingdom also had more than 229 tons of gold, $25 billion in foreign currency, and $32 billion in foreign bank accounts. Wisely, Saudi Arabia has saved an enormous amount of money for the lean years that will inevitably follow this fabulous but fleeting oil boom.

Creating a New Business Climate

Because Saudi Arabia's population continues to double every twenty-five years, the government estimates that during the next two decades, it will need to build more than $600 billion worth of new housing, roads, ports, power stations, water works, petrochemical plants, telecommunications lines, and other infrastructure projects. Since not even an oil boom can pay for all this, it is vital that the kingdom begin to attract more foreign investment.

Until recently, it was rare for foreigners to invest in anything other than petrochemical plants and retail outlets because Saudi Arabia was a difficult place to collect debts or enforce contracts. Islamic courts were unpredictable, and princes were beyond the law. Not surprisingly, in the 1980s and the 1990s, Saudi Arabia received only one-eighth as much foreign investment as Malaysia, a Muslim country with about the same number of people that had a much better business climate.

In the twenty-first century, however, King Abdullah and his advisers have been determined to integrate Saudi Arabia into the world economy. To make its legal system more predictable, the Saudi government began to publish new laws, regulations, and administrative decisions, both online and in an official gazette, *before* they took effect so that a business affected by a new law or regulation can have a reasonable time to make comments. In a sharp departure from past practice, Abdullah has asked that companies seeking government contracts refrain from hiring princes to represent them. In April 2007, he also set up internal control units in every government department to try to guard against corruption. Today, the substance of a company's business plan is often more important than the clout of the Saudis connected with it.

The Saudi Arabian General Investment Authority (SAGIA), which by 2001 had already reduced the period needed to obtain a business license from several months to thirty days, used the Internet to shrink the waiting period again to just three days by 2005. SAGIA issued more than three thousand business licenses between 2003 and 2006, and foreign investment in the kingdom increased to $18 billion in 2006, seven times what it was in 2003. In 2007, to encourage more foreign entrepreneurs to visit the kingdom, the Saudi Foreign Ministry began to issue yearlong, multiple-entry business visas in only twenty-four hours.

As part of Saudi Arabia's long and detailed negotiations to join the World Trade Organization (WTO), the kingdom signed several international treaties on arbitration, insurance law, and the protection of patents and copyrights. The copyright protections were particularly necessary because by 2005, duplication piracy accounted for more than 50 percent of the kingdom's business software and 90 percent of its government and entertainment software. Under a new law the kingdom passed to enforce the copyright treaty, the Saudi police can now raid a pirate's workplace, confiscate his equipment and inventory, and imprison him for a year. In 2005, the police seized 27 million illegally copied computer disks, 2.3 million in one raid alone.

The kingdom also created new commercial courts in order to protect foreign companies from the caprice of Islamic judges who were ignorant of world commerce. One notorious example of Islamic justice occurred in 2001 when a *sharia* judge ruled that Pokemon cards were un-Islamic because they had Zionist influences and encouraged gambling. In fact, Pokemon cards are Japanese, but they were taken off store shelves anyway, and the distributor had no legal means to contest his loss. Today, the distributor could plead his case before a Saudi commercial court and, if necessary, an international panel of arbitrators. The new commercial courts and treaties are bitterly opposed by Islamic extremists such as Osama bin Laden, however, because they feel that the *sharia*, the law of God, is being replaced by a poor substitute, the laws of men.

The new courts have specific jurisdiction over insurance companies because many Islamic judges do not regard insurance as a legitimate business, thinking that it is a sin to insure oneself or one's business against God's will. By 2007, the government licensed twenty-two foreign insurers to start doing business in the kingdom and more than thirty Saudi insurers, too. Most of the Saudi companies will insure their clients according to Islamic tradition, owning a percentage of the insured's company and sharing his risks, rather than collecting premiums.

The kingdom has also let ten foreign banks open branches in Saudi Arabia: four from the Gulf states, three from Europe, and one each from India, Pakistan, and the United States (J. P. Morgan Chase). Other industries formerly closed to non-Saudis that are now open to foreign investment include mining, printing, wholesaling, health care, air transport, telecommunications, and natural gas exploration.

Drinking water, however, is too heavily subsidized to attract foreign investors. Two-thirds of the tap water in Saudi cities comes from thirty desalinization plants, many along the Red Sea, and the water they distill is excellent but expensive. Most Saudis pay only one-seventh of the cost of distillation and piping.

Saudi Arabia's many efforts to create a better business climate won praise in a September 2007 report titled *Ease of Doing Business* by the International Finance Corporation, a division of the World Bank. In a survey of 178 countries, the report rated Saudi Arabia as the twenty-third-best place to do business, a ranking higher than that of France or Austria.

A closer look at the organization's recent reports shows that Saudi Arabia's economic progress is uneven. The kingdom is still a hard place to enforce a contract. It has typically taken forty-four steps and eleven and a half months and cost 20 percent of the amount of the original debt. Not surprisingly, the kingdom has ranked below average in this category.[13]

Even so, the report was cause for celebration. Saudi Arabia moved from sixty-seventh to twenty-third place in just three years and earned the highest ranking in the Middle East. The Saudi Arabian General Investment Authority is not content with the kingdom being number twenty-three, however. In 2006, the agency announced a "10 by 10" program: a drive to shrink the kingdom's bureaucracy further so that by 2010, Saudi Arabia will become one of the world's ten best places to do business.

Closer Ties to the Other Gulf States

One reason it is so important for Saudi Arabia to create a better business climate is that it faces stiff competition from its neighbors for investment dollars. If a businessman cannot get what he wants in the kingdom, he may choose instead to build a plant or start a company in one of the other five states of the Gulf Cooperation Council (GCC): Kuwait, Bahrain, Qatar, Oman, and especially the United Arab Emirates (UAE). In contrast to Saudi Arabia, where until recently the government's business decisions were often slow and arbitrary, the UAE's bureaucracy moves quickly and predictably, following precise and public regulations that make arbitrary decisions rare. And while Saudi Arabia cut its corporate income tax to 20 percent in 2004, the UAE has no corporate tax at all.

With roughly the same size and population as South Carolina, the UAE has 8 percent of the world's proven oil reserves, a volume triple that of the United States. With just eight hundred thousand citizens, however, the UAE has more than five times more oil per citizen than Saudi Arabia does, so the average family income in the UAE is almost triple what it is in Saudi Arabia.

The UAE today is booming, and much of its surplus capital goes to Saudi Arabia. Because the kingdom's business climate has improved, foreign investment in Saudi Arabia more than tripled between 2004 and 2006, and at least 40 percent of this new money came from the UAE.[14]

Money flows freely between Saudi Arabia and the UAE because the Gulf states have developed extraordinarily close ties. By 2007, the citizens of the six nations of the GCC no longer needed passports to cross one another's boundaries or permits to work in one another's countries. The GCC nations have also standardized many of their commercial and labor regulations and began a tariff-free customs union on January 1, 2008.

Highways between the GCC countries are excellent. Goods from Europe are shipped through the Suez Canal to Jeddah and trucked east to Kuwait and the UAE, and goods from Asia are shipped to Dubai and trucked west to Saudi Arabia. By 2010, the GCC nations will also connect their electricity grids, making power failures less likely because engineers will be able to send electricity wherever it is most needed. If things go smoothly, there may even be a pan-Arab grid stretching from Morocco to Oman by 2015.

Five of the six GCC states (but not Oman) plan to have a common currency sometime in the 2010s, perhaps pegged to a "basket" of dollars, euros, and yen. If the Saudi riyal, the Kuwaiti dinar, and the UAE dirham do merge, the new money will instantly become the leading currency of the Muslim world. For this merger to work, however, the five countries will have to keep their interest and inflation rates within about 3 percent of each other, a difficult but achievable goal, and also create a new bank to oversee the joint currency.

To become more integrated with the world economy, Kuwait, Bahrain, Qatar, and the UAE have recently changed their weekend from Thursday and Friday to Friday and Saturday, and today many businessmen in Saudi Arabia want the kingdom to follow their lead. "We are cut off from the rest of the world for four days Thursday, Friday, Saturday and Sunday," complained Dr. Abdullah Saati of King Abdul Aziz University in Jeddah, so if international business is not concluded by Wednesday afternoon, it has to wait until Monday morning.[15]

The United States has rewarded its allies in the Middle East with free-trade agreements that allow these nations to sell their goods to the United States duty free. An unintended effect of these well-intentioned treaties, however, is that they are making the GCC's economic unification more difficult. America's first three treaties, with Israel, Jordan, and Morocco, did no harm to the GCC. But in 2004, the United States signed a free-trade agreement with Bahrain, a New York City–sized island that is the home of the U.S. Navy's Fifth Fleet and is connected to Saudi Arabia by a sixteen-mile-long causeway. The United States also signed a free-trade agreement in 2006 with Oman, a Utah-sized nation that hosts both a U.S. Air Force base and some U.S. special forces.

The Saudis and their neighbors in Kuwait and the UAE approve of free trade but fear that these new agreements will prevent Bahrain and Oman from charging the 5 percent duty that GCC states are supposed to levy against non-GCC products. Nothing today prevents a businessman in Bahrain or Oman from importing U.S. goods duty free and exporting them again, duty free, to Saudi Arabia, although so far the merchants in Bahrain and Oman have not been that aggressive.

The only realistic solution to this odd state of affairs is for the four other GCC nations to sign free-trade agreements with the United

States, too. Qatar and the UAE have already begun talks with the United States, and Saudi Arabia just spent a decade in detailed trade negotiations with the United States as part of its successful effort to join the WTO in December 2005. As part of its trade agreement with the United States, Saudi Arabia promised to reduce most of its tariffs on U.S. goods to 3.2 percent.

The lesson the six GCC states have learned from all of this is to negotiate as a bloc in future trade talks. The UAE, for example, had begun its own trade negotiations with Australia in 2005, but in 2006, it asked the Australians to widen the scope of the talks to include trade with all six GCC states. The GCC states also began unified trade talks with China in 2004 and with Japan in 2006. As a result, the GCC will soon lower its 5 percent tariff on Asian cars, machinery, and clothing, and China and Japan will buy more Saudi, Kuwaiti, and UAE petrochemicals. In addition, the GCC is engaged in advanced trade talks with India, Turkey, and the European Union.

The most dynamic city in the Middle East is Dubai, one of the seven city-states that merged to form the UAE in 1971, the year that Britain ended its naval protection of the principalities. Unlike neighboring Abu Dhabi, however, Dubai is running out of oil. It receives only about 6 percent of its revenue today from petroleum, and sometime in the 2010s, its wells will simply run dry. Yet in Dubai, oil has become almost irrelevant. The city's economy has nearly tripled in size in the last decade because it has become one of the world's great trading centers, with a government that places almost no restrictions on business activity.

Dubai is one of the ten largest ports in the world, attracts more than five million tourists a year (more than India), and is the Middle East headquarters for more than a thousand U.S. and European corporations. "Dubai has been trying to prove to the rest of the Arab world that there is life after oil, and that in fact it is a better life," said Abdulkhaleq Abdulla, a professor of political science at Emirates University. "The good news is that there is room for a second and a third Dubai."[16]

In Saudi Arabia, a third of the people are foreign workers. In Dubai, almost 90 percent of the people are foreign laborers (nearly two-thirds of them are from India, Pakistan, Sri Lanka, and Bangladesh), and the city's financial district does its business in English, not Arabic.

Dubai is also one of the world's most architecturally striking cities. It has almost as many skyscrapers as New York City does, and visually, the buildings in Dubai are more interesting. One building under construction, the Burj Dubai (Dubai Tower), will be the tallest building in the world when it is completed in 2009. It will be more than two thousand feet high, twice as tall as New York's Chrysler Building.

Other attractions in Dubai that were recently finished or are nearing completion include the Dubai Sunny Mountain Ski Dome, a twenty-five-story indoor ski slope; Hydropolis, an underwater hotel; Restless Planet, an amusement park where tourists will fight replicas of dinosaurs; the Ibn Battuta Mall, a shopping center with 250 stores and restaurants in six wings designed to look like North Africa, Egypt, Persia, India, China, and medieval Spain; and several enormous resort developments with artificial islands that are shaped like palm trees, Arabic letters, and real islands such as Hawaii, Britain, and Cuba.

Although the local press is tame and still censors itself, Dubai built Media City for foreign newspapers, television networks, and magazines. Inside Media City, they are free to broadcast or print anything they like as long as it is not pornographic or blasphemous.

Commercially, Dubai is the freest city in the Arab world, the Singapore of the Middle East. Even its grossly underpaid foreign laborers, who on average make less than $8 a day, won a limited right to bargain collectively (but not to unionize or strike) in 2006.

Less than two hundred miles from Saudi Arabia, Dubai is a model for forward-looking Saudis and for entrepreneurial Muslims everywhere. In the words of Abdulrahman al-Rashid, the Saudi journalist in charge of the Al Arabiya satellite news network, "People are beginning to ask their governments: 'If Dubai can do it, why can't we?'"[17]

Joining the World Trade Organization

By far the most important step Saudi Arabia has taken to improve its business climate was to join the World Trade Organization as its 149th member on December 11, 2005. The organization oversees more than 97 percent of the world's trade. Among the world's leading economic nations, only Russia and Iran have yet to become members. Of the six GCC states, Saudi Arabia was the last to join.

Membership in the WTO gives Saudi Arabia "most favored nation" status (also known as Permanent Normal Trade Relations). This means that U.S. and European tariffs on Saudi petrochemicals, for example, cannot be any higher than their tariffs on petrochemicals from any other country. WTO membership will also lead to more foreign investment in the kingdom because businessmen know that in order to join the WTO, Saudi Arabia had to sign dozens of commercial treaties that made its commercial laws conform to international standards, which has made Saudi Arabia a much safer place to invest.

Saudi Arabia's negotiations to join the WTO took twelve years and involved 314 rounds of talks with trade representatives from other countries. The Saudis prepared more than 7,000 pages of documents to answer more than 3,400 trade-related questions over the course of these negotiations. Saudi Arabia signed 38 trade agreements with various countries that covered 7,177 separate tariffs on agricultural and manufactured goods and 155 different kinds of services.[18]

The Saudis won fifty-nine exemptions that permit them to continue to ban pork, alcohol, pornography, and slot machines from the kingdom; prohibit non-Muslims from traveling to Mecca and Medina; limit the percentage of foreign ownership in some industries; subsidize farmers; and allow government buyers to favor local manufacturers.[19]

Most important, the Saudis made fifty-eight separate commitments to honor previous WTO agreements on arbitration, fiscal transparency, the elimination of barriers to foreign investment, and the protection of intellectual property—in short, to abide by the norms of international business. Beginning in 2000, the kingdom passed forty-two laws to implement these commitments, covering subjects from fertilizer-making to integrated circuits.[20]

In the 1990s, talks to join the WTO got bogged down over the details of farm subsidies, petrochemical tariffs, and foreign access to the kingdom's businesses. The pace of the talks picked up in 2003 when the United States began to negotiate free-trade agreements with Bahrain, Oman, and the UAE, and the Saudis realized that their petrochemicals could be priced out of the U.S. and other markets unless they became serious about lowering their tariffs. Abdullah encouraged his negotiators to move quickly because he saw membership in the WTO as a prerequisite for the increased foreign investment that was needed to create more jobs and reduce the kingdom's unemployment.

In exchange for lower Western tariffs on petrochemicals and other Saudi goods, the kingdom agreed to open its markets to foreign agricultural products and to foreign services such as banking, retailing, express delivery, and telecommunications. The Saudis also agreed to remove their tariffs on U.S. pharmaceutical products as soon as they joined the WTO and on computer hardware and software by January 2008. (In 2004, the kingdom's top imports from the United States were, by value, cars, aircraft parts, car and truck engines, and cigarettes.)[21]

Negotiations with the European Union were particularly complex, but the day that Saudi Arabia joined the WTO, the European Union's tariff on Saudi petrochemicals fell by almost half, from 11.5 percent to just 6.5 percent, and the United States followed Europe's lead.

Until recently, Saudi Arabia exported more than half of its petrochemicals to East Asia because the Asian nations did not levy any tariffs on Saudi petrochemical products. Now, reduced U.S. and European tariffs will allow Saudi petrochemical companies to compete in Western markets, too. They can sell petrochemicals more cheaply than U.S. and European petrochemical companies can because they pay less for natural gas, the main ingredient in petrochemicals, so in the next few years the sales of Saudi petrochemicals in the West will probably increase dramatically.

The biggest beneficiary of Saudi Arabia's membership in the WTO is the kingdom's largest petrochemical company, the Saudi Arabian Basic Industries Corporation (SABIC), which should be able to increase its share of the world's petrochemical market from about 9 to 10 percent today to 15 percent by 2015. By then, if trends continue, SABIC may be the largest petrochemical company in the world. Other Saudi petrochemical firms will also prosper.

The biggest losers will be Saudi Arabia's grain, dairy, and poultry farmers. Under WTO rules, the Saudi government's large subsidies to them must gradually decrease, while the 20 percent tariff on food that protected them from foreign competition has already fallen to only 5 percent. The government is reducing its buying of wheat from Saudi farmers 12.5 percent a year in order to save water. By 2016 its purchases will stop completely.

Some entrepreneurs are frightened that free trade will lead to a massive influx of cheap foreign goods that will put them out of business. "SABIC will gain and the rest of us will lose," a Saudi pharmaceutical importer told me. Another businessman, an American who has lived in the kingdom for thirty years, is equally skeptical of the benefits of WTO membership because even the largest petrochemical plants rarely employ more than a few hundred people.

Other businessmen, including a majority of the members of Saudi Arabia's chambers of commerce, are more optimistic. First, they feel that the hundreds of improvements the government made to the kingdom's commercial and legal systems in order to win WTO membership are good for business and good for growth. Foreign investment tripled the very first year that Saudi Arabia joined the WTO, and the non-oil economy, which had grown just 2 percent annually in the 1990s, started to grow 6 to 7 percent a year from 2003 onward.

Second, many women hope that as the economy grows, more women will have jobs and that these women will demand and win more rights and a gentler form of gender segregation. Third, many entrepreneurs feel that the new oil boom has given them the time they need to make their businesses leaner, more efficient, and better able to face foreign competition.

Finally, many businessmen agree with Khan Zahid, the chief economist of the Riyad Bank, who said that if Saudi Arabia is to diversify its economy and reduce its dependence on oil, joining the WTO is not a choice but a necessity. The kingdom's petrochemical, fertilizer, cement, and aluminum companies can only sell their products abroad, he said, if foreign tariffs are low and the kingdom's rules of trade are predictable.[22]

Prince Abdullah bin Faisal bin Turki, the energetic leader of the Saudi Arabian General Investment Authority (SAGIA) from 2000 to 2004, conceded that joining the WTO will force Saudi businesses to make painful changes but also said that membership is a necessity: "Many Saudi businesses have been subsidized and spoiled. Only hard work will protect our industries now, but we are part of the human race and cannot isolate ourselves forever. The royal family wants Saudi Arabia to be integrated with the world."[23]

A Booming Economy, a Stock Market Bubble, and Some Profitable Public Offerings

Saudi Arabia's efforts to improve its business climate paid off quickly. The kingdom's non-oil economy, which had been sluggish through 2003, grew 5.7 percent in 2004, 6.6 percent in 2005, and 6.4 percent in 2006. But oil drives the Saudi economy, and rising prices have created a boom. Saudi Arabia's nominal GDP climbed from $189 billion in 2002 to $349 billion in 2006. Even allowing for inflation, which climbed from less than 1 percent a year from 1996 to 2005, to 6 percent annually during the last quarter of 2007, the Saudi economy still nearly doubled in size in only four years.[24]

Saudi GDP per person grew almost 80 percent during this period, from $8,728 in 2002 to about $15,500 in 2006. This is the highest income per person since 1981, when the last oil boom was at its peak. Because foreign workers, who make up one-third of the population, earn very little money, income per person for Saudi citizens is probably more than $20,000 a year, a level comparable to that of Spain or South Korea. The Saudis are wealthier today than they have been in a quarter of a century, and at least a few Saudi women are worried that their husbands have become rich enough to afford second wives.[25]

Until 2006, stocks soared. When the price of oil was low, stocks rose just 3.6 percent in 2002. As the price of oil increased, however, stocks climbed 76 percent in 2003, 85 percent in 2004, and 103 percent in 2005. The Saudi Tadawul Index, which barely peeped above 2,500 in December 2002, soared to 16,713 by the end of 2005, a sevenfold increase in three years.

The first reason for Saudi Arabia's bull market was the classic one: rising corporate profits. In 2004, the average profit of a company on the Saudi exchange climbed 45 percent. The largest companies enjoyed even bigger profits. At SABIC, the petrochemical giant, profits skyrocketed 110 percent in 2004, and several large banks doubled their profits too, driving the entire market upward.

The second reason for the kingdom's bull market was that many Saudis began to move their money from the United States back home. Saudi investors were already discouraged by the dot-com bust in 2000 and early 2001, having lost more than $100 billion in Western and Asian stocks. Then came September 11 and the shocking news that fifteen of the 9/11 hijackers were Saudi. Many Saudis wondered whether U.S. courts might freeze or even seize their assets, especially after 3,600 relatives of the 9/11 victims filed a $1 trillion lawsuit in a U.S. district court in Washington, D.C., in August 2002.

Under a 1992 U.S. law that allows terror victims to sue for damages, the 3,600 plaintiffs in *Burnett v. Al Baraka Investment and Development Corporation* sued 205 defendants, including 6 Saudi princes, 3 Saudi banks, and 7 Saudi charities. Many of the claims, including every one against the Saudi princes, have since been dismissed, but others are still pending. More suits by different sets of 9/11 plaintiffs have also been filed, with some suits dismissed and others delayed. For many Saudis, the damage was done as soon as the suits were filed. They no longer felt that their U.S. assets were secure, and they began to sell much of their U.S. stocks and real estate and to invest in Saudi shares and land instead. The *Financial Times* estimates that Saudi investors sold up to $200 billion worth of their U.S. assets, about a third of their total U.S. holdings.

The third reason for the Saudi bull market was that a great deal of money was being invested in a small number of companies. Of the 11,622 limited liability companies in Saudi Arabia in 2002, only 121 were joint stock firms, and only about 70 of these were listed on the Saudi stock exchange.[26] Today, the number of companies on the exchange is still barely over 100, because most Saudi businessmen do not want to lose control of their firms by going public, even if staying private means doing without the vast sums of money a public offering can raise. Worse, the Saudi government and its pension funds own about 30 percent of the Saudi stock market because the government has been too slow to sell its shares of SABIC, Saudi Telecom, and other large companies. Saudi banks own another 40 percent of the market, which leaves the ordinary Saudi investor with fewer shares to buy, and the scarcity of shares drives up prices.[27]

By the winter of 2005–2006, the bull market had become a bubble. But before that happened, it had been climbing for years. At the end of 2002, the Tadawul Index was 2,530; it hit 4,450 in 2003, 8,206 in 2004, and 16,713 on December 31, 2005. In January and February 2006, the market leaped another 4,253 points, peaking at 20,966 on February 25, 2006, only a year after the market had first climbed above 10,000. More than five million Saudis had bought stock by the end of 2005, which amounts to more than half of the kingdom's adults. As the market roared, both teachers and their students pulled out cell phones during class breaks to buy stock, and banks opened lounges where women could follow their stocks minute by minute. Some cocky investors even took out loans to buy more shares.

By 2006, stock prices were far beyond anything that could be justified by corporate earnings, and on February 26, the bubble finally burst. The market dropped 1,895 points in two days, then fell another 9,373 points over the next ten weeks. By May 10, the market had lost more than half its value, and the Tadawul Index was just 9,698. In an attempt to lift stock prices, the government changed its rules and allowed foreigners living in the kingdom and GCC-based pension funds to buy Saudi stock. This didn't help. From November 2006 through January 2007, the market plunged another 28 percent, to 6,923—wiping out all the gains that investors had made since October 2004—and it stayed below 8,000 until August and below 10,000 into 2008. On paper, the Saudis lost more than $450 billion, but experienced investors who had been in the market since 2003 were unhurt because they were still far ahead of their initial investment.

Many ordinary Saudis took a beating. Few had understood that a stock's price is dependent on its earnings; they had hoped only to double their money as other investors had the previous year. Those who bought stock at the peak of the market lost more than half of their savings, and the brash few who had borrowed money to buy more stock were ruined.

Because record oil revenues continued to pour into the kingdom, the crash of 2006 had almost no effect on the kingdom's booming economy, but it did make many Saudis aware of the need for more financial reform. The government had already created the Capital Market Authority (CMA) in June 2004, modeling the agency on both the U.S. and the Malaysian Securities Exchange Commissions.

Within a year and a half, the CMA had fined forty-four Saudis for insider trading, executives and directors from half of the firms listed on the Saudi stock exchange, which proved that the problem of insider trading was endemic, not isolated. Unfortunately, the maximum fine for the offense at this time was only U.S. $27,000, far too small to discourage such trading, nor did the Capital Markets Law specify any jail time for the offenders. The CMA did, however, make Saudi companies much more transparent. By 2004, more than 85 percent of the kingdom's joint stock companies were releasing quarterly balance sheets, and by 2006, they all were, without exception.[28] The CMA strengthened its enforcement of the laws against manipulation and insider trading in 2006 and punished twenty-eight offenders, including three traders who were fined $45 million.

Since the stock market crash, a growing number of Saudis have urged the government to accelerate the arrival of independent brokers, securities analysts, and investment bankers in the kingdom because these professionals will demand more detailed and precise financial statements from Saudi companies. As Khan Zahid, the chief economist at the Riyad Bank, wrote in the *Arab News* after the crash began, "We know what the solutions are but they need to be implemented quickly . . . increase the supply of shares, increase market knowledge and transparency through the introduction of independent analysts and advisors, and impose severe and public punishment for market manipulation and insider trading."[29]

Although several hundred thousand Saudis lost a great deal of money in the crash of 2006, almost ten million Saudis have made enormous profits by participating in the kingdom's initial public offerings (IPOs). As recently as 2002, only forty thousand Saudis owned stock, but this changed in December of that year when the Saudi Telecommunications Company (previously the Ministry of Posts, Telephones, and Telegraphs) raised $2.7 billion by selling 30 percent of its shares to pension funds and to the Saudi public, shares that more than doubled in value the following year. The word was out: There was money to be made in buying IPOs.

When the next IPO became available in June 2004, for shares in the Sahara Petrochemical Company, 552,000 Saudis participated. Sahara's stock nearly quadrupled in just six months, so when an IPO for a cell phone company, Ettihad Etisalat, took place in November and December, 4.2 million Saudis bought shares—half of the adult population.[30]

These shares, which were probably offered too cheaply, leaped sevenfold by the end of 2004, so when 50 percent of the shares of Al Bilad Bank became available in March 2005, 8.3 million Saudis bought shares—virtually the entire adult population. Another 8 million Saudis bought shares of the Yanbu National Petrochemicals Company in an IPO in December. This time, almost 40 percent of the shares were purchased through ATMs or the Internet.[31]

The stock market crash of 2006 did not dampen the public's enthusiasm for IPOs. More than fifty IPOs took place in 2006 and 2007, and the CMA is reviewing plans for many more.

IPOs have been enormously profitable for Saudi investors. Despite the crash, an investor who bought shares during Saudi Telecom's IPO had still more than tripled his money. Similar investments in Sahara Petrochemicals had grown sixfold; in cell phone giant Ettihad Etisalat, eightfold; and in Al Bilad Bank, ninefold. Even the initial shares of a relative dud, Al-Marai Dairy, were still worth 50 percent more after the crash than they had been at the time of the offering.[32] The new boom was making millions of Saudis wealthier.

A "Great Meeting" in Crawford, Texas

On April 25, 2005, Crown Prince Abdullah became the first head of state to visit President George W. Bush's ranch in Crawford, Texas, a second time. Only half a dozen world leaders had visited the ranch even once, so it was a high honor. In the afternoon, the two leaders held hands in front of photographers, a gesture that let the whole world know that in spite of 9/11, the sixty-year friendship between the United States and Saudi Arabia was still strong.

During the crown prince's visit, the Saudis promised to increase their maximum oil production capacity from 10.5 million barrels a day to 12.5 million barrels a day by the end of 2009, an effort that will probably cost them about $20 billion. Because the world's demand for oil was rising and the kingdom's production in 2005 was already near its maximum, the only way the Saudis could continue to have a buffer of 1 to 2 million barrels of oil a day above their daily production was to increase their production capacity further. Without this extra margin, the Saudis would not be able to increase their oil production during troubled times, such as the week after 9/11 or the week before the U.S. invasion of Iraq. Without more spare capacity, the Saudis would not be able to bring the price of oil down. In fact, they would have no control over the price of oil at all.

President Bush, Vice President Dick Cheney, and Secretary of State Condoleezza Rice were extremely pleased by Abdullah's pledge, and in return, they promised to train more Saudi military officers, increase the number of meetings between midlevel U.S. and Saudi officials, and ease the visa process so that more young Saudis could study in the United States. The Americans also agreed to wind up the U.S.-Saudi trade talks that had been one of Saudi Arabia's final hurdles before it could join the WTO.

Happily, both nations kept their promises. Within eight months, Saudi Arabia had joined the WTO, and the number of Saudi students at U.S. universities had tripled. And the Saudis, as the next section describes in detail, began to spend $4 billion a year to increase their oil-production capacity. Abdullah's flights to Texas and back had taken thirty hours, a long way for an eighty-two-year-old man to travel. But when Abdullah returned home, he told an adviser, "It wasn't a good meeting, it was a great meeting."[33]

The Need and the Struggle to Produce More Oil

When the new oil boom began in 2003, the Saudis had not increased their oil-production capacity since the 1970s because, during most of the years since then, there had been a glut of oil, not a shortage. Even when the demand for oil began to climb in 2003, the Saudis were reluctant to increase their capacity; the memory of oil at $10 a barrel in 1985 and 1998 was still too strong. By the autumn of 2004, however, the world's demand for oil had grown so much that the Saudis were no longer worried about new discoveries or alternative fuels pushing the price of oil back down. The world seemed to need all the energy it could find.

In addition to wanting more control over the price of oil, the Saudis had two other reasons to increase their production capacity: first, as insurance. As Saudi oil minister Ali al-Naimi explained at a news conference in Washington on May 2, 2006, "It has been and will continue to be our policy to maintain 1.5 to 2 million barrels a day of spare crude oil production capacity . . . to lessen the negative impact on prices of wars, strikes and natural disasters."[34]

Second, the Saudis would like to check Iran's growing power. In the 2010s, the Iranians may build, test, and deploy nuclear weapons, thinking that the world will not apply any meaningful sanctions against them because a boycott of Iranian oil might cause the price of crude to surge well above $150 a barrel. But if the Saudis can increase their production capacity to 12.5 million barrels a day (while still pumping only about 9 million barrels a day, as they do today), then their spare capacity will be more than 3 million barrels a day—considerably more than the 2.3 million barrels a day that Iran exports. By enlarging its production capacity, Saudi Arabia could temporarily make up for the loss of Iranian oil, which might give the world the courage to apply tougher sanctions against Iran should its regime act irresponsibly. The Saudis might even have enough spare capacity left to cover a second shortfall of oil arising from instability in Iraq, Venezuela, or Nigeria—assuming, of course, that the kingdom's extra new capacity is not simply devoured by Asia's steadily growing demand for oil.

Finding new oil is expensive. The process of exploring, building rigs, drilling, injecting water, separating oil from gas, and building storage tanks, pumping stations, and miles of pipelines costs many millions of dollars. Running an offshore rig with only six or seven wells, for example, costs more than $40 million a year, yet Saudi Aramco spends the money. Between 2004 and 2006, the number of drilling rigs in the kingdom doubled, and the number of offshore rigs tripled.

To raise Saudi Arabia's production capacity from 10.5 to 12.5 million barrels a day, it is not enough just to find new wells that can produce 2 million barrels a day. Old wells become depleted, and their production has to be replaced. When King Abdullah pledged to increase Saudi Arabia's production capacity, he was really committing the kingdom to finding *3 million* new barrels of oil a day—the equivalent of another Kuwait or Venezuela—because only then, with the depletion of old wells subtracted, would the kingdom's production capacity reach 12.5 million barrels a day.

The kingdom is increasing its capacity in stages. By 2004, Saudi Aramco had already developed two new fields at Qatif and Abu Safah to increase its production capacity to about 10.5 million barrels a day. In the spring of 2006, a field at Haradh added 300,000 more barrels a day to the kingdom's production, and late in 2008, a fourth new field at Khursaniyah will add another 500,000 barrels a day. A fifth field at Shaybah will produce 750,000 barrels a day by the end of 2008, but subtracting depletions, the five fields combined will have raised the kingdom's production capacity to only 11.8 million barrels of oil a day.

Saudi Aramco has saved the development of its biggest new field for last. At a cost of $6 billion, with help from Halliburton, geologists are reviving a massive old field named Khoreis that had been too difficult to drill in the 1970s. Now, with the help of more than three hundred horizontal wells tapping dozens of previously hidden reservoirs, geologists expect Khoreis to produce more than 1 million barrels a day by the end of 2009, which will bring the kingdom's production capacity up to 12.5 million barrels a day, as promised.

Saudi Aramco is thinking about expanding its field at Shaybah further and developing new offshore fields at Manifa by 2012, but only if the global demand for oil continues to increase. Together, the Shaybah and Manifa fields would add more than 1 million barrels a day to the kingdom's oil production, which, minus depletion, would increase Saudi Arabia's production capacity to 13.1 million barrels of oil a day by 2012, with luck enough to allow for several emergencies.

The Saudis are not only increasing their oil production capacity, they are increasing their refining capacity, too. At present, the kingdom has eight refineries: four on the Red Sea, three on the Persian Gulf, and one in Riyadh. Together, they refine about 2 million barrels of oil a day into gasoline and diesel fuel, almost a quarter of the kingdom's production. The Saudis use about 80 percent of this fuel themselves and export the rest.

Because the Saudis would like to make more money by refining even more of their oil, Saudi Aramco, ConocoPhillips, and Total, the French oil company, are spending $12 billion to build two huge new refineries that will turn 800,000 barrels of oil a day into gasoline and diesel fuel by 2012. In contrast to most refineries, however, these plants will be able to refine "sour" crude, oil that is heavier and more sulfuric than "sweet crude."

One refinery, in Yanbu, on the Red Sea, is a joint venture between Saudi Aramco and ConocoPhillips. Kellogg, Brown and Root, a division of Halliburton, is building the plant, and the gasoline it produces will be shipped west to the United States and Europe. The other refinery is in Jubail, on the Persian Gulf, and is a joint venture between Saudi Aramco and Total. Technip, the Italian engineering firm, is building the plant, and the gasoline it produces will be shipped east to Asia. The Saudis also co-own refineries in China, Greece, South Korea, the Philippines, and Port Arthur, Texas.

Using Gas to Save Oil

Saudi Arabia has 4 percent of the world's natural gas. (Russia has 27 percent; Iran, 15 percent; Qatar, 14 percent; the UAE, 3.5 percent; and the United States, 3 percent).[35] The kingdom's vast reserves make up more than 252 trillion cubic feet. If it were all in one place, it would fill a cube 12.8 miles on each side. Unlike oil, natural gas is expensive to store and ship because liquefaction requires frigid containers with temperatures hundreds of degrees below zero. Saudi Arabia therefore exports very little of its natural gas.

Domestically, however, natural gas accounts for a quarter of the Saudis' energy use. Pipelines send natural gas directly into petrochemical complexes, electric power plants, cement factories, and the thirty desalinization plants that furnish 70 percent of the kingdom's drinking water and 20 percent of its electricity. Using a cubic meter of natural gas saves roughly a cup of crude oil. Across the kingdom, the Saudis' daily use of more than 160 million cubic meters of natural gas saves them about 250,000 barrels of oil a day, oil that can be exported instead of consumed at home. In other words, the use of natural gas lets the Saudis earn an extra $4 to $6 billion a year, roughly $100 million a week.

"Only 15 percent of Saudi Arabia has been adequately explored for gas," says Saudi Aramco's vice president for new development, Khalid al-Falih. Since 1999, however, Saudi Aramco has spent nearly $2 billion a year on natural gas exploration and processing, a level of spending that it intends to continue at least until 2025. Its goal is to increase the kingdom's gas reserves 2 to 4 percent a year and eventually to triple its annual production.

In 2003, the government passed a law that allows foreign companies to look for natural gas in the kingdom in return for a 35 percent tax on their profits. In July, Saudi Aramco started a joint venture with Shell and Total to try to find natural gas in the Empty Quarter. It was the first time that Saudi Arabia had allowed foreign companies to look for oil and gas since the 1970s.

Six months later, in January 2004, the Saudis started three more joint ventures—with Sinopec, the Chinese oil company; Lukoil, the Russian oil company; and ENI, the Italian oil company, and Repsol, the Spanish oil company—to look for natural gas in the Empty Quarter. In each case, Saudi Aramco owned 20 percent of the venture, and the companies agreed to pay a 35 percent tax on their profits. (In essence, the split was 52 percent for the foreign oil companies and 48 percent for the Saudis.) Exploration and drilling in a region as harsh as the Empty Quarter take time. The companies do not expect to produce commercial volumes of natural gas until 2009 at the earliest.

Not one of the kingdom's gas deals is with a U.S. oil company. Talks with ExxonMobil and other U.S. companies broke down in

2002 over the issues of how much land the companies could explore and how much profit they could earn. By 2002, the Saudis were also angered and hurt by the many hostile articles about the kingdom in the U.S. press after 9/11, and they wanted to be less dependent on U.S. technical expertise. The desire for energy independence is a two-way street.

A Growing Petrochemical Industry

Petrochemical is an intimidating word, but the process of turning natural gases into useful materials is a big part of our everyday lives. Ethane is an ingredient in paint, ink, detergent, adhesives, plastic, polyester, antifreeze, and de-icers; methane is used in vinyl, fertilizers, and animal feed; and propane is used in making solvents and insulation.

Saudi Arabia manufactured almost sixty million tons of petrochemicals in 2006, more than three thousand pounds a second. The kingdom is the eighth- or ninth-largest producer of petrochemicals in the world but may become the number-one or -two producer by 2015 because it is spending billions of dollars a year building new plants to double its production and because the demand for its low-cost products, especially in Asia, is high. Methane, ethane, and other natural gases are seven to ten times cheaper in Saudi Arabia than they are on the New York Mercantile Exchange, so Saudi Arabia's finished petrochemical products are much cheaper than petrochemicals made in Germany or the United States.

The kingdom's largest petrochemical company, SABIC, earned profits of $5.1 billion in 2005, $5.4 billion in 2006, and $7.2 billion in 2007, making it by far the most profitable petrochemical company in the world. The government still owns 70 percent of the privately managed enterprise and does not seem to want to sell any more shares of this wonderful cash cow.

In addition to its own plants, SABIC bought General Electric's plastics division in the summer of 2007 and is also the part-owner of more than a dozen joint ventures with foreign oil and chemical companies. Saudi Chevron Petrochemical, for example, makes benzene, while the Arabian Chemical Company, a subsidiary of Dow Chemical, makes latex.

Half of the kingdom's petrochemical plants are in Jubail, the industrial port of a hundred thousand people that the government built on the Persian Gulf in the 1970s and the 1980s. Today, it is the leading industrial city on the Arabian peninsula, with a giant oil refinery, a lubricants plant, a steel mill, a natural gas processing facility, and three fertilizer plants, in addition to the city's many petrochemical complexes. By itself, Jubail employs a quarter of the kingdom's industrial workers and receives almost half of the kingdom's foreign investment. In fact, Jubail's enterprises have been so successful that in 2002, the government began to build a second industrial city next door in the hopes of employing another fifty thousand people.[36]

Five more petrochemical plants are in Yanbu, the industrial city of seventy thousand people that the government built on the Red Sea about two hundred miles north of Jeddah. One of them, a joint venture between ExxonMobil and the Saudi government, is the world's largest manufacturer of polyethylene, a key ingredient in plastics and insulation. Yanbu also has three oil refineries.

In 2004, Saudi Aramco decided to compete with SABIC and make its own petrochemicals. Two years later, it signed a contract with Japan's Sumitomo Chemical Company to build the world's largest petrochemical complex at Rabigh, a city on the Red Sea north of Jeddah. The new plant, PetroRabigh, is costing about $10 billion and will be complete in 2009. Seventeen Japanese and Western banks lent the joint venture $4.8 billion, and it raised an additional $1.2 billion by selling twenty-five percent of the venture to the Saudi public in an IPO in January 2008. Once PetroRabigh begins running, it will produce more than four thousand tons a day of ethylene, an important ingredient in paints and plastics.[37]

On the other side of the kingdom, Saudi Aramco signed a preliminary agreement with Dow Chemical in May 2007 to form a joint venture that will build and run a $20 billion petrochemical and plastics complex at Ras Tanura on the Persian Gulf by 2013. The two companies plan to raise most of the money they need through corporate bonds.

Saudi Arabia's petrochemical industry is a huge success story, but two notes of caution are in order. First, even the largest petrochemical complexes employ only a few thousand people, so no matter how much the industry grows, it will do little to solve the kingdom's perennial problem of unemployment. Second, because Saudi Arabia exports more than half of its oil and petrochemicals to Asia, the country is becoming increasingly sensitive to the ups and downs of the Asian economy.

As the table on page 489 makes clear, Saudi Arabia's economy is completely dependent on oil and petrochemicals, commodities whose prices change constantly in a world of jittery markets. If the Saudis

Saudi Arabia's Top Imports and Exports (by Value) to China, Japan, and India in 2004[38]

China Exports To	China Imports From	Japan Exports To	Japan Imports From	India Exports To	India Imports From
oil	men's clothes	oil	large cars	oil	rice
propane	women's clothes	propane	jeeps	propane	men's suits
polyethylene	tile	refined oil	tires	styrene	black tea
styrene	tugboats	gasoline	pickup trucks	ammonium nitrate	cathodes
ethylene glycol	computer parts	methanol	small cars	gasoline	skin cream

are ever to control their own destiny—if they can maintain their standard of living even during a severe Asian or U.S. recession—they must develop a non-oil economy, too. Petrochemicals are lucrative, but they do not reduce the kingdom's huge need for economic diversification.

Creating a Non-Oil Economy

Saudi Arabia's non-oil economy employs 98.6 percent of its workforce, yet it accounts for just 60 percent of its GDP and only 12 percent of its exports. Since 2003, however, record oil revenues have led to increased private investments, bigger government loans, and even gifts of free land by the Saudi Authority for Industrial Estates and Technology Zones. Together, these spending increases helped the kingdom's non-oil economy to grow an impressive 30 percent between 2003 and 2007.

Much of this growth was in construction, as private developers and government agencies spent billions of dollars repairing or replacing aging roads, schools, clinics, sewage plants, apartments, and shopping malls that had been quickly but cheaply built during the first oil boom in the 1970s and the early 1980s. The kingdom is also spending about $6 billion a year to double its production of electricity by 2025. The construction boom has created smaller booms in the steel, tile, glass, cable, granite, and marble industries, and the kingdom's eight cement companies have been operating at full capacity.

The new construction is particularly visible in Riyadh, which now has two skyscrapers almost a thousand feet high, only slightly shorter than New York's Chrysler Building. Both buildings have ultramodern shopping malls on their first three floors. A government agency also began the construction of a financial district in Riyadh in 2007. The area will have not only new office buildings, hotels, and shopping malls, but a monorail and a business school, too.

One of the most promising areas for diversifying the Saudi economy is mining. Mines have been operating in Saudi Arabia for thousands of years; King Solomon's largest gold mine may have been just a few miles southeast of Medina. The Mahd Ad' Dahab, as the mine is called today, still produces thirty to forty pounds of gold a day, along with about 20,000 to 30,000 pounds of zinc.

Ma'aden, a mostly government-owned mining company, is spending hundreds of millions of dollars a year developing new mines to extract bauxite, zinc, copper, and phosphate, which is the key ingredient in fertilizer. Each mine also brings roads, railroads, power plants, and, most important, jobs, to a rural area.

In July 2006, Ma'aden signed a contract with a Dutch company, Litwin, to build the largest fertilizer plant in the world, at Ras Az Zawr Mineral City, a new port on the Persian Gulf, by 2010. By 2016, some analysts think that Saudi Arabia will be the world's third-largest producer of fertilizer. "The world will depend on Saudi Arabia for food the same way it depends on it for energy," said Abdallah Dabbagh, Ma'aden's president.[39]

More important than phosphate is bauxite, the core ingredient in aluminum. The recent development of large bauxite mines in the kingdom's far north and deep south has led Ma'aden to sign multibillion-dollar agreements with Alcan, a Canadian company, to build a bauxite refinery and an aluminum smelter at Ras Az Zawr Mineral City by 2011, and with two Chinese companies to build a second refinery and smelter at Jizan in the south. Each of the giant smelters will convert more than ten thousand tons of bauxite a day into almost two thousand tons of aluminum and may create as many as ten thousand jobs.[40]

Bauxite is also abundant in the other GCC states. The six states currently smelt about 7 percent of the world's aluminum, but this percentage will probably rise to 10 percent in the next decade because Qatar and Oman are also building aluminum smelters, and Bahrain and Dubai are enlarging existing plants.

Ironically, because aluminum makes up about a third of most automobile frames, the world will soon be almost as dependent on the Gulf States for aluminum, the car's most basic ingredient, as it is for oil.

The Saudis have been manufacturing building materials since the 1970s, but only recently have they begun to make more sophisticated items. In Riyadh, General Motors has built a factory to assemble trucks and buses. The engines are made in the United States and Europe, but Saudis put the vehicles together on an assembly line. In Jeddah, Daimler-Benz has built a similar factory to assemble Mercedes trucks and buses. A Saudi company, Zamil Industrial Investment, manufactures batteries for General Motors and air conditioners for General Electric and Sanyo, and in 2007, a Korean company, LG Electronics, built a factory in Riyadh that makes five thousand air conditioners a week.[41]

A Saudi computer company, Bitcom, has opened a factory in Riyadh that makes notebook computers, desktop computers, and LCD screens. Saudi firms also export about $80 million worth of switches, amplifiers, and other electronic components annually.[42]

A less promising portion of Saudi Arabia's non-oil economy is nonreligious tourism. Religious tourism, of course, is a huge moneymaker. Roughly three million pilgrims travel to Mecca and Medina every year, and they spend more than $8 billion. But the government wants to attract non-Muslim tourists to scuba dive in the Red Sea and visit several archaeological sites. Unfortunately, it is highly doubtful that the kingdom can ever attract more than a trickle of Westerners and Asians, at least in the next decade or two.

The most obvious factors that discourage non-Muslims from coming to Saudi Arabia are the inability to buy alcohol and the necessity for men and especially women to dress modestly. Women must cover all of their arms, legs, and hair, and if they are under thirty, they cannot enter the kingdom at all unless they are accompanied by a father, a husband, or a brother.

Even more frustrating for non-Muslims is the disruption that prayer times cause to schedules. If you arrive at a museum even one minute after a prayer has begun, you will have to wait twenty minutes before the gatekeeper can return from his mosque to let you in. If you are in a store when a prayer call begins, you must go to the cash register immediately to pay for what you are buying before the owner closes his shop to go pray—and then sit outside and wait twenty minutes before his store or any other store opens again.

The two evening prayers, the first at sunset and the second an hour after sunset, can be the most frustrating for non-Muslims because it is impossible to relax at a café or have a non–fast food dinner before nine o'clock, for cafes and restaurants also close for prayers. Drinking and eating are what most tourists do between six and nine, and Saudi Arabia simply cannot accommodate them.

Until 2006, photography was also a problem in Saudi Arabia. Once, after I took a picture of some veiled women waiting in line at a Dunkin' Donuts, a Saudi told me that I was lucky that no policeman had seen me, and he warned me not to do it again. Another time I took a picture of the Ministry of the Interior headquarters from a car window and was stopped just seconds later by a friendly policeman who nevertheless insisted that I open my camera and give him the film. It did not matter that the architecturally striking building is on many postcards.

I got into the most trouble when I took a picture of a soldier sitting behind a mounted machine gun under some camouflage netting. I was a block away when I took the picture, but he saw me, took my passport and camera, and led me to his superior officer. For the next two hours, the soldiers argued among themselves about what to do with me. One said to me angrily in halting English, "You took picture my family!" Finally, the soldiers called the police, and a friendly, easy-going officer put me into the back of his patrol car and drove me to his station, occasionally saying, "No problem." I spent the next three and a half hours sitting in a plastic chair in a dingy, fluorescent-lit waiting room but was treated courteously and given a bottle of water. At last, an officer asked me to write a statement, and I explained what I was doing in Saudi Arabia and promised not to take any more unauthorized pictures. Five minutes later, I was free to leave with my passport and camera, minus another roll of film.

To promote tourism, the government announced in August 2006 that photography that is not specifically forbidden is legal. But there is still an ingrained hostility to photography among uniformed officers, and this will probably only change slowly. In any case, pictures of soldiers, government buildings, and women, if the women have not agreed to be photographed, are still taboo.

I had a wonderful time living in Saudi Arabia, but the kingdom is a long way from being a tourist-friendly country.

Tourists and Saudis alike will soon have better transportation. Two new Saudi airlines are buying dozens of jets in a variety of sizes for budget flights on more than twenty domestic routes by the end of the decade.

On the ground, the Saudi Railway Organization is financing a "Landbridge" to build nine hundred miles of new railroads in the western part of the kingdom, to connect the city of Jeddah to Riyadh, Mecca, and Medina. When the Landbridge is complete, it will be the first time that the Persian Gulf and the Red Sea have been connected by rail. Several companies, including the Saudi Binladin Group, are submitting bids for the rails' construction. The winning firm will build both high-speed lines for passengers and slower-moving rails for cargo, but even freight trains will be able to travel from one shore to the other in twenty-four hours. A Saudi steel company, Al Tuwairqi, will begin to forge most of the railroad tracks for the Landbridge in 2009, and twenty U.S. companies are supplying engines, coaches, equipment, and spare parts. The U.S. firms are also teaching young Saudis how to operate and maintain the engines and the equipment.

Saudi Arabia's most ambitious and risky non-oil ventures are the six new "economic cities" that developers are starting to build in different parts of the kingdom under the guidance of SAGIA. By far the largest venture is King Abdullah Economic City, a $27 billion construction project that is planned, when finished, to be a thriving city of more than a million people near the town of Rabigh, two hours north of Jeddah on the Red Sea. By 2015, the new city may include a seaport as big as Rotterdam's; a long row of petrochemical factories called Plastics City; a "financial island" of skyscrapers with fully wired offices for tens of thousands of bankers, brokers, and clerks; a retail district with thousands of stores; and three residential areas with 100,000 apartments, 14,000 seaside villas, and 300 mosques. KAEC, as the new city is called for short, is being built by a joint venture that includes the Saudi Binladin Group and the Dubai-based Emaar Properties, the largest real estate developer in the world.[43]

The most unusual feature of the new city will be its new coed college, King Abdullah University of Science and Technology, where, with the king's full support, men and women will attend the same classes, professors will enjoy complete academic freedom, and the religious police will be barred from the campus. At first, the university's president and most of its professors and graduate students will be non-Saudis, but slowly officials hope to create a "Saudi MIT." The university is being endowed with a staggering $10 billion, and it is scheduled to open in the fall of 2009.

Developers are building a second economic city near Hail, about 350 miles northwest of Riyadh. The region around Hail grows 90 percent of Saudi Arabia's corn and 30 percent of its potatoes and barley, so the new city is designed to be the largest trucking, rail, logistics, and food-processing hub in northern Arabia. Saudi, Kuwaiti, and UAE financiers may invest as much as $8 billion in the city and will pave superhighways to the borders of Jordan and Iraq, making Hail the "northern gateway" to the kingdom.

A third metropolis, Knowledge City, outside Medina, will be connected by monorail to the Prophet's Mosque downtown. The new city will include an institute for information technology; a campus for medical, biological, and pharmacological research; and residential areas and shopping districts for tens of thousands of new residents. It will cost more than $6.5 billion.

A fourth economic city will be built just north of Jizan, a seaport on the Red Sea near Yemen. It will have a steel mill, an oil refinery, a copper smelter, an aluminum smelter, a desalinization plant, a seafood storage facility, and several state-of-the-art shipping docks. The city will also include new factories to make building materials because Jizan is located near large deposits of limestone, marble, gypsum, and silica. The two firms that will build most of the metropolis are the Saudi Binladin Group and the MMC Corporation, Malaysia's biggest construction contractor.

A fifth new economic city is planned near Tabuk, in the northwest corner of the kingdom, and may also be geared toward minerals. A sixth economic city is envisioned along the shore of the Persian Gulf, but its precise location and core industry have yet to be determined.[44]

Whether the Saudis can simply create new cities from scratch remains to be seen. When the Brazilians built their capital, Brasilia, deep in their country's interior in the 1950s, they hoped that their new city would lure millions of people from the crowded Atlantic coast to a vibrant inland frontier. Instead, fifty years later, Brasilia is a center only of government, not business, and has just one-fifth the population of Rio de Janeiro, the former capital.

One of the main reasons Saudi Arabia is building these economic cities is to create jobs. "These huge projects will employ thousands of young Saudis and . . . cover all the kingdom's provinces," said Crown Prince Sultan. "Every job seeker will find an employment opportunity in the region where he lives. We are optimistic that in the next five years unemployment will no longer be a problem, God willing."[45]

The desire to reduce unemployment is admirable, but estimates that the six cities will create more than 1.5 million new jobs seem wildly overoptimistic. The Saudi Arabian General Investment Authority, for example, usually one of the government's most efficient and level-headed agencies, estimates that 150,000 people will eventually work in the research and development facilities at King Abdullah Economic

City. But Saudi Arabia simply does not have that many scientists and graduate-level technicians, and even California's Silicon Valley probably does not have many more research and development jobs than this.

Still, money talks. If Saudi and UAE investors really do spend more than $70 billion to build these cities during the next decade—more than $500 million a month—then factories, jobs, support services, and more jobs will surely follow. If the economic cities do grow as planned, they will go a long way toward reducing the kingdom's enormous dependence on oil. Brad Bourland, the knowledgeable chief economist of Jadwa Investments, said, "There will not be any white elephants built in the desert, [because] decisions will be driven by businessmen."[46] Perhaps, but the construction of the six cities is still a huge gamble.

The Momentum of Economic Reform

Saudi Arabia's great challenge today is to make its private sector vigorous enough so that if the price of oil falls sharply, income and employment will not have to plummet, too. The Saudis know that if they want their economy to grow faster than their population, they must spend their oil money more wisely than they have in the past, and even the most conservative clerics understand that in the long run, the financial cost of postponing economic reforms is greater than the social nuisance of adjusting to them.

In the last few years, King Abdullah has reformed the Saudi economy faster than a democracy could have. With his approval, the government has run budget surpluses, paid off most of its debts, encouraged financial transparency, increased its foreign assets, and vastly improved the business climate for foreign investors. It has joined the WTO; strengthened its ties to the other Gulf states; increased its oil-production capacity; encouraged the growth of its petrochemical, natural gas, and non-oil sectors; and built dozens of new universities, hundreds of new vocational training centers, and thousands of new schools.

The government deserves special praise for pushing these reforms during an oil boom, when it would have been easy to relax, and for continuing to spend a quarter of its skyrocketing budget on education and technical training. If Saudi Arabia can continue to maintain its happy combination of economic reform and fiscal discipline, and if Asia's growing economies keep the price of oil high, Saudi Arabia's next decade will be bright indeed because the oil boom that began in 2003 is still going strong.

Abdullah was eighty when the oil boom began and was eighty-five when this book went to press. Because his time as king is limited, he and his advisers have been in a race against time to create enough economic momentum so that no matter who follows him, Saudi Arabia's drive to improve its business climate will continue.

In all likelihood, Abdullah has succeeded. It is hard to imagine the kingdom suddenly reversing its pro-business policies, and this has broad implications. Growing businesses will need women workers, and women with incomes will insist on being treated as equals. As the Saudi people grow more prosperous, better educated, and more widely traveled, they will also become more open to new ideas about religious tolerance and gender equality. Westerners who want to change Saudi Arabia are therefore much more effective when they focus on economic reform, an area where Western expertise is welcomed, than they are when they comment too directly on social issues, a subject where outside opinions are often resented. In the words of Prince Muhammad al-Faisal, a Harvard Business School graduate who runs a high-tech dairy farm that employs many Saudi women, "Economic reform is the chariot that will drive all the other reforms."[47]

22

Abdullah Becomes King,
Iran Becomes a Threat
(2005–)

O N AUGUST 1, 2005, King Fahad, who had been physically and mentally incapacitated for more than nine years, died of pneumonia at eighty-four. Within hours, the senior princes pledged their allegiance to Abdullah, the country's new king. The next day, in keeping with Wahhabi simplicity, a prayer for King Fahad lasted just two minutes before his body, wrapped tightly in a white shroud, was driven to a small cemetery outside Riyadh. Following Saudi custom, the royal family did not place a headstone at King Fahad's grave, only a bit of crushed stone to mark the location.

The day after the funeral, Saudi Arabia's top leaders gathered at Abdullah's palace in Riyadh for the *bayah*, the traditional Muslim ceremony of loyalty. Each member of the Council of the Senior Clergy shook Abdullah's hand and said, "I express my allegiance to you. I hear and obey, except in what would disobey God."[1] Then, one by one, tribal chiefs; top government officials; senior army, navy, and air force officers; and more clerics shook Abdullah's hand and gave him the same oath. Later in the day, the new king opened his doors to thousands of well-wishers who streamed into his palace to recite the oath in unison. In other Saudi cities, people flocked to the palaces of their provincial governors and also, in unison, pledged their loyalty to King Abdullah. After twenty-three years as Saudi Arabia's crown prince and nine years as its de facto leader, Abdullah could finally rule in his own name.

Abdullah's First Months as King

One of Abdullah's first acts as king was to end the Saudi custom of kissing the monarch's hand. From now on, shaking hands would be sufficient and much more in line with Muslim and Wahhabi egalitarianism. Abdullah also declared September 23 "National Day," to commemorate the day in 1932 when the different regions of Arabia united to become the Kingdom of Saudi Arabia. Many conservative clerics did not like the idea of a nonreligious holiday, but ordinary Saudis loved it. Abdullah also dropped the title "His Majesty." Like King Fahad, he preferred to be called "the Custodian of the Two Holy Mosques."

With oil revenues surging, Abdullah ended a nineteen-year freeze on government salaries that was imposed when the price of oil fell to $9 a barrel in 1986. Every soldier and civil servant (except cabinet ministers) received a 15 percent pay raise, and enlisted men and lower-grade employees received an extra month's pay as a bonus.

Abdullah decided to remain commander of the National Guard but has relied on his second-oldest son, Prince Mitab, to run the guard's day-to-day affairs. Officially, this Sandhurst-educated prince is the guard's number-three man, but actually he is its de facto commander.

In his first month as king, Abdullah donated $100 million to help the victims of Hurricane Katrina as a gesture of the kingdom's long friendship with the United States. The Saudis suffered a disaster of their own on January 12, 2006, when a stampede at Mecca's Jamarat Bridge caused 363 people, including 36 Saudis, to be trampled to death. Every year, 2.5 million pilgrims cross this bridge in a single afternoon to throw pebbles at three pillars that represent the devil. The bridge, a notorious bottleneck, was the site of 119 deaths in 1998, 35 fatalities in 2001, and 245 deaths in 2004. In 2006, as soon as the pilgrimage ended, the Saudi Binladin Group, the giant construction company, tore the bridge down and began to build a new, much safer, four-story bridge that cost the government more than $1 billion.

The kingdom gave $92 million in annual aid to the Palestinian Authority in the spring of 2006, up from $84 million in 2005, and pledged $250 million for the reconstruction of Gaza and the West

Bank after the war between Israel and Hezbollah ended in August. The Saudi money went to the Palestinian Authority rather than to Hamas, the Palestinian political party that won a parliamentary majority in January 2006, because the United States and many other Western governments regard Hamas as a terrorist organization. Iran, however, does give money to Hamas.

During the winter of 2006–2007, gunmen loyal to Hamas and to the Palestinian Authority began to fight street battles in the West Bank and Gaza. To stop this, King Abdullah invited the leaders of the two Palestinian groups to Mecca in February 2007 to settle their differences. After two days of negotiations, with the Saudis greatly displeasing the Bush administration by acting as mediators, Mahmoud Abbas, the president of the Palestinian Authority, appointed the leader of Hamas, Ismail Haniya, to be the prime minister of a new national unity government. While Hamas supports terrorism and does not recognize Israel's right to exist, it did agree to "respect" the Palestinian Authority's prior agreements with Israel. The unity government collapsed four months later when ski-masked Hamas gunmen took control of the Gaza Strip in June.

Abdullah Talks to Barbara Walters about Women Driving

In Abdullah's third month as king, he surprised everyone by granting his first television interview to a woman, journalist Barbara Walters. It took place on October 14, 2005, and excerpts were broadcast on *20/20* and *Nightline* that evening.

King Abdullah began by assuring Americans that President George W. Bush is a leader "whose friendship I value and treasure," and that "Saudi Arabia's oil reserves are sufficient to provide supplies for longer than sixty or seventy years."[2]

Barbara Walters then asked the king, "Would you support allowing women to drive?"

Abdullah replied, "My daughter is a woman. My wife is a woman. I believe the day will come when women will drive. In fact if you look at the areas of Saudi Arabia, the desert, and in the rural areas, you will find that women do drive. The issue will require patience. In time I believe that it will be possible. I believe that patience is a virtue."[3]

Walters asked, "You cannot just make a decree that women can drive? You are the king!"

Abdullah responded, "It is impossible that I would do anything that is not acceptable to my people. . . . It will require a little bit of time."[4]

Saudi opinions about women driving vary widely. One blogger, "Saudi Jeans," said that the men who do not want their wives and daughters to drive should not be allowed to prevent everyone else from driving. The people against women driving, he said, are using "the same lame excuses" as the people who opposed girls' education in the early 1960s, "when King Faisal said: We will open the schools anyway, and if you don't want your daughters to study at our schools, then don't let them."[5]

By contrast, 118 judges and professors, all men, signed a petition in July 2005 that called those who favor women driving "the enemies of Islam" because the "closing of doors" [that is, creating places where women can be alone with men] "leads to corruption."[6] Early in 2006, when a member of the national consultative council, Muhammad al-Zulfa, proposed legislation to end the ban on women driving, the council's speaker refused to schedule any time to discuss the subject. Several days later, some militants approached al-Zulfa and shouted, "Do you want to face God on Judgment Day with women's driving next to your name?"[7]

In 2006 and 2007 more than 3,000 women petitioned King Abdullah asking for the right to drive, but more than 500 other women sent a petition to the king that described women driving as "un-Islamic."

One poll revealed that a third of the kingdom's women already know how to drive, having learned the skill in the desert, in neighboring states such as Kuwait and the United Arab Emirates, or in the United States and Europe.[8] Most Saudi women were pleased that King Abdullah publicly approved of the concept of women driving, even if he did not think the kingdom was ready to accept it yet, because the cause immediately became much more respectable. Many women point out that the Quran, a seventh-century scripture, makes no mention of motor vehicles, and that in Muhammad's time, women rode camels and horses.

When I lived in Saudi Arabia, women groaned if I asked them about driving because they resent the Western stereotype that Saudi women are repressed and unhappy. "Driving is just a method of transportation," a young woman named Wafa from the Eastern Province told me, "it is not a big deal. Expanding career opportunities is much more important."

"I like being chauffeured," concurred Sherrifa, a housewife in Riyadh. "I wouldn't want to drive until people here have had some driver's education first. There are too many crazy people behind the wheel."

"Child custody after a divorce is much more important for us," said Noura, an economist. "I would be happy with a monorail and more buses."

After King Abdullah's television interview, however, and after his daughter, Princess Adela, publicly supported women driving, Saudi women began to talk about the issue more often. Suddenly, driving was no longer a dim dream a generation or more in the future; it was a real possibility, perhaps less than a decade away.

When Saudi women do start driving, one difficult issue the government will have to resolve is whether a policeman who stops a vehicle can ask a female driver to remove the veil that covers her face. If he can, the kingdom will be relaxing its standards of modesty. If he cannot, the kingdom will have to hire female police officers. Either way, allowing women to drive involves sweeping social changes beyond the mere fact of women driving.

For this reason, Saudi Arabia is likely to move slowly. In March 2008, for example, the national consultative council recommended that the kingdom allow women over thirty to drive, but only on weekdays from 7:00 a.m. to 8.00 p.m. and only with the permission of a male relative.

Abdullah and China's Hu Jintao Visit

In January 2006, King Abdullah flew to Beijing for a three-day summit, the first time that a Saudi king had visited China. The kingdom provides China with one-sixth of its oil imports, and Chinese contractors and geologists are working throughout Saudi Arabia drilling gas wells and building cement plants and telecommunications towers. It was therefore not surprising that China's premier, Hu Jintao, called Abdullah "a respected and familiar old friend."

In April, three months later, Premier Hu visited Saudi Arabia. He was immensely pleased when King Abdullah made a written promise to double the amount of oil that Saudi Arabia sells to China to one million barrels a day by 2010. Abdullah also agreed to send extra oil to China to help it build a strategic petroleum reserve to protect both nations from a sudden cutoff of oil shipments due to war or terrorism. By the end of 2008, the Chinese plan to have a storage capacity of a hundred million barrels of oil at four different sites, but even this will cover only about five weeks of China's imports.

Relations between China and Saudi Arabia today are particularly warm because the Chinese, unlike the Americans, do not press the Saudis to make democratic, educational, or feminist reforms. They just want to do business. Of course, China cannot guarantee Saudi Arabia's security, as the United States can. In the words of Omar Bahlaiwa, the top trade official at Saudi Arabia's Chamber of Commerce, "We are in a Catholic marriage with America [that is, divorce is out of the question], but we are also Muslims. We can have more than one wife."[9]

Iran: A Growing Geopolitical Threat

Although President Bush identified Iran as part of an "axis of evil" in his State of the Union speech in January 2002, the United States actually increased Iran's power when it overthrew Iran's biggest enemy, Saddam Hussein, a Sunni Muslim, in May 2003. Iraq's Shi'ites, who make up nearly 65 percent of Iraq's population, immediately became the dominant force in the country, and the change in their status has also emboldened Shi'ites in Lebanon, Bahrain, and, to a much lesser extent, Saudi Arabia.

In the axis of evil speech, President Bush warned Iran, which was beginning to enrich uranium, that the United States "will not permit the world's most dangerous regimes to threaten us with the world's most dangerous weapons." Yet later in 2002, the U.S. State Department assured North Korea, which may already have built one or two nuclear weapons, that the United States had "no plans to invade." By contrast, after the fall of Saddam Hussein in April 2003, an unidentified top U.S. official told a *Los Angeles Times* reporter that Iran should "take a number," implying that Iran's government would be the next to fall.[10]

The Iranian government noted the difference in the U.S. attitudes toward North Korea and Iran and decided to continue its drive to enrich uranium. Iran has therefore become a growing threat to Saudi Arabia, both politically in Iraq, Lebanon, and other countries with large Shi'ite populations and militarily, as the Saudis face the prospect of a hostile nuclear power just across the Persian Gulf.

The "Shi'ite Crescent"

Of the 360 million people who live between Lebanon and Pakistan, 140 million are Shi'ite Muslims. (Shi'ites, also known as Shias, pray to saints as intermediaries between God and man, while Sunnis condemn this practice as idol worship. Shi'ites also revere Ali, Muhammad's adopted son, and his descendants. See chapters 3 and 4.) Another 30 million Shi'ites live in India and Bangladesh, for a global total of 170 million. Despite this enormous figure, the troubled democracy that began in Iraq in 2005 was the first Shi'ite-led government in Arab territory since the fall of Egypt's Fatimid dynasty in AD 1171.

Shi'ites make up 90 percent of the people of Iran; about 65 percent of the population of Iraq, Bahrain, and Azerbaijan; almost 45 percent of the people in Lebanon; more than 25 percent of those in Kuwait; 20 percent of Pakistan's population; and more than 15 percent of the people in Qatar, Afghanistan, and Bangladesh. They also make up 9 percent of the people of Saudi Arabia, including nearly 50 percent of the population of the kingdom's oil-rich Eastern Province. Today, the fiery Iraqi cleric Moqtada al-Sadr is a popular figure among Saudi Shi'ites, and Saudi officials worry that chaos in Iraq could spread across the border and inspire uprisings by the Shi'ite minority.

The prospect of millions of Shi'ites becoming more powerful in Iraq, Lebanon, and elsewhere is disconcerting for many Sunnis, including Jordan's King Abdullah, who in a December 2004 television interview with NBC News's Chris Matthews warned of an Iranian-backed Shi'ite "crescent" waxing across the Middle East. In April 2006, Egyptian president Hosni Mubarak told the Al-Arabiya television network, almost certainly incorrectly, that "Shi'ites are mostly always loyal to Iran and not to the countries where they live."[11]

It is true that in Bahrain—the island in the Persian Gulf that is home to the U.S. Navy's Fifth Fleet and is connected to Saudi Arabia by a causeway—there are many posters of Iran's supreme leader, Sayyed Ali Khamenei. But Bahrain is a special case because the monarchy is Sunni, even though two-thirds of the people are Shi'ite. Still, if President Mubarak is even partly right, and a small percentage of Shi'ites do feel more loyalty to Iran than they do to their home countries, it happens that the Shi'ites live in strategic areas, not only along Israel's northern border but in every state on the Persian Gulf. If the Saudis or the Kuwaitis decided to hurt Iran economically, Iran might be able to retaliate by mobilizing Shi'ite supporters in the kingdom's Eastern Province or in Kuwait City. To prepare for this and other contingencies, Saudi Arabia has increased the number of troops in its military services by 25 percent since the United States first invaded Iraq in 2003.

Iraq

To the Saudis, who are 91 percent Sunni, the U.S. war in Iraq has been a disaster because it not only destroyed Iraq's army, the only force in the Middle East capable of containing Iran, but it also transferred political power in Iraq to Shi'ites, who receive money and weapons from Iran. As Saudi Arabia's foreign minister, Prince Saud al-Faisal, lamented in a speech in New York in September 2005, "We fought a war [in the 1980s] to keep Iran out of Iraq; now we are handing the whole country to Iran without reason."[12]

Iraq's lengthy, six-hundred-mile border with Iran makes it easy for Iran's Quds Force—the overseas special operations arm of Iran's Islamic Revolutionary Guard Corps that the United States has called a terrorist organization—to smuggle weapons and money to Shi'ite militias in Iraq. The weapons include sniper rifles, mortar shells, rocket-propelled grenade launchers, shoulder-fired antiaircraft missiles, and, most lethal of all, the motion-triggered roadside bombs that fling speeding discs of molten copper that can pierce both armored Humvees and $4 million Abrams tanks. These explosively formed penetrators, or EFPs, have killed more than two hundred U.S. soldiers, and wounded more than eight hundred.

To date, Iraq's Sunni insurgents have killed more people, including U.S. troops, than Iraq's Shi'ite militias have. The Shi'ite militias became more deadly only after Sunni terrorists blew up the Golden Mosque in Samarra, one of the most sacred Shi'ite sites, in February 2006. The Golden Mosque is where Shi'ites believe their twelfth *imam*, Muhammad al-Mahdi, was last seen before he disappeared in 874. Al-Mahdi and Jesus, Shi'ites believe, will return to Earth to establish peace and justice shortly before Judgment Day.

After the Golden Mosque was destroyed, sectarian and ethnic violence between Sunnis and Shi'ites rose sharply, killing more than eighty people a day during the rest of 2006 and the first half of 2007, a rate of more than thirty thousand people a year before the rate fell substantially at the end of 2007.[13] Fearing for their lives, 60,000 to 90,000 Iraqis a month fled their homes in 2006 and the first three quarters of 2007, although the rate slowed to 30,000 to 40,000 Iraqis a month in the fall. Most of these one million Iraqis were Sunnis driven from their ethnically mixed neighborhoods in Baghdad and other cities by vengeful Shi'ite militias.

These Shi'ite forces have included:

- The Mahdi Army, a ten-thousand-man militia that is loyal to the young cleric Moqtada al-Sadr, which fought U.S. troops twice in 2004 and can quickly call on fifty thousand additional fighters when needed.

- The Badr Organization for Reconstruction and Development (aka the Badr Brigade), a twenty-five-thousand-man militia that is loyal to Iraq's largest Shi'ite political party, the Supreme Islamic Iraqi Council, a party that receives large amounts of money from Iran.

- Fadhila, a militia of several thousand men in the southern provinces that is loyal to the Fadhila (Islamic Virtue) Party.

- Smaller, less disciplined, and sometimes criminal Shi'ite militias and gangs that have splintered off from the Mahdi Army and, to a lesser extent, from the Badr Brigade. Together, these militias have at least fifteen thousand men.

Nawaf Obaid, a prominent Saudi expert on national security issues, has claimed that officers in Iraq's Ministry of the Interior coordinate the smuggling of weapons from Iran to the Shi'ite militias.[14]

Ties between the Shi'ites in Iraq and Iran are deep. Many of Iraq's top Shi'ite politicians spent years in exile in Iran, married Iranian women, and raised Persian-speaking children. Even some officers in Iran's Revolutionary Guard Corps are Iraqi Shi'ites who fled Saddam Hussein's tyranny. This is also true of some of Iran's top clerics. One Iraqi exile is a longtime adviser to Iran's supreme leader, Ayatollah Sayyed Ali Khamenei. Another exile is Iran's chief justice.[15]

Many analysts agree that Iranian intelligence informants have infiltrated every government ministry, army division, and police force in Iraq, and that most of Iraq's policemen feel more loyalty to the Mahdi Army or the Badr Brigade than they do to their own units. Thousands of men in these militias have been trained by Iranians on how to carry out ambushes, kidnappings, and assassinations. Iraqi Shi'ites killed an average of about a hundred Sunni lawyers, engineers, teachers, and other professionals a month in 2005 and 2006, causing many thousands more Sunni professionals to leave the country.[16]

Of course, Iraq's Sunni insurgents have killed tens of thousands of Shi'ites, including more than five thousand Shi'ite police officers. Shi'ites in Iraq are therefore much more worried about Sunni violence than they are about possible domination by Iran. To the Shi'ites, the Mahdi Army and the Badr Brigade offer some long-term protection against the Sunnis, while the security offered by U.S. troops is merely temporary. (Similarly, Iraq's Sunnis see their own insurgents as a force protecting them against both the Shi'ite militias and the Shi'ite-dominated army and police.)

Many Saudi clerics have expressed outrage at the Shi'ites' "murder, torture and displacement of Sunnis" in Iraq, and according to the Iraq Study Group led by former U.S. secretary of state James Baker, several Saudi businessmen have sent cash to the Sunni insurgents. Some of this cash is smuggled into Iraq by pilgrims returning home from Mecca.

Many Saudis want their government to send money and weapons to Iraq's Sunnis, but although King Abdullah has called the U.S. presence in Iraq an "illegitimate foreign occupation," he also gave his word to President Bush that the kingdom would not assist the Sunni insurgency while U.S. soldiers are fighting there, so for now these requests have been denied. Abdullah has also publicly asked both the Sunnis and the Shi'ites to refrain from violence, and Foreign Minister Saud al-Faisal has said that Saudi Arabia is not "the guardian of any one group or sect. We cooperate with all those who want a united, independent and sovereign Iraq."[17]

The Saudis are deeply concerned about the safety of their fellow Sunnis in Iraq and worry that they could be massacred because they comprise just one-fifth of the nation's population. If U.S. troops leave Iraq, Saudi Arabia, as the center of Sunni Islam, might feel a duty to intervene if Iraq's predominantly Shi'ite army and police forces fail to protect the Sunni Arab minority from Iraq's Shi'ite militias. Jordan might also send troops into western Iraq to prevent the already huge influx of more than four hundred thousand Iraqi refugees into Jordanian territory from growing even larger. Even Turkey has put two hundred thousand soldiers on its border with Iraq and has threatened a full-scale invasion of the country to prevent the creation of an independent Kurdish state because such a state would destabilize southeastern Turkey, where Kurds are a majority.

During a two-hour meeting in Riyadh in November 2006, King Abdullah told U.S. vice president Dick Cheney that Saudi Arabia strongly opposed a total U.S. withdrawal from Iraq or the start of any U.S. talks with Iran. Prince Bandar bin Sultan, who was the kingdom's ambassador to the United States from 1983 to 2005 and now serves as the king's national security adviser, flew to Washington several times in the middle of the night to give the same message to President Bush and Secretary of State Rice. (Because Prince Bandar bypassed his successor as ambassador—Prince Turki al-Faisal, who had advocated talks between the United States and Iran—Prince Turki resigned as Saudi Arabia's ambassador to the United States on December 11, 2006. One week later, King Abdullah appointed one of his closest aides, Adel al-Jubeir, a Georgetown University–educated commoner, to be the kingdom's new ambassador to the United States.)

In Riyadh, King Abdullah reportedly told Vice President Cheney that if U.S. forces leave Iraq entirely, Saudi Arabia would "intervene aggressively" to prevent a Shi'ite massacre of Sunnis. Abdullah also told Cheney that Saudi Arabia might even pump more oil to try to lower the price and reduce Iran's oil revenues, which would make it harder for Iran to send money to Iraq's Shi'ites.[18]

If the Saudis increased their oil production to their new maximum capacity, that is, raised their output from their usual 8 to 9 million barrels a day to the 12.5 million barrels a day that they will be capable of pumping by the end of 2009, the price of oil might decline considerably. If it does fall, Saudi Arabia, which has just eighteen million citizens, could easily draw on its $250 billion in U.S. Treasury bonds and other foreign accounts to build plenty of new roads, schools, clinics, and power plants and continue all its social welfare programs, too.

Iran, by contrast, has seventy-five million people, exports less than a third of the oil that Saudi Arabia does, and holds almost no foreign bonds. In 2005, it spent more than half of its oil income subsidizing food, education, housing, medical care, and gasoline, which in Iran is only 40 cents a gallon. A return of the price of oil to the pre-boom level of $30 a barrel would hurt Iran deeply because after paying for its subsidies, there would be almost no money left for foreign adventures.

Pumping oil at maximum capacity would be a last resort for the Saudis. The action would significantly shrink Iran's ability to project military power abroad, but it would also force the kingdom to give up many of the benefits of the new oil boom.

Hezbollah

Iran also troubles Saudi Arabia because since 1982 it has formed branches of Hezbollah (the Party of God) in every country with a significant Shi'ite population. The most successful branch by far is in Lebanon.

In 1982, Israel intervened in a Lebanese civil war and began an eighteen-year occupation of a six-mile stretch of southern Lebanon next to its border. Hezbollah started as a Lebanese resistance movement fighting the Israeli occupation. Iran's Revolutionary Guards Corps trained more than two thousand Hezbollah fighters, who then taught thousands more Lebanese laborers, shopkeepers, and office workers how to use guns, detonate bombs, and fire missiles. The Iranians helped Hezbollah to build a maze of underground bunkers and tunnels. For a quarter of a century, Iran has sent about $10 million a month to Hezbollah, so Hezbollah also runs schools, clinics, and a large charity for needy Shi'ites.

In the 1980s and the 1990s, Hezbollah suicide bombers killed more than 900 people, including 241 U.S. Marines and 56 French paratroopers stationed in Lebanon. In 2000, when Israel finally withdrew from southern Lebanon, Hezbollah claimed victory. Unlike Syria and Jordan in 1967, Hezbollah had driven the Israelis from Arab land,

and unlike Egypt in 1978, it had done so without signing a peace treaty. Today, Hezbollah is a political party as well as an armed force, controlling nearly every office in southern Lebanon and enjoying the loyalty of about a third of the Lebanese army.

In a speech in May 2005, Sheikh Hassan Nasrallah, who has led Hezbollah since 1992, announced that Hezbollah possessed more than twelve thousand missiles, a number that confirmed earlier estimates by U.S. and Israeli analysts. Every one of these missiles came from Iran. Most are small, inaccurate Katyusha rockets that can carry only forty pounds of explosives seven to twelve miles, barely enough to harass Israeli border towns. But Iran also sent Hezbollah about five hundred Fajr rockets with a range of twenty-eight to forty-three miles, enough to hit Haifa, northern Israel's largest city, and several dozen massive Zelzal missiles that can carry thirteen hundred pounds of explosives sixty-two miles, enough to destroy entire neighborhoods in Tel Aviv.[19]

During its war with Israel in the summer of 2006, Hezbollah did not fire one Zelzal rocket. Probably Iran, which almost certainly makes the final decisions as to which missiles Hezbollah can launch, did not wish to escalate the war further. Zelzal missiles also require giant launchers that are easy for Israeli jets to find and destroy. By contrast, a Katyusha missile can be stored in a house, carried on a donkey, and fired from a small tripod that can be set up in only ten minutes.

Iran has also given Hezbollah many laser-guided TOW antitank missiles that have proved effective against Israeli tanks and armored vehicles because they can fly up to a mile from a shoulder-held launcher. Hezbollah also has some C-802 antiship cruise missiles, an Iranian-made version of the Chinese Silkworm. Two of these missiles damaged Israeli navy ships off the coast of Lebanon in July 2006. "Never before in history has a terrorist organization had such state-of-the-art military equipment," complained one Israeli general.[20]

The Saudis worry about Hezbollah's effect on Lebanon's stability and fear that Iran might someday try to create a similar force among Shi'ites in Saudi Arabia's Eastern Province. To the Israelis, however, Hezbollah was no longer merely a cause for concern. With twelve thousand missiles and a well-trained militia, it had become a mortal danger.

The 2006 War between Hezbollah and Israel

When Hezbollah fighters crossed Israel's northern border in July 2006 and kidnapped two Israeli soldiers, Saudi Arabia surprised many people around the world by condemning Hezbollah's action.

The hostilities actually began in Gaza two weeks earlier. Although Israel had evicted more than seven thousand Jewish settlers and had withdrawn from Gaza in 2005, in June 2006 several members of Hamas tunneled into Israel, killed two Israeli soldiers, and kidnapped a third. In response, the Israeli army moved back into parts of Gaza, and on July 12, Hezbollah showed its support for Hamas by kidnapping two more Israeli soldiers in the north. Israeli troops chased Hezbollah's raiding party back into Lebanon, but during the chase, a mine destroyed an Israeli tank. As Israeli soldiers frantically tried to rescue the men inside, Hezbollah troops fired on them, killing eight.

Two days later, the Saudi Press Agency, with the approval of the Foreign Ministry, said, "A difference should be drawn between legitimate resistance [against Israel] and miscalculated adventures carried out . . . without consultation with the legitimate authority [in Lebanon] or coordination with the Arab countries."[21]

At a meeting of Arab foreign ministers in Cairo on July 15, Saudi Arabia's foreign minister, Prince Saud al-Faisal, called Hezbollah "undisciplined and irresponsible" and said that its "uncalculated adventure is categorically rejected."[22] The Saudi government was defying the opinion of its own public, which was thrilled to see Hezbollah firing rockets into Israeli cities. Other Arab nations criticized Hezbollah, too, including Egypt, Jordan, Iraq, Kuwait, Bahrain, and the United Arab Emirates. They all saw Hezbollah as an unpredictable and dangerous tool in the hands of Iran.

For the first time, the Arab foreign ministers also endorsed UN Security Council Resolution 1559, which was passed the previous year and which not only demanded that Syria withdraw its troops from Lebanon, but required every Lebanese militia, including Hezbollah, to disarm. In other words, Saudi Arabia and six other Arab nations no longer felt that Hezbollah had a right to arm itself since, after all, it was not a government. The Saudis were particularly angry at Hezbollah for engaging in what the Saudis regarded as a senseless piece of aggression utterly counterproductive to the Palestinians' goal of negotiating a separate state for themselves.

In contrast to Iran, whose president, Mahmoud Ahmadinejad, told a crowd in October 2005 that "the occupying regime of Jerusalem must be wiped off the map," Saudi Arabia has sought peace between Israel and Palestine. In March 2002, King Abdullah, when he was still the crown prince, proposed a "comprehensive peace" and "the establishment of normal relations" with Israel, in return for a "full Israeli withdrawal from all the Arab territories occupied since June 1967," a "just and fair" solution to the plight of the Palestinian refugees, and "an independent Palestinian state with East Jerusalem as its capital."[23] Neither Israel nor the United States gave Abdullah's plan for "normal relations" the response it deserved, probably because the prospect of evicting a quarter of a million Israeli settlers from the West Bank did not seem realistic, and because a Hamas suicide bomber killed twenty-nine Israelis celebrating Passover at a hotel just days later. The plan's very existence, however, showed that in the long run, the Saudis are willing to live with Israel if the Israelis can achieve peace with the Palestinians. In a delayed recognition of this fact, Israeli prime minister Ehud Olmert told kibbutz farmers in March 2007 that the Saudi plan "contains many parts I would be ready to accept."

When Hezbollah launched its raid into Israel on July 12, 2006, Israel took the attack as an opportunity to destroy as many of Hezbollah's twelve thousand missiles and other weapons as it could. The Israelis destroyed the runways at Beirut's airport, imposed a naval blockade from the Mediterranean, and bombed Hezbollah's strongholds in the Shi'ite suburbs of Beirut and throughout southern Lebanon. Except for a few stray bombs, the Israelis left Christian and Sunni Muslim neighborhoods alone, but in Shi'ite areas, hundreds of civilians died and tens of thousands lost their homes.

Like the Israelis, the Bush administration saw the war as an opportunity to weaken Hezbollah, so it approved of Israel's intensive bombing. The Saudis did not expect this. When they criticized Hezbollah's raid on July 14 and again on July 15, they hoped that international pressure would compel Israel and Hezbollah to end hostilities immediately and would force a chastened Hezbollah to abandon military action and work instead as a political party.

Israel's massive bombing of Lebanon changed the political situation completely. Al Jazeera and other Arab television networks broadcast the destruction of southern Lebanon almost twenty-four hours a day. To the Saudis and to Arabs everywhere, Hezbollah's initial raid paled in comparison with the enormity of Israel's response. It was no longer possible for the Saudis or any other Arabs to oppose Hezbollah. The Iranian-backed fighters had turned into an army of heroes, a scrappy Arab underdog challenging the full might of Israel's army, navy, and air force.

When the United States not only supported Israel's bombing but even sped up weapons shipments, the Saudis felt that they had done all that they could to restrain Hezbollah. Now it was more important for the Saudis to show their solidarity with the victims of Israel's bombing in southern Lebanon. "We cannot tolerate that Israel plays with the lives of civilians—women, old people and children," Crown

Prince Sultan told reporters on July 20, a week after the bombing began.[24] The next day, a top cleric at Mecca's Grand Mosque spoke even more passionately. After criticizing "the savage and barbaric Israeli bombing of the Lebanese and Palestinian people," he asked, "What happened to those people who shout slogans of democracy and world peace? Was it all just propaganda and false statements to shed Muslim blood?"[25]

On July 23, Saudi Arabia's foreign minister, Prince Saud al-Faisal, spent an hour with President Bush at the White House and delivered a letter from King Abdullah that called for an immediate cease-fire in Lebanon. But President Bush and Secretary of State Condoleezza Rice did not ask Israel to stop its bombing because they did not feel that a cease-fire would last until Hezbollah was weakened further. In exasperation, the Saudi Royal Court issued a warning two days later, on July 25: "Should the option of peace fail as a result of the Israeli arrogance, only the option of war will remain . . . the evil of which will spare no one, not even those whose military power is now pushing them to play with fire."[26]

The royal statement was unanimously supported by the members of the Majlis al-Shura, by the national consultative council, and by journalists across the kingdom. In an editorial on August 4, the *Arab News* summed up the feelings of most Saudis:

> If the US continues its policy of slavish support for Israel it will reap a harvest of hatred that will last for generations. . . . It is difficult to remain friends with someone who does not listen to what you have to say, who is patronizing and arrogant, who wants to change you. . . .
>
> Unless Washington stops being so patronizing and so obsessively supportive of Israeli brutality, it will lose every last shred of credibility and respect among Muslims and Arabs the world over.[27]

Finally, on August 11, three weeks after King Abdullah had first called for a cease-fire in his letter to President Bush, the United Nations Security Council unanimously passed Resolution 1701, which ended the war between Israel and Hezbollah, effective August 13. It directed Lebanon's army and a force of almost ten thousand UN troops led by France and Italy to enter southern Lebanon as soon as Israeli forces withdrew. On August 12, the last day of the war, Hezbollah fired 246 missiles into northern Israel and still had more than 8,000 when the war ended. Since then, according to Israel's chief of military intelligence, Major General Amos Yadlin, "Hezbollah has almost totally rebuilt its arsenal" of the easy-to-hide short-range rockets, in defiance of Security Council Resolution 1701, "thanks to the traffic of arms from Iran and Syria."[28] Hezbollah's leader, Sheikh Hassan Nasrallah, confirmed this in a speech in February 2007, when he said, "We had 12,000 rockets [before the war] and used 4,000. Now we have 20,000."[29]

The war between Israel and Hezbollah lasted a month and a day. Hezbollah fired more than 4,000 missiles into Israel, mostly at random, and killed 116 Israeli soldiers and 43 Israeli civilians. The Israeli air force made 8,700 bombing runs (an average of 11 an hour), and the Israeli army and air force together killed 530 Hezbollah fighters in Lebanon and about 150 Palestinians in Gaza. It destroyed roughly two-thirds of Hezbollah's medium- and long-range missiles. Lebanese civilians suffered the worst losses. Israel's bombing killed more than 1,200 Lebanese civilians and wounded 3,500 more. Tens of thousands of Lebanese homes were destroyed, along with at least 50 factories, 74 major roads, and 149 bridges. In addition, more than 900,000 Lebanese, half of the country's Shi'ite population, had to flee their homes and live with relatives for several months.[30]

The war did not kill any Saudis, but Saudi investors in Lebanon's tourism, industry, and real estate lost much more than $1 billion in income and structural damage. In addition, more than twenty thousand Saudis vacationing on the Mediterranean had to cut their trips short, take buses to Damascus, and fly home on government-chartered jets.

Israel did not come close to its original and unrealistic goal of crippling Hezbollah, and as a result, Hezbollah's reputation among the Arabs rose considerably. Unlike the Egyptian, Jordanian, and Syrian armies, Hezbollah actually fought the Israelis and survived to fight again. But Hezbollah paid a heavy price for its new prestige. The cost of rehousing the 130,000 people that the war made homeless is enormous, and many Lebanese Shi'ites, although not a majority, feel that Iran has become a disruptive influence in their country, and that Hezbollah's leader, Sheikh Hassan Nasrallah, has led them to ruin. Even Sheikh Nasrallah conceded that the kidnapping of two Israeli soldiers on July 12, 2006, was a misjudgment. "We just wanted to capture prisoners for exchange purposes," he told the *New Yorker*'s Seymour Hersh. "We never wanted to drag the region into war."[31]

What is most troubling about the war's aftermath is the possibility that other groups in Lebanon that disarmed in the early 1990s—the Christians, the Druze, and Sunni Muslims—may now decide that they need to rearm to prevent Hezbollah from becoming too dominant since Hezbollah openly defies UN Security Council Resolution 1559, which demands that every Lebanese militia disarm. The fifteen-year civil war that Lebanon endured between 1975 and 1990 was devastating: one out of twenty Lebanese was killed or wounded. Today, unfortunately, the risk of civil war erupting in Lebanon again has grown substantially, and some Christian militias have already begun to stockpile weapons.

As soon as the war ended in August 2006, Hezbollah sent volunteers with calculators, clipboards, and walkie-talkies from one house to another in southern Lebanon to assess the damage. An Iranian official pledged that Iran would give Hezbollah plenty of money for reconstruction. Sheikh Nasrallah promised to rebuild war-torn areas by the end of 2008 and gave every family that had lost a home an initial payment of $12,000 for food, a year's rent, and "decent and suitable furniture." Hezbollah also sent construction crews to bulldoze the rubble away and patch up cratered roads. International charities sent water trucks, and Iran supplied thousands of small generators to restore electric power. Unfortunately, the Lebanese government was seldom present because it had long been almost nonexistent in southern Lebanon, Hezbollah's stronghold. In the autumn, however, the government started to repair bridges and sewer lines and began to finance the rebuilding of about two-thirds of the many homes destroyed, although in 2007, the pace of both government- and Hezbollah-financed reconstruction was slow.

The Saudis were upset both by the suffering of Lebanon's people and by the rise of Iran's influence in the southern part of the country. Sending money to Lebanon was therefore an act of both idealism and practical politics. In July 2006, when the war was just two weeks old, Saudi Arabia deposited $1 billion in Lebanon's central bank to stabilize Lebanon's currency at a time when many people were sending their money abroad. The kingdom also pledged $500 million for Lebanon's postwar reconstruction.

In August, the Saudis sent four cargo planes to deliver five ambulances, six mobile clinics, and a state-of-the-art field hospital with eighteen doctors and forty-three nurses and technicians. Even before the war ended, the doctors had already treated more than three thousand people. Once the cease-fire began, forty-two trucks left Saudi Arabia for Lebanon with more than eight hundred tons of food, medicine, and medical supplies.

In 2007, the Saudis pledged an additional $1.1 billion in loans and grants to the Lebanese government. They have also paid for most of the cost of the Lebanese and UN troops in southern Lebanon and for the education of Lebanese children whose schools were destroyed by Israeli bombs. The Saudis hope that the Lebanese people will see that, unlike Iran, Saudi Arabia is trying to help all of the Lebanese people, not only the Shi'ites, and that the size of its aid dwarfs Iran's.

The Iranian Nuclear Threat

On August 14, 2002, the Saudis and the rest of the world were shocked when the National Council of Resistance, a group of Iranian exiles, revealed the existence of two previously secret Iranian nuclear facilities: a heavy-water reactor in Arak, 200 miles southwest of Tehran, that theoretically could make plutonium and, more ominous, a uranium-enrichment plant at Natanz, 150 miles southeast of Tehran, which suggested that Iran was actually trying to build a nuclear bomb.

In nature, less than 1 percent of uranium is radioactive. For an atom bomb to explode, 90 percent of its uranium must be radioactive. The problem is how to separate radioactive uranium from nonradioactive uranium when they are both the same element. Scientists use a method called "enrichment." First, they combine uranium with fluorine to make a gas, then they funnel the gas into high-speed centrifuges where the nonradioactive uranium, weighing about 1 percent more than the radioactive uranium, slowly moves to the outside of each centrifuge. The rotors in these centrifuges spin about three thousand times a second, so the slightest smudge or fingerprint can cause a rotor to wobble, fly off, and smash other centrifuges. It takes about forty pounds of radioactive uranium to make an atomic bomb, and this requires not only that hundreds and preferably thousands of centrifuges work properly, but also that the funneling of the gas in and out of them be synchronized together in a "cascade."

Iran Spars with the UN and the IAEA

In 2002, the Iranians admitted that they had failed to inform the International Atomic Energy Agency (IAEA) about their secret uranium-enrichment and heavy-water plants. They denied that the enrichment was in violation of the Nuclear Non-Proliferation Treaty (ratified by Iran in 1970) because Brazil, Japan, and about thirty other nations enrich uranium, too. The Iranians said that they built the Natanz and Arak plants in secret because otherwise the United States would have found a way to prevent them from finishing the complexes.

To try to prove to the world that their nuclear program was peaceful, Iran allowed IAEA officials to inspect every one of its nuclear plants in 2003 and in December signed an Additional Protocol that allowed the IAEA to make unannounced and more intrusive inspections. In November 2004, Iran temporarily stopped its enrichment of uranium as negotiations began with the foreign ministers of Britain, France, and Germany.

Finally, in August 2005, the three European nations offered Iran a wide variety of economic incentives, including limited nuclear technology, increased trade, much-needed aircraft parts, and faster admission to the World Trade Organization, if Iran would agree to permanently stop its production of enriched uranium and trace amounts of plutonium. But during this same month, the conservative Islamist Mahmoud Ahmadinejad was elected president of Iran, and only two days after he assumed office, he rejected the European offer and resumed Iran's manufacture of the uranium hexafluoride gas that is funneled into centrifuges. In September, the IAEA found that Iran had violated sixteen provisions of the Nuclear Non-Proliferation Treaty. Iran responded to the accusations by removing the IAEA's seals from the enrichment plant at Natanz and two other nuclear facilities.

In October, President Ahmadinejad made Iran's nuclear program seem much more alarming when he told a group of students, "The occupying regime of Jerusalem must be wiped off the map." Blunt as this was, however, the world is used to harsh speeches about Israel.

What really shocked the world, and especially the European public, was Ahmadinejad's statement to a crowd in the city of Zahedan on December 14 that Europeans "created a myth called the Holocaust" to justify the creation of a Jewish state in Palestine. That a leader seeking nuclear weapons could be so dismissive of history's greatest evil frightened nearly everyone, especially when Iran resumed its enrichment of uranium a few weeks later in January 2006.

On February 4, 2006, by a margin of twenty-seven to three, the IAEA's Board of Governors voted to report Iran's sixteen treaty violations to the UN Security Council. The only nations voting against the report were Syria, Cuba, and Venezuela. The resolution also demanded that Iran stop enriching uranium and resume its previous cooperation with the IAEA's inspectors.

After this meeting, Iran said that it would no longer allow IAEA inspectors to make unannounced searches of its nuclear facilities or take soil samples nearby, and it defiantly declared that it intended to build thousands of new centrifuges at Natanz. This only aroused more suspicion. France's foreign minister, Philippe Douste-Blazy, told a television reporter, "No civilian plan can explain Iran's nuclear program. Therefore it's a secret military operation."[32] Supporting this hypothesis was a Pakistani document that IAEA inspectors found in Iran that explained how to mold uranium into perfect spheres, a shape that is unnecessary for civilian reactors but crucial in an atomic bomb. Iran also ignored a Russian proposal that would have allowed the Iranians to enrich uranium under Russian supervision.

On April 11, President Ahmadinejad proudly announced, "Iran has joined the nuclear countries of the world." Two days earlier, its scientists had successfully run a cascade of 164 centrifuges and enriched uranium to a point where 3.5 percent of it was radioactive, enough to start a controlled chain reaction and generate electric power. Ahmadinejad's claim to have joined the world's nuclear club may have been premature, but as Hans Blix, the UN's former chief weapons inspector, told a French journalist, "If you can enrich [uranium] to 5 percent you can enrich it to 85 percent."[33] Ahmadinejad also announced that Iran was studying how to build P-2 (now known as IR-2) centrifuges, Pakistani-designed machines that enrich uranium four times faster than previous models have. In the autumn, Iran also began to run a second cascade of 164 centrifuges and confirmed that it planned to build 3,000 more centrifuges soon.

On July 31, 2006, three and a half months after President Ahmadinejad's announcement that Iran had run a cascade, the United Nations Security Council passed Resolution 1696, demanding that Iran "suspend all enrichment-related and [plutonium] reprocessing activities, including research and development, to be verified by the IAEA," by August 31, or face unspecified UN sanctions.[34] The resolution passed fourteen to one. Only Qatar voted against the UN demand because the tiny emirate is only 150 miles from Iran's coast and therefore did not want to be on record as pressuring Iran.

Although Iran ignored the Security Council's August 31 deadline and continued to enrich uranium, Russia and China were reluctant to enact sanctions. Finally, on December 23, the Security Council unanimously passed Resolution 1737, which banned the export to Iran of all "materials, equipment, goods and technology which could contribute to Iran's enrichment-related, reprocessing or heavy water–related activities, or to the development of nuclear weapons delivery systems." The resolution also froze the foreign assets of ten Iranian corporations and twelve individuals engaged in these activities and allowed the Security Council to freeze the assets of more men and more companies in the future. The resolution did not include any sanctions against Iran's nonmilitary economy.[35]

In the first week of 2007, President Ahmadinejad responded by declaring that Iran will ignore "the bullying of the decadent powers." The day after this statement, China's president, Hu Jintao, urged Iran to "make a serious response" to the UN vote. Ignoring this plea, Iran's supreme religious leader, Ayatollah Ali Khamenei, praised Iran's uranium enrichment on January 8 and told a crowd in Qum, "The Iranian people will definitely not give up . . . this great achievement."[36]

On February 22, an IAEA report said that Iran was defying UN Security Council Resolution 1737 by operating 690 centrifuges at Natanz, with another 328 in the "final stages" of completion and still another 2,000 under construction. The report surprised many observers because it gave credence to President Ahmadinejad's claim just weeks later that Iran was enriching uranium "on an industrial scale."[37]

On March 24, the Security Council responded to the IAEA's findings by unanimously voting for a worldwide boycott of Iranian arms and called on UN member states to exercise "vigilance and restraint" when selling Iran tanks, aircraft, and artillery. The Russians also delayed sending low-enriched uranium to the nuclear power reactor that Russian engineers had built at Bushehr until December 2007. The $1 billion reactor was originally scheduled to begin running in 2007, but at present, even an autumn 2008 startup seems optimistic.

By the middle of November 2007, according to a subsequent IAEA report, Iran was operating 2,952 centrifuges but was using them to enrich uranium at just 10 to 20 percent of their capacity. Iran also had the components to build at least another 5,000 centrifuges.

When Will Iran Have a Nuclear Bomb?

If Iran's first three thousand centrifuges run at one-eighth speed around the clock, it will take the country only a little longer than two years to make the forty pounds of 90 percent enriched uranium that is needed to make one atomic bomb. It is a rare cascade of centrifuges that can run twenty-four hours a day, but Iran is trying to make up for this deficiency by building tens of thousands of additional centrifuges.

In 2007, Mohamed ElBaradei, the director general of the International Atomic Energy Agency and a winner of the Nobel Peace Prize, said that Iran was three to eight years away from building a bomb. The most detailed estimate of Iran's nuclear capabilities has come from David Albright, a former UN weapons inspector who now heads the Institute for Science and International Security in Washington. Albright said that if Iran can operate fifteen hundred centrifuges soon at high capacity, as seems likely, it could enrich enough uranium to build its first bomb by the end of the decade. It will happen this fast, however, only if its centrifuges run day and night without breaking.

It is possible, of course, that Iran has an underground facility unknown to the West, perhaps with thousands of the high-speed IR-2 centrifuges. When China exploded its first atomic bomb in 1964 and India detonated one in 1974, Western intelligence agencies had no idea that the Chinese and Indian nuclear programs had advanced so quickly. At present, however, the CIA says that it has no convincing evidence that Iran has a large parallel nuclear weapons program, and it has measured the radioactivity of smoke, streams, and soil at suspect sites throughout the country.

In December 2007 the United States intelligence agencies collectively issued a report, the National Intelligence Estimate (NIE), that said that Iran had stopped the "design and weaponization work" involved with building nuclear weapons in 2003. The headlines this report created made the Russians and Chinese less inclined to vote for new United Nations sanctions against Iran, in spite of the fact that the NIE report also said that Iran had achieved the technical capacity to build nuclear weapons "if it decides to do so."

Almost as troubling as Iran's nuclear program is the fact that Iran has increased the range of its ballistic missiles. Since the 1990s, Iran has had more than 200 Shahab-2 (Shooting Star) missiles, which can deliver a one-ton warhead 300 miles—far enough to hit most Saudi Arabian oil facilities. In August 2004, Iran successfully tested the Shahab-3, a 56-foot-tall, North Korean–designed missile that can carry a 2,200-pound warhead 800 to 1,250 miles, far enough to hit Riyadh, Jeddah, or Tel Aviv. In parades in Tehran, these missiles have been draped with banners saying, "We Will Crush America" and "Wipe the Zionist Entity off the Map." Iran also successfully tested a more accurate, Chinese-designed, solid-fuel version of the Shahab-3 in 2005, and on January 7, 2006, it test-fired a Fajr-5 missile that, the Iranians claim, can carry multiple warheads.

The Iranian View

Many Westerners wonder why Iran needs nuclear power when it has so much oil. But with seventy-five million people, Iran barely exports enough oil to pay for its many government programs. It actually makes sense for Iran to develop nuclear power as a substitute for the consumption of oil at home. The use of nuclear power would enable Iran to ship more oil abroad and significantly increase its export revenues. Under the Nuclear Non-Proliferation Treaty, Iran is entitled to build as many reactors as it wants if their purpose is to produce electric power, and the scientists at Iran's more than forty universities with nuclear physics departments are keen to build them.

As for the desire for nuclear weapons, even U.S. secretary of defense Robert Gates has conceded that Iranians may want a bomb "as a deterrent. They are surrounded by powers with nuclear weapons—Pakistan to their east, the Russians to the north, the Israelis to the west and us [U.S. air force and navy bases] in the Persian Gulf."[38] The Iranians probably also feel that having nuclear weapons would increase their influence in countries with large Shi'ite populations such as Iraq, Bahrain, and Lebanon.

Iran's nuclear program is popular with the Iranian people. A 2005 poll of sixteen thousand Iranians found that 77 percent of them support President Ahmadinejad's nuclear policies.[39] Even most of the opposition groups in exile support the government on this issue. Iranians everywhere claim the right to enrich uranium, at least to generate power, as a matter of national pride. Confident of his people's support for his program, President Ahmadinejad laughed when he asked a retired U.S. diplomat, "Why doesn't America stop enriching uranium? We'll enrich it for you and sell it to you at a fifty-percent discount."[40]

Shi'ite Apocalypticism: Daft, or Just Different?

No one knows what Iran's clerics would do with nuclear weapons. In 2001, former Iranian president Hashemi Rafsanjani noted that "even one nuclear bomb inside Israel will destroy everything," while an Israeli retaliation "will only harm [a small part of] the Islamic world."[41]

In August 2005, President Ahmadinejad, in one of his first television interviews after taking office, asked, "Is there an art that is more beautiful, more divine, more eternal than the art of the martyr's death?"[42] Three months later, at a theology conference, Ahmadinejad said, "The most important task of our Revolution is to prepare the way for the return of the Twelfth Imam" (who will, with Jesus, prepare the world for Judgment Day).[43]

When President Ahmadinejad spoke to the United Nations General Assembly in September 2005, he asked God "to hasten the emergence" of the Twelfth Imam, "the promised one, that perfect and pure human being who will fill this world with justice and peace."[44] Later, Ahmadinejad told his associates that while giving his speech, he felt immersed in a mysterious green light. At the United Nations, Ahmadinejad also asked the French foreign minister, Philippe Douste-Blazy, "Do you know why we should wish for chaos at any price? Because, after the chaos, we can see the greatness of Allah."[45]

Shi'ite millennialism today worries many scholars and military analysts, both Western and Saudi. Since the 1950s, none of the world's nuclear powers has ever used an atomic weapon because of "mutual assured destruction," the certainty that a retaliatory strike meant death. But if Iran's leaders think martyrdom is "beautiful" and Judgment Day is imminent, do they fear death? What if mutual destruction holds no fear for them and thus has no deterrent effect? In the words of Bernard Lewis, the great scholar of Islam who is also a staunch neoconservative, "For people with this mindset, mutual assured destruction is not a constraint; it is an inducement."[46]

The Iranian mind-set is a particular cause for concern because in the 1980s, Iran's leaders showed a willingness to incur massive casualties when they sent more than a hundred thousand teenage boys to march to their deaths in "human waves" through Iraqi minefields. Also troubling is the recent weakening of the ancient Muslim restrictions against killing women, children, and other Muslims in wartime. First, in the mid-1990s, Palestinian suicide bombers began to kill Israeli women and children. Then, in 1998, al-Qaeda started to kill U.S. civilians. If innocent Muslims have also died in the African embassy bombings, at New York's World Trade Center, or in Iraq today, this is permissible, according to the terrorists, because "Allah knows his own" and sends dead Muslims directly to paradise.

The weakening of the taboo against killing Muslims in wartime raises a question: If Iran's leaders believe that innocent Muslims killed in war go straight to paradise, would they be willing to sacrifice several million Iranians and Palestinians to destroy Israel once and for all? The possibility disturbs the Israelis, and given the high percentage of fanatics in the Middle East, it cannot be completely dismissed. Yet there is little evidence that the Shi'ite reverence for martyrdom has degenerated into a widespread desire for mass suicide. Iran has been a Shi'ite nation for more than five hundred years but has not invaded a foreign country since 1739, when it sent an army to India, nor started a war since 1850, when it overthrew a hostile Afghan warlord just across its border. And however crazy an individual president or *ayatollah* might be, power in Iran is more diffuse than most Westerners realize. The president is subordinate to the supreme leader, and even the supreme leader can be removed by an elected body of eighty-six clerics called the Assembly of Experts. A single Iranian's fanaticism is unlikely to be enough to launch a nuclear strike.

In the words of Jehangir Amugezar, a former finance minister to the shah who is no friend of Ahmadinejad's:

> The new president may be a political amateur, occasionally making dimwitted statements, but he is neither a fool nor a suicide bomber. Some pundits argue that a Shi'ite belief in martyrdom, coupled with

the Iranian regime's extremist ideology, could render deterrence meaningless. Such people know neither Shi'ite martyrdom nor the regime leaders' instinct for self-preservation, nor even the mullah's *bazaari* habit of always looking for the best deal.[47]

Iran's clerics probably want the bomb for the same reason that North Korea does: as insurance against regime change.

Israeli Alarm

Because Iran could destroy most of Israel with just one or two nuclear missiles, and because President Ahmadinejad has said that the "the occupying regime of Jerusalem must be wiped off the map," the Israelis are understandably much more alarmed than other nations are by the progress of Iran's nuclear program. Meir Dagan, the director of Mossad, Israel's intelligence agency, told Israel's parliament in January 2005 that Iran's nuclear program was nearly "at the point of no return . . . [because] the moment you have the technology for enrichment, you are home free," for then the building of an atomic bomb is just a mechanical process.[48]

Former prime minister Benjamin Netanyahu, the hawkish leader of Israel's conservative Likud Party, thinks that Israel should attack Iran's nuclear facilities immediately, while there is still time to stop the program. "It's 1938," Netanyahu told an audience in Los Angeles in November 2006, "and Iran is Germany."[49] As if to confirm Netanyahu's bleak assessment, President Ahmadinejad held a global conference of Holocaust deniers in Tehran a month later with a motley crew of Ku Klux Klansmen, European anti-Semites, and the American ex-Nazi David Duke.

Ephraim Sneh, Israel's deputy minister of defense and a member of Israel's Labor Party, offered a more subtle but equally alarming view of Iran's nuclear threat in an interview, also in November, with the *Jerusalem Post*:

> The danger isn't as much Ahmadinejad's deciding to launch an attack but Israel's living under a dark cloud of fear from a leader committed to its destruction. . . . [M]ost Jews would prefer not to come here with their families, and Israelis who can live abroad will. . . . I am afraid Ahmadinejad will be able to kill the Zionist dream without pushing a button. That's why we must prevent this regime from obtaining nuclear weapons at all costs.[50]

The Israelis have had nuclear weapons since 1967 but neither confirm nor deny their existence. They have also assured the United States that they will not launch a conventional (or nuclear) air attack against Iran's nuclear facilities without America's go-ahead. In April 2006, President Bush hinted at the possibility of a preventive strike when he said, "All options are on the table." Even Democratic senators Hillary Clinton and Barack Obama have agreed, saying, "We cannot take any option off the table."[51]

Because an attack on Iran's nuclear facilities is fraught with danger, as the next section makes clear, the most effective way for Israel to deal with a nuclear-armed Iran is to develop a secure "second-strike" nuclear capability. The Israelis have done this in two ways. First, they keep about fifty Jericho-2 missiles in caves outside Tel Aviv that are far enough underground to withstand a nuclear attack by Iran or any other nation. Each of these missiles carries a nuclear warhead and has a range of eleven hundred miles, far enough to strike Tehran or any other target in western or central Iran.

Second, the Israelis have recently acquired five submarines capable of launching nuclear missiles. In 2007, Israel took delivery of its fourth and fifth German-made Dolphin-class submarines, each capable of launching ten computer-guided, nuclear-armed, long-range cruise missiles from underwater. The new thirty-five-sailor, diesel-fueled vessels cost $650 million each and can stay submerged for a month at a time, but their real function is to let Iran's leaders know that if they ever fire a nuclear missile at Israel, the destruction of Iran's largest cities and military bases is assured. Israel bought its first two Dolphin submarines from Germany in 1999 and successfully tested some cruise missiles in the Indian Ocean in 2000. Now that Israel has five submarines, it can deploy one in the Mediterranean and another in the Persian Gulf at all times.[52]

The Difficulties of Attacking Iran's Nuclear Facilities

In 1981, an attack by eight Israeli jets on Iraq's Osirak nuclear reactor complex outside Baghdad completely destroyed Iraq's nuclear weapons program because all of Iraq's nuclear facilities were in one place. Iran learned from this mistake and has dispersed its facilities. According to Colonel Sam Gardiner, who taught at the U.S. National War College before retiring from the air force, U.S. or Israeli bombers attacking Iran today would need to strike more than four hundred targets— nuclear facilities, missile sites, and navy bases—to prevent Iran from attacking ships in the Persian Gulf. A strike this big would have more than fifteen hundred different "aim points," but as one White House official told a reporter for *Time* magazine, "We don't know where it all is, so we can't get it all." The most important target, Iran's centrifuge plant at Natanz, is fifty to seventy-five feet underground—deep enough to be impervious to anything but nuclear weapons since the facility is reinforced with concrete.[53]

Iran has also moved some of its most sensitive nuclear facilities to urban areas, so an attack on them will not succeed unless Americans or Israelis are willing to kill many Iranian civilians. It is also the CIA's opinion that without better intelligence about where Iran's nuclear facilities are, even a massive strike would not stop Iran's nuclear program but would only delay it a few years.[54]

This cautious view was confirmed by the difficulties Israel had in pinpointing Hezbollah's missile sites in Lebanon in the summer of 2006. Southern Lebanon is smaller than Rhode Island, yet after a month of intensive bombing, Israel was able to destroy only about two-thirds of Hezbollah's long-range missiles and just a small fraction of its short-range missiles. When the bombing ended, Hezbollah's missile-launching capability was still very much intact. Unlike Southern Lebanon, however, Iran is huge—the size of the U.S. South minus Texas—and mountainous, which makes an attack that much harder.

In addition, as Yahya Salavi, the former commander of Iran's Revolutionary Guard Corps, has pointed out, if the United States attacks Iran, more than a hundred thousand U.S. soldiers in Iraq, Afghanistan, Kuwait, Qatar, Bahrain, and the United Arab Emirates will be highly vulnerable to retaliation. The troops would not only be subject to direct Iranian attacks, but could also suffer from a disruption of the truck convoys and the shipping lanes that provide them with food, fuel, and ammunition. "American warships are heavy," warned Admiral Sejad Kouchaki, Iran's naval commander, "have no maneuverability, and are easily sunk."[55] U.S. counterterrorism experts also worry that Iran may have "sleeper" agents inside the United States who could spread terror on a moment's notice.

The drawbacks of attacking Iran are not only military but political. Iran's theocracy is deeply unpopular, especially with the young, most of whom hate the clerics and admire the West. But a U.S. or Israeli attack could turn President Ahmadinejad and the supreme leader, Ayatollah Sayyed Ali Khamenei, into heroes, rally the Iranian people to their defense, prolong the Iranian regime's survival, and guarantee that Iran would actually build nuclear weapons, rather than just develop the capability to make them. This is not a price worth paying if bombing can merely delay, rather than destroy, Iran's nuclear program. In the words of Jahangir Amugezar, formerly the shah's finance minister, "the military option" involves "lots of pain for not much gain."[56]

One final and devastating argument against the United States going to war with Iran is that the group with the most to gain from such a conflict is al-Qaeda. Al-Qaeda would like nothing better than to see its two biggest enemies, the "Crusaders" and the Shi'ites, fight a full-scale war. It would anger Muslims around the world, increase the number of al-Qaeda recruits, and merge several theaters of war into one giant battlefield stretching from Iraq's border with Syria in the west to Afghanistan's porous border with Pakistan to the east. Together, these countries have three hundred million Muslims.

Saudi Opposition to Attacking Iran

The Saudis oppose any U.S. military action against Iran because they worry that Iran would retaliate not only against U.S. forces, but against Saudi Arabia and the other Gulf Cooperation Council (GCC) nations, too. Although Iran's air force is running out of spare parts, its navy has dozens of patrol boats, high-speed catamarans, and shore-based mobile missile launchers, each of which can fire missiles twenty-five to sixty miles and wreak havoc on Saudi Arabia's desalinization plants, oil terminals, offshore oil platforms, and, further inland, the operation of its largest oil field, Ghawar. If the Ghawar field shut down for even a few months, the kingdom's economy would quickly shrink by half. Of course, Iran's oil facilities are equally vulnerable.

Iran has three submarines that can release mines in the Strait of Hormuz, the twenty-one-mile-wide bottleneck between the Persian Gulf and the Indian Ocean. Almost a quarter of the world's daily oil supply passes through this strait; mines there would temporarily prevent Saudi Arabia, Kuwait, Iraq, and the United Arab Emirates from exporting much of their oil and could immediately send the price of petroleum as high as $200 a barrel. Although U.S. Navy minesweepers and helicopters dragging magnetic minesweeping "sleds" could almost certainly keep the Strait of Hormuz open, Iran's catamarans, which are too small to be detected by shipborne radar, could harass the minesweepers and probably sink some. The UAE is thinking about building a 200-mile-long underground pipeline that would bypass the Strait of Hormuz and send 1.5 million barrels of oil a day from Abu Dhabi to a port on the Indian Ocean instead, but it would take several years to complete.

Iran also has a "Martyrdom Brigade" that early in 2007 had fifty-six volunteers willing to be suicide bombers. The brigade's female commander, Firooz Rajai, was one of the students who took fifty-two Americans as hostages at the U.S. embassy in Tehran in 1979. Twenty-seven years later, in the fall of 2006, she warned that if the United States attacks Iran, its allies in the Gulf "should not expect to have security while we enjoy none."[57] On March 3, 2007, President Ahmadinejad flew to Riyadh and reportedly gave King Abdullah the same message.[58] Undoubtedly, Ahmadinejad simply told King Abdullah that a war between the United States and Iran would be disastrous for the entire Middle East, not just Iran, and did not go into detail. But an organized group of Iranian suicide bombers could not only blow up Saudi oil facilities, they could also release nerve gas, spread disease, or detonate "dirty" bombs filled with radioactive material. (After listening to President Ahmadinejad, King Abdullah reportedly asked him, "What is the rush? Why do you have to enrich uranium this year and not next year or the year after?"[59])

In the end, the Saudis think that even if Iran builds nuclear weapons, it is unlikely to use them. By contrast, the Saudis fear that if the United States or Israel attacks Iran, it is likely, even probable, that war—ruthless, twenty-first-century war—will spread throughout the Gulf. "We have two nightmares," the Saudi foreign minister, Prince Saud al-Faisal, told President Bush in May 2006. "One is that Iran will develop a nuclear bomb, and the other is that America will take military action to prevent Iran from getting a nuclear bomb."[60]

The Problem with Sanctions

While military strikes against Iran are unlikely to succeed, economic sanctions are also difficult to enact and unlikely to work. Because Russia and China have a veto in United Nations Security Council, the United Nations cannot impose sanctions against Iran without their approval. But Iran is one of the biggest buyers of Russian-made weapons. In 2006, it bought $700 million worth of Russian antiaircraft missiles, among other items. Iran also sells China about 12 percent of the oil that China imports, and Chinese engineers are currently building a subway system in Tehran and developing two giant natural gas fields in Pars Province. Neither Russia nor China will therefore easily agree to UN sanctions that hurt their economic interests.

Even if the Russians and the Chinese can be persuaded to agree to some limited sanctions against Iran's nonenergy exports, the measures would hurt only carpet weavers and pistachio growers, not the government. Only a worldwide boycott of Iranian oil is likely to change Tehran's behavior, since 85 percent of Iran's foreign exchange and 70 percent of its budget come from its oil revenues. But in an era of high demand, a boycott would be painful. Merely a discussion of UN sanctions caused the price of oil to soar above $75 a barrel in the spring of 2006, although it also caused Iran's stock exchange to fall 30 percent. Actually passing sanctions against Iranian oil could easily push the price of petroleum to more than $160 a barrel, which would devastate China's oil-importing economy. The Chinese are therefore highly unlikely to vote for effective sanctions against Iran.

Economic Hardball, if Necessary

Even without UN sanctions, Iran is vulnerable to a number of economic measures that don't require the assent of the whole world. First, Iran is dependent on the price of oil. Although its oil revenues have quintupled since 1998, its population has ballooned to seventy-five million, and its unemployment rate is as high as Saudi Arabia's. In 2005, Iran spent 56 percent of its oil revenues on government subsidies and welfare programs.[61] If the price of oil were to fall to pre-2003 levels, to $30 a barrel, for example, Iran would face a stark choice. It could either trim its nuclear program, military budget, and aid to Hezbollah and Hamas or, alternatively, cut the food, housing, gasoline, medical, and other subsidies that it gives to its people, cuts that would make the ruling clerics even more unpopular than they already are.

By 2009, Saudi Arabia will have a spare production capacity greater than the 2.3 to 2.5 million barrels of oil a day that Iran exports. If necessary, the kingdom can sell the world a lot of new oil. Pumping an extra 2.5 million barrels of oil a day would not cause the price of oil to fall in half, but even a smaller decline in the price would cause Iran great harm because Iran has three times as many people as Saudi Arabia does, yet exports only one-third as much oil.

Iran, aware of this vulnerability, has taken precautions to ensure that its nuclear program will continue even if the price of oil plummets. In 2007, the government based its budget on the extremely conservative assumption that the price of oil would fall to $34 a barrel, even though the year began with the price at $56 a barrel. "It is a signal to our enemies," said President Ahmadinejad. "We are ready, and we will manage the country even if you lower the oil prices."[62]

Another one of Iran's vulnerabilities is its reliance on foreign gasoline. Iran refines only 60 percent of its gasoline; the other 40 percent is imported from India, France, the United Arab Emirates, and several nearby Arab countries. An embargo of gasoline sales to Iran would seriously weaken Iran's economy and would force the government to impose rationing even more severe than the "temporary" rationing that began in June 2007, when the government limited private vehicles to twenty-five gallons of gasoline per month. This would make intercity transportation in Iran even more difficult than it already is and would further increase popular discontent with the ruling clerics. Iran is currently spending more than $15 billion to build four new oil refineries and is also buying extra gasoline from Venezuela in an attempt to stockpile. At the beginning of 2007, however, Iran had only a forty-five-day supply of gasoline.[63]

Iran's greatest vulnerability is its need for foreign geologists and engineers to discover new oil fields and revive old ones. At present, Iran pumps about 4 million barrels of oil a day and uses 1.5 million for its own needs. But its old fields are declining at a rate of 8 to 10 percent a year, and its domestic consumption is rising 8 to 10 percent a year. Even if Iran can meet its goal and find 500,000 new barrels of oil a day by 2010, it will still face a crunch. In another decade, Iran's growing population, which may number a hundred million by 2020, will need much more oil than before for its own use. If Iran's production remains stagnant, its oil exports could easily fall to half of their current level by 2020 and could stop completely by 2030. Even if energy-hungry countries such as China import all the oil from Iran that they want, as long as they don't help Iran to *increase* its production, Iran's economy may collapse within a generation.

Saudi Diplomacy

In August 2006, Foreign Minister Saud al-Faisal visited Tehran and declared that Iran has a right under the Nuclear Non-Proliferation Treaty to develop nuclear energy for peaceful purposes. The statement was not merely diplomacy; it reflected the opinion of the Saudi people. Polls by the Al Jazeera television network and Zogby International earlier in the year had shown that more than 60 percent of Saudis opposed the West's efforts to stop Iran's pursuit of peaceful nuclear energy.[64]

What Saudi Arabia and the other Gulf states want is for Iran to let the IAEA resume its inspections of Iran's nuclear facilities. This is why the Saudis have been cool to United Nations Security Council sanctions. They feel that negotiations are a much more promising means of getting Iran to agree to renewed inspections than a public confrontation that leaves the world in the dark about Iran's nuclear activities.

Iran has sent several diplomats to Riyadh to reassure the Saudis that its nuclear program is not directed against the kingdom. But because for years Iran had often called on the Saudi people to overthrow the royal family, and because President Ahmadinejad once called the states of the GCC "gas stations, not real countries," the Saudis remain suspicious. In December 2006, the six GCC states called on Israel to sign the Nuclear Non-Proliferation Treaty and make the Middle East a nuclear weapons–free region but also demanded that Iran not only cooperate with the IAEA but consider the environmental consequences of its nuclear program, since Iran is one of the most earthquake-prone countries on Earth.

Iran's Russian-built nuclear power reactor at Bushehr sits on a peninsula in the Persian Gulf just 150 miles from the Saudi industrial port of Jubail. In fact, Bushehr is three times closer to Jubail and to Kuwait City than it is to Tehran, so once the reactor begins to run, an earthquake, a meltdown, or a radiation leak could easily do more damage to the Persian Gulf than to the Iranian mainland. Saudi Arabia and the other five GCC countries have asked Iran whether they can send a team of safety experts to inspect the Bushehr reactor, but so far, Iran has refused this request. The refusal makes the Saudis suspicious because if the reactor begins to operate, one of its by-products can easily be converted to plutonium if Iran should order the Russian engineers who work at the plant or the IAEA inspectors who visit it regularly to go home.

Possible Resolutions

The outcome the Saudis would most like to see is the one least likely to happen: a nuclear-free Middle East with neither Israel nor Iran possessing atomic weapons. In February 2006, Prince Turki al-Faisal, then the kingdom's ambassador to the United States, asked the United States to adopt this goal, "instead of picking and choosing whose nuclear weapons to oppose."[65] Of course, the chance of Israel dismantling its nuclear weapons when it is surrounded by such hostile neighbors is nil.

A somewhat more likely resolution of the dispute between Iran and the West could involve promises by the United States not to attack Iran and an end to sanctions. The Europeans could also promise Iran economic incentives such as the sale of badly needed aircraft parts; assistance in the construction of modern, Western-designed nuclear power reactors; and faster negotiations for Iran to join the World Trade Organization. In return for its reintegration into the world economy, Iran would have to suspend all of its large-scale uranium enrichment, although perhaps it could continue to run a lone cascade of 164 centrifuges. Iran would also have to agree to unannounced and intrusive inspections by the IAEA, to cooperate fully with investigations of past violations of the Non-Proliferation Treaty, and to freeze the construction of new centrifuges.

The chances of the United States giving Iran a security guarantee and Iran agreeing to renewed IAEA searches are slim. It is more likely that Iran will try to draw out the negotiation process until it has fully mastered the technology of uranium enrichment, at which point it will no longer make sense for the West to offer Iran economic incentives or security guarantees, since Iran will have given little in return.

In the meantime, the United States has succeeded in persuading many European banks, such as Barclays, HSBC, UBS, Deutsche Bank, Credit Lyonnais, and Credit Suisse First Boston, as well as Japan's Bank of International Cooperation, not to make any new loans to Iran until its nuclear program is in compliance with UN and IAEA standards, for fear that sham companies might secretly use the foreign money for nuclear purposes. Public employee pension funds in California, New York, Illinois, and North Carolina have also asked European oil companies not to invest in Iran, and French president Nicolas Sarkozy's government has similarly asked French companies not to tender bids for any new contracts in Iran. The increase in Iran's economic isolation has led Iranian businessmen to send more than $100 billion to Dubai, Malaysia, and Europe.

The Saudi Future: Nuclear Weapons or a Security Guarantee?

If Iran builds nuclear weapons, Saudi Arabia has three options: It can start to build a bomb of its own, which would take many years; it can give massive aid to Pakistan, a longtime ally, and become a partner in its nuclear program, assuming that Pakistan would be willing; or, like many other nations around the world, it can seek a nuclear guarantee from the United States. If the Saudis' goal is to limit nuclear proliferation in the Middle East, the third option—an assurance that the United States would use nuclear weapons to protect Saudi Arabia—is clearly the best choice. It is possible that the Saudis might prefer such a U.S. guarantee to be secret in order to appear more nonaligned, but, obviously, a public guarantee is a more effective deterrent against potential enemies.

Saudi Arabia ratified the Nuclear Non-Proliferation Treaty in 1970. Under the treaty, it can build nuclear reactors for research and for electric power, but if it started to build bombs, it would have to withdraw from the treaty, something that Iran has threatened to do if the United Nations Security Council enacts harsh sanctions.

In Barbara Walters's interview with King Abdullah on October 14, 2005, she asked the king, "If Iran gets those [nuclear] weapons, would Saudi Arabia have to have them, too?" The king replied, "The Kingdom of Saudi Arabia, like other countries in the region, rejects the acquisition of nuclear weapons by anyone, especially nuclear weapons in the Middle East. We hope that such weapons will be banned or eliminated from the region."[66]

Iran is still several years away from acquiring a nuclear weapons capability, and even if it builds bombs, it does not appear to want to turn Saudi Arabia into an enemy. So the Saudis have some time. They do not have to decide yet whether to build a bomb of their own.

To show its support for Saudi Arabia and to help deter Iran, the United States announced on July 27, 2007, that it intends to sell Saudi Arabia $20 billion worth of advanced weapons over the next ten years, including fighter jet upgrades, air-to-air missiles, and satellite-guided "smart" bombs. The planned sale, which must be approved by Congress, has been criticized by more than one hundred members of the U.S. House of Representatives, who worry that Saudi weapons would someday be used against Israel or Iraq, rather than against Iran.

Surprisingly, Israel's prime minister, Ehud Olmert, praised the U.S. arms plan as a way to create a united front against Iran. This was partly because the United States simultaneously announced a $30.4 billion arms package for Israel, but also because the Saudis have expressed a willingness not to deploy their most advanced weapons at bases near Israel.

An abundance of conventional weapons does not necessarily mean that Saudi Arabia will forgo its nuclear options. At a summit of the GCC in Riyadh on December 11, 2006, the kings and the emirs of Saudi Arabia, Kuwait, Qatar, Bahrain, Oman, and the United Arab Emirates ordered a technical study of how "to form a joint program in the field of nuclear technology for peaceful purposes, in keeping with international standards and regulations."[67] "We hope our statement will not be misunderstood," Saudi Arabia's foreign minister, Prince Saud al-Faisal, told the press. "This is not secret and we are doing this out in the open. Our aim is to obtain the technology for peaceful purposes, no more, no less."[68]

Two months later, Russia's president, Vladimir Putin, met King Abdullah in Riyadh and offered to sell the Saudis a wide range of nuclear technology.

The announcement of the GCC study and the occasion of Abdullah's summit with Putin were clearly designed to win Iran's attention. For better and for worse, Saudi Arabia and its neighbors can also rub the nuclear genie's lamp.

The Uncertain Saudi Succession

Saudi Arabia's biggest problems are high unemployment, chaos in Iraq, a resurgent Iran, and the need to develop an economy that is less dependent on oil. How well or how badly the Saudis handle these challenges will depend on who rules the country. Abdullah has been an unusually good king, but as he and his brothers grow older, Saudi Arabia runs the risk of being led by men who lack the energy and imagination to tackle the future's unpredictable challenges.

The Chernenko Syndrome

When the Soviet Union's communist dictator Leonid Brezhnev died at age seventy-six in 1982, he was succeeded by Yuri Andropov, age sixty-eight, who died just two years later. Andropov's successor was another old man: an already-sick party hack, Konstantin Chernenko, for whom the "Chernenko Syndrome" is named. At age seventy-two, he ruled only one year (1984–1985) before he, too, died of illness— the third elderly ruler to die in three years. By then, even the long-fearful Russian people openly expressed contempt for their decrepit leadership, and the communist government fell just six years later.

Today Saudi Arabia is ruled by King Abdullah, who was almost eighty-five as this book was published, and a crown prince, Sultan, who was nearly eighty-four. The two men most likely to succeed them are Prince Nayef, seventy-five, and Prince Salman, seventy-two. It is vital that the royal family transfer power soon to the next generation, but even many of the grandsons of King Abdul Aziz are now in their sixties.

Publicly, the royal family refuses to recognize the problem. In May 2006, I asked Prince Turki al-Faisal, then the kingdom's ambassador to the United States, whether he was worried that Saudi Arabia might suffer from the "Chernenko Syndrome":

> Prince Turki: Not at all. As you know, we have great respect for our elders, and we think of them as seasoned, practiced, and wise. So any succession that takes place will be within that context.
>
> Author: So even if, God forbid, there should be a new leader every year or two, it would still be all right?
>
> Prince Turki: Yes, if that is God's will.
>
> The Author: Have there been any serious discussions about transferring power from the sons of King Abdul Aziz to the grandsons of Abdul Aziz?
>
> Prince Turki: No. Nor do I think there is a need. There are enough sons of King Abdul Aziz who are alive and well, who are quite capable of carrying on the succession.[69]

In fact, the three youngest sons of King Abdul Aziz are already sixty-one, sixty-five, and sixty-six years old, which suggests that after

Abdullah and Sultan, there is time for no more than one final king from among Abdul Aziz's sons if the kingdom is to avoid its own version of the Chernenko Syndrome.

Prince Nayef

The problem of succession is particularly troublesome today because after King Abdullah and Crown Prince Sultan, the brother who is the "eldest able" to serve as king is Prince Nayef, a powerful but ultra-conservative monarch who may not have the flexibility a king needs to handle the future's many challenges.

Prince Nayef has been Saudi Arabia's minister of the interior since 1975, commanding an enormous force of 250,000 men, including 95,000 police officers, 30,000 emergency troops, more than 20,000 oil facilities troops, 20,000 border guards, 20,000 drug enforcement officers, 15,000 prison guards, and 10,000 men each in the Special Security Forces and the Coast Guard, as well as a still-classified number of men in the General Security Service, Saudi Arabia's equivalent of the FBI.[70] More people work for the Ministry of the Interior than for all the branches of the military combined, and little happens in the kingdom without the ministry's knowledge. Its annual budget is at least $9 billion; the Saudi government spends more than 35 percent of its budget on defense and security, compared to an average of 22 percent elsewhere in the Middle East and 10 percent around the world.[71]

The Ministry of the Interior is the largest employer in Saudi Arabia, and since 2001, it has been instrumental in finding, attacking, arresting, and often killing hundreds of members of al-Qaeda. Much of the credit for this must go to Nayef's younger brother, Prince Ahmad, the deputy minister of the interior, and to one of Nayef's sons, Prince Muhammad, the deputy minister for security affairs. Together, the father, the brother, and the son are extremely popular among the men in the ministry's uniformed forces. This is partly because the princes pay large bonuses for jobs well done, but also because Nayef, Ahmad, and Muhammad have a reputation for being hardworking and for not using government contracts to enrich themselves.

Prince Nayef is one of the most conservative Saudi monarchs. He has called the deaths of people detained by the religious police "minor mistakes," has dismissed calls for reform as "useless barking," and does not even like to use the words *reform* or *change* because they imply that the kingdom's system of government needs fixing. Nayef prefers the word *development*, as he told the *Saudi Gazette* in March 2003: "I have said it clearly—no to change . . . however, there is scope for development—development that does not clash with the principles of the nation."[72]

In the spring of 2002, despite a national uproar, Prince Nayef refused to punish the religious policemen who had stopped Mecca's firemen from rescuing girls fleeing a burning school because the girls were not wearing their *abayas*. In November of that year, Prince Nayef also told a Kuwaiti reporter that he thought the Israelis were behind 9/11 because they were going to benefit the most when the United States invaded Iraq. In fairness to Nayef, most Saudis in 2002 were still in denial about the role of the fifteen Saudi hijackers; nevertheless, it is deeply troubling that a man as informed as Prince Nayef could have clung to such a distorted view of reality a full year after 9/11.

A more recent example of Prince Nayef's lack of sympathy with the need for reform took place on February 2, 2007, when police-men from the Ministry of the Interior arrested nine Saudis and a Moroccan legal assistant for "collecting donations for terrorist activi-ties in neighboring countries," that is, Iraq. Although one of the men had recently been to Iraq to help refugees, at least seven others were lawyers and human rights activists who were highly unlikely to have helped the terrorists' cause. While it is possible that Prince Nayef has evidence of the accused men's guilt that he has not released, it seems more likely that he ordered the arrests because of a petition at least four of the men had presented to King Abdullah the day before.

It was no ordinary petition. In addition to the usual calls for an elected parliament, the document's nineteen signers asked that the local police and the national police be split into two separate min-istries, and that the kingdom's investigators and prosecutors also be placed under two separate jurisdictions, with the prosecutors moving from the Ministry of the Interior to the Office of the Prime Minister (that is, the king).[73] In other words, the petition proposed to substan-tially reduce Prince Nayef's power.

Because petitions are legal in Saudi Arabia, Prince Nayef arrested the signers on charges of terror funding instead. The ruse has had two advantages. First, it confused the issue and made it much less likely that Western governments would take an interest in the case. Second, the terror-funding charges also made pardons from King Abdullah less likely. A year after their arrests, nine of the men are still in jail without any formal charges, and a blogger who publicized their cause is also in prison.

King Abdullah Keeps the Number-Three Post Vacant

According to one foreigner who knows the kingdom's senior princes, "Abdullah and Nayef don't like each other." Perhaps King Abdullah agrees with the *Economist*, which reported that Prince Nayef "is widely regarded as moody, abrasive, capricious, and prone to intrigue."[74]

It was therefore highly significant that when Abdullah became king in August 2005 and Sultan became crown prince, Abdullah let the position of second deputy prime minister—the third-most powerful post in the kingdom—stay vacant. Despite the humdrum name, the second deputy prime minister is second in line to the throne, next in line to be crown prince. There had been a second deputy prime minister for thirty-eight years, since King Faisal first made the royal succession crystal clear by creating the number-three post for Fahad in 1967. When Fahad became king and Abdullah became crown prince after Khalid died in 1982, Fahad appointed Sultan as second deputy prime minister. Prince Sultan served as the number-three monarch for twenty-three years until King Fahad died in August 2005 and Sultan became the crown prince.

In 2005, however, King Abdullah declined to name anyone second deputy prime minister. The natural choice for the job would have been Prince Nayef, the "eldest able" of the surviving sons of King Abdul Aziz. Some people speculate that Abdullah may think that Nayef is simply too reactionary to lead the kingdom in a new era when citizens need more democracy, women need more freedom, and the economy needs more foreign investment. In the words of newspaper editor Jamal Khashoggi in August 2005, "If Nayef is appointed [Second] Deputy Prime Minister, it's 'game over,' but if you leave the post open, and that's what everybody is hoping for, then a younger generation will have an opportunity."[75]

The Allegiance Institution
On October 20, 2006, King Abdullah abolished the post of second deputy prime minister and created an entirely new body to pick heirs to the throne, the Allegiance Institution. This powerful new council consists of representatives of the sons of the founding king, Abdul Aziz: either the sons themselves, if they are still living, or, if not, then grandsons appointed by the king to represent each of the other branches of the family. The Allegiance Institution thus has thirty-five princes—at present, sixteen sons and nineteen grandsons of Abdul Aziz. Together, they will help the next king choose his crown prince.

The new law is an amendment to the Basic Law of 1992 and undoubtedly is the product of many discussions among the senior princes. It will take effect the next time the post of crown prince is vacant. No longer will the king choose an heir after only a few discussions with his brothers. Instead, within ten days of assuming office, the king will formally nominate one or maybe two men as possible heirs to the throne. The Allegiance Institution's thirty-five princes will then, within ten days, vote for one of the king's nominees, although they have the right to reject the nominees and pick someone of their own choosing as crown prince.

The royal decree also created a medical committee of five doctors. If the doctors conclude that a king cannot do his job, they can invite the crown prince to rule instead. This ensures that there will never again be another period like 1996–2005, when King Fahad was mentally and physically unable to govern. The new law also says that if the king and the crown prince should both die or both be incapacitated, then a temporary council of senior princes shall govern the kingdom for one week and shall choose the ablest of King Abdul Aziz's sons and grandsons to rule as king. The meetings of the Allegiance Institution and the doctors' committee will not be public, nor will the Allegiance Institution include any tribal chiefs, senior clerics, business leaders, members of the Consultative Council, or anyone else outside the royal family.

Speculation about the Allegiance Institution and about Prince Salman

The following is merely speculation. No one outside the Saudi royal family really knows how the family makes its decisions or how much or how little sibling rivalries come into play. Even the most informed speculation is conjecture. In the words of the ancient Taoist philosopher Lao-Tzu, "Those who know don't say, and those who say don't know."

The senior princes may have created the Allegiance Institution for five reasons. First, it formalizes the process of choosing an heir to the throne, which may be important if the princes cannot reach a consensus. Second, it makes fitness for the office of crown prince a more important factor than seniority. Third, it gives the most prominent grandsons of King Abdul Aziz a say in choosing their ruler. Fourth, it makes it difficult for a future king to pick a son as crown prince.

Finally, by abolishing the post of second deputy prime minister, the new law probably makes it harder for Prince Nayef to become king. It is no longer enough for Nayef merely to be the eldest able among his brothers; he will now have to win a plurality of votes from thirty-five princes, a difficult task for an abrasive man, especially if nineteen of the princes are from the next generation.

It is possible that the next king could submit two nominees to the Allegiance Institution, one of whom is Prince Nayef. Nayef would then have the honor of being a royal nominee, which he could graciously decline if he is unable to win a majority of the Allegiance

Institution's thirty-five votes. It is also possible that events in Iran, Iraq, or Palestine could cause the royal family to turn sharply to the right and choose Prince Nayef as crown prince after all.

Did King Abdullah create the Allegiance Institution as a way to transfer power from the sons of Abdul Aziz to the grandsons of the founding king? Perhaps, but at present there does not seem to be any agreement within the royal family on which grandson should be the first king from the new generation. One of the most likely candidates is the kingdom's foreign minister, Prince Saud al-Faisal, but he is already sixty-eight and suffers from Parkinson's disease.

If the Allegiance Institution does bypass Prince Nayef, the man most likely to become the next crown prince is Prince Nayef's (and Crown Prince Sultan's) younger full brother, Prince Salman. Salman is seventy-two, is reasonably healthy, and has been the governor of Riyadh Province since 1962. He was only twenty-six when Faisal gave him the job, and he has held it for nearly half a century. By all accounts, Salman both looks and acts like a king, and for decades, he has been a calm and tactful arbitrator of family disputes. A man of contradictions, he is both open-minded and fundamentalist, anti-Israeli and pro-American, and he favors educational reform even though he is close to many conservative clerics.

The Future

Although ninety-five percent of the Saudi people have a favorable opinion of King Abdullah, according to a December 2007 poll by the Center for Public Opinion, it is still true that no dynasty holds power forever. Sooner or later, every royal family either accepts constitutional monarchy or gets swept away by a revolution. The Saudi view of constitutional monarchy, of course, is different from the European view. When I asked Prince Turki al-Faisal, then the kingdom's ambassador to the United States, whether members of the royal family see themselves becoming constitutional monarchs in the far future, Prince Turki replied, "We are already constitutional monarchs. We follow the constitution of the Quran and the sayings of the Prophet."[76]

Five months later, in October 2006, Prince Turki elaborated on this theme in a speech at a conference of Middle East experts in Washington: "Saudi Arabia's constitutional evolution is homegrown and consistent with the traditions of its people and the tenets of Islam. . . . We are not in a hurry to experiment with foreign interpretations of democracy or methods of government. . . . We will make mistakes along the way, we can be sure of that, but they will be our mistakes, not someone else's."[77]

Few would argue with Prince Turki that the structure of Saudi Arabia's government should be "homegrown" and consistent with Muslim tradition. But when the government "makes mistakes along the way," who will be blamed? Suppose, a generation from now, half of the following scenarios come true: Saudi oil production peaks, the price of oil falls as alternative fuels become more economical, a war in a nearby Arab country goes badly, unemployment stays high, aquifers decline, and water becomes costly. A Saudi king handling these tough problems could grow increasingly unpopular.

Wouldn't it be better for a king to let a prime minister take the blame, accept his resignation, and appoint another politician to take his place? It is easy to disburse money during an oil boom. It will be much harder to govern when the fat years turn lean again. In the future, if the royal family gives more power to the people, it will be blamed for fewer mistakes when times become tougher.

By 2044—the three hundredth anniversary of the Saudi-Wahhabi alliance—if the royal family has made the transition to a modern constitutional monarchy, it will most likely continue to command the loyalty of the Saudi people as it begins to reign (not rule) for a fourth century.

Conclusion

SAUDI ARABIA, for all its shortcomings, is a country on the move. Young women are receiving college educations and working in new fields. Young men are studying abroad in record numbers. Foreigners are investing billions of dollars in the kingdom as the government cuts red tape and Saudi businesses become better managed. At home, people are watching satellite television, surfing the Internet, and reading less-censored newspapers. Two human rights commissions have begun to hear and investigate complaints.

The kingdom is not a democracy. The Saudis do not choose their leaders, and they lack many freedoms. But King Abdullah is grappling with the nation's most important issue: either Saudi Arabia develops a diversified non-oil economy in the next half-century, or it will return to poverty when the kingdom runs out of oil or the world turns to new, alternative fuels. Indeed, in the last few years. King Abdullah has modernized Saudi Arabia's economy at a much faster pace than a democratically elected government that is indebted to special interests could have.

The king and his brothers consult an enormous number of businessmen, clerics, professors, tribal leaders, and diplomats before they make a decision because Saudi Arabia's political tradition is one of consensus. In the United States, when a political party wins 51 percent of the vote, it passes as much of its legislative program as it can. In Saudi Arabia, by contrast, social changes must usually wait until the royal family feels that two-thirds or even three-quarters of the people support the changes.

The royal family mediates between conservative clerics and Western-educated businessmen and professors. Neither group is satisfied—clerics warn of the danger of changing too fast, liberals warn of the peril of moving too slowly—which suggests that the royal family performs its mediation with care and skill.

Through business loans, public works, and cradle-to-grave welfare payments, the royal family has skillfully, if unevenly, spread the nation's oil money to every region and class. Most Saudis regard the monarchy favorably, and King Abdullah, who has made many more changes than his predecessor, Fahad, is especially popular. "Western-educated Saudis want constitutional reform," Dr. Saleh al-Kathlan, a professor of political science at King Saud University, told me. "Ordinary Saudis don't want to change the political system. They just want the government to be more responsive and efficient."

Most Saudis not only approve of the monarchy, they also prefer their austere Wahhabi lifestyle to our looser way of life in the West. Wahhabism, of course, is just one of several puritanical Muslim movements, which include the Muslim Brotherhood in Egypt, the Deobandi movement in India, and the religious Jamaat-i-Islam political party in Pakistan. To lump them together and condemn Wahhabism as the key influence behind global terrorism is a common but serious mistake.

The Saudi people are deeply conservative. Too much change too quickly can spur thousands of angry clerics to take to the streets, as happened in 1990 when forty-seven women drove cars in downtown Riyadh and set their cause back a generation. It is fine for Westerners to call for democracy in Saudi Arabia, but even the kingdom's liberals concede that they are greatly outnumbered by fundamentalists. If democracy comes too quickly to the kingdom, a militantly Islamic regime could control a quarter of the world's oil, stop women's progress cold, and create enormous trouble for the West.

Often, the same people who want instant democracy in Saudi Arabia also call for changes that the Saudi people do not want, such as the right of foreign Christians to build churches in the kingdom, an idea most Saudis are not ready for and are unlikely to support for decades. It would help if more U.S. legislators and reporters visited Saudi Arabia and could see for themselves that the majority of Saudis are devout Muslims who are content with their monarchy and its slow but steady pace of change. Unfortunately, between late 2001 and early 2006, an average of only four U.S. congressmen a year visited the kingdom, although it is our most important Muslim ally.

At present, what Saudi Arabia needs more than elections is the rule of law, including the enforcement of a new but frequently ignored code of criminal procedure that requires the police to obtain warrants for searches and arrests, detainees to be told what their charges are, and defendants to receive public trials. In business, the kingdom needs to continue its ongoing efforts to ensure that every purchase, sale, contract, deed, and permit is subject to written laws or regulations, rather than an official's whim.

Most important, Saudi Arabia needs to guarantee its people the right to openly criticize the government and the clergy. "If we can talk without fear," a history professor told me, "the centrists will win the day because they are more rational than the fundamentalists. But if we are not so open, then the Islamists will control the discussion."

Despite many positive changes since 2001, Saudi Arabia is still run by only a dozen or so princes, although, according to Robert Lacey, a British historian, "The ones I've spoken to know that the old days of authority, owning the country as if it were a personal possession, are long gone." A Saudi historian, Dr. Muhammad al-Zulfa, told me, "The slow pace of democratization is okay, as long as it is constant." Al-Zulfa is optimistic about the kingdom's future but does fear a possible "Talibanization of Saudi Arabia" if the nation's Islamic militants are not checked. "The best way to fight militancy," he said, "is to prepare the people for democracy through education and participation, so that they will not listen to the militants when they say that democracy is un-Islamic."

It may be too soon for full democracy in Saudi Arabia, but in just a few years, the public will be ready to elect a third or even half of the members of the nascent national legislature, the Majlis al-Shura. Limited elections would give the Saudis some experience with democracy and, more important, would give the royal family some valuable guidance about when to make controversial social reforms such as allowing women to drive, work with men, and travel alone. If the government moves too quickly on these issues, clerics and other conservatives will revolt. But if it waits until 80 percent of the people are ready for these changes, the kingdom's economy will suffer because so few women work outside the home. Elections make it clear how the people feel and can help the royal family mediate between conservatives and reformers.

Around the world, monarchies often serve as guarantors of electoral fairness, ensuring that officials count the votes properly and that the winners of an election will not change the rules before the next ballot. This is especially important in a Muslim country where a political or religious faction might feel that its interpretation of the *sharia*, God's law, is more important than existing election statutes.

If the royal family gave the Majlis al-Shura some genuine power over parts of the national budget, it would also free the princes from having to make the unpopular cuts in spending that will be inevitable when, sooner or later, the price of oil falls.

Unfortunately, the royal family has not given even the municipal councils any power, despite the fact that Saudi men voted for half of the councils' members in local elections in 2005. The municipal councils present the royal family with a tremendous opportunity to create a kind of laboratory, a place where highly conservative Muslims can take power without doing too much damage. In the next election, if, instead of choosing only half of the municipal council members, the voters could elect *all* of the men on these councils, and if the councils were given some real power over local budgets and local issues, the Saudi people could vote for different kinds of governments in different cities and see what life is like in each of them. Saudis who vote for ultraconservative Muslims in one city could compare their governments to more secular-minded councils in another city.

After a few years, if the religious conservatives seemed tiresome, the Saudis (unlike the Iranians) could vote them out of office because the royal family would still hold power at the national and provincial levels. To appeal to the electorate, which will probably include women in 2009, the fundamentalists might even become more flexible on social issues.

Political reform has been slow, but the government deserves great credit for taking on nearly all of the kingdom's economic challenges. These include the need to encourage foreign investment; join the World Trade Organization; strengthen ties to the other Gulf states; reduce debt; increase foreign assets; streamline bureaucracy; establish commercial courts; promote fiscal transparency; boost oil production capacity; finance petrochemical plants; build roads, hospitals, power stations, and other infrastructure; and improve the quality of universities, vocational training centers, and tens of thousands of schools.

One issue has been ducked: Saudi Arabia's population has grown one-third larger every decade, yet the government has done nothing to try to reduce this crippling growth rate. Today, half of the Saudi people are under twenty. In just ten years, 2.5 million Saudi men will reach adulthood and will need jobs and housing, and hundreds of thousands of women will need jobs, too. The most careful business plans will do little good if most of the kingdom's economic growth is swallowed up by a population surge, for there will be too little additional growth to raise the standard of living.

The probability that Saudi Arabia's population will increase 50 to 70 percent in the next twenty years is a much greater threat to the country's stability and well-being than the slim possibility of an Iranian nuclear strike. The kingdom's future will be much brighter if some courageous men or, more likely, brave women can persuade both the country's senior clergy and its many young people of the nation's pressing need for voluntary birth control.

A genuine dialogue about the need for birth control will be possible only if the Saudis have more freedom to discuss religion and its role in modern life. The first Saudis to raise the issue may be condemned by conservatives for trying to spread "Western values" and may even be intimidated into silence. But is the ability to freely discuss religion, sex, and politics really a Western value? As Vartan Gregorian asked in his informative short book *Islam, a Mosaic Not a Monolith*, "Are 'Western' values really Western—or are they universal values similar to those that prevailed in the Golden Age of Islam?" Caliph Umar, after all, constantly told his followers, "I am your servant and you should question my actions."

The problem with Muslim fundamentalists, said Theodore Dalrymple in London's *City Journal* in 2004, "is that they want the power that free inquiry confers, without either the free inquiry or the philosophy and institutions that guarantee that free inquiry." Recently, for example, a Saudi militant told author Madawi al-Rasheed that his aim was to embrace Western science and technology, while rejecting Western values. But as Saudi Arabia's current minister of labor, Ghazi al-Gosaibi, wrote in an essay almost thirty years ago, "Arabs and Western Civilization," Western society "does not begin and end with long hair, sex shows and drug addiction." Arabs who study the West's science must also find "in its intellectual heritage those areas which we may need to adopt or acquire." "It is an insult to our faith," al-Gosaibi said, "to suggest that the adoption of positive aspects of Western civilization will damage our religion."

Fortunately, neither governments nor clerics today can limit the flood of information and discussion pouring into every Muslim home. Just as the printing press broke the lock that the Catholic Church had on reading and knowledge before the fifteenth century, the Internet and satellite television have ended the monopoly on discussion that Muslim clerics and officials maintained until the twenty-first century.

For the first time, Saudis are watching how Egyptians, Lebanese, and other Muslims live. They are seeing that women can be good

Muslims without having to live apart from men. "Saudi Arabia's gender segregation is unnatural and will dissolve," said Saudi novelist Turki al-Hamad. Even the kingdom's archconservative minister of the interior, Prince Nayef, told a gathering of media executives in 2007 that the "segregation of men and women is not correct," and that he hoped it "would be reduced." The future of gender segregation, of course, is something that the Saudis must decide for themselves. Westerners who work with Saudis should respect their culture and be patient, mindful that people everywhere take years to change their customs.

The issue of how much or how little the Saudis should adapt to foreign ways was expressed quite simply by my friend Hammad al-Roqi, a graduate student from a village in the western desert, when he explained why he does not like to argue with his fundamentalist brother. "My brother sees everything as either for or against Islam. I'm not like that. I think we have to be open to new things, even if they come from non-Muslims. We have to be open to the world."

Years ago, at my home in suburban New York, my family invited two of our oldest, dearest, and most interesting friends to dinner. Unfortunately, during coffee after the meal, a lively political discussion suddenly turned into a personal quarrel, and it became obvious that except for a wedding or a funeral, we might never have these two men in the same room again. "We love you both," my sister said, as one of them rose to leave, and years later, we continue to be close friends with both men and their families.

This is the way the United States must be with Israel and Saudi Arabia, for each country has been our friend and ally for sixty years.

Clearly, the two nations loathe each other. In 2003, Dore Gold, Ariel Sharon's foreign minister, wrote *Hatred's Kingdom: How Saudi Arabia Supports the New Global Terrorism*, the best-researched of the one-sided books attacking Saudi Arabia after 9/11. In his conclusion, Gold mistakenly said that the Wahhabis "generate a unique anti-Western hatred," as if his own country's struggle with the Palestinians were not a factor, then added that the Saudi government was "the delivery system to carry that hatred worldwide."

Israelis can at least say the words *Saudi Arabia*. Saudis, like most Arabs, usually will not even speak the name Israel or write it on a map. They refer to the country instead as "Occupied Palestine" or "the Zionist state." (A Saudi peace plan for the region, however, uses the word *Israel*.) Saudis continue to give money to the Palestinian Authority and sometimes meet with leaders of Hamas, Israel's mortal enemy.

Given the bitterness of the dispute between Israel and Palestine, it is natural that Israel and Saudi Arabia should regard each other with suspicion and even hostility. But there is no reason for the United States not to remain friends with both nations. The United States has moral and spiritual reasons for its ties to Israel and political and economic reasons for its ties to Saudi Arabia. The many recent books and articles by U.S. neoconservatives that condemn Saudi Arabia cannot negate the simple fact that a friendship and an alliance with the Saudi kingdom is unquestionably in America's national interest.

The countries that surround the Persian Gulf have two-thirds of the world's oil. Saudi Arabia, the largest of them, has nearly as much oil as Iran, Iraq, and Kuwait combined. While it is true that the United States could probably make up for a shortfall of Saudi oil by importing more petroleum from Canada, Mexico, and Venezuela, a shortage of Saudi crude would be a crippling blow to the nations of Europe and East Asia, and the United States is as dependent on the manufactured goods of these countries as they are on Saudi oil. Without Saudi Arabia's oil exports, a shortage of petroleum would cause the price of oil to skyrocket and would plunge the world's economy into a recession.

As Saudi Arabia is vital to global stability, the royal family is essential to Saudi stability. Few Westerners know anything about the kingdom's historical regions: Najd, Hejaz, Al-Hasa, and Asir, but Saudis are keenly aware that even today, their accents, occupations, and outlooks are determined to a large extent by geography. "If an elected leader came from one region, the other regions would chafe," said a young Saudi reporter who asked not to be named. "The royal family is the glue that holds Saudi Arabia together." Dr. Sulaiman al-Hattlan, a media consultant who used to be the editor in chief of *Forbes Arabia*, agreed. "Almost no one challenges the legitimacy of the royal family," he told me, "because the family is the symbol of Saudi Arabia's unification." In al-Hattlan's opinion, King Abdul Aziz's unification of the country in the 1910s and the 1920s is "a much more important part of the royal family's legitimacy today" than its 260-year alliance with the Wahhabi clergy. Others agree, and this is why even Western-educated Saudis who dislike Wahhabism do not question the al-Saud family's right to rule.

The United States is fortunate to have a six-decade friendship with this family, for it gives the United States an extra influence in the Middle East that otherwise it would not have. Most of us, when we think of allies, think of countries that we share many values with, such as Britain, Canada, and the Netherlands. Obviously, Saudi Arabia, as a gender-segregated monarchy governed by Muslim law, does not fit this mold. But should the United States have allies only in North America and Europe? Isn't it more useful to have an ally in a hostile region where the United States sorely needs a friend?

The Saudis do share three fundamental beliefs with the West: they worship the same God we do, they are capitalists, and they oppose terrorism. (Often, I heard Saudis call the terrorists "uneducated savages.") To cite cultural differences, however large, as a reason to end our long-standing alliance with the kingdom makes no sense when the prospect of another government friendlier to the United States assuming power in Saudi Arabia is nil. The many Americans on both the right and the left who want the monarchy to fall are shortsighted and naive; they imagine that Arabia's next government will somehow be more sympathetic to women's rights and U.S. interests, and they ignore the hard fact that the Saudi people are both more conservative and more anti-American than the ruling family is. Israelis, too, need to understand that Saudi Arabia is about as moderate as an Arab country can be as long as Israel's lengthy dispute with the Palestinians continues.

The United States cannot win the war against Islamic terror alone. It is essential that we have the support of moderate Arabs and Muslims because without them we could wind up fighting a long and exhausting struggle across a quarter of the planet. Of the eleven Arab nations that are allied with the United States today, eight are monarchies: Saudi Arabia, Morocco, Jordan, Kuwait, Bahrain, Qatar, Oman, and the United Arab Emirates.

It is natural for Americans to be suspicious of kings because our nation rebelled against one in 1776. But if the United States is to have any Arab allies at all, we cannot spurn the support of monarchies. Saudi Arabia, with a quarter of the world's oil, is one of America's two most important non-Western allies (Japan is the other). It has been a reliable friend since the 1940s. Even during the Arab oil embargo in 1973, when tension between the United States and Saudi Arabia was at its highest, the Saudis made sure that plenty of oil was shipped to U.S. troops in Vietnam. Today, contrary to widespread belief, the fifteen Saudis who hijacked airplanes and killed nearly three thousand Americans on 9/11 are not representative of the Saudi people, the vast majority of the Saudi clergy, or even Wahhabi doctrine.

America's sixty-year friendship with Saudi Arabia needs to be nurtured, not censured.

When I lived in Riyadh, I walked past a Saudi soldier every day. He had a machine gun and wore a uniform of beige-and-brown desert camouflage; his job was to help guard an apartment complex where foreign university professors lived. After two weeks of waving to each other, he asked me a question: "Are you a Muslim?"

The answer I gave him was a variation of part of the Muslim prayer call. "There is but one God," I said, "Moses and Jesus and Muhammad are His prophets." The soldier liked this answer. He smiled from ear to ear, nodded several times, and shook my hand vigorously. Muslims revere Moses and Jesus. The Quran mentions Moses 130 times and Jesus several dozen.

If more people could agree that God is One and that a number of religions have had great prophets, there might be slightly less fighting. Christians could still believe that Jesus is the Son of God, Jews could still believe that they are a chosen people, and Muslims could still believe that Muhammad is the last and the greatest of the prophets. But at a minimum, as Vartan Gregorian said, "the time has come for the world to recognize that Jews, Christians, and Muslims are the children of Abraham." We don't need to concede that other religions are as miraculous as our own, but in the interest of peace we need to acknowledge our common heritage.

Jews and Christians revere Obadiah and Haggai as prophets, even though their books at the end of the Old Testament are just twenty-one verses and thirty-eight verses long. Yet many would balk at granting the same honor to Muhammad, although he has nearly doubled the number of people who believe in one God. Ironically, it is the Muslims—except, of course, for their murderous, lunatic fringe—who may have the easiest time accepting religious differences.

In Sura (chapter) 5 of the Quran, God affirms that he has sent mankind the Torah, the Gospel, and the Quran as guidance and light: "For every one of you, We have appointed a path and a way. If God had willed, He would have made you but one community; but that [He has not done, in order that] He may try you in what has come to you. So compete with one another in good works."[1]

Here is a divine vision: the world's people engaged not in a struggle for territory or weapons, but in a friendly competition to do good. Perhaps this is a dream we can achieve sooner rather than later.

Insha'allah. (If it is God's will.)

Acknowledgments

I want to start by thanking Ambassador Wyche Fowler Jr. for encouraging me to write this book and for writing the book's foreword.

Many people helped me with *Prophets and Princes*. My agents, Peter Rubie and Bob Shuman, edited my proposals and were remarkably patient as a short book on the early Muslims evolved into a long history of Saudi Arabia. Peter Ginna, at Bloomsbury Press, introduced me to Peter Rubie.

I especially want to thank my editor, Stephen Power, who helped me tighten this book, and his hardworking assistant, Ellen Wright. I would also like to thank production editor Lisa Burstiner, copy editor Patti Waldygo, and proofreader Rima Weinberg for their help.

Author Sandra Mackey was invaluable in getting me started with my research, steering me to valuable Web sites, and suggesting that I meet Ambassador Fowler.

John West, the former governor of South Carolina who was President Carter's ambassador to Saudi Arabia, encouraged me from the very beginning and allowed me to use his name in letters I wrote to several Saudi princes. One of them, Prince Turki al-Faisal, made it possible for me to become a Visiting Scholar at the King Faisal Institute for Research and Islamic Studies in Riyadh. Later, as Saudi Arabia's ambassador to the United States, Prince Turki was kind enough to grant me a lengthy interview at his office in May 2006, some of which is excerpted at the end of chapter 22. At the Royal Embassy in Washington I am also indebted to Rima Hassan for providing dozens of photographs.

My stay as a Visiting Scholar at the King Faisal Institute was one of the most fascinating and rewarding experiences of my life. The director of the institute, Dr. Yahya Mahmoud ibn Junaid, and his deputy, Dr. Awadh al-Badi, went out of their way to make me feel welcome and make my time productive. They introduced me to many of the Saudis I quote in this book.

I owe a great debt to John and Rebecca Langford, who invited me to their home in Riyadh on numerous occasions. Rebecca introduced me to a remarkable Saudi woman, who must remain unnamed, but I want to thank her for the dinner she arranged on my behalf, where I got to meet many more Saudi women.

Sulaiman al-Hattlan lent me his car and driver so that I could meet Prince Abdullah bin Faisal bin Turki, the director of the Saudi Arabian General Investment Authority, who granted me a long interview. Samiha al-Haydar, the director of social services at King Abdulaziz Medical City, invited me to her hospital and improved my understanding of some of the difficulties many Saudi women face.

Students Marzoq Alotaibi and Hammad al-Roqi had coffee with me many evenings and let me know what young Saudis think about today's issues. My book is richer because of their insights.

I am grateful to the staff of the New York Public Library and to the libraries at the University of Georgia, the University of Virginia, Dartmouth College, and the State University of New York at Albany. I am also indebted to Andy and Yijing Robertson for their business expertise and helpful comments on chapter 21 and to Abigail Baglione for all her encouragement.

I could not have written this book without regular visits to two quiet and supportive colonies for writers. At the Dorset Colony House in Dorset, Vermont, I want to thank the directors, John and Paula Nassivera, for their warmth and support. At the Hambidge Center in Rabun Gap, Georgia, I am grateful to an equally warm and encouraging group: Dimmie Ziegler, Kim Waters, and Judy Morris Lampert, the executive directors; and Fran Lanier and Bob Thomas, the residency directors.

My deepest thanks go to Marybeth Weston Lobdell, a loving mother and an excellent writer. She taught me to respect the core truth in all religions, and respect is the first requirement for anyone trying to understand another culture.

Notes

Introduction

1. Niccolo Machiavelli, *The Prince and the Discourses*, trans. Christian E. Detmold (New York: Random House Modern Library, 1950), p. 103.

1. Muhammad: Islam's Prophet

The unsourced quotations in this chapter derive from traditional accounts, which are found in the works listed in the bibliography; in some cases I have simplified the wording in these sources.

1. *The Koran*, trans. J. M. Rodwell (New York: E. P. Dutton, [1861] 1953), p. 29 (Sura 112). Although J. M. Rodwell completed his translation of the Quran in 1861, I use it throughout this book. After carefully comparing his work to a number of contemporary translations, I feel that he has given the English-language Quran a majesty that other versions lack. No doubt this is because I grew up listening to the words of the King James Bible; to me, scripture sounds better if some of the words are archaic.
2. Ibid., p. 94 (Sura 20, verses 1–7).
3. Sayyid Qutb, *In the Shade of the Qur'an*, Volume 30, trans. M. Adil Salahi and Ahaur A. Shamis (New Delhi: Islamic Book Service, 2001), p. 225.
4. Karen Armstrong, *Muhammad: A Biography of the Prophet* (San Francisco: HarperCollins, 1992), pp. 207–208.
5. *The Excellent Sayings of the Prophet Muhammad and Hazrat Ali*, trans. Charles I. Campbell (New York: Maleknia Naseralishah, 1978), pp. 18, 25, 33, 37, 41, 52.
6. *The Koran*, trans. Rodwell, p. 28 (Sura 1), p. 265 (Sura 29, verse 45), p. 31 (Sura 107), p. 29 (Sura 112), pp. 66–69 (Sura 56, verses 22–23, 27–35, and 92–97).

2. The Successors Who Preserved the Faith and Began the Conquests: Abu Bakr and Umar (632–644)

The unsourced quotations in this chapter derive from traditional accounts, which are found in the works listed in the bibliography; in some cases I have simplified the wording in these sources.

1. Sir John Bagot Glubb, *The Great Arab Conquests* (Englewood Cliffs, NJ: Prentice-Hall, 1963), pp. 72, 179.
2. Fazl Ahmad, *Omar, the Second Caliph of Islam* (Lahore: Sh. Muhammad Ashraf, 1975), p. 100; and Abdur Rahman Shad, *Umar Faruq* (Lahore: Kazi, 1979), pp. 85, 87.

3. Expansion, Civil War, and the Sunni-Shi'ite Split: Uthman and Ali (644–661)

The unsourced quotations in this chapter derive from traditional accounts, which are found in the works listed in the bibliography; in some cases I have simplified the wording in these sources.

1. Abdul Ali, *Caliph Ali, His Life and Times* (Madras: Diocesan Press, 1964), p. 85.
2. Karen Armstrong, *Muhammad: A Biography of the Prophet* (San Francisco: HarperCollins, 1992), p. 258.
3. Philip K. Hitti, *Makers of Arab History* (New York: St. Martin's, 1968), p. 49; and Anthony Nutting, *The Arabs: A Narrative History from Mohammed to the Present* (New York: Clarkson Potter, 1964), p. 63.
4. *The Excellent Sayings of the Prophet Muhammad and Hazrat Ali*, trans. Charles I. Campbell (New York: Maleknia Naseralishah, 1978), pp. 71, 88; and Ali, *Caliph Ali*, pp. 87–88.

4. The Beginning of Monarchy: Muawiya, the Fifth Caliph, His Son Yazid, and the Martyrdom of Hussein (661–683)

The unsourced quotations in this chapter derive from traditional accounts, which are found in the works listed in the bibliography; in some cases I have simplified the wording in these sources.

1. G. R. Hawting, *The First Dynasty of Islam* (London: Croom Helm, 1986), p. 42; and Philip K. Hitti, *Makers of Arab History* (New York: St. Martin's, 1968), p. 51.
2. Reynold A. Nicholson, *A Literary History of the Arabs* (Cambridge, UK: Cambridge University Press, 1930), p. 195, modified slightly to keep the poem from sounding archaic.

5. The Founder of Wahhabism: Muhammad ibn Abdul Wahhab (1703–1792)

1. Uwaidah M. Al-Juhany, *Najd before the Salafi Reform Movement* (Reading,UK: Ithaca Press, 2002), p. 148.
2. Natana J. Delong-Bas, *Wahhabi Islam: From Revival and Reform to Global Jihad* (New York: Oxford University Press, 2004), pp. 230–233.
3. *The Koran*, trans. J. M. Rodwell (New York: E. P. Dutton, [1909] 1953), pp. 202 and 417 (Sura 16, verse 36, and Sura 4, verse 51).
4. Muhammad Bin Abdul-Wahhab, *Kitab At-Tauhid*, trans. the Compilation and Research Department of Dar-us-Salam Publications (Riyadh: Dar-us-Salam Publications, [c. 1740] 1996), pp. 96, 110.
5. Delong-Bas, *Wahhabi Islam*, p. 61.
6. Ibid., pp. 127, 136, 191, 286.
7. *The Koran*, trans. Rodwell, p. 399 (Sura 3, verse 134).
8. Delong-Bas, *Wahhabi Islam*, p. 76.
9. Sheikh Mohammad Iqbal, *Saudi Arabia: Landmarks in Islamic Solidarity* (Srinagar, Kashmir: Barzalla Bridge, 1986), p. 55.

6. Nineteenth-Century Saudi Arabia (1792–1887)

1. Alexei Vassiliev, *The History of Saudi Arabia* (New York: New York University Press, 2000), p. 144.
2. Abdulaziz H. Al-Fahad, "From Exclusion to Accommodation: Doctrinal and Legal Evolution of Wahhabism," *New York University Law Review* 79, no. 2 (May 2004): 496, 500.

3. Sheikh Mohammad Iqbal, *Saudi Arabia: Landmarks in Islamic Solidarity* (Srinagar, Kashmir: Barzalla Bridge, 1986), pp. 39–40.
4. Willard A. Beling, ed., *King Faisal and the Modernization of Saudi Arabia* (Boulder, CO: Westview Press, 1980), p. 23.

7. Exile and Return (1876–1902)

1. Sheikh Mohammad Iqbal, *Saudi Arabia: Landmarks in Islamic Solidarity* (Srinagar, Kashmir: Barzall Bridge, 1986), pp. 84–85, modified slightly to sound less archaic.

8. Expanding the Kingdom (1902–1926)

1. Leslie McLoughlin, *Ibn Saud, Founder of a Kingdom* (New York: St. Martin's, 1993), p. 26.
2. Robert Lacey, *The Kingdom* (New York: Harcourt Brace Jovanovich, 1981), p. 104.
3. Mohammed Almana, *Arabia Unified: A Portrait of Ibn Saud* (London: Hutchinson Benham, 1980), p. 233; Lacey, *The Kingdom*, p. 105; and McLoughlin, *Ibn Saud*, p. 44.
4. Lacey, *The Kingdom*, p. 112.
5. Ibid., p. 136.
6. Ibid., p. 160.
7. Alexei Vassiliev, *The History of Saudi Arabia* (New York: New York University Press, 2000), p. 258, quoting interpreter H. R. P. Dickson.
8. Lacey, *The Kingdom*, p. 211.
9. Sheikh Mohammad Iqbal, *Saudi Arabia: Landmarks in Islamic Solidarity* (Srinagar, Kashmir: Barzalla Bridge, 1986), p. 86.

9. Powerful but Poor (1926–1945)

1. David Howarth, *The Desert King: A Life of Ibn Saud* (London: Collins, 1964), p. 148.
2. Mohammed Almana, *Arabia Unified: A Portrait of Ibn Saud* (London: Hutchinson Benham, 1980), p. 104.
3. Ibid., p. 223.
4. Leslie McLoughlin, *Ibn Saud, Founder of a Kingdom* (New York: St. Martin's, 1993), p. 131.
5. Ibid., p. 137; and Robert Lacey, *The Kingdom* (New York: Harcourt Brace Jovanovich, 1981), p. 259.
6. Sheikh Mohammad Iqbal, *Saudi Arabia: Landmarks in Islamic Solidarity* (Srinagar, Kashmir: Barzalla Bridge, 1986), p. 78, modified slightly to sound less archaic.

10. The Influx of Oil Money (1945–1953)

1. Robert Lacey, *The Kingdom* (New York: Harcourt Brace Jovanovich, 1981), p. 271.
2. Winston S. Churchill, *The Second World War, Vol. 6, Triumph and Tragedy* (Boston: Houghton Mifflin, 1952), pp. 397–398.
3. Lacey, *The Kingdom*, p. 280.
4. Lawrence Wright, *The Looming Tower: Al-Qaeda and the Road to 9/11* (New York: Knopf, 2006), pp. 64–68.
5. David Howarth, *The Desert King: A Life of Ibn Saud* (London: Collins, 1964), pp. 117–118.

11. The Young Prince and Foreign Minister (1905–1953)

1. Interview with Dr. Muhammad al-Zulfa, a leading historian of Asir, in Riyadh, May 12, 2004.
2. K. J. Ahmad, *A Hundred Great Muslims* (Chicago: Kazi, 1987), p. 426.

3. Gerald De Gaury, *Faisal, King of Saudi Arabia* (London: Arthur Barker, 1966), p. 141.
4. Robert Lacey, *The Kingdom* (New York: Harcourt Brace Jovanovich, 1981), p. 288.

12. The Struggle between the Brothers (1953–1964)

1. David Holden and Richard Johns, *The House of Saud: The Rise and Rule of the Most Powerful Dynasty in the Arab World* (New York: Holt, Rinehart and Winston, 1981), pp. 192–193.
2. Willard A. Beling, ed., *King Faisal and the Modernization of Saudi Arabia* (London: Croom Helm, 1980), pp. 58–59.
3. Jeffrey Robinson, *Yamani: The Inside Story* (New York: Atlantic Monthly Press, 1988), p. 47.
4. Gordon Gaskill, "King Faisal: Saudi Arabia's Modern Monarch," *Reader's Digest*, January 1967, p. 122.
5. Gerald De Gaury, *Faisal, King of Saudi Arabia* (London: Arthur Barker, 1966), p. 133.
6. Ibid., p. 138.

13. The King in Full Control (1964–1972)

1. David Holden and Richard Johns, *The House of Saud: The Rise and Rule of the Most Powerful Dynasty in the Arab World* (New York: Holt, Rinehart and Winston, 1981), p. 262.
2. Robert Lacey, *The Kingdom* (New York: Harcourt Brace Jovanovich, 1981), p. 371.
3. Ibid., p. 345.
4. Jeffrey Robinson, *Yamani: The Inside Story* (New York: Atlantic Monthly Press, 1988), p. 16.

14. Oil as Political Power (1973–1975)

1. Steven A. Schneider, *The Oil Price Revolution* (Baltimore: Johns Hopkins University Press, 1983), p. 219.
2. Ibid., p. 220.
3. Anthony Sampson, *The Seven Sisters: The Great Oil Companies and the World They Made* (New York: Viking Press, 1975), p. 248.
4. Jeffrey Robinson, *Yamani: The Inside Story* (New York: Atlantic Monthly Press, 1988), p. 73.
5. Robert Lacey, *The Kingdom* (New York: Harcourt Brace Jovanovich, 1981), p. 424.

15. The Boom Years of King Khalid (1975–1982)

1. Dore Gold, *Hatred's Kingdom: How Saudi Arabia Supports the New Global Terrorism* (Washington, DC: Regnery, 2003), p. 108.
2. Robert Lacey, *The Kingdom* (New York: Harcourt Brace Jovanovich, 1981), p. 512.
3. Sandra Mackey, *The Saudis: Inside the Desert Kingdom* (New York: W. W. Norton, 1987), p. 345.
4. Daniel Yergin, *The Prize: The Epic Quest for Oil, Money and Power* (New York: Free Press, 1991), p. 711.
5. Joseph A. Kechichian, *Succession in Saudi Arabia* (New York: Palgrave, 2001), p. 57.

16. The Lean Years of King Fahad (1982–1990)

1. Elsa Walsh, "The Prince," *New Yorker*, March 24, 2003, p. 53, quoting Prince Bandar bin Sultan.
2. *The Koran*, trans. J. M. Rodwell (New York: E. P. Dutton, 1953), p. 496.
3. Peter W. Wilson and Douglas F. Graham, *Saudi Arabia: The Coming Storm* (Armonk, NY: M. E. Sharpe, 1994), p. 61.

4. Anders Jerichow, *The Saudi File: People, Power, Politics* (New York: St. Martin's, 1998), p. 195.

5. Peter L. Bergen, *Holy War, Inc.: Inside the Secret World of Osama bin Laden* (New York: Free Press, 2001), p. 52.

6. Ibid., p. 53.

7. Mamoun Fandy, *Saudi Arabia and the Politics of Dissent* (New York: St. Martin's, 1999), p. 180.

8. Peter Bergen, "The Long Hunt for Osama," *Atlantic Monthly*, October 2004, p. 99.

9. Jeffrey Robinson, *Yamani: The Inside Story* (New York: Atlantic Monthly Press, 1988), p. 278.

10. Ibid., p. 281.

11. Anthony Cordesman, *Saudi Arabia: Guarding the Desert Kingdom* (Boulder, CO: Westview, 1997), p. 73.

12. Sandra Mackey, *The Iranians: Persia, Islam and the Soul of a Nation* (New York: Plume [Penguin], 1996, 1998), p. 331; and Yergin, *The Prize*, p. 766.

13. General H. Norman Schwarzkopf, with Peter Petre, *It Doesn't Take a Hero: General H. Norman Schwarzkopf, the Autobiography* (New York: Bantam, 1992), p. 305.

14. Ibid., p. 306.

17. The Persian Gulf War (1990–1991)

1. Sandra Mackey, *Passion and Politics: The Turbulent World of the Arabs* (New York: Dutton, 1992), p. 242.

2. Joshua Teitelbaum, *Holier Than Thou: Saudi Arabia's Islamic Opposition* (Washington, DC: Washington Institute for Near East Policy, 2000), p. 30.

3. Joseph Kostiner, ed., *Middle East Monarchies: The Challenge of Modernity* (Boulder, CO: Lynne Rienner, 2000), p. 141.

4. Teitelbaum, *Holier Than Thou*, p. 29.

5. Colin L. Powell, with Joseph E. Persico, *My American Journey* (New York: Random House, 1995), p. 474.

6. Ibid.

7. Geraldine Brooks, *Nine Parts of Desire: The Hidden World of Islamic Women* (New York: Random House, 1995), p. 200.

8. Peter W. Wilson and Douglas F. Graham, *Saudi Arabia: The Coming Storm* (Armonk, NY: M. E. Sharpe, 1994), p. 116.

9. Ibid., p. 190.

10. Anders Jerichow, *The Saudi File: People, Power, Politics* (New York: St. Martin's, 1998), p. 325; and Schwarzkopf, *It Doesn't Take a Hero*, p. 420.

11. George Herbert Walker Bush and Brent Scowcroft, *A World Transformed* (New York: Knopf, 1998), p. 489.

12. General H. Norman Schwarzkopf, with Peter Petre, *It Doesn't Take a Hero: General H. Norman Schwarzkopf, the Autobiography* (New York: Bantam, 1992), p. 488.

13. Ibid., p. 489.

14. Richard Cohen and Claudio Gatti, *In the Eye of the Storm: The Life of General H. Norman Schwarzkopf* (New York: Farrar, Straus and Giroux, 1991), p. 305.

15. Ibid., p. 315.

16. Gerald Posner, *Secrets of the Kingdom: The Inside Story of the Saudi–U.S. Connection* (New York: Random House, 2005), pp. 124–132.

18. The Rise of Militant Fundamentalism (1991–1996)

1. Joseph A. Kechichian, *Succession in Saudi Arabia* (New York: Palgrave, 2001), appendix 11.

2. Ibid., appendix 12.
3. Peter Molan, ed. and trans., *Arabic Religious Rhetoric: The Radical Saudi Sheikhs, A Reader* (Kensington, Md.: Dunwoody, 1997), p. 128; and Joshua Teitelbaum, *Holier Than Thou: Saudi Arabia's Islamic Opposition* (Washington, DC: Washington Institute for Near East Policy, 2000), pp. 37–38.
4. Peter W. Wilson and Douglas F. Graham, *Saudi Arabia: The Coming Storm* (Armonk, NY: M. E. Sharpe, 1994), p. 74.
5. Asad Abukhalil, *The Battle for Saudi Arabia—Royalty, Fundamentalism, and Global Power* (New York: Seven Stories, 2004), p. 70.
6. Madawi Al-Rasheed, *A History of Saudi Arabia* (Cambridge, UK: Cambridge University Press, 2002), p. 179.
7. Teitelbaum, *Holier Than Thou*, p. 55.
8. Elizabeth Rubin, "The Jihadi Who Kept Asking Why," *New York Times Magazine*, March 7, 2004, p. 62.
9. Leslie and Andrew Cockburn, "Royal Mess," *New Yorker*, November 28, 1994, p. 69.
10. Steve Coll, *Ghost Wars: The Secret History of the CIA, Afghanistan, and bin Laden, from the Soviet Invasion to September 10, 2001* (New York: Penguin, 2004), p. 223.
11. Ibid., p. 601.
12. Lawrence Wright, "The Man behind Bin Laden," *New Yorker*, September 16, 2002, p. 77.
13. Craig Unger, *House of Bush, House of Saud: The Secret Relationship between the World's Two Most Powerful Dynasties* (New York: Scribner, 2004), pp. 150–151.
14. Geoff Simons, *Saudi Arabia: The Shape of a Client Feudalism* (New York: St. Martin's, 1998), p. 323; and Lawrence Wright, *The Looming Tower: Al-Qaeda and the Road to 9/11* (New York: Knopf, 2006), p. 195.
15. Dore Gold, *Hatred's Kingdom: How Saudi Arabia Supports the New Global Terrorism* (Washington, DC: Regnery, 2003), p. 171.
16. Mamoun Fandy, *Saudi Arabia and the Politics of Dissent* (New York: St. Martin's, 1999), p. 187.
17. Gold, *Hatred's Kingdom*, p. 171.
18. Anthony Cordesman, *Saudi Arabia Enters the Twenty-First Century*, Volume 1 (Westport, CT: Praeger, 2003), p. 75.
19. Eleanor Abdella Doumato, "Women and Work in Saudi Arabia: How Flexible Are Islamic Margins?" *Middle East Journal* (Fall 1999): 579.
20. Najam Sethi, "Musharraf's Problem—and Opportunity," *Wall Street Journal*, July 16, 2007, p. A-13; and Pervez Musharraf, president of Pakistan, interviewed by Peter Jennings, *ABC World News Tonight*, broadcast September 20, 2004.
21. Peter L. Bergen, *Holy War, Inc.: Inside the Secret World of Osama bin Laden* (New York: Free Press, 2001), p. 88.
22. Cordesman, *Saudi Arabia Enters the Twenty-First Century*, Volume 1, p. 193.
23. Ibid., p. 205.

19. Abdullah Begins Reform, bin Laden Steps Up Terror (1996–August 2001)

1. William Powell, *Saudi Arabia and Its Royal Family* (Secaucus, NJ: Lyle Stuart, 1982), p. 366.
2. Gulf Wire e-newsletter, February 4, 2001, interview of Abdullah by John Duke Anthony, publisher.
3. Thirty-Fifth Annual Report (1999), Saudi Arabian Monetary Agency Research and Statistics Department, Riyadh, pp. 202, 205, 206.
4. Craig Unger, *House of Bush, House of Saud: The Secret Relationship between the World's Two Most Powerful Dynasties* (New York: Scribner, 2004), p. 105.

5. Steve Coll, *Ghost Wars: The Secret History of the CIA, Afghanistan, and bin Laden, from the Soviet Invasion to September 10, 2001* (New York: Penguin, 2004), p. 400; National Commission on Terrorist Attacks upon the United States, *The 9/11 Report* (New York: St. Martin's Paperbacks, 2004), p. 98; and Peter L. Bergen, *Holy War, Inc.: Inside the Secret World of Osama bin Laden* (New York: Free Press, 2001), p. 90.

6. "Bin Laden's Fatwa," PBS Online Newshour, www.pbs.org/newshour/terrorism/international/fatwa/_1996.html, pp. 5, 10, 16, 17, accessed October 19, 2004.

7. Ibid., pp. 23, 24.

8. Ibid., p. 27; and *The Koran*, trans. J. M. Rodwell (New York: E. P. Dutton, 1953), p. 471.

9. Natana J. Delong-Bas, *Wahhabi Islam: From Revival and Reform to Global Jihad* (Oxford, UK: Oxford University Press, 2004), pp. 274, 275, 277, 279.

10. Dore Gold, *Hatred's Kingdom: How Saudi Arabia Supports the New Global Terrorism* (Washington, DC: Regnery, 2003), pp. 100, 267; and Gilles Kepel, *The War for Muslim Minds: Islam and the West* (Cambridge, MA: Harvard University Press, 2004), pp. 94, 98.

11. Brynjar Lia, *The Society of the Muslim Brothers in Egypt* (Reading, UK: Ithaca Press, 1998), p. 36.

12. David Remnick, "Going Nowhere," *New Yorker*, July 12, 2004, p. 76.

13. Ibid.

14. David Von Drehle, "A Lesson in Hate," *Smithsonian*, February 2006, p. 96.

15. "A Tide of Islamic Fury," *New York Times*, January 30, 2005, section 4, p. 5; and Ahmad S. Moussalli, *Radical Islamic Fundamentalism: The Ideological and Political Discourse of Sayyid Qutb* (Beirut: American University of Beirut, 1992), p. 28.

16. Sayyid Qutb, *Islam and World Peace* (Plainfield, IN: American Trust, 1993), p. xi.

17. Lawrence Wright, *The Looming Tower: Al-Qaeda and the Road to 9/11* (New York: Knopf, 2006), p. 31.

18. Paul Berman, *Terror and Liberalism* (New York: W. W. Norton, 2003), p. 67.

19. Sayyid Qutb, *In the Shade of the Quran*, Volume 30 (New Delhi: Islamic Book Service, 2001), pp. 31, 32.

20. Sayyid Qutb, *Milestones* (Karachi: International Islamic Publishers, 1988), p. 119.

21. Sayyid Qutb, *Milestones* (New Delhi: Islamic Book Service, 2001), p. 56.

22. Ibid., pp. 80, 81.

23. Youssef M. Choueiri, *Islamic Fundamentalism* (London: Pinter, 1990), p. 124.

24. Qutb, *Milestones* (Islamic Book Service, 2001 edition), pp. 98 and 139.

25. Ibid., p. 76.

26. Ibid., p. 82.

27. Qutb, *In the Shade of the Quran*, Volume 30, p. 306.

28. Qutb, *Milestones* (Islamic Book Service, 2001 edition), pp. 11–12.

29. Berman, *Terror and Liberalism*, p. 117.

30. Qutb, *In the Shade of the Quran*, Volume 30, p. 352.

31. Qutb, *Milestones* (Islamic Book Service, 2001 edition), p. 71.

32. Ibid., p. 72.

33. William E. Shepard, *Sayyid Qutb and Islamic Activism: A Translation and Critical Analysis of Social Justice in Islam* (Leiden, Netherlands: E. J. Brill, 1996), p. 353.

34. Bernard Lewis, "License to Kill: Usama bin Ladin's Declaration of Jihad," *Foreign Affairs* 77, no. 6 (November–December 1998): 14.

35. See Shaykh Usamah Bin-Muhammad Bin-Ladin, Ayman al-Zawahiri, Abu-Yasir Rifa'i Ahmad Taha, Shaykh Mir Hamzah, and Fazlul Rahman, "Jihad Against Jews and Crusaders," www.library.cornell.edu/colldev/mideast/wif.htm, pp. 1, 2, last accessed February 4, 2008.

36. Lewis, "License to Kill," p. 19.

37. Jonathan Mahler, "The Bush Administration vs. Salim Hamdan," *New York Times Magazine*, January 8, 2006, p. 49.

38. Anonymous (Now known to be Michael Scheuer), *Through Our Enemies' Eyes: Osama bin Laden, Radical Islam and the Future of America* (Washington, DC: Brassey's, 2002), p. 197.
39. Coll, *Ghost Wars*, p. 414 (quoting Prince Turki on ABC News's *Nightline*, December 10, 2001).
40. Ibid., p. 414.
41. Ibid., p. 529.
42. Unger, *House of Bush, House of Saud*, p. 231, quoting the *Los Angeles Times*, May 22, 2001.
43. Daryl Champion, *The Paradoxical Kingdom: Saudi Arabia and the Momentum of Reform* (New York: Columbia University Press, 2004), p. 211.
44. Eleanor Abdella Doumato, "Women and Work in Saudi Arabia: How Flexible Are Islamic Margins?" *Middle East Journal* (Fall 1999): 578.
45. "Saudi Arabia: A Secret State of Suffering," *Amnesty International USA* (New York: 2000), p. 8.
46. "The Kingdom of Saudi Arabia, Information on Current Issues, 2003" (Washington, DC: Royal Embassy of Saudi Arabia), p. 17.
47. Anthony Cordesman, *Saudi Arabia Enters the Twenty-First Century*, Volume 1 (Westport, CT: Praeger, 2003), p. 234.
48. "School for Suicide," *Atlantic*, May 2007, p. 33.
49. Henry Munson, "Islam, Nationalism and Resentment of Foreign Domination," *Middle East Policy* 10, no. 2 (Summer 2003): 45.
50. Ibid., p. 46.
51. Cordesman, *Saudi Arabia Enters the Twenty-First Century*, Volume 1, p. 91.
52. Elsa Walsh, "The Prince," *New Yorker*, March 24, 2003, p. 58.
53. Cordesman, *Saudi Arabia Enters the Twenty-First Century*, Volume 1, p. 90.
54. Unger, *House of Bush, House of Saud*, p. 235.
55. Ibid., p. 243.
56. Walsh, "The Prince," p. 59.
57. Ibid.
58. Interview with Dr. Muhammad al-Zulfa in Riyadh, May 12, 2004.
59. National Commission on Terrorist Attacks upon the United States, *The 9/11 Report*, p. 564.
60. John Miller and Michael Stone, with Chris Mitchell, *The Cell: Inside the 9/11 Plot, and Why the FBI and CIA Failed to Stop It* (New York: Hyperion, 2003), pp. 294–295.
61. Ibid., p. 306.
62. Kepel, *The War for Muslim Minds*, p. 106.
63. Coll, *Ghost Wars*, p. 560.
64. Ibid.

20. Fighting Terror, Fostering Reform (2001–2007)

1. Page 6 of an interview with Mai Yamani, November 5, 2001, posted online to accompany a broadcast of "The House of Saud," PBS *Frontline*, February 8, 2005, David Fanning, executive producer, www.pbs.org/wgbh/pages/frontline/shows/saudi/interviews/yamani.html, accessed February 4, 2008; and page 4 of an interview with Bassim Alim, December 6, 2004, accompanying the same broadcast, www.pbs.org/wgbh/pages/frontline/shows/saudi/interviews/alim.html, accessed February 4, 2008.
2. *Saudi Arabia* (Royal Embassy of Saudi Arabia, Washington, DC) Vol. 19, no. 2 (Summer 2002): 5.
3. Ibid.
4. The National Commission on Terrorist Attacks upon the United States, *The 9/11 Report* (New York: St. Martin's, 2004), pp. 471–472.

5. Eric Lichtblau, article in the *International Herald Tribune*, March 28, 2005, p. 8.
6. Page 5 of an interview with Foreign Minister Saud al-Faisal, December 15, 2004, posted online to accompany a broadcast of "The House of Saud," PBS *Frontline*, February 8, 2005, David Fanning, executive producer, www.pbs.org/wgbh/pages/frontline/shows/saudi/interviews/saud.html, accessed February 4, 2008.
7. Dore Gold, *Hatred's Kingdom: How Saudi Arabia Supports the New Global Terrorism* (Washington, DC: Regnery, 2003), p. 193.
8. Letter dated September 10, 2002, reprinted in a full-page advertisement in the *New York Times* (and other papers) on September 15, 2002, section 1, p. 23.
9. Lawrence Wright, *The Looming Tower: Al Qaeda and the Road to 9/11* (New York: Knopf, 2006), p. 370.
10. Middle East Media Research Institute (MEMRI), Special Dispatch Series, no. 446, December 3, 2002, pp. 1–2.
11. Gold, *Hatred's Kingdom*, p. 206.
12. Thomas E. Ricks, "Briefing Depicted Saudis as Enemies," *Washington Post*, August 6, 2002, p. 1.
13. "Saudi-European Relations: Towards a Reliable Partnership," speech distributed by the Royal Embassy of Saudi Arabia, Washington, DC, February 2004.
14. Gerald Posner, *Secrets of the Kingdom: The Inside Story of the Saudi-U.S. Connection* (New York: Random House, 2005), p. 167.
15. *The 9/11 Report*, pp. 246–247.
16. Lisa Beyer, article quoting U.S. ambassador W. Jordan, *Time*, September 15, 2003, p. 46.
17. Gold, *Hatred's Kingdom*, p. 190.
18. MEMRI, no. 343, February 8, 2002, p. 2.
19. See "Khutbah," www.alminbar.com, nos. 819 and 892; and Asra Q. Nomani, *Standing Alone in Mecca* (San Francisco: HarperSanFrancisco, 2005), p. 261.
20. MEMRI, no. 752, July 23, 2004, p. 2.
21. MEMRI, Special Report, no. 12, December 20, 2002, p. 3, quoting *The One God and the Prophet's Sayings* (Riyadh: Ministry of Education, 1999), p. 34.
22. Posner, *Secrets of the Kingdom*, p. 174.
23. Gold, *Hatred's Kingdom*, p. 176.
24. MEMRI, Inquiry and Analysis Series, no. 195, November 9, 2004, p. 11.
25. Nina Shea, "This Is a Saudi Textbook," *Washington Post*, May 21, 2006, p. B-4.
26. Eleanor Abdella Doumato, "Manning the Barricades: Islam According to Saudi Arabia's School Texts," *Middle East Journal* 57, no. 2 (Spring 2003): 244.
27. "Saudi Textbooks Lack Global Dimension," *Arab News*, May 23, 2003.
28. MEMRI, no. 1080, January 27, 2006, p. 2.
29. Doumato, "Manning the Barricades," p. 242.
30. MEMRI, Inquiry and Analysis Series, no. 247, October 13, 2005, p. 10.
31. Maureen Dowd, *New York Times*, November 6, 2002, p. A23.
32. James Wynbrandt, *A Brief History of Saudi Arabia* (New York: Facts on File, 2004), p. 285.
33. Page 4 of an interview with Nasser al-Omar, December 17, 2004, posted online to accompany a broadcast of "The House of Saud," PBS *Frontline*, February 8, 2005, David Fanning, executive producer, www.pbs.org/wgbh/pages/frontline/shows/saudi/interviews/alomar.html, accessed February 4, 2008.
34. Andrew Hammond, "Saudi 'Corrects' Ideas of 700 Qaeda Sympathizers," Reuters, August 28, 2006.
35. *Can Saudi Arabia Reform Itself?* International Crisis Group Middle East Report, no. 28 (Cairo and Brussels), July 14, 2004, p. 25.
36. MEMRI, no. 840, January 5, 2005, p. 1.
37. Ibid., p. 1; also, "Scars of 9/11 Show No Signs of Healing" (team reporting), *Arab News*, September 12, 2006.

38. Interview with Prince Turki al-Faisal in Washington, D.C., May 30, 2006.

39. Christopher Dickey and Rod Nordland, "The Fire That Won't Die Out," *Newsweek* online, July 22, 2002.

40. Ibid.

41. See "Saudi Obesity Alarm," January 23, 2007, *www.ameinfo.com*, accessed February 4, 2008; and *Pocket World in Figures, 2007 Edition* (London: The Economist, in association with Profile Books), p. 87.

42. MEMRI, no. 448, December 11, 2002, pp. 1–2.

43. Ned Parker, "Saudis' Role in Iraq Insurgency Outlined," latimes.com, July 15, 2007; and Richard A. Oppel Jr., "Foreign Fighters in Iraq Are Tied to Allies of U.S.," www .nytimes.com, November 22, 2007.

44. *Saudi Arabia Backgrounder: Who Are the Islamists?* International Crisis Group Middle East Report. no. 31, Amman/Riyadh/Brussels, September 21, 2004, p. 10; and MEMRI, no. 956, August 12, 2005, p. 6.

45. MEMRI, no. 896, April 21, 2005, p. 4.

46. Ibid., p. 5.

47. Craig Hoyle, "Saudi Arabia Commits to Typhoon," *Flight International*, http://info. flightinternational.com, January 3, 2006; Philip Aldrick and Stephen Seawright, "BAE Takes Off on Saudi Jet Deal," *Telegraph* (London), www.telegraph.co.uk, August 18, 2006; Stephen Fidler, "Saudis Confirm £4bn Typhoon Deal," *Financial Times*, www.ft.com, September 17, 2007; and Tom Ripley, "Saudi Typhoon Buy," *Jane's*, http://defence.janes.com, September 18, 2007.

48. David Leppard, "Bid to End Saudi Probe over Arms Deal Threat," (London) *Times*, www.the-times.co.uk, March 26, 2006.

49. MEMRI, Inquiry and Analysis Series, no. 247, October 13, 2005, p. 1; and "Address to the Nation—Crown Prince Abdullah Bin Abdulaziz," May 13, 2003, public statements by senior Saudi officials condemning extremism and promoting moderation (Washington, DC: Royal Embassy of Saudi Arabia, September, 2004), pp. 19–20.

50. Faye Bowers, quoting Mohammed al-Hulwah, "How an Al Qaeda Hotbed Turned Inhospitable," in the online edition of the *Christian Science Monitor*, January 8, 2004, reprinted January 9, 2004, by the Saudi-US Relations Information Service (Washington, DC), quotation on p. 2.

51. Saudi-US Relations Information Service (SUSRIS), www.susris.org (Washington, DC), November 8, 2005, p. 4.

52. Amir Taheri, "To Kill or Not to Kill," *New York Post*, June 10, 2005, p. 34.

53. Gilles Kepel, *Jihad: On the Trail of Political Islam* (Cambridge, MA: Harvard University Press), 2002, p. 376.

54. Colin Wells, *The Complete Idiot's Guide to Understanding Saudi Arabia* (Indianapolis: Alpha-Penguin, 2003), p. 266.

55. Gilles Kepel, *The War for Muslim Minds: Islam and the West*, trans. Pascale Ghazaleh (Cambridge, MA: Harvard University Press, 2004), p. 193.

56. MEMRI, October 13, 2005, p. 3; and *Saudi Arabia Backgrounder: Who Are the Islamists?* p. 8, n. 51.

57. MEMRI, no. 665, February 20, 2004, p. 4.

58. SUSRIS, July 20, 2004, p. 10, quoting a speech by Dr. Jamal al-Lail given May 31, 2004.

59. Amir Taheri, "What 'Fueled' the Saudi Raid," *New York Post*, December 7, 2004, p. 29.

60. MEMRI, no. 706, May 3, 2004, p. 1.

61. Neil MacFarquhar, "Kidnappers of American Threaten to Kill Him in 3 Days," *New York Times*, June 16, 2004, p. A13.

62. Niles Lathem and Andy Soltis, "Post Vile Photos before Saudi Gang Chief Is Slain," *New York Post*, June 19, 2004, p. 5.

63. Peter C. Valenti, "Saudi Arabia—Tragedy and Triumph," *Washington Report on Middle East Affairs*, September 2004, p. 32.

64. *Saudi Arabia Backgrounder: Who Are the Islamists?* p. 18.

65. MEMRI, no. 838, December 30, 2004, pp. 1, 5, 65.

66. *Saudi Arabia Backgrounder: Who Are the Islamists?* p. 20.

67. MEMRI, no. 886, March 30, 2005, p. 3.

68. Anthony Cordesman and Nawaz Obaid, *National Security in Saudi Arabia: Threats, Responses and Challenges* (Westport, CT: Praeger, 2005), p. 390; and *Country Reports on Human Rights Practices—Saudi Arabia 2005*, U.S. Department of State, Washington, D.C., March 8, 2006, www.state.gov/g/drl/rls/hrrpt/2005/61698.htm, p. 10, accessed February 4, 2008.

69. Page 6 of an interview with Bassim Alim, December 6, 2004, posted online to accompany a broadcast of "The House of Saud," PBS *Frontline*, February 8, 2005, David Fanning, executive producer, www.pbs.org/wgbh/pages/frontline/shows/saudi/interviews/alomar.html, accessed February 4, 2008.

70. Elizabeth Rubin, "A Saudi Response on Reform: Round Up the Usual Dissidents," *New York Times*, March 21, 2004, section 4, p. 3.

71. *Can Saudi Arabia Reform Itself?* p. 18.

72. Ibid.

73. Anthony Shadid and Steve Coll, "At a Crossroads, Saudi King Tests the Winds of Reform," *Washington Post*, August 18, 2005, p. A1.

74. U.S. State Department, *Country Reports on Human Rights Practices—Saudi Arabia 2006*, Washington, D.C., March 6, 2007, p. 8.

75. Editorial, "Saudi Arabia's Meager Election," *New York Times*, February 18, 2005, p. A28.

76. Neil MacFarquhar, "For Many Saudi Men, a Day to Cherish," *New York Times*, February 11, 2005, p. A6.

77. Dr. Khaled Batarfi, "Why I Welcome Municipal Polls," SUSRIS, February 21, 2005, p. 2, reprinting an article from the *Arab News* published on the same day.

78. Raid Qusti, "Saudi Women Are Making Strides: Crown Prince," SUSRIS, April 14, 2005, p. 2, reprinting an article published in the *Arab News* on the same day.

79. Paul Aarts and Gerd Nonneman, eds., *Saudi Arabia in the Balance: Political Economy, Society, Foreign Affairs* (London: Hurst, 2004), p. 448.

80. *Charlie Rose*, PBS Television, February 13, 2006.

81. Interview with Prince Turki al-Faisal at his office in Washington, D.C., May 30, 2006.

82. SUSRIS, January 21, 2004, p. 6.

83. Saudi-American Forum, February 11, 2004, p. 4; Judith Barnett, "A Mind-Bending Venture into Saudi Gender Politics," originally in the *Washington Post*, "Outlook," January 25, 2004.

84. "Saudi Arabia's Top Cleric Condemns Calls for Women's Rights" (article by Reuters), *New York Times*, January 22, 2004, p. A13.

85. Kathy Sheridan, "Change Comes Slowly for Out-of-Sight Saudi Women," *Irish Times*, www.ireland.com, February 13, 2006.

86. Intisar Al-Yamani, "Shocking Child Abuse," *Saudi Gazette*, May 27, 2004, p. 2.

87. MEMRI, no. 937, July 20, 2005, pp. 1–7.

88. Amr Hamzawy, "The Saudi Labyrinth: Evaluating the Current Political Opening," Washington, D.C., Carnegie Papers, no. 68, April 2006, p. 5.

89. Lubna Mohammed, letter in the *Arab News*, May 10, 2004, p. 14.

90. "Attitudes of Arabs: 2005," Zogby International, December 2005, p. 10.

91. Sheridan, "Change Comes Slowly for Out-of-Sight Saudi Women."

92. Sarah Kershaw, "Saudi Arabia Awakes to the Perils of Inbreeding," *New York Times*, May 1, 2003, p. A3; and Colin Wells, *The Complete Idiot's Guide to Understanding Saudi Arabia* (Indianapolis: Alpha Books [Penguin], 2003), p. 171.

93. Aarts and Nonneman, *Saudi Arabia in the Balance*, pp. 196–197, chapter by Madawi Al-Rashid.

94. Ebtihal Mubarak, "Fans and Rebuke Greet Women Writers," *Arab News*, March 3, 2006.

95. "King Abdullah on the Issues," SUSRIS, August 29, 2006.

96. Aarts and Nonneman, *Saudi Arabia in the Balance*, p. 70, chapter by Michaela Prokop.

97. Thomas Lippman, *Inside the Mirage: America's Fragile Partnership with Saudi Arabia* (Boulder, CO: Westview, 2004), p. 331.

98. "Saudis Put Cinema Ban in the Frame," Al Jazeera.Net, http://english.aljazeera.net, February 23, 2006.

99. "Saudi TV Newscaster Buthayna Nasser Slams Islamists," MEMRI TV Monitor Project, March 25, 2007, clip no. 1420.

100. Marc Lynch, "Watching al-Jazeera," *Wilson Quarterly* (Summer 2005): 36.

101. Ibid.

102. L. Azuri, "Public Debate in Saudi Arabia on Employment Opportunities for Women," Middle East Media Research Institute (MEMRI), Inquiry and Analysis Series, no. 300, November 17, 2006, pp. 3, 4.

103. "Gosaibi Answers Back," *Saudi Gazette*, June 5, 2006.

104. Pascal Menoret, *The Saudi Enigma: A History* (London: Zed Books, 2003), pp. 165, 164.

105. Anthony Cordesman, *Energy Developments in the Middle East* (Westport, CT: Praeger, 2004), p. 282.

106. Anthony Cordesman, *Saudi Arabia Enters the Twenty-First Century*, Volume 1 (Westport, CT: Praeger, 2003), p. 306; and Anthony Cordesman, *Beyond Anger and Counterterrorism: A New Grand Strategy for US and Arab Relations* (Washington, DC: Center for Strategic and International Studies, September 13, 2004), p. 10.

107. *Can Saudi Arabia Reform Itself?* p. 10, note 36.

108. Andrew Hammond, "Saudi Arabia Takes First Steps on Path to Reform," Reuters Foundation AlertNet, www.alertnet.org, February 2, 2006.

109. Christian Chaise, "Saudi Arabia Discreetly Presses Ahead with Reform," Middle East Online, www.middle-east-online.com/english, March 1, 2006, p. 3.

110. *Charlie Rose*, PBS Television, February 13, 2006.

21. A New Oil Boom, a New Business Climate (2003–)

1. "China's Big Appetite for Oil Is High on Agenda for U.S.," *New York Times*, April 19, 2006, p. A8.

2. Peter Maass, "The Breaking Point," *New York Times Magazine*, August 21, 2005, p. 34.

3. Matthew Simmons, *Twilight in the Desert: The Coming Saudi Oil Shock and the World Economy* (Hoboken, NJ: John Wiley & Sons, 2005), p. 161.

4. Anthony H. Cordesman, *Energy Developments in the Middle East* (Westport, CT: Praeger, 2004), p. 9.

5. Peter Maass, "The Breaking Point," p. 56.

6. Pitpundit, September 28, 2005, www.resourceinvestor.com/pebble.asp?relid=13232, accessed February 6, 2008.

7. Cordesman, *Energy Developments in the Middle East*, pp. 160, 164–166.

8. "Special Report: The Oil Industry," *Economist*, April 22, 2006, p. 67.

9. "Oil in Troubled Waters: A Survey of Oil," *Economist*, April 30, 2005, pp. 16, 19.

10. Simmons, *Twilight in the Desert*, p. 279.

11. "Special Report: The Oil Industry," pp. 66, 67.

12. Jad Mouawad, "Saudi Arabia Looks Past Oil," *New York Times*, December 13, 2005, pp. C1, C5.

13. Wael Mahdi, "Doing Business in Saudi Arabia: The World Bank Perspective," *Arab News*, December 6, 2005; and "World Bank Recognizes Saudi Arabia's Economic Reforms," Asharq Al-Awsat, http://asharqalawsat.com/english, September 26, 2007.

14. "UAE Dominates Foreign Investment in Saudi Arabia," DubaiCityGuide.com, www.dubaicityguide.com/geninfo/news, June 17, 2006.

15. P. K. Abdul Ghafour, "Call to Change Weekly Holidays to Friday–Saturday," *Arab News*, September 25, 2006.

16. Hassan M. Fattah, "Emirate Wakes Up Famous. Thank You, America," *New York Times*, March 2, 2006, p. A4.

17. Afshin Molavi, "Sudden City," *National Geographic*, January 2007, pp. 100, 102.

18. Brad Bourland, "Saudi Arabia and the WTO," SAMBA Financial Group, Riyadh, February 2006, p. 6.

19. Ibid., p. 40.

20. Ibid.; and Andrea H. Pampanini, *Saudi Arabia: Moving towards a Privatized Economy* (New York: Turnaround Associates, 2005), pp. 125, 126.

21. Bourland, "Saudi Arabia and the WTO," p. 7

22. Khan H. Zahid, "Why Does Saudi Arabia Need the WTO?" *Arab News*, December 26, 2005.

23. Interview with Prince Abdullah bin Faisal bin Turki at his home in Riyadh, June 12, 2004.

24. Brad Bourland, "The Saudi Economy at Mid-Year 2006," SAMBA Financial Group, Riyadh, June 30, 2006, pp. 2, 15, 16, 21; and Asharq Al-Awsat, "Saudi Economy Enters 2007 on High Note," December 31, 2006.

25. Marcia Smith, "For Women, Saudi Reality Is Harsh," *Atlanta Journal-Constitution*, November 30, 2005, p. A-15.

26. Mohammed A. Ramady, *The Saudi Arabian Economy: Policies, Achievements and Challenges* (New York: Springer, 2005), p. 188.

27. Bourland, "The Saudi Economy at Mid-Year 2006," p. 9; and Cordesman, *Saudi Arabia Enters the Twenty-First Century*, Volume 1, p. 439.

28. Mariam Al Hakeem, "Saudi Joint Stock Firms 'Are 100 Percent Transparent,'" gulfnews.com, www.gulfnews.com/business/Markets/10080704.html, November 8, 2006.

29. Khan H. Zahid, "What We Know and Don't Know about the Saudi Stock Market," *Arab News*, March 13, 2006.

30. Ramady, *The Saudi Arabian Economy*, p. 152.

31. Paul Aarts and Gerd Nonneman, eds., *Saudi Arabia in the Balance: Political Economy Society, Foreign Affairs* (London: Hurst, 2004), p. 169; and Saleh Al-Hamamy, "Yansab IPO Closes," *Arab News*, December 20, 2005.

32. Bourland, "The Saudi Economy at Mid-Year 2006," p. 9.

33. Rachel Bronson and Isobel Coleman, "The Need for Education Reform—Saudi System Is the Problem," Saudi-U.S. Information Service, May 31, 2005.

34. "The Future of US-Saudi Relations—Ali I. Al-Naimi," SUSRIS, May 3, 2006, p. 6.

35. Russell Gold and Gregory White, "Russia and Iran Discuss a Cartel for Natural Gas" (citing the *British Petroleum Statistical Review of World Energy*, 2006), *Wall Street Journal*, February 2, 2007, p. A17.

36. Pampanini, *Saudi Arabia—Moving towards a Privatized Economy*, pp. 41–47; and Andrea H. Pampanini, *Cities from the Arabian Desert—The Building of Jubail and Yanbu in Saudi Arabia* (New York: Turnaround Associates, 1997), pp. 125, 142.

37. Bourland, "The Saudi Economy at Mid-Year 2006," p. 19.
38. Bourland, "Saudi Arabia and the WTO," pp. 9, 15, 30.
39. Jad Mouawad, "Saudi Arabia Looks Past Oil," *New York Times*, December 13, 2005, p. C5.
40. "Saudi Aluminum Industry Takes Off," AME Info, www.ameinfo.com/118793.html, May 2, 2007; and "Saudi Signs $1.9 bn Rail Contract," ArabianBusiness.Com, www.arabianbusiness.com, April 4, 2007.
41 Ramady, *The Saudi Economy*, p. 328; David A. Andelman, "The Sino-Saudi Connection," *Forbes*, April 17, 2006; and Cho Jin-seo, "LG to Build Saudi Air Conditioner Factory," SUSRIS, April 9, 2006, reprinting an article of the same day from the *Korea Times*.
42. "Bitcom Computer Plant Opens in Saudi Arabia," AME Info, www.ameinfo.com/87883.html, June 4, 2006; and Saeed AlAbyad, "Export of SR300m Worth of Electronic Goods Likely," *Arab News*, August 23, 2006.
43. P. K. Abdul Ghafour, "Emaar to Offer 255 Million Shares in Largest IPO," *Arab News*, May 6, 2006; "Record 10 Million Saudis Subscribe to SR2.55 Billion Emaar the Economic City IPO," *Property World*, August 7, 2006; and "EEC Expands KAEC Project Size," *Arab News*, October 12, 2006.
44. "New Economic City in Saudi Arabia Set to Become the Largest Transportation and Logistics Hub in the Middle East," AME Info, www.ameinfo.com/90042.html, June 27, 2006; "Saudi Plans $8bn Economic City in North," TradeArabia, www.tradearabia.com, June 14, 2006; and "MMC Develop Jizan Economic City in Saudi Arabia," SUSRIS, November 5, 2006, citing an article published the same day by Bernama (Malaysian National News Agency).
45. Interview with Crown Prince Sultan by Tariq Alhomayed, *Asharq Al-Awsat*, January 8, 2007, http://aawsat.com/english/printasp?artid=id7587, accessed February 6, 2008.
46. "Saudi Economy Becomes Less Dependent on Oil," AME Info, www.ameinfo.com/113150.html, March 11, 2007.
47. Afshin Molavi, "Young and Restless," *Smithsonian*, April 2006, pp. 74, 77.

22. Abdullah Becomes King, Iran Becomes a Threat (2005–)

1. "Saudi Arabia: King Abdullah Receives Oaths of Loyalty," *Al Bawaba*, www.albawaba.com, August 3, 2005.
2. "King Abdullah Interview," excerpt from *20/20*, broadcast October 14, 2006, SUSRIS, October 22, 2005.
3. Ibid.
4. Ibid.
5. See Saudi Jeans (blogger), www.saudijeans.org, "Women's Driving: Do We Need Another King Faisal?" July 18, 2005.
6. Ibid.
7. See Saudi Jeans (blogger), www.saudijeans.org, "Exclusive: Riyadh International Book Fair," February 25, 2006.
8. "A Long Walk: A Survey of Saudi Arabia," *Economist*, January 7, 2006, p. 8.
9. Hassan M. Fattah, "Avoiding Political Talk, Saudis and Chinese Build Trade," *New York Times*, April 23, 2006, section 1, p. 12.
10. Scott D. Sagan, "How to Keep the Bomb from Iran," *Foreign Affairs* 85, no. 5 (September–October 2006): 56.
11. Vali Nasr, "When the Shi'ites Rise," *Foreign Affairs* 85, no. 4 (July–August 2006): 62.
12. Nawaf Obaid, *Meeting the Challenge of a Fragmented Iraq: A Saudi Perspective* (Washington, DC: Center for Strategic and International Studies [CSIS], April 6, 2006), p. 3.

13. Sabrina Tavernise, "Iraqi Death Toll Exceeded 34,000 in 2006, U.N. Says," *New York Times*, January 17, 2007, pp. A1, A7; and J. Campbell, M. O'Hanlon, and A. Unikewicz, "Op-Chart," *New York Times*, September 4, 2007, p. A19.

14. Obaid, "Meeting the Challenges of a Fragmented Iraq," pp. 11–12, 16–17.

15. Nasr, "When the Shi'ites Rise," p. 62.

16. Obaid, "Meeting the Challenge of a Fragmented Iraq," pp. 15–17.

17. Reuters, "Saudi King Condemns U.S. Occupation of Iraq," www.nytimes.com, March 28, 2007; P. K. Abdul Ghafour, "Kingdom Won't Take Sides in Iraq, Says Saud," *Arab News*, December 20, 2006; and *Charlie Rose*, PBS-TV, September 25, 2007, interview with Prince Saud al-Faisal.

18. Hassan M. Fattah (citing several unnamed Saudi officials familiar with the king's conversation), "Bickering Saudis Struggle for an Answer to Iran's Rising Influence in the Middle East," *New York Times*, December 22, 2006, p. A14.

19. "Special Report—Crisis in the Middle East," *Economist*, July 22, 2006, p. 30; and "Hezbollah's Arsenal" (chart), *New York Times*, July 18, 2006, p. A8.

20. Steven Erlanger and Thom Shanker, "Israel Finds Fighting Tougher Than Planned," *New York Times*, July 26, 2006, p. A8.

21. See "Saudi Official Comments on Latest Events in Lebanon and Palestine," www.SaudiEmbassy.net/2006News/News/AraDetail.asp?cIndex=6356, July 14, 2006, accessed February 7, 2008.

22. See "Hasty Decisions Only Escalate Crisis—Saud," www.saudigazette.com.sa/index.php?option=com_content&task=view&id=10507&Itemid=146, July 17, 2006, accessed February 7, 2008.

23. See "The Arab Peace Initiative, 2002," www.al-bab.com/arab/docs/league/peace02.htm, accessed February 7, 2008.

24. Reuters, "Saudi Protest Bombing of Lebanon," *Gulf Times*, www.gulf-times.com (Qatar), July 21, 2006.

25. Mariam Al-Hakeem, "Disaster 'Has No Parallel,' Warns Al-Sudais," *Gulf News*, http://archive.gulfnews.com/articles/06/07/21/10054005.html, July 22, 2006; and "Makkah's Imam Questions World Response to ME Crisis," *Arab News*, July 22, 2006.

26. SUSRIS, "Saudi Arabia's View on the Crisis in Lebanon—Statement of the Royal Court," July 26, 2006.

27. "Heed the Warnings," *Arab News*, August 4, 2006.

28. Agence France-Presse, "Lebanon: Israel Says Hezbollah Is Rearming," *New York Times*, January 10, 2007, p. A14.

29. H. Varulkar, "Lebanese Media Discusses Hizbullah's Status in Lebanon," MEMRI, Inquiry and Analysis Series, no. 333, March 12, 2007, p. 4.

30. "The Search for Peace," *Economist*, August 12, 2006, p. 37; "The Blame Game," *Economist*, August 19, 2006, p. 43; and "Hizbullah's New Offensive," *Economist*, September 16, 2006, p. 55; Seymour M. Hersh, "Watching Lebanon," *New Yorker*, August 21, 2006, p. 32; John Kifner, "Hezbollah Leads Work to Rebuild, Gaining Stature," *New York Times*, August 16, 2006, pp. A1, A8; and Farnaz Fassihi, "A Lebanese Militant Group Launches a Rebuilding Project," *Wall Street Journal*, September 17, 2007, p. A-1.

31. Seymour M. Hersh, "The Redirection," *New Yorker*, March 5, 2007, p. 63.

32. Jahangir Amugezar, "Nuclear Iran: Perils and Prospects," *Middle East Policy* 8, no. 2 (Summer 2006): 96.

33. Anthony H. Cordesman and Khalid R. Al-Rodhan, *Iran's Weapons of Mass Destruction: The Real and Potential Threat* (Washington, DC: Center for Strategic and International Studies, 2006), p. 75.

34. UN Security Council, Resolution 1696 (2006), July 31, 2006, http://daccess-ods .un.org/TMP/9895017.html, accessed February 7, 2008.

35. Elissa Goodman, "Security Council Approves Sanctions against Iran over Nuclear Program," *New York Times*, December 24, 2006, sec. 1, p. 8; and Nimrod Raphaeli, "The Middle East on a Collision Course: The Saudi Oil Weapon," MEMRI, February 14, 2007, p. 1.

36. Nazila Fathi, "Iran's President Promises More Nuclear Fuel and a Celebration," *New York Times*, January 4, 2007, p. A3; Associated Press, "Iran Should Give Sanctions 'Serious Response,' China Says," *New York Times*, January 6, 2007, p. A6; and Nazila Fathi, "Iranian Leader Vows to Resist UN Sanctions," *New York Times*, January 9, 2007, p. A9.

37. David Sanger and William Broad, "Report Finds Iran in Breach of U.N. Order," *New York Times*, February 23, 2007, pp. A1, A11; and Nazila Fathi, "Iran Says It Can Enrich Uranium on an Industrial Scale," *New York Times*, April 10, 2007, p. A3.

38. Associated Press, "Saudi Intelligence Chief Says Israeli Nuclear Arsenal Is Provoking Arms Race," *International Herald Tribune*, www.iht.com, December 8, 2006.

39. Amugezar, "Nuclear Iran," p. 111, n. 102.

40. Seymour M. Hersh, "The Next Act," *New Yorker*, November 27, 2006, p. 107.

41. Matthias Kuntzel, "Ahmadinejad's Demons," *New Republic*, April 24, 2006, p. 23.

42. Ibid.

43. Ibid.

44. Masood Farivar, "Armageddon and the Mahdi," *Wall Street Journal*, March 16, 2007, p. W11.

45. Nimrod Raphaeli (citing Foreign Minister Douste-Blazy's memoir), "The Middle East on a Collision Course: The Saudi Oil Weapon," Middle East Media Research Institute (MEMRI), February 14, 2007, p. 1.

46. Bernard Lewis, "August 22," *Wall Street Journal*, August 8, 2006, p. A10.

47. Amugezar, "Nuclear Iran," p. 98.

48. Cordesman and Al-Rodhan, *Iran's Weapons of Mass Destruction*, p. 220.

49. Hersh, "The Next Act," pp. 104, 106.

50. Ibid., p. 104.

51. Sagan, "How to Keep the Bomb from Iran," p. 56; Hersh, "The Next Act," p. 106; and "Obama vs. Clinton," debate, ABC television, April 16, 2008.

52. Ramit Plushnick-Masti of the Associated Press, "In Clear Message to Iran, Israel Adds Submarines," *Atlanta Journal-Constitution*, August 25, 2006, p. C4; and "Israeli Nuclear Forces, 2002" (numerous authors), *Bulletin of the Atomic Scientists* 58, no. 5 (September–October 2002): 73–75.

53. Seymour M. Hersh, "The Iran Plans," *New Yorker*, April 17, 2006, p. 32; and "What Would War with Iran Look Like (and How to Avoid It)," *Time*, September 25, 2006, p. 41, cover story on Iran by numerous authors.

54. Hersh, "The Next Act," p. 102.

55. "Top Iranian Military Commanders: In Case of Attack on Iran, We'll Target U.S. Troops in Gulf," MEMRI, no. 1378, December 6, 2006.

56. Amugezar, "Nuclear Iran," p. 104.

57. "Top Iranian Military Commanders," MEMRI.

58. Hassan M. Fattah, "Iran President Meets Saudi to Discuss Mideast Issues," *New York Times*, March 4, 2007, p. A10.

59. Christopher Dickey (citing the Saudi foreign minister, Prince Saud al-Faisal, as his source), "Flexing Their Muscles," *Newsweek*, March 26, 2007.

60. Christopher Dickey, "A Desert's Lion in Winter," *Newsweek*, April 9, 2007.

61. Thomas Friedman, "The Oil-Addicted Ayatollahs," *New York Times*, February 2, 2007, p. A19.

62. Nazila Fathi, "Iran's Leader Stands by Nuclear Plans," *New York Times*, January 22, 2007, p. A4.

63. Ilan Berman, "An Economic Coalition of the Willing," *Wall Street Journal*, September 26, 2006, p. A14.

64. Amugezar, "Nuclear Iran," p. 111, n. 94; and Emile El-Hokayem and Matteo Legrenzi, "The Arab Gulf States in the Shadow of the Iranian Nuclear Challenge" (Working Paper), The Henry L. Stimson Center, May 26, 2006, p. 6.

65. Amanda Lee Myers, "Saudi Ambassador Decried Iran Nuke Program," Associated Press, February 8, 2006, as reported the same day in the *Seattle Post Intelligencer*, http://seattlepi.nwsource.com.

66. King Abdullah interview, excerpt from ABC Television's *20/20*, broadcast October 14, 2006, p. 4, Saudi-U.S. Information Service (SUSRIS), October 22, 2005.

67. Raid Qusti, "GCC to Develop Civilian Nuclear Energy," *Arab News*, December 12, 2006.

68. Diana Elias, "Gulf States Commission Study for Possible Shared Nuclear Program," *International Herald Tribune*, www.iht.com, December 10, 2006.

69. Interview with Prince Turki al-Faisal in Washington, D.C., May 30, 2006.

70. Anthony H. Cordesman, "Saudi Energy Security: A Global Perspective" (Washington, DC: Center for Strategic and International Studies, November 10, 2006), p. 34; Cordesman and Obaid, *National Security in Saudi Arabia*, pp. 286–287; and Bill Farren-Price, "For Oil Producers, Energy Security Rises Up the Political Agenda," *International Herald Tribune*, www.iht.com/bin/printfriendly .php?id=8079140, accessed February 7, 2008.

71. Aarts and Nonneman, eds., *Saudi Arabia in the Balance*, p. 106, chapter by Monica Malik and Tim Niblock.

72. Toby Jones, "Seeking a 'Social Contract' for Saudi Arabia," *Middle East Report*, no. 228 (Fall 2003): 47.

73. "Saudi Petition Calling for Reforms Issued by Islamists Who Support Terrorism," MEMRI, no. 1467, February 16, 2007.

74. "A Long Walk: A Survey of Saudi Arabia," *Economist*, January 7, 2006, p. 6.

75. Anthony Shadid and Steve Coll, "At a Crossroads, Saudi King Tests the Winds of Reform," *Washington Post*, August 18, 2005. p. A1.

76. Interview with Prince Turki al-Faisal in Washington, D.C., May 30, 2006.

77. Speech by Prince Turki al-Faisal, then ambassador to the United States, to the Arab-U.S. Policymaker's Conference in Washington, D.C., October 30, 2006, SUSRIS, November 6, 2006, pp. 3–5.

Conclusion

1. *The Quran*, Sura 5, versa 48 (verse 53 in some other translations), as translated in Abdulaziz Sachedina, *Islamic Roots in Democratic Pluralism* (Oxford: Oxford University Press, 2001), p. 63.

Selected Bibliography

Part One. The Birth of Islam in the Seventh Century

Books about Muhammad

Armstrong, Karen. *Muhammad: A Biography of the Prophet*. San Francisco: HarperCollins, 1992.

Glubb, Sir John Bagot. *The Life and Times of Muhammad*. New York: Stein and Day, 1970.

Lings, Martin. *Muhammad: His Life Based on the Earliest Sources*. New Delhi: Saaed International (originally published by Inner Traditions International in 1983, no date given for this paperback edition).

Oliver, Marilyn Tower. *Muhammad*. San Diego: Lucent Books, 2003.

Peters, F. E. *Muhammad and the Origins of Islam*. Albany: State University of New York Press, 1994.

Ramadan, Tariq. *In the Footsteps of the Prophet: Lessons from the Life of Muhammad*. Oxford, UK: Oxford University Press, 2007.

Rodinson, Maxime. *Muhammed*. Trans. from the French by Anne Carter. New York: Vintage Books, 1961, 1974.

Rogerson, Barnaby. *The Prophet Muhammad*. London: Little, Brown, 2003.

Watt, W. Montgomery. *Muhammad at Mecca*. London: Oxford University Press, 1953.

———. *Muhammad at Medina*. London: Oxford University Press, 1956.

Weinberger, Eliot. *Muhammad*. London, New York: Verso, 2006.

Books on Early Islam

Aslan, Reza. *No God but God: The Origins, Evolution and Future of Islam*. New York: Random House, 2005.

Bulliet, Richard. *Conversion to Islam in the Medieval Period: An Essay in Quantitative History*. Cambridge, MA: Harvard University Press, 1979.

Crone, Patricia, and Martin Hinds. *God's Caliph: Religious Authority in the First Centuries of Islam*. Cambridge, UK: Cambridge University Press, 1986.

Donner, Fred McGraw. *The Early Islamic Conquests*. Princeton, NJ: Princeton University Press, 1981.

Gabrieli, Francesco. *Muhammad and the Conquests of Islam*. Trans. from the Italian by Virginia Luling and Rosamund Linell. New York: McGraw-Hill, 1968.

Glubb, Sir John Bagot. *The Empire of the Arabs*. London: Hodder and Stoughton, 1963.

———. *The Great Arab Conquests*. Englewood Cliffs, NJ: Prentice-Hall, 1963.

Hinds, Martin. *Studies in Early Islamic History*. Princeton, NJ: Darwin Press, 1996.
Hodgson, Marshall G. S. *The Venture of Islam: Conscience and History in a World Civilization*, Vol. I. Chicago: University of Chicago Press, 1974.
Madelung, Wilfred. *The Succession to Muhammad: A Study of the Early Caliphate*. Cambridge, UK: Cambridge University Press, 1999.
Muir, Sir William. *The Caliphate: Its Rise, Decline and Fall*. London: Smith Elder, 1898.
Watt, W. Montgomery. *Early Islam: Collected Articles*. Edinburgh: Edinburgh University Press, 1990.

Books about the Umayyad

Hawting, G. R. *The First Dynasty of Islam: The Umayyad Caliphate AD 661–750*. London: Croom Helm, 1986.
Kennedy, Hugh. *The Prophet and the Age of the Caliphates*. London: Longman, 1986.
Saunders, J. J. *A History of Medieval Islam*. New York: Barnes & Noble, 1965.
Shaban, M. A. *Islamic History A.D. 600–750: A New Interpretation*. Cambridge, UK: Cambridge University Press, 1971.
Wellhausen, J. *The Arab Kingdom and Its Fall*. Trans. Margaret Weir. Beirut: Khayats, 1963.
Zaydan, Jurji. *Umayyads and Abbasids*. Trans. David Margoliuth. Westport, CT: Hyperion, 1981.

General Works on Arab History

Armstrong, Karen. *Islam: A Short History*. New York: Modern Library, 2000.
Esposito, John, ed. *The Oxford History of Islam*. Oxford: Oxford University Press, 1999.
Gabrieli, Francesco. *The Arabs: A Compact History*. Trans. Salvator Attanasio. New York: Hawthorn Books, 1963.
Hitti, Philip K. *History of the Arabs, from the Earliest Times to the Present*. New York: St. Martin's, 1970.
———. *Islam: A Way of Life*. Minneapolis: University of Minnesota Press, 1970.
———. *Makers of Arab History*. New York: St. Martin's, 1968.
Hourani, Albert. *A History of the Arab Peoples*. Cambridge, MA: Harvard University Press, 1991.
Lewis, Bernard. *The Arabs in History*. London: Hutchinson University Library, 1962.
Nutting, Anthony. *The Arabs: A Narrative History from Mohammed to the Present*. New York: Clarkson Potter, 1964.

South Asian Pamphlets on the Early Muslims

Ahmad, Fazl. *Abu Bakr: The First Caliph of Islam*. Lahore: Sh. Muhammad Ashraf, 1975.
———. *Aisha, the Truthful*. Lahore: Sh. Muhammad Ashraf, 1976.
———. *Omar, the Second Caliph of Islam*. Lahore: Sh. Muhammad Ashraf, 1975.
———. *Othman, the Third Caliph of Islam*. Lahore: Sh. Muhammad Ashraf, 1987.
Ali, Abdul. *Caliph Ali: His Life and Times*. Madras: Diocesan Press, 1964.
Aziz, A. *Abu Bakr, the Caliph*. Karachi: Ghazanfar Academy, 1978.
Bahadur, Nawab Sadr Yar Jung, and M. Habibur Rahman Khan Sherwani. *Life of Abu-Bakr, First Caliph of Islam*. Trans. Syed Moin-ul Haq. Lahore: Sh. Muhammad Ashraf, 1993.
Shad, Abdur Rahman. *Umar Faruq*. Revised by Abdul Hameed Siddiqui. Lahore: Kazi, 1979.

Ancient Sources (in Translation)

The Essential Koran: The Heart of Islam. Translated and presented by Thomas Cleary. San Francisco: HarperSanFrancisco, 1993.
The Excellent Sayings of the Prophet Muhammad and Hazrat Ali. New York: Maleknia Naseralishah, 1978.

Guillaume, Alfred. *The Life of Muhammad: A Translation of Ibn Ishaq's "Sirat Rasul Allah."* London: Oxford University Press, 1970.

The History of al-Tabari (c. 915), Vols. 6–19. Vol. 6, Muhammad at Mecca. Trans. W. Montgomery Watt and M. V. McDonald. Albany: State University of New York Press, 1988.

The History of al-Tabari (c. 915), Vols. 6–19. Vol. 7, The Foundation of the Community. Trans. W. Montgomery Watt and M. V. McDonald. Albany: State University of New York Press, 1987.

The History of al-Tabari (c. 915), Vols. 6–19. Vol. 8, The Victory of Islam. Trans. Michael Fishbein. Albany: State University of New York Press, 1997.

The History of al-Tabari (c. 915), Vols. 6–19. Vol. 10, The Conquest of Arabia. Trans. Fred M. Donner. Albany: State University of New York Press, 1993.

The History of al-Tabari (c. 915), Vols. 6–19. Vol. 11, The Challenge to the Empires. Trans. Khalid Yahya Blankinship. Albany: State University of New York Press, 1993.

The History of al-Tabari (c. 915), Vols. 6–19. Vol. 12, The Battle of al-Qadisiyyah and the Conquest of Syria and Palestine. Trans. Yohanan Friedman. Albany: State University of New York Press, 1992.

The History of al-Tabari (c. 915), Vols. 6–19. Vol. 13, The Conquest of Iraq, Southwest Persia and Egypt. Trans. Gautier H. A. Juynboll. Albany: State University of New York Press, 1989.

The History of al-Tabari (c. 915), Vols. 6–19. Vol. 15, The Crisis of the Early Caliphate. Trans. R. Stephen Humphreys. Albany: State University of New York Press, 1990.

The History of al-Tabari (c. 915), Vols. 6–19. Vol. 16, The Community Divided. Trans. Adrian Brockett. Albany: State University of New York Press, 1997.

The History of al-Tabari (c. 915), Vols. 6–19. Vol. 17, The First Civil War. Trans. G. R. Hawting. Albany: State University of New York Press, 1996.

The History of al-Tabari (c. 915), Vols. 6–19. Vol. 18, The Caliphate of Muawiya. Trans. Michael G. Morony. Albany: State University of New York Press, 1987.

The History of al-Tabari (c. 915), Vols. 6–19. Vol. 19, The Caliphate of Yezid b. Muawiya. Trans. I. K. A. Howard. Albany: State University of New York Press, 1990.

Ibn Sa'd, Muhammad. *The Women of Medina.* Trans. Aisha Bewley. London: Tà-Ha Publishers, 1995.

The Koran Interpreted. Trans. Arthur J. Arberry. London: Oxford University Press, 1964.

The Koran. Trans. J. M. Rodwell. New York: E. P. Dutton, 1953.

The Qur'an. Trans. N. J. Dawood. London: Penguin, 1990.

Part Two. The First and Second Saudi States (1744–1887)

Books on Saudi Arabia and Ibn Abdul Wahhab

Al-Dakhil, Khalid. *Understanding Wahhabism.* Ann Arbor: University of Michigan Press, 2007.

Al-Fahad, Abdulaziz H. "From Exclusion to Accommodation: Doctrinal Evolution of Wahhabism." *New York University Law Review* 79, no. 2 (May 2004): 485–519.

Burckhardt, John Lewis. *Notes on the Bedouins and Wahabys Collected during His Travels in the East by John Lewis Burckhardt.* 2 vols. London: Colburn & Bentley, 1930.

Commins, David. *The Wahhabi Mission and Saudi Arabia.* London, New York: I. B. Tauris, 2006.

Delong-Bas, Natana J. *Wahhabi Islam: From Revival and Reform to Global Jihad.* New York: Oxford University Press, 2004.

Facey, William. *Dir'iyyah and the First Saudi State.* London: Stacey International, 1996.

Helms, Christine Moss. *The Cohesion of Saudi Arabia: Evolution of Political Identity.* Baltimore: Johns Hopkins University Press, 1981.

Philby, H. St. John. *Sa'udi Arabia.* New York: Praeger, 1955.

Rentz, George S. *The Birth of the Islamic Reform Movement in Saudi Arabia: Muhammad b. 'Abd al-Wahhab (1703/4–1792) and the Beginnings of Unitarian Empire in Arabia*. Edited by William Facey. London: Arabian Publishing, 2004.

Sabini, John. *Armies in the Sand: The Struggle for Mecca and Medina*. London: Thames and Hudson, 1981.

Vassiliev, Alexei. *The History of Saudi Arabia*. New York: New York University Press, 2000.

Winder, R. Bayly. *Saudi Arabia in the Nineteenth Century*. New York: St. Martin's, 1965.

South Asian Biographies of Ibn Abdul Wahhab

Iqbal, Sheikh Mohammad. *Sheikh Muhammad Bin Abdul Wahhab: The Wonder of Modern Islam*. Srinagar, Kashmir: Barzalla Bridge, 1988.

Nadwi, Masood Alam. *Mohammad Bin Abdul Wahab: A Slandered Reformer*. Trans. M. Rafiq Khan. Varanasi, India: Idaratul Buhoosil Islamia, 1983.

Ancient Sources (in Translation)

Bin Abdul-Wahhab, Muhammad. *Kitab At-Tauhid*. Trans. the Compilation and Research Department, Dar-us-Salam Publications. Riyadh: Dar-us-Salam Publications, 1996.

De Corancez, Louis Alexandre Olivier. *The History of the Wahabis from Their Origin until the End of 1809*. Reading, UK: Garnet Publications, 1995.

Ibn Abd al-Wahhab, Shaykh Muhammad. *Kitab Al Tawhid*. Trans. Ismail Raji al Faroqi. Riyadh: International Islamic Publishing House, 1991.

Ibn Taimiyah, Sheikh-ul-Islam. *Sharh Al-Aqeedat-il-Wasitiyah: Text on the Fundamental Beliefs of Islam and Rejection of the False Concepts of Its Opponents*. Commentary by Muhammad Khalil Harras. Trans. Muhammad Rafiq Khan. Riyadh: Dar-us-Salam Publications, 1996.

Ibn Taymiyyah, Taqi ad-Din. *Ibn Taymiyyah Expounds on Islam: Selected Writings of Shaykh al-Islam Taqi ad-Din Ibn Taymiyyah on Islamic Faith, Life and Society*. Compiled and translated by Muhammad Abdul-Haqq Ansari. Riyadh: General Administration of Culture and Publication, Kingdom of Saudi Arabia Ministry of Higher Education, 2000.

Stauch, Sameh. *Kitab At-Tawheed Explained*. Riyadh: International Islamic Publishing House, 2000.

Part Three. The Creation of Modern Saudi Arabia: The Life of King Abdul Aziz (1876–1953)

Biographies of Abdul Aziz

Almana, Mohammed. *Arabia Unified: A Portrait of Ibn Saud*. London: Hutchinson Benham, 1980.

Armstrong, Harold C. *Lord of Arabia: Ibn Saud*. London: Arthur Barker, 1934.

Howarth, David. *The Desert King: A Life of Ibn Saud*. London: Collins, 1964.

McLoughlin, Leslie. *Ibn Saud, Founder of a Kingdom*. New York: St. Martin's, 1993.

Philby, Harold St. John. *Arabian Jubilee*. London: Robert Hale, 1952.

Rihani, Ameen. *Ibn Sa'oud of Arabia*. London: Constable, 1928.

Sander, Nestor. *Ibn Saud: King by Conquest*. Tucson, AZ: Hats Off Books, 2001.

Van Der Meulen, Daniel. *The Wells of Ibn Sa'ud*. New York: Praeger, 1957.

Williams, Kenneth. *Ibn Sa'ud: The Puritan King of Arabia*. London: Jonathan Cape, 1933.

Histories of Saudi Arabia

Al-Rasheed, Madawi. *A History of Saudi Arabia*. Cambridge, UK: Cambridge University Press, 2002.

Facey, William. *The Story of the Eastern Province of Saudi Arabia*. London: Stacey International, 1994.

Helms, Christine Moss. *The Cohesion of Saudi Arabia: Evolution of Political Identity.* Baltimore: Johns Hopkins University Press, 1981.

Holden, David, and Richard Johns. *The House of Saud.* New York: Holt, Rinehart and Winston, 1981.

Lacey, Robert. *The Kingdom.* New York: Harcourt Brace Jovanovich, 1981.

Philby, Harold St. John. *Sa'udi Arabia.* New York: Praeger, 1955.

Twitchell, K. S., with Edward J. Jurji and R. Bayly Winder. *Saudi Arabia: With an Account of the Development of Its Natural Resources.* New York: Greenwood, 1969.

Vassiliev, Alexei. *The History of Saudi Arabia.* New York: New York University Press, 2000.

Books on Portions of Abdul Aziz's Life

Alangari, Haifa. *The Struggle for Power in Arabia: Ibn Saud, Hussein and Great Britain.* Reading, UK: Ithaca Press, 1998.

Al-Rashid, Ibrahim, ed. *The Struggle between the Princes: The Kingdom of Saudi Arabia in the Final Days of Ibn Saud.* Chapel Hill, NC: Documentary Publications, 1985.

Al-Semmari, Fahd, and Jill A. Roberg, eds. *Forever Friends.* Riyadh: King Abdul Aziz Foundation, 2000.

Anscombe, Frederick F. *The Ottoman Gulf: The Creation of Kuwait, Saudi Arabia and Qatar.* New York: Columbia University Press, 1997.

Glubb, Sir John Bagot. *Britain and the Arabs: A Study of Fifty Years, 1908–1959.* London: Hodder and Stoughton, 1959.

———. *War in the Desert: An R.A.F. Frontier Campaign.* New York: W. W. Norton, 1961.

Goldberg, Jacob. *The Foreign Policy of Saudi Arabia: The Formative Years, 1902–1918.* Cambridge, MA: Harvard University Press, 1986.

Habib, John S. *Ibn Sa'ud's Warriors of Islam: The Ikhwan of Najd and Their Role in the Creation of the Saudi Kingdom, 1910–1930.* Leiden, The Netherlands: E. J. Brill, 1978.

Kostiner, Joseph. *The Making of Saudi Arabia 1916–1936: From Chieftancy to Monarchial State.* New York: Oxford University Press, 1993.

Leatherdale, Clive. *Britain and Saudi Arabia 1925–1939: The Imperial Oasis.* London: Frank Cass, 1983.

Niblock, Tim, ed. *State, Society and Economy in Saudi Arabia.* London: Croom Helm, 1982.

Stegner, Wallace. *Discovery! The Search for Arabian Oil.* Vista, California: Selwa Press, 2007.

Troeller, Gary. *The Birth of Saudi Arabia: Britain and the Rise of the House of Saud.* London: Frank Cass, 1976.

Wilkinson, John C. *Arabia's Frontiers: The Story of Britain's Boundary Drawing in the Desert.* London: I. B. Tauris, 1991.

Biographies of Contemporaries of Abdul Aziz

Alghanim, Salwa. *The Reign of Mubarak al Sabah, Sheikh of Kuwait, 1896–1915.* London: I. B. Tauris, 1998.

Al Yahya, Eid, ed. *Travellers in Arabia: British Explorers in Saudi Arabia.* London: Stacey International, 2006.

Baker, P. Randall. *King Husain and the Kingdom of the Hijaz.* Cambridge, UK: Oleander, 1979.

Graves, P. *The Life of Sir Percy Cox.* London: Hutchinson, 1940.

Howell, Georgina. *Daughter of the Desert: The Remarkable Life of Gertrude Bell.* New York: Farrar, Straus and Giroux, 2007.

Lukitz, Liora. *A Quest in the Middle East: Gertrude Bell and the Making of Modern Iraq.* London: I. B. Tauris, 2006.

Morris, James. *The Hashemite Kings.* London: Faber and Faber, 1959.

Wallach, Janet. *Desert Queen: The Extraordinary Life of Gertrude Bell.* New York: Random House Anchor, 1999.

Winstone, H. V. F. *Captain Shakespear: A Portrait.* London: Jonathan Cape, 1976.

Part Four. Oil Brings Power: The Life of King Faisal (1905–1975)

Books Specifically about Faisal and His Years in Power

Beling, Willard A., ed. *King Faisal and the Modernization of Saudi Arabia*. London: Croom Helm, 1980.

De Gaury, Gerald. *Faisal, King of Saudi Arabia*. London: Arthur Barker, 1966.

Gause, F. Gregory. *Saudi-Yemeni Relations: Domestic Structures and Foreign Influence*. New York: Columbia University Press, 1990.

Sheean, Vincent. *Faisal: The King and His Kingdom*. Tavistock, England: University Press of Arabia, 1975.

Stefoff, Rebecca. *Faisal*. New York: Chelsea House, 1989.

Yizraeli, Sarah. *The Remaking of Saudi Arabia: The Struggle between King Sa'ud and Crown Prince Faysal, 1953–1962*. Tel Aviv: Moshe Dayan Center for Middle Eastern and African Studies, 1997.

Books about Oil Policies

Kayak, Alawi D. *The Control of Oil: East-West Rivalry in the Persian Gulf*. London: Kegan Paul, 2002.

Robinson, Jeffrey. *Yamani: The Inside Story*. New York: Atlantic Monthly Books, 1988.

Sampson, Anthony. *The Seven Sisters*. New York: Viking, 1975.

Schneider, Steven A. *The Oil Price Revolution*. Baltimore: Johns Hopkins University Press, 1983.

Terzian, Pierre. *OPEC: The Inside Story*. Trans. Michael Pallis. London: Zed Books, 1985.

Yergin, Daniel. *The Prize: The Epic Quest for Oil, Money and Power*. New York: Free Press, 1991.

Histories and Economic Surveys of Saudi Arabia That Cover Faisal's Reign

Abir, Mordechai. *Saudi Arabia in the Oil Era: Regime and Elites, Conflict and Collaboration*. Boulder, CO: Westview, 1988.

Aburish, Said K. *The Rise, Corruption and Coming Fall of the House of Saud*. London: Bloomsbury, 1994.

Bligh, Alexander. *From Prince to King: Royal Succession in the House of Saud in the Twentieth Century*. New York: New York University Press, 1984.

Halliday, Fred. *Arabia without Sultans: A Political Survey of Instability in the Arab World*. New York: Random House Vintage, 1975.

Hart, Peter T. *Saudi Arabia and the United States: Birth of a Security Partnership*. Bloomington: Indiana University Press, 1998.

Holden, David, and Richard Johns. *The House of Saud*. New York: Holt, Rinehart and Winston, 1981.

Kechichian, Joseph A. *Succession in Saudi Arabia*. New York: Palgrave, 2001.

Knauerhause, Ramon. *The Saudi Arabian Economy*. New York: Praeger, 1975.

Lacey, Robert. *The Kingdom*. New York: Harcourt Brace Jovanovich, 1981.

Lackner, Helen. *A House Built on Sand: A Political Economy of Saudi Arabia*. London: Ithaca Press, 1978.

Moliver, Donald M., and Paul J. Abbondante. *The Economy of Saudi Arabia*. New York: Praeger, 1980.

Niblock, Tim, ed. *State, Society and Economy in Saudi Arabia*. New York: St. Martin's, 1982.

Safran, Nadav. *Saudi Arabia: The Ceaseless Quest for Security*. Cambridge, MA: Harvard University Press, 1985.

Vassiliev, Alexei. *The History of Saudi Arabia*. New York: New York University Press, 2000.

Wilson, Peter W., and Douglas F. Graham. *Saudi Arabia: The Coming Storm*. Armonk, NY: M. E. Sharpe, 1994.

Biographies of Abdul Aziz with Information about Faisal's Youth

Almana, Mohammed. *Arabia Unified: A Portrait of Ibn Saud*. London: Hutchinson Benham, 1980.
Howarth, David. *The Desert King: A Life of Ibn Saud*. London: Collins, 1964.
McLoughlin, Leslie. *Ibn Saud, Founder of a Kingdom*. New York: St. Martin's, 1993.
Sander, Nestor. *Ibn Saud: King by Conquest*. Tucson, AZ: Hats Off Books, 2001.

Part Five. Modern Saudi Arabia (1975–2001)

Histories and General Books about Modern Saudi Arabia

Abir, Mordechai. *Saudi Arabia: Government, Society and the Gulf Crisis*. London: Routledge, 1993.
———. *Saudi Arabia in the Oil Era: Regime and Elites, Conflict and Collaboration*. Boulder, CO: Westview, 1988.
AbuKhalil, Asad. *The Battle for Saudi Arabia: Royalty, Fundamentalism and Global Power*. New York: Seven Stories, 2004.
Al-Rasheed, Madawi. *A History of Saudi Arabia*. Cambridge, UK: Cambridge University Press, 2002.
Baer, Robert. *Sleeping with the Devil: How Washington Sold Our Soul for Saudi Crude*. New York: Crown, 2003.
Bronson, Rachel. *Thicker Than Oil: America's Uneasy Partnership with Saudi Arabia*. New York: Oxford University Press, 2006.
Champion, Daryl. *The Paradoxical Kingdom: Saudi Arabia and the Momentum of Reform*. New York: Columbia University Press, 2004.
Holden, David, and Richard Johns. *The House of Saud*. New York: Holt, Rinehart and Winston, 1981.
Lacey, Robert. *The Kingdom*. London: Hutchinson, 1981.
Lippman, Thomas W. *Inside the Mirage: American's Fragile Partnership with Saudi Arabia*. Boulder, CO: Westview Press, 2004.
Long, David E. *The Kingdom of Saudi Arabia*. Gainesville: University Press of Florida, 1997.
———. *The United States and Saudi Arabia: Ambivalent Allies*. Boulder, CO: Westview, 1985.
Mackey, Sandra. *The Saudis: Inside the Desert Kingdom*. New York: W. W. Norton, 1987, 2002.
Metz, Helen Chapin, ed. *Saudi Arabia: A Country Study*. Washington, DC: Library of Congress, 1992.
Simons, Geoff. *Saudi Arabia: The Shape of a Client Feudalism*. New York: St. Martin's, 1998.
Wilson, Peter W., and Douglas F. Graham. *Saudi Arabia: The Coming Storm*. Armonk, NY: M. E. Sharpe, 1994.
Wynbrandt, James. *A Brief History of Saudi Arabia*. New York: Facts on File, 2004.

Books about Oil

Aperjis, Dmitri. *The Oil Market in the 1980s: OPEC Oil Policy and Economic Development*. Cambridge, MA: Ballinger (Harper & Row), 1982.
Golub, David B. *When Oil and Politics Mix: Saudi Oil Policy 1973–1985*. Cambridge, MA: Harvard University Center for Middle Eastern Studies, 1985.
Johany, Ali D. *The Myth of the OPEC Cartel: The Role of Saudi Arabia*. New York: John Wiley & Sons, 1980.
Noreng, Oystein. *Crude Power: Politics in the Oil Market*. London: I. B. Tauris, 2002.

Obaid, Nawaf. *The Oil Kingdom at 100: Petroleum Policymaking in Saudi Arabia.* Washington, DC: Washington Institute for Near East Policy, 2000.

Robinson, Jeffrey. *Yamani: The Inside Story.* New York: Atlantic Monthly Press, 1988.

Schneider, Steven A. *The Oil Price Revolution.* Baltimore: Johns Hopkins University Press, 1983.

Yergin, Daniel. *The Prize: The Epic Quest for Oil, Money and Power.* New York: Free Press, 1991.

Yetiv, Steve. *Crude Awakenings: Global Oil Security and American Foreign Policy.* Ithaca, NY: Cornell University Press, 2004.

Books about the Saudi Royal Family

Bligh, Alexander. *From Prince to King: Royal Succession in the House of Saud in the Twentieth Century.* New York: New York University Press, 1984.

Gause, F. Gregory. *Oil Monarchies: Domestic and Security Challenges in the Arab Gulf States.* New York: Council on Foreign Relations, 1994.

Henderson, Simon. *After King Fahd: Succession in Saudi Arabia.* Washington, DC: Washington Institute for Near East Policy, 1994.

Kechichian, Joseph A. *Succession in Saudi Arabia.* New York: Palgrave, 2001.

Kostiner, Joseph, ed. *Middle East Monarchies: The Challenge of Modernity.* London: Lynne Rienner, 2000.

Powell, William. *Saudi Arabia and Its Royal Family.* Secaucus, NJ: Lyle Stuart, 1982.

Sabri, Sharaf. *The House of Saud in Commerce: A Study of Royal Entrepreneurship in Saudi Arabia.* New Delhi: IS Publications, 2001.

Unger, Craig. *House of Bush, House of Saud.* New York: Scribner, 2004.

Books about Saudi Defense

Cordesman, Anthony H. *Saudi Arabia: Guarding the Desert Kingdom.* Boulder, CO: Westview, 1997.

Kechichian, Joseph A. *Political Dynamics and Security in the Arabian Peninsula through the 1990s.* Santa Monica, CA: RAND, 1993.

Peterson, J. E. *Saudi Arabia and the Illusion of Security.* New York: Oxford University Press, 2002.

Quandt, William B. *Saudi Arabia in the 1980s: Foreign Policy, Security and Oil.* Washington, DC: Brookings Institution, 1981.

Safran, Nadav. *Saudi Arabia: The Ceaseless Quest for Security.* Cambridge, MA: Harvard University Press, 1985.

Books on the 1991 Gulf War

Atkinson, Rick. *Crusade: The Untold Story of the Persian Gulf War.* New York: Houghton Mifflin, 1993.

Bush, George Herbert Walker, and Brent Scowcroft. *A World Transformed.* New York: Knopf, 1998.

Cohen, Roger, and Claudio Gatti. *In the Eye of the Storm: The Life of General H. Norman Schwarzkopf.* New York: Farrar, Straus and Giroux, 1991.

Gordon, Michael R., and General Barnard E. Trainor. *The Generals' War.* Boston: Back Bay Books, 1995.

Lehrack, Otto J. *America's Battalion: Marines in the First Gulf War.* Tuscaloosa: University of Alabama Press, 2005.

Means, Howard. *Colin Powell: Soldier/Statesman, Statesman/Soldier.* New York: Donald I. Fine, 1992.

Powell, Colin L., with Joseph E. Persico. *My American Journey.* New York: Random House, 1995.

Schwarzkopf, General H. Norman, written with Peter Petre. *It Doesn't Take a Hero*. New York: Bantam, 1992.

Sifrey, Micah L., and Christopher Cerf, eds. *The Gulf War Reader: History, Documents, Opinions*. New York: Times Books, 1991.

Sultan, HRH General Khaled bin, written with Patrick Seale. *Desert Warrior: A Personal View of the Gulf War by the Joint Forces Commander*. New York: HarperCollins, 1995.

Books about Human Rights in the 1990s

An-Naim, Abdullahi Ahmed. *Towards an Islamic Reformation: Civil Liberties, Human Rights, and International Law*. Syracuse, NY: Syracuse University Press, 1990.

Fandy, Mamoun. *Saudi Arabia and the Politics of Dissent*. New York: St. Martin's, 1999.

Jerichow, Anders. *Saudi Arabia: Outside Global Law and Order*. Richmond, UK: Curzon, 1997.

————. *The Saudi File: People, Power, Politics*. New York: St. Martin's, 1998.

Vogel, Frank E. *Islamic Law and Legal System: Studies of Saudi Arabia*. Boston and Leiden, The Netherlands: Brill, 2000.

Books about Women in Saudi Arabia

Al-Munajjed, Mona. *Women in Saudi Arabia Today*. Houndmills, UK: Macmillan, 1997.

Altorki, Soraya. *Women in Saudi Arabia*. New York: Columbia University Press, 1986.

Doumato, Eleanor Abdella. *Getting God's Ear: Women, Islam and Healing in Saudi Arabia and the Gulf*. New York: Columbia University Press, 1986.

Yamani, Mai. *Changed Identities: The Challenge of a New Generation in Saudi Arabia*. London: Royal Institute of International Affairs, 2000.

————. *Feminism and Islam: Legal and Literary Perspectives*. New York: New York University Press, 1996.

Books on Modern Wahhabism

Al-Yassini, Ayman. *Religion and State in the Kingdom of Saudi Arabia*. Boulder, CO: Westview, 1985.

Commins, David. *The Wahhabi Mission and Saudi Arabia*. London, New York: I. B. Tauris, 2006.

Delong-Bas, Natana J. *Wahhabi Islam: From Revival and Reform to Global Jihad*. New York: Oxford University Press, 2004.

Gold, Dore. *Hatred's Kingdom: How Saudi Arabia Supports the New Global Terrorism*. Washington, DC: Regnery, 2003.

Hunter, Shireen T., ed. *The Politics of Islamic Revivalism: Diversity and Unity*. Bloomington: Indiana University Press, 1988.

Molan, Peter, ed. and trans. *Arabic Religious Rhetoric: The Radical Saudi Sheikhs, a Reader*. Kensington, MD: Dunwoody, 1997.

Teitelbaum, Joshua. *Holier Than Thou: Saudi Arabia's Islamic Opposition*. Washington, DC: Washington Institute for Near East Policy, 2000.

Books on Terrorism, Osama bin Laden, and His Two Key Fatwas (for Both Parts Five and Six)

Benjamin, Daniel, and Steven Simon. *The Age of Sacred Terror*. New York: Random House, 2002.

Bergen, Peter L. *Holy War, Inc.: Inside the Secret World of Osama bin Laden.* New York: Free Press, 2001.

———. *The Osama bin Laden I Know: An Oral History of al Qaeda's Leader.* New York: Free Press, 2006.

Bin Laden, Osama. "Declaration of War against the Americans Occupying the Land of the Two Holy Places." 1996. www.pbs.org/newshour/terrorism/international/fatwa_1996.html, accessed October 19, 2004.

Bin Laden, Osama, and Ayman al-Zawahiri (and three additional authors). "Jihad against Jews and Crusaders." 1998. www.library.cornell.edu/colldev/mideast/wif.htm.

Coll, Steve. *Ghost Wars: The Secret History of the CIA, Afghanistan, and bin Laden, from the Soviet Invasion to September 10, 2001.* New York: Penguin, 2004.

Ferguson, Amanda. *The Attack on U.S. Servicemen in Saudi Arabia on June 25, 1996.* New York: Rosen, 2003.

Fuller, Graham E., and Bernard Lewis. *The Crisis of Islam: Holy War and Unholy Terror.* New York: Random House, 2003.

Georges, Fawaz A. *The Far Enemy: Why Jihad Went global.* Cambridge, UK: Cambridge University Press, 2005.

———. *Journey of the Jihadist: Inside the Muslim Militancy.* Orlando, FL: Harcourt, 2006.

Gold, Dore. *Hatred's Kingdom: How Saudi Arabia Supports the New Global Terrorism.* Washington, DC., Regnery, 2003.

Kepel, Gilles. *Jihad: On the Trail of Political Islam.* Trans. from the French by Anthony F. Roberts. Cambridge, MA: Harvard University Press, 2002.

———. *The War for Muslim Minds: Islam and the West.* Trans. Pascale Ghazaleh. Cambridge, MA: Harvard University Press, 2004.

Lawrence, Bruce, ed. *Messages to the World: The Statements of Osama bin Laden.* Trans. James Howarth. London: Verso, 2005.

McDermott, Terry. *Perfect Soldiers, The Hijackers: Who They Were, Why They Did It.* New York: HarperCollins, 2005.

Miller, John, and Michael Stone, with Chris Mitchell. *The Cell: Inside the 9/11 Plot, and Why the FBI and CIA Failed to Stop It.* New York: Hyperion, 2003.

The 9/11 Report: The National Commission on Terrorist Attacks upon the United States. New York: St. Martin's Paperbacks, 2004.

Randal, Jonathan. *Osama: The Making of a Terrorist.* New York: Knopf, 2004.

Wright, Lawrence. *The Looming Tower: Al Qaeda and the Road to 9/11.* New York: Knopf, 2006.

Selected Books by Sayyid Qutb

Qutb, Sayyid. *In the Shade of the Qur'an.* Trans. from Arabic by M. Adil Salahi and Ahaur A. Shamis. Vol. 1, Nairobi: Islamic Foundation, 1999; Vol. 30, New Delhi: Islamic Book Service, 2002.

———. *Islam and Universal Peace.* (No translator listed.) Plainfield, IN: American Trust, 1993.

———. *Islam, the Religion of the Future.* (No translator listed.) Kuwait: International Islamic Federation of Student Organizations, 1977.

———. *The Islamic Concept and Its Characteristics*, Vols. 1 and 2. Trans. Mohammed Moinuddin Siddiqui. Plainfield, IN: American Trust, 1991.

———. *Milestones.* (No translator from Arabic listed.) New Delhi: Islamic Book Service, 2002.

———. *Social Justice in Islam.* Trans. from Arabic by John B. Hardie. Oneonta, NY: Islamic Publications International, 2000.

Books about Sayyid Qutb and the Muslim Brotherhood

Abu-Rabi, Ibrahim M. *Intellectual Origins of Islamic Resurgence in the Modern Arab World*. Albany: State University of New York Press, 1996.

Berman, Paul. *Terror and Liberalism*. New York: W. W. Norton, 2003.

Choueiri, Youssef M. *Islamic Fundamentalism*. London: Pinter, 1990.

Esposito, John L., ed. *Voices of a Resurgent Islam*. (Chapter by Yvonne Haddad.) New York: Oxford University Press, 1983.

Habeck, Mary R. *Knowing the Enemy: Jihadi Ideology and the War on Terror*. New Haven, CT: Yale University Press, 2006.

Hasan, S. Badrul. *Syed Qutb Shaheed*. Karachi: International Islamic Publications, 1980.

Lia, Brynjar. *The Society of the Muslim Brothers in Egypt: The Rise of an Islamic Mass Movement 1928–1942*. Reading, UK: Ithaca Press, 1998.

Mitchell, Richard P. *The Society of the Muslim Brothers*. London: Oxford University Press, 1969.

Moussalli, Ahmad S. *Radical Islamic Fundamentalism: The Ideological and Political Discourse of Sayyid Qutb*. Beirut: American University of Beirut, 1992.

Shepard, William E. *Sayyid Qutb and Islamic Activism: A Translation and Critical Analysis of Social Justice in Islam*. Leiden, The Netherlands, and New York: E. J. Brill, 1996.

Other Books

Al Salloom, Hamad. *Education in Saudi Arabia*. Beltsville, MD: Amana, 1995.

Heller, Mark, and Nadav Safran. *The New Middle Class and Regime Stability in Saudi Arabia*. Cambridge, MA: Harvard Middle East Papers, 1985.

Ibrahim, S. E. *The New Arab Social Order: A Study of the Social Impact of Oil Wealth*. Boulder, CO: Westview, 1982.

Katakura, Joseph A. *Bedouin Village: A Study of a Saudi Arabian People in Transition*. Tokyo: University of Tokyo Press, 1977.

Pampanini, Andrea H. *Cities from the Desert: The Building of Jubail and Yanbu in Saudi Arabia*. New York: Turnaround Associates, 1997.

Part Six. Saudi Arabia since 9/11

Histories and General Books about Contemporary Saudi Arabia

Aarts, Paul, and Gerd Nonneman, eds. *Saudi Arabia in the Balance: Political Economy, Society and Survival*. London: Hurst & Company, 2005.

AbuKhalil, Asad. *The Battle for Saudi Arabia: Royalty, Fundamentalism and Global Power*. New York: Seven Stories, 2004.

Bradley, John R. *Saudi Arabia Exposed: Inside a Kingdom in Crisis*. New York: Palgrave Macmillan, 2005.

Bronson, Rachel. *Thicker Than Oil: America's Uneasy Partnership with Saudi Arabia*. New York: Oxford University Press, 2006.

Champion, Daryl. *The Paradoxical Kingdom: Saudi Arabia and the Momentum of Reform*. New York: Columbia University Press, 2004.

Cordesman, Anthony H. *Saudi Arabia Enters the Twenty-First Century*, Vols. 1 and 2. Westport, CT: Praeger, 2003.

Cordesman, Anthony, and Nawaf Obaid. *National Security in Saudi Arabia: Threats, Responses and Challenges*. Westport, CT: Praeger, 2005.

Menoret, Pascal. *The Saudi Enigma: A History*. Trans. Patrick Camiller. London: Zed Books, 2005.

Niblock, Tim. *Saudi Arabia: Power, Legitimacy and Survival*. London, New York: Routledge, 2006.

Peterson, J. E. *Saudi Arabia and the Illusion of Security*. New York: Oxford University Press, 2002.

Posner, Gerald. *Secrets of the Kingdom: The Inside Story of the Saudi-U.S. Connection*. New York: Random House, 2005.

Ramady, Mohamed A. *The Saudi Arabian Economy: Policies, Achievements and Challenges*. New York: Springer, 2005.

Wilson, Rodney. *Economic Development in Saudi Arabia*. London: Routledge-Curzon, 2004.

Books about Oil

Cordesman, Anthony, and Khalid R. Al-Rodhan. *The Changing Dynamics of Energy in the Middle East*, Vols. 1 and 2. Westport, CT: Praeger, 2006.

———. *The Global Oil Market*. Westport, CT: Praeger, 2006.

Maugeri, Leonardo. *The Age of Oil: The Mythology, History and Future of the World's Most Controversial Resource*. Westport, CT: Praeger, 2006.

Simmons, Matthew. *Twilight in the Desert: The Coming Saudi Oil Shock and the World Economy*. Hoboken, NJ: John Wiley & Sons, 2005.

Tertzakian, Peter. *A Thousand Barrels a Second: The Coming Oil Break Point and the Challenges Facing an Energy Dependent World*. New York: McGraw-Hill, 2006.

Victor, David, Amy Jaffe, and Mark Hayes, eds. *Natural Gas and Geopolitics: From 1970 to 2040*. Cambridge, UK: Cambridge University Press, 2006.

Yetiv, Steve. *Crude Awakenings: Global Oil Security and American Foreign Policy*. Ithaca, NY: Cornell University Press, 2004.

Books about the Saudi Royal Family

Kechichian, Joseph A. *Succession in Saudi Arabia*. New York: Palgrave, 2001.

Khan, Riz. *Alwaleed: Businessman, Billionaire, Prince*. New York: William Morrow (HarperCollins), 2005.

Kostiner, Joseph, ed. *Middle East Monarchies: The Challenge of Modernity*. London: Lynne Rienner, 2000.

Simpson, William. *The Prince: The Secret Story of the World's Most Intriguing Royal*. New York: Regan (HarperCollins), 2006.

Unger, Craig. *House of Bush, House of Saud*. New York: Scribner, 2004.

Books on Iran's Nuclear Threat

Chubin, Shahram. *Iran's Nuclear Ambitions*. Washington, DC: Carnegie Endowment for International Peace, 2006.

Cordesman, Anthony H., and Khalid R. Al-Rodhan. *Iran's Weapons of Mass Destruction: The Real and Potential Threat*. Washington, DC: Center for Strategic International Studies Press, 2006.

Cordesman, Anthony, and Martin Kleiber. *Iran's Military Forces and Warfighting Capabilities: The Threat in the Northern Gulf*. Westport, CT: Praeger, 2007.

Jafarzadeh, Alireza. *The Iran Threat: President Ahmadinejad and the Coming Nuclear Crisis*. New York: Palgrave Macmillan, 2007.

Takeyh, Ray. *Hidden Iran: Paradox and Power in the Iranian Republic*. New York: Henry Holt, 2006.

Other Books

Al-Rasheed, Madawi. *Contesting the Saudi State: Islamic Voices from a New Generation*. Cambridge, UK: Cambridge University Press, 2007.

Arkin, William. *Divining Victory: Air Power in the 2006 Israel-Hezbollah War*. Montgomery, AL: Air University Press, Maxwell Air Force Base, 2007.

Caudill, Mark A. *Twilight in the Kingdom: Understanding the Saudis*. Westport, CT: Praeger, 2006.

Ibrahim, Fouad. *The Shi'is of Saudi Arabia*. London: Saqi, 2006.

Long, David E. *Culture and Customs in Saudi Arabia*. Westport, CT: Greenwood, 2005.

Miles, Hugh. *Al-Jazeera*. New York: Grove, 2005.

Norton, Augustus. *Hezbollah: A Short History*. Princeton, NJ: Princeton University Press, 2007.

Pampanini, Andrea H. *Saudi Arabia: Moving towards a Privatized Economy*. New York: Turnaround Associates, 2005.

Rugh, William. *Arab Mass Media: Newspapers, Radio and Television in Arab Politics*. Westport, CT: Praeger, 2004.

Wells, Colin. *The Complete Idiot's Guide to Understanding Saudi Arabia*. Indianapolis: Alpha Books, 2003.

Zirinsky, Roni. *Ad Hoc Arabism: Advertising, Culture and Technology in Saudi Arabia*. New York: P. Lang, 2005.

Selected Periodicals, Journals, Web Sites, and Reports

Periodicals

Al-Hayat
Arab News
Asharq Al-Awsat
Atlantic Monthly
Business Week
Christian Science Monitor
Daily Star
Economist
Financial Times
Forbes
Gulf News
Gulf Times
Khaleej Times
Middle East
Middle East Times
National Geographic
New Republic
Newsweek
New Yorker
New York Times
New York Times Magazine
Peninsula
Saudi Aramco World
Saudi Gazette
Time
Times of Oman
Trade Arabia
USA Today
Wall Street Journal
Washington Post

Journals

Foreign Affairs
Foreign Policy
International Journal of Middle East Studies
Middle East Journal
Middle East Policy
Middle East Quarterly
Middle East Report
The Washington Report on Middle East Affairs

Selected Web Sites

http://saudiblogs.blogspot.com (list of Saudi blogs)
www.arabinsight.com
www.arabnews.com
www.memri.org
www.samba.com
www.saudiaramco.com
www.saudiembassy.net
www.saudijeans.org (blog)
www.susris.org
www.xrdarabia.org

Two YouTube videos of a Saudi wife showing her home, and a female Saudi doctor showing her office, can be found at:
   http://youtube.com/watch?v=_kbvvZs_OZc
   http://youtube.com/watch?v=vnWroPVmAQE

Selected Reports by Anthony H. Cordesman

Cordesman, Anthony H. *Beyond Anger and Counterterrorism: A New Grand Strategy for US and Arab Relations.* Washington, DC: Center for Strategic and International Studies. September 13, 2004.
———. *Global Oil Security: Risks by Region and Supplier.* Washington, DC: Center for Strategic and International Studies. November 13, 2006.
———. *Iran, Oil and the Strait of Hormuz.* Washington, DC: Center for Strategic and International Studies. March 26, 2007.
———. *Iran's Nuclear Program: UN and IAEA Reporting and Developments.* Washington, DC: Center for Strategic and International Studies, November 27, 2007.
———. *Saudi Energy Security: A Global Perspective.* Washington, DC: Center for Strategic and International Studies. November 10, 2006.

Other Reports

Can Saudi Arabia Reform Itself? International Crisis Group Middle East Report No. 28. Brussels, July 14, 2004.
Saudi Arabia Backgrounder: Who Are the Islamists? International Crisis Group Middle East Report No. 31. Brussels, September 21, 2004.
Campagna, Joel. *Princes, Clerics and Censors.* Committee to Protect Journalists. New York, May 9, 2006.
Hamzawy, Amr. *The Saudi Labyrinth: Evaluating the Current Political Opening.* Carnegie (Endowment) Papers, No. 68. Washington, D.C., April 2006.

Human Rights Watch. Periodic reports on Saudi Arabia. www.hrw.org.

Obaid, Nawaf. *Meeting the Challenge of a Fragmented Iraq: A Saudi Perspective*. Washington, DC: Center for Strategic and International Studies, April 6, 2006.

SAMBA (Saudi American Bank). Annual and quarterly reports on the Saudi economy by the Financial Group in Riyadh. www.samba.com.

SAMBA Financial Group. *Saudi Arabia and the WTO*. Riyadh, February 2006.

U.S. Department of State. Annual reports on human rights practices in Saudi Arabia by the department's Bureau of Democracy, Human Rights and Labor, in Washington, D.C.

Index

References in *italics* refer to illustrations.

p29 hostage treatment. Mhd accuses Jewish tribe of plotting to kill him
p31 mary. Mhd slept w/ Christian concubine, named mary
p32 Qurayzah. largest Jewish tribe in Medina, assassinated
p33 Safiyah, one of mhd's wife. Jewish before their marriage
p36 7 sayings of Mhd & history of spread of Islam p39